February 27–March 1, 2011
Monterey, California, USA

Association for
Computing Machinery

Advancing Computing as a Science & Profession

FPGA'11

Proceedings of the 2011 ACM/SIGDA International Symposium on
Field Programmable Gate Arrays

Sponsored by:
ACM SIGDA

Supported by:
Altera, Xilinx, Microsemi, & BEEcube

With logistical support from:
The Trimberger Family Foundation

Association for
Computing Machinery

Advancing Computing as a Science & Profession

The Association for Computing Machinery
2 Penn Plaza, Suite 701
New York, New York 10121-0701

Notice to Past Authors of ACM-Published Articles
ACM intends to create a complete electronic archive of all articles and/or other material previously published by ACM. If you have written a work that has been previously published by ACM in any journal or conference proceedings prior to 1978, or any SIG Newsletter at any time, and you do NOT want this work to appear in the ACM Digital Library, please inform permissions@acm.org, stating the title of the work, the author(s), and where and when published.

ISBN: 978-1-4503-0554-9

Additional copies may be ordered prepaid from:

ACM Order Department
PO Box 30777
New York, NY 10087-0777, USA

Phone: 1-800-342-6626 (USA and Canada)
+1-212-626-0500 (Global)
Fax: +1-212-944-1318
E-mail: acmhelp@acm.org
Hours of Operation: 8:30 am – 4:30 pm ET

ACM Order Number 480110548102

Printed in the USA

Foreword

We welcome you to the 19th annual ACM International Symposium on Field-Programmable Gate Arrays. This is premier venue for disseminating research advances in a wide range of topic areas related to FPGAs and FPGA-like technologies.

In response to the FPGA 2011 Call for Papers, 82 papers were submitted. From these, the program committee accepted 21 full-length papers (25.6% acceptance rate). We also continued the practice started in 2010 of accepting a number of short (four-page) papers in order to broaden the participation in the conference, and highlight interesting new projects. The authors of these papers are given the opportunity to give a five-minute oral presentation, followed by a poster presentation to spur discussion. This year we have 16 short papers. Additionally, there are over 20 poster-only presentations that allow authors to interact with attendees more directly.

This year's symposium features a pre-conference workshop, "The Role of FPGAs in a Converged Future with Heterogeneous Programmable Processors", run by Jonathan Rose (University of Toronto) and Guy Lemieux (University of British Columbia). All FPGA 2011 attendees are encouraged to participate. We will also have an evening panel, organized by John Wawrzynek (UC Berkeley), entitled "Should the Academic Community Launch an Open Source FPGA Device and Tools Effort?"

We thank all of the authors who contributed and presented interesting new work to the conference, and the reviewers who identified the top papers to include in this year's program. Constructive reviewer feedback is one of the keys to a high-quality conference year after year, because it encourages each of us, as researchers, to make our work more complete, or to reach a little further.

The conference would also not be possible without the help of the ACM and ACM SIGDA, as well as the generosity of the corporate supporters: Altera, Microsemi, Xilinx, and BEECube. We also thank the Trimberger Family Foundation for additional logistical support.

Welcome to FPGA 2011!

John Wawrzynek
FPGA'11 General Chair
UC Berkeley, USA

Katherine Compton
FPGA'11 Program Chair
University of Wisconsin-Madison, USA

Table of Contents

Session 3: FPGA Architectures and Technology

Session 4: CAD

Session 5: CAD, Measurement, and Estimation

Session 6: Applications II

Session 7: FPGA CAD and Architecture

Session 8: Networking and Security

Poster Session 1

Poster Session 2

Poster Session 3

Author Index

FPGA 2011 Symposium Organization

General Chair: John Wawrzynek *(University of California, Berkeley, USA)*

Program Chair: Katherine Compton *(University of Wisconsin-Madison, USA)*

Publicity Chair: Satnam Singh *(Microsoft Cambridge Research, UK)*

Finance Chair: Peter Cheung *(Imperial College London, UK)*

Workshop Chairs: Jonathan Rose *(University of Toronto, Canada)*
Guy Lemieux *(University of British Columbia, Canada)*

Panel Chair: John Wawrzynek *(University of California, Berkeley, USA)*

Program Committee: Jason Anderson *(University of Toronto, Canada)*
Vaughn Betz *(Altera, Canada)*
Chen Chang *(BEEcube, USA)*
Deming Chen *(University of Illinois at Urbana-Champaign, USA)*
Peter Cheung *(Imperial College London, UK)*
Derek Chiou *(University of Texas, Austin, USA)*
Katherine Compton *(University of Wisconsin at Madison, USA)*
Jason Cong *(University of California at Los Angeles, USA)*
Carl Ebeling *(University of Washington, USA)*
Jonathan Greene *(Actel, USA)*
Scott Hauck *(University of Washington, USA)*
Mike Hutton *(Altera, USA)*
Lei He *(University of California at Los Angeles, USA)*
Brad Hutchings *(Brigham Young University, USA)*
Ryan Kastner *(University of California, Santa Barbara, USA)*
Martin Langhammer *(Altera, UK)*
Miriam Leeser *(Northeastern University, USA)*
Guy Lemieux *(University of British Columbia, Canada)*
Philip Leong *(University of Sydney, Australia)*
David Lewis *(Altera, Canada)*
John Lockwood *(Algo-Logic Systems, USA)*
Wayne Luk *(Imperial College London, UK)*
Patrick Lysaght *(Xilinx, USA)*
Stephen Neuendorffer *(Xilinx, USA)*
Jonathan Rose *(University of Toronto, Canada)*
Lesley Shannon *(Simon Fraser University, Canada)*
Satnam Singh *(Microsoft Cambridge Research, UK)*
Juergen Teich *(University of Erlangen, Germany)*
Russell Tessier *(University of Massachusetts at Amherst, USA)*
Steve Trimberger *(Xilinx, USA)*
John Wawrzynek *(University of California, Berkeley, USA)*
Steve Wilton *(Veridae Systems, Canada)*

FPGA 2011 Sponsor & Supporters

Sponsor:

Supporters:

With logistical support from:

The Role of FPGAs in a Converged Future with Heterogeneous Programmable Processors

Chair: Jonathan Rose
University of Toronto

Co-Chair: Guy Lemieux
University of British Columbia

The battle of fixed function devices vs. programmable devices has been won by the programmables. The question facing us now is to determine what kinds of programmability to place on next generation systems/devices. Research and development on many applications has shown that different kinds of hardware and software programmability succeed for different application classes: powerful, single-thread-optimized CPUs continue to do very well for many applications; the General Purpose GPU is carving a niche in high throughput, parallel floating point codes in addition to its home turf of graphics; the FPGA is particularly good at variable bit-size computations and data steering, as well as parallel distributed control of networks. Future systems may well need all three types of these types of engines, and perhaps interesting mixtures of them. This is particularly true when we deal with the combined goals of optimizing cost, performance and energy.

In this workshop, we will look to the future of the FPGA within these types of 'converged' programmable computing engines, and reflectively ask ourselves: What role can the FPGA play? What future applications in areas such as networking, mobile, and artificial intelligence can be driven by FPGAs? How do FPGAs fit into the architecture realm of CPUs, general purpose GPUs, and DSPs? How should the designer/programme express their intent in the most effective way possible? What are the requirements for a compilation and optimization environment that allow FPGAs to intermix within a heterogeneous and converged future?

The intent of this workshop is to open a discussion on these questions. There will be a series of short, invited talks interspersed with free and open discussion.

Categories and Subject Descriptors: C.3 [Computer Systems Organization]: Special-Purpose and Application-based Systems

General Terms: Design

Keywords: FPGA, Reconfigurable Computing, Signal Processing, DSP, High Level Programming Models, Heterogeneity, Heterogeneous Computing Systems

Evening Panel

Should the Academic Community Launch an Open-Source FPGA Device and Tools Effort?

Chair: John Wawrzynek
UC Berkeley

Panelists: To Be Announced

For years, many academic researchers in reconfigurable computing have been frustrated by their reliance on commercial FPGAs and tools. Commercial FPGAs have highly complex micro-architectures, come with undocumented binary interfaces, have no compatibility between generations, and come with difficult to use proprietary place and route tools. The FPGA vendors are making the right moves for serving their commercial customer base, but it seems at times these moves are in conflict with the needs of the academic research community.

These problems make it difficult for academics to teach FPGA design and to participate in relevant research related to FPGAs. Complex FPGA fabrics and undocumented proprietary interfaces make it nearly impossible to build new tools to target actual commercial devices. University researchers are now hesitant to participate in FPGA architecture research because the level of complexity of FPGAs is beyond what is possible to implement in an academic setting. Reconfigurable computing application developers are at the mercy of complex FPGA devices and closed-source place and route tools—not optimized for computing applications.

Some argue that the time is right for academia to break away and create an open source FPGA device. Such an effort would enable university researchers to take an active role in architecture design, and promote an open source community effort in developing and advancing the state of the art of tools.

A similar situation existed in the early 80's surrounding processor design. As a result of competition among the big computer companies, microprocessor designs had evolved from very simple beginnings to highly complex architectures and equally complex compilers. Universities were largely on the sidelines, as they couldn't compete at the level of industrial designs of the day. "RISC" changed all that. By adopting simple architectures, universities were once again able to actually design and implement their own processors and to innovate with micro-architecture and compilers.

Is it time for a "RISC" revolution for FPGAs? FPGA companies might argue that FPGA platforms are necessarily complex and out of the realm of what's possible to implement within an academic setting, and would say that an open source effort in not necessary, as they are helping to promote academic research by collaborations with universities, and donation of tools, and hardware platforms.

This panel will discuss the pros and cons of an academic community led open FPGA device and tools development effort.

Categories and Subject Descriptors: C.3 [Computer Systems Organization]: Special-Purpose and Application-based Systems

General Terms: Design, Documentation, Standardization

Keywords: FPGA, Signal Processing, DSP, High Level Programming Models, Open Source, Design Tools, Reconfigurable Computing

Copyright is held by the author/owner(s).
FPGA'11, February 27–March 1, 2011, Monterey, California, USA.
ACM 978-1-4503-0554-9/11/02.

Comparing FPGA vs. Custom CMOS and the Impact on Processor Microarchitecture

Henry Wong
Department of Electrical and
Computer Engineering
University of Toronto
henry@eecg.utoronto.ca

Vaughn Betz
Altera Corp.
vbetz@altera.com

Jonathan Rose
Department of Electrical and
Computer Engineering
University of Toronto
jayar@eecg.utoronto.ca

ABSTRACT

As soft processors are increasingly used in diverse applications, there is a need to evolve their microarchitectures in a way that suits the FPGA implementation substrate. This paper compares the delay and area of a comprehensive set of processor building block circuits when implemented on custom CMOS and FPGA substrates. We then use the results of these comparisons to infer how the microarchitecture of soft processors on FPGAs should be different from hard processors on custom CMOS.

We find that the ratios of the area required by an FPGA to that of custom CMOS for different building blocks varies significantly more than the speed ratios. As area is often a key design constraint in FPGA circuits, area ratios have the most impact on microarchitecture choices. Complete processor cores have area ratios of 17-27× and delay ratios of 18-26×. Building blocks that have dedicated hardware support on FPGAs such as SRAMs, adders, and multipliers are particularly area-efficient (2-7× area ratio), while multiplexers and CAMs are particularly area-inefficient (> 100× area ratio), leading to cheaper ALUs, larger caches of low associativity, and more expensive bypass networks than on similar hard processors. We also find that a low delay ratio for pipeline latches (12-19×) suggests soft processors should have pipeline depths 20% greater than hard processors of similar complexity.

Categories and Subject Descriptors

B.7.1 [**Integrated Circuits**]: Types and Design Styles

General Terms

Design, Measurement

Keywords

FPGA, CMOS, Area, Delay, Soft Processor

1. INTRODUCTION

Custom CMOS silicon logic processes, standard cell ASICs, and FPGAs are commonly-used substrates for implementing digital circuits, with circuits implemented on each one having different characteristics such as delay, area, and power. In this paper, we compare custom CMOS and FPGA substrates for implementing processors and explore the microarchitecture trade-off space of soft processors in light of the differences.

FPGA soft processors have mostly employed single-issue in-order microarchitectures due to the limited area budget available on FPGAs [1–3]. We believe that future soft processor microarchitecture design decisions can benefit from a quantitative understanding of the differences between custom CMOS and FPGA substrates. Another reason to revisit the soft processor microarchitecture trade-off space is that the increased capacity of modern FPGAs can accommodate much larger soft processors if it results in a performance benefit.

Previous studies have measured the relative delay and area of FPGA, standard cell, and custom CMOS substrates as an average across a large set of benchmark circuits [4,5]. While these earlier results are useful in determining an estimate of the size and speed of circuit designs that can be implemented on FPGAs, we need to compare the relative performance of various types of "building block" circuits in order to have enough detail to guide microarchitecture design decisions.

This paper makes two contributions:

- We compare delay and area between FPGA and custom CMOS implementations of a set of building block circuits. While prior work gave results for complete systems, we show specific strengths and weaknesses of the FPGA substrate for the different building blocks.

- Based on the delay and area ratios of building block circuits on FPGAs vs. custom CMOS, we discuss how processor microarchitecture design trade-offs change on an FPGA substrate and the suitability of existing processor microarchitecture techniques when used on FPGAs.

We begin with background in Section 2 and methodology in Section 3. We then present our comparison results and their impact on microarchitecture in Sections 4 and 5, and conclude in Section 6.

2. BACKGROUND

2.1 Technology Impact on Microarchitecture

Studies on how process technology trends impact microarchitecture are essential for designing effective microarchitectures that take advantage of ever-changing manufacturing processes. Issues currently facing CMOS technology include poor wire delay scaling, high power consumption, and more recently, process variation. Microarchitectural techniques that respond to these challenges include clustered processor microarchitectures and chip multiprocessors [6,7].

FPGA-implemented circuits face a very different set of constraints. Power consumption is not currently the dominant design constraint due to lower clock speeds, while area is often the primary constraint due to high area overheads of FPGA circuits. Characteristics such as inefficient multiplexers and the need to map RAM structures into FPGA hard SRAM blocks are known and generally adjusted for by modifying circuit-level, but not microarchitecture-level, design [8–11].

2.2 Measurement of FPGAs

Kuon and Rose have measured the area, delay, and power overheads of FPGAs compared to a standard cell ASIC flow on 90 nm processes [4] using a benchmark set of complete circuits to measure the overall impact of using FPGAs compared to ASICs and the effect of FPGA hard blocks. They found that circuits implemented on FPGAs consumed $35\times$ more area than on standard cell ASIC for circuits that did not use hard memory or multiplier blocks, to a low of $18\times$ for those that used both types. Minimum cycle time of the FPGA circuits were not significantly affected by hard blocks, ranging from 3.0 to $3.5\times$ greater than ASIC. Chinnery and Keutzer [5] made similar comparisons between standard cell and custom CMOS and reported a delay ratio of 3 to $8\times$. Combined, these reports suggest that the delay of circuits implemented on an FPGA would be 9 to $28\times$ greater than on custom CMOS. However, data for full circuits are insufficiently detailed to guide microarchitecture-level decisions.

3. METHODOLOGY

We seek to measure the delay and area of FPGA building block circuits and compare them against their custom CMOS counterparts, resulting in *area ratios* and *delay ratios*. We define these ratios to be the area or delay of an FPGA circuit divided by the area or delay of the custom CMOS circuit. A higher ratio means the FPGA implementation has more overhead. We compare several complete processor cores and a set of building block circuits against their custom CMOS implementations, then observe which types of building block circuits have particularly high or low overhead on FPGA.

As we do not have the expertise to implement highly-optimized custom CMOS circuits, our building block circuit comparisons use data from custom CMOS implementations found in the literature. The set of building block circuits is generic enough so that there are sufficient published delay and area data. We focus mainly on custom designs built in 65 nm processes, because it is the most recent process where design examples are readily available in the literature, and compare them to the Altera Stratix III 65 nm FPGA. In most cases, we implemented the equivalent FPGA circuits for comparison. Power consumption is not compared due to the scarcity of data in the literature and the difficulty in standardizing testing conditions such as test vectors, voltage, and temperature.

We normalize area measurements to a 65 nm process using an ideal scale factor of $0.5\times$ area between process nodes. We normalize delay using published ring oscillator data, with

	90 nm	65 nm	45 nm
Area	0.5	1.0	2.0
Delay	0.78	1.0	1.23

Table 1: Normalization Factors Between Processes

Resource	Relative Area (Equiv. LABs)	Tile Area (mm²)
LAB	1	0.0221
ALUT (half-ALM)	0.05	0.0011
M9K memory	2.87	0.0635
M144K memory	26.7	0.5897
DSP block	11.9	0.2623
Total core area	18 621	412

Table 2: Estimated FPGA Resource Area Usage

the understanding that these reflect gate delay scaling more than interconnect scaling. Intel reports 29% FO1 delay improvement between 90 nm and 65 nm, and 23% FO2 delay improvement between 65 nm and 45 nm [12,13]. The area and delay scaling factors used are summarized in Table 1.

Delay is measured as the longest register to register path or input to output path in a circuit. In papers that describe CMOS circuits embedded in a larger unit (e.g., a shifter inside an ALU), we conservatively assume that the subcircuit has the same cycle time as the larger unit. In FPGA circuits, delay is measured using register to register paths, with the register delay subtracted out when comparing circuits that do not include a register (e.g., wire delay).

To measure FPGA resource usage, we implement circuits on the Stratix III FPGA and use the "logic utilization" metric as reported by Quartus II to account for lookup tables (LUT) and registers, and count partially-used memory and multiplier blocks as entirely used since it is unlikely another part of the design can use them. Table 2 shows the areas of the Stratix III FPGA resources. The FPGA tile areas include routing area so we do not track routing separately. The core of the the largest Stratix III (EP3LS340) FPGA contains 13 500 LABs of 10 ALMs each, 1 040 M9K memories, 48 M144K memories, and 72 DSP blocks, for a total of 18 621 LAB equivalent areas and 412 mm² core area.

We implemented FPGA circuits using Altera Quartus II 10.0 SP1 using the fastest speed grade of the largest Stratix III. Circuits containing MLABs used Stratix IV due to hardware[1] issues. Registers delimit the inputs and outputs of our circuits under test. We set timing constraints to maximize clock speed, reflecting the use of these circuits as part of a larger circuit in the FPGA core.

3.1 Additional Limitations

The trade-off space for a given circuit structure on custom CMOS is huge and our comparison circuit examples may not all have the same optimization targets. Delay, area, power, and design effort can all be traded-off, resulting in vastly different circuit performance. We assume that designs published in the literature are optimized primarily for delay with reasonable values for the other metrics and we implement our FPGA equivalents with the same approach.

Another source of imprecision results from the differences in performance between chip manufacturers. For example,

---

[1] A Stratix III erratum halves the MLAB capacity to 320 bits and is fixed in Stratix IV. See Stratix III Device Family Errata Sheet

transistor drive strength impacts logic gate delay and is voltage- and process-dependent. At 100 nA/μm leakage current, Intel's 65 nm process [14] achieves 1.46 and 0.88 mA/μm at 1.2 V for NMOS and PMOS, respectively, and 1.1 and 0.66 mA/μm at 1.0 V, while TSMC's 65 nm process [15] achieves 1.01 and 0.48 mA/μm at 1.0 V. The choice of supply voltage results from both the power-performance trade-off and the transistor reliability the manufacturer can achieve.

Finally, we note that high-performance microprocessor designs tend to have generous power budgets that FPGAs do not enjoy, and this has an impact that is embedded in the area and speed comparisons.

4. FPGA VS. CUSTOM CMOS

4.1 Complete Processor Cores

We begin by comparing complete processor cores implemented on an FPGA vs. custom CMOS to provide context for the building block measurements. Table 3 shows a comparison of the area and delay of four commercial processors that have both custom CMOS and FPGA implementations and includes in-order, multithreaded, and complex out-of-order processors. The FPGA implementations are synthesized from RTL code for the custom CMOS processors, with some FPGA-specific circuit-level optimizations. However, the FPGA-specific optimization effort is smaller than for custom CMOS designs and could inflate the area and delay ratios slightly. Overall, custom processors have delay ratios of 18-26× and area ratios of 17-27×, with no obvious trends with processor complexity.

The OpenSPARC T1 and T2 cores are derived from the Sun UltraSPARC T1 and T2, respectively [21]. Both cores are in-order multithreaded, and use the 64-bit SPARC V9 instruction set. The OpenSPARC T2 has the encryption unit from the UltraSPARC T2 removed, although we believe the change is small enough to not significantly skew our measurements.

The Intel Atom is a reduced-voltage dual-issue in-order 64-bit x86 processor with two-way multithreading. The FPGA synthesis by Wang et al. includes only the processor core without L2 cache, and occupies 85% of the largest 65 nm Virtex-5 FPGA (XC5VLX330) [10]. Our FPGA area metric assumes the core area of the largest Virtex 5 is the same as the Stratix III, 412 mm².

The Intel Nehalem is a high-performance multiple-issue out-of-order 64-bit x86 processor with two-way multithreading. The Nehalem's core area was estimated from a die photo. The FPGA synthesis by Schelle et al. does not include the per-core L2 cache, and occupies roughly 300% of the largest Virtex-5 FPGA [19]. Because the FPGA synthesis is split over multiple chips and runs at 520 kHz, it is not useful for estimating delay ratio.

4.2 SRAM Blocks

SRAM blocks are commonly used in processors for building caches and register files. SRAM performance can be characterized by latency and throughput. Custom SRAM designs can trade latency and throughput by pipelining, while FPGA designs are typically limited to the types of hard SRAM blocks that exist on the FPGA. SRAMs on the Stratix III FPGA can be implemented using two sizes of hard block SRAM, LUTRAM, or in registers and LUTs. Their throughput and density are compared in Table 4 to five high-performance custom SRAMs in 65 nm processes.

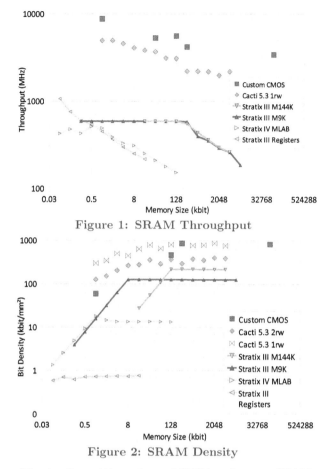

Figure 1: SRAM Throughput

Figure 2: SRAM Density

The density and throughput of FPGA and custom SRAMs is plotted against memory size in Figures 1 and 2. The plots include data from CACTI 5.3, a CMOS memory performance and area model [27]. The throughput ratio between FPGA memories and custom is 7-10×, lower than the overall delay ratio of 18-26×, showing that SRAMs are relatively fast on FPGAs. It is surprising that this ratio is not lower because FPGA SRAM blocks have little programmability. The FPGA data above use 32-bit wide data ports that slightly underutilize the native 36-bit ports. The raw density of an FPGA SRAM block is listed in Table 4.

Below 9 kbit, the bit density of FPGA RAMs falls off nearly linearly with reducing RAM size because M9Ks are underutilized, and the MLAB density is low. For larger arrays with good utilization, FPGA SRAM arrays have a density ratio of only 2-5× vs. single read-write port (1rw) CMOS (and CACTI) SRAMs, far below the full processor area ratio of 17-27×.

As FPGA SRAMs use dual-ported (2rw) arrays, we also plotted CACTI's 2rw model for comparison. For arrays of similar size, the bit density of CACTI's 2rw models are 1.9× and 1.5× the raw bit density of fully-utilized M9K and M144K memory blocks, respectively. This suggests that half of the bit density gap between FPGA and custom in our single-ported test is due to FPGA memories paying the overhead of dual ports.

For register file use where latency may be more important than memory density, custom processors have the option of trading throughput for area and power by using faster and larger storage cells. The 65 nm Pentium 4 register file trades 5× bit density for 9 GHz single-cycle performance

Processor	Custom CMOS		FPGA		Logic Utilization (ALUT)	Ratios	
	f_{max} (MHz)	Area (mm^2)	f_{max} (MHz)	Area (mm^2)		f_{max}	Area
OpenSPARC T1 (90 nm) [16]	1800	6.0	79	100	86 597	23	17
OpenSPARC T2 (65 nm) [17]	1600	11.7	88	294	250 235	18	25
Atom (45 nm) [10,18]	>1300	12.8	50	350	85%	26	27
Nehalem (45 nm) [19,20]	3000	51	-	1240	300%	-	24
Geometric Mean						22	23

Table 3: Complete Processor Cores. Area and delay normalized to 65 nm.

Design	Ports	Size (kbit)	f_{max} (MHz)	Area (mm^2)	Bit Density (kbit/mm^2)	Ratios	
						f_{max}	Density
IBM 6T 65 nm [22]	2r or 1w	128	5600 1.2 V	0.276	464	9.5	2.1
Intel 6T 65 nm [23]	1rw	256	4200 1.2 V	0.3	853	7.6	3.9
Intel 6T 65 nm [14]	1rw	70 Mb	3430 1.2 V	110 [24]	820	–	–
IBM 8T 65 nm SOI [25]	1r1w	32	5300 1.2 V	–	–	9.0	–
Intel 65 nm Regfile [26]	1r1w	1	8800 1.2 V	0.017	59	18	3.3
Registers	1r1w	-	-	-	0.77		
MLAB	1r1w	640 b	~600	0.033	23		
M9K	1r1w	9	590	0.064	142		
M144K	1r1w	144	590	0.59	244		

Table 4: Custom and FPGA SRAM Blocks

Ports	CACTI 5.3		FPGA		Ratios	
	f_{max} (MHz)	Density ($\frac{kbit}{mm^2}$)	f_{max} (MHz)	Density ($\frac{kbit}{mm^2}$)	f_{max}	Density
2r1w	4430	109	501	15.7	9	7
4r2w	4200	35	320	0.25	13	143
6r3w	3800	17	286	0.20	13	89
8r4w	3970	9.8	269	0.15	15	65
10r5w	3740	6.3	266	0.10	14	61
12r6w	3520	4.5	249	0.090	14	51
14r7w	3330	3.4	237	0.080	14	43
16r8w	3160	2.7	224	0.068	14	39
Live Value Table (LVT)						
4r2w			420	1.50	10	23
8r4w			345	0.41	12	24

Table 5: Multiported 2 kbit SRAM. LVT data from LaForest et al. [28].

[26]. FPGA RAMs lack this flexibility, and the delay ratio is even greater (18×) for this specific use.

4.3 Multiported SRAM Blocks

FPGA hard SRAM blocks can typically implement up to two read-write ports (2rw). Increasing the number of read ports can be achieved reasonably efficiently by replicating the memory blocks but increasing the number of write ports cannot. A multi-write port RAM can be implemented using registers for storage, but it is inefficient. A more efficient method using hard RAM blocks for most of the storage replicates memory blocks for each write and read port and uses a live value table (LVT) to indicate for each word which of the replicated memories holds the most recent copy [28]. We present data for multiported RAMs implemented using registers, LVT-based multiported memories [28], and CACTI 5.3 models of custom CMOS multiported RAMs. We focus on a 64×32-bit (2 kbit) memory array with twice as many read ports as write ports (2N read, N write) because it is similar to register files in processors. Table 5 shows the throughput and density comparisons.

The custom vs. FPGA bit density ratio is 7× for 2r1w, and increases to 23× and 143× for 4r2w LVT- and register-based memories, respectively. The delay ratio is 9× for 2r1w, and increases to 10× and 13× for 4r2w LVT- and register-based memories, respectively, a smaller impact than the area ratio increase.

4.4 Content-Addressable Memories

A Content-Addressable Memory (CAM) is a logic circuit that allows associative searches of its stored contents. Custom CMOS CAMs are implemented as dense arrays using 9T to 11T cells compared to 6T in SRAM, and are about 2-3× less dense than SRAMs. Ternary CAMs use two storage cells per "bit" to store three states (0, 1, and don't-care), a capability often used for longest prefix searches in network packet routers. In processors, CAMs are used in tag arrays for high-associativity caches and TLBs. CAM-like structures are also used in out-of-order instruction schedulers. CAMs in processors require both frequent read and write capability, but not large capacities. Pagiamtzis and Sheikholeslami give a good overview of the CAM design space [29].

There are several methods of implementing CAM functionality on FPGAs [30]. CAMs implemented in soft logic use registers for storage and LUTs to read, write, and search the stored bits. Another proposal, which we call BRAM-CAM, stores one-hot encoded match-line values in block RAM to provide the functionality of a $w \times b$-bit CAM using a $2^b \times w$-bit block RAM [31]. The soft logic CAM is the only design that provides one-cycle writes, while the BRAM-CAM offers improved bit density with two-cycle writes. We do not consider CAM implementations with even longer write times.

Table 6 shows a variety of custom CMOS and FPGA CAM designs. Figures 3 and 4 plot these and also 8-bit

	Size	Search Time	Bit Density	Ratios	
	(bits)	(ns)	$(\frac{kbit}{mm^2})$	Delay	Density
Ternary CAMs					
IBM 64×72 [32]	4 608	0.6	-	5.0	-
IBM 64×240 [32]	15 360	2.2	167	1.7	205
Binary CAMs					
POWER6 8×60 [33]	480	<0.2	-	14	-
Godson-3 64×64 [34]	4 096	0.55	76	5	99
Intel 64×128 [35]	8 192	0.25	167	14	209
FPGA Binary CAMs					
Soft logic 64×72	4 608	3.0	0.82		
Soft logic 64×240	15 360	3.8	0.81		
Soft logic 8×60	480	2.1	0.83		
Soft logic 64×64	4 096	2.9	0.77		
Soft logic 64×128	8 192	3.4	0.80		
MLAB-CAM 64×20	1 280	4.5	1.0		
M9K-CAM 64×16	1 024	2.0	2.0		

Table 6: CAM Designs

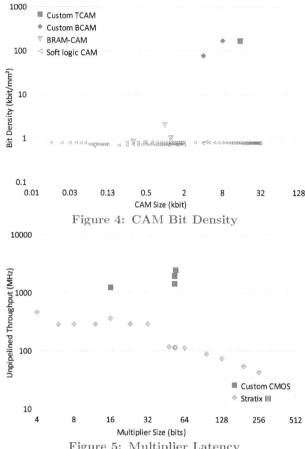

Figure 4: CAM Bit Density

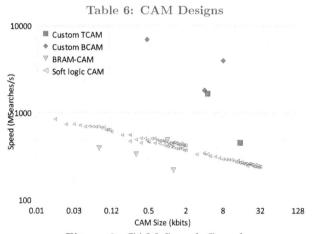

Figure 3: CAM Search Speed

Figure 5: Multiplier Latency

4.5 Multipliers

Multiplication is an operation performed frequently in signal processing applications, but not used as often in processors. Multiplier blocks can also be used to inefficiently implement shifters and multiplexers [39].

Figure 5 shows the latency of multiplier circuits on custom CMOS and on FPGA using hard DSP blocks. Latency is the product of the cycle time and the number of pipeline stages, and does not adjust for unbalanced pipeline stages or pipeline latch overheads. Table 7 shows details of the design examples. The two IBM multipliers have latency ratios comparable to full processor cores. Intel's 16-bit multiplier design has much lower latency ratios as it appears to target low power instead of delay. Because custom multiplier de-

and 128-bit soft logic CAMs of varying depth. Because of high power consumption, CAMs often have three competing design goals: delay, density, and energy per bit per search. CAMs can achieve delay comparable to SRAMs but at a high cost in power. Both the POWER6 TLB and Intel's 64×128 BCAM achieve at least 4 GHz, but the latter uses 13 fJ/bit/search while IBM's 450 MHz 64×240 TCAM uses 1 fJ/bit/search. While Intel's BCAM and the Godson-3 TLB are both 64-entry full-custom designs, Intel achieves twice the bit density and half the cycle time at equal energy per bit per search, highlighting the impact of good circuit design, layout, and process technology.

As shown in Table 6, soft logic CAMs have poor 100-210× bit density ratios vs. custom CAMs. Despite the low density, the delay ratio is only 14×. BRAM-CAMs built from M9Ks can offer 2.4× better density than soft logic CAMs but halved write bandwidth. Despite the higher port-width/depth aspect ratio, MLAB BRAM-CAMs have bit density worse than M9K-CAMs because of control logic overhead. The halved write bandwidth of BRAM-CAMs make them unsuitable for performance-critical uses, such as tag matching in instruction schedulers and L1 caches.

We observe that the bit density of soft logic CAMs is nearly the same as using registers to implement RAM (Table 4), suggesting that the area inefficiency comes from using registers for storage, not the associative search itself.

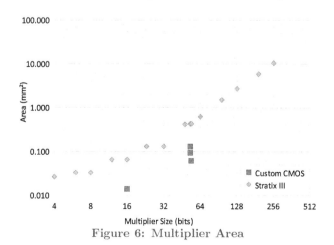

Figure 6: Multiplier Area

Design	Size	Stages	Latency (ns)	Area (mm²)	Ratios Latency	Ratios Area
Intel 90 nm 1.3 V [36]	16×16	1	0.81	0.014	3.4	4.7
IBM 90 nm SOI 1.4 V [37]	54×54	4	0.41	0.062	22	7.0
IBM 90 nm SOI 1.3 V [38]	53×53	3	0.51	0.095	17	4.5
Stratix III	16×16	1	2.8	0.066		
Stratix III	54×54	1	8.8	0.43		

Table 7: Multiplier area and delay, normalized to 65 nm process. Unpipelined latency is pipelined cycle time×stages.

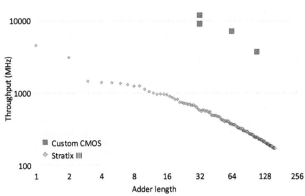

Figure 7: Adder Delay

signs are often more deeply pipelined (3 and 4 stages) than the hard multipliers on FPGAs (2 stages), throughput ratios are higher than latency ratios.

The area of the custom CMOS and FPGA multipliers are plotted in Figure 6. The area ratios of 4.5-7.0× are much lower than for full processor cores.

4.6 Adders

Custom CMOS adder circuit designs can span the area-delay trade-off space from slow ripple-carry adders to fast parallel adders. On an FPGA, adders are usually implemented using hard carry chains that implement variations of the ripple-carry adder, although carry-select adders have been also been used. Although parallel adders can be implemented with soft logic and routing, the lack of dedicated circuitry means parallel adders are bigger and slower than the ripple-carry adder with hard carry chains [44].

Figure 7 plots a comparison of adder delay, with details in

Design	Size (bit)	f_{max} (MHz)	Area (mm²)	Delay Ratio	Area Ratio
Agah et al. [40]	32	12 000 1.3 V	-	20	-
Kao et al. 90 nm [41]	64	7 100 1.3 V	0.016	19	4.5
Pentium 4 [42]	32	9 000 1.3 V	-	16	-
IBM [43]	108	3 700 1.0 V	0.017	15	6.9
Stratix III	32	593	0.035		
	64	374	0.071		
	108	242	0.119		

Table 8: Adders. Area and delay normalized to 65 nm process.

Mux Inputs	FPGA Area (mm²)	FPGA Delay (ps)	Custom Delay (ps)	Delay Ratio
2	0.0011	210	2.8	74
4	0.0011	260	4.9	53
8	0.0022	500	9.1	54
16	0.0055	680	18	37
32	0.0100	940	29	32
64	0.0232	1200	54	21

Table 9: Analytical model of passive tree multiplexers [45] normalized to 65 nm process.

Table 8. The Pentium 4 delay is conservative as the delay is for the full integer ALU. FPGA adders achieve delay ratios of 15-20× and a low area ratio of around 4.5-7×.

4.7 Multiplexers

Multiplexers are found in many circuits, yet we have found little literature that provides their area and delay in custom CMOS. Instead, we estimate delays of small multiplexers using an RC analytical model and the delays of the Pentium 4 shifter unit and the Stratix III ALM. Our area ratio estimate comes from an indirect measurement using the ALM.

Table 9 shows a delay comparison between FPGA and an analytical model of switch-based tree multiplexers [45]. This passive switch model is pessimistic for larger multiplexers, as active buffer elements can reduce delay. On an FPGA, small multiplexers can often be combined with other logic with minimal extra delay and area, so multiplexers measured in isolation are likely pessimistic. For small multiplexers, the delay ratio is high, roughly 40-75×. Larger multiplexers appear to have decreasing delay ratios, but we believe this is largely due to the unsuitability of passive designs.

The 65 nm Pentium 4 integer shifter datapath [42] is dominated by small multiplexers (sizes 3, 4, and 8), but not in isolation. We implemented the datapath (Figure 8) excluding control logic on the Stratix III, with results shown in Table 10. The delay ratio of 20× is smaller than suggested by the isolated multiplexer comparison, but may be optimistic if Intel omitted details from their shifter circuit diagram. Another delay ratio estimate can be made by examining the Stratix III Adaptive Logic Module itself, as its delay consists mainly of multiplexers. Configuration RAM hold static values and do not affect delay. We implemented a circuit equivalent to an ALM as described in the Stratix III Handbook [46], comparing delays of the FPGA implementation to custom CMOS delays of the ALM given by the Quartus timing models. Internal LUTs are modeled as multiplexers. Each ALM input pin is modeled as a 21-to-1 multiplexer, as 21 to 30 are reasonable sizes according to Lewis et al. [47].

We examined one long path and one short path out of many possible timing paths through the ALM. The long and short timing paths begin after the input multiplexers for pins datab0 and dataf0, respectively, both terminating at the LUT register. We placed these two paths into separate clock domains to ensure they were independently optimized. Table 10 shows delay ratios of 7.1× and 11.7× for the long and short paths, respectively. These delay ratios are lower compared to previous examples due to the lower power and area budgets preventing custom FPGAs from being as aggressively delay-optimized as custom processors, and to

Circuit	FPGA Delay (ps)	Custom Delay (ps)	Ratio
65 nm Pentium 4 Shifter	2260	111	20
Stratix III ALM			
Long path	2500	350	7.1
Short path	800	68	11.7

Table 10: Delay of Multiplexer-Dominated Circuits

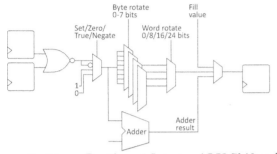

Figure 8: 65 nm Pentium 4 Integer ALU Shifter [42]

Design	Register Delay (ps)	Delay Ratio
Sprangle et al. [48]	35 (90 ps in 180 nm)	12
Hartstein et al. [49]	32 (2.5 FO4)	14
Hrishikesh et al. [50]	23 (1.8 FO4)	19
Geometric Mean	29.5	15
Stratix III	436	-

Table 11: Pipeline Latch Delay

extra circuit complexity not shown in the Stratix III Handbook.

We estimate the multiplexer area ratio indirectly by again implementing the equivalent circuit of an ALM on a Stratix III. We find that our equivalent ALM consumes 104 ALUTs, or roughly 52 ALMs. An area ratio of 52× is the ratio of the area of the FPGA equivalent circuit (52 ALMs) compared to the silicon area of the custom circuit (1 ALM equivalent). The real area ratio is substantially greater, as we implemented only the ALM's input and internal multiplexers and did not include global routing resources or configuration RAM. A rule of thumb is that half of an FPGA's core area is spent in the programmable global routing network, for an area ratio estimate of 104×. We expect this to be even higher once configuration RAM and other ALM complexities are accounted for.

Groups of multiplexers have delay ratios below 20×, with small isolated multiplexers being worse (40-75×). However, multiplexers are particularly area-intensive with an area ratio greater than 100×. Thus we find that the intuition that multiplexers are expensive is justified, especially from an area perspective.

4.8 Pipeline Latches

In synchronous circuits, the maximum clock speed of a circuit is typically limited by a register-to-register delay path from a pipeline latch[2], through a pipeline stage's combinational logic, to the next set of pipeline latches. The delay of a pipeline latch (setup and clock-to-output times) impacts the speed of a circuit and the clock speed improvement when increasing pipeline depth.

The "effective" cost of inserting an extra pipeline register into LUT-based pipeline logic is measured by observing the increase in delay as the number of LUTs between registers increases, then extrapolating the delay to zero LUTs. Table 11 shows estimates of the delay cost of a custom CMOS pipeline stage. The 180 nm Pentium 4 design assumed 90 ps of pipeline latch delays including clock skew [48], which we

---

[2]Latch refers to pipeline storage elements. This can be a latch, flip-flop, or other implementation.

scaled according to the FO1 ring oscillator delays for Intel's processes (11 ps at 180 nm to 4.25 ps at 65 nm) [14]. Hartstein et al. and Hrishikesh et al. present estimates expressed in FO4 delays, which were scaled to an estimated FO4 delay of 12.8 ps for Intel's 65 nm process.

The delay ratio for a pipeline latch is 10-15×. Although we do not have area comparisons, registers are considered to occupy very little FPGA area because more LUTs are used than registers in most FPGA circuits, yet FPGA logic elements include at least one register for every LUT.

4.9 Point-to-Point Routing

Interconnect delay comprises a significant portion of the total delay in both FPGAs and modern CMOS processes. Figure 9 plots the point-to-point wire delays for three classes of interconnect (local, intermediate, and global), and FPGA routing delay both in absolute distance and normalized for decreased FPGA area efficiency.

We model each buffered segment as an RC delay as illustrated in Figure 10 and Equation 1, where h is the buffer transistor size and R_{tr} is the linearized buffer resistance. Buffered wires are modeled as multiple identical segments with the number of segments chosen to minimize delay, while minimum-delay buffer transistor sizing can be found by differentiating Equation 1 with respect to h. Equation 1 is modified from Bakoglu and Meindl to include transistor gate (C_g) and junction (C_d) lumped capacitances and to model 50%-to-50% delay instead of 0-to-90% delay [51].

$$T = R_{tr}C_d + (\frac{1}{h}R_{tr} + \frac{1}{2}R_{int})C_{int} + (\frac{1}{h}R_{tr} + R_{int})hC_g \quad (1)$$

We use interconnect and transistor parameters from the International Technology Roadmap for Semiconductors (ITRS) 2007 report [52]. We model the minimum pitch for each class of wiring (local, intermediate, global). Buffers are assumed to be inverters with 2:1 PMOS to NMOS transistor size ratio, and junction capacitance is approximated as half of gate capacitance. Gate and junction capacitances are modeled as lump capacitances and wires are modeled as distributed RC. Interconnect delays using ITRS 2007 data may be pessimistic, as Intel's 65 nm process reports lower delays using larger pitch and wire thicknesses [14].

The point-to-point delay on FPGA is measured using the delay between two manually-placed registers, with the delay of the register itself subtracted out, and includes the overhead of routing programmability. Assuming LABs have an aspect ratio (the vertical/horizontal ratio of delay for each LAB) of 1.6 gives a good delay vs. Manhattan distance fit. The physical distance is calculated from LAB coordinates using the aspect ratio and area of a LAB (Table 2).

In Figure 9, the delay of the CMOS load and driving buffers (one FO1) dominates the delay for CMOS short wire lengths under 20 μm. FPGA short local wires (100 μm) have a delay ratio around 9×. Long global wire delay is quite close

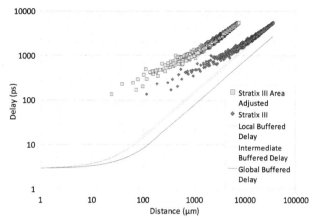

Figure 9: Point-to-Point Routing Delay

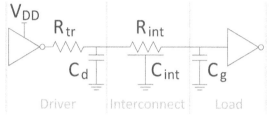

Figure 10: RC Model of Wire Delay

	Custom CMOS	FPGA [53]	Ratio
DDR2 Frequency (MHz)	533	400	1.3
DDR3 Frequency (MHz)	800	533	1.5
Read Latency (ns)	55-65	100-133	2

Table 12: Off-Chip DRAM Latency and Throughput. Latency assumes closed-page random accesses.

Design	Delay Ratio	Area Ratio
Processor Cores	18 - 26	17 - 27
SRAM 1rw	7 - 10	2 - 5
SRAM 4r2w LUTs / LVT	13 / 10	143 / 23
CAM	14	100 - 210
Multiplier	17 - 22	4.5 - 7.0
Adder	15 - 20	4.5 - 7.0
Multiplexer	20 - 75	> 100
Pipeline latch	12 - 19	-
Routing	9 - 20	-
Off-Chip Memory	1.3 - 2	-

Table 13: Delay and Area Ratio Summary

($2\times$) to CMOS for the same length of wire.

Routing delays are more meaningful when "distance" is normalized to the amount of "logic" that can be reached. To approximate this metric, we adjust the FPGA routing distance by the square-root of the FPGA's overall area overhead vs. custom CMOS ($\sqrt{23\times} = 4.8\times$). Short local FPGA wires (100 µm) have a logic density-normalized delay ratio $20\times$, while long global wires (7 500 µm) have a delay ratio of only $9\times$. The short wire delay ratio is comparable to the overall delay overhead for full processors, but the long wire delay ratio is half that, suggesting that FPGAs are less affected by long wire delays than custom CMOS.

4.10 Off-Chip Memory

Table 12 gives a brief overview of off-chip DRAM latency and bandwidth as commonly used in processor systems. Random read latency is measured on Intel DDR2 and DDR3 systems with off-chip (65 ns) and on-die (55 ns) memory controllers. FPGA memory latency is the sum of the memory controller latency and closed-page DRAM access time. While these estimates do not account for real access patterns, they are enough to show that off-chip latency and throughput ratios between custom CMOS and FPGA are far lower than for in-core circuits like complete processors.

4.11 Summary of Building Block Circuits

A summary of our estimates for the FPGA vs. custom CMOS delay and area ratios can be found in Table 13. The range of delay ratios ($8-75\times$) is smaller than the range of area ratios ($2-210\times$). Multiplexers have the highest delay ratios and hard blocks only have a small impact on delay ratios. Hard blocks are particularly area-efficient (SRAM, adders, multipliers), while multiplexers and CAMs are particularly area-inefficient.

In previous work, Kuon and Rose reported an average of $3.0-3.5\times$ delay ratio and $18-35\times$ area ratio for FPGA vs. standard cell ASIC for a set of complete circuits [4]. Al-

though we expect both ratios to be higher when comparing FPGA against custom CMOS, our processor core delay ratios are higher but area ratios are slightly lower, likely due to custom processors being optimized more for delay at the expense of area compared to typical standard cell circuits.

5. IMPACT ON MICROARCHITECTURE

The area and delay differences between circuit types and substrates measured in Section 4 affects the microarchitectural design of circuits targeting custom CMOS vs. targeting FPGAs. As FPGA designs often have logic utilization (area) as a primary design constraint, we expect that area ratios will have more impact on microarchitecture than delay ratios.

5.1 Pipeline Depth

Pipeline depth is one of the fundamental choices in the design of a processor microarchitecture. Increasing pipeline depth results in higher clock speeds, but with diminishing returns due to pipeline latch delays. The analysis by Hartstein et al. shows that the optimal processor pipeline depth for performance is proportional to $\sqrt{\frac{t_p}{t_o}}$, where t_p is the total logic delay of the processor pipeline, and t_o is the delay overhead of a pipeline latch [49].

Section 4.8 showed that the delay ratio of registers (i.e., t_o FPGA vs. t_o custom CMOS, $\sim 15\times$) on FPGAs is lower than that of a complete processor (approximately t_p FPGA vs. t_p custom CMOS, $\sim 22\times$), increasing t_p/t_o on FPGA. The change in t_p/t_o is roughly $(22/15)$, suggesting soft processors should have pipeline depths roughly 20% longer compared to an equivalent microarchitecture implemented in custom CMOS. Today's soft processors prefer short pipelines [54] because soft processors are simple and have low t_p, and not due to a property of the FPGA substrate.

5.2 Partitioning of Structures

The portion of a chip that can be reached in a single clock cycle is decreasing with each newer process, while transistor switching speeds continue to improve. This leads to microarchitectures that partition large structures into smaller ones and partition the design into clusters or multiple cores to avoid global communication [7].

In Section 4.9, we observed that after adjustment for the reduced logic density of FPGAs, long wires have a delay ratio roughly half that of a processor core. The relatively faster long wires lessen the impact of global communication, reducing the need for aggressive partitioning of designs for FPGAs. In practice, FPGA processors have less logic complexity than high-performance custom processors, further reducing the need to partition.

5.3 ALUs and Bypassing

Multiplexers consume much more area on FPGAs than custom CMOS (Section 4.7), making bypass networks that shuffle operands between functional units more expensive on FPGAs. The functional units themselves are often composed of adders and multipliers and have a lower 4.5-7× area ratio. The high cost of multiplexers reduces the area benefit of using multiplexers to share these functional units.

There are processor microarchitecture techniques that reduce the size of operand-shuffling networks relative to the number of ALUs. "Fused" ALUs that perform two or more dependent operations at a time increase the amount of computation relative to operand shuffling, such as the common fused multiply-accumulate unit and interlock collapsing ALUs [55,56]. Other proposals cluster instructions together to reduce the communication of operand values to instructions outside the group [57,58]. These techniques may benefit soft processors even more than hard processors.

5.4 Cache Organization

Set-associative caches have two common implementation styles. Low associativity caches replicate the cache tag RAM and access them in parallel, while high associativity caches store tags in CAMs. High associativity caches are more expensive on FPGAs because of the high area cost of CAMs (100-210× bit density ratio). In addition, custom CMOS caches built from tag CAM and data RAM blocks can have the CAM's decoded match lines directly drive the RAM's word lines, while an FPGA CAM must produce encoded outputs that are then decoded by the SRAM, adding a redundant encode-decode operation that was not included in the circuits in Section 4.4. In comparison, custom CMOS CAMs have minimal delay and 2-3× area overhead compared to RAM allowing for high-associativity caches to have an amortized area overhead of around 10%, with minimal change in delay compared to set-associative caches [59].

CAM-based high-associativity caches are not area efficient in FPGA soft processors and soft processor caches should have lower associativity than similar hard processors. Soft processor caches should also be higher capacity than similar hard processors because of the area efficiency of FPGA SRAMs (2-5× density ratio).

5.5 Memory System Design

The lower area cost of block RAM encourages the use of larger caches, reducing cache miss rates and lowering the demand for off-chip bandwidth to DRAM main memory. The lower clock speeds of FPGA circuits further reduce off-chip bandwidth demand. The latency and bandwidth of off-chip memory is only slightly worse on FPGAs than on custom CMOS processors.

Low off-chip memory system demands suggest that more resources should be dedicated to improving the performance of the processor core than improving memory bandwidth or tolerating latency. Techniques used to improve the memory system in hard processors include DRAM access scheduling, non-blocking caches, prefetching, memory dependence speculation, and out of order memory accesses.

5.6 Out-of-Order Microarchitecture

Section 4.1 suggests that processor complexity does not have a strong correlation with area ratio, so out-of-order microarchitectures seem to be a reasonable method for improving soft processor performance. There are several styles of microarchitectures commonly used to implement precise interrupt support in pipelined or out-of-order processors and many variations are used in modern processors [60,61]. The main variations between the microarchitecture styles concern the organization of the reorder buffer, register renaming logic, register file, and instruction scheduler and whether each component uses RAM- or CAM-based implementations.

FPGA RAMs have particularly low area cost (Section 4.2), but CAMs are area expensive (Section 4.4). These characteristics favour microarchitecture styles that minimize the use of CAM-like structures. Reorder buffers, register renaming logic, and register files are commonly implemented without CAMs. There are CAM-free instruction scheduler techniques that are not widely implemented [6,62], but may become more favourable in soft processors.

If a traditional CAM-based scheduler is used in a soft processor, its capacity would tend to be smaller than on hard processors due to area, but the delay ratio of CAMs (15×) is not particularly poor. Reducing scheduler area can be done by reducing the number of entries or the amount of storage required per entry. Schedulers can be data-capturing where operand values are captured and stored in the scheduler, or non-data-capturing where the scheduler tracks only the availability of operands, with values fetched from the register file or bypass networks when an instruction is finally issued. Non-data-capturing schedulers reduce the amount of data that must be stored in each entry of a scheduler.

On FPGAs, block RAMs come in a limited selection of sizes, with the smallest commonly being 4.5 kbit to 18 kbit. Reorder buffers and register files are usually even smaller but are limited by port width or port count so processors on FPGAs can have larger capacity ROBs, register files, and other port-limited RAM structures at little extra cost. In contrast, expensive CAMs limit soft processors to small scheduling windows (instruction scheduler size). Microarchitectures that address this particular problem of large instruction windows with small scheduling windows may be useful in soft processors [63].

6. CONCLUSIONS

We have presented area and delay comparisons of processors and their building block circuits implemented on custom CMOS and FPGA substrates. In 65 nm processes, we find FPGA implementations of processor cores have 18-26× greater delay and 17-27× greater area usage than the same processors implemented using custom CMOS. We find that the FPGA vs. custom delay ratios of most processor building block circuits fall within the delay ratio range for complete processor cores, but that area ratios vary more. Building block circuits such as adders and SRAMs that have dedicated hardware support on FPGAs are particularly area-efficient, while multiplexers and CAMs are particularly area-inefficient. The measurements' precision is limited by the availability of custom CMOS design examples in the literature. The measurements can also change as both CMOS technology and FPGA architectures evolve and may lead to different design choices.

We have discussed how our measurements impact microarchitecture design choices: Differences in the FPGA substrate encourage soft processors to have larger, low-associativity caches, deeper pipelines, and fewer bypass networks than similar hard processors. Also, out-of-order execution is a valid design option for soft processors, although scheduling windows should be kept small.

7. REFERENCES

[1] Altera. Nios II processor. http://www.altera.com/products/ip/processors/nios2/.

[2] Xilinx. MicroBlaze soft processor. http://www.xilinx.com/tools/microblaze.htm.

[3] ARM. Cortex-M1 processor. http://www.arm.com/products/processors/cortex-m/cortex-m1.php.

[4] I. Kuon and J. Rose. Measuring the Gap Between FPGAs and ASICs. *IEEE Trans. Computer-Aided Design of Integrated Circuits and Systems*, 26(2), Feb. 2007.

[5] D. Chinnery and K. Keutzer. *Closing the Gap Between ASIC & Custom, Tools and Techniques for High-Performance ASIC Design.* Kluwer Academic Publishers, 2002.

[6] S. Palacharla et al. Complexity-Effective Superscalar Processors. *SIGARCH Comp. Arch. News*, 25(2), 1997.

[7] V. Agarwal et al. Clock Rate versus IPC: The End of the Road for Conventional Microarchitectures. *SIGARCH Comp. Arch. News*, 28(2), 2000.

[8] P. Metzgen and D. Nancekievill. Multiplexer Restructuring for FPGA Implementation Cost Reduction. In *Proc. DAC*, 2005.

[9] P. Metzgen. A High Performance 32-bit ALU for Programmable Logic. In *Proc. FPGA*, 2004.

[10] P. H. Wang et al. Intel Atom Processor Core Made FPGA-Synthesizable. In *Proc. FPGA*, 2009.

[11] S.-L. Lu et al. An FPGA-based Pentium in a Complete Desktop System. In *Proc. FPGA*, 2007.

[12] S. Tyagi et al. An Advanced Low Power, High Performance, Strained Channel 65nm Technology. In *Proc. IEDM*, 2005.

[13] K. Mistry et al. A 45nm logic technology with high-k+metal gate transistors, strained silicon, 9 cu interconnect layers, 193nm dry patterning, and 100% pb-free packaging. In *Proc. IEDM*, 2007.

[14] P. Bai et al. A 65nm Logic Technology Featuring 35nm Gate Lengths, Enhanced Channel Strain, 8 Cu Interconnect Layers, Low-k ILD and 0.57 μm^2 SRAM Cell. In *Proc. IEDM*, 2004.

[15] S.K.H. Fung et al. 65nm CMOS High Speed, General Purpose and Low Power Transistor Technology for High Volume Foundry Application. In *Proc. VLSI*, 2004.

[16] A. S. Leon et al. A Power-Efficient High-Throughput 32-Thread SPARC Processor. *IEEE Journal of Solid-State Circuits*, 42(1), 2007.

[17] U.G. Nawathe et al. Implementation of an 8-Core, 64-Thread, Power-Efficient SPARC Server on a Chip. *IEEE Journal of Solid-State Circuits*, 43(1), 2008.

[18] G. Gerosa et al. A Sub-2 W Low Power IA Processor for Mobile Internet Devices in 45 nm High-k Metal Gate CMOS. *IEEE Journal of Solid-State Circuits*, 44(1), 2009.

[19] G. Schelle et al. Intel Nehalem Processor Core Made FPGA Synthesizable. In *Proc. FPGA*, 2010.

[20] R. Kumar and G. Hinton. A Family of 45nm IA Processors. In *Proc. ISSCC*, 2009.

[21] Sun Microsystems. OpenSPARC. http://www.opensparc.net/.

[22] J. Davis et al. A 5.6GHz 64kB Dual-Read Data Cache for the POWER6 Processor. In *Proc. ISSCC*, 2006.

[23] M. Khellah et al. A 4.2GHz 0.3mm² 256kb Dual-V_{cc} SRAM Building Block in 65nm CMOS. In *Proc. ISSCC*, 2006.

[24] P. Bai. Foils from "A 65nm Logic Technology Featuring 35nm Gate Lengths, Enhanced Channel Strain, 8 Cu Interconnect Layers, Low-k ILD and 0.57 0.57 μm^2 SRAM Cell". IEDM, 2004.

[25] L. Chang et al. A 5.3GHz 8T-SRAM with Operation Down to 0.41V in 65nm CMOS. In *Proc. VLSI*, 2007.

[26] S. Hsu et al. An 8.8GHz 198mW 16x64b 1R/1W Variation-Tolerant Register File in 65nm CMOS. In *Proc. ISSCC*, 2006.

[27] S. Thoziyoor et al. CACTI 5.1. Technical report, HP Laboratories, Palo Alto, 2008.

[28] C. E. LaForest and J. G. Steffan. Efficient Multi-Ported Memories for FPGAs. In *Proc. FPGA*, 2010.

[29] K. Pagiamtzis and A. Sheikholeslami. Content-Addressable Memory (CAM) Circuits and Architectures: A Tutorial and Survey. *IEEE Journal of Solid-State Circuits*, 2006.

[30] K. McLaughlin et al. Exploring CAM Design For Network Processing Using FPGA Technology. In *Proc. AICT-ICIW*, 2006.

[31] J.-L. Brelet and L. Gopalakrishnan. Using Virtex-II Block RAM for High Performance Read/Write CAMs. http://www.xilinx.com/support/documentation/application_notes/xapp260.pdf, 2002.

[32] I. Arsovski and R. Wistort. Self-Referenced Sense Amplifier for Across-Chip-Variation Immune Sensing in High-Performance Content-Addressable Memories. In *Proc. CICC*, 2006.

[33] D. W. Plass and Y. H. Chan. IBM POWER6 SRAM Arrays. *IBM Journal of Research and Development*, 51(6), 2007.

[34] W. Hu et al. Godson-3: A Scalable Multicore RISC Processor with x86 Emulation. *IEEE Micro*, 29(2), 2009.

[35] A. Agarwal et al. A Dual-Supply 4GHz 13fJ/bit/search 64×128b CAM in 65nm CMOS. In *Proc. ESSCIRC 32*, 2006.

[36] S.K. Hsu et al. A 110 GOPS/W 16-bit Multiplier and Reconfigurable PLA Loop in 90-nm CMOS. *IEEE Journal of Solid-State Circuits*, 41(1), 2006.

[37] W. Belluomini et al. An 8GHz Floating-Point Multiply. In *Proc. ISSCC*, 2005.

[38] J.B. Kuang et al. The Design and Implementation of Double-Precision Multiplier in a First-Generation CELL Processor. In *Proc. ICIDT*, 2005.

[39] P. Jamieson and J. Rose. Mapping Multiplexers onto Hard Multipliers in FPGAs. In *IEEE-NEWCAS*, 2005.

[40] A. Agah et al. Tertiary-Tree 12-GHz 32-bit Adder in 65nm Technology. In *Proc. ISCAS*, 2007.

[41] S. Kao et al. A 240ps 64b Carry-Lookahead Adder in 90nm CMOS. In *Proc. ISSCC*, 2006.

[42] S. B. Wijeratne et al. A 9-GHz 65-nm Intel Pentium 4 Processor Integer Execution Unit. *IEEE Journal of Solid-State Circuits*, 42(1), 2007.

[43] X. Y. Zhang et al. A 270ps 20mW 108-bit End-around Carry Adder for Multiply-Add Fused Floating Point Unit. *Signal Processing Systems*, 58(2), 2010.

[44] K. Vitoroulis and A.J. Al-Khalili. Performance of Parallel Prefix Adders Implemented with FPGA Technology. In *Proc. NEWCAS Workshop*, 2007.

[45] M. Alioto and G. Palumbo. Interconnect-Aware Design of Fast Large Fan-In CMOS Multiplexers. *IEEE Trans. Circuits and Systems II*, 2007.

[46] Altera. *Stratix III Device Handbook Volume 1*. 2009.

[47] D. Lewis et al. The Stratix II Logic and Routing Architecture. In *Proc. FPGA*, 2005.

[48] E. Sprangle and D. Carmean. Increasing Processor Performance by Implementing Deeper Pipelines. *SIGARCH Comp. Arch. News*, 30(2), 2002.

[49] A. Hartstein and T. R. Puzak. The Optimum Pipeline Depth for a Microprocessor. *SIGARCH Comp. Arch. News*, 30(2), 2002.

[50] M. S. Hrishikesh et al. The Optimal Logic Depth per Pipeline Stage is 6 to 8 FO4 Inverter Delays. In *Proc. ISCA 29*, 2002.

[51] H.B. Bakoglu and J.D. Meindl. Optimal Interconnection Circuits for VLSI. *IEEE Trans. Electron Devices*, 32(5), 1985.

[52] International Technology Roadmap for Semiconductors. http://www.itrs.net/Links/2007ITRS/Home2007.htm, 2007.

[53] Altera. *External Memory Interface Handbook, Volume 3*. 2010.

[54] Peter Yiannacouras et al. The Microarchitecture of FPGA-based Soft Processors. In *Proc. CASES*, 2005.

[55] N. Malik et al. Interlock Collapsing ALU for Increased Instruction-Level Parallelism. *SIGMICRO Newsl.*, 23(1-2), 1992.

[56] J. Phillips and S. Vassiliadis. High-Performance 3-1 Interlock Collapsing ALU's. *IEEE Trans. Computers*, 43(3), 1994.

[57] P. G. Sassone and D. S. Wills. Dynamic Strands: Collapsing Speculative Dependence Chains for Reducing Pipeline Communication. In *Proc. MICRO 37*, 2004.

[58] A. W. Bracy. *Mini-Graph Processing*. PhD thesis, University of Pennsylvania, 2008.

[59] M. Zhang and K. Asanovic. Highly-Associative Caches for Low-Power Processors. In *Kool Chips Workshop, Micro-33*, 2000.

[60] J.E. Smith and A.R. Pleszkun. Implementing Precise Interrupts in Pipelined Processors. *IEEE Trans. Computers*, 37(5), 1988.

[61] G.S. Sohi. Instruction Issue Logic for High-Performance, Interruptible, Multiple Functional Unit, Pipelined Computers. *IEEE Trans. Computers*, 39:349–359, 1990.

[62] F. J. Mesa-Martínez et al. SEED: Scalable, Efficient Enforcement of Dependences. In *Proc. PACT*, 2006.

[63] M. P. et al. A Decoupled KILO-Instruction Processor. *Proc. HPCA*, 2006.

VEGAS: Soft Vector Processor with Scratchpad Memory

Christopher H. Chou
cchou@ece.ubc.ca

Aaron Severance
aaronsev@ece.ubc.ca

Alex D. Brant
alexb@ece.ubc.ca

Zhiduo Liu
zhiduol@ece.ubc.ca

Saurabh Sant
ssant@ece.ubc.ca

Guy Lemieux
lemieux@ece.ubc.ca

Dept. of Elec. and Comp. Eng.
Univ. of British Columbia
Vancouver, Canada

ABSTRACT

This paper presents VEGAS, a new soft vector architecture, in which the vector processor reads and writes directly to a scratchpad memory instead of a vector register file. The scratchpad memory is a more efficient storage medium than a vector register file, allowing up to 9× more data elements to fit into on-chip memory. In addition, the use of fracturable ALUs in VEGAS allow efficient processing of bytes, halfwords and words in the same processor instance, providing up to 4× the operations compared to existing fixed-width soft vector ALUs. Benchmarks show the new VEGAS architecture is 10× to 208× faster than Nios II and has 1.7× to 3.1× better area-delay product than previous vector work, achieving much higher throughput per unit area. To put this performance in perspective, VEGAS is faster than a leading-edge Intel processor at integer matrix multiply. To ease programming effort and provide full debug support, VEGAS uses a C macro API that outputs vector instructions as standard NIOS II/f custom instructions.

Categories and Subject Descriptors

C.1.2 [**Multiple Data Stream Architectures (Multiprocessors)**]: Array and vector processors; C.3 [**Special-purpose and Application-based Systems**]: Real-time and Embedded systems

General Terms

Design, Experimentation, Measurement, Performance

Keywords

vector, SIMD, soft processors, scratchpad memory, FPGA

1. INTRODUCTION

FPGA-based embedded systems often use a soft processor for control purposes, but they use RTL blocks for performance-critical processing. Transferring some of these processing-intensive tasks onto a soft processor offers productivity, cost, and time-to-market advantages by reducing the amount of RTL design. In particular, soft processors allow algorithms to be easily modified without changing the FPGA bitstream, which could otherwise lead to convergence issues such as timing closure.

Unfortunately, traditional soft processors are too slow for most processing-intensive tasks. However, vector processing is known to accelerate data-parallel tasks. The VIRAM architecture [9] demonstrated that embedded tasks such as the EEMBC benchmark suite [1] can be accelerated with vectors. Embedded vector architectures SODA [12] and Ardbeg [18] were developed for low-power wireless applications which are also rich in data parallelism. VIRAM, SODA and Ardbeg were all developed for ASIC implementation, but the VESPA [20] and VIPERS [24, 23] processors demonstrate that soft vector architectures can be implemented efficiently and offer significant speedups on an FPGA as well.

This paper develops a new soft vector processor architecture called VEGAS. The two key distinguishing features of VEGAS are a cacheless scratchpad memory and the ability to fracture a 32-bit ALU into two 16-bit or four 8-bit ALUs at run-time. Combined, these two features make VEGAS more efficient with limited on-chip memory resources, allowing up to 9× more vector data elements to be stored on-chip and 4× more ALU engines. Benchmark results demonstrate that VEGAS offers up to 68% smaller area-delay product than VIPERS and VESPA, meaning it provides up to 3.1× the performance per unit area.

Scratchpads enable several performance enhancements. Instead of using traditional RISC-like vector load/store instructions, direct memory-memory operations are executed using the scratchpad. Source and destination operands are specified by vector address registers, each of which holds a scalar representing the starting address of the vector. To reduce loop overhead, VEGAS supports very large vector lengths, up to the full size of the scratchpad. Auto-increment of the address registers make it efficient to iterate through very long vectors or 2D arrays in a blocked fashion. Auto-increment allows very compact loops to achieve the same 3–5× performance advantage as the loop-unrolled examples in VIPERS, without the code bloat. Compact loops are also easier to program than unrolled loops. Finally, the scratchpad and external memory can tranfer data asynchronously with double-buffering to hide memory latency.

To conserve on-chip memory resources, VEGAS is cacheless and double-clocks the scratchpad, providing four

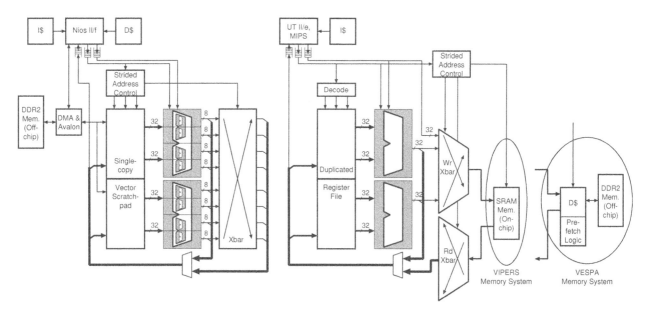

Figure 1: VEGAS (left) compared to VIPERS and VESPA (right)

read/write ports per cycle. Two read ports and one write port are used for vector instruction execution, while the fourth read/write port is used as a dedicated DMA channel between the scratchpad and off-chip memory. Efficient use of on-chip memory reduces the need to spill vector data to off-chip memory. This leads to significant performance advantages in some applications.

The VEGAS soft vector processor is attached to a standard Nios II/f. We encode each vector instruction as a single Nios II custom instruction by fitting the vector instruction bits into the available fields. Vector instructions are dispatched by Nios to a vector instruction queue. Since many vector instructions are multi-cycle, this allows Nios II to run ahead and asynchronously execute scalar code, such as loop bounds checking and control flow instructions. The Nios also issues scratchpad DMA transfer requests asynchronously as custom instructions. This means DMA transfers, vector instructions, and Nios instructions can all execute concurrently. A few special synchronization instructions cause Nios to wait, such as reading a scalar result from the vector scratchpad. The use of a standard Nios II/f gives users full debug capability using the Altera IDE as well.

A common concern for soft vector processors is compiler support. VESPA and VIPERS require hand-written or inline assembly code, translating vector instructions with a modified GNU assembler (gasm). Researchers have investigated the autovectorizing capability of gcc, but have not yet used it successfully [21]. Instead of an autovectorizing compiler, VEGAS uses C macros exclusively to emit Nios custom instructions on demand without modifying gcc or gasm. The macros are more readable, and the system is much simpler to program because the user doesn't need to track the scalar (control flow) values as register numbers. Instead, users track only vector scratchpad addresses stored in the vector address registers, and initiate DMA transfers explicitly. We also provide some convenience routines to simplify allocating and deallocating scratchpad memory. The macros are easier to program than pure assembly, and still gives explicit control over the hardware for maximum performance.

2. BACKGROUND AND RELATED WORK

Vector processing has been applied in supercomputers on scientific and engineering workloads for decades. It exploits the data-level parallelism readily available in scientific and engineering applications by performing the same operation over all elements in a vector or matrix.

2.1 Vector Processing Overview

Classically, execution of a vector instruction is done by sending a stream of values into a pipelined ALU at a rate of one element per clock cycle. Parallelism is obtained through pipelining, allowing high clock issue rates. Additional parallelism is obtained by vector chaining, where the output of one ALU is passed directly to the input of another ALU which is executing a separate vector instruction. Chaining requires complex register files with multiple write ports to support writeback by several ALUs each clock cycle, and multiple read ports to feed several ALUs each cycle.

Alternatively, several ALUs can operate in lockstep SIMD mode to execute the same vector instruction, thus shortening the time to process a long vector. In this mode, multiple ALUs each write back to their own independent partition of the vector register file, so parallelism can be achieved without the multiple write ports required by chaining.

Modern microprocessors are augmented with SIMD processing instructions to accelerate data-parallel workloads. These operate on short, fixed-length vectors (e.g., only four 32-bit words). Significant overhead comes from instructions to load/pack/unpack these short vectors and looping.

There are two key distinguishing traits of vector processors that set them apart from SIMD processing instructions. First is the use of the vector length (VL) control register, which can be changed at run-time to process arbitrary-length vectors up to a certain maximum vector length (MVL). Second is the use of complex addressing modes, such as walking through memory in strides instead of complex pack/unpack instructions. For example, strided access simplifies columnwise traversal of a 2D array.

2.2 Soft Vector Architectures

The VIPERS soft vector architecture [23, 24] demonstrated that programmers can explore the area-performance tradeoffs of data-parallel workloads without any hardware design expertise. Based on results from three benchmark kernels, VIPERS provides a scalable speedup of 3–30× over the scalar Nios II processor. Moreover, an additional speedup factor of 3–5× can be achieved by fully unrolling the vector assembly code. VIPERS uses a Nios II-compatible multithreaded processor called UT-IIe [7], but control flow execution is hindered by the multithreaded pipeline. The UT-IIe is also cacheless; it contains a small, fast on-chip instruction memory and accesses all data through the vector read/write crossbars to fast, on-chip memory. VIPERS instructions are largely based on VIRAM [9].

The VESPA soft vector architecture [20, 21] is a MIPS-compatible scalar core with a VIRAM [9] compatible vector coprocessor. The original VESPA at 16 lanes can acheive an average speedup of 6.3× over six EEMBC benchmarks. Furthermore, VESPA demonstrated improved performance by adding support for vector chaining with a banked register file and heterogeneous vector lanes [22]. Over the 9 benchmarks tested, the improved VESPA averages a speedup of 10× at 16 lanes and 14× at 32 lanes. The MIPS core uses a 4kB instruction cache, and shares a data cache with the vector coprocessor. Smaller (1- or 2-lane) vector coprocessors use an 8kB data cache, while larger ones use 32kB.

Both VIPERS and VESPA offer a wide range of configurability. For example, the parallel vector lanes can be specified at FPGA compile-time to be 8, 16 or 32 bits wide. However, when mixed-width data is required, the vector engine must be built to the widest data. Therefore, when processing smaller data, load instructions will zero-extend or sign-extend to the full width, and store instructions will truncate the upper bits. Since the vector register file must store all data (even byte-sized data) at the widest width, VIPERS and VESPA can be very inefficient: byte-wide data is stored in the on-chip main memory or data cache, then expanded to word-wide inside the registerfile. On top of that, to implement dual read ports, VIPERS and VESPA duplicate the vector register file. Hence, a single byte of data may occupy up to 9 bytes of on-chip storage.

Both VIPERS and VESPA also share a similar design for striding through memory. The vector register file is connected to an on-chip memory (VIPERS) or on-chip data cache (VESPA) through *separate* read and write crossbars. These crossbars are used when striding through memory during vector loads and stores; they must shuffle bytes/halfwords/words from their byte-offset in memory into word size at a new byte-offset in the vector register file. The size of the crossbars are constrained on one end by the overall width of the vector register file, and on the other side by the overall width of the on-chip memory/cache. As the vector processor is scaled to contain more lanes, one end of the crossbars increases in size while the other end is fixed by the memory width. To quickly load a large register file, the on-chip memory/cache width must be similarly increased to match. The area to implement these crossbars is significant, and grows as the product of the two widths.

2.3 Scratchpad Memory

Many recent embedded processors in academia and industry supoprt private scratchpad memories. The CELL pro-

cessor [16, 5, 6] from IBM, which is designed for streaming multimedia computations, features 8 synergistic processor elements (SPEs), each operating on fixed-width (128-bit) vectors with private SRAM scratchpads which are filled using DMA operations. The Signal-processing On-Demand Architecture (SODA) [11, 12] for 3G wireless protocols has a global scratchpad memory and local scratchpad memory for each of its 4 SIMD processors. ARM, Nios II and MicroBlaze processors also support both cache and scratchpad memory, so users can tune the system design based on the needs of a specific application.

As an architectural feature, researchers have also investigated ways to automatically utilize scratchpad memories. For a joint cache and scratchpad system, [14] presents a scheme for partitioning the scalar and array variables to minimize cache misses. In [3], a technique for static data allocation to heterogeneous memory units at compile-time is presented. Dynamic allocation approaches are also discussed in [8, 13].

2.4 Address Registers

Address registers have long been used in processors for indirect accessing of memories, where the effective address of an operand is computed based on the address register content and the addressing mode. Indirect access of memory via address registers can also be found in vector processors. The Cray-1 [17] uses eight dedicated address registers for memory accesses. The Torrent-0 [2] supports unit-stride (with auto-increment) and strided memory accesses by computing the effective address from its scalar registers, and indexed memory accesses by computing the effective address from its vector registers. The VIRAM [9, 10] also supports unit-stride, strided, and indexed accesses, but the base addresses and stride values are stored in a separate register file to comply with the MIPS ISA. In all of these cases, the address registers are dedicated for use with load or store instructions.

The register pointer architecture (RPA) [15] proposed using register pointers to indirectly access a larger register file without modifying the instruction set architecture. It also demonstrated that by changing the register pointer contents dynamically, the need for loop unrolling can be reduced. The same technique is exploited by the vector address registers in VEGAS.

3. VEGAS ARCHITECTURE

Similar to VESPA and VIPERS, the new VEGAS architecture offers scalable performance and area. Without any RTL design effort, users can configure the high-level design parameters to tune the VEGAS soft processor for a given application, providing productivity, cost, and time-to-market advantages. Moreover, VEGAS achieves better performance per unit area over the existing soft vector designs from its major design features:

1. Decoupled vector architecture,

2. Vector scratchpad memory,

3. Address registers,

4. Fracturable ALUs,

5. Data alignment crossbar network (DACN), and

6. Simplified C-macro programming.

The subsequent sections provide details on each feature.

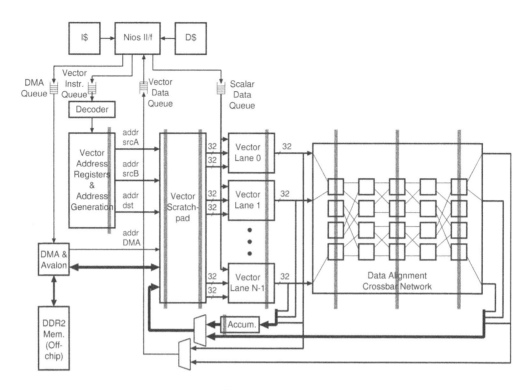

Figure 2: VEGAS Architecture (gray vertical bars indicate pipeline registers)

3.1 Decoupled Vector Architecture

VEGAS evolved from three key observations concerning VESPA and VIPERS: Nios II is small and fast and has plenty of debug support; the soft vector processors run about half the speed of Nios II/f; and vector data register files are huge while on-chip memory capacity in FPGAs is strictly limited. We wanted to design a vector processor that could scale to fill the entire FPGA, e.g. use all of the FPGA multipliers while still leaving memory blocks left over, or use all memory efficiently for applications with large datasets. We also looked at the loop-unrolled code examples presented in VIPERS and thought there must be a way to capture the performance without unrolling.

Figure 1 provides a high-level comparison of VEGAS, VIPERS and VESPA. A more detailed view of VEGAS is provided in Figure 2. VEGAS consists of a standard Nios II/f processor, a vector core, a DDR2 controller plus external memory, and a DMA engine. All of these blocks are capable of running concurrently.

The vector core does not access the Nios II instruction memory directly; vector and DMA instructions are implemented as custom instructions in the regular Nios II instruction stream. When 'executed' by Nios, these instructions are typically deposited into an appropriate queue for later asynchronous execution by the other core; if the target queue is full, the Nios II processor stalls until there is space. There are two separate 16-entry queues: one for vector instructions, and another for DMA block-transfer operations. Since vector and DMA operations usually take multiple cycles, this allows Nios II to run ahead to enqueue several instructions. This usually allows the overhead of control flow instructions to be hidden.

Some vector instructions include a scalar operand, which is deposited into a separate scalar data queue. Likewise,

some vector instructions demand a response word from the vector core, such as reading a scalar value from the scratchpad memory or querying the current DMA queue length. Currently, instructions that demand a response block the Nios II, resulting in a flushed vector instruction queue. In the future, we plan to implement a non-blocking version, where the response is deposited into a vector data queue to be picked up by a later 'read vector queue' instruction. This pipelining avoids instruction queue flushes and hides the latency of crossing clock domain boundaries twice (two directions), but there is a risk of deadlock if the vector data queue fills up.

The DMA engine processes block transfers by issuing read or write operations between the DDR2 controller and the fourth port of the scratchpad memory; data movement between the scratchpad and DDR2 controller uses Altera's Avalon system fabric.

In our implementation, the Nios II/f uses a 4kB instruction cache and a 4kB data cache. The Nios II, Avalon fabric, and DMA engine run at 200MHz, and the vector core runs at 100MHz. The clock ratios need not be strictly 2:1, as dual-clock FIFOs are used to cross clock domain boundaries. Timing analysis reports indicate that VEGAS can run up to 130MHz. VIPERS and VESPA achieve similar clock rates, but they lock the scalar processor clock to the vector clock. To avoid ambiguity, we report performance results by measuring wall-clock time and reporting this elapsed time in terms of 100MHz cycles.

VEGAS encodes register values, auto-increment, and operand size in the upper 16 bits of the Nios II custom instruction. It uses 6 bits of the 8-bit N field for encoding the function to be performed, allowing up to 4 VEGAS vector cores to share a Nios II, or allowing VEGAS to coexist with other coprocessors.

3.2 Vector Scratchpad Memory

Instead of a traditional vector register file, VEGAS uses a scratchpad memory to store the working set of vector data. Eight vector address registers are used to access the scratchpad memory. Data read from vector scratchpad memory are sent directly to the vector lanes for processing, and the results are written back into the same memory. This direct coupling of the scratchpad memory and vector lanes is very efficient when the vector data operands are aligned to the lane structure. When vectors are not aligned, a data alignment crossbar network is used to correct the situation. The scratchpad enhances the VEGAS design in terms of performance, memory efficiency, and flexibility.

3.2.1 Performance

The traditional vector register file requires explicit load/store operations to transfer the data from/to memory before any vector operations can be performed. These data transfers can be time consuming. A 3–5× speedup over the original vector code is possible by fitting the primary working set into the 64-entry vector register file. As demonstrated in the VIPERS median filter example [23], this was only possible by fully unrolling two nested loops, leading to 225 unrolled iterations.

In VEGAS, data vectors are stored in the scratchpad memory and accessed via address registers. Most vector instructions specify 3 address registers: 2 source, and 1 destination. Each register specifies the starting location of a vector in the scratchpad. The number of elements in the vector is determined by a separate dedicated vector length register, VL.

When data needs to be loaded from the external DDR2 memory, the DMA engine will transfer the data into the vector scratchpad memory. This is done in parallel with vector operations, usually in a double-buffered fashion, so memory transfer latency is often completely hidden from the vector core. The programmer must explicitly ensure the DMA transfer is complete by polling or blocking before issuing any dependant vector instructions.

Performance gained by the elimination of load/store operations is maximized when the vector sources and destination reside in aligned locations and the working set fits entirely in the scratchpad memory. If the working set does not fit, vectors must be spilled to memory, degrading performance. Also, if the vectors are not aligned, additional data movement using the data alignment crossbar network (Section 3.5) is necessary to temporarily restore alignment. If unaligned accesses are predictable and occur more than once, an explicit vector move instruction to bring the data into alignment helps restore performance.

3.2.2 Memory Efficiency

In typical soft processor implementations, the register file is duplicated to provide dual read ports. However, for a vector processor, the vector data store is much larger, making the cost of duplication extremely high in terms of memory usage. In the VEGAS architecture, we take advantage of the high speed memory that is readily available in modern FPGAs and operate the memory at twice the clock frequency of the vector processor to provide the dual read ports. Therefore, the VEGAS vector processor needs just one set of data to reside in the on-chip memory, resulting in improved storage efficiency.

Moreover, instead of zero/sign-extending the vector elements to match the vector lane width, VEGAS stores vector data in the scratchpad memory at their natural length of 8 bits, 16 bits, or 32 bits. This maximizes the utilization of limited on-chip memory. As these smaller data elements are fetched directly from the scratchpad, fracturable ALUs are used to operate on elements with varying sizes. Details on the fracturable ALUs are presented in Section 3.4.

3.2.3 Flexibility

The scratchpad memory is also a more flexible form of storage than traditional vector register files. A typical vector register file is fixed in size, limiting both the number of vectors and the maximum vector length. In VEGAS, there is greater flexibility in dividing the scratchpad up into different vector lengths and the number of vectors stored. The maximum vector length is limited only by the availability of scratchpad memory. Although there are only eight address registers, reloading an address register is far faster than reloading an entire vector of data. Hence, the number of vectors resident in the scratchpad is not artificially limited by the instruction set architecture bit encoding. This flexibility allows the use of long vectors, or many vectors, depending upon the needs of the application.

It should be noted that using long vectors is encouraged: it requires fewer iterations to compute a given task, lowers loop overhead, and prepares an application for scalable execution on wider vector processor instances. The configurability of the FPGA allows the scratchpad memory to be scaled up to provide as much storage space as allowed by the device without changing the instruction set. Since there is little waste, it is easy for users to predict the total storage capacity of VEGAS for each FPGA device. If the required scratchpad memory size does not fit in a particular FPGA device, there is the option to migrate to a device with higher capacity. The flexibility of the vector scratchpad memory allows the VEGAS architecture to tackle many different applications.

3.3 Address Registers

VEGAS contains 8 vector address registers. Each of these registers points an address in the scratchpad which holds the beginning of a vector (element 0). We found 8 address registers to be sufficient for all of our benchmarks. If more than 8 vectors are needed, a new value can be written to an existing address register very quickly (one clock cycle).

In addition, address registers have an auto-increment feature. Encoded in each instruction is a bit for each source and the destination operand which indicates whether the register should be incremented after use. The increment amount is determined by a set of 8 increment registers, one for each address register. If the same register specifier appears in multiple operand fields, it is only incremented once after the instruction completes.

The use of auto-increment helps lower loop overhead in tight vector code. The ability to specify arbitrary increment amounts is useful because the amount of increment can vary: for example, it may equal 1 element, turning the vector into a shift register, or it may equal VL elements to iterate over a long sequence of data VL elements at a time, or it may equal the row length of a 2-dimensional array to traverse the array columnwise. Although the incremented address can be computed by Nios II, this adds loop overhead (e.g., several address registers are incremented in a tight loop).

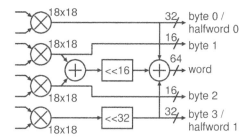

Figure 3: Fracturable Multiplier

When used with auto-increment, it is possible to obtain the equivalent performance of fully unrolled code without unrolling the loop. Our rolled-up median filter kernel is shown in Figure 6. In comparison, the original VIPERS code examples unrolled these nested loops and used 25 vector registers to hold the entire filter window. While this avoided all loads and stores in the innermost loop, the 225 loop iterations had to be *fully* unrolled (not partially) because the vector data can only be addressed by static register names. In VEGAS, unrolling is not necessary. The entire filter window is stored in the scratchpad, and data is addressed dynamically by address register. In the example, the address register V2 is auto-incremented to the next vector of data in each inner loop iteration.

The VIPERS unrolling approach is limited by the number of iterations required, the number of vector registers in the ISA, the size of the vector register file, and the amount of instruction memory available. In contrast, using address registers with auto-increment, VEGAS can automatically cycle through the data in the scratchpad with a loop without any unrolling or reloading of the address register. Only scratchpad capacity limits the length and number of vectors that can be stored. The added efficiency of natively storing bytes or halfwords without extending them to 32-bits in the scratchpad magnifies this advantage.

3.4 Fracturable ALUs

To execute on input data of different sizes, each lane must be subdivided into sub-lanes of appropriate width. This requires a *fracturable* ALU which can be subdivided to operate on four bytes, two halfwords, or one word for every 32 bits of data. Furthermore, each instruction must specify the operand size so the ALUs can be configured to an appropriate width. With fracturing, a 4-lane VEGAS processor offers the performance potential of a 16-lane VIPERS/VESPA processor when operating on byte-size vector elements.

Fracturing works together with the scratchpad to help it preserve limited on-chip memory. In VIPERS, an implementation capable of operating on all three data sizes would require each lane to have a 32-bit register file and 32-bit ALU, so both the storage efficiency and processing power is wasted when operating on vectors of halfwords or bytes. In VEGAS, the fracturable ALUs allow vectors to be stored at their natural lengths, so memory efficiency remains high.

The fracturable ALUs require a fracturable adder and fracturable multiplier. A fracturable adder is four 8-bit adders which can dynamically cascade their carry chains for wider operation. While the interrupted carry chain does cause some area overhead, the implementation is simple. In contrast, a fracturable multiplier is more complex and must

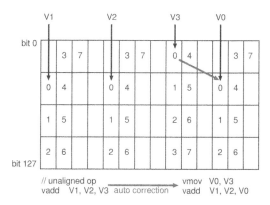

Figure 4: Example of Misaligned VEGAS Operation

support both signed and unsigned modes. In Stratix III, the embedded multiplier blocks cannot be dynamically resized or reconfigured for signed/unsigned operation. In VEGAS, we designed a fracturable multiplier around four 18×18 hardware multiplier blocks which fit nicely into a single DSP block plus additional logic. The basic design is shown in Figure 3. With careful input multiplexing, as well as output selection, this design becomes a signed/unsigned fracturable multiplier. With additional input selection logic, these multipliers are turned into fracturable shifters as well.

The ALUs support absolute-difference and sum-of-absolute-difference instructions. Also, we have an accumulate function like VIPERS, but our implementation is significantly different. Instead of instantiating more DSP blocks and using the built-in accumulators, we build our own fracturable accumulators in logic placed near the write-back port of the scratchpad.

3.5 Data Alignment Crossbar Network

Since the scratchpad memory couples directly to the vector lanes in VEGAS as shown in Figure 2, all vectors involved in a single vector instruction (two sources and one destination) must reside in aligned locations. When vectors are not aligned, the input to the vector lanes is mismatched and would produce an incorrect result. When misalignment occurs, an extra instruction is necessary to move the data into alignment as shown in Figure 4.

To help lower the learning curve in software development, misalignment detection and auto-correction logic is implemented in VEGAS. If two source vectors are misaligned, a vector move instruction is automatically inserted into the pipeline. The automatic-move makes use of the data alignment crossbar network to align the one operand, and stores the result at a reserved location determined by vector address register V0. Then the original instruction is re-issued, using V0 to replace the misaligned source. If the destination is also misaligned, the result is re-aligned on the fly prior to writing back the result in the correct location.

Although the auto-correction is convenient, it represents lost performance. To help tune software, performance counters are implemented for each of three misalignment cases that occur while running the vectorized code. The user can retrieve the counter values via control registers, and utilize this information to optimize their application.

In addition to alignment, variations of the move instruction called scatter and gather provide strided access through

```
#include "vegas.h"

int dotprod( int *v1, int *v2,
             int const1, int const2, int vec_len)
{
  int result;
  int *vegas_v1,*vegas_v2,*vegas_result;

  //Allocate two vectors in scratchpad
  vegas_v1 = vegas_malloc( vec_len*sizeof(int) );
  vegas_v2 = vegas_malloc( vec_len*sizeof(int) );
  vegas_result  = vegas_malloc( sizeof(int) );

  //Start the DMA transfers to VEGAS
  vegas_dma_to_vector(vegas_v1,v1,vec_len*sizeof(int));
  vegas_dma_to_vector(vegas_v2,v2,vec_len*sizeof(int));

  //Set VEGAS VL and set address registers
  vegas_set( VCTRL, VL, vec_len );
  vegas_set( VADDR, V1, vegas_v1 );
  vegas_set( VADDR, V2, vegas_v2 );
  vegas_set( VADDR, V3, vegas_result );

  //Zero the accumulators before using them; whatever was
  //in them will be written to V3 which will be overwritten
  //with the result later
  vegas_vvw( VCCZACC, V3, VUNUSED, VUNUSED );

  //Wait for memory transfer to complete before computation
  vegas_wait_for_dma();

  //Multiply vector by scalar words
  vegas_vsw( VMULLO, V1, V1, const1 );
  vegas_vsw( VMULLO, V2, V2, const2 );

  //Multiply the two vectors together and accumulate the
  //result of the multiply will be written back to V2 while
  //the accumulation happens in the external accumulators
  vegas_vvw( VMAC, V2, V2, V1 );

  //Store result in first word of V3 and zero the accumulators
  vegas_vvw( VCCZACC, V3, VUNUSED, VUNUSED );

  //Extract the result.  This also syncs Nios II and VEGAS
  vegas_vsw( VEXT, result, V3, VUNUSED );

  //Free all scratchpad memory
  vegas_free();

  return result;
}
```

Figure 5: Example Dot Product

```
  //Bubble sort up to halfway
  for( j = 0; j < FILTER_SIZE/2; j++ ) {
    vegas_set( VADDR, V1, v_temp+j*IMAGE_WIDTH );
    vegas_set( VADDR, V2, v_temp+(j+1)*IMAGE_WIDTH );

    for( i = j+1; i < FILTER_SIZE; i++ ) {
      vegas_vvb( VMAXU, V4, V1, V2 );
      vegas_vvb( VMINU, V1, V1, V2 );
      vegas_vvb( VMOVA, V2INC, V4, V4 );
    }
  }
```

Figure 6: Example Median Filter Kernel

the scratchpad. Scatter takes a densely packed vector as the source, and writes a new vector with elements separated by gaps of $n - 1$ elements, where n is called the stride. Gather works in the opposite direction. Furthermore, both scatter and gather are capable of converting elements of one data size into any other data size (words, halfwords, and bytes) through sign-extension, zero-extension, or truncation.

The alignment, scatter, and gather operations are achieved using a data alignment corssbar network (DACN). Instead of using a full crossbar, which is costly in resource usage, VEGAS employs a Benes network [4]. This network can realize all of the required permutations, but requires only $O(N \log N)$ instead of $O(N^2)$ logic in the switching network. However, the multistage nature of this network requires complex control algorithms. The control must first generate the output ports for each input data element, then the control values for each layer of the switch. Our current control logic is inefficient for scatter and gather operations with certain strides, and this limits the speedup achieved with certain applications.

3.6 Programming VEGAS

VEGAS is programmed in a manner similar to inline assembly in C. However, C macros are used to simplify programming and make VEGAS instructions look like C functions without any run time overhead. The sample code in Figure 5 multiplies two vectors by separate scalars and then computes their dot product.

To add byte vectors pointed by address registers V2 to V1, increment V1 and store the result in V3 the required macro would be vegas_vvb(VADD,V3,V1INC,V2). Vector register specifiers can take on any value V0 through V7, but special register V0 is also used by the system for temporary storage during automatic alignment operations. A register specifier written as V7INC, for example, post-increments the register by a signed amount previously stored in its respective increment register. A placeholder value VUNUSED can be used with certain instructions. In the function name, the vvb suffix refers to 'vector-vector' operation (vv) on byte-size data (b). Other combinations are scalar-vector (sv) or vector-scalar (vs), where the first or second source operand is a scalar value provided by Nios instead of a vector address register. These may be combined with data sizes of bytes (b), halfwords (h) and words (w). For example, computing a vector of halfwords in V7 by subtracting a vector V2 from the integer scalar variable k would be written as vegas_svh(VSUB,V7,k,V2). In addition, conditional execution of individual vector elements is achieved via a vector mask, where a mask is a vector of 1-bit results from a vector comparison.

Data can be allocated in vector scratchpad memory using special vegas_malloc(num_bytes) which returns an aligned pointer. By default, V0 tracks the end of the allocated scratchpad memory, allowing the use of all remaining space as an alignment buffer. The vegas_free() call simply frees all previous scrachpad allocations. DMA transfers and instruction synchronization are handled by macros as well.

While this approach requires programmers to manually manage vector address registers, it should be straightforward to create a compiler to manage register allocation and allow the programmer to deal with pointers directly. Such a compiler could also infer data size from the pointer type.

Num. Lane	VEGAS				VIPERS				VESPA			
	ALM	DSP	M9K	Fmax	ALM	DSP	M9K	Fmax	ALM	DSP	M9K	Fmax
1	3,831	8	40	131					5,556	10	46	133
2	4,881	12	40	131					6,218	14	48	130
4	6,976	20	40	130	5,825	25	16	106	7,362	22	76	128
8	11,824	36	40	125	7,501	46	25	110	12,565	39	98	124
16	19,843	68	40	122	10,995	86	41	105	20,179	79	98	113
32	36,611	132	40	116					34,471	175	196	98

Table 1: Resource Usage Comparison

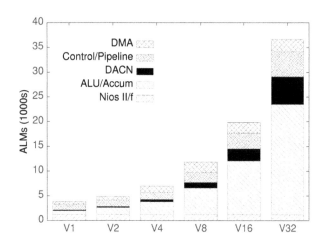

Figure 7: VEGAS Area Breakdown (ALM count)

4. RESULTS

In this section, the resource usage, performance, and area-delay product of the new VEGAS soft vector architecture is compared against existing soft vector architectures VESPA and VIPERS.

4.1 Resource Usage

Different configurations of the VEGAS architecture are compiled using Quartus II to measure their resource usage and compare them against the equivalent VESPA/VIPERS designs. VEGAS is compiled targeting the Stratix III EP3SL150F1152C3ES device that is found on the Altera DE3-150 development board. Since all three architectures target Altera's Stratix III devices on a DE3 platform, comparisons are easy.

The logic usage is summarized by the number of adaptive logic modules (ALMs) and DSP 18x18 elements, while memory usage is summarized by the number of M9K blocks. Table 1 lists the ALM/DSP/M9K usage for all three architectures with various number of lanes, as well as the maximum clock frequency of the design. The V1, V2, V4 labels indicate 1, 2, 4 vector lanes (each lane is 32 bits in width), respectively. For VEGAS, this means V4 can run instructions on byte-wide data using 16 vector sub-lanes. For these results, VEGAS was configured to use a 32kB scratchpad.

In terms of logic resources, the ALM usage of VEGAS typically settles between VIPERS and VESPA, except VEGAS surpasses VESPA in the 32-lane configuration. The breakdown of ALM usage in Figure 7 shows that ALUs account for the majority of ALM use. This is partly explained by the complexity of the fracturable ALUs, and partly by the complex min/max/absolute-difference instructions. The multiplier also requires significant ALM resources for its many modes and shifting operations. Future work should reduce ALM usage in the ALUs.

In terms of multiplier resources, the fracturable ALUs were carefully designed to limit use of DSP blocks, and we avoided using multipliers in address calculations. As a result, VEGAS is slighty better than both VIPERS and VESPA in DSP usage.

In terms of memory, the number of M9K memory blocks consumed by VEGAS is similar to that of both VIPERS and VESPA. However, it is much more efficient, allowing up to 8× more vector data elements to be stored in the same number of M9K blocks.

4.2 Performance

For performance comparisons, we adopted benchmarks from VIPERS (motion estimation, median filter), VESPA (EEMBC benchmarks autocor, conven, fbital plus VIRAM benchmarks imgblend and filt3x3), and also added a classic fir filter with 16 taps on 4096 halfword samples.

We compiled all applications using gcc with -O3 optimization and ran them on the Nios II/f processor at 200MHz to establish the baseline performance. Next, we recoded the benchmarks by hand using the VEGAS C macros and attempted to maximize the vector lengths, use the smallest data elements needed by each benchmark, and overlap DMA with computation. We compiled VEGAS vector core instances ranging from 1 to 16 lanes with 256kB, and 32 lanes with 128kB scratchpad memory.[1] The vector core was run at 100MHz. Performance was then measured using hardware timestamp counters running at 100MHz. The number of 100MHz clock cycles required for each configuration is shown in Table 2. For VEGAS, we also calculated the highest speedup over Nios II on these benchmarks. For VIPERS and VESPA results, we extracted cycle counts from published works [19, 23].

Compared to VIPERS, VEGAS matches it on the median filter benchmark, and beats it by 2× on motion estimation. However, we also see that VEGAS achieves peak performance with fewer lanes than VIPERS because of the fracturable ALUs. This gives VEGAS an area advantage. Also, the VIPERS results were achieved through aggressive loop unrolling in both benchmarks, but VEGAS does not use any loop unrolling.

Compared to VESPA, VEGAS matches it on imgblend and filt3x3, beats it on autocor and fbital, but runs more slowly on conven. The slower performance of conven is due to strided scatter/gather operations which do not yet execute at full speed in VEGAS due to complex DACN control. We are actively working to address this limitation. However, we note that VEGAS always achieves better perfor-

---

[1]The fbital benchmark requires a 256kB scratchpad for a lookup table, so we could not collect V32 performance data.

CPU Name	Benchmark Name							
	fir	motest	median	autocor	conven	fbital	imgblend	filt3x3
Nios II/f	509,919	1,668,869	1,388	124,338	48,988	240,849	1,231,172	6,556,592
	VIPERS			VESPA				
V1				125,376	17,610	358,070	1,127,965	2,754,216
V2				64,791	9,821	191,054	677,856	1,432,396
V4		157,792	189	32,556	4,479	106,911	229,014	608,222
V8		88,288	95	16,896	2,103	69,186	112,937	271,252
V16		55,328	48	10,287	1,638	47,303	64,176	145,729
V32				7,062	984	39,372	33,953	72,966
	VEGAS							
data size	halfword	byte	byte	word	byte	halfword	halfword	halfword
VL	dynamic	256	dynamic	1024	512	256	320	317
V1	85,549	82,515	185	45,027	3,462	165,839	175,890	813,471
V2	47,443	47,249	93	26,512	2,690	90,114	99,666	419,589
V4	25,346	30,243	47	14,470	2,154	52,278	61,169	219,816
V8	13,536	29,643	24	7,941	1,976	33,166	40,231	122,072
V16	7,690	27,344	12	4,563	1,924	23,999	35,656	75,776
V32	4,693	24,717	7	2,822	1,897	–	35,485	75,349
Speedup	108×	67×	208×	44×	25×	10×	34×	87×

Table 2: Performance Comparison (100MHz clock cycles)

CPU Name	Benchmark Name							
	fir	motest	median	autocor	conven	fbital	imgblend	filt3x3
Nios II/f	1.00	1.00	1.00	1.00	1.00	1.00	1.00	1.00
VIPERS		(V16) 0.31	(V16) 0.41					
VESPA				(V16) 1.37	(V8) 0.44	(V8) 2.95	(V32) 0.78	(V32) 0.31
VEGAS	(V16) 0.24	(V4) 0.10	(V16) 0.14	(V16) 0.60	(V2) 0.22	(V4) 1.24	(V4) 0.28	(V8) 0.18
Improvement		3.1×	2.9×	2.3×	2×	2.4×	2.8×	1.7×

Table 3: Best Area-Delay Product (Normalized to Nios II/f, lower=better)

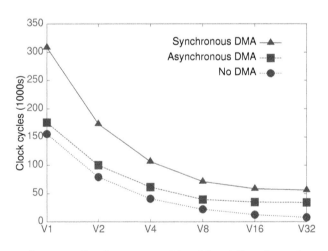

Figure 8: Performance of imgblend Benchmark

	Clock speed	1024×1024	4096×4096
Nios II/f	200MHz	77.78	5406.81
Intel Core 2	2.66GHz	1.09	71.66
VEGAS	100MHz	0.72	43.77

Table 4: Integer Matrix Multiply Runtime (seconds)

be hidden. To demonstrate this, we ran the imgblend application in three modes: synchronous DMA, asynchronous DMA, and no DMA. The runtime of these three modes is shown in Figure 8. With synchronous DMA, we block waiting for each DMA operation to finish before performing any computation. With no DMA, we skipped the DMA transfer entirely, so runtime is entirely computational (and uses incorrect data). The asynchronous DMA result allows computation to occur while the DMA operates in parallel. The figure shows that most of the transfer latency is successfully hidden up to V8. Hiding the latency at V16 and V32 is difficult because the computation is so fast.

Finally, using integer matrix multiply, Table 4 shows that VEGAS outperforms a 2.66GHz Intel Xeon X5355 processor. We believe this is the first time a soft processor has outperformed a leading-edge hard processor in similar (65nm) technology. The Nios II and Intel versions ran individually tuned single-threaded C programs that used various loop orderings and tile sizes compiled with gcc -O3. Note that Intel SSE instructions were not used. The VEGAS version was the fastest code written among a graduate class of 10 students; the slowest code was roughly 2× slower.

mance when using a smaller number of lanes (V1 to V8, and often V16). In particular, VEGAS-V2 is 6.8× faster than VESPA-V2 on imgblend.

Table 3 reports the best area-delay product achieved by each vector processor. For VEGAS, this is often at a small number of lanes. A lower area-delay is better, as greater throughput performance can be obtained by replicating these vector cores across the chip. The VEGAS area-delay product is up to 68% lower than VIPERS and up to 64% lower than VESPA, giving it up to 3.1× better throughput per unit area.

The ability to run DMA operations concurrently in a double-buffered fashion often allows all memory latency to

5. CONCLUSIONS

Previous work on VIPERS and VESPA have demonstrated that soft vector processors can scale and accelerate data-parallel embedded applications on FPGAs. Vector processoring offers an easier way to explore the area-performance tradeoffs than designing custom logic accelerator in VHDL or Verilog.

This paper introduces VEGAS, a new soft vector architecture that optimizes use of limited on-chip memory in modern FPGAs. An on-chip scratchpad memory serves as the vector data storage medium and is accessed using vector address registers. This eliminates traditional restrictions on the maximum vector length and number of vectors. Instead of traditional vector load/store operations, double-buffered asynchronous DMA can potentially hide all memory latency. Better storage efficiency (up to $9\times$) allows more vector data to reside on-chip, avoiding the need to spill vector data. Additional performance enhancement is achieved by fracturable ALUs, which increases processing power up to $4\times$ on byte-size data.

The VEGAS architecture supports very long vector lengths. Together with the auto-increment feature of the address registers, this can reduce overhead in tight loops. The address registers achieve the performance of unrolled code without doing any unrolling, making it easier to program and debug and reducing code bloat.

Using area-delay product on selected benchmarks, VEGAS provides up to $3.1\times$ higher throughput per unit area than VIPERS, and up to $2.8\times$ higher than VESPA. In raw performance, VEGAS is $10\times$ to $208\times$ faster than Nios II on the same benchmarks. Using integer matrix multiply, VEGAS is faster than a 2.66GHz Intel X5355 (Clovertown) processor. This may be the first time a soft processor has surpassed a leading-edge hard processor in performance.

Finally, the C-based macro system is easier to program than assembly language. While not offering the full convenience of an autovectorizing compiler, it relieves the programmer of scalar assembly instructions yet still allows explicitly scheduled data movement and vector instructions.

6. ACKNOWLEDGMENTS

Funding for this work was provided by NSERC and hardware donations by Altera Corp. We thank the following graduate students for coding their own matrix multiply algorithms and providing usability feedback: Kyle Balston, Stuart Dueck, Abdullah Gharaibeh, Jeffrey Goeders, Ziaeddin Jalali, Tim Rogers, Emalayan Vairavanathan, and Jiesheng Wei (the other 2 students are co-authors Alex and Zhiduo). Finally, thanks are due to Tor Aamodt, Philip Brisk, Philip Leong, Satnam Singh, and Greg Steffan for their useful feedback on this work, as well as Christos Kozyrakis for providing VIRAM-coded versions of EEMBC benchmarks for analysis.

7. REFERENCES

[1] The embedded microprocessor benchmark consortium. http://www.eembc.org/.

[2] K. Asanovic. *Vector microprocessors*. PhD thesis, University of California, Berkeley, 1998.

[3] O. Avissar, R. Barua, and D. Stewart. An optimal memory allocation scheme for scratch-pad-based embedded systems. *ACM TECS*, 1(1):6–26, 2002.

[4] V. E. Benes. Optimal rearrangeable multistage connecting networks. *Bell Systems Technical Journal*, 43(7):1641–1656, 1964.

[5] S. H. Dhong, O. Takahashi, et al. A 4.8 GHz fully pipelined embedded SRAM in the streaming processor of a CELL processor. In *ISSCC*, pages 486–487, 2005.

[6] B. Flachs, S. Asano, et al. A streaming processing unit for a CELL processor. In *ISSCC*, pages 134–135, 2005.

[7] B. Fort, D. Capalija, Z. G. Vranesic, and S. D. Brown. A multithreaded soft processor for SoPC area reduction. In *FCCM*, pages 131–142, 2006.

[8] M. Kandemir, J. Ramanujam, M. J. Irwin, N. Vijaykrishnan, I. Kadayif, and A. Parikh. A Compiler-Based approach for dynamically managing Scratch-Pad memories in embedded systems. *IEEE TCAD*, 23(2):243–260, 2004.

[9] C. Kozyrakis. *Scalable Vector Media Processors for Embedded Systems*. PhD thesis, University of California at Berkeley, May 2002. Technical Report UCB-CSD-02-1183.

[10] C. E. Kozyrakis and D. A. Patterson. Scalable vector processors for embedded systems. *IEEE Micro*, 23(6):36–45, 2003.

[11] Y. Lin, H. Lee, Y. Harel, M. Woh, S. Mahlke, T. Mudge, and K. Flautner. A system solution for High-Performance, low power SDR. In *SDR Technical Conference*, 2005.

[12] Y. Lin, H. Lee, M. Woh, Y. Harel, S. Mahlke, T. Mudge, C. Chakrabarti, and K. Flautner. SODA: a low-power architecture for software radio. *SIGARCH Comput. Archit. News*, 34(2):89–101, 2006.

[13] B. Mathew and A. Davis. An energy efficient high performance scratch-pad memory system. *DAC*, 2004.

[14] P. R. Panda, N. D. Dutt, and A. Nicolau. On-chip vs. off-chip memory: the data partitioning problem in embedded processor-based systems. *ACM TODAES*, 5(3):704, 2000.

[15] J. Park, S. Park, J. D. Balfour, D. Black-Schaffer, C. Kozyrakis, and W. J. Dally. Register pointer architecture for efficient embedded processors. In *DATE*, pages 600–605. EDA Consortium, 2007.

[16] D. Pham, E. Behnen, M. Bolliger, H. P. Hofstee, C. Johns, J. Kahle, A. Kameyama, J. Keaty, B. Le, Y. Masubuchi, et al. The design methodology and implementation of a first-generation CELL processor: a multi-core SoC. In *CICC*, pages 45–49, 2005.

[17] R. M. Russell. The CRAY-1 computer system. *Commun. ACM*, 21(1):63–72, 1978.

[18] M. Woh, Y. Lin, S. Seo, S. Mahlke, T. Mudge, C. Chakrabarti, R. Bruce, D. Kershaw, A. Reid, M. Wilder, and K. Flautner. From SODA to scotch: The evolution of a wireless baseband processor. In *MICRO 41*, pages 152–163, 2008.

[19] P. Yiannacouras. *FPGA-Based Soft Vector Processors*. PhD thesis, Dept. of ECE, Univ. of Toronto, Canada, 2009.

[20] P. Yiannacouras, J. G. Steffan, and J. Rose. VESPA: portable, scalable, and flexible FPGA-based vector processors. In *CASES*, pages 61–70. ACM, 2008.

[21] P. Yiannacouras, J. G. Steffan, and J. Rose. Data parallel FPGA workloads: Software versus hardware. In *FPL*, pages 51–58, Progue, Czech Republic, 2009.

[22] P. Yiannacouras, J. G. Steffan, and J. Rose. Fine-grain performance scaling of soft vector processors. In *CASES*, pages 97–106, Grenoble, France, 2009. ACM.

[23] J. Yu, C. Eagleston, C. H. Chou, M. Perreault, and G. Lemieux. Vector processing as a soft processor accelerator. *ACM TRETS*, 2(2):1–34, 2009.

[24] J. Yu, G. Lemieux, and C. Eagleston. Vector processing as a soft-core CPU accelerator. In *FPGA*, pages 222–232, Monterey, California, USA, 2008.

LEAP Scratchpads: Automatic Memory and Cache Management for Reconfigurable Logic *

Michael Adler[†]   Kermin E. Fleming[¶]   Angshuman Parashar[†]   Michael Pellauer[¶]   Joel Emer[†¶]

[†]Intel Corporation
VSSAD Group
{michael.adler, angshuman.parashar,
joel.emer}@intel.com

[¶]Massachusetts Institute of Technology
Computer Science and A.I. Laboratory
Computation Structures Group
{kfleming, pellauer, emer}@csail.mit.edu

ABSTRACT

Developers accelerating applications on FPGAs or other reconfigurable logic have nothing but raw memory devices in their standard toolkits. Each project typically includes tedious development of single-use memory management. Software developers expect a programming environment to include automatic memory management. Virtual memory provides the illusion of very large arrays and processor caches reduce access latency without explicit programmer instructions.

LEAP scratchpads for reconfigurable logic dynamically allocate and manage multiple, independent, memory arrays in a large backing store. Scratchpad accesses are cached automatically in multiple levels, ranging from shared on-board, RAM-based, set-associative caches to private caches stored in FPGA RAM blocks. In the LEAP framework, scratchpads share the same interface as on-die RAM blocks and are plug-in replacements. Additional libraries support heap management within a storage set. Like software developers, accelerator authors using scratchpads may focus more on core algorithms and less on memory management.

Categories and Subject Descriptors

C.5.m [**Computer System Implementation**]: Miscellaneous

General Terms

Algorithms, Performance

Keywords

FPGA, memory management, caches

---

*An extended version of this paper showing experimental results is available as MIT Technical Report MIT-CSAIL-TR-2010-054

1. INTRODUCTION

FPGAs are increasingly employed as coprocessors alongside general purpose CPUs. The combination of large memory and ease of programming a general purpose machine along with the abundant parallelism and low communication latency in an FPGA make the pair attractive for *hybrid* algorithms that split computation across both engines.

Memory management in software development is supported by a rich set of OS and library features. Software designers targeting general purpose hardware long ago accepted that the gain in programmer efficiency from using compilers, support libraries and operating systems outweighs possible performance gains of hand-coding raw instructions.

The memory subsystem in general purpose hardware offers a hierarchy of storage, ranging from fast but small caches embedded in the processor to large external RAM arrays on memory buses, and to swap files on disks. Management of cache state is controlled by fixed hardware algorithms chosen for their overall performance. Explicit, hand-tuned cache management instructions are typically added only to the most performance-sensitive programs. Tremendous effort has been spent building compilers capable of automatic cache-management, e.g. [6, 7]. As general purpose processors add more parallel processing, language designers continue to add abstract memory management to design tools in order to split algorithmic design from the grunt work of memory management [2].

The gap between the programming environment on the general purpose half and the reconfigurable half of a hybrid machine is stark. Most FPGA developers still code in low level languages equivalent to assembly language on general purpose machines. Those optimizing a set of loop kernels may use C or Java-like languages [4, 5, 8] and a handful are beginning to use languages such as Bluespec [1, 11] that support language-based static elaboration and polymorphic module definitions.

The state of memory management on reconfigurable logic is similarly primitive. FPGA synthesis tools support relatively easy management of on-die memory arrays. The interface to on-die RAM blocks is simple: a method for writing a value to an address and a two-phase pair of read request and response methods. This interface may be made timing insensitive by predicating the methods with *ready* and *enable* flags and buffering state on pipeline stalls [3].

1.1 Scratchpad memory hierarchies

What if an algorithm needs more memory than is available on-die? At best, designers are offered low-level device drivers for embedded memory controllers, PCIe DMA controllers or some other bus. Building an FPGA-side memory hierarchy is treated as an application-specific problem. Even methods for mapping memory management as basic as malloc and free to on-die RAM for C-like synthesis languages are a very recent innovation [12]. On general purpose hardware the memory hierarchy is invisible to an application, except for timing. A similar memory abstraction, identical to the interface to on-die RAM blocks but implementing a full storage hierarchy, is equally useful for a range of FPGA-based applications.

Our project began as an effort to accelerate processor microarchitecture timing models using FPGAs. We quickly realized that some effort writing a general programming framework would make our task more tractable. The resulting platform is in active use for timing models and has been adopted for other algorithmic accelerators, such as an H.264 decoder.

We have written LEAP *(Logic-based Environment for Application Programming)* [9], a platform for application development on reconfigurable logic. LEAP runs on any set of reconfigurable logic connected to general purpose machines. Like an operating system, LEAP is layered on top of device-specific drivers. It presents a consistent virtual platform on any hardware. Application writers may then target the virtual platform, rendering their code portable across communication fabrics. LEAP presents the same interface over connections as diverse as FPGAs plugged directly into Intel Front Side Bus sockets and FPGAs connected to a host over a JTAG cable. The virtual platform provides a rich set of services, including streaming I/O devices, application control primitives, and an asynchronous hybrid procedural interface similar to remote procedure calls [10]. The platform also provides automatic instantiation of processor-like memory hierarchies, ranging from private caches, through shared caches and down to host memory. In this paper we focus on the automatically constructed memory stack.

LEAP defines a single, timing insensitive, interface to scratchpad memory hierarchies. The same write, read request and read response interface methods are used for any memory implementation defined by the platform, along with the predicates governing whether the methods may be invoked in a given FPGA cycle. The simplest memory device allocates an on-die RAM block. However, LEAP memory stacks sharing the same interface can be configured for a variety of hierarchies. The most complicated has three levels: a large storage region such as virtual memory in a host system, a medium sized intermediate latency memory such as SDRAM controlled by an FPGA, and fast, small memories such as on-FPGA RAM blocks. Converting a client from using on-die memory to a complex memory hierarchy is simply a matter of instantiating a different memory module with identical connections.

For a given set of hardware, low-level device drivers must be provided for each level in a physical hierarchy. Virtual devices and services are layered on top of these physical device drivers, thus providing a consistent programming model independent of the underlying physical devices. Our goal is to make programming an FPGA more like software development on general purpose hardware. Programmers target an abstract set of virtual services similar to general purpose kernel and user-space libraries. Like general purpose hardware, programmers may get an algorithm working with generic code and then, optionally, tune their application for specific hardware latencies and sizes.

1.2 Related work

Many researchers have considered the problem of cache hierarchies in reconfigurable logic and embedded systems. For a review of related work and analysis of workloads using LEAP scratchpads please see the extended version of this paper, released as MIT Technical Report MIT-CSAIL-TR-2010-054.

2. SCRATCHPAD ARCHITECTURE

2.1 FPGA On-Die RAM Blocks

On-die FPGA RAM blocks can be configured quite flexibly. Xilinx RAM blocks are organized as 18Kb or 36Kb blocks in data widths of 1, 2, 4, 9, 18 or 36 bits [13]. Altera RAM blocks have similar widths. Synthesis tools automatically provide the illusion of arbitrary size and width by grouping multiple blocks into a single logical block and mapping into the closest available bit width. A large Xilinx Virtex 6 FPGA has about 32Mb of RAM.

Access to RAM blocks is simple: a single cycle write operation and a two phase read request / read response protocol. Even a naïve implementation can be dual ported, permitting simultaneous reads and writes. RAM blocks are fast, flexible and easy to access as private storage within a module. Unfortunately, they are finite. What are we to do for algorithms with memory footprints too large for on-FPGA RAM?

2.2 On-Board RAM

Many FPGA platforms have on-board RAM and have memory controllers available as logic blocks. Compared to an FPGA's internal RAM blocks, on-board memory is plentiful: typically measured in megabytes or gigabytes. Unlike FPGA RAM blocks, on-board memory is a monolithic resource. At most only a few banks are available, managed by individual controllers. In order to share on-board RAM among multiple clients the memory must be partitioned and managed by a central controller. We call this service the *scratchpad controller*. The controller is responsible for partitioning a large memory into individual *scratchpads*, corresponding to private memories requested by clients. The controller then routes requests from scratchpads to their unique memory segments. This is implemented using an indirection table, mapping scratchpads to memory base offsets.

Except for latency, moving storage to a different level in the memory hierarchy is invisible to software written for general purpose hardware. The change could range from missing in an L1 cache to suffering a page fault and swapping data in from a disk. While not an absolute requirement for FPGA-based scratchpads, having the ability to express memory I/O operations independent of their underlying implementation and latency is equally convenient on reconfigurable logic. In our implementation, the difference between a client using a private on-die RAM block and a scratchpad in a shared memory is only a single source line. The client using a RAM block invokes a module that instantiates on-die memory. To use a scratchpad instead, the client replaces this instantiation with a module that connects itself to the scratchpad controller.

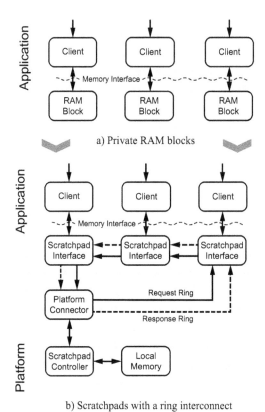

a) Private RAM blocks

b) Scratchpads with a ring interconnect

Figure 1: Transforming private RAM blocks to scratchpads. The memory interface between clients and storage is unchanged following the transformation. Only timing is different.

Each client requesting a scratchpad memory instantiates a *scratchpad interface*. This interface is private to a single client, transforming client-side references to requests in the scratchpad controller. The scratchpad controller is a shared resource. Connecting multiple clients to the controller requires an interconnect and arbitration. For a small number of scratchpads, a set of point-to-point connections from scratchpad interfaces to the controller along with a round-robin arbiter works perfectly well. As the number of clients grows, the burden on FPGA routing becomes too great and a more sophisticated network is required. We have built a pair of token rings, using self-assembling rings described in [11]. The transformation from private RAM blocks to scratchpad memories is illustrated in Figure 1. Deadlocks are avoided by assigning requests to one ring and responses to the other. A pair of rings was chosen instead of a single ring with virtual request and response channels both to increase network bandwidth and because the FPGA overheads of channel buffering and multiplexing are similar to the simpler, multi-ring, solution. One ring stop is responsible for forwarding messages between the rings and the scratchpad controller.

2.3 Marshaling

Astute readers will have noticed a problem in our transformation of RAM block clients to scratchpad clients. Synthesis tools permit FPGA RAM allocation in any bit width. While the underlying hardware does not support arbitrary width, it

is sufficiently flexible that memory is allocated relatively efficiently. In contrast, on-board memory is presented in chunks of words and lines, with some hardware adding write masks to support byte-sized writes.

An easy, but unacceptably inefficient solution would be fixed mapping of RAM block addresses to word-sized on-board memory chunks. The fixed mapping would not support data widths larger than a memory word. It would also waste nearly the entire word for small data widths, turning a dense 1024 x 1-bit RAM block into a 64KB chunk, assuming a 64 bit word!

To solve this mapping problem, the scratchpad interface interposes a marshaling layer between the client and requests to the platform interface. When objects are smaller than the memory word size, multiple objects are grouped into a single memory word. When objects are larger than the memory word size, the marshaling layer spreads objects across multiple words. In the first case the marshaler is forced to request read-modify-write operations in order to update an entry. In the second case the marshaler must emit multiple read or write requests in order to reference all memory words corresponding to a scratchpad location. From the client's perspective, the word size remains the size originally requested.

The LEAP platform provides a marshaling library module. Compile-time parameters declare the memory word size along with the desired scratchpad width and number of elements. The marshaler computes the dimensions of an on-board-memory-sized container for holding the equivalent data and determines whether read-modify-write or group reads and writes are required. It also exports read and write methods that act on the requested array's data type. The methods automatically trigger either read-modify-write or group reads and writes when needed.

2.4 Private Caches

With the addition of marshaling we now have an architectural description for replacing RAM blocks with on-board memory scratchpads that is fully functional. Unfortunately, it will perform terribly. RAM block references that were formerly single cycle references and parallel for each block have been converted into a shared, high contention, higher latency resource. A cache is needed, both to provide lower latency and to reduce the number of requests that reach on-board memory. LEAP provides low latency, direct mapped, caches, though developers may specify their own cache implementations optimized for particular access patterns.

The position of the cache, above or below the marshaler, is a compromise. Choosing to insert the cache between the client and the marshaler would eliminate many read-modify-write operations in the marshaler. However, read-modify-write operations are required because the data width above the marshaler is small. Consider a scratchpad of boolean values. Caching above the marshaler would require tag sizes to cover the address space but would have only one bit data buckets. This ratio of meta-data to actual cache data is unacceptable.

In our implementation, both the private cache and the marshaler present the same interface to the client. The relative order of the marshaler and a cache is invisible to the scratchpad client. A compile-time heuristic could choose a locally optimal topology based on a scratchpad's size and data type, placing the cache either above or below the marshaler. In our current implementation the cache is always inserted below the marshaler.

2.5 Host Memory

The hierarchy has now expanded available FPGA-side memory from the capacity of on-die RAM blocks to the capacity of on-board RAM. This solution is fully functional on both stand-alone FPGAs and on FPGAs connected to a host computer. For scratchpad memories, on-die RAM block usage is reduced to fixed sized caches. Now we face the same question asked at the end of Section 2.1: What are we to do for algorithms with memory footprints too large for on-board RAM?

If the FPGA is connected via a high speed bus to a host computer, the solution is the same as when we ran out of on-die memory: push the backing storage one level down in the hierarchy, using host memory as the home for scratchpad data. Instead of reading and writing data from on-board memory, the scratchpad controller reads and writes host memory using either direct memory access or a protocol over an I/O channel.

2.6 Central Cache

Moving the backing storage from on-board RAM to host memory offers more space at the expense of access time. Configuring the now unused on-board RAM as a last-level cache can reduce this penalty. Because only one central cache controller is instantiated we can afford a more complicated controller. The platform's central cache controller is set associative with LRU replacement.

Like the scratchpad controller, the central cache constructs a unique address space for each client by concatenating client IDs and address requests from clients. This internal address space enables the central cache to associate entries with specific clients.

Clients connecting to the central cache must provide functions for spilling and filling memory lines. Pushing the details of spills and fills out of the central cache allows a variety of clients to connect, all sharing the same on-board RAM, each with unique methods of reading and writing their backing storage. The LRU central cache policy automatically optimizes the footprint of each client in the central cache based on the global access pattern of all clients.

3. CONCLUSION

Automatic cache instantiation frees the FPGA application developer to concentrate more on algorithmic design and less on memory management. A platform-provided memory hierarchy automatically partitions the on-board memory among competing clients. Without it, application writers would be forced to manage access to on-die RAM blocks and shared DDR RAM explicitly. Designers would most likely hard partition memory among clients. Like application development on general purpose machines, core algorithms may be written and then tuned for their particular memory access patterns.

LEAP scratchpads are in active use in projects as diverse as H.264 decoders and micro-architectural timing models. We have found them to be particularly useful for managing storage in applications that require multiple, large, random access buffers.

4. REFERENCES

[1] Arvind. Bluespec: A Language for Hardware Design, Simulation, Synthesis and Verification. In *MEMOCODE '03: Proceedings of the First ACM and IEEE International Conference on Formal Methods and Models for Co-Design*, page 249. IEEE Computer Society, 2003.

[2] Z. Budimlic, A. M. Chandramowlishwaran, K. Knobe, G. N. Lowney, V. Sarkar, and L. Treggiari. Declarative Aspects of Memory Management in the Concurrent Collections Parallel Programming Model. In *DAMP '09: Proceedings of the 4th Workshop on Declarative Aspects of Multicore Programming*, pages 47–58. ACM, 2008.

[3] N. Dave, M. C. Ng, M. Pellauer, and Arvind. A design flow based on modular refinement. In *Formal Methods and Models for Codesign (MEMOCODE), 2010 8th IEEE/ACM International Conference on*, pages 11 –20, Jul. 2010.

[4] M. B. Gokhale, J. M. Stone, J. Arnold, and M. Kalinowski. Stream-Oriented FPGA Computing in the Streams-C High Level Language. In *FCCM '00: Proceedings of the 2000 IEEE Symposium on Field-Programmable Custom Computing Machines*, page 49. IEEE Computer Society, 2000.

[5] S. S. Huang, A. Hormati, D. F. Bacon, and R. Rabbah. Liquid Metal: Object-Oriented Programming Across the Hardware/Software Boundary. In *ECOOP '08: Proceedings of the 22nd European conference on Object-Oriented Programming*, pages 76–103. Springer-Verlag, 2008.

[6] W. W. Hwu and P. P. Chang. Achieving High Instruction Cache Performance with an Optimizing Compiler. *SIGARCH Comput. Archit. News*, 17(3):242–251, 1989.

[7] C.-K. Luk and T. C. Mowry. Cooperative Prefetching: Compiler and Hardware Support for Effective Instruction Prefetching in Modern Processors. In *MICRO 31: Proceedings of the 31st Annual ACM/IEEE International Symposium on Microarchitecture*, pages 182–194. IEEE Computer Society Press, 1998.

[8] W. A. Najjar, W. Böhm, B. A. Draper, J. Hammes, R. Rinker, J. R. Beveridge, M. Chawathe, and C. Ross. High-Level Language Abstraction for Reconfigurable Computing. *Computer*, 36(8):63–69, 2003.

[9] A. Parashar, M. Adler, K. Fleming, M. Pellauer, and J. Emer. LEAP: A Virtual Platform Architecture for FPGAs. In *CARL '10: The 1st Workshop on the Intersections of Computer Architecture and Reconfigurable Logic*, 2010.

[10] A. Parashar, M. Adler, M. Pellauer, and J. Emer. Hybrid CPU/FPGA Performance Models. In *WARP '08: The 3rd Workshop on Architectural Research Prototyping*, 2008.

[11] M. Pellauer, M. Adler, D. Chiou, and J. Emer. Soft Connections: Addressing the Hardware-Design Modularity Problem. In *DAC '09: Proceedings of the 46th Annual Design Automation Conference*, pages 276–281. ACM, 2009.

[12] J. Simsa and S. Singh. Designing Hardware with Dynamic Memory Abstraction. In *FPGA '10: Proceedings of the 18th Annual ACM/SIGDA International Symposium on Field Programmable Gate Arrays*, pages 69–72. ACM, 2010.

[13] Xilinx, Inc. UG363: Virtex-6 FPGA Memory Resources User Guide. 2010.

NetTM: Faster and Easier Synchronization for Soft Multicores via Transactional Memory

Martin Labrecque and J. Gregory Steffan
University of Toronto, Canada
{martinl,steffan}@eecg.utoronto.ca

ABSTRACT

We propose NetTM: support for hardware *transactional memory* (HTM) in an FPGA-based soft multithreaded multicore that matches the strengths of FPGAs. We evaluate our system using the NetFPGA [6] platform and four network packet processing applications that are threaded and share memory. Relative to NetThreads [5], an existing two-processor four-way-multithreaded system with conventional lock-based synchronization, we find that adding HTM support (i) maintains a reasonable operating frequency of 125MHz with an area overhead of 20%, (ii) can transactionally execute lock-based critical sections with no software modification, and (iii) achieves 6%, 55% and 57% increases in packet throughput for three of four packet processing applications studied, due to reduced false synchronization.

Categories and Subject Descriptors

C.1.4 [**Processor architectures**]: Parallel Architectures; C.3 [**Special-purpose and application-based systems**]: Real-time and embedded systems

General Terms

Design, Performance

1. INTRODUCTION

FPGA-based systems are increasingly used to implement larger and more complex systems-on-chip composed of multiple processor and acceleration cores that must synchronize and share data. While systems based on shared memory can ease communication between cores, they require correct synchronization (i.e. lock and unlock operations). Consequently, threads executing in parallel wanting to enter the same *critical section* (i.e. a portion of code that accesses shared data delimited by synchronization) at the same time will be serialized, thus losing the parallel advantage of such a system. Therefore designers face two important challenges: (i) writing parallel programs with manually inserted lock-based synchronization is error-prone and difficult to debug, and (ii) multiple processors need to share memory, communicate, and synchronize without serializing the execution.

Transactional memory (TM, see references in [4]) offers a potential solution to both challenges as it (i) offers an

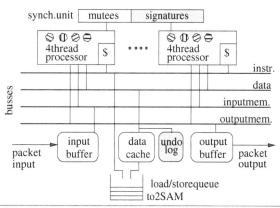

Figure 1: The NetTM architecture, which supports TM by extending NetThreads with signatures and an undo-log.

easier programming model for synchronization, and (ii) can reduce the contention on critical sections. With transactional execution, a programmer is free to employ coarser critical sections, spend less effort minimizing them, and not worry about deadlocks since a properly implemented TM system does not suffer from them. A TM system optimistically allows multiple threads inside a critical section—hence TM can improve performance when the parallel critical sections access independent data locations. To guarantee correctness, the underlying system dynamically monitors the memory accesses of each transaction (the *read set* and *write set*) and detects *conflicts* between them. While TM can be implemented purely or partly in software (STM), an FPGA-based system can be extended to support TM in hardware (HTM) with much lower performance overhead than an STM. Our goal is to use HTM to improve synchronization for FPGA-based multicores, by which we mean interconnected processor or accelerator cores that synchronize and share memory. There are many known methods for implementing HTM for an ASIC multicore processor, although they do not necessarily map well to FPGA-based processors. In this paper we introduce NetTM, which adds support for HTM to the NetThreads [5] system, an FPGA-based multithreaded multicore for high-throughput packet processing.

2. BASE ARCHITECTURE: NETTHREADS

In this work our starting point architecture for comparison is the NetThreads [5] multithreaded multicore architecture that supports only lock-based critical sections, shown in Figure 1. Each NetThreads processor is a single-issue, in-order, 5-stage pipelined processor. In a single core, instructions from four hardware threads are issued in a round-robin fashion to hide pipeline hazards and cache miss latency [5]. The SDRAM controller services a merged load/store queue of up to 64 entries in-order; since this queue and the data cache are shared by all processors, they serve as a single point of serialization and memory consistency, hence threads need only block on pending loads but not stores. Each processor has a 16KB instruction cache. Packets are received into the 10-slot input buffer memory, and written out via the output buffer. There is also a shared data cache capable of 32-bit line-sized data transfers with the DDR2 SDRAM controller. All three of these memories are 16KB. To implement lock-based synchronization, NetThreads provides a synchronization unit containing 16 hardware mutexes (sufficient for our applications). In the NetThreads ISA, each lock/unlock operation specifies a unique identifier, indicating one of these 16 mutexes.

Benchmark Applications For 2009, both Altera and Xilinx reported that communications comprised 44% of their net revenues. NetThreads targets network packet processing applications, in particular those that require deeper packet inspection. We focus on *stateful* applications—i.e., applications in which shared, persistent data structures are modified during the processing of most packets. To take full advantage of the software programmability of our processors, our focus is on the control-flow intensive applications described in detail in earlier work [5]. Note that each of these is a full application, with significant numbers of loads and stores, designed for the NetFPGA platform and integrated with a host.

3. PROGRAMMING NETTM

Specifying Transactions TM semantics imply that any transaction will appear to have executed atomically with respect to any other transaction. To denote the start and end of a transactional critical section, NetTM uses the same instruction API as the lock-based synchronization for NetThreads—i.e., lock(ID) can mean "start transaction" and unlock(ID) can mean "end transaction". Hence existing programs need not be modified, since NetTM can use existing synchronization in the code and simply interpret critical sections as transactional. We next describe how the lock identifier, ID, is interpreted by NetTM.

Locks vs Transactions NetTM supports both lock-based and TM-based synchronization, since a code region's access patterns can favor one approach over the other. For example, lock-based critical sections are necessary for I/O operations since they cannot be undone in the event of an aborted transaction: specifically, for processor initialization, to protect the sequence of memory-mapped commands leading to sending a packet, and to protect the allocation of output memory (Figure 1). We use the software identifier associated with lock/unlock operations to distinguish whether a given critical section should be executed via a transaction or via traditional lock-based synchronization: this mapping of the identifiers is provided by the designer as a parameter to the hardware synchronization unit (Figure 1). When using locks, a programmer would typically need to worry about which identifier encloses accesses to which shared variables. NetTM simplifies the programmer's task when using transactions: NetTM enforces the atomicity of all transactions regardless of the lock identifier value. Therefore

only one identifier can be designated to be of the transaction type, and doing so frees the remaining identifiers/mutexes to be used as traditional locks. However, to support legacy software, a designer is also free to designate multiple identifiers to be of the transaction type.

4. IMPLEMENTING NETTM

Version Management Version management refers to the method of segregating transactional modifications from other transactions and regular memory. For a simple HTM, the two main options for version management are *lazy* [2] versus *eager* [9]. In an eager approach, writes modify main memory directly and are not buffered—therefore any conflicts must be detected before a write is performed. To support rollback for aborts, a backup copy of each modified memory location must be saved in an *undo-log*. Hence when a transaction aborts, the undo-log is flushed to regular memory, and when a transaction commits, the undo-log is discarded. A major benefit of an eager approach is that reads proceed unhindered and can directly access main memory, and hence an undo-log is much simpler than a write-buffer since the undo-log need only be read when flushing to regular memory on abort. Because eager schemes modify regular memory directly: (i) they cannot support multiple transactions writing to the same location (this results in a conflict), (ii) conflict detection must be performed on every memory access, (iii) aborts are slow because the undo-log must be flushed to regular memory, and (iv) commits are fast because the undo-log is simply discarded.

After serious consideration of the lazy and eager approaches, we concluded that eager version management was the best match to FPGA-based systems such as NetTM for several reasons. First, while requiring a similar minimum amount of storage, a write buffer is necessarily significantly more complex than an undo-log since it must support fast reads via indexing and a cache-like organization. Our preliminary efforts found that it was extremely difficult to create a write-buffer with single-cycle read and write access. To avoid replacement from a cache-organized write-buffer (which in turn must result in transaction stall or abort), it must be large or associative or both, and these are both challenging for FPGAs. Second, an eager approach allows spilling transactional modifications from the shared data cache to the next level of memory (in this case off-chip), and our benchmarks exhibit large write sets. Third, via simulation, we observed that disallowing multiple writers to the same memory location(s) (a limitation of an eager approach) resulted in only a 1% increase in aborts for our applications in the worst case. Fourth, we found that transactions commit in the common case for our applications, and an eager approach is fastest for commit.

Conflict Detection A key consequence of our decision to implement eager version management is that we must be able to detect conflicts with every memory access; hence to avoid undue added sources of stalling in the system, we must be able to do so in a single cycle. This requirement led us to consider implementing conflict detection via *signatures*, which are bit-vectors that track the memory locations accessed by a transaction via hash indexing, with each transaction owning two signatures to track its read and write sets. Signatures can represent an unbounded set of addresses,

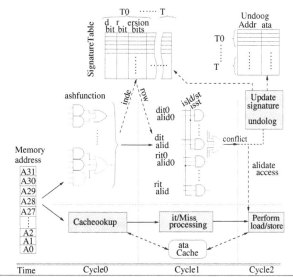

Figure 2: Integration of conflict detection hardware with the processor pipeline for a memory access.

Table 1: NetFPGA Implementation of NetTM.

Aspect	Description
Compilation	Modified gcc 4.0.2 for 32-bit MIPS-I ISA
Platform	NetFPGA 2.1 [6] with 4 x 1GigE links
FPGA	Virtex II Pro 50 speed grade 7ns
Synthesis	Xilinx ISE 10.1.03, high effort for speed
Off-chip memory	64 Mbytes 200MHz DDR2 SDRAM
Processor clock	125MHz, same as Ethernet MACs
Packet stimulus	Packet traces sent by modified Tcpreplay 3.4.0 via a Broadcom NetXtreme II GigE NIC to a NetFPGA port. A different NetFPGA port is used for output.

they decouple conflict detection from version management, and provide an opportunity to capitalize on the bit-level parallelism of FPGAs. Previous work [4] explored the design space of signature implementations for an FPGA-based two-processor system (i.e., for two total threads), and proposed a method for creating application-specific hash functions to reduce signature size without impacting their accuracy. We extended this prior scheme to support a multithreaded multicore for eight total threads.

Signature Table In contrast with prior work [4], in NetTM we store signatures in BRAMs. As shown in Figure 2, the hash function indexes a row of the BRAM, and we map the corresponding read and write bits for every transaction/thread-context on the same memory row. Therefore with one BRAM access, we can read all of the read and write signature bits for a given address for all transactions in parallel. Note in Figure 2 that memory instructions undergo an extra pipeline stage (*cycle 1*) to allot for the hashing and conflict detection. A challenge is that we must clear the signature bits for a given transaction when it commits or aborts, and it would be too costly to visit all of the rows of the BRAM to do so. Instead we add a version number per transaction (incremented on commit or rollback), that we can compare to a register holding the true version number of the current transaction for that thread context. Comparing version numbers produces a `Valid` signal (Figure 2) that is used to ignore the result of comparing signature bits when appropriate. We clear signature bits lazily: for every memory reference, a row of the signature table is accessed, and we clear the corresponding signature bits for any transaction with mismatching version numbers. This lazy-clear works well in practice, although it is possible that the version number may completely wrap-around before there is an intervening memory reference to cause a clear, resulting in a false conflict (which hurts performance but not correctness). We are hence motivated to support version numbers that are as large as possible.

Our target device has 36-bit-wide BRAMs, and we determined experimentally that a signature table composed of

at most two block RAMs could be integrated in the NetTM CPU pipeline while preserving the 125MHz target frequency. We could combine the BRAMs horizontally to allow larger version numbers, or vertically to allow more signature bits; we determined experimentally that the vertical option produced the fewest false conflicts. Hence in NetTM, each BRAM row contains a read bit, a write bit, and two version bits (four bits total) for each of eight transactions/thread-contexts, for a total of 32 bits (slightly under-utilizing the available 36 bit width). For our applications, we implement signatures of maximum length ranging from 618 to 904 bits (limited by the speed of the hash function).

Undo-Log The undo-log is implemented as a single physical structure logically divided equally for each thread context. On a transaction commit, a per-thread undo-log is cleared in one cycle by resetting a write-pointer. On a transaction abort, the undo-log requests exclusive access to the shared data cache, and flushes its contents to the cache in reverse order. This flush is performed atomically with respect to any other memory access, although processors can continue to execute non-memory-reference instructions during an undo-log flush. We buffer data in the undo-log at a word granularity because that matches our conflict detection resolution. In NetTM, the undo-log must be provisioned to be large enough to accommodate the longest transactions. We save undo-log capacity via a filtering mechanism that ignores the uninitialized portion of the stack.

5. EVALUATING NETTM

In this section, we report the maximum sustainable packet rate for a given application with the configuration in Table 1 as the packet rate with 90% confidence of not dropping any packet over a five-second run—thus our results are conservative given that network appliances are typically allowed to drop a small fraction of packets.

Resource Utilization In total, with two four-threaded processors, NetTM consumes 32 more BRAMs than NetThreads, so its BRAM utilization is 71% (161/232) compared to 57% (129/232) for NetThreads. The additional BRAMs are used as follows: 2 for the signature bit vectors, 4 for the log filters (to save last and checkpoint stack pointers) and 26 for the undo-log (1024 words and addresses for 8 threads). NetThreads consumes 18980 LUTs (out of 47232, i.e. 40% of the total LUT capacity) when optimized with high-effort for speed; NetTM design variations range from 3816 to 4097 additional LUTs, an overhead of roughly 21% over NetThreads.

NetTM Throughput NetTM improves packet throughput by 57%, 6% and 55% for `Classifier`, `NAT`, and `UDHCP` re-

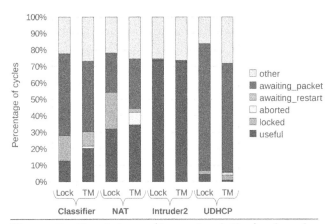

Figure 3: Breakdown (from simulation) of cycles spent: on pipeline hazards, and data and instruction misses (*other*); de-scheduled or busy-waiting for a packet (*awaiting_packet*); waiting to re-start a transaction (*awaiting_restart*); on instructions canceled due to transaction aborts (*aborted*); de-scheduled waiting for a lock (*locked*); or executing useful instructions (*useful*).

spectively, by exploiting the optimistic parallelism available in critical sections. The TM speedup is the result of reduced time spent awaiting locks, but moderated by the number of conflicts between transactions and the time to recover from them. `Classifier` has occasional long transactions that do not always conflict, providing an opportunity for reclaiming the corresponding large wait times incurred with locks. Similarly, `UDHCP` has a significant fraction of read-only transactions that do not conflict. `NAT` has a less pronounced speedup because of shorter transactions and higher abort rates. For `Intruder2`, despite having a high average commit rate, TM results in an 8% lower throughput due to bursty periods of repeated transaction aborts, leading to a reduced parallelism and packet rate.

Processor utilization To provide a detailed view of processor activity, we profile the execution of our applications using our cycle-accurate simulator. While it is unable to faithfully model the timing of DRAM refreshes and packet arrivals, our simulator gives predicted speedups of 1.6 for `Classifier`, 1.1 for `NAT`, 1.6 for `UDHCP` and 1.0 for `Intruder2`—i.e., a maximum error of 8% and a mean error of 4%. Figure 3 gives the breakdown of how time (in cycles) is spent for each application for both NetThreads and NetTM. `NAT` and `Classifier` experience a significant fraction of cycles waiting for locks in NetThreads, e.g. 22% for `NAT`. In our 4-way multithreaded cores, this is indicative of high lock contention because the thread scheduler could hide `locked` cycles, instruction hazards (included in the *other* category) and wait times for packets and transaction restarts, if there was any other thread context to schedule on those cycles. Compared to `Classifier`, `NAT` has a smaller speedup due to a considerable fraction of aborted work. Also, we can see that `UDHCP` spends most of the time waiting for packets despite functioning at its fixed maximum packet rate, indicating the highest variability in critical section size across our benchmarks. Comparatively, `Intruder2` has the highest CPU utilization, meaning that wait times for synchronization are smaller and data dependences across

transactions will be harmful because of transaction aborts. This case demonstrates that TM isn't necessarily the best option for every region of code or application.

6. RELATED WORK

The goal of most previous FPGA implementations of HTM [1, 7, 8] was to prototype ASIC attempts at TM—as opposed to targeting the strengths of an FPGA as a final product. To provide a low-overhead implementation, our work distinguishes itself in the type of TM that we implement and in the way that we perform conflict detection. To track transactional speculative state, prior FPGA implementations [1,3,8] use (i) extra bits per line in a private cache per thread or in a shared cache, and (ii) *lazy version management* (i.e., regular memory is modified only upon commit), and (iii) *lazy conflict detection* (i.e., validation is only performed at commit time). These approaches are not a good match for product-oriented FPGA-based systems because of the significant cache storage overhead required. Rather than using off-the-shelf soft cores requiring the programmer to explicitly mark each transactional access in the code as in other work [1,7,8], in NetTM we integrate TM with each soft processor pipeline and automatically and seamlessly handle loads and stores within transactions or lock-based critical sections appropriately.

7. CONCLUSIONS

We have shown that NetTM, an eager TM with application-specific signatures and contention management, matches the strengths and limitations of an FPGA, and can be integrated into a multithreaded processor pipeline without impacting clock frequency by adding a pipeline stage. NetTM makes synchronization (i) easier, by allowing more coarse-grained critical sections and eliminating deadlock errors, and (ii) faster, by exploiting the optimistic parallelism available in many concurrent critical sections, especially for software packet processing. For multithreaded applications that share and synchronize, we demonstrated that NetTM can improve throughput by 6%, 55%, and 57% over a locks-only system, but that TM is inappropriate for some applications where the cost of occasional aborts negates the wait times reclaimed.

8. REFERENCES

[1] S. Grinberg and S. Weiss. Investigation of transactional memory using FPGAs. In *EEEI*, Nov. 2006.

[2] L. Hammond, V. Wong, M. Chen, B. D. Carlstrom, J. D. Davis, B. Hertzberg, M. K. Prabhu, H. Wijaya, C. Kozyrakis, and K. Olukotun. Transactional memory coherence and consistency. *SIGARCH Comput. Archit. News*, 32(2):102, 2004.

[3] C. Kachris and C. Kulkarni. Configurable transactional memory. In *FCCM*, 2007.

[4] M. Labrecque, M. Jeffrey, and J. G. Steffan. Application-specific signatures for transactional memory in soft processors. In *ARC*, 2010.

[5] M. Labrecque and J. G. Steffan. The case for hardware transactional memory in software packet processing. In *ANCS*, 2010.

[6] J. W. Lockwood, N. McKeown, G. Watson, et al. NetFPGA - an open platform for gigabit-rate network switching and routing. In *MSE*, 2007.

[7] R. Teodorescu and J. Torrellas. Prototyping architectural support for program rollback using FPGAs. *FCCM*, 2005.

[8] S. Wee, J. Casper, N. Njoroge, et al. A practical FPGA-based framework for novel CMP research. In *FPGA*, 2007.

[9] L. Yen, J. Bobba, M. R. Marty, et al. LogTM-SE: Decoupling hardware transactional memory from caches. In *HPCA*, 2007.

LegUp: High-Level Synthesis for FPGA-Based Processor/Accelerator Systems

Andrew Canis[1], Jongsok Choi[1], Mark Aldham[1], Victor Zhang[1], Ahmed Kammoona[1],
Jason Anderson[1], Stephen Brown[1], and Tomasz Czajkowski[‡]

[1]ECE Department, University of Toronto, Toronto, ON, Canada
[‡]Altera Toronto Technology Centre, Toronto, ON, Canada
legup@eecg.toronto.edu

ABSTRACT

In this paper, we introduce a new open source high-level synthesis tool called *LegUp* that allows software techniques to be used for hardware design. LegUp accepts a standard C program as input and automatically compiles the program to a hybrid architecture containing an FPGA-based MIPS soft processor and custom hardware accelerators that communicate through a standard bus interface. Results show that the tool produces hardware solutions of comparable quality to a commercial high-level synthesis tool.

Categories and Subject Descriptors

B.7 [**Integrated Circuits**]: Design Aids

General Terms

Design, Algorithms

1. INTRODUCTION

Two approaches are possible for implementing computations: software (running on a standard processor) or hardware (custom circuits). A hardware implementation can improve speed and energy-efficiency versus software implementation (e.g. [3]). However, hardware design requires writing complex RTL code, which is error prone and difficult to debug. Software design, on the other hand, is more straightforward, and mature debugging and analysis tools are freely accessible. Despite the potential energy and performance benefits, hardware design is too difficult and costly for most applications, and a software approach is preferred.

In this paper, we propose *LegUp* – an open source high-level synthesis (HLS) framework we have developed that provides the performance and energy benefits of hardware, while retaining software ease-of-use. LegUp automatically compiles a C program to target a hybrid FPGA-based software/hardware system, where some program segments execute on an FPGA-based 32-bit MIPS soft processor and other program segments are automatically synthesized into FPGA circuits – *hardware accelerators* – that communicate and work in tandem with the soft processor. Since the first FPGAs appeared in the mid-1980s, access to the technology has been restricted to those with hardware design skills.

However, according to labor statistics, software engineers outnumber hardware engineers by more than 10X in the U.S. [10]. An overarching goal of LegUp is to broaden the FPGA user base to include software engineers, thereby expanding the scope of FPGA applications and growing the size of the programmable hardware market.

LegUp includes a soft processor because not all program segments are appropriate for hardware implementation. Inherently sequential computations are well-suited for software (e.g. traversing a linked list); whereas, other computations are ideally suited for hardware (e.g. addition of integer arrays). Incorporating a processor also offers the advantage of increased high-level language coverage. Program segments that use restricted C language constructs can execute on the processor (e.g. recursion).

LegUp is written in modular C++ to permit easy experimentation with new HLS algorithms. The LegUp distribution includes a set of benchmark C programs [6] that can be compiled to pure software, pure hardware, or a hybrid system. In this paper, we present an experimental study demonstrating that LegUp produces hardware implementations of comparable quality to a commercial tool [13], and we give results demonstrating the tool's capabilities for hardware/software co-design.

2. RELATED WORK

Among prior academic work, the *Warp Processor* proposed by Vahid, Stitt and Lysecky bears similarity to our framework [12]. The Warp Processor profiles software running on a processor. The profiling results guide the selection of program segments to be synthesized to hardware. Such segments are disassembled from the software binary to a higher-level representation, which is then synthesized to hardware [9]. We take a somewhat similar approach, with key differences being that we compile hardware from the high-level language source code and our tool is open source.

On the commercial front is Altera's C2H tool [1]. C2H allows a user to partition a C program's functions into a hardware set and a software set. The software-designated functions execute on a Nios II soft processor, and the hardware-designated functions are synthesized into custom hardware accelerators. The C2H system architecture closely resembles that targeted by LegUp.

3. LEGUP FLOW AND ARCHITECTURE

The LegUp design flow comprises first compiling and running a program on a standard processor, profiling its execution, selecting program segments to target to hardware, and then re-compiling the program to a hybrid hardware/software system. Fig. 1 illustrates the detailed flow. Referring to the labels in the figure, at step ①, a C compiler compiles a program to a binary executable [7]. At ②, the executable

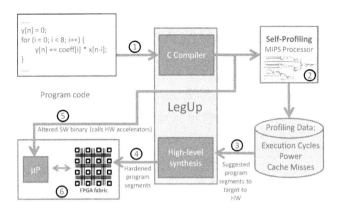

Figure 1: Design flow with LegUp.

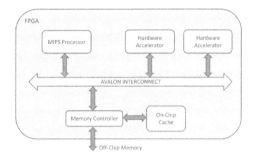

Figure 2: Target system architecture.

runs on an FPGA-based MIPS processor. We evaluated several publicly-available MIPS processor implementations and selected the Tiger MIPS processor from the University of Cambridge [11], based on its full support of the MIPS instruction set, established tool flow, and well-documented modular Verilog.

The MIPS processor has been augmented with extra circuitry to profile its own execution. Using its profiling ability, the processor is able to identify sections of program code that would benefit from hardware implementation. Specifically, the profiling results drive the selection of program code segments to be re-targeted to custom hardware from the C source. Profiling a program's execution in the processor itself provides the highest possible accuracy. Presently, we profile program run-time at the function level.

Having chosen program segments to target to custom hardware, at step ③ LegUp is invoked to compile these segments to synthesizeable Verilog RTL. LegUp's hardware synthesis and software compilation are part of the same compiler framework. Presently, LegUp HLS operates at the function level: entire functions are synthesized to hardware from the C source. The RTL produced by LegUp is synthesized to an FPGA implementation using standard commercial tools at step ④. In step ⑤, the C source is modified such that the functions implemented as hardware accelerators are *replaced* by wrapper functions that *call* the accelerators (instead of doing computations in software). This new modified source is compiled to a MIPS binary executable. Finally, in step ⑥ the hybrid processor/accelerator system executes on the FPGA.

Our long-term vision is to fully automate the flow in Fig. 1, thereby creating a *self-accelerating adaptive processor* in which profiling, hardware synthesis and acceleration happen transparently without user awareness. In the first release of our tool, however, the user must manually examine the profiling results and place the names of the functions to be accelerated in a file that is read by LegUp.

Fig. 2 elaborates on the target system architecture. The processor connects to one or more custom hardware accelerators through a standard on-chip interface. As our initial hardware platform is the Altera DE2 Development and Education board (containing a 90 *nm* Cyclone II FPGA), we use the Altera Avalon interface for processor/accelerator communication [2]. A shared memory architecture is used, with the processor and accelerators sharing an on-FPGA data cache and off-chip main memory. The on-chip cache memory is implemented using block RAMs within the FPGA fabric (M4K blocks on Cyclone II). Access to memory is handled by a memory controller. The architecture in Fig. 2 allows

processor/accelerator communication across the Avalon interface or through memory.

The architecture depicted in Fig. 2 represents the target system most natural for an initial release of the tool. The architecture of processor/accelerator systems is an important direction for future research.

4. DESIGN AND IMPLEMENTATION
4.1 High-Level Hardware Synthesis

High-level synthesis has traditionally been divided into three steps [4]: allocation, scheduling and binding. Allocation determines the amount of hardware resources available for use, and manages other hardware constraints (e.g., speed, area, and power). Scheduling assigns each operation in the program being synthesized to a particular clock cycle (state) and generates a finite state machine. Binding saves area by sharing functional units between operations, and sharing registers/memories between variables.

LegUp leverages the low-level virtual machine (LLVM) compiler framework. At the core of LLVM is an intermediate representation (IR), which is essentially machine-independent assembly language. C code is translated into LLVM's IR then analyzed and modified by a series of compiler optimization passes. LLVM IR instructions are simple enough to directly correspond to hardware operations (e.g., an arithmetic computation). Our HLS tool operates directly with the LLVM IR, scheduling the instructions into specific clock cycles. LegUp HLS algorithms have been implemented as LLVM passes that fit neatly into the existing framework. Implementing the HLS steps as distinct passes also allows easy experimentation with different HLS algorithms; for example, one could modify LegUp to "plug in" a new scheduling algorithm.

The initial release of LegUp uses as-soon-as-possible (ASAP) scheduling [5], which assigns an operation to the first state after its dependencies are available. In some cases, we can schedule an instruction into the *same* state as one of its dependencies. This is called *operation chaining*. Chaining can reduce hardware latency (# of cycles for execution) without impacting the clock period.

Binding consists of two tasks: assigning operators from the program being synthesized to specific hardware units, and assigning program variables to registers (register allocation). When multiple operators are assigned to the same hardware unit, or when multiple variables are bound to the same register, multiplexers are required to facilitate the sharing. We make two FPGA-specific observations in our approach to binding. First, multiplexers are relatively expensive to implement in FPGAs using LUTs. A 32-bit multiplexer implemented in 4-LUTs is the same size as a 32-bit adder. Consequently, there is little advantage to sharing all but the largest functional units, namely, multipliers and dividers. Likewise, the FPGA fabric is *register rich* and sharing registers is rarely justified. The initial relase of LegUp uses a weighted bipartite matching heuristic to solve the binding problem [8]. We minimize the number of multiplexer inputs required, thereby minimizing area.

4.2 Processor/Accelerator Communication

Functions selected for hardware implementation are automatically replaced with a wrapper by the LegUp framework. The wrapper function passes the function arguments to the corresponding hardware accelerator, and receives the returned data over the Avalon interconnect. While waiting for the accelerator to complete its work, the MIPS processor can do one of two things: 1) continue to perform computations and periodically poll a memory-mapped register whose value is set when the accelerator is done, or, 2) stall until a done signal is asserted by the accelerator. The advantage of polling is that the processor can execute other computations while the accelerator performs its work. The advantage of stalling is reduced energy consumption – the processor is in a low-power state while the accelerator operates. In our initial LegUp release, both modes are functional; however, we use stalling for the results in this paper.

4.3 Language Support and Benchmarks

LegUp supports a large subset of ANSI C for synthesis to hardware including: control flow statements, all integer arithmetic and bitwise operations, and integer types. Program segments that use unsupported language features are required to remain in software and execute on the MIPS processor. LegUp also supports functions, arrays, structs, global variables and pointer arithmetic. Dynamic memory, floating point and recursion are unsupported in the initial release.

With the LegUp distribution, we include 13 benchmark C programs. Included are all 12 programs in the CHStone high-level synthesis benchmark suite [6], and Dhrystone – a standard integer benchmark. A key characteristic of the benchmarks is that inputs and expected outputs are included in the programs themselves. The presence of golden outputs for each program gives us assurance regarding the correctness of our synthesis results.

5. EXPERIMENTS

The goals of our experimental study are three-fold: 1) to demonstrate that the quality of result (speed, area, power) produced by LegUp HLS is comparable to that produced by a commercial HLS tool (eXCite [13]), 2) to demonstrate LegUp's ability to effectively explore the hardware/software co-design space, and 3) to compare the quality of hardware vs. software implementations of the benchmark programs.

We map each benchmark program using 5 different flows, representing implementations with increasing amounts of computation happening in hardware vs. software: 1) A software only implementation running on the MIPS soft processor (*MIPS-SW*); 2) A hybrid software/hardware implementation where the *second most* compute-intensive function (and its descendants) in the benchmark is implemented as a hardware accelerator (*LegUp-Hybrid2*); 3) A hybrid software/hardware implementation where the *most* compute-intensive function (and its descendants) is implemented as a hardware accelerator (*LegUp-Hybrid1*); 4) A pure hardware implementation produced by LegUp (*LegUp-HW*); 5) A pure hardware implementation produced by eXCite (*eXCite-HW*). The two hybrid flows correspond to a system that includes the MIPS processor and a single accelerator, where the accelerator implements a C function and all of its descendant functions. For the back-end of all flows, we use Quartus II ver. 9.1 SP2 to target the Cyclone II FPGA.

Three metrics are employed to gauge quality of result: 1) circuit speed, 2) area, and 3) energy consumption. For circuit speed, we consider the cycle latency, clock frequency and total execution time. Cycle latency refers to the number of clock cycles required for a complete execution of a benchmark. Clock frequency refers to the reciprocal of the post-routed critical path delay reported by Altera timing analysis. Total execution time is simply the cycle latency multiplied by the clock period. To measure energy, we use Altera's PowerPlay power analyzer tool, applied to the routed design. We use switching activity data gathered from a full delay simulation with Mentor Graphics' ModelSim.

Table 1 presents speed performance results for all circuits and flows. Three data columns are given for each flow: *Cycles*, *Freq* in MHz, and *Time* in μS (*Cycles/Freq*). The second last row of the table contains geometric mean results for each column. The *dhrystone* benchmark was excluded from the geomean calculations, as eXCite was not able to compile this benchmark. The last row of the table presents the ratio of the geomean relative to the software flow (*MIPS-SW*).

For the *MIPS-SW* flow, Table 1 indicates that the processor runs at 74 MHz on the Cyclone II and the benchmarks take between 6.7K-29M cycles to complete their execution. In the *LegUp-Hybrid2* flow, the number of cycles needed for execution is reduced by 50% compared with software, on average. The *Hybrid2* circuits run at 6% lower frequency than the processor, on average. Overall, *LegUp-Hybrid2* provides a 47% (1.9×) speed-up in program execution time vs. software (*MIPS-SW*). In the *LegUp-Hybrid1* flow, cycle latency is 75% lower than software alone. However, clock speed is 9% worse for this flow, which results in a 73% reduction in program execution time vs. software (a 3.7× speed-up over software). Looking broadly at the data for *MIPS-SW*, *LegUp-Hybrid1* and *LegUp-Hybrid2*, we observe a trend: execution time decreases substantially as more computations are mapped to hardware.

Benchmark programs mapped using the *LegUp-HW* flow require 12% of the clock cycles of the software implementations, on average, yet they run at about the same speed in MHz. Benchmarks mapped using *eXCite-HW* require even fewer clock cycles – just 8% of that required for software implementations. However, implementations produced by eXCite run at 45% lower clock frequency than the MIPS processor, on average. LegUp produces heavily pipelined hardware implementations, whereas, we believe eXCite does more operation chaining, resulting in fewer cycles yet longer critical path delays. Considering total execution time of a benchmark, LegUp and eXCite offer similar results. *LegUp-HW* provides an 88% execution time improvement vs. software (8× speed-up); *eXCite-HW* provides an 85% improvement (6.7× speed-up).

It is worth highlighting a few results in Table 1. Comparing *LegUp-HW* with *eXCite-HW* for the benchmark *aes*, LegUp's implementation provides a nearly 5× improvement over eXCite in terms of execution time. Conversely, for the *motion* benchmark, LegUp's implementation requires nearly 4× more cycles than eXCite's implementation. We believe such differences lie in the extent of pipelining used by LegUp vs. eXCite.

Average area results are provided in Table 2. For each flow, three columns provide the number of Cyclone II logic elements (*LEs*), the number of memory bits used (*# bits*), as well as the number of 9x9 multipliers (*Mults*). The numbers in parentheses represent ratios relative to the *MIPS-SW* flow. The hybrid flows include *both* the MIPS processor, as well as custom hardware, and consequently, they consume considerably more area. The *LegUp-HW* flow implementa-

Table 1: Speed performance results.

Benchmark	MIPS-SW			LegUp-Hybrid2			LegUp-Hybrid1			LegUp-HW			eXCite-HW		
	Cycles	Freq.	Time	Cycles	Freq.	Time	Cycles	Freq.	Time	Cycles	Freq.	Time	Cycles	Freq.	Time
adpcm	193607	74.26	2607	159883	61.61	2595	96948	57.19	1695	36795	45.79	804	21992	28.88	761
aes	73777	74.26	993	55014	54.97	1001	26878	49.52	543	14022	60.72	231	55679	50.96	1093
blowfish	954563	74.26	12854	680343	63.21	10763	319931	63.7	5022	209866	65.41	3208	209614	35.86	5845
dfadd	16496	74.26	222	14672	83.14	176	5649	83.65	68	2330	124.05	19	370	24.54	15
dfdiv	71507	74.26	963	15973	83.78	191	4538	65.92	69	2144	74.72	29	2029	43.95	46
dfmul	6796	74.26	92	10784	85.46	126	2471	83.53	30	347	85.62	4	223	49.17	5
dfsin	2993369	74.26	40309	293031	65.66	4463	80678	68.23	1182	67466	62.64	1077	49709	40.06	1241
gsm	39108	74.26	527	29500	61.46	480	18505	61.14	303	6656	58.93	113	5739	41.82	137
jpeg	29802639	74.26	401328	16072954	51.2	313925	15978127	46.65	342511	5861516	47.09	124475	3248488	22.66	143358
mips	43384	74.26	584	6463	84.5	76	6463	84.5	76	6443	90.09	72	4344	76.25	57
motion	36753	74.26	495	34859	73.34	475	17017	83.98	203	8578	91.79	93	2268	42.87	53
sha	1209523	74.26	16288	358405	84.52	4240	265221	81.89	3239	247738	86.93	2850	238009	62.48	3809
dhrystone	28855	74.26	389	25599	82.26	311	25509	83.58	305	10202	85.38	119	-	-	-
Geomean:	173332.0	74.26	2334.1	86258.3	69.98	1232.6	42700.5	67.78	630.0	20853.8	71.56	291.7	14594.4	40.87	357.1
Ratio:	1	1	1	0.50	0.94	0.53	0.25	0.91	0.27	0.12	0.96	0.12	0.08	0.55	0.15

Table 2: Area results (geometric mean).

Flow	#LEs	# bits	Mults
MIPS-SW	12243 (1)	226009 (1)	16 (1)
LegUp-Hybrid2	27248 (2.23)	258526 (1.14)	43 (2.68)
LegUp-Hybrid1	33629 (2.75)	261260 (1.16)	51 (3.18)
LegUp-HW	15646 (1.28)	28822 (0.13)	12 (0.72)
eXCite-HW	13101 (1.07)	496 (0.00)	5 (0.32)

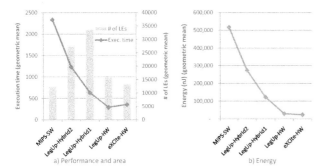

Figure 3: Performance, area and energy results.

tions require 28% more LEs than the MIPS processor on average; the *eXCite-HW* implementations require 7% more LEs than the processor. In terms of memory bits, both the *LegUp-HW* flow and the *eXCite-HW* flow require much fewer memory bits than the MIPS processor alone. For the benchmarks that require embedded multipliers, the *LegUp-HW* implementations use more multipliers than the *eXCite-HW* implementations, which we believe is due to more extensive multiplier sharing in the binding phase of eXCite.

Fig. 3(a) summarizes the speed and area results. The left vertical axis represents geometric mean execution time; the right axis represents area (number of LEs). Observe that execution time drops as more computations are implemented in hardware. While the data shows that pure hardware implementations offer superior speed performance to pure software or hybrid implementations, the plot demonstrates LegUp's usefulness as a tool for exploring the hardware/software co-design space. One can multiply the delay and area values to produce an *area-delay product*. On such a metric, *LegUp-HW* and *eXCite-HW* are nearly identical (∼4.6M μS-LEs vs. ∼4.7M μS-LEs) – *LegUp-HW* requires more LEs vs. *eXCite-HW*, however, it offers better speed, producing a roughly equivalent area-delay product.

Fig. 3(b) presents the geometric mean energy results for each flow. Energy is reduced drastically as more computa-

tions are implemented in hardware vs. software. The *LegUp-Hybrid2* and *LegUp-Hybrid1* flows use 47% and 76% less energy than the *MIPS-SW* flow, respectively. With *LegUp-HW*, the benchmarks use 94% less energy than if they are implemented with the *MIPS-SW* flow (an 18× reduction). The eXCite energy results are similar to LegUp.

6. CONCLUSIONS

In this paper, we introduced LegUp – a new high-level synthesis tool that compiles a standard C program to a hybrid processor/accelerator architecture. Using LegUp, one can explore the hardware/software design space, where some portions of a program run on a processor, and others as custom hardware circuits. LegUp, along with its suite of benchmark C programs, is a powerful open source platform for HLS research that we expect will enable a variety of research advances in hardware synthesis, as well as in hardware/software co-design. LegUp is available for download at: http://www.legup.org.

7. REFERENCES

[1] Altera, Corp. *Nios II C2H Compiler User Guide*, 2009.
[2] Altera, Corp. *Avalon Interface Specification*, 2010.
[3] J. Cong and Y. Zou. FPGA-based hardware acceleration of lithographic aerial image simulation. *ACM Trans. Reconfigurable Technol. Syst.*, 2(3):1–29, 2009.
[4] P. Coussy, D. Gajski, M. Meredith, and A. Takach. An introduction to high-level synthesis. *IEEE Design Test of Computers*, 26(4):8 – 17, jul. 2009.
[5] D. Gajski and et. al. Editors. *High-Level Synthesis - Introduction to Chip and System Design*. Kulwer Academic Publishers, 1992.
[6] Y. Hara, H. Tomiyama, S. Honda, and H. Takada. Proposal and quantitative analysis of the CHStone benchmark program suite for practical C-based high-level synthesis. *Journal of Information Processing*, 17:242–254, 2009.
[7] http://www.llvm.org. *The LLVM Compiler Infrastructure Project*, 2010.
[8] C.Y. Huang, Y.S. Che, Y.L. Lin, and Y.C. Hsu. Data path allocation based on bipartite weighted matching. In *Design Automation Conference*, volume 27, pages 499–504, 1990.
[9] G. Stitt and F. Vahid. Binary synthesis. *ACM Transactions on Design Automation of Electronic Systems*, 12(3), 2007.
[10] United States Bureau of Labor Statistics. *Occupational Outlook Handbook 2010-2011 Edition*, 2010.
[11] Univ. of Cambridge, http://www.cl.cam.ac.uk/teaching/0910/ECAD+Arch/mips.html. *The Tiger "MIPS" processor.*, 2010.
[12] F. Vahid, G. Stitt, and Lysecky R. Warp processing: Dynamic translation of binaries to FPGA circuits. *IEEE Computer*, 41(7):40–46, 2008.
[13] Y Explorations (XYI), San Jose, CA. *eXCite C to RTL Behavioral Synthesis 4.1(a)*, 2010.

Automatic SoC Design Flow on Many-core Processors: a Software Hardware Co-Design Approach for FPGAs

Ling Liu
Computer Systems Institute
ETH, Zurich
Zurich, Switzerland
ling.liu@inf.ethz.ch

Oleksii Morozov
Physics in Medicine Research
University Hospital of Basel
Basel, Switzerland
MorozovA@uhbs.ch

Yuxing Han
Dept. of Electrical Engineering
UCLA
Los Angeles, USA
ericahan@ee.ucla.edu

Jürg Gutknecht
Computer Systems Institute
ETH, Zurich
Zurich, Switzerland
gutknecht@inf.ethz.ch

Patrick Hunziker
Physics in Medicine Research
University Hospital of Basel
Basel, Switzerland
PHunziker@uhbs.ch

ABSTRACT

Traditional FPGA-based system-on-chip (SoC) design in general is accomplished via separate software and hardware design flows. With such a separate design methodology, extra development overhead has to be paid to meet the final system's performance, size and power consumption requirements. To overcome this development overhead which usually leads to significant increase of the time-to-market, a unified and efficient SoC design flow is needed. The current work addresses this problem via a SoC design flow which allows automatic building of a complete autonomous system on an FPGA in accordance with the need of a specific application. In the proposed design flow the architecture of the generated hardware is tailored to match the parallelism granularity and communication structure of the application. This, in turn, allows the application developer to meet the system's performance, size and power consumption requirements with a short time-to-market. To prove the applicability of the proposed approach, a monitor for real-time electrocardiographic (ECG) signal analysis and a motion detection algorithm have been implemented.

Categories and Subject Descriptors

B.6.3 [**Hardware**]: LOGIC DESIGN—*Design Aids*

General Terms

design, languages, experimentation

Keywords

automatic design flow, many-core architecture, software-hardware co-design, FPGA

1. INTRODUCTION

Embedded streaming systems or streaming systems on a chip usually consist of processors that execute domain-specific real-time applications, in which functions of the applications are organized in pipeline-like computation chains, and data are streamed through the pipeline in a sequential order.

The traditional streaming system design involves separate software and hardware design flows. With such a separate design methodology, the architecture of the target hardware in general does not reflect the computation granularity and the communication structure of a particular application. That is, the number of processor cores and the interconnection among the cores do not match the number of concurrent computation tasks and the communication paths among these tasks. Therefore, in order to meet the system's requirements, the application developers have to map the concurrency granularity (number of concurrent tasks) in the application into the concurrency granularity (number of processor cores) in the target hardware via time-sharing of a processor core. In addition, it is also necessary to implement message packaging and management to map the communication paths among the concurrent tasks in the application into the interconnect architecture in the hardware. Moreover, the target hardware's built-in I/O controllers and the connection among I/O controllers and processor cores do not necessarily match the need of an application, which can also lead to the increase of the development and power consumption overhead.

Facing the contrary between the stringent requirements and the design complexity/cost for a streaming system, we propose in this paper a unified and efficient SoC design flow for FPGAs. To achieve this design flow, a process-oriented system design paradigm, SystemSpec, and a toolchain which can automatically map the application structure onto the hardware architecture have been developed.

The rest of this paper is organized as follows: Section 2 summarizes and compares the proposed design approach with related work; Section 3 describes SystemSpec design flow. Section 4 describes the case study results of a complete electrocardiographic (ECG) system and a motion detection algorithm implementation; Section 5 concludes the paper.

2. RELATED WORK

Research in automation of the streaming system design has been carried out for decades. Most of this research targets the final system on a platform with FPGAs as co-processors [8, 11] or a pre-implemented many-core architecture [7, 9]. However, the mismatch between the amount of concurrent processes in an application and the amount of independent processors in the target platform introduces the need for processor time-sharing. In addition, the interconnect architecture in the target many-core processor normally does not reflect the communication paths in the application. This mismatch between the structure of the application and the structure of the target hardware usually introduces performance overhead, therefore, requires more development work to overcome this overhead and to meet the performance requirements of the final system.

Recently, as FPGAs have become larger and more sophisticated, an increasing number of automatic system design environments take a single FPGA or a set of FPGAs as the target platform [2, 3, 4, 5, 6]. In these solutions, the hardware abstraction reflects a much finer parallelism granularity compared to the task-level parallelism. To accomplish this, application developers usually have to manually annotate the code with regard to its mapping to the hardware. This manual annotation work usually requires application developers to master the hardware design, and therefore increases the development difficulty, the system's time-to-market and hinders the design reuse.

Comparing to the streaming system design environments mentioned above, the main advantages of the proposed SystemSpec design approach are:

- A pre-implemented hardware library abstracts away the cycle-accurate implementation details, and bridges the big semantic gap between software and hardware. Therefore, the hardware library allows the compiler to automatically map an application onto a many-core architecture.

- The entire system can be developed with a high-level language - SystemOberon, with **no hardware design work involved**. Therefore, our approach increases the potential for system reuse and decreases the time-to-market.

3. SYSTEMSPEC DESIGN FLOW

The SystemSpec design flow is mainly supported by four components: SystemOberon language, a run-time library, a hardware library implemented on an FPGA, and a compiler to automate the system design flow. With the support of these components, the system design flow can be divided into four phases: write the specification of a streaming application in our high-level language SystemOberon; compile the SystemOberon program to Verilog; synthesis, routing and finally the configuration phase. In the "compile the SystemSpec application to Verilog" phase, the SystemOberon compiler automatically generates the Verilog code of a many-core processor from the system specification. It also compiles process bodies to generate instruction image and data image, *.mem* files, for each processor core. A TCL script file *make.tcl* and block memory configuration file *ram.bmm* are also generated by the compiler to automate the synthesis, routing and configuration steps. In the "configuration" phase, if the resource and timing requirements for the target can be met, a bit stream file for the target machine will be generated. Otherwise, the application programmer may have to adjust the specification of the system e.g. number or the size of buffered channels.

```
SYSTEM AddAccu;
   IMPORT Source, Adder, Accumulator, Sink;

   CHANNEL (D = 32) c1, c2, c3, c4;
   PROCESS (IM = 2, DM = 1) p1(c1, c2): Source;
   PROCESS (IM = 2, DM = 1) p2(c1, c2, c3): Adder;
   PROCESS (IM = 2, DM = 1) p3(c3, c4): Accumulator;
   PROCESS (IM = 2, DM = 1) p4(c4): Sink;
END AddAccu.
```

```
MODULE Source (OUTPUT out1, out2: INTEGER);
IMPORT RS232;
VAR
   a, b: INTEGER;
BEGIN
   REPEAT
      RS232.RecInt(a); RS232.RecInt(b);
      Write(out1, a); Write(out2, b);
   UNTIL FALSE
END Source.
```

```
MODULE Adder (INPUT in1, in2: INTEGER; OUTPUT out: INTEGER);
VAR
   a, b, c: INTEGER;
BEGIN
   REPEAT
      Read(in1, a); Read(in2, b);
      c := a+b;
      Write(out, a);
   UNTIL FALSE
END Adder.
```

```
MODULE Sink (INPUT in: INTEGER);
IMPORT LCD;
VAR
   a: INTEGER;
BEGIN
   REPEAT
      Read(in, a);
      LCD.Clear; LCD.WriteInt(a);
   UNTIL FALSE
END Sink.
```

```
MODULE Accumulator (INPUT in: INTEGER; OUTPUT out: INTEGER);
VAR
   sum, a: INTEGER;
BEGIN
   sum := 0;
   REPEAT
      Read(in, a);
      sum := sum + a; Write(out, sum);
   UNTIL FALSE
END Accumulator.
```

Figure 1: The SystemOberon program of "AddAccu"

3.1 SystemOberon Language

SystemOberon is designed to allow application developers to specify a streaming system as a set of processes and buffered channels. A process is defined by a SystemOberon construct called a module. Each process is attached to its dedicated channels via its ports.

Ports are defined as formal parameters of the modules. Each port is defined by a direction - input or output, and a type. The directions of each pair of ports decide the direction of the connected channel. The type of connected ports defines the type of tokens passing through the channel, and it must be same. If a channel connects two ports of different types, a compilation error will occur.

Fig. 1 gives the SystemOberon description of a stream "AddAccu". In this example, two integers are read from the UART port in process "p1" and flow into process "p2" which adds them together. The results of process "p2" flow into process "p3" to be summed up. The results of process "p3" then flow into process "p4" to be displayed on an LCD. The system specification "AddAccu" consists of four processes and four channels. **SYSTEM**, **CHANNEL**, **PROCESS** and **MODULE** are reserved words.

3.2 The run-time library

A run-time library has been developed to support the channel operations and I/O device operations. The operations on channels are Read(ch, x), Read(ch, x, res) and Write(ch, x), meaning read/write "x" from/into channel "ch". Operation Read(ch, x) is blocked when the channel "ch" is empty. Operation Read(ch, x, res) returns the status "res" and the token "x" read from the channel "ch", and is not blocked when the channel is empty. Providing a non-blocking read allows programmers to model non-determinism in streaming applications.

The run-time library also includes operations on I/O devices, for example, the drivers for UART, Compact Flash card, LCD, DDR2 memory etc.

3.3 The hardware library

The target machine for a SystemSpec application is a many-core processor. This many-core processor is built from the hardware library implemented on an FPGA. This hardware library includes the following components.

- **Computation components** consist of **a tiny register machine (TRM)** and **a vector processor VTRM**. TRM is designed as a general purpose minimal machine to execute the code of a process. VTRM is used to support the data parallelism required by the applications.

- **Storage component - a processor TRMDMA** has been implemented to support direct data transfers from DDR2 to computation components.

- **Communication components** consist of buffered channels implemented as **FIFOs** with different width and depth configurations. These channels are used to transfer data from one processor core to another.

- **IO components** consist of a processor TRMIO and I/O controllers. TRMIO is used for efficient serialization/deserialization to ensure the required performance and data throughput.

The hardware library is implemented in behavioral Verilog and can be compiled for a specific target FPGA by using conventional behavioral synthesis tools. The behavioral Verilog code uses no device-specific libraries, and is portable to any Xilinx Virtex FPGA. However, it uses idioms that infer particular efficient structures on Xilinx Virtex FPGAs, e.g. DSPs and BRAMs.

3.4 SystemOberon Compiler

Fig. 2 shows the process of building a SystemOberon application. The SystemOberon compiler reads the SystemOberon program, for example, the "AddAccu" system specification, generates the Verilog code, *top.v*, of the top module, the TCL script *make.tcl* for building the many-core processor via ISE tools, the BRAM location specification file *ram.bmm* and the downloading batch file *flash.bat*. It also compiles process functions (modules) to generate instruction and data memory image files, *.mem* files, for each processor core. The generated top module of the many-core processor instantiates processor cores, channel FIFOs, and I/O controllers that are used in the application. If a process definition module imports an I/O module, for example, "RS232", in "Source" module of the "AddAccu" example, an I/O controller will be instantiated and connected to the processor core that will run the process. All hardware components are designed to run at the same clock speed, 116MHz. To check the maximum size of a SystemSpec application that can run on the Virtex-5LX50T FPGA, a processor consisting of 30 TRM cores was successfully built.

4. CASE STUDY

To show the applicability of the SystemSpec design flow, an electrocardiographic (ECG) signal analysis system and a motion detection application have been implemented on a Virtex-5 FPGA.

The ECG system performs the analysis of the electrical activity of the heart, including detection of the waves, analysis

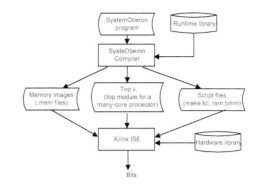

Figure 2: Building a SystemOberon application

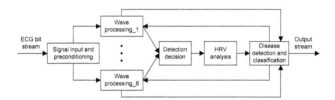

Figure 3: The ECG program structure

of their morphology, heart rate variability (HRV) analysis, detection and classification of disease. The analyzed signal represents a standard set of 8 physical channels recorded by a conventional monitoring device with a sampling rate $F_s = 500$ Hz.

We implemented the ECG analysis application in Fig. 3 in the SystemOberon language. Fig. 4 shows the corresponding output platform generated using the SystemSpec design flow. The architecture of the many-core processor in the target platform is consistent with structure of the application. It consists of 12 TRM cores, 34 FIFOs, a UART controller, a compact flash (CF) card controller and an LCD controller.

We applied our SystemSpec ECG implementation to record I01 from the St.-Petersburg Institute of Cardiological Technics 12-lead Arrhythmia Database [1]. The performance measurements of our ECG implementation show that each sample of the raw ECG data is processed in $\sim 30\mu s$, which is about 1.6% of the interval between two subsequent samples (2 ms for $F_s = 500$ Hz). The time cost for the analysis of a single ECG beat is $\sim 5.2ms$, which for very high heart rates of 200 bpm is about 1.5% of the interval between subsequent heart contractions. It is clear from the obtained measurements that the hardware used still offers plenty of spare computation power to meet the performance requirement of more sophisticated algorithms.

To compare the results of SystemSpec design flow with a generally designed hardware platform, we implemented the same desired algorithm shown in Fig. 3 on a generally pre-designed 12-core processor - TRM12 [10]. It contains 12 TRMs connected via an on-chip network implemented on a Virtex-5XC5VLX50T FPGA chip. Our first experience with the implementation of the ECG application on the TRM12 took about one month to get a working solution. Much faster result was achieved using the SystemSpec approach where we got the working application in a few days. Here the process-oriented system design paradigm with channel-based communication abstraction increased productivity by

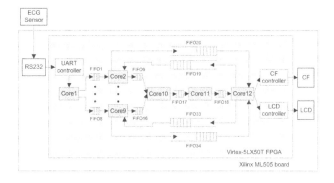

Figure 4: The generated ECG hardware target

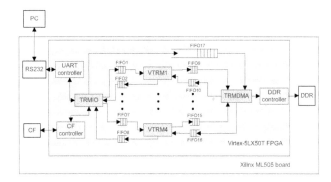

Figure 5: The generated hardware for the motion detection application

a factor of 10. Moreover, the ECG system implemented using the SystemSpec allowed to save 86% quiescent power and 17% dynamic power when compared to TRM12, which is due to more specific use of the hardware resources and a simpler interconnect.

To test the SystemSpec design approach with other hardware components, an algorithm for motion detection from a sequence of images has been implemented. In this application, an I/O process loads input images from CF and stores them to DDR2 memory. Then, the data from DDR2 is loaded and processed in parallel by vector processes. The result of the processing is streamed back to the DDR2. Using the same I/O process the resulted data from DDR2 is stored to CF for checking for correctness on a PC. Fig. 5 shows the generated hardware for the implemented algorithm. Using SystemSpec design flow, the development time for the motion detection application including the time for implementing a DMA driver, a library for array-based data access, and debugging, took only a few days which is much faster than building a customized system.

5. CONCLUSIONS

This paper presents a streaming system design paradigm called SystemSpec which allows developers to model streaming applications and their FPGA-based many-core hardware architectures as processes and channels. A programming language called SystemOberon, a run-time library, a hardware library, and a compiler have been developed to automate the system design flow. A real-time ECG monitor system and a motion detection application have been implemented to show that the process abstraction and the

streaming computation support in our paradigm can offer good performance, better size and power consumption results compared to a pre-implemented many-core architecture, and can improve productivity by a factor of 10.

6. ACKNOWLEDGMENTS

The authors thank Prof. Niklaus Wirth for his idea and great support in configurable interconnect architecture implementation, especially his work on TRM processor core design, implementation and compiler development. We also acknowledge Dr. Charles Thacker of Microsoft Research for his invaluable help with ISE tools and hardware development. Finally, we would like to thank Tacu Dan for his 2-stage pipelined implementation of TRM which improved the clock rate of the whole system to 116MHz. This project is supported by funding from Microsoft innovation cluster for embedded software (ICES).

7. REFERENCES

[1] St.-Petersburg Institute of Cardiological Technics 12-lead Arrhythmia Database. http://www.physionet.org/physiobank/database/.

[2] Handel-C. http://celoxica.com/technology/c design/handel-c.asp, 2005. Software from Celoxica, Inc.

[3] Ptolemy II. http://ptolemy.eecs.berkeley.edu/ptolemyII/, 2005. Software from UC Berkeley.

[4] System generator for DSP. http://www.xilinx.com/ise/optional prod/system generator.htm, 2005. Software from Xilinx, Inc.

[5] S. S. Bhattacharyya, G. Brebner, J. W. Janneck, J. Eker, C. von Platen, M. Mattavelli, and M. Raulet. OpenDF: a dataflow toolset for reconfigurable hardware and multicore systems. *SIGARCH Comput. Archit. News*, 36(5):29–35, 2008.

[6] E. Caspi, M. Chu, R. Huang, J. Yeh, J. Wawrzynek, and A. DeHon. Stream Computations Organized for Reconfigurable Execution (SCORE). In *FPL '00: Proceedings of the The Roadmap to Reconfigurable Computing, 10th International Workshop on Field-Programmable Logic and Applications*, pages 605–614, 2000.

[7] E. de Kock, G. Essink, W. Smits, R. van der Wolf, J.-Y. Brunei, W. Kruijtzer, P. Lieverse, and K. Vissers. YAPI: application modeling for signal processing systems. pages 402–405, 2000.

[8] M. Gokhale, J. Stone, J. Arnold, and M. Kalinowski. Stream-oriented FPGA computing in the Streams-C high level language. pages 49–56, 2000.

[9] M. I. Gordon, W. Thies, M. Karczmarek, J. Lin, A. S. Meli, A. A. Lamb, C. Leger, J. Wong, H. Hoffmann, D. Maze, and S. P. Amarasinghe. A stream compiler for communication-exposed architectures. pages 291–303, 2002.

[10] L. Liu. A 12-Core Processor Implementation on FPGA. http://www.inf.ethz.ch/research/disstechreps/techreports, 2009. ETH technical report. No. 646.

[11] T. Stefanov, C. Zissulescu, A. Turjan, B. Kienhuis, and E. Deprette. System design using Kahn process networks: the Compaan/Laura approach. volume 1, pages 340–345 Vol.1, feb. 2004.

Torc: Towards an Open-Source Tool Flow

Neil Steiner[1]
neil.steiner@isi.edu

Aaron Wood[1,2]
awood@isi.edu

Hamid Shojaei[1,3]
shojaei@wisc.edu

Jacob Couch[4]
jacouch@vt.edu

Peter Athanas[4]
athanas@vt.edu

Matthew French[1]
mfrench@isi.edu

[1]Information Sciences Institute
University of Southern California
3811 N Fairfax Dr, Ste 200
Arlington, VA 22203

[2]Department of Electrical Engineering
University of Washington
185 Stevens Way
Seattle, WA 98195

[3]Dept of Electrical and Computer Engenering
University of Wisconsin-Madison
1415 Engineering Drive
Madison, WI 53706

[4]Dept of Electrical and Computer Engeneering
Virginia Tech
302 Whittemore Hall
Blacksburg, VA 24061

ABSTRACT

We present and describe Torc—*Tools for Open Reconfigurable Computing*—an open-source infrastructure and tool set, provided entirely as C++ source code and available at http://torc.isi.edu. Torc is suitable for custom research applications, for CAD tool development, and for architecture exploration.

The Torc infrastructure can (1) read, write, and manipulate generic netlists—currently EDIF, (2) read, write, and manipulate physical netlists—currently XDL, and indirectly NCD, (3) provide exhaustive wiring and logic information for commercial devices, and (4) read, write, and manipulate bitstream packets (but not configuration frame *contents*). Torc furthermore provides routing and *unpacking* tools for full or partial designs, soon to be augmented with BLIF support, and with packing and placing tools.

The architectural data for Xilinx devices is generated from non-proprietary XDLRC files, and currently supports 140 devices in 11 families: Virtex, Virtex-E, Virtex-II, Virtex-II Pro, Virtex4, Virtex5, Virtex6, Virtex6L, Spartan3E, Spartan6, and Spartan6L. We believe that Altera architectures and designs could be similarly supported if the necessary data were available, and we have successfully used Torc internally with custom architectures.

Categories and Subject Descriptors: J.6 [Computer Applications]: Computer-Aided Engineering

General Terms: Algorithms, Design, Standardization.

Keywords: C++, FPGA, place, route, unpack, EDIF, XDL, XDLRC.

1. INTRODUCTION

Modern FPGAs are complex devices, and the designs targeting them are often described in complex file formats. As a result, researchers either have to work with simplified files and models, or have to invest significant development effort into parsers, object models, and large routing graphs.

Special requirements on a large project forced us to develop custom tools for internal use, which we are now repackaging and releasing to the research community as an open-source project. One aim is to provide *real* device data, and thereby increase the relevance of the CAD tools that are frequently developed by researchers. Another aim is to provide a framework for device and design data, allowing researchers to focus on the unique and novel aspects of their work, instead of being waylaid by infrastructure development.

Device manufacturer data is often sensitive and proprietary, and we ensure that the data and capabilities underlying Torc—including exhaustive device databases—are derived from publicly available sources. As a result of this, Torc can manipulate bitstream packets and configuration frames, but does not understand frame *contents*.

We divide Torc into a collection of Application Programming Interfaces (APIs) and Tools: The *generic netlist* API supports unmapped netlists, most commonly EDIF. The *physical netlist* API supports mapped netlists, with or without placement or routing information, most commonly XDL. The *device architecture* API provides exhaustive wiring and logic information for supported commercial or experimental devices. And the *bitstream* API supports Xilinx bitstream packets and frames.

The *router* tool creates connections for anything from individual wires to entire designs. And the *unpacker* tool expands compound blocks such as SLICEs into constituent Look-Up Tables (LUTs), flip-flops, and muxes. Two tools still in development are the *packer* tool, which recombines what the unpacker has expanded, and the *placer* tool, which assigns physical locations to design logic elements.

We provide background information in Section 2, and then describe the Torc design in Section 3, the API in Section 4, and the associated CAD tools in Section 5. We finally consider applicability in Section 6 and conclude in Section 7.

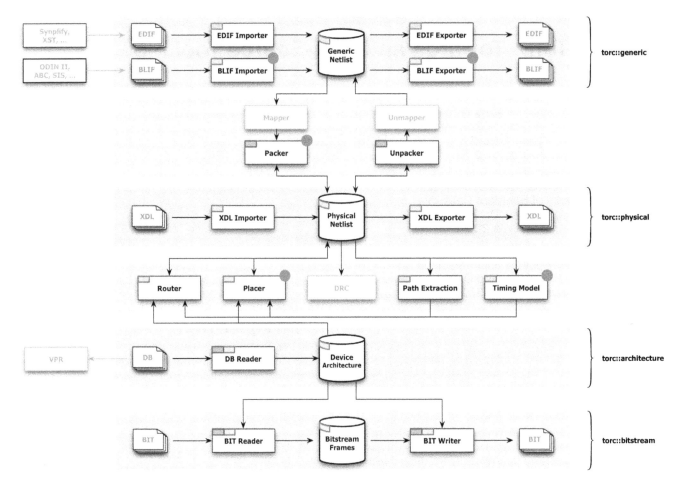

Figure 1: Torc block diagram. *Red dots indicate components still under development.*

2. BACKGROUND

Torc functionality is heavily based on prior work, much of it previously unreleased for reasons beyond our control. Torc's Device Database is a direct descendant of ADB [11], originally developed in conjunction with the JBits [5] project, and later to become the foundation of a completely rewritten but unreleased version of JBits.

We know of no other API or tool set comparable to Torc, other than friendly competition from our collaborators at Brigham Young University (BYU) [6]. There are however a number of important related tools, some of which we hope to interface with to mutual advantage. In doing so, we believe we can usefully expand the number of research tool flows described on the fpgaCAD web site [4].

At the mapped netlist level, VPR [1] is the de facto place-and-route tool for research, and has been used for modeling in the development of recent Altera architectures [7]. At the mapped netlist level, many groups have dabbled with XDL designs or XDLRC device data, but few if any of those efforts have resulted in open toolsets.

Torc aims to be reasonably architecture independent, but is strongly influenced by the disparity in device and design information available for Xilinx and Altera architectures. While Xilinx provides insertion points and architecture data necessary for changes after synthesis, after mapping, after place-and-route, and even after bitstream generation, the available insertion points and architecture data for Altera devices are insufficient for our needs.

Despite the limited access to Altera wiring data and low-level implementation files, we believe that Torc's architecture API could represent Altera architectures, and that the physical netlist API could probably describe low-level Altera circuit implementations. The same is not true for the bitstream API, which is derived almost entirely from configuration information in Xilinx device user guides.

3. DESIGN

Torc's major components are depicted in Figure 1. The APIs are shaded in blue and are designated on the right according to their respective C++ namespaces. The tool sets are shaded in gray, and are positioned between the APIs that they depend upon. Input and output file types are labeled in green. The components still undergoing development or integration have red dots in their upper right corners, while the components not yet scheduled for development are grayed out. The remainder of the color coding reflects internal task assignments for ISI, Virginia Tech, and Interra Systems.

Also present on the left of the diagram are groups of tools that we hope to interface with, including commercial synthesis engines by way of EDIF files, and academic synthesis and optimization tools by way of BLIF files. We also hope to supply routing graphs for real devices to VPR, further confirming and extending its usefulness.

4. API

The core functionality of Torc is encapsulated in the four databases depicted in Figure 1: The generic netlist API, the physical netlist API, the device architecture API, and the bitstream API.

4.1 Generic Netlist

The generic netlist API supports netlists that are not mapped to physical primitives in a target device. The API supports the ubiquitous EDIF 2 0 0 Level 0 [3], and can manipulate the NETLIST view type. Support for the academically popular BLIF format is still under development, and is intended to provide compatibility between Torc and existing research tools and flows.

The API includes EDIF importers and exporters, and is built around an internal *netlist object model*. The EDIF support and the object model were developed for us by Interra Systems, Inc., a company with significant expertise in front-end language analyzers, and with a customer base that includes some of the largest EDA vendors.

The generic netlist API can be used to access all of the circuit design elements, including libraries, cells, views, ports, instances, nets, and more. These elements can be queried, added, modified, or removed, and entirely new designs can be created from scratch. In addition to circuit manipulation, the API can also flatten netlists, and can provide a foundation for synthesis or mapping algorithms.

4.2 Physical Netlist

The physical netlist API supports netlists that have been mapped to physical primitives in the target device. Physical netlists may include partial or full placement and routing information, or may be devoid of any such information.

In a manner similar to the generic netlist API, the physical netlist API can be used to access all circuit elements, including designs, modules, nets, and instances, along with their configuration settings and any placement and routing information.

There are two reasons why physical netlist capabilities give the user exceptional control over their design: (1) Unlike the ISE place-and-route tool, Torc allows users to strictly enforce their requirements, making it possible to generate and retain arbitrary routes, or to reserve arbitrary resources or regions of the device. (2) There are no subsequent mapping or transformation steps performed before bitstream generation, so the user is guaranteed that any changes will be retained as applied. Comparable assurances are much more elusive at the generic netlist level.

4.3 Device Architecture

The device architecture API is built upon proven methods and representations for very large and irregular devices [11]. A precursor to this code was successfully used in an embedded system, allowing that system to autonomously place and route new circuitry within itself while continuing to run [10].

The Device Database includes exhaustive knowledge of the device wiring and logic, and makes all of that information available through the API. It also tracks wire and arc usage, to prevent contention with existing nets or logic, or simply to inform routers of resource availability. Furthermore, it provides the physical and bitstream APIs with tile maps, logic site maps, and usage information.

For router research, including tools such as VPR which may expect to work within a fully expanded routing graph, we note that one could expand the graph ahead of time, at the cost of significant memory overhead.

4.4 Bitstream Interface

The bitstream API supports reading, modifying, and writing bitstream packets and frames for supported Xilinx architectures. We note again that the API can work with configuration frames but lacks any understanding of frame contents, since that information is proprietary and undocumented. Unfortunately, no comparable information is available for Altera architectures.

5. TOOLS

Torc includes CAD tools to perform unpacking and routing, with packing and placing tools still being developed or integrated. The tools are provided as source code, rather than executables, and can serve as guides for working with the physical netlist API and the device architecture API. If compiled as standalone executables they can be substituted into the regular design implementation flow, with a few stipulations pertaining to timing and to multiple clock domains.

5.1 Unpacker and Packer

The configurable computing community generally speaks of *packing* in the sense of combining logic functions or gates into LUTs, or of combining LUTs and flip-flops into simple logic blocks or clusters, mindful of the impact on circuit performance, but with very few physical rules to constrain such operations. We use the term here to describe the process of combining LUTs, flip-flops, muxes, carry chains, and other elements into logic block primitives—Virtex SLICEs for example—while generating the corresponding configuration settings, and respecting device rules.

The value of a logic block packer is that it allows the user to work with circuitry much more naturally, in terms of LUTs, flip-flops, and other basic elements. In the common case of a user working from an existing design, it makes sense to first unpack it, modify the circuit as needed, and then incrementally re-pack, re-place, and re-route it. With the packer still under development, the unpacker nevertheless plays an important role by exposing synchronous and asynchronous circuit elements, to facilitate combinational path analysis. These combinational paths are then ordered according to logic level depth, and are used by the placer and router when prioritizing nets and resources.

5.2 Router

The router constructs paths that connect sources to sinks for every net, with final results that must meet timing requirements and be free from contention. The Torc routing capability includes an optional preliminary router, along with a global PathFinder [8] implementation to resolve net contention, and an underlying signal router based on an A* search [9]. We note that it is possible to bypass the preliminary router, and that it is also possible to invoke the signal router directly on nets or arbitrary device wires.

Regrettably absent from the available Xilinx architecture data is any timing information, and even ISE's timing analysis tool reports delays for nets rather than their constituent wires and arcs. Consequently neither the Device Database nor the router can accurately analyze or guarantee timing. We alleviate the issue in part by prioritizing long combinational paths and thus reducing the delay of the likely critical paths. We have also had considerable success modeling wiring delays based on technology process nodes, but have not yet integrated the resulting timing data into Torc.

6. APPLICATIONS AND FUTURE WORK

Torc is useful for any application that requires very fine-grained programmatic control over design implementation. Sometimes it is necessary to constrain a design in ways that are not possible with the vendor implementation tools. Taking the AREA_GROUP constraint as an example, although a user may wish to strictly constrain routing inside or outside of a specified boundary, the tools do not always produce the desired results. But Torc permits the user to allow, disallow, or even require the use of arbitrary routing resources. The user could also programmatically generate some portion of their design with the physical netlist API, and add highly structured placement in the manner of Lava [2].

Torc is also useful as a platform for CAD tool research. The possibility of broadly linking design information—at the HDL, generic netlist, and physical netlist levels—opens the possibility of tightly-coupled interactive incremental debug and development. We note growing interest in parallel tool research, but entirely new approaches may also emerge: It may be feasible to partition designs at the generic netlist level, and then to perform combined mapping, placing, and routing on each partition concurrently.

Torc tools still under development include the packer and placer. Additional capabilities that we hope to add in time include timing models, constraint file support, design rule checks, TCL scripting, parallelization, mapping, and support for other architectures.

7. CONCLUSION

Torc is an open-source C++ infrastructure for reconfigurable computing, suitable for custom research applications, for CAD tool development, and for architecture exploration. Its primary purpose is to promote and facilitate research, by providing a framework for device and design data, allowing researchers to focus on the truly novel and unique aspects of their work.

The Torc infrastructure can (1) read, write, and manipulate generic netlists—currently EDIF, (2) read, write, and manipulate physical netlists—currently XDL, and indirectly NCD, (3) provide exhaustive wiring and logic information for commercial devices, and (4) read, write, and manipulate bitstream packets (but not frame contents). Torc's use of standard file formats also allows complete simulation and timing analysis with standard commercial tools.

Torc furthermore provides unpacking and routing tools, with packing and placing tools still under development. Packing and unpacking allow users to more naturally work with basic architecture-independent elements, instead of working with more complex physical primitive instances. And though we are not yet deploying device timing models, we have had good initial success with our internal efforts.

The architectural data included with Torc is derived entirely from non-proprietary sources. We presently support 140 Xilinx devices in 11 families, and are interested in adding Altera support if the necessary data can be obtained.

Torc is available at http://torc.isi.edu.

8. ACKNOWLEDGMENTS

ISI wishes to thank our project sponsor. Thanks also to our collaborators, including the Virginia Tech Configurable Computing Lab; Brad Hutchings, Brent Nelson, and the Brigham Young University Configurable Computing Lab; and Vijeta Kashyap and the team at Interra Systems.

9. REFERENCES

[1] V. Betz and J. Rose. VPR: A new packing, placement and routing tool for FPGA research. In W. Luk, P. Y. K. Cheung, and M. Glesner, editors, *Proceedings of the 7th International Workshop on Field-Programmable Logic and Applications, FPL 1997, (London), September 1–3*, volume 1304 of *Lecture Notes in Computer Science*, pages 213–222. Springer Verlag, 1997.

[2] P. Bjesse, K. Claessen, M. Sheeran, and S. Singh. Lava: hardware design in Haskell. In *ACM SIGPLAN Notices*, volume 34, pages 174–184, New York, NY, 1999. ACM.

[3] Electronic Industries Association. *Electronic Design Interchange Format*, 1988.

[4] fpgaCAD. http://fpgacad.ece.wisc.edu.

[5] S. Guccione, D. Levi, and P. Sundararajan. JBits: Java based interface for reconfigurable computing. In *Proceedings of the Second Annual Military and Aerospace Applications of Programmable Devices and Technologies Conference, MAPLD 1999, (Laurel, Maryland), September 28–30*, 1999.

[6] C. Lavin, M. Padilla, J. Lamprecht, P. Lundrigan, B. Nelson, B. Hutchings, and M. Wirthlin. A library for low-level manipulation of partially placed-and-routed FPGA designs. Technical report, Brigham Young University, 2010.

[7] D. Lewis, E. Ahmed, G. Baeckler, V. Betz, et al. The Stratix II logic and routing architecture. In *Proceedings of the 2005 ACM/SIGDA 13th Annual International Symposium on Field-Programmable Gate Arrays, FPGA 2005 (Monterey, California), February 20–22*, pages 14–20, 2005.

[8] L. McMurchie and C. Ebeling. PathFinder: A negotiation-based performance-driven router for FPGAs. In *Proceedings of the 1995 ACM 3rd International Symposium on Field-Programmable Gate Arrays, FPGA 1995, (Monterey, California), February 12–14*, pages 111–117, 1995.

[9] N. J. Nilsson. *Principles of Artificial Intelligence*. Tioga Publishing Company, Palo Alto, California, 1980.

[10] N. Steiner and P. Athanas. Hardware autonomy and space systems. In *Proceedings of the 2009 IEEE Aerospace Conference, (Big Sky, Montana), March 7–14*, 2009.

[11] N. J. Steiner. A standalone wire database for routing and tracing in Xilinx Virtex, Virtex-E, and Virtex-II FPGAs. Master's thesis, Virginia Tech, August 2002.

FPGASort: A High Performance Sorting Architecture Exploiting Run-time Reconfiguration on FPGAs for Large Problem Sorting

Dirk Koch and Jim Torresen
Department of Informatics, University of Oslo, Norway
Email: {koch, jimtoer@ifi.uio.no

ABSTRACT

This paper analyses different hardware sorting architectures in order to implement a highly scaleable sorter for solving huge problems at high performance up to the GB range in linear time complexity. It will be proven that a combination of a FIFO-based merge sorter and a tree-based merge sorter results in the best performance at low cost. Moreover, we will demonstrate how partial run-time reconfiguration can be used for saving almost half the FPGA resources or alternatively for improving the speed. Experiments show a sustainable sorting throughput of 2GB/s for problems fitting into the on-chip FPGA memory and 1 GB/s when using external memory. These values surpass the best published results on large problem sorting implementations on FPGAs, GPUs, and the Cell processor.

Categories and Subject Descriptors

B.0 [**Hardware**]: GENERAL

General Terms

Design, Experimentation, Performance

1. INTRODUCTION

Large problem sorting is a process that is heavily used in database systems [8]. In this paper we introduce a highly optimized sorter implementation for FPGAs that has the potential to scale to sort problem sizes of several GB of data. The data items to be sorted are commonly referred as *keys*. Keys can be integer, floating-point numbers or any other sortable data type. Throughout this paper we focus on 64-bit integers.

Sorting a huge amount of data means that the whole sorting problem cannot fit into on-FPGA memory. Consequently external memory is required to store intermediate values. This also means that the sort keys have to be transferred to the FPGA multiple times, according to the actual problem size and the used sorter architecture.

For the following observations, let us assume the system illustrated in Figure 1. The System provides an FPGA that includes the basic infrastructure, consisting of a host interface (e.g., PCIe or a front-side bus), memory controllers,

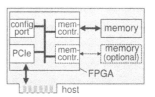

Figure 1: Assumed system with host connection and local memory.

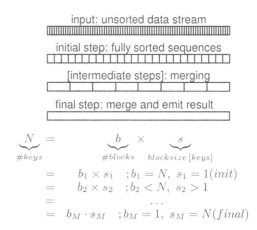

Figure 2: Sorting N keys in M steps.

and logic to perform run-time reconfiguration. At first, let us consider only one local memory channel. Then, the sort keys arrive via the host interface to the FPGA from where they are stored in external memory attached to the FPGA. We assume that the local on-board memory provides sufficient capacity to host the whole search problem and that it provides the same throughput as the host interface.

While the sort keys arrive from the host, a first sorting step can be performed such that the local memory will store blocks of fully sorted sequences. As illustrated in Figure 2, these sequences will then be merged to fewer but larger fully sorted sequences in one or more successive sorting steps. Note that throughout the whole paper, we assume that the input sort keys are fully random.

Similar to performing some of the sorting during arrival of the data, a final sort step might be performed when writing the result back to the host. Independent of the problem size, this can only start after the arrival of all sort keys. This is obvious as the last input key from the host could be the first key of the result.

The following sections first discuss the compare-swap el-

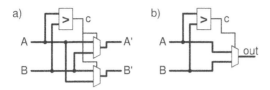

Figure 3: Basic sorting elements: a) compare-swap element, b) select-value element.

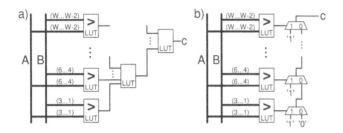

Figure 4: Magnitude comparator implemented with 6-input LUTs. a) tree-based, b) carry-chain logic.

Table 1: Latency of a carry-chain comparator implemented on a Virtex-5 XC5VLX50-3 device.

Operand width (W)	8	16	32	48	64
latency [ns]	0.57	0.65	1.15	1.3	1.42
LUT count	4	8	16	24	32

ement, which is the basic building block of a sorter. After this, various sorter architectures are analyzed with respect of their applicability of sorting the different steps.

1.1 Basic Sorting Elements

The basic building block for most sorting architectures is a compare-swap element that compares two input values and swaps the values at the output, if required. A compare-swap element is depicted in Figure 3 a). Another widely used basic building block is a select-value element shown in Figure 3 b). The function of this element is to provide the smaller (larger) value if the task is a ascending (descending) sorting. Typically, the selected value will be consumed at the input while leaving the other (not selected) value for a comparison in the next cycle.

1.1.1 Comparators

While a multiplexer contributes only one logic level to the latency, the comparator is typically the critical part of the compare-swap element with respect to latency. Depending on the FPGA synthesis tool, comparators are commonly mapped to tree-based structures or implementations using the carry chain logic that is commonly provided in FPGA architectures. Figure 4 shows examples of how comparators for natural numbers ($\mathbb{N}_0$) can be mapped to 6-input LUT-based FPGAs.

Assuming 6-input LUTs, which are common for all recent high-density FPGAs, the amount of logic levels in a tree-based comparator is for W bit wide operands $1 + \lceil log_6 W \rceil$ levels. For 32-bit or 64-bit operands this results in three logic levels only for the comparator. The corresponding carry chain would be $\lceil \frac{W}{3} \rceil$ LUTs or $\lceil \frac{W}{(3 \cdot 4)} \rceil$ Xilinx Virtex-5 slices long. On recent Xilinx devices (such as Virtex-5/6 or Spartan-6 FPGAs), one slice comprises a cluster of four 6-input look-up tables. For 32-bit (64-bit) operands, this results in a chain being 3 (6) slices long. Consequently, carry-chains result in lower latency for wide operands. However, tree-based comparator architectures are still an option for Spartan-6 devices where only half the amount of LUTs provide attached carry chain logic.

We found that the recent vendor logic synthesis and mapping tools (XST 12.1) were only able to compare two operand

bits per 6-input LUT, in spite of the FPGA fabric allowing the implementation of a comparator with three operand bits exactly as shown in Figure 4 b). For investigating a denser fitting, we explored the physical implementation results achieved for a Xilinx Virtex-5 device. The results listed in Table 1 denote only the latency of a combinatory comparator chain and the values do not include any further elements such as the routing latency for connecting the comparator. Exploiting all six look-up table inputs would reduce the length of the carry chain to $\frac{2}{3}$ times the size of what is required when using the Xilinx vendor tools. This would allow implementing the 64-bit comparator with the latency that is listed for the 48-bit case in Table 1. However, the saving is then only 120 ps or roughly 5% of the slack available in a data path running at 250 MHz. To take advantage of the more compact comparators when using the Xilinx vendor tools, it is possible to instantiate hard macros that have to be manually created.

1.1.2 Multiplexers

In the basic compare-swap element, the result of the comparator is used to control a multiplexer pair for adjusting the input operands in order to deliver a sorted result. Therefore, the basic element demands two look-up tables per signal bit of the operand, which is $2 \times W$ LUTs in total. Consequently, the multiplexers contribute to the majority of the implementation cost in terms of LUTs. When using the Xilinx vendor tools, this results in 80% of the logic cost just for the multiplexers when implementing a basic compare swap element (see also Table 1 for the comparator logic cost). However, this value can be improved by utilizing the second look-up table output in order to implement a single bit multiplexer pair inside the same LUT. Then the total logic cost for implementing the compare-swap element can be reduced to 60% as compared to the baseline implementation when using the standard VHDL operators and the Vendor tools. A second LUT output is available on 6-input LUT devices from Xilinx and Altera. In case of Xilinx devices, this technique is typically only suited for Spartan-6 or Virtex-6 series FPGAs, because these devices provide a flip-flop for both LUT outputs whereas the older Virtex-5 device only allowed one result to be registered. Despite the benefit and low cost of the look-up table sharing, the Xilinx vendor synthesis and mapping tools (XST 12.1) do not make use of the second LUT output when implementing multiplexers. Again, this can be exploited by instantiating corresponding LUT primitives or manually implemented hard macros.

Depending on the sorter architecture, it can be beneficial to sort more than two values within a basic compare-swap element at the same time. For example, by sorting 4 input vectors simultaneously, the work of 6 (5) two-value compare-swap elements can be done in one step when considering bitonic (even-odd) merge sorting networks (see Section 2.1 for more details on sorting networks). This approach does not help to reduce the number of comparators, but it helps to save logic for the multiplexers that contribute to the majority of the logic cost within a compare-swap element. Combining multiple sorter stages is particularly useful when considering the select-value element with only one

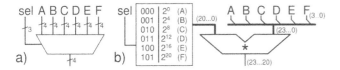

Figure 5: Multiplexer implementation using a dedicated multiplier primitive.

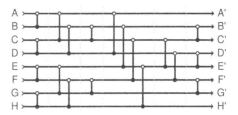

Figure 6: Even-Odd sorting network. The operator represents a compare-swap cell from Figure 3b).

output multiplexer for picking the entire smallest or largest sort key as the result.

While single 6-input LUTs permit directly implementing 4:1 multiplexers, wider multiplexers comprise more logic levels and thus result in higher latency. As one solution to this problem, dedicated hard-IP multipliers (found in all high-density FPGAs), can be used to efficiently implement wide input multiplexers [1]. This approach costs nothing as these primitives would otherwise be unused in our sorting application. An example of a 4-bit wide 6:1 multiplexer implemented using a single multiplier is depicted in Figure 5. The same multiplier would allow a 2-bit (1-bit) wide 12:1 (24:1) multiplexer implementation with the same latency (when not further considering the select encoding).

1.1.3 Wide and Fast Operand Sorting

Large problem sorting is often performed in databases. Here, the search keys typically represent not only simple integer numbers, but structs concatenating multiple sub-keys of arbitrary type, including integer, floating point numbers, or even strings. The size of a single key can exceed a hundred bytes or even more.

For biased floating-point number representations (such as IEEE 754 floating point numbers), the comparator design is very similar to the integer case when firstly comparing the exponent lexicographical and secondly taking the comparison of the mantissa into account. The comparison of strings can be very difficult and we will bound our investigation to integer numbers. Strings are more difficult to handle as there exist different text codes (e.g., ASCII, UTF-x) and different language and even context dependent rules for sorting [17].

Considering fully random search keys allow in more than 99% ($\frac{1}{2^8}$) of all comparisons stopping the comparison after processing the most significant byte. However, in databases, search keys might posses a common prefix that has to be verified (e.g., when sorting a date field). For this reason, we consider the whole key at once.

It can be seen from the basic compare-swap element in Figure 3a) that the sorting of wide operands can easily be done in multiple consecutive time steps processing only a subword per step. Then we must add a simple state machine to each compare-swap element that keeps track of the present compare state. When arranging the keys from most significant subword to least significant subword, the compare-swap element can start emitting the result with only one cycle latency. This is possible because the output will either be the same (in the case of a common prefix) or can be determined within the same clock cycle.

At an extreme, the size of the subwords could be reduced to a single bit, allowing the implementation of the basic compare-swap element in a single Virtex-5 slice. This would result in a low throughput of a single element but would allow parallel processing with many tens of thousands compare-swap elements in parallel on the largest available devices.

To enhance the throughput of a single compare-swap element, the data path of a single subword must be wider. For

instance, when targeting a sort key throughput of 2GB/s, the data paths of the sorting elements must be 64-bits (128-bits) wide, assuming a key fillrate of 250 MHz (125 MHz). As both operands within a compare-swap element traverse the data path at the same speed, a compare-swap element (see Figure 3a)) can be easily pipelined. As opposed to this, only one operand moves in a select-value element (see Figure 3b)), while backpressing the entire other operand input stream. Such a structure is more difficult to implement for wide data paths because of the logic latency and the routing latency between the different sorting elements (see also Table 1 for the latency of a comparator).

2. SORTER ARCHITECTURES

Hardware implementations using different kinds of sorting architectures have been presented multiple times before. This section gives an overview of common approaches.

2.1 Sorting Networks

Sorting networks are mathematical models of networks with compare-swap elements designed to sort a set of input values very fast by exploiting a high degree of parallelism. Common architectures include bitonic merge sorter networks and the more efficient even-odd networks [2]. Figure 6 illustrates an even-odd network for eight input operands. The network could operate fully combinatory, but it is common to add a pipeline register after each compare-swap element. Then a set of N search keys can be sorted in $\frac{log_2N}{2}(log_2N + 1)$ clock cycles ($\frac{3}{2} \cdot 4 = 6$ in the shown example). The hardware cost of such a sorting network is $\frac{N}{4}(log_2N)^2$ compare-swap elements.

Sorting Networks have been used for sorting large problems using vector operations, for example, using the Cell Broadband Engine Architecture [6] or GPUs [7]. On FPGAs, sorting networks are typically applied to smaller problem classes, for example, to compute a median value [15]. For large problems, sorting networks require greater I/O throughput as they consume more sort keys and produce a huge amount of result data at the same time. This leads to alternating operation between I/O bursts and processing bursts and consequently in poor utilization of the I/O interface and the logic fabric. However, in [11] symmetries within the even-odd network have been used to solve larger problems using multiple runs on smaller networks.

2.2 Insertion Sorting

Hardware implementations of insertion sorting provide a shift register for storing the search keys. As illustrated in Figure 7, the shifting of each individual register is controlled by attached comparator logic. By comparing the input value with the current register content, a free position will be generated at the right position within the register by shifting

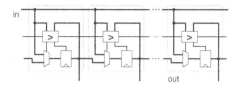

Figure 7: Insertion sorter.

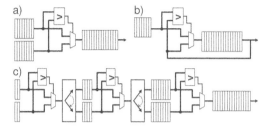

Figure 8: FIFO-based merge sorter. a) baseline approach [12], b) circulating merge sorter [13], c) cascading FIFO-based merge sorters.

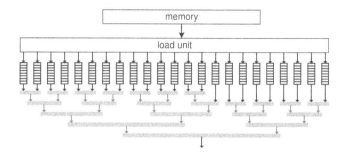

Figure 9: Merge sorter tree with key load unit. Each horizontal bar constitutes a select-value element.

all larger sort keys one position further. The resource requirements are N comparators and N registers for sorting N keys in N operation cycles.

The basic architecture of a insertion sorter would not allow fast and large implementations with many comparators because the input signal has to be broadcasted to all comparator instances. However, in [3], a systolic merge sorter implementation is presented that achieved with 128 processing elements a 66 MHz operation speed on a Xilinx Virtex XCV-1000-4 FPGA. Because of the relatively high implementation cost and because the search keys have to be stored in registers instead of using dedicated on-chip memory blocks, we consider insertion sorting only for smaller problem sizes.

2.3 FIFO-Based Merge Sorter

FIFO-based merge sorters consist of a select value element (see Figure 3b)) that is surrounded by FIFOs at the input and output ports. As illustrated in Figure 8a), this allows the generation of an output stream possessing the combined size of the two input FIFOs.

In [13], only one shared FIFO was used by feeding back the output FIFO to one input, as depicted in Figure 8b). We do not consider this approach, as it results in a data-dependent execution time with quadratic time complexity for random input data.

For generating longer fully sorted sequences, multiple FIFO-based merge sorters can be cascaded, as shown in Figure 8c). At the cost of doubling the amount of local on-chip memory in each sorter stage, the size of the sorted sequence is doubled as well. A drawback of the shown data path is that it is not suitable for sorting on a continuous stream. For example, consider only the last output stage: in an initial step, the sorter fills one FIFO. After this, the sorter can immediately start to merge the keys with the arrival of the second input stream. When the second stream is fully written to the input FIFO, it cannot be guaranteed that a new sort sequence will fit in one of the input FIFOs because the processing of the actual sort job is data dependent and consequently also the free space in the input FIFOs.

2.4 Merge Sorter Trees

Select-value elements can alternatively be arranged in a tree based structure for merging multiple sorted subsequences to one combined sequence that will be fully sorted. As illustrated in Figure 9, this can be used to merge long sequences from external memory. Then, small FIFOs attached to the inputs of the first sorter stage can be used to hide the latency of the external memory.

With M inputs at the first sorter stage, the tree structure can merge M streams together in one run with linear time complexity, thus reducing the total amount of streams to $\frac{1}{M}$ for possible further runs. In each run, the whole data is streamed once through the sorting tree.

An interesting property of a tree sorting structure is its little switching activity. Even through the implementation cost scales linearly with M, only $log_2 M$ select-value elements are active within one operation cycle. Besides the reduced power consumption, this results in a homogenous distribution of memory load requests over time. This simplifies to achieve sustained high throughput with the external memory.

A merge sorter with a tree-like network-on-chip architecture has been demonstrated in [18] and points out that NoCs are too slow for high throughput merge sorter implementations.

2.5 Bucket Sort

Bucket sort follows a divide and conquer strategy by splitting the whole search problem into buckets containing fewer search keys than the original problem. This can be recursively repeated until the remaining problem fits into local on-chip memory for fast sorting of the different buckets. The most famous application for bucket search is the Postman's sort, where all letters are consecutively sorted into buckets for countries, states, cities, and streets. For hardware-accelerated sorting, different pivot elements are selected to define the buckets. In the case of uniform distributed search keys, buckets can be defined by the most significant bits (MSBs) of the search keys. This has been demonstrated on GPUs for an implementation of quicksort [16].

In a special case of bucket sort known as radix sort, both the size of the keys and the number of buckets are a power of two, thus requiring inspection of only a prefix of the binary encoding of the key in order to find the corresponding bucket. This was used in the fastest published papers on sorting using GPUs [9, 10].

Bucket sort is an interesting candidate for implementations on FPGAs, where an input stream of search keys might be stored in different regions of attached memory. However, when taking two buckets in each step and recursively sorting each buckets again into two smaller buckets, bucket sort is basically identical to quicksort. As a consequence, bucket sort might perform poorly (with in the worst case quadratic time complexity), if the problem is not equally distributed

Table 2: Benchmarking different sort architectures. N denotes the problem size in terms of keys and M the amount of parallel processed memory blocks. The marked (*) architectures involve bursting I/O traffic.

architecture	time complexity	space complexity logic	memory
bitonic networks*	$\frac{log_2 N}{2}(log_2 N + 1)$	$\frac{N}{4}(log_2^2 N + log_2 N)$	$> N$
even-odd networks*	$\frac{log_2 N}{2}(log_2 N + 1)$	$\frac{N}{4}(log_2 N)^2$	$> N$
insertion sorter*	N	N	N
FIFO merge sorter	N	$log_2 N$	N
merge sorter trees	N (one run)	$M - 1$	M+buffer
bucket sort	N (one run)	M	M+buffer

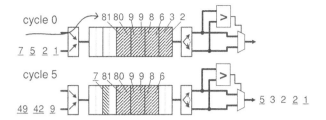

Figure 10: FIFO-based merge sorter using a shared memory block for both input streams.

or if the pivot elements haven't been properly chosen. This problem can especially occur when sorting database keys as they often share a common prefix, posses bounded ranges, or represent text. As we want in particular to address also database applications, we do not further consider bucket sort.

2.6 Architecture Benchmarking

In order to allow a direct comparison of the different sorting architectures, we list all candidates together with the entire complexity in both space (implementation cost) and time (throughput) in Table 2. As all data has to be streamed sequentially via an interface (e.g., memory or PCIe) to and from the FPGA, a better than linear time complexity will result at some point in time in idling the sorter hardware. Because of this and the bursting I/O traffic, sorting networks are only appropriate for relatively small problems, when implemented on FPGAs.

The most effective architecture is the FIFO-based merge sorter that achieves a linear throughput at only logarithmic logic cost. Moreover, it can use dedicated on-chip memory (block RAM) to solve larger problems fully on-chip. If the problem size exceeds the local memory, external memory is required to temporarily host blocks containing fully sorted sub-problems. Depending on the number of blocks, one or more additional runs through a tree-based merge sorter may be required.

As the FIFO-based merge sorter requires already-sorted streams at the input and because it requires only little logic cost, other sorting architectures can be used to generate fully sorted initial streams. Here insertion sorters will be most effective because of their linear implementation cost.

3. DESIGN FACTORS

With the knowledge of the right sorting architecture, we now discuss design factors that impact implementation and performance when considering relatively large problem classes. The great advantage of using an FPGA to implement a sorter is that it can implement any combination of sorting algorithms that can be perfectly scaled to the resources provided by the entire target platform. As opposed to GPUs or the Cell processor, FPGAs don't rely on a particular memory hierarchy, a special instruction set, or a communication architecture; they can directly implement the most suitable operands and link them arbitrarily together using a perfectly tailored interconnection network.

The following sections address again the most promising sorting architectures, this time focusing on a highly optimized FPGA implementation. After this, we discuss further issues that impact the overall sorting system, including architecture partitioning to FPGA resources, I/O throughput performance, and the benefits of applying partial run-time reconfiguration for sorting.

3.1 Efficient FIFO Merge Sorters

The merge sorter is the heart of the sorting accelerator and has to accomplish the following two main objectives: 1) high throughput and 1) efficient use of the on-chip memory. The design of a pipelined select-value element is presented in the next section, while we concentrate on the memory in the following paragraphs.

By studying Figure 8 again, we can identify that only one input FIFO will be read in each operation cycle of the sorter. Furthermore, as already stated in Section 2.3, the sort operation can start immedatly upon fully receiving the first stream and with the arrival of the first value of the second stream. Then, assuming a streaming operation at maximum speed, one value will arrive at the input and one value will be emitted to the output in each clock cycle. As a consequence, the combined fill level of both input FIFOs will remain constant and one proprietary FIFO using one memory block for both streams is sufficient as sketched in Figure 10.

To allow zero-overhead iterations with the next set of two input streams, we have to allow that data can be written during the time the FIFO is flushed (i.e., the phase after the arrival of the last key in the second stream). As it is not possible to predict when a certain part of the FIFO will be flushed, due to the data-dependent merge sort process, we tile the memory block into multiple smaller blocks. To manage these blocks, we developed an address computation unit that organizes the different blocks as linked lists. This allows fragmentation among the blocks and permits a continues stream of sort keys.

Figure 11 illustrates the fill-phase of a FIFO merge sorter. Always two streams share one linked-list FIFO and during the time a FIFO is flushed, it stores simultaneously the next input stream. In the last select-value stage of a FIFO-based merge sorter, we can directly store the results in external on-board memory, hence not requiring a larger output FIFO. Then the largest fully sorted sequence that can be generated by this sorter is twice the size of the shared combined input FIFO. As the total amount of FIFO storage in all other preceding sorter stages is approximately the size of the last FIFO, the sorted sequence size is equal to the total on-chip memory that can be spent on FIFO storage. This holds under the assumption that both streams are of the same size. Our address computation unit is capable of handling any given input stream size, thus simplifying the partitioning of FIFOs to on-FPGA memory block primitives.

As we have to leave at least two blocks in our FIFO implementation unused and because we are not fully utilizing the

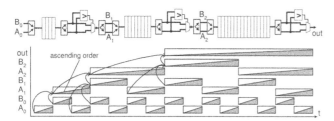

Figure 11: Fill phase of a FIFO-based merge sorter.

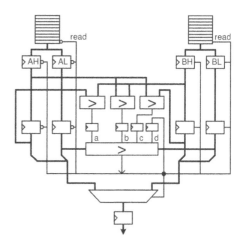

Figure 12: Pipelined select-value compare element. For the sake of readability, the example hides details on the control flow, filling the pipeline, and flushing out correctly all values from the compare element.

memory blocks in the first merge sorter stages, we achieved only an 80% efficiency out of the memory, which is still much better than the achieved 33% efficiency by the baseline approach using multiple parallel FIFOs. This value results from the fact that the baseline approach in Figure 8c) requires a third additional FIFO for storing the next initial sequence while the preceding iteration is flushed.

3.2 Throughput Optimized Tree Merge Sorter

Whenever the problem size exceeds the FPGA on-chip memory capacity, we have to perform one or more further merging steps that are best performed with a tree-based merge sorter, like the one depicted in Figure 9. The main difficulty in the design of a merge sorter tree is the backpressure flow control in the network. If we run through the operation of the tree sorter example, we see that the final root select-value element consumes one of the two input values while backpressing the entire other part. The same situation will recursively repeat on the entire selected branch of the tree in the next level until we reach the input layer to the sort tree. As a consequence, a baseline tree sorter would demand single-cycle flow control from the root sorter to every other sorter. This would consequently hinder fast operation or scaling to larger trees.

To solve this issue, we propose to decouple the operation between the different layers by adding small FIFOs between the different layers of the sorting tree. Then the propagation of the flow control against the data flow direction can take multiple clock cycles without risking the loss of any sort key value. These decoupling FIFOs can be efficiently implemented using distributed memory (i.e., using look-up tables as small memory blocks or shift register primitives); consequently leaving the much larger dedicated block RAMs for implementing input FIFOs for hiding the latency from external memory.

Due to the relatively low operation clock frequency of an FPGA as compared to CPU or GPU chips that have been manufactured in the same process technology, wide data paths must be used to sustain high sorting throughput. However, wide data paths require deep pipelining to avoid a break-down in the clock speed. The afore mentioned backpressure problem also applies within the pipeline. For example, let us assume that we pipeline the compare block of a select-value element into two parts, one for comparing the upper part of the two input operands (AH, BH) and one for the lower part (AL, BL). Then, there is the problem that the temporal results will be invalid because in each clock cycle one operand has to be shifted while leaving the other one behind.

Nevertheless, as illustrated in Figure 12, it is still possible to pipeline the compare operation. For this reason, the circuit provides three independent comparators for comparing the most significant subwords (AH, BH) in a first clock cycle. The state stored in register b is for determining the

initial compare value when filling the pipeline. The registers a and c denote the speculative high word comparison in the case that either value B or value A is shifted to the output. Then, depending on the last sort decision (stored in register d), the corresponding state is considered together with the low word (AL, BL) to compute the final compare state.

This proposed speculative comparison is suitable for even more deeply pipelined (and consequently wider) data paths. This approach can also be used if the path is wider than the search key in order to reorder elements inside the stream, for instance, when sorting 64-bit keys in a 128-bit data path. With these optimizations, high throughput merge sorter trees are possible on FPGAs.

3.3 Optimal Resource Partitioning

With the knowledge of the right sorter modules and their efficient implementation, we have to allocate the FPGA resources for the different modules. In the case of both the FIFO-based merge sorter and the tree merge sorter, the dedicated block RAM memories will be the limiting resource on the FPGA. In the following, we compute an optimal partition of the BRAM resources that maximize the possible problem size N that can be sorted with one initial run of the FIFO-based merge sorter and a following final merging in a sort tree. Ignoring the latency required to flush the FIFO-based merge sorter and the time to initially fill the sort tree, the result can be read back from the FPGA board immediately after the last sort key was sent to the FPGA. Consequently, a two stage sorter provides lowest possible latency and should be used as far as it it possible concerning N.

Given an estimate η denoting the memory efficiency, the cost c_F to implement a FIFO-based merge sorter in terms of memory blocks (where each block can store k keys), is for a problem size N_F:

$$c_F = \frac{N_F}{\eta \cdot k} \qquad (1)$$

Where $\eta \cdot k$ expresses the number of keys that effectively fit in one memory block.

When considering one memory block per stream input, the implementation cost c_t of a tree merge sorter being capable of simultaneously merging M streams is:

$$c_t = M \qquad (2)$$

The implementation cost of both sorter modules must fit onto the total number B of available on-FPGA memory blocks:

$$B \le c_F + c_t = \frac{N_F}{\eta \cdot k} + M \qquad (3)$$

The largest problem size N that can be solved with the two modules is therefore:

$$N = N_F \cdot M = (B \cdot k \cdot \eta - M \cdot k \cdot \eta) \cdot M \qquad (4)$$

The optimal size for M is found by setting the derivative of N with respect to M equal to zero:

$$\frac{\partial N}{\partial M} = B \cdot k \cdot \eta - 2M \cdot k \cdot \eta = 0 \qquad (5)$$

Finally, the optimal memory block partition is:

$$M = \frac{1}{2}B \qquad (6)$$

Equation 6 points out that regardless of the size of a memory block or the efficiency of the FIFO-based merge sorter implementation, the available memory resources should be equally balanced among the two sorter modules. Note that this result is valid for an implementation on any target FPGA.

3.4 The Impact of I/O Capacity

With respect to the system depicted in Figure 1, we assumed that for the first run through the FIFO-based merge sorter, the host interface provides sufficient throughput to deliver the operands and that the memory interface provides sufficient throughput to store the intermediate sorted blocks. When running the second tree-based merge sorting step, the data flow will be in the opposite direction (towards the host PC), as sketched in Figure 13a).

If we now consider a second memory channel that is fast enough to simultaneously read and write the stream of sort keys, a merging step can be performed in parallel to the first run, as depicted in Figure 13b). Then, instead of solving a problem size of $N_1^S = \frac{1}{4}B^2k\eta$ (see also Equation 4), it is possible to sort up to $N_2^S = \frac{4}{27}B^3k\eta$ keys in linear time complexity, when allocating one third of the memory resources for the FIFO-based merge sorter and the remaining on-FPGA memory for the merge sorter tree. Again, the result can be read almost immediately after the arrival of the last key (with a small latency for flushing and filling the pipelines).

Figure 13b) shows the dataflow in a simplified manner. It must be mentioned that each of the memory blocks is not required to provide sufficient space to store the whole problem. By swapping between the two memory blocks during the run of each step, it is sufficient when both memories together are capable to host the problem.

The comparison between the two approaches does not take the additional logic overhead for a second memory channel and the slightly more advanced flow control into account, but proves that especially for implementations on larger FPGAs a second memory channel should be utilized for sorting. For very large problem sizes with several GB of sort key data, adding further memory channels is recommended if not considering a reconfiguration of the present sorter architecture.

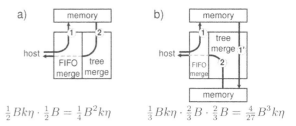

$$\frac{1}{2}Bk\eta \cdot \frac{1}{2}B = \frac{1}{4}B^2k\eta \qquad\qquad \frac{1}{3}Bk\eta \cdot \frac{2}{3}B \cdot \frac{2}{3}B = \frac{4}{27}B^3k\eta$$

Figure 13: Data flow in a static sorting system. a) one memory channel, b) two memory channels.

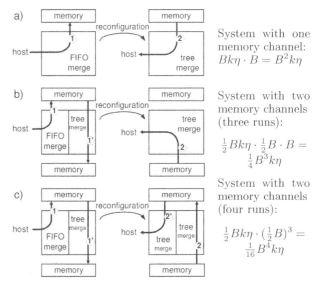

System with one memory channel: $Bk\eta \cdot B = B^2k\eta$

System with two memory channels (three runs): $\frac{1}{2}Bk\eta \cdot \frac{1}{2}B \cdot B = \frac{1}{4}B^3k\eta$

System with two memory channels (four runs): $\frac{1}{2}Bk\eta \cdot (\frac{1}{2}B)^3 = \frac{1}{16}B^4k\eta$

Figure 14: Data flow in a sorting system using partial run-time reconfiguration.

3.5 Using Partial Run-time Reconfiguration

Throughout the last sections, we have proven that the problem that can be solved by a sorting module within one run of a particular sort module scales linear with the amount of allocated FPGA area, which in particular comprises the On-FPGA memory resources. When assuming the case that a FIFO-based merge sorter and a tree-based merger sorter have to share the same FPGA resources, each module can only solve half the problem size per run. (see also Section 3.3). Let us assume a large sort problem that should be accomplished as fast as possible by starting a single run on the FIFO-based merger sorter followed by the tree-based sorter. Then we can identify, that during the first run of the FIFO-based merge sorter the tree sorter is idle while in the second phase the FIFO-based merge sorter will be idle. For enhancing the FPGA device utilization, it is then an option to allocate the same FPGA resources for both sorter modules and using partial runtime reconfiguration to swap from the FIFO-based merge sorter to the tree-based sorter module, as depicted in Figure 14a).

3.5.1 Reconfiguration Overhead

However, for a fair comparison, we also have to consider the required reconfiguration time. The configuration time of a sorter module is directly proportional to its size. Our case study has shown that a partially reconfigurable module with 100 memory blocks (B=100) on a Xilinx Virtex-5 FPGA results in roughly 3 MB of configuration data for the surrounding logic resources and the routing, which is 30KB

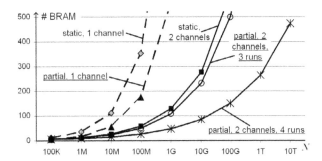

Figure 15: Memory block requirements of the different sorter architectures. The values are for the case that reading the result can be started directly after transferring all search keys to the FPGA.

Table 3: Configuration selection for different problem sizes (one memory channel).

#Keys (N)	remark	ex. time	figure
$0 \ldots Bk\eta$	only on-chip memory	$\approx N$	14a) left
$Bk\eta \ldots \frac{1}{4}Bk\eta$	static & off-chip mem.	$\approx 2N$	13a)
$> \frac{1}{4}Bk\eta$	partial reonf.	$> 2N$	14a)

per memory block. As we do not demand special initial values for the configuration of the memory blocks, their content is excluded from the configuration. Furthermore, the maximum specified configuration speed is with $400\,\mathrm{MB/s}$ five time slower than the expected throughput of the sorter hardware. See Section 4.3 for the exact throughput measures for the configuration speed and the sorter modules.

With this information, we can state the reconfiguration time overhead by means of sort processing time. Given the 100 memory block example, a single configuration would take as long as sorting $5 \cdot 3\,\mathrm{MB} = 15\,\mathrm{MB}$ within a single run, because of the five times lower configuration throughput. By multiplying this value with the number of configuration swaps and dividing the result by the pure processing time, the relative overhead can be computed. Considering the example on the Xilinx Virtex-5 FPGA with $B = 100$ memory blocks and one memory channel, the problem size that can be solved within one run of both the FIFO-bsed merge sorter and the tree-based merge sorter is: $B^2k\eta$ (see Figure 14a)). Given that a single memory block provides $k = 4\,\mathrm{KB}$ capacity and that the FIFO implementation efficiency is $\eta = 80\%$, this sorter can process up to $32\,\mathrm{MB}$ in two runs. This data will be transferred two times through the FPGA, once when receiving the sort keys (and when simultaneously running the FIFO-based merge sorter) and once more for writing the result back directly from the tree-based merge sorter. Consequently, for this example, the configuration overhead is roughly an additional $\frac{15}{2 \cdot 32} = 23\%$. Solving the identical problem on the same FPGA in a fully static implementation (see Figure 13a)) would require an additional run through the tree-based merge sorter and results in a respective time overhead of an additional 50%.

This does not mean that the partial version will be always outperform the static only implementation. Partial reconfiguration basically permits to adjust the resource allocation for adapting the sorter hardware to varying problem sizes as listed in Table 3.

3.5.2 Reconfiguration with Additional I/O Capacity

In Section 3.4, we have presented how an additional memory channel permits to run a tree merge step in parallel to

any other sorting step. This raises the problem size to higher power. By utilizing partial reconfiguration for swapping from the FIFO-based merge sorter to the tree-based merge sorter, as shown in Figure 14c), two times two parallel runs can be performed to solve problems up to $N_2^R = \frac{1}{16}B^4k\eta$. Given the example with $B = 100$ available memory blocks on a Xilinx Virtex-5 FPGA results in sortable problem sizes up to $20\,\mathrm{GB}$.

This requires streaming the key data four times through the FPGA, while two streams can be processed in parallel (with a small delay to generate sufficient fully sorted blocks for starting the next tree-based sorter). Given a host interface with $2\,\mathrm{GB/s}$ and assuming a sufficient fast sorter and memory, the whole sorting process takes theoretically only slightly more than 20 seconds. Meaning that the sort throughput is roughly $1\,\mathrm{GB/s}$ up to the problem size of $20\,\mathrm{GB}$. This requires a corresponding amount of on-board memory but comprises only moderate demands on the logic resources and the I/O throughput. Note that the reconfiguration involves only half the amount of resources that have been allocated for the sorting hardware, because only one sorter module is being swapped while keeping one tree-based merge sorter statically in the system. For large sorting problems, the configuration overhead can be ignored.

The introduction of partial run-time reconfiguration permits to sort much larger sequences at a throughput of $1\,\mathrm{GB/s}$ than it would be possible in a static only system. Given the two sorting systems shown in Figure 13b) and Figure 14c) providing two memory channels each, the extension λ is:

$$\lambda = \frac{N_2^R}{N_2^S} = \frac{\frac{1}{16}B^4k\eta}{\frac{4}{27}B^3k\eta} = \frac{27}{64}B \qquad (7)$$

For the example, this results in a theoretical $\lambda_{(B=100)} = 42$ times longer sequence that can be sorted by the reconfigurable sorter at $1\,\mathrm{GB/s}$, while the static implementation would only achieve $666\,\mathrm{MB/s}$ because of the additional run for the final merge step. Figure 15 denotes the number of BRAMs required to solve a particular problem size at $1\,\mathrm{GB/s}$ using any of the proposed sorter architectures in this paper.

3.5.3 Discussion on Using Reconfiguration

As the amount of BRAM is the main limiting FPGA resource, someone can think to multiplex memory blocks between sorter architectures, instead of using partial run-time reconfiguration. This is virtually impossible as the FIFO-based merge sorter requires memory block interfaces with small word sizes to implement the relatively large interfaces, while the memory blocks in the tree-based merge sorter demand bigest word sizes. Furthermore, the memory block multiplexing would add additional logic into the sorter designs and will also affect the routing that has to meet the requirements of the combined data path. Moreover, the design would be very difficult as memory block multiplexing Requires the instantiation of memory blocks at the top level of the design and not encapsulated in the design hierarchy.

An interesting further option is a hierarchical reconfiguration of the sorter with partially exchangeable comparators to adapt the system to different data types with the help of run-time reconfiguration.

4. CASE STUDY

4.1 Implementation and Design Flow

We implemented a test system for hosting all proposed single memory channel sorter architectures using the Xilinx XUPV5 Board. This board provides a XC5VLX110T-1

FPGA, a PCIe host interface, and 250 MB of DDR2-memory. We implemented the three configurations listed in Table 3 each as partially reconfigurable modules.

We haven't considered the partial design flow provided by Xilinx that interfaces reconfigurable modules via look-up table resources (which are called 'proxy logic' by Xilinx [19]). This approach comprises a latency penalty for passing the LUTs and a resource overhead of roughly 300 LUTs in our system. Moreover, the Xilinx vendor flow restricts the routing of reconfigurable modules not to cross regions outside from any module bounding box (i.e., signals of a partial module crossing the static system). This was defined as a requirement to achieve high performance also for the reconfigurable sorter modules.

To overcome these restrictions, we implemented the static system only with placement constraints such that all static resources fit into *configuration rows* A reconfiguration row contains four BRAM memory blocks or 20 configurable logic blocks (CLBs) that contain a cluster of eight 6-input LUTs each. Such a configuration row is the smallest piece of configuration logic that can be partially updated. By separating the static logic and memory resources into strict separated rows, it is ensured that the partial reconfiguration process is not corrupting any logic state. Note that both the static design and the reconfigurable sorter modules make heavily use out of distributed memory, meaning that look-up tables are used as shift registers that would be corrupted if logic is updated within the same configuration row of the distributed memory primitive. We haven't defined restrictions on the routing resources as the routing can be updated independent from the logic, because the configuration rows are written in multiple data items (called *frames*) and there exist separate frames for routing and logic.

If a routed net exists in all partial configuration bitstreams, it will not glitch during the configuration process. In order to guarantee this for the static routing, we converted the static design into a *hard macro* that is instantiated during the implementation of a sorter module. Hard macros are modules that can contain any kind of logic or routing. The routing of a macro can be preserved, hence ensuring for our static design that always identical routing resources will be used. For activating all clock drivers in the reconfigurable region, we instantiated dummy primitives (BRAMs and LUTs) and connected them to the global clock net. After this, we generated the configuration bitstream for the static design. Next we removed the dummy logic and converted the design into a hard macro. In this hard macro, we labeled specific primitive pins as I/O pins. These pins correspond to the top-level entities in the HDL-code of the sorting modules.

4.2 Demo System

The demo system provides a Microblaze soft-core processor connected to a multi-port DDR-2 memory controller module (MPMC) that is provided by Xilinx. The processor controls the operation of the system and permits to verify or initialize the memory. A PCIe core was integrated as the host interface. For ensuring fast FPGA reconfiguration, one port of the MPMC has been connected to the internal configuration access port ICAP. At system start, the processor is used to cache all partial bitfiles in the DDR memory. The partial reconfiguration process itself is then a DMA transfer of the corresponding configuration bitstream to the ICAP port. By running the configuration port at 125 MHz, we configured the device faster than specified, what has been studied in [5].

The sorter modules communicate via command FIFOs with the static system. This was in particular used to de-couple the clock of the CPU/memory sub-system from the sorting accelerators.

A weak point of the system is the poor I/O performance of the XUPV5 system based on the MPMC memory core and the single lane PCIe interface. For testing our sorters at full speed, we added I/O emulation modules into the static system. PCIe read access was emulated by supplying random data (from a LFSR), while memory read data was generated by a counter for the upper half of the key data and a random data generator for the lower half. This emulates the reading of pre-sorted blocks as they would have been generated by a FIFO-based merge sorter. For all write operations, the emulators verified an ascending order of the keys. All data paths and the keys have been set to be 64-bit wide.

4.3 Experimental Results

When setting the target clock frequency to 250 MHz for the sorter modules, we achieved the synthesis results listed in Table 4. The table lists also the chosen design parameters and the sort throughput for the different sorter modules. The values do not include the configuration overhead, that is 27 ms for 3.12 MB configuration data. Given a 4 M key sorting problem (which is 32 MB data), the configuration overhead is considerable $(1 + \frac{27ms}{32\,MB \cdot 2\,s/2\,GB})^{-1} = 46\%$ of the total time. However, given a 400 M key problem (which is 3.2 GB data), the configuration overhead can be neglected. Note that partial reconfiguration is the only option to sort such large problems in only three runs on the XUPV5 board (assuming a sufficient large memory module). If implementing the sorter with less resources, partial run-time reconfiguration becomes much more benefitial also for the small sorting example. Assuming an implementation with one half the logic, the reconfiguration overhead is only 22%.

For rating our approach, we compared it with state-of-the-art alternatives. A Cell processor implementation of SIMD bitonic sorting reports a maximum problem size of 128 KB (32-bit keys) that is being processed on one PPE SIMD unit in 2.5 ms [6]. This results in a sorting throughput of 51.2 MB/s or $\frac{1}{39}$ times the throughput of the FIFO-based merge sorter. Consequently, even utilizing all 16 available PPEs of the two Cell processors within the used Cell-Blade system cannot compete with the FPGA solution.

The best published result on sorting using a GPU reports a speed of 178 M keys/s, which is 720 MB/s [10]. But it must be mentioned that this performance is available for up to 16 M keys or (64 MB key storage) where we require three times of streaming the problem through the FPGA, what is then slightly slower. However, by adding a second memory port to the system and using partial run-time reconfiguration, the FPGA will outperform the GPU in speed. This would allow 1GB/s on problems beeing two orders of magnitude larger than the 35 MB result. Note that the required memory throughput of that FPGA solution is only about 6.2% of the memory throughput that is available on the GeForce GTX260 that was used in [10].

[6] lists results for a Quicksort reference implementation running on a 2-core 3.2 GHz Xeon system. For 1M keys (32 bit), the throughput is only 40.4 MB/s (31.7 MB/s for 128M keys) which is almost two orders of magnitude slower than our FPGA solution.

To the best of our knowledge, there is no published FPGA implementation that would allow a direct comparison. Most related FPGA implementations have been done on relatively small sorting problems, e.g. for median filtering in video processing systems and are also not designed for a throughput in the GB/s domain. In a recent publication, the authors

Table 4: Throughput and physical implementation results. $\#N$ states the number of 64-bit keys.

module	clock	# slices	# BRAMs	B	$\# N_F$ / [(KB)]	M	$\# N$ / [(KB)]	throughput	figure
FIFO-merge	252 MHz	10646 (74%)	103 (98%)	99	43 K (344 KB)		43 K (344 KB)	2 GB/s ; $N < 43\,K$	14a) left
tree-merge	273 MHz	12983 (90%)	105 (100%)	102		102	4.39 M 35.1 MB	1 GB/s ; $N < 4.4\,M$	14a) right
Fifo & tree	258 MHz	12254 (85%)	105 (100%)	100	21.5 K (172 KB)	50	1.08 M (8.6 MB)	1 GB/s ; $N < 2.1\,M$	13a)
one run of the FIFO merge sorter and two runs of the tree merge sorter							448 M 3.58 GB	667 MB/s ; $N < 3.5\,G$	

reported a throughput of less than 100 MB/s when fully utilizing a XC2VP30 FPGA on a problem size of 256 MB [14]. However, the chosen XC2VP30 device provides sufficient on-chip memory for solving a 250 MB problem in three runs, when using our sorting architecture. We estimate that our sorter hardware will work with 200 MHz on that device. We can summarize, that our FPGA solution surpasses any GPU, Cell processor or existing FPGA solution in both problem size and throughput, when considering an architecture with two memory channels.

5. CONCLUSIONS

In this paper, we carefully analyzed existing sorting architectures and tuned them into a highly optimized implementation that outperforms the best published results on the Cell processor and GPUs. The system is highly scalable and has the potential to dramatically further improve by introducing second memory channel. Moreover, this paper demonstrated considerable rises in performance as well as in resource efficiency by introducing partial run-time reconfiguration. It must be mentioned that the results have been achieved for the sort kernels but not for a complete system, as the available XUPV5 board provides only a single lane PCIe host interface. However, there exist commercial as well as academic systems that would fulfill our I/O requirements (e.g., the BEE3 system [4]).

Future work will demonstrate the performance with a real host interface and two memory channels to prove our theoretical observations by experiments. A further topic that will be investigated is a hierarchical reconfiguration for only swapping comparator functions.

Acknowledgment

This work is supported in part by the Norwegian Research Council under grant 191156V30

6. REFERENCES

[1] P. Alfke. Take Advantage of Leftover Multipliers and Block RAMs. *Xcell Journal*, 2:48–49, 2001.

[2] K. E. Batcher. Sorting networks and their applications. In *Proceedings of the April 30–May 2, 1968, spring joint computer conference (AFIPS 68)*, pages 307–314. ACM, 1968.

[3] M. Bednara, O. Beyer, J. Teich, and R. Wanka. Tradeoff Analysis and Architecture Design of a Hybrid Hardware/Software Sorter. In *Proceedings of the IEEE International Conference on Application-Specific Systems, Architectures, and Processors (ASAP)*, pages 299–308. IEEE Computer Society, 2000.

[4] Berkeley Wireless Research Center. BEEcube Homepage, 2010. http://www.beecube.com/platform.html.

[5] C. Claus, R. Ahmed, F. Altenried, and W. Stechele. Towards Rapid Dynamic Partial Reconfiguration in Video-Based Driver Assistance Systems. In *Reconfigurable Computing: Architectures, Tools and Applications (ARCS)*, volume 5992 of *LNCS*, pages 55–67. Springer, 2010.

[6] B. Gedik, R. R. Bordawekar, and P. S. Yu. CellSort: High Performance Sorting on the Cell Processor. In *Proceedings of the 33rd international conference on Very large data bases (VLDB)*, pages 1286–1297. VLDB Endowment, 2007.

[7] N. K. Govindaraju, J. Gray, R. Kumar, and D. Manocha. GPUTeraSort: High Performance Graphics Coprocessor Sorting for Large Database Management. In *Proceedings of the ACM international conference on management of data (SIGMOD)*, pages 325–336. ACM, 2006.

[8] G. Graefe. Implementing sorting in database systems. *ACM Comput. Surv.*, 38(3):10, 2006.

[9] L. K. Ha, J. Krüger, and C. T. Silva. Fast Four-Way Parallel Radix Sorting on GPUs. *Comput. Graph. Forum*, 28(8):2368–2378, 2009.

[10] J. K. L. Ha and C. Silva. Implicit radix sorting on GPUs, 2010. GPU GEMS volume 2, to appear, www.sci.utah.edu/ csilva/papers/ImplSorting.pdf.

[11] C. Layer and H.-J. Pfleiderer. A Reconfigurable Recurrent Bitonic Sorting Network for Concurrently Accessible Data. In *Proceedings of the International Conference on Field Programmable Logic and Applications (FPL)*, pages 648–657, 2004.

[12] R. Marcelino, H. Neto, and J. Cardoso. Sorting Units for FPGA-Based Embedded Systems. In *Distributed Embedded Systems: Design, Middleware and Resources*, volume 271 of *IFIP International Federation for Information Processing*, pages 11–22. Springer Boston, 2008.

[13] R. Marcelino, H. Neto, and J. Cardoso. Unbalanced FIFO Sorting for FPGA-Based Systems. In *16th IEEE International Conference on Electronics, Circuits, and Systems, (ICECS)*, pages 431–434, dec 2009.

[14] R. Mueller, J. Teubner, and G. Alonso. Data processing on fpgas. *Proc. VLDB Endow.*, 2(1):910–921, 2009.

[15] Y. Seddiq, S. Alshebeili, S. Alhumaidi, and A. Obied. FPGA-Based Implementation of a CFAR Processor Using Batcher's Sort and LUT Arithmetic. In *Design and Test Workshop (IDT), 2009 4th International*, pages 1 –6, nov. 2009.

[16] S. Sengupta, M. Harris, Y. Zhang, and J. D. Owens. Scan Primitives for GPU Computing. In *Proceedings of the 22nd ACM SIGGRAPH/EUROGRAPHICS Symposium on Graphics Hardware*, pages 97–106, Aire-la-Ville, Switzerland, Switzerland, 2007.

[17] The Unicode Consortium. About the Unicode Standard, 2010. http://www.unicode.org.

[18] S. Wong, S. Vassiliadis, and J. Hur. Parallel Merge Sort on a Binary Tree On-Chip Network. In *Proceedings of the 16th Annual Workshop on Circuits, Systems and Signal Processing (ProRISC)*, pages 365–368, November 2005.

[19] Xilinx Inc. Partial Reconfiguration User Guide, May 2010. Rel 12.1.

Real-Time High-Definition Stereo Matching on FPGA

Lu Zhang
Delft University of Technology
Mekelweg 4, 2600GA Delft
The Netherlands
lu.zhang@live.com

Ke Zhang
IMEC
Kapeldreef 75, B-3001 Leuven
Belgium
zhangke@imec.be

Tian Sheuan Chang
National Chiao Tung University
1001 Ta Hsueh Rd., Hsinchu
Taiwan
tschang@dragons.ee.nctu.edu.tw

Gauthier Lafruit
IMEC
Kapeldreef 75, B-3001 Leuven
Belgium
lafruit@imec.be

Georgi Kuzmanov
Delft University of Technology
Mekelweg 4, 2600GA Delft
The Netherlands
g.k.kuzmanov@tudelft.nl

Diederik Verkest
IMEC
Kapeldreef 75, B-3001 Leuven
Belgium
diederik.verkest@imec.be

ABSTRACT

Although many fast stereo matching designs have been proposed in the past decades, it is still very challenging to achieve real-time speed at high definition resolution while maintaining high matching accuracy. In this paper, we propose a real-time high definition stereo matching design on FPGA. By using the Mini-Census transform and the Cross-based cost aggregation, the proposed algorithm is robust to radiometric differences and produces accurate disparity maps. The algorithm modules have been optimized for efficient hardware implementations and instantiated in an SoC environment. Implemented on a single EP3SL150 FPGA, our design achieves 60 frames per second for 1024 × 768 stereo images. Evaluated with the Middlebury stereo benchmark, the proposed design also delivers leading stereo matching accuracy among prior related work.

Categories and Subject Descriptors

B.5.1 [**Register-Transfer-Level Implementation**]: Design; I.4.8 [**Image Processing and Computer Vision**]: Scene Analysis—*Stereo*

General Terms

Algorithms, Design, Performance

Keywords

Stereo Matching, High-Definition, Parallel Computing, FPGA

1. INTRODUCTION

Stereo matching has been one of the most active research topics in computer vision with many applications, such as multiview interpolation, object detection, etc. The task of stereo algorithms is to match the images taken from a pair of stereo cameras and extract depth information of captured objects. A *disparity* is estimated for each pixel of the reference image by searching for its correspondence in the target image. Recently proposed stereo matching implementations utilize various processing platforms such as GPU, FPGA and ASIC to achieve real-time performance. However, these designs rarely attain the target of producing high-resolution and accurate disparity maps at real-time speed.

In this paper, we propose a robust and accurate stereo matching design on FPGA. We employed state-of-the-art Mini-Census [2] and Variable-Cross [14] algorithms. Our design preserves high matching accuracy and robustness to radiometric differences. We have designed a fully pipelined architecture and parallelized all the algorithm modules on the FPGA. With efficient hardware-oriented optimizations, the proposed design achieves 60 frames per second when matching 1024 × 768 high-definition stereo images. Summarized contributions of the paper are:

- We combined the Mini-Census and the Variable-Cross algorithms to achieve high matching accuracy and robustness to radiometric distortions and bias differences.

- We implemented our improved stereo matching algorithm in a fully pipelined and scalable hardware design.

- We developed a prototype of the proposed design on an Altera EP3SL150 FPGA, which achieves real-time stereo matching independent on the disparity range at various resolutions e.g., 75FPS @ 640 × 480, 75FPS @ 800 × 600 and 60FPS @ 1024 × 768.

The remainder of this paper is organized as follows: Section 2 reviews related work. Section 3 introduces our modified stereo matching algorithm. Section 4 presents the proposed hardware implementation. Section 5 shows the experimental results and the comparisons to related work. Finally, Section 6 concludes the paper.

2. RELATED WORK

To enable real-time applications of stereo matching, various approaches have been developed recently with the primary targets to improve the matching accuracy and/or to increase the execution speed. We categorize them according to the implementation platforms as follows.

General purpose CPUs are flexible and suitable for complex algorithm-level optimizations. Tombari et al. [10] proposed an efficient segmentation-based cost aggregation strategy, which achieves a frame rate of 5 FPS for 384×288 images with 16 disparity range on an Intel Core Duo clocked at 2.14 GHz. Salmen et al. [9] optimized a dynamic programming algorithm on a 1.8 GHz PC platform and achieves a frame rate of 5 FPS for 384×288 and 16 disparity range stereo matching. Kosov et al. [8] combined a multi-level adaptive technique with a multi-grid approach that allows the variational method to reach 3.5 FPS with 450×375 images and a disparity range of 60. Zhang et al. [14] proposed the Variable-Cross algorithm and an orthogonal integral image technique to accelerate the aggregation over irregularly shaped regions, achieving 1.11 FPS with 384×288 and a disparity range of 16.

Recently, GPUs have been effectively utilized to accelerate stereo matching algorithms. Yang et al. [13] implemented a hierarchical belief propagation on a GeForce 7900 GTX GPU, which reached 16 FPS for 320×240 images with 16 disparities. Wang et al. [12] used an adaptive aggregation method and dynamic programming, reaching 43 FPS for 320×240 images and 16 disparity levels on an ATI Radeon XL1800 GPU. Zhang et al. [15] implemented a cross-based algorithm on GeForce GTX 8800, which achieves 100.9 FPS with 384×288 images and a disparity range of 16. Most recently, Humenberger et al. [6] optimized the Census transform on GeForce GTX 280 GPU, and reaches 105.4 FPS with 450×375 resolution and 60 disparity levels. Although GPU implementations have attained considerable speedup by parallel computing, they are still far from achieving real-time performance at high definition resolution.

Chang et al. [1] investigated the performance of using DSP as the implementation platform. In this work, the authors proposed a 4×5 jigsaw matching template and the dual-block parallel processing technique to enhance the stereo matching performance on a VLIW DSP. The DSP implementation achieves 50 FPS with a disparity range of 16 for 384×288 stereo matching. Nevertheless, its accuracy is heavily undermined.

To obtain higher computational efficiency, several hard-wired implementations of stereo matching are introduced to facilitate high performance embedded applications. Chang et al. [2] proposed a VLSI design of stereo matching algorithm with Mini-Census and Adaptive Support Weight (MCADSW). It reaches 42 FPS with 352×288 images and a disparity range of 64 while preserves desirable matching accuracy. Jin et al. [7] proposed a fully pipelined hardware design using Census transform and sum of Hamming distances. It has achieved 230 FPS with 640×480 resolution and 64 disparities. However, the produced disparity maps are not very accurate.

In all of the above references, high performance is achieved at the cost of lower matching accuracy and moderate frame resolution. Our design goal is, contrary to related work, to achieve high-definition real-time performance without compromising the matching accuracy. The proposed design is illustrated in the following sections.

3. THE STEREO MATCHING ALGORITHM

Our proposed algorithm is based on the Mini-Census transform [2] and the Variable-Cross [14] approach.

The **Mini-Census** transform is a hardware-friendly cen-

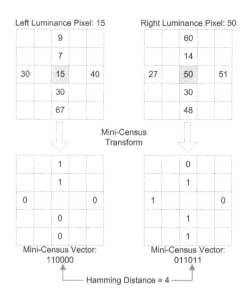

Figure 1: The Mini-Census transform and cost

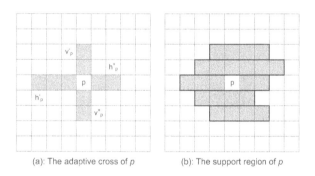

(a): The adaptive cross of p (b): The support region of p

Figure 2: Adaptive cross and support region

sus transform, which makes the matching cost robust to radiometric differences. It extracts the neighborhood information of a certain pixel and encodes the information in a vector. As shown in Figure 1, each square in the transform window represents an 8-bit luminance pixel and only the pixel locations with values are considered. If the luminance of a neighbor pixel is larger than that of the anchor pixel, the corresponding bit is set to '0', otherwise it is set to '1'. The matching cost is defined as the Hamming distance among the output vectors. The derived cost function is proved to be robust to radiometric distortions [5]. In addition, the Mini-Census transform significantly reduces the memory utilization due to less storage bits required by the transformed vectors and matching cost values.

The **Variable-Cross** approach constructs an appropriate support region for each pixel based on adaptive crosses. As shown in Figure 2(a), the cross of each anchor pixel p is defined by a quadruple $\{h_p^-, h_p^+, v_p^-, v_p^+\}$ that denotes the left, right, up, and bottom *adaptive arm* length, respectively. To decide the four arms, luminance difference evaluations are performed in the four directions on its consecutive neighboring pixels. Based on the crosses, the support region for p is constructed by merging the horizontal arms of its vertical neighbors, as shown in Figure 2(b). Detailed Variable-Cross algorithm implementation is found in [14].

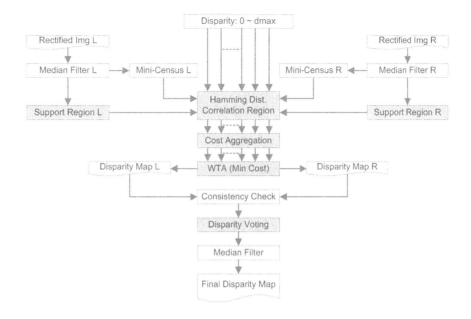

Figure 3: Overview of the proposed algorithm

Proposed Algorithm: We propose to merge the Mini-Census and the Variable-Cross algorithms, as suggested in Figure 3. Thus, we obtain potentially higher robustness and hardware efficiency due to the Mini-Census transform, and higher matching accuracy due to the Variable-Cross approach. To estimate the optimal disparity for pixel $p(x, y)$ in the left image, the algorithm searches in a segment of pixels $p'(x', y')$ in the right image. The matching cost between $p(x, y)$ and $p'(x', y')$ is the aggregated *raw matching cost*, Hamming distance, over the support regions that are constructed using the Variable-Cross method. The disparity producing the minimum matching cost is selected as the initial result. The initial disparity map is refined using a voting scheme (see [14] for details).

Hardware-oriented Algorithm Modifications: Besides combining the Mini-Census and Variable-Cross, we have also made modifications to enable an efficient parallel-computing hardware implementation. The shaded blocks in Figure 3 represent parts where we have introduced our modifications. The contributions of our modifications are twofold: enabling parallel computing hardware design and reducing the possible hardware resource utilization.

Given a pair of hypothetical correspondences, i.e., $p(x, y)$ in the left image and $p'(x', y')$ in the right image, we define the following variables to simplify our explanations:

- *Raw Matching Cost*: the Hamming distance between their Mini-Census vectors i.e., $RawCost(x, y, d)$

- *Correlation Region*: the overlapped area of the two pixels' support regions

- *Aggregated Matching Cost*: the accumulated raw matching costs in their correlation region i.e., $AggCost(x, y, d)$

- *Aggregated Pixel Count*: the total number of pixels in their correlation region i.e., $PixCount(x, y, d)$

- *Averaged Matching Cost*: the aggregated cost divided

by the aggregated pixel count in their correlation region i.e.,

$$AvgCost(x, y, d) = \frac{AggCost(x, y, d)}{PixCount(x, y, d)} \quad (1)$$

Here the coordinates of p and p' are correlated with a hypothetical disparity d ranging from 0 to d_{max} (the maximum disparity under consideration), i.e., $x' = x - d$ and $y' = y$.

Using the Luminance Only: The original Variable-Cross algorithm uses R-G-B color to decide the four arms and perform cost aggregations, but here we only make use of the luminance channel. This modification reduces potential bandwidth and storage requirements to one third of the case using three R-G-B channels. Combined with the Mini-Census transform, this modification does not degrade the resulting disparity maps.

Limited Support Region Radius: In the original Variable-Cross algorithm, the maximum support region radius L_{max} is not limited and adjustable in software. But for hardware implementation, this parameter determines the silicon resource utilization. From our experiments we found that the proposed stereo matching algorithm produces high accuracy with L_{max} ranging from 15 to 20. To save storage requirements, we set L_{max} to 15, which ensures each arm of the quadruple $\{h_p^-, h_p^+, v_p^-, v_p^+\}$ to be fully represented by a 4-bit word.

Parallelized Disparity Estimations: One of the major contributions of this paper is the parallelization of the cost aggregation computation. To obtain the minimum averaged cost $AvgCost(x, y, d)$ in the disparity range $[0, d_{max}]$, the original Variable-Cross algorithm, implemented on CPU, uses nested loops to compute the disparity at each pixel location and to track the minimum $AvgCost(x, y, d)$ in the disparity range. Obviously, these nested loops introduce the major bottleneck that prevents fast processing. With our parallelized cost aggregation, the $RawCost(x, y, d)$ values with different disparity hypotheses are accumulated in par-

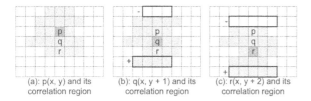

(a): p(x, y) and its correlation region   (b): q(x, y + 1) and its correlation region   (c): r(x, y + 2) and its correlation region

Figure 4: Vertical cost aggregation data reuse

allel, independently of each other. Therefore the number of parallel computing threads is in accordance with the disparity range, and each of the threads presents $AggCost(x, y, d)$ and $PixCount(x, y, d)$ associated with a unique d.

With $AggCost(x, y, d)$ and $PixCount(x, y, d)$ in the disparity range $[0, d_{max}]$ computed concurrently, the minimum $AvgCost(x, y, d)$ is attainable through a tree-structure WTA (*Winner-Takes-All*) module. To avoid the division computation indicated by (1), we use a multiply-subtract technique to track the minimum $AvgCost(x, y, d)$. This proposed technique is according to the fact indicated by (2).

$$\frac{AggCost(x, y, d_0)}{PixCount(x, y, d_0)} < \frac{AggCost(x, y, d_1)}{PixCount(x, y, d_1)}$$
$$\Longleftrightarrow$$
$$AggCost(x, y, d_0) \times PixCount(x, y, d_1)$$
$$<$$
$$AggCost(x, y, d_1) \times PixCount(x, y, d_0)$$
(2)

Therefore we let two of the parallel threads compete with each other according to (2), and the winner thread enters the next stage. Such competitions repeat until the final winner is selected.

Fixed Vertical Aggregation Span: In the cost aggregation step, we adopt the orthogonal integral image technique [14] proposed in the Variable-Cross algorithm, which decomposes the aggregation over a 2D correlation region into 2 × 1D aggregation steps i.e., *horizontal aggregation* and *vertical aggregation*. In Variable-Cross, costs are aggregated over fully adaptive correlation regions in both steps. In our proposed algorithm, the vertical aggregation step uses a fixed aggregation span for each pixel instead of using the adaptive vertical arms. This approach significantly reduces the line buffers needed for each vertical aggregation module, with negligible influence on the disparity map quality. Based on our investigation, a vertical aggregation span of 5 (see Figure 4) gives the best trade-off between matching accuracy and hardware complexity. The 5-line vertical aggregation covers the anchor pixel's scanline and the adjacent ±2 lines.

Moreover, with fixed vertical aggregation span, a more efficient data reuse technique is applicable. The concept of this technique is illustrated in Figure 4, where pixels $p(x, y)$, $q(x, y + 1)$ and $r(x, y + 2)$ are located in the same vertical column, and their correlation regions are shaded. Obviously, the aggregated costs of pixel $q(x, y + 1)$ and $r(x, y + 2)$ fulfill the following equation. In (3) the $AggCost_h(\cdot)$ returns the horizontally aggregated cost in the bordered region. Therefore, the vertically aggregated cost is reused for vertically adjacent pixels. The similar scheme is also applied to the

$PixCount(x, y, d)$ calculations.

$$AggCost(x, y + 1, d) = AggCost(x, y, d)$$
$$+ AggCost_h(x, y + 3, d)$$
$$- AggCost_h(x, y - 2, d)$$
$$AggCost(x, y + 2, d) = AggCost(x, y + 1, d)$$
$$+ AggCost_h(x, y + 4, d)$$
$$- AggCost_h(x, y - 1, d)$$
(3)

Decomposed Disparity Voting: Although the correlation regions are truncated in the vertical aggregation step, the fully adaptive support region is still applied to the disparity voting step. Like cost aggregations, the disparity voting also performs on an arbitrarily shaped 2D support region, which complicates the hardware design. To simplify this problem, here we again decompose a 2D region voting into 2 × 1D voting processes (see Figure 5); i.e., the *horizontal disparity voting* step first searches for the majority disparity in each horizontal segment in the support region of pixel $p(x, y)$, then the *vertical disparity voting* picks out the majority one in the vertical segment. Our experiments show that this

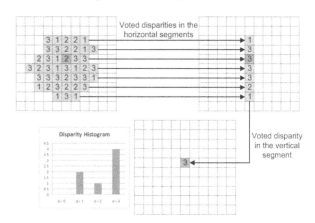

Figure 5: 2 × 1D orthogonal voting method

modification only provides a slightly different disparity map compared with the 2D voting result.

4. HARDWARE IMPLEMENTATION

In accordance with the algorithm flow illustrated in Figure 3, the hardware implementation of the proposed algorithm is decomposed into three processor blocks i.e., *Pre-Processor*, *Stereo-Matcher* and *Post-Processor*.

The key to best processing throughput is to fully pipeline all processing steps, i.e. with source image pixels come progressively in scanline order, a new income pixel gets its disparity at the end of the pipeline after a certain pipeline latency, and valid disparities also come successively in scanline order, synchronized with the input pixel rate. To enable fully pipelined implementation, massive data-level parallelizations are mainly implemented in the Stereo-Matcher processor, where matching costs with different hypothetical disparities are computed and aggregated mutually independently. In the other two co-processors, data and bit level parallelism are also applied. For example, the left and right images are processed in parallel whenever possible.

The Pre-Processor Implementation: This processor does not deal with any disparity information. It performs

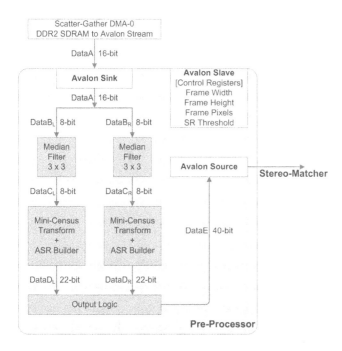

Figure 6: The Pre-Processor pipeline

median filter, Mini-Census transform, and support region construction on the left and right images independently (see Figure 6). Because these functions are all window-based processing, line buffer memories and register matrices are employed to provide pipelined window content. The line buffer and register matrix used in the *Median Filter 3 × 3* module are illustrated in Figure 7. This module prepares all the required pixels for computing the median for the center pixel $p(x, y)$, buffered in *WinReg4*. As pixels come in continuously, the 3 × 3 pixel window also slides over the whole frame in scanline order. The 9 luminance values in a filter window are captured by a systolic sorting module to get the median. We have adopted the median sorting structure proposed by Vega-Rodríguez et al. in [11] and implemented suitable pipeline stages. With this structure, the output median pixel rate is synchronized with the input pixel rate. The depth of a line buffer is determined by the maximum allowed frame width. A 1024 × 8 SRAM block supports any frame width up to 1024. In practice, we use 1 of the M9K blocks in EP3SL150 FPGA to construct a line buffer, which is configured to 1024 × 8bits.

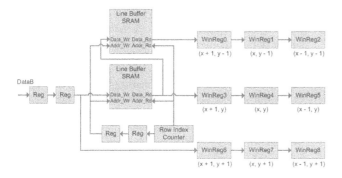

Figure 7: Median filter Line buffers and registers

The median filter implementation conveys the fundamental technique we have used to construct a fully pipelined processing module for window-based functions. In follow-up steps, variations of this structure are widely implemented.

The filtered left and right image streams are separately operated by corresponding *Mini-Census Transform* and *Adaptive Support Region Builder* modules (ASR Builder); they are designed to share the same line and window buffers. The Mini-Census transform is computed straightforwardly using the 6 selected neighbor pixels. The adaptive arm computations are implemented with priority encoders. The dimension of the register matrix is $(2 \cdot L_{max} + 1) \times (2 \cdot L_{max} + 1)$.

The Stereo-Matcher Implementation: The processing pipeline structure of the Stereo-Matcher processor is sketched in Figure 8. This processor operates on the transformed image data stream coming from the Pre-Processor and computes the left and right disparity maps accordingly. Once the L-R disparities are available, the Stereo-Matcher sends them to the Post-Processor. In Figure 8, before the vertical aggregation step there are two major data paths, denoted by *Front* and *Delay* respectively. They work for the data reuse technique implemented in the vertical aggregation. After the vertical aggregation step, there are still two major data paths, but now they are associated with the left and right disparity map respectively. In each path, there are a number of parallel computing threads in accordance with the maximum allowed disparity range; each thread deals with the cost aggregations for a unique disparity hypothesis d. In practice, the number of parallel threads can be arbitrary, only limited by the available hardware resources.

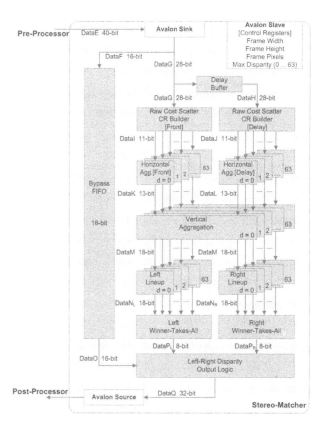

Figure 8: The Stereo-Matcher pipeline

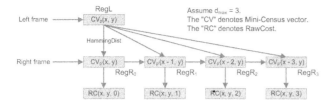

Figure 9: The Raw Cost Scatter logic

The Stereo-Matcher starts with the *Raw Cost Scatter*, which receives transformed image data words in scanline order and distributes raw costs to different cost aggregation threads. The *Correlation Region Builder* (CR Builder) works similarly to generate correlation region information from the quadruple arms. *Horizontal Aggregation* modules calculate $AggCost_h(x, y, d)$ (see Figure 4) for each pixel and each module is responsible for an assigned hypothetical disparity. According to (3), $AggCost_h(x, y + 3, d)$ from the *Front* data path and $AggCost_h(x, y - 2, d)$ from the *Delay* data path are used in *Vertical Aggregation* modules together with $AggCost(x, y, d)$ to compute $AggCost(x, y+1, d)$. The calculated $AggCost(x, y, d)$ values of a scanline are stored in a line buffer to enable the data-reuse technique. Similar computation logic is applied to the $PixCount(x, y, d)$. Following the vertical aggregation step, the *Lineup* modules are used to synchronize left-right disparity estimations. Thereafter the $AggCost(x, y, d)$ and $PixCount(x, y, d)$ values enter the tree-structure *WTA* modules and the estimated disparity for each pixel is computed according to (2).

The *Bypass FIFO* in Figure 8 is used to preserve the adaptive arms associated with each pixel in the left image, which are also consumed in the cost aggregation steps. The adaptive arms still have to be used in the disparity voting step. The output of the Stereo-Matcher is the data stream that consists of 16-bit L-R disparities and 16-bit adaptive arms of each pixel in the left image.

The Post-Processor Implementation: The internal processing pipeline of the Post-Processor is depicted in Figure 10. It takes the left and right disparity maps and adaptive arms $\{h_p^-, h_p^+, v_p^-, v_p^+\}$ of the left image pixels. The right disparity map is used to check disparity consistency, and correct mismatched correspondences in the left disparity map. The double-checked left disparity map is sent to the following disparity voting modules to further refine its quality. The right disparity map can also be refined and output finally, but in our target application, the right disparity map is not used and discarded after the L-R consistency check. Finally the refined left disparity map passes through a median filter to remove its speckles. The median filter gives the final disparity map output, which is used for higher level applications such as view interpolation or feature detection.

The task of the *L-R Consistency Check* module is to verify whether the two disparity maps satisfy (4).

$$d_{p'}\big(x - d_p(x, y), y\big) = d_p(x, y) \qquad (4)$$

Here $d_p(x, y)$ and $d_{p'}(x', y')$ denote the disparity of $p(x, y)$ and $p'(x', y')$, respectively. If $d_p(x, y)$ and the corresponding $d_{p'}\big(x - d_p(x, y), y\big)$ satisfy this equation, $d_p(x, y)$ is considered as a valid disparity; otherwise $d_p(x, y)$ is regarded as a mismatch. In the latter case $d_p(x, y)$ is replaced by a closest valid disparity.

The decomposed disparity voting scheme is implemented

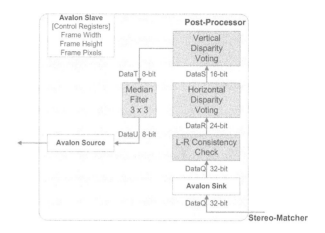

Figure 10: The Post-Processor pipeline

in the *Horizontal Disparity Voting* module and the *Vertical Disparity Voting* module respectively. The horizontal disparity voting module is comprised of $(d_{max}+1)$ voting units. Each of them is responsible for building the histogram bin over $[h_p^-, h_p^+]$ for a certain disparity d. Therefore, the disparity associated with the histogram peak is attainable using a pipelined tree-structure maximum value search module. The vertical disparity voting module works similarly, but line buffers are used first to form vertical vectors i.e., $[v_p^-, v_p^+]$ before the voting units take effect.

SoC Implementation on FPGA: To verify and evaluate the whole stereo matching pipeline design, we have instantiated the three co-processors in an SoC environment with DMA engines, DDR2-SDRAM controllers etc. The system diagram is given by Figure 11, which has been implemented on a Terasic DE3 main board with EP3SL150 FPGA and peripheral daughter cards, as illustrated in Figure 12. Cameras shown in the figure will be used for target application developments, but in this implementation we use DMA to emulate the progressive scanline data stream of a stereo camera pair, which moves benchmark images stored in the external DDR2-SDRAM to the processing pipeline. Pixels in the left and right images are synchronized and transferred in a packed data word.

In this implementation, the disparity maps are rendered on a standard DVI monitor, and tested with a number of common pixel clocks. In another implementation of ours, the disparity maps are uploaded to a PC to verify the hardware implementation results and perform benchmarks. We use the *Avalon Memory-Mapped* [3] interface to control some parameters in the processor blocks and the *Avalon Streaming* [3] interface to transfer pipelined data stream between them. The data transfers on Avalon Streaming interconnections follow *Avalon-ST Video Protocol* [4]. Although the DDR2-SDRAM is used as source image buffer, it is not accessed during the stereo matching processing. To match the refresh rate required by the DVI monitor, the DMA has to provide valid data in real-time. The whole system is controlled by the Nios-II soft processor, which regulates data flows but it is not directly involved in the stereo matching computations.

The FPGA hardware is split in two clock domains: the CPU clock domain and the peripheral clock domain. In our implementation, the CPU clock domain is working at

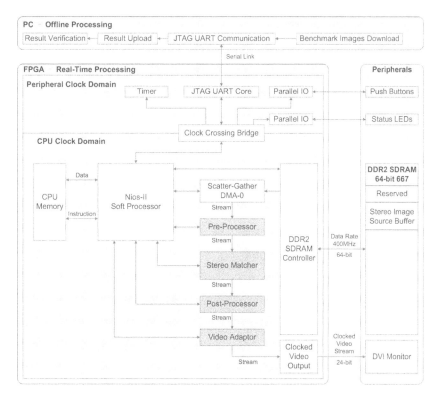

Figure 11: The SoC implementation
Shaded blocks are developed by this work

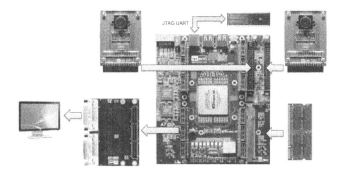

Figure 12: The implementation platform

100MHz, which contains more time-critical components than those in the 50MHz peripheral clock domain. This split allows Quartus-II synthesis to optimize the hardware placement and routing. Components in the two clock domains communicate with each other through a clock crossing bridge. The stereo matching processing is fully synchronous and pipelined. Pixel output of the *Clocked Video Output* module is synchronized with desired pixel clocks and this module also contains a FIFO to buffer the data from the stereo matching pipeline, which works at 100MHz. When the FIFO is almost full, it back-pressures the stereo matching pipeline to make it stall.

Implementation Report: The whole system depicted in Figure 11 is synthesized using Quartus-II 9.1 and implemented in a single EP3SL150 FPGA. In the stereo matching pipeline, the Pre-Processor is not aware of any dispar-

ity range and the Post-Processor is only slightly affected by the maximum disparity range. In contrast, utilized hardware resources by the Stereo-Matcher are mainly determined by the maximum allowed disparity range. As suggested in Figure 8, the number of processing threads in the Stereo-Matcher scales with the maximum allowed disparity range. In practice, the disparity range is determined by the distance between the scene objects and the stereo camera baseline, and the length of the baseline itself. It hence varies with the target application and corresponding camera setup. In our implementation, the Post-Processor is set to deal with a maximum disparity range of 64, and the Stereo-Matcher is tested with maximum disparity range of 16, 32 and 64 respectively. The implementation report is shown in Table 1.

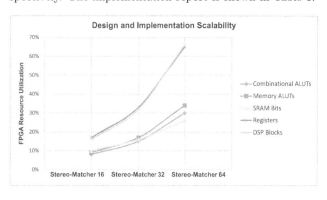

Figure 13: The Stereo-Matcher design scalability

The Stereo-Matcher design scalability is illustrated in Figure 13. The scalability figure shows that the implementation

	Combinational ALUTs		Memory ALUTs		Registers		DSP Blocks		SRAM Bits	
	Total: 113,600	Util.	Total: 56,800	Util.	Total: 113,600	Util.	Total: 384	Util.	Total: 5,630,976	Util.
Pre-Processor	3,310	3%	288	1%	2,075	2%	0	0%	417,792	7%
Post-Processor	12,211	11%	536	1%	10,263	9%	0	0%	393,216	7%
Stereo-Matcher 16	8,874	8%	4,864	9%	18,813	17%	60	16%	589,824	10%
Stereo-Matcher 32	17,136	15%	9,728	17%	37,245	33%	124	32%	884,736	16%
Stereo-Matcher 64	33,639	30%	19,456	34%	74,109	65%	252	66%	1,474,560	26%
Stereo-Matcher 64 SoC	60,296	53%	20,288	36%	94,891	84%	257	67%	3,771,247	67%

Table 1: EP3SL150 utilization report

complexity scales nearly linearly with the number of parallel computing threads, but there are different scaling factors associated with the corresponding hardware resource. In the current implementation, the required registers (flip-flops) and dedicated DSP blocks are limiting resources for a larger scale implementation. Balancing techniques include replacing some dedicated hardware DSPs with LUTs, and reducing the usage of pipeline registers.

5. EXPERIMENTAL RESULTS

The benchmark disparity maps produced by our proposed algorithm are presented in Figure 15. Comparisons of benchmarked error rates with related work are listed in Table 3. To enable efficient hardware implementation, we have introduced the Mini-Census transform and made some trade-off modifications as described in Section 3. Therefore, the averaged accuracy is reasonably a bit worse than the original software Variable-Cross. Nevertheless, the modified algorithm still demonstrates even better performance than Variable-Cross on the *Teddy* and *Cones* image sets, which feature higher resolution and disparity range.

(a)   (b)

(c)   (d)
Error: 98.4%   Error: 7.80%

Figure 14: Luminance biased results

The improved algorithm robustness is illustrated in Figure 14, where (a) and (b) present the Teddy stereo image set with a luminance bias of +50 on the right image. The resulting disparity map Figure 14(c) is computed by the Variable-Cross algorithm, which is severely degraded by the bias. In contrast, Figure 14(d) is the result computed by our proposed algorithm, which is only slightly affected.

We have tested the SoC implementation with several commonly used pixel clocks and corresponding standard display resolutions. The developed stereo matching system successfully fulfills the specifications listed in Table 2. Table 4 contains the processing speed comparisons between our implementation and other reported real-time implementations. The processing speed of different systems is given in frames per second (FPS) and million disparity evaluations per second (MDE/s), which equals to (image width × image height × disparity range × FPS). Obviously, our implementation demonstrates very high frame rates compared to other implementations. Our implementation and the one proposed by Jin et al. [7] are both fully pipelined designs and the frame rates are not limited by the computing pipeline itself. The frame rate difference between the two implementations is caused by different measurement methods. In addition, our implementation achieves higher matching accuracy compared with Jin's work. For FPGA implementations, the achievable resolution is usually limited by the available on-chip memories, used as line buffers etc. Thanks to the Mini-Census transform, the required on-chip matching cost storage is significantly reduced. Moreover, we have also applied data-reuse technique in the cost aggregation step to further reduce the memory consumption. CPU and GPU based implementations do not have resolution limitations, however, they hardly achieve real-time performance with higher definition images.

Resulted Frame Rates (FPS) for Common Pixel Clocks					
Frame Sizes	640 × 480	640 × 480	800 × 600	800 × 600	1024 × 768
Pixel Clock (MHz)	25.17	31.5	40	49.5	65
Frame Rates (FPS)	60	75	60	75	60

Table 2: Resulted FPS for common pixel clocks

6. CONCLUSIONS

This paper has proposed an improved stereo matching algorithm suitable for hardware implementation using the Mini-Census transform and the Variable-Cross stereo matching algorithm. Furthermore, we provide fully pipelined parallel computing hardware design and implementation of the proposed algorithm. The experimental results suggest that our work has achieved high speed real-time processing with programmable video resolutions, while preserving high stereo matching accuracy. The combination of Mini-Census and Variable-Cross is proved to be suitable for parallelization and pipelined systolic array processing. We have also proposed modifications, which make our algorithm more efficient for hardware implementations than the Variable-Cross algorithm, without degrading the matching accuracy. There is still room for further optimizing the design and implementation, and its ASIC counterpart is in the process of being developed which will provide feasible solutions for promising 3DTV and viewpoint interpolation applications.

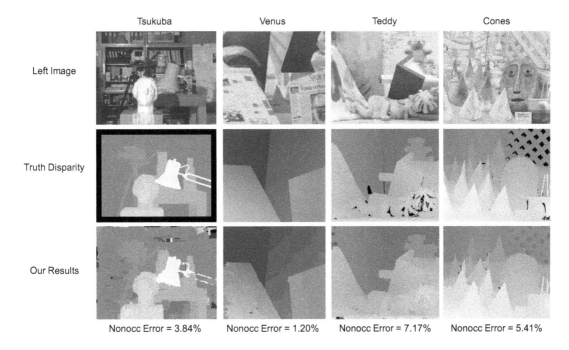

	Tsukuba	Venus	Teddy	Cones
Left Image				
Truth Disparity				
Our Results				
	Nonocc Error = 3.84%	Nonocc Error = 1.20%	Nonocc Error = 7.17%	Nonocc Error = 5.41%

Figure 15: Truth disparity maps and our results

Stereo Matching Algorithm Error Rates (Bad Matches%)													
Image Set	Tsukuba			Venus			Teddy			Cones			Average Bad Pixel Rate
Image Size	384 x 288			434 x 383			450 x 375			450 x 375			
Disparity Range	16			20			60			60			
Evaluation Method	nonocc	all	disc	nonocc	all	disc	nonocc	all	disc	nonocc	all	disc	
VariableCross [14]	1.99	2.65	6.77	0.62	0.96	3.20	9.75	15.1	18.2	6.28	12.7	12.9	7.60
RealtimeBFV [15]	1.71	2.22	6.74	0.55	0.87	2.88	9.90	15.0	19.5	6.66	12.3	13.4	7.65
RealtimeBP [13]	1.49	3.40	7.87	0.77	1.90	9.00	8.72	13.2	17.2	4.61	11.6	12.4	7.69
Chang et al. 2010 [2]	N/A	2.80	N/A	N/A	0.64	N/A	N/A	13.7	N/A	N/A	10.1	N/A	N/A
Proposed	**3.84**	**4.34**	**14.2**	**1.20**	**1.68**	**5.62**	**7.17**	**12.6**	**17.4**	**5.41**	**11.0**	**13.9**	**8.20**
FastAggreg [10]	1.16	2.11	6.06	4.03	4.75	6.43	9.04	15.2	20.2	5.37	12.6	11.9	8.24
OptimizedDP [9]	1.97	3.78	9.80	3.33	4.74	13.0	6.53	13.9	16.6	5.17	13.7	13.4	8.83
RealtimeVar [8]	3.33	5.48	16.8	1.15	2.35	12.8	6.18	13.1	17.3	4.66	11.7	13.7	9.05
RTCensus [6]	5.08	6.25	19.2	1.58	2.42	14.2	7.96	13.8	20.3	4.10	9.54	12.2	9.73
RealTimeGPU [12]	2.05	4.22	10.6	1.92	2.98	20.3	7.23	14.4	17.6	6.41	13.7	16.5	9.82
Jin et al. 2009 [7]	9.79	11.56	20.29	3.59	5.27	36.82	12.5	21.5	30.57	7.34	17.58	21.01	17.24
Chang et al. 2007 [1]	21.5	21.7	48.7	16.5	17.8	29.9	26.3	33.6	35.1	24.2	32.4	31.0	N/A

Table 3: Stereo matching algorithm error rates
The algorithms are ordered by the averaged bad pixel rate.

Stereo Matching Implementation Frame Rates (FPS)					
		Implementation	Disparity Range	Frame Rates	MDE/s
Jin et al. 2009 [7]	1 x FPGA	Virtex-4 XC4VLX20	64	230 @ 640 x 480	4521
Proposed	**1 x FPGA**	**EP3SL150**	**64**	**60 @ 1024 x 768**	**3019**
RTCensus [6]	GPU	GeForce GTX 280	60	105.4 @ 450 x 375	1067
Chang et al. 2010 [2]	ASIC	UMC 90nm	64	42 @ 352 x 288	272
RealtimeBFV [15]	GPU	GeForce GTX 8800	64	12 @ 450 x 375	129
Chang et al. 2007 [1]	DSP	TMS320C64x	60	9.1 @ 450 x 375	92
RealTimeGPU [12]	GPU	Radeon XL1800	16	43 @ 320 x 240	53
RealtimeVar [8]	CPU	Pentium 2.83GHz	60	3.5 @ 450 x 375	35
RealtimeBP [13]	GPU	GeForce GTX 7900	16	16 @ 320 x 240	20
FastAggreg [10]	CPU	Core Duo 2.14GHz	60	1.67 @ 450 x 375	17
OptimizedDP [9]	PC	1.8GHz	60	1.25 @ 450 x 375	13
VariableCross [14]	CPU	Pentium IV 3.0GHz	60	0.63 @ 450 x 375	13

Table 4: Stereo matching implementation FPS
The implementations are ordered by the MDE/s.

7. ACKNOWLEDGMENTS

The authors would like to thank the IMEC Taiwan Innovation Center (ITIC), Li-Hsin Road 1, Hsinchu, Taiwan, for their ideas and support in the system design and RTL synthesis.

8. REFERENCES

[1] N. Chang, T. Lin, T. Tsai, Y. Tseng, and T. Chang. Real-time DSP implementation on local stereo matching. *Multimedia and Expo, 2007 IEEE International Conference on*, pages 2090–2093, 2007.

[2] N. Chang, T. Tsai, B. Hsu, Y. Chen, and T. Chang. Algorithm and Architecture of Disparity Estimation With Mini-Census Adaptive Support Weight. *Circuits and Systems for Video Technology, IEEE Transactions on*, 20(6):792–805, 2010.

[3] Altera Corporation. *Avalon Interface Specifications*, April 2009.

[4] Altera Corporation. *Video and Image Processing Suite User Guide*, July 2010.

[5] H. Hirschmueller and D. Scharstein. Evaluation of stereo matching costs on images with radiometric differences. *IEEE transactions on pattern analysis and machine intelligence*, pages 1582–1599, 2008.

[6] M. Humenberger, C. Zinner, M. Weber, W. Kubinger, and M. Vincze. A fast stereo matching algorithm suitable for embedded real-time systems. *Computer Vision and Image Understanding*, 2010.

[7] S. Jin, J. Cho, X. Pham, K. Lee, S. Park, M. Kim, and J. Jeon. FPGA Design and Implementation of a Real-time Stereo Vision System. *IEEE Transactions on Circuits and Systems for Video Technology*, 2010.

[8] S. Kosov, T. Thormahlen, and H. Seidel. Accurate real-time disparity estimation with variational methods. *Advances in Visual Computing*, pages 796–807, 2009.

[9] J. Salmen, M. Schlipsing, J. Edelbrunner, S. Hegemann, and S. Luke. Real-Time Stereo Vision: Making More Out of Dynamic Programming. In *Computer Analysis of Images and Patterns*, pages 1096–1103. Springer, 2009.

[10] F. Tombari, S. Mattoccia, L. Di Stefano, and E. Addimanda. Near real-time stereo based on effective cost aggregation. In *19th International Conference on Pattern Recognition*, pages 1–4, 2008.

[11] M. Vega-Rodríguez, J. Sánchez-Pérez, and J. Gómez-Pulido. An FPGA-based implementation for median filter meeting the real-time requirements of automated visual inspection systems. In *Proceedings of the 10th Mediterranean Conference on Control and Automation*, Citeseer, 2007.

[12] L. Wang, M. Liao, M. Gong, R. Yang, and D. Nister. High-quality real-time stereo using adaptive cost aggregation and dynamic programming. In *Third International Symposium on 3D Data Processing, Visualization, and Transmission*, 2006

[13] Q. Yang, L. Wang, R. Yang, S. Wang, M. Liao, and D. Nister. Real-time global stereo matching using hierarchical belief propagation. In *The British Machine Vision Conference*, pages 989–998, 2006.

[14] K. Zhang, J. Lu, and G. Lafruit. Cross-based local stereo matching using orthogonal integral images. *IEEE Transactions on Circuits and Systems for Video Technology*, 19(7):1073–1079, 2009.

[15] K. Zhang, J. Lu, G. Lafruit, R. Lauwereins, and L. Van Gool. Real-time accurate stereo with bitwise fast voting on CUDA. *5th IEEE workshop on embedded computer vision, held in conjunction with ICCV*. 2009.

Eliminating the Memory Bottleneck: An FPGA-based Solution for 3D Reverse Time Migration

Haohuan Fu
Center for Earth System Science
Tsinghua University
Beijing, China
haohuan@gmail.com

Robert G. Clapp
Center for Computational Earth and
Environmental Science
Stanford University
Stanford, CA, US
bob@sep.stanford.edu

ABSTRACT

Memory-related constraints (memory bandwidth, cache size) are nowadays the performance bottleneck of most computational applications. Especially in the scenario of multiple cores, the performance does not scale with the number of cores in many cases. In our work, we present our FPGA-based solution for the 3D Reverse Time Migration (RTM) algorithm. As the most computationally demanding imaging algorithm in current oil and gas exploration, RTM involves various computational challenges, such as a high demand for storage size and bandwidth, and a poor cache behavior. Combining optimizations from both the algorithmic and architectural perspectives, our FPGA-based solution manages to remove the memory constraints and provide a high performance that can scale well with the amount of computational resources available. Compared with an optimized CPU implementation using two quad-core Intel Nehalem CPUs, our solution achieves 4× speedup on two Virtex-5 FPGAs, and 8× speedup on two Virtex-6 FPGAs. Our projection demonstrates that the performance will continue to scale with the future increase of FPGA capacities.

Categories and Subject Descriptors

B.7.1 [**INTEGRATED CIRCUITS**]: Types and Design Styles—*Algorithms implemented in hardware*

General Terms

Algorithm, Design, Performance

Keywords

Field Programmable Gate Arrays (FPGA), Reverse Time Migration (RTM)

1. INTRODUCTION

Through the last two decades, memory-related constraints (memory bandwidth, cache size) have gradually become the performance bottleneck in most computationally-intensive applications. While the speed of the processor increases by 70% every year, the memory speed increases by a much smaller 7% [9]. The exponentially-increasing gap between the processor speed and the memory speed brings a tough challenge in feeding enough data to keep the processors busy. The multi-level cache hierarchy in current processors partly solves the memory constraints by pre-fetching and storing parts of the data closer to the processors. However, when the consecutive read/write instructions cover a wide range of memory locations, or the memory access pattern is too random to predict, the application will suffer from a high ratio of cache misses and the memory bottleneck re-emerges.

In the current trend of fitting more and more cores into a processing unit (such as the 32 cores in Intel Knights Ferry CPUs and up to 512 cores in NVIDIA Fermi GPUs), feeding enough data for the processing cores becomes an even tougher challenge. With the memory capacity being the main constraint, performance does not scale well with the number of cores, which make it difficult for existing application to take advantage of the increase of computation density in newly-released silicon chips.

In this paper, we present our FPGA-based solution for the Reverse Time Migration (RTM) algorithm [14], which is the most computationally-demanding imaging algorithms in oil and gas exploration. The RTM algorithm generally needs to deal with source and receiver 3D wave field arrays at thousands of different time steps, which brings the requirement to manipulate terabytes of data in disk or in memory. The kernel of the RTM algorithm, which applies a large 3D stencil over a 3D data cube, needs to access a wide range of memory locations while computing the result of one point. In many cases, the computation incurs a large number of cache misses and reduces the performance significantly. These highly demanding memory access characteristics of RTM form a 'memory wall' that keeps us from achieving high throughput in common computer clusters.

In our work, by utilizing the enormous internal memory bandwidth of the FPGA and performing the computation in a streaming pattern, we manage to remove the memory bottleneck from our RTM computation engine, and to achieve a solution that scales linearly with the amount of computation resources available. Our major contributions are as follows:

- by adding randomness into the boundaries of the problem, we minimize the storage requirement of the RTM algorithm, and encapsulate the entire computation into the FPGA device (detailed in Section 3).

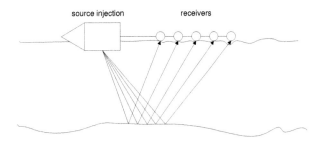

Figure 1: A typical scenario of a marine based seismic exploration.

- by customizing the FPGA's Block RAMs into a window buffer, we achieve perfect data reuse in the stencil computation (detailed in Section 4).

- by switching to a stencil that involves more computations, we achieve a better memory behavior and reduce the required Block RAM size significantly (detailed in Section 5).

- by cascading multiple stencil operators to process multiple time steps in one pass, we manage to remove the memory bandwidth constraint and to form a design that scales almost linearly with the amount of computational resources available (detailed in Section 6).

By applying all the above optimizations in our FPGA-based computation engine, compared with an optimized CPU implementation that uses two quad-core Intel Nehalem CPUs, we achieve 4× speedup with two Xilinx Virtex-5 FPGAs, and a projected 8× speedup with two Virtex-6 FPGAs. We also demonstrate that the performance is going to scale for future FPGA devices with more hardware resources.

The rest of the paper is organized as follows. Section 2 provides a brief introduction about the RTM algorithm, discusses about existing FPGA-based solutions for stencil operations, and describes the FPGA hardware used in our work. Section 3 to 6 present the above four techniques we apply to remove the 'memory wall' in the RTM algorithm. Section 7 shows the general structure of our FPGA-based RTM solution and some further optimization techniques we can apply. Section 8 presents results and discussions. Section 9 concludes the paper.

2. BACKGROUND

2.1 The Reverse Time Migration Algorithm

In oil and gas exploration projects, the seismic data is collected by recording the reflected seismic waves generated from controlled source injections. Figure 1 shows a typical scenario of a marine based seismic exploration, which involves a controlled source that injects waves into the sea, and an array of receivers that record the seismic signals reflected from different earth layers below the sea water. During the exploration, dragged by a ship, the source and the receiver array normally traverse a large 2D plane, and produce a recorded 5D (source coordinates, receiver coordinates, and time) data set that can be terabytes in size.

The RTM algorithm uses the velocity of sound waves through the earth's subsurface as an input. After an initial velocity

estimation, the RTM algorithm is performed to create an image of the earth from the recorded data set. Figure 2 shows the pseudo code of RTM. In this example, we apply a simple second order stencil operator to approximate the derivatives. In practical code, much higher order stencil operators are used.

As shown in Figure 2, the RTM algorithm consists of different levels of loops (lines 5 to 10, and lines 25 to 28). We need to loop over different shots (i.e. different source locations), different time steps, and different grids in the 3D domain. The computations for different shots are completely independent of each other. For the scenario of multiple computer nodes, we can simply scale the solution by assigning each computer node with the signals related to one single source. Based on the above consideration, in this paper, the discussion focuses on the optimizations we apply within a single computer node.

The computation inside the shot loop consists of two major parts. In the first part (lines 7 to 22), we propagate the source wave fields from time step 0 to time step $nt - 1$. In the second part (lines 25 to 43), we reverse-propagate the receiver wave fields from time step $nt - 1$ to time step 0. While reverse-propagating the receiver wave fields, we cross-correlate the source and receiver wave fields of the same time step, and accumulate the results to the imaging result.

Besides applying the finite-difference based stencils, the forward and reverse propagation loops also need to add the recorded source and receivers signals to the corresponding locations, and to deal with the boundary conditions. The forward and reverse propagations simulate the propagation of the seismic wave in the model. As the simulated domain in RTM has a limited size compared to the actual landscape, the simulation generates artifacts of reflections from the boundaries of the simulated domain. To remove the artifacts, we need to keep a buffering zone near the boundary, and to absorb the reflections through a simple damping or a more complicated Perfect Match Layer (PML) [1].

2.2 Computational Challenges in Reverse Time Migration

The first challenge of RTM comes from the workflow of the algorithm. The final result of RTM, the image, comes from the cross correlation of source and receiver wave fields at the same time step (as shown in line 42). However, in the RTM algorithm, the source and receiver wave fields get computed in different directions in time (source from time step 0 to time step $nt - 1$ and receiver from time step $nt - 1$ to time step 0). Depending on the problem dimension size (nx, ny, nz), the typical size of the source wave fields for one time step can be 0.5 to 4 GB. As the algorithm normally involves up to several thousand time steps, storing the source wave fields of all the time steps requires terabytes of space, which is impractical to be stored in memory and leads to performance bottleneck in I/O if stored in hard disk. In previous work, this problem is usually solved with a check-pointing approach [13], which stores the source wave fields of one time step in disk for every 10 to 20 time steps, and then uses the stored check points to reconstruct the source wave fields of the time step needed for cross correlation.

The second challenge comes from the memory access pattern in the convolution kernel. In both the forward and reverse propagation loop, most of the computing cycles are consumed for convolving the 3D finite-difference based sten-

```
0   // s(nt, nz, ny, nx) : source wave field array
1   // r(nt, nz, ny, nx) : receiver wave field array
2   // v(nz, ny, nx) : velocity array
3   // res(nz, ny, nx) : the resulting image array, initialized as zeros
4
5   for ( ishot = 0; ishot < nshot; ishot++ ){
6       //forward migration
7       for ( it = 0; it < nt; it++ )
8           for ( iz = 0; iz < nz; iz++ )
9               for ( iy = 0; iy < ny; iy++ )
10                  for ( ix = 0; ix < nx; ix++ ){
11                      s(it,iz,iy,ix)=2*s(it-1,iz,iy,ix)-s(it-2,iz,iy,ix)+v(iz,iy,ix)*v(iz,iy,ix)*dt*dt*(
12                          s(it-1,iz,iy,ix)*(2/dx/dx+2/dy/dy+2/dz/dz)+
13                          (-s(it-1,iz,iy,ix-1)-s(it-1,iz,iy,ix+1))/dx/dx+
14                          (-s(it-1,iz,iy-1,ix)-s(it-1,iz,iy+1,ix))/dy/dy+
15                          (-s(it-1,iz-1,iy,ix)-s(it-1,iz+1,iy,ix))/dz/dz);
16
17                      if ( (iz, iy, ix) corresponds to the current source location )
18                          s(it,iz,iy,ix) += recorded_source(it,iz,iy,ix);
19
20                      if ( (iz, iy, ix) is in the boundary range )
21                          process_boundary_condition();
22                  }
23
24      //reverse migration
25      for ( it = nt-1; it >= 0; it-- )
26          for ( iz = 0; iz < nz; iz++ )
27              for ( iy = 0; iy < ny; iy++ )
28                  for ( ix = 0; ix < nx; ix++ ){
29                      r(it-2,iz,iy,ix)=2*r(it-1,iz,iy,ix)-r(it,iz,iy,ix)+v(iz,iy,ix)*v(iz,iy,ix)*dt*dt*(
30                          r(it-1,iz,iy,ix)*(2/dx/dx+2/dy/dy+2/dz/dz)+
31                          (-r(it-1,iz,iy,ix-1)-r(it-1,iz,iy,ix+1))/dx/dx+
32                          (-r(it-1,iz,iy-1,ix)-r(it-1,iz,iy+1,ix))/dy/dy+
33                          (-r(it-1,iz-1,iy,ix)-r(it-1,iz+1,iy,ix))/dz/dz);
34
35                      if ( (iz, iy, ix) corresponds to the one of the receiver locations )
36                          r(it-2,iz,iy,ix) += recorded_receiver(it-2,iz,iy,ix);
37
38                      if ( (iz, iy, ix) is in the boundary range )
39                          process_boundary_condition();
40
41                      //correlate the source and receiver wave fields into the imaging results
42                      res(iz,iy,ix) += s(it-2,iz,iy,ix)*r(it-2,iz,iy,ix);
43                  }
44  }
```

Figure 2: Pseudo code of the RTM algorithm.

cil over the 3D data array(lines 12 to 15 for forward propagation and lines 30 to 33 for reverse propagation). Computing the 3D stencil normally involves multiplications and additions on a number of adjacent points and constant coefficients. While the points are neighbors to each other in a 3D geometric perspective, they are stored in different rows, different columns, or even different slices, and can be far apart in the memory space. The requirement of accessing data points that are far away from each other incurs a lot of cache misses when the domain gets large, and decreases the efficiency of the computation.

Our work investigates the above design challenges in RTM, and provides a customized FPGA-based solution that removes the memory constraints and provides a high performance that scales with the amount of resources available.

2.3 Existing FPGA-based Convolution Engines

On the FPGA platforms, there exist a lot of projects that accelerate the stencil operations with FPGA's parallel computation capacity and distributed memory storage.

Most of early work focus on accelerating electromagnetic simulations on FPGAs. W. Chen et al. [2] present an FPGA-based design for a 2D finite-difference time-domain (FDTD) algorithm used in electromagnetic simulations. Due to the resource constraints of FPGAs at that time, the Block RAMs are only used as the memory interface to the onboard memory. J. Durbano et al. [4] demonstrate an FPGA-based solution for a 3D FDTD problem in electromagnetic simulations. Taking advantage of a high-speed memory hierarchy that consists of onboard DRAM, SRAM, and Block RAMs (serving as the cache), the solution achieves significant speedup against CPU-based solutions.

C. He et al. [7] propose an FPGA-based computation platform for 2D and 3D time domain simulation in seismic applications. By taking full advantage of FPGA's computational potential, the platform computes 1.5 to 4 times faster than a single-core CPU station. As floating-point arithmetic is expensive for previous and even the current FPGAs, C. He et al. [6] later propose a method to combine the normalization and addition of multiple floating-point operands into one unit to reduce the area cost.

A recent work by M. Shafiq et al. [11] focuses on tackling the memory problem and proposes a multi-layer memory hierarchy to load different slices, different columns of the data and feed the required values to the computation engine.

While almost all the published FPGA designs utilize the distributed Block RAMs to maximize the data reuse and sustain a fast speed to feed the data into computational units, most of them use the Block RAMs to implement a similar hierarchy to the CPU cache. In our work, we use a buffering mechanism that is completely based on the streaming computation approach of the FPGA devices. As detailed in Section 4, the buffering mechanism achieves a perfect cache behavior and is straightforward to design and implement.

2.4 Our FPGA Acceleration Platform

In our work, we use the Maxeler MAX2 acceleration card [5], which contains two Virtex-5 LX330T FPGAs, 12 GB onboard memory with 28 GB/s memory bandwidth, and a PCI-Express x16 interface (4 GB/s bandwidth) to the host PC. Each Virtex-5 LX330T FPGA contains 51,840 logic slices (each slice contains 4 registers and 4 look-up tables), 196 DSP48E units that can perform 18×25 multiplications, and 324 36-KBit Block RAMs (BRAMs).

The 648 36-KBit BRAMs in the two FPGAs provide 2.8 MB of storage. Meanwhile, as each of the 648 BRAMs has its own read/write ports that can be used concurrently, the BRAMs in the FPGAs provide up to 1518 GB/s bandwidth. The large size and high bandwidth of the BRAMs make it possible to build a customized cache for the stencil computation in RTM, which can effectively solve the problem of poor cache efficiency related to the stencil operators (a more detailed discussion in section 4). The 12 GB onboard memory provides enough space to fit in large-size seismic problems.

3. RANDOM BOUNDARIES

As mentioned in Section 2.2, one major challenge in implementing the RTM algorithm comes from the cross-correlation of the source and receiver wave fields of the same time step (line 42 in Figure 2). As the source and receiver wave fields are computed in different orders in time, we need to either store the source wave fields at different time steps or recompute them when they are needed. The dimension size of current 3D RTM problems makes it impractical to store the source wave fields of all different time steps in memory. Storing all the wave fields in hard disk can lead to a performance bottleneck in I/O operations. Therefore, most existing designs take the checkpointing approach [13] to store the source wave fields at certain time steps, and then recompute the rest time steps based on the checkpointed time steps.

Although the checkpointing approach significantly reduces the storage requirement of the RTM algorithm, the size of the checkpoints is still too large to fit into the memory, and the checkpoints are usually stored in disk. Besides, during the computation, we need a memory buffer large enough to store all the source wave fields for the time steps between two consecutive checkpoints. In a CPU-based solution, by overlapping the disk I/O and the computation, we can generally achieve good performance. However, for an FPGA-based solution, the checkpointing would bring extra memory transfers between the host and the FPGA device through the 4 GB/s PCI-Express interface, which has a much lower bandwidth than the onboard memory and downgrades the performance of the entire system.

To minimize the data transfer between the host and the FPGA card, our approach propagates the source wave fields to the maximum simulation time, and then reverses the propagation to produce the source wave fields in the same time sequence as the receiver wave fields. The stencil operations (lines 11 to 15 in Figure 2) and the injection of recorded source signals (lines 17 to 18 in Figure 2) in the propagation

```
for all x,y,z do
    if within boundary region then
        d=distance within boundary
        found=false
        while found==false do
            select random number r
            vtest = v(x, y, z) + r * d
            if vtest meets stability constraint then
                v(x, y, z) = vtest
                found=true
            end if
        end while
    end if
end for
```

Figure 3: The algorithm for adding randomness into the boundaries.

process are both reversible in time. However, the processing of boundary conditions (lines 20 to 21 in Figure 2), either achieved by damping or PML, can only be computed in one direction in time.

To solve the above problem, we take a different approach on handling boundary condition. Ideally, we want to eliminate all reflections from the computational domain boundaries. However, only coherent reflections in both source and receiver wave fields affect the imaging result. If we can distort the reflections in the source wave fields so that the reflections do not coherently correlate with the receiver wave fields, we will accomplish the same goal of removing reflection artifacts from the imaging result.

In acoustic modeling, one way to manipulate the boundaries while still allowing a reversed propagation in time, is to introduce a random component to the velocity fields (the array of v in Figure 2) at the boundaries. In the process of adding randomness into the velocity fields, there are two basic rules: one is that the modified velocity values must still stay within the stability constraint of our finite difference method; the other is that we should slowly introduce the random numbers to avoid an immediate reflection off the randomized zone. The basic algorithm for constructing the random boundaries is described in Figure 3.

By using the pseudo-random boundary conditions, we effectively distort the reflection artifacts of the source wave fields. We use these boundary conditions to propagate the source wave fields in both the forward and the reverse order. The distorted reflection parts correlate poorly with the receiver wave fields, which minimizes boundary artifacts. Meanwhile, the random boundary approach eliminates the need to store the checkpoints in hard disk, and minimizes the requirement for memory storage. We only need to store one copy of the source wave fields and one copy of the receiver wave fields, thus being able to encapsulate the entire computation of RTM into the FPGA card.

4. A CUSTOMIZED WINDOW BUFFER

4.1 Perfect Data Reuse with A Window Buffer

Different from the classical Von Neumann computer architecture, the FPGA usually takes a streaming approach to perform the computation. In the Von Neumann architecture, we normally achieve parallel computation by using

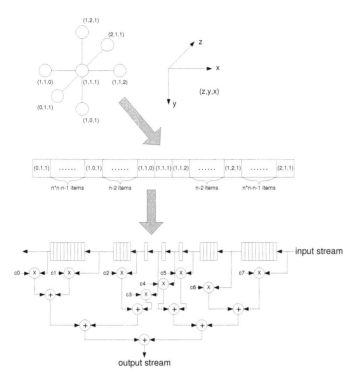

Figure 4: A streaming design of a 3D convolution engine using a window buffer.

multiple identical threads to process different data, i.e. the Single Instruction Multiple Data (SIMD) approach. In the streaming architectures of FPGAs, we achieve parallelism by streaming the same data item through different processing units, i.e. the Multiple Instruction Single Data (MISD) approach. By fully pipelining the FPGA design, at a given cycle, we would have different data items processed at different processing units, which gives us the parallelism in a Multiple Instruction Multiple Data (MIMD) approach.

As discussed in Section 2.2, one of the challenges of a convolution design comes from the cache misses caused by memory access of the points in different rows, different columns, or even different slices of a 3D array. In our FPGA design, we use block RAMs to store a window of the input stream. As shown in Figure 4, suppose we are applying a second order in space stencil on data item $(1, 1, 1)$ in a 3D $n \times n \times n$ array, the stencil operation involves 7 different points. In a streaming design, the 3D array is pushed in as a sequential stream. Therefore, the 7 points correspond to 7 different locations in the data stream. The points on the same row correspond to locations next to each other, while the points on different rows or different slices correspond to locations that are $n - 2$ or $n \cdot n - n - 1$ data items away. Using block RAMs and registers to implement FIFOs of the corresponding distances between the 7 locations, we achieve a window buffer that covers the 7 different points.

Considering the block RAMs and registers as the 'cache' of the FPGA design, the above window buffer mechanism provides a perfect 'cache' behavior: (1) the data item gets streamed into the window buffer when it is needed for the computation for the first time; (2) the data item gets streamed out of the window buffer as soon as it is no longer needed for the computation; (3) all the data items needed for the sten-

cil operations can be read out in the same cycle to perform the computations in parallel.

4.2 Domain Decomposition and Its Related Cost

For the second-order-in-space stencil shown in Figure 4, in order to cover all the seven points, the window buffer needs a storage size of roughly $2n^2$ data points, and each data point takes a four-byte floating-point number to represent. For a problem size of $512 \times 512 \times 512$, the storage requirement amounts to $2 \times 512 \times 512 \times 4 = 2$ MB. In practical application, we usually apply higher order stencils, which requires a larger buffer size. For example, a 6th-order-in-space stencil with 19 points requires a storage size of around $6 \times 512 \times 512 \times 4 = 6$ MB. Therefore, in most cases, the required storage size of the window buffer will be larger than the 1.4 MB storage available on the Virtex-5 FPGA. In order to fit the problem into the FPGA chip, we need to perform a 2D domain decomposition of the original problem to achieve smaller dimension sizes.

While reducing the storage size to fit into the BRAMs, domain decomposition brings the cost of redundant processing of the overlapping halos. Figure 5 shows that, for a stencil with d points on each side of the center point, we need to stream in both the central block and the halos around ($nx \cdot ny$ points) to compute the convolution results of the central block (($nx - 2d)(ny - 2d)$ points). With domain decomposition, a large part of the halos get redundantly processed in different sub-blocks.

Suppose that we are decomposing a n^3 data cube into smaller data cubes of size $nx \times ny \times n$. The relative cost for redundantly processing the overlapping halos can be estimated as follows:

$$cost = \frac{\left\lceil \frac{n-2d}{nx-2d} \right\rceil \cdot \left\lceil \frac{n-2d}{ny-2d} \right\rceil \cdot nx \cdot ny}{n^2} - 1 \qquad (1)$$

Therefore, the design problem in domain decomposition becomes finding the nx, ny values that minimizes the cost value in Equation 1, under the constraint that slices of size $nx \times ny$ are small enough to fit into the BRAMs, i.e. $4 \cdot 2d \cdot nx \cdot ny < 1.4$MB. A close approximation of Equation 1 comes as follows:

$$
\begin{aligned}
cost &= \frac{nx \cdot ny}{(nx - 2d) \cdot (ny - 2d)} - 1 \\
&= \frac{2d \cdot (nx + ny) - 4d^2}{nx \cdot ny - 2d \cdot (nx + ny) + 4d^2} \qquad (2)
\end{aligned}
$$

As $nx \cdot ny$ should be smaller than a certain value, the optimal solution is to use equal nx, ny values.

Another underlying constraint comes from the memory controller interface provided by the MAX2 card. The memory controller supports a 2D-blocking memory access mode, which fits the 2D domain decomposition perfectly. However, to achieve a similar memory performance to linear mode, the number of bytes on x axis (the fast axis) should be multiples of 96. Therefore, nx shall be multiples of 24.

5. EXPLORING DIFFERENT STENCILS

To achieve a 6th order in space accuracy, we can use either a 19-point 'star' stencil or a 27-point 'cube' stencil [12]. Figure 6 shows the shapes of these two different stencils. Most

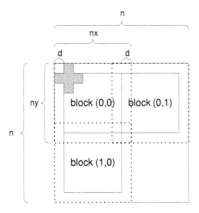

Figure 5: An example of 2D domain decomposition in a stencil operation.

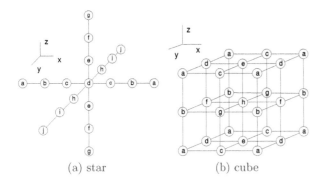

(a) star   (b) cube

Figure 6: 6th order in space 'star' and 'cube' stencils.

of the existing applications choose to use the 'star' stencil, mainly because it requires a fewer number of arithmetic operations. In a naive implementation, the 'star' one requires 19 multiplications and 18 additions, while the 'cube' one requires 27 multiplications and 26 additions, around 40% more computations to perform than the 'star' stencil.

As both stencils are computing space derivatives, the points that have the same distance from the center point will have equivalent mathematical properties and share the same coefficients. As shown in Figure 6, the points labeled with the same characters have the same coefficients.

By considering the symmetry of coefficients in the stencils, the computation cost of the 'star' stencil is reduced from 19 multiplications and 18 additions to 10 multiplications and 18 additions, while the computation cost of the 'cube' stencil is reduced from 27 multiplications and 26 additions to 8 multiplications and 26 additions. For the reduced versions, compared with the 'star' stencil, the 'cube' saves one multiplications, but still requires 40% more additions.

On the other hand, the costs for implementing the window buffers are also different between the 'star' and the 'cube' stencils. To store all the values for a 19-point 'star' stencil, we need a window buffer that covers 6 slices of the 3D data cube. While for the 'cube' stencil, as the 27 points fall into three consecutive slices, the window buffer only needs to cover 2 slices, which is one third of the 'star' stencil cost.

As the 'cube' stencil requires much less storage than the

'star' stencil, under the same BRAM size constraint, the 'cube' stencil can have a larger dimension size for the decomposed blocks, which leads to a smaller cost for processing overlapping halos. For example, for a $512 \times 512 \times 512$ problem size, using the 'star' stencil, we need to decompose the data set into $4 \times 4 = 16$ blocks with the size of 144×133. According to Equation 1 the related cost for processing overlapping halos equal to $(4 \times 4 \times 144 \times 133)/(512 \times 512) - 1 = 16.9\%$. On the other hand, using 'cube' stencil, we can decompose the same data set into $2 \times 3 = 6$ blocks with the size of 264×172. According to Equation 1, the cost for processing overlapping halos is $(2 \times 3 \times 264 \times 172)/(512 \times 512) - 1 = 3.9\%$, which is much lower than the 'star'.

Therefore, in the cases that the BRAM size becomes the constraint of the performance (which is usually the case), we can switch from the 'star' stencil to the 'cube' stencil to significantly reduce the storage requirement.

6. CASCADING MULTIPLE TIME STEPS

6.1 Processing Multiple Points in Parallel

A 'star' or a 'cube' stencil requires less than 10 multipliers and 30 adders. The Virtex-5 LX330 FPGA has the capacity for over hundred multipliers and adders, which are enough to implement multiple stencil operators.

A straightforward method to further improve the performance is to fit multiple stencil operators into the FPGA to compute multiple points concurrently (shown in Figure 7(a)). The advantage is that multiple points can share the same window buffer structure. The disadvantage is that the memory bandwidth requirement gets multiplied by the number of points processed in parallel, and can easily hit the memory bandwidth constraint of the system.

6.2 Processing Multiple Time Steps in One Pass

To circumvent the memory bandwidth constraint, we adopt another approach to further parallelize the computation. As described in Section 2.1, we usually need to convolve the source and receiver wave fields for thousands of time steps. Therefore, after the data is processed for the first time step, we can forward the result to another window buffer and continue to process the data for the second time step (shown in Figure 7(b)). This approach shares a similar idea as the FPGA's general MISD (Multiple Instruction Single Data) approach, which accommodate more computation by extending the pipeline. The advantage is that we can perform more computation without requiring more memory bandwidth. The disadvantage is that we need multiple copies of the window buffer for different time steps. We can also combine the two options to process multiple time steps for multiple points (shown in Figure 7(c)).

In our designs, the combined approach is used in most cases. As long as there is available memory bandwidth, we take the first option to compute multiple points in parallel. After the memory bandwidth is saturated, we compute multiple time steps to make full utilization of both the FPGA resources and the memory bandwidth.

6.3 Domain Decomposition for Multiple Time Steps

Section 4.2 describes the extra cost of processing overlapping halo regions in decomposed blocks. In the case that we

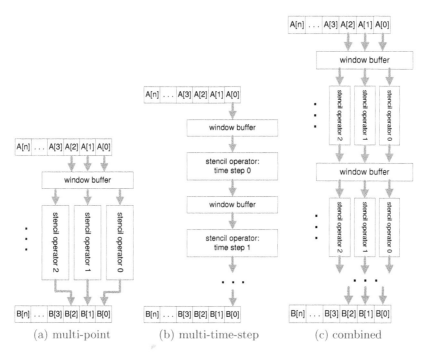

(a) multi-point   (b) multi-time-step   (c) combined

Figure 7: Different ways to parallelize the computation: (a) process multiple points concurrently; (b) process multiple time steps in one pass; (c) a combined approach that process multiple time steps for multiple points.

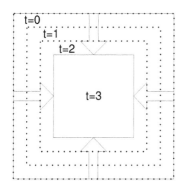

Figure 8: The expanded halo regions when we process multiple time steps in one pass.

process multiple time steps in one pass, the cost for processing the halos gets multiplied by the number of time steps.

As shown in Figure 8, when processing multiple time steps, for each extra time step processed, we need an extra layer of halo. Therefore, to process three time steps in one pass, for a decomposed block of size $nx \times ny \times n$, we need to stream in $nx \times ny \times n$ points to get $(nx - 6d) \times (ny - 6d) \times n$ results (d denotes the number of points on each side of the center point of the stencil). In the multiple-time-step case, the relative cost for redundantly processing the overlapping halos can be estimated as follows:

$$cost = \frac{\left\lceil \frac{n-2d \cdot nt}{nx-2d \cdot nt} \right\rceil \cdot \left\lceil \frac{n-2d \cdot nt}{ny-2d \cdot nt} \right\rceil \cdot nx \cdot ny}{n^2} - 1 \quad (3)$$

Meanwhile, we need multiple copies of the window buffer for multiple time steps. Under the same BRAM size con-

straint, the storage for each window buffer becomes smaller, and we need to reduce nx and ny accordingly.

Assume we are processing three time steps for a $512 \times 512 \times 512$ data cube with 6th order in space stencil. Using the 'star' stencil, we need to decompose the data set into $7 \times 7 = 49$ blocks with the size of 96×91. According to Equation **??** the related cost for processing overlapping halos equal to $(7 \times 7 \times 96 \times 91)/(512 \times 512) - 1 = 63.3\%$. On the other hand, using 'cube' stencil, we can decompose the same data set into $4 \times 4 = 16$ blocks with the size of 144×134. According to Equation **??**, the cost for processing overlapping halos is $(4 \times 4 \times 134 \times 144)/(512 \times 512) - 1 = 17.8\%$, which increases much slower than the 'star' stencil.

7. AN FPGA-BASED RTM DESIGN

7.1 General Structure

Combining all the different techniques described in Sections 3, 4, 5, and 6, we manage to fit the RTM design into the MAX2 acceleration card, which has two Xilinx Virtex-5 LX330 FPGAs and 12 GB onboard memory.

Figure 9 shows the general structure of our FPGA-based RTM design. The MAX2 card connects to the host through the 4 GB/s PCI-Express interface. In the beginning of the computation, the wave fields, the velocities, and the recorded source and receiver signals are transferred into the card through the PCI-Express interface. After that, the entire computation happens within the card, and no data communication is further needed between the card and the host. Each FPGA chip connects to 6 GB of DRAM with a bandwidth of 14 GB/s. Inside each FPGA chip, we implement the long pipelines that process multiple time steps in one pass for multiple points in parallel. The original problem is

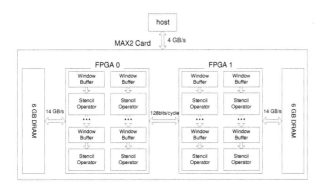

Figure 9: The general structure of our RTM Design.

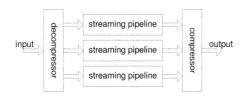

Figure 10: Streaming the data in a compressed format.

decomposed into two parts for the two FPGAs. The decomposition requires communication between the two FPGAs about the overlapping halos, which is performed through the 128 bits/cycle interconnect between the two FPGAs. As the halo only takes a relative small part of the decomposed block, the communication latency can be completely hidden in the computation for the current time step.

7.2 Further Optimization Techniques

Besides the optimization techniques we have discussed in Sections 3, 4, 5, and 6, there are still other optimization techniques we can apply to alleviate the memory constraints and improve the computation performance.

The first technique is to use a compressed format for the data stored in the memory. As shown in Figure 10, we can add a decompressor and a compressor to the beginning and the end of the FPGA design, which will fit more input and output streams into the same memory bandwidth. On the FPGA platform, the computation is generally fully-pipelined. Therefore, adding a decompressor and compressor only consumes more resources of the FPGA chip, and does not affect the computation throughput. In contrast, the compression and decompression procedures consume extra clock cycles on CPU or GPU platforms.

The second technique is to use a customized number representation. One of FPGA's inherent advantages is the freedom of using arbitrary number representation formats. On the CPU or GPU platforms, the available number formats are largely determined by the underlying processor architecture. On these platforms, adjusting the number representation at the bit level is impractical and does not bring any performance benefits. On the FPGA platform, the reconfigurability in both arithmetic and data path implementations enables application-specific number representations. By using a reduced number precision or switching from floating-point to fixed-point format, the cost for implementing arithmetic and storage units is significantly reduced, while the

bandwidth requirement for streaming the same amount of inputs and outputs also becomes much lower. Therefore, with the same amount of FPGA resources and the same memory bandwidth constraint, we can fit a larger number of processing units and stream in and out a larger number of input and output values, thus multiplying the computation throughput of the application.

8. RESULTS AND DISCUSSIONS

8.1 Performance Results

In this section, we describe the throughput as the number of wave field points that get updated in every second.

As a base case for the performance comparison, we implement a CPU version of the RTM algorithm that uses one to eight Nehalem cores (each running at 2.27 GHz). To make a fair comparison, we apply a set of optimization techniques to improve the performance, such as loop tiling [10], different levels of blocking [3, 8], and loop permutation that improves the vectorization efficiency. After a careful optimization, our single-core CPU version provides a throughput of 90 MPoints/Sec (million points per second). The eight-core CPU version achieves a throughput of 378 MPoints/Sec, which only scales four times for using eight times more cores.

On the FPGA platform, we have several different approaches to parallelize the stencil computation: the multiple-point approach, which computes the stencil operation for multiple points in parallel; the multiple-time-step approach, which cascades the computation of multiple time steps for one point; and the combined approach, which cascades the computation of multiple time steps for multiple points.

Figure 11 shows the performance results of the multiple-point approach. Using the resources on the Virtex-5 LX330 FPGA chip, we can compute eight points in parallel for the 'star' stencil, or six points for the 'cube' stencil. However, with the number of points computed in parallel increasing to four, the computation throughput stops to improve. The flat lines after four points demonstrate that four stencil operators already saturate the memory bandwidth available, and memory becomes the bottleneck of performance. In this approach, the 'cube' stencil performs on average 15% better than the 'star' stencil, as the 'cube' has a lower storage cost for implementing the window buffer and a higher efficiency in the domain decomposition.

The multiple-point approach achieves a throughput of 1.02 BPoints/Sec (billion points per second) for the 'cube' stencil, which provides around 2.7× speedup compared with the eight-core CPU implementation.

Figure 12 shows the performance results of the multiple-time-step approach and the combined approach. Using the multiple-time-step approach, we can cascade six time steps of one point for the 'cube' stencil, and observe an almost linear increase to around 1.2 BPoints/Sec (3.2× speed up compared with an 8-core CPU implementation). For the 'star' stencil, we have resources enough for seven time steps. However, due to the significant cost for processing the large overlapping boundaries in decomposed domains (detailed in Section 6.3), the performance starts to drop when the number of time steps increases to four.

The best performance is achieved using the combined approach. For the 'cube' stencil, we can compute two time steps for three points in parallel, which provides a throughput of 1.36 BPoints/Sec. For the 'star' stencil, we can com-

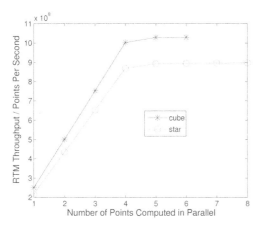

Figure 11: Throughput for computing multiple points in parallel.

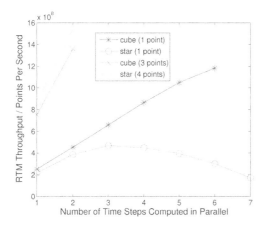

Figure 12: Throughput for cascading multiple time steps for single or multiple points.

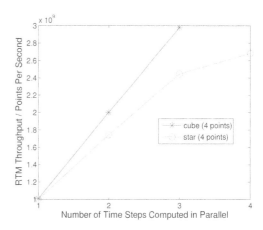

Figure 13: Throughput for cascading multiple time steps for single or multiple points on a Virtex-6 FPGA card.

pute two time steps for four points in parallel, and achieve a throughput of 1.54 BPoints/Sec (4× speedup compared with an 8-core CPU implementation). Although the 'cube' stencil has a lower cost for processing overlapping boundaries in domain decomposition, the 'star' stencil wins slightly as more stencil operators can be fit into the card.

The card with the Virtex-5 FPGAs reflects the FPGA technology of the year 2008, while the Intel Nehalem cores come out in the year of 2009. To make a more fair comparison of the two technologies, Figure 13 shows the projected performance results of the combined approach on the more recent Virtex-6 SX475T FPGAs. With the increased resources, we can now fit three time steps for four points in the 'cube' case, and four time steps for four points in the 'star' case. Although the 'star' stencil fits 33.3% more computation units, the performance scalability degrades significantly after the number of time steps increases to four. Therefore, the 'cube' provides a better performance of 3 BPoints/Sec (around 8× speedup compared with an 8-core CPU implementation), due to its better memory properties.

In both the multiple-time-step and the combined approaches, we demonstrate that the FPGA-based solution is capable of

removing the memory bottleneck and producing throughput from all the available computation resources.

Compared with the 'star' stencil, the 'cube' stencil provides the option to achieve a better memory property by performing more computations. For the cases that we can fit more than 3 time steps, the 'cube' stencil demonstrates a clear performance superiority to the 'star' stencil.

The projection of performance from Virtex-5 to Virtex-6 FPGAs has partly demonstrated the performance scalability of our approach. In Figure 14, we demonstrate the experimental and projected performance results for different FPGA platforms with continuously increasing hardware resources. Besides the Virtex-5 LX330 and Virtex-6 SX475T FPGAs, we also project performance results for virtual devices that have twice or four times resources as the Virtex-6 FPGA. For the 'star' stencil, although we can fit more time steps into one pipeline, the heavy cost on processing overlapping boundaries of decomposed domains will cancel out a large part of the performance benefits achieved from processing multiple time steps. Therefore, the performance scalability of the 'star' stencil is far from linear.

For the 'cube' stencil, the penalty for processing the overlapping boundaries is much less. As a result, the 'cube' stencil demonstrates a performance that scales well with the amount of available resources on the FPGAs. For the cases that we have twice or even four times resources as the Virtex-6 FPGAs, the increase in BRAM resources will allow a larger size of the decomposed domain, thus significantly reducing the cost related to the processing of overlapping halos. In those cases, we observe a even better scalability.

8.2 Discussions

In general, we achieve significant performance improvement on the RTM algorithm through customization on the FPGA platform. The success of the customization process demonstrates the necessity to optimize from both the perspectives of the algorithm and the architecture. We can modify the algorithms (such as random boundary technique introduced in Section 3, and the exploration of different stencils described in Section 5) to fit into the characteristics of the underlying hardware architecture. On the other hand, the reconfigurability of the FPGA platforms also enable us

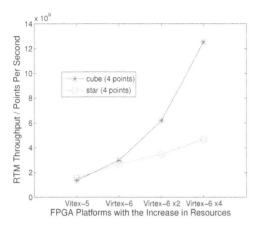

Figure 14: Throughput on different FPGA platforms with an increase in hardware resources.

to customize the cache-like storage (such as the window buffer introduced in Section 4) and computation data flow (such as the cascaded pipeline described in Section 6) for the specific algorithm. Combining both algorithmic and architectural optimizations for a specific application, we manage to provide an FPGA-based solution that removes the memory bottleneck, achieves a high performance, and scales well with the computation resources available.

9. CONCLUSION

This paper presents our FPGA-based solution for the Reverse Time Migration algorithm, which is the most computationally demanding algorithm in oil and gas exploration operations. By utilizing the reconfigurability of the FPGA device and optimizing from both the algorithmic and the architectural perspective, our RTM design manages to remove the memory bottleneck, and to provide a high performance that scales with the amount of computational resources available. When comparing to two Nehalem quad-core CPUs, our solution achieves 4× speedup with two Virtex-5 FPGAs, and a projected 8× speedup with two Virtex-6 FPGAs.

With abundant computation and storage resources on the FPGA boards, we think that FPGA-based solutions are becoming efficient HPC solution alternatives to CPU and GPU clusters. The stream computing approach, which is the natural choice for most FPGA solutions, parallelize the computation by adding more processing units into the pipeline. The approach removes the memory constraints and provides a performance that scales well with the available reconfigurable resources. Meanwhile, the customization that users can perform on various aspects of the design provide another boost to the performance. These unique properties make FPGAs a preferable choice for many computationally-intensive applications.

10. ACKNOWLEDGEMENT

The funding support from the Stanford Center for Computational Earth and Environmental Science (CEES) and Stanford Earth Sciences Algorithm & Architectures Initiative (SESAAI) is gratefully acknowledged. We would also like to thank Maxeler Technologies for providing the MAX2 card and software.

11. REFERENCES

[1] J. Berenger. A Perfectly Matched Layer for the Absorption of Electromagnetic Waves. *Journal of Computational Physics*, 114:185–200, 1994.

[2] W. Chen, P. Kosmas, M. Leeser, and C. Rappaport. An FPGA Implementation of the Two-dimensional Finite-Difference Time-Domain (FDTD) Algorithm. In *Proc. International Symposium on Field Programmable Gate Arrays*, pages 213–222, 2004.

[3] K. Datta, M. Murphy, V. Volkov, S. Williams, J. Carter, L. Oliker, D. Patterson, J. Shalf, and K. Yelick. Stencil Computation Optimization and Auto-Tuning on State-of-the-Art Multicore Architectures. In *Proc. Supercomputing*, pages 1–12, 2008.

[4] J. P. Durbano, F. E. Ortiz, J. R. Humphrey, P. F. Curt, and D. W. Prather. FPGA-Based Acceleration of the 3D Finite-Difference Time-Domain Method. In *Proc. IEEE Symposium on Field-Programmable Custom Computing Machines (FCCM)*, pages 156–163, 2004.

[5] M. Flynn, R. Dimond, O. Mencer, and O. Pell. Finding Speedup in Parallel Processors. In *Proc. International Symposium on Parallel and Distributed Computing*, pages 3–7, 2008.

[6] C. He, G. Qin, M. Lu, and W. Zhao. An Efficient Implementation of High-Accuracy Finite Difference Computing Engine on FPGAs. In *Proc. International Conference on Application-specific Systems, Architectures and Processors (ASAP)*, pages 95–98, 2006.

[7] C. He, W. Zhao, and M. Lu. Time Domain Numerical Simulation for Transient Waves on Reconfigurable Coprocessor Platform. In *Proc. IEEE Symposium on Field-Programmable Custom Computing Machines*, pages 127–136, 2005.

[8] V. W. Lee, C. Kim, J. Chhugani, M. Deisher, D. Kim, A. D. Nguyen, N. Satish, M. Smelyanskiy, S. Chennupaty, P. Hammarlund, R. Singhal, and P. Dubey. Debunking the 100X GPU vs. CPU myth: an evaluation of throughput computing on CPU and GPU. In *Proc. International Symposium on Computer Architecture*, pages 451–460, 2010.

[9] S. A. McKee. Reflections on the memory wall. In *Proc. Conference on Computing frontiers*, page 162, 2004.

[10] G. Rivera and C. Tseng. Tiling Optimizations for 3D Scientific Computations. In *Proc. Supercomputing*, 2000.

[11] M. Shafiq, M. Pericas, R. de la Cruz, M. Araya-Polo, N. Navarro, and E. Ayguade. Exploiting Memory Customization in FPGA for 3D Stencil Computations. In *Proc. International Conference on Field Programmable Technology (FPT)*, pages 38–45, 2009.

[12] W. Spotz and G. Carey. A High-Order Compact Formulation for the 3D Poisson Equation. *Numerical Methods for Partial Differential Equations*, 1996.

[13] W. Symes. Reverse Time Migration with Optimal Checkpointing. *Geophysics*, 72:SM213–SM221, 2007.

[14] K. Yoon, C.Chin, S. Suh, L. Lines, and S. Hong. 3D Reverse-time Migration Using the Acoustic Wave Equation: An Experience with the SEG/EAGE Data Set. *The Leading Edge*, 22(1):38–41, 2003.

A Platform for High Level Synthesis of Memory-Intensive Image Processing Algorithms

Tim Papenfuss
Fraunhofer Institute for Integrated Circuits
Am Wolfsmantel 33
91058 Erlangen, Germany
tim.papenfuss@iis.fraunhofer.de

Holger Michel
Technical University Braunschweig
Hans-Sommer-Strasse 66
38106 Braunschweig, Germany
michel@ida.ing.tu-bs.de

ABSTRACT

For high-end industrial image processing applications with real-time requirements, FPGAs are often used as custom accelerators. High level synthesis tools, such as CatapultC, provide a compelling means of speeding up the algorithmic hardware design. However, increasing image resolutions make it ever more difficult to obtain sufficient throughput from external SDRAM frame buffers while providing simple, low-latency memory resources for the data path. To address these issues, this paper proposes a platform-based design with a custom memory system of buffers, caches and an optimized commercial memory controller that improves available SDRAM bandwidth by up to 4x. This greatly facilitates the high level synthesis flow, which is demonstrated by implementing two memory-intensive algorithms using 47.0 Gbit/s and 5.7 Gbit/s of on-chip and off-chip memory bandwidth respectively.

Categories and Subject Descriptors

B.6.3 [**Logic Design**]: Design Aids—*automatic synthesis*; B.3.2 [**Memory Structures**]: Design Styles—*primary memory, cache memory*; C.3 [**Special-Purpose and Application-Based Systems**]: Real-time and embedded systems

General Terms

Design, Languages, Performance

Keywords

SDRAM, fpga, high level synthesis, image processing

1. INTRODUCTION

Industrial machine vision systems for defect recognition often use a 16bit-grayscale camera that streams pixels to a PC, where software analyses the images. This analysis depends on input images having previously been corrected of

camera imperfections and image artifacts. As image resolutions have risen to the order of 2048x2048 pixels delivered at up to 30fps, offloading the data-intensive correction algorithms to a FPGA ensures a reliable throughput, avoids that the PC is saturated with image correction and therefore enables real-time analysis. The use of high level synthesis (HLS) tools allows for faster design of the image processing data path in C/C++ and makes it accessible to algorithm designer without in-depth hardware knowledge. However, external SDRAMs for frame buffering have complex controllers and large latencies, which creates the dual challenge of supplying adequate memory throughput while maintaining a high abstraction level for the designer. This paper explores the design of a flexible hardware platform enabling rapid integration of memory-intensive image processing algorithms generated with the HLS tool CatapultC [6]. The memory system architecture includes local buffers, low-latency image caches, and a Xilinx memory controller core [9] further optimized for high throughput.

2. RELATED WORK

A related design flow with CatapultC has been described in [1]. To the best of our knowledge, creating interfaces between CatapultC data paths and SDRAM has not been reported. Sliding window buffering techniques in FPGAs have been proposed in [8]. In [11], traditional CPU caches were implemented on FPGAs, but these do not prefetch large memory blocks as required in image processing. The authors in [5] proposed a useful n-dimensional cache with active prefetching and our work integrates these concepts into a complete platform. The FlexWAFE project [4] also employed large external memories but could not comment on Xilinx SDRAM controller cores like MIG [9] and MPMC [10] that are currently available. Although MPMC offers multiple user ports, we based this work on MIG in order to better control data prefetching processes and the interface to HLS. An excellent study on improving SDRAM controller bandwidth for media stream processing can be found in [7].

3. PLATFORM OVERVIEW

A platform overview is given in Figure 1. The input pixel stream of an industrial camera with standard *CameraLink* interface enters the FPGA processing board containing a Xilinx Virtex-5 FPGA XC5VFX100T. The stream runs through the image processing chain and via *CameraLink* to the user PC, which runs the image analysis software. Optionally, Gigabit transceivers cascade the processing chain over multiple boards cased in the host PC. Both PCs are

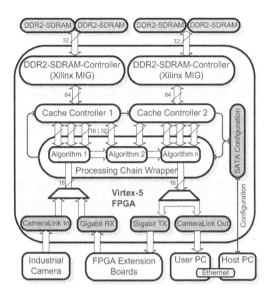

Figure 1: Platform overview

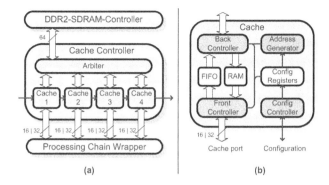

(a)   (b)

Figure 3: (a) Cache controller (b) Cache module

linked by Ethernet. For system initialization and run-time control, the host PC uses the SATA interface to feed a configuration channel as described below.

The memory system is built around four 16bit DDR2-400 SDRAM components. Two of each form a 32bit wide memory channel with 256MB density and peak bandwidth of 12.8Gbit/s, served by a controller generated from Xilinx MIG 3.0 [9] with throughput optimizations as detailed in Section 4. Two cache controllers provide a total of eight cache ports, parametrizable to either 16 or 32bit data width. Adhering to platform-based design principles, the processing functionality should be easily interchangeable. This is achieved by the generic processing chain which can wrap any number of uniform algorithms as shown in Figure 2. Each algorithm has 16bit streaming channel with handshake and can use cache ports as required. It contains the dedicated image processing core described in C/C++ for CatapultC or alternatively in a HDL, plus a configuration controller, register set and optional bypass. Run-time parameters are written into registers by using the configuration channel.

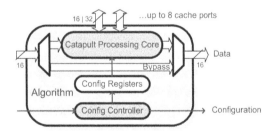

Figure 2: Generic algorithm module

4. MEMORY SYSTEM DESIGN

Memory system performance is paramount in an application where most algorithms are memory bandwidth-limited. In this section, we propose a custom, hierarchical memory system for image processing and highlight its integration into HLS.

Sliding window buffers

Sliding window buffers are commonly used in image processing hardware for algorithms whose processing area moves deterministically and references several input image lines concurrently. Using the FPGA's on-chip block RAMs as line buffers, this greatly reduces the total number of external memory accesses. For this work, we created synthesizable, templatized C++ classes `RingBuffer` and `WindowBuffer` to be instantiated within the CatapultC algorithm. The former acts as standard line buffer and the latter is a composition of `RingBuffer` objects and a 2D *sliding window* array. During HLS, buffers and window are respectively mapped to dualport RAM and registers, making all window pixels immediately available to the data path. Pixels can be written once per cycle and both buffer width and window size can be reprogrammed at run-time.

Cache controller

The cache controller of Figure 3(a) adds an extra level in the memory hierarchy between external SDRAM and local algorithm buffers. An arbiter maps each cache to a separate SDRAM bank and performs round-robin scheduling with one SDRAM burst per cache, hence enforcing *bank interleaving* at the SDRAM physical layer, which is essential to high throughput. The cache controller is particularly significant for the platform because it decreases the read latency from a minimum of 26 cycles at the MIG user interface to 2 cycles for a cache hit, which enables scheduling of heavily pipelined algorithms. Also, it reduces the transaction size from 64 to a user-friendly 16 or 32bits without losing throughput by data masking. Finally, it decouples SDRAM and algorithm clocks and enables reuse of fetched read if required.

Cache module

In the cache module of Figure 3(b), the write path is a simple FIFO because the system uses in-order pixel streaming. The read path is targeted to a class of image processing algorithms that have a deterministic read pattern between successive frames, but with small random displacements within each frame. We define an image *tile* as that two-dimensional processing area which moves through the buffered input frame deterministically, for every output frame. The cache is designed to *prefetch* two currently required tiles from SDRAM and store them in its RAM, without data tags. Algorithm-specific tile size, start position and stride vector are programmed into registers at run-time and processed by

4-bank interleaving access patterns Transaction length N=4-word burst				DQ bus utilization	
Pattern name	Bank cycle	Row cycle	DQ bus cycle	Original ctrl	Custom ctrl
84R	8N	4N	Read	47%	55%
84W	8N	4N	Write	38%	53%
84RW	8N	4N	4N	41%	47%
14R	1N	4N	Read	39%	71%
14W	1N	4N	Write	38%	70%
14RW	1N	4N	4N	32%	57%
11R	1N	1N	Read	19%	48%
11W	1N	1N	Write	12%	48%
11RW	1N	1N	1N	16%	33%

Table 1: Memory controller throughput

the address generator. This simpler version of the generator in [2] suffices for current algorithms. The front controller translates addresses, searches for hits in tiles and invalidates them depending on the read address. The back controller executes write-backs and prefetches through the arbiter. Read latency is just two cycles for a hit and user commands can be issued every cycle. During a miss, the cache stalls the algorithm with handshake signals. For transparent HLS integration, we defined a SRAM-like cache port interface with *virtual address space* of 2048x2048 pixels. As shown in Section 5, cache ports are used as simple 2D pixel arrays, requiring no active management. The cache characteristics are read from a CatapultC custom object library and corresponding interface controllers are instantiated for every port.

Memory controller

Enforcing *bank interleaving* is only useful if the memory controller achieves a high throughput in this mode, which largely depends on its row-management policy. In SDRAM, a *row conflict* means having to switch the active row within a bank, which incurs many overhead cycles due to precharge, activate and read/write commands. Basic controller policies to alleviate this are *open-row* for repeated accesses to same rows or *close-row* which pre-emptively closes rows [7]. We tested data bus (DQ) utilization for specific bank interleaving accesses with Virtex-5 MIG as shown in Table 1. For instance, the 84RW pattern generates four bursts, a row conflict, change in DQ direction, four more bursts, then a change in bank and DQ direction. MIG does not support *close-row* but has a strict *in-order* policy with weak throughput because row conflicts are handled at the latest possible moment, stalling the data bus. We therefore added a custom *row conflict prediction logic* with an extra 6-deep shift register to the original user command FIFO. Because the cache controller fixes the bank cycle at one burst, the logic can predict conflicts for a future bank-row. In this case, a read/write with auto-precharge is issued *as soon as possible* to the concerned bank-row and the required bank-row is activated ahead of time. The optimization offers substantially more bandwidth as bank and row cycles become shorter and services up to 4x as many transactions in the 11W case. The worst case of 11RW translates to a guaranteed bandwidth for each cache port of 1.0Gbit/s. Hardware cost is 1260 registers and 1230 LUTs as opposed to 238 registers and 257 LUTs for the original ddr2_ctrl. This is only an additional 2% of logic resources for this device.

```
1  typedef ac_int<16,false> t_pixel;
2  void processing (
3  ac_channel<t_pixel> &DataInput,
4  ac_channel<t_pixel> &DataOutput,
5  t_pixel CachePort[2048][2048]) {
6  t_pixel InputPixel,BufferPixel,OutputPixel;
7  static WindowBuffer<2048,t_pixel,5,5> myBuf;
8  DataInput.read(InputPixel);
9  OutputPixel = InputPixel + CachePort[y][x];
10 myBuf.Write(InputPixel);
11 for(int i=0;i<5;i++)
12  for(int j=0;j<5;j++){
13   MyBuf.ReadWindow(i,j,BufferPixel);
14   OutputPixel += BufferPixel;}
15 DataOutput.write(OutputPixel);)
```

Table 2: Example use of platform features in HLS

5. ALGORITHMIC STUDY

Having discussed the memory system details, this section examines how to use platform features from within a CatapultC algorithm. Table 2 shows a template which omits control statements and uses the synthesizable *Algorithmic C Data Types* from MentorGraphics. The 16bit pixel streaming channels described as *ac_channel* objects in Lines 3-4 synthesize to handshake interface controllers. A cache port is declared and accessed like a simple 2D pixel array in Lines 5 and 9. A sliding window buffer object is instantiated for 2048 image width and 5x5 window size in Line 7, then used in Lines 10 and 13. Mapping the window pixels to registers enables the loops of Lines 11-14 to be *fully unrolled* in the HLS schedule. Finally, the result is streamed out in Line 15.

2D FIR Filter

Filtering operations such as edge detection can be described by the 2D convolution of the input image $X(i,j)$ with the kernel $h(n,m)$ of size NxN giving the output image $Y(i,j)$:

$$Y(i,j) = \sum_{n=1}^{N}\sum_{m=1}^{N} h(n,m) \cdot X(i - \left\lfloor \frac{N}{2} \right\rfloor + n, j - \left\lfloor \frac{N}{2} \right\rfloor + m) \quad (1)$$

The hardware implementation exploits a WindowBuffer instance with a maximum window size of 7x7. Kernel coefficients $h(n,m)$ are mapped to configuration registers of Figure 2, enabling run-time programming of arbitrary filter functionality with kernel sizes 3x3, 5x5, or 7x7.

Geometric Correction

Every camera lens causes a certain degree of image distortion, for instance *barrel distortion* [3]. To correct the distortion, a reference matrix of dots is recorded without any image correction applied and analyzed in software outside this platform. This results in an address matrix mapping corrected output image pixel coordinates $Y(i,j)$ to distorted input image pixel coordinates $X(k,l) : Y(i,j) = X(k,l)$. As the coordinates k, l are real numbers, bilinear interpolation with four adjacent pixels is used:

$$Y(i,j) = a_{i,j} \cdot X(\lfloor k \rfloor, \lfloor l \rfloor) + b_{i,j} \cdot X(\lceil k \rceil, \lfloor l \rfloor) \quad (2)$$
$$+ c_{i,j} \cdot X(\lfloor k \rfloor, \lceil l \rceil) + d_{i,j} \cdot X(\lceil k \rceil, \lceil l \rceil) \quad (3)$$

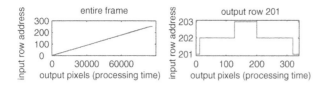

Figure 4: Locality of reference example

Wherein the weights $a_{i,j}, b_{i,j}, c_{i,j}$ and $d_{i,j}$ can be determined by:

$$a_{i,j} = (\lceil k \rceil - k)(\lceil l \rceil - l) \quad b_{i,j} = (k - \lfloor k \rfloor)(\lceil l \rceil - l) \quad (4)$$

$$c_{i,j} = (\lceil k \rceil - k)(l - \lfloor l \rfloor) \quad d_{i,j} = (k - \lfloor k \rfloor)(l - \lfloor l \rfloor) \quad (5)$$

The hardware implementation must fetch four required input pixels given by the address matrix and then apply the bilinear interpolation with the weight matrix. For this platform, address and weight matrices are loaded into SDRAM through cache ports `Addr` and `Weights` respectively. The difficulty is that the memory access pattern given by `Addr` is not known *a priori* at synthesis. Therefore, the algorithm always buffers an entire frame by using four 16bit cache ports `RAM1` to `RAM4` as ping-pong buffers, swapping read and write directions after each frame period. The caching strategy must then consider the locality of reference implicit in the address matrix, and Figure 4 gives a typical example. The access pattern over an entire frame is linear and deterministic, but within an output row, required pixels oscillate between input rows, which would cause SDRAM row conflicts in an uncached system. Here, synthesizing caches of 10 full image rows with linear tile movement eliminates cache misses for virtually all practical address matrices.

6. RESULTS

Area and throughput results are listed in Table 3, where algorithm resources show the CatapultC core only. C algorithms were developed in Microsoft VisualStudio 2008. MentorGraphics CatapultC 2009a.110 and PrecisionRTL 2008a.93 were used for HLS and RTL synthesis of algorithms respectively, and Xilinx ISE11.5 for platform implementation. The SDRAM domain was clocked at 196MHz. The algorithms were aggressively pipelined to 2 and 3 throughput cycles. At maximum kernel size of N=7, the filter computes 2.94 GMACs[1] and draws 47.0 Gbit/s of bandwidth from the on-chip window buffer (49 16bit-registers). The geometric correction transfers 144 external memory bits (64 matrix bits, 64 read bits, 16 write bits) per output pixel. This represents a bandwidth of 5.7 Gbit/s, which is in line with the 6.0 Gbit/s that the six cache ports provide at a minimum.

7. CONCLUSION

This paper has presented a flexible FPGA platform for image processing data paths synthesized with CatapultC. A custom memory system alleviating the usual bottlenecks of low throughput and high latency has been proposed, featuring common window buffers, autonomously prefetching caches, and an optimized SDRAM controller. The latter services up to 4x as many transactions as the original core, enabling each cache to provide 1.0Gbit/s at 2 cycle read

---

[1]A GMAC is 10^9 multiply and accumulate operations per second.

Design unit	Filter	Geometric correction	Cache controller
Clock rate (MHz)	120	120	120 (front) 196 (back)
Throughput (cycles)	2	3	1 (front)
Pipeline stages	25	4	1 (write) 2 (read)
Pixel rate (MHz)	60	40	-
fps at 2048x2048	14	9	-
fps at 1024x1024	57	38	-
FFs	14576	728	4981
LUTs (6-input)	10105	717	7264
DSP48E slices	27	4	-
18kb BRAMs	6	0	71

Table 3: Area and throughput of major design units

latency. The C implementation of filtering and geometric correction has shown that a real-time throughput on the order of 10fps is achievable at 2048x2048 resolution.

8. ACKNOWLEDGMENTS

We thank Philippe Grosse, Robert Koch, Hussein Chokr, Daniel Ziener and Thomas Siegmund for their contributions.

9. REFERENCES

[1] R. Beun, K. Irek, and M. Ditzel. C++ based design flow for reconfigurable image processing systems. In *Field Programmable Logic and Applications. FPL*, 2007.

[2] A. do Carmo Lucas and R. Ernst. An image processor for digital film. In *Application-Specific Systems, Architecture Processors. ASAP*, 2005.

[3] K. Gribbon, C. Johnston, and D. Bailey. A real-time fpga implementation of a barrel distortion correction algorithm with bilinear interpolation. In *Image and Vision Computing New Zealand*, 2003.

[4] S. Heithecker, A. do Carmo Lucas, and R. Ernst. A high-end real-time digital film processing reconfigurable platform. *EURASIP J. Embedded Syst.*, 2007(1), 2007.

[5] Z. Larabi, Y. Mathieu, and S. Mancini. Efficient data access management for fpga-based image processing socs. In *Rapid System Prototyping. RSP*, 2009.

[6] MentorGraphics Inc. *CatapultC Synthesis User's and Reference Manual*, 2009a update2 edition, 2010.

[7] S. Rixner, W. Dally, U. Kapasi, P. Mattson, and J. Owens. Memory access scheduling. In *Computer Architecture. ISCA*, 2000.

[8] M. Weinhardt and W. Luk. Memory access optimisation for reconfigurable systems. In *Computers and Digital Techniques, IEE Proceedings*, volume 148, pages 105–112, 2001.

[9] Xilinx Inc. *Memory Interface Solutions User Guide UG086*, 3.0 edition, 2009.

[10] Xilinx Inc. *Multi-Port Memory Controller DS643*, 6.01a edition, 2010.

[11] P. Yiannacouras and J. Rose. A parameterized automatic cache generator for fpgas. In *Field-Programmable Technology. FPT*, 2003.

Improved Double Angle Complex Rotation QRD-RLS

Qiang Gao and Robert W Stewart

DSP enabled Communications (DSPeC) Group
Department of Electrical and Electronic Engineering
University of Strathclyde, 204 George Street
Glasgow, Scotland, United Kingdom
+44 (0) 141 548 2605
{qiang.gao, r.stewart}@eee.strath.ac.uk

ABSTRACT

In recent years, the classic method of Coordinate Rotation by Digital Computer (CORDIC) arithmetic has been widely implemented as part of the computational requirements of the well known QR-RLS (Recursive Least Squares) algorithm. In order to operate Givens rotation on a complex number system, double angle complex rotation (DACR) was adopted to simplify the computational requirement of Complex Givens Rotation. This paper presents a new architecture of high speed CORDIC based single Processor Element (PE) that can be used to accomplish the complex value QR update based RLS. The implementation results on Xilinx FPGA implementaton demonstrates that the proposed structure results in a lower latency and lower cost.

Categories and Subject Descriptors

C.3 [**Special-purpose and application-based systems**] : Signal processing systems

General Terms

Design

Keywords

CORDIC, QR-RLS, FPGA

1. INTRODUCTION

Within the area of wireless communications, the increasing requirement of communication speed means that there is sustained demand for implementation of high speed data equalisers, beamsteerers and Multiple Input Multiple Output (MIMO) antenna systems. Over recent years, one widely used method of high speed (parallel) implementation has been the QR Decomposition (QRD)-RLS algorithm [1] [2] [4] given its fast convergence and and its good fixed point numerical properties [2] [4]. Furthermore from an FPGA implementation point of view, the QR can be mapped to a very regular triangular systolic type array implementation [2] [1] [6].

The QR Decomposition can be performed through a sequence of unitary transformations. Among the various unitary transformations, Givens rotation [2] have the advantage that it can be easily parallelised and therefore more appropriate frequently used arithmetic technique that performs the Givens rotation is the CORDIC algorithm, which was first developed by Volder [2] in the 1950s. CORDIC performs a series of microrotations with an architecture comprised almost entirely of shift and add operations, and hence results in an easy to implement hardware design.

2. QR-RLS ARRAY WITH DOWNDATING

Based on [3], the QR-RLS recursive algorithm derived for weight extraction (i.e. the downdating method) is summarized as:

$$Q(k)\begin{bmatrix} \lambda^{1/2}R(k-1) & \lambda^{1/2}u(k-1) & \lambda^{-1/2}R^{-H}(k-1) \\ x^T(k) & d(k) & 0 \end{bmatrix} = \begin{bmatrix} R(k) & u(k) & R^{-H}(k) \\ 0 & a(k) & b(k) \end{bmatrix} \tag{1}$$

Where $Q(k)$ is the orthogonal rotation matrix, which triangularises the left hand side matrix of Eq. (1), λ is the *forgetting factor* (set to a value just less than 1), $x(k)$ is the input data vector, $d(k)$ is the desired data vector, and $a(k)$ is the *posteriori* Least-Square residual.

Figure 1 shows a simple Signal Flow Graph (SFG) representation of the QR-RLS systolic array [3] aiming to find the weights of an $N = 3$ weights FIR filter (this small dimension is used to keep the SFG diagrams simple). This array uses the Givens rotation to convert the input data into an upper triangular matrix R [1]. Each r_{ij} stored and updated inside of the array is one element of this upper triangular matrix, where the subscript (i,j) represents the location of the element in the R matrix and u vector. The definitions of the Boundary Cell (BC) and Internal Cell (IC) of QR-RLS array are also described in Figure 1. s and c are used to express the Givens rotation values (often denoted Sine & Cosine) calculated with in a boundary cell. The column on the right hand side of u_{ij} elements generates the product of the cosines γ. The posteriori error $e(k)$ can be found from the multiplier $\otimes$ [1].

In many implementations ([1], [4]) the final coefficient weight vector is derived from the outputs of the QR decomposition algorithm using backsubstitution. To implement a systolic structure for back-substitution, one approach is to append a linear array to the upper triangular QR-RLS array (on the left of dash line) [4]. However it is not easy to interface the backsubstitution array, which requires the R values to be first "shifted" out from the QR array [4]. Also, the maximum data throughput of the linear array is lower than that of the

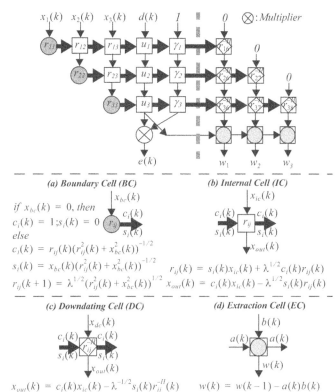

(a) Boundary Cell (BC) *(b) Internal Cell (IC)*

if $x_{bc}(k) = 0$, then
$c_i(k) = 1; s_i(k) = 0$
else
$c_i(k) = r_{ij}(k)(r_{ij}^2(k) + x_{bc}^2(k))^{-1/2}$
$s_i(k) = x_{bc}(k)(r_{ij}^2(k) + x_{bc}^2(k))^{-1/2}$
$r_{ij}(k+1) = \lambda^{1/2}(r_{ij}^2(k) + x_{bc}^2(k))^{1/2}$

$r_{ij}(k) = s_i(k)x_{ic}(k) + \lambda^{1/2}c_i(k)r_{ij}(k)$
$x_{out}(k) = c_i(k)x_{ic}(k) - \lambda^{1/2}s_i(k)r_{ij}(k)$

(c) Downdating Cell (DC) *(d) Extraction Cell (EC)*

$x_{out}(k) = c_i(k)x_{ic}(k) - \lambda^{-1/2}s_i(k)r_{ij}^{-II}(k)$
$r_{ij}^{-1}(k) = s_i(k)x_{ic}(k) + \lambda^{-1/2}c_i(k)r_{ij}^{-II}(k)$

$w(k) = w(k-1) - a(k)b(k)$

Figure 1. Systolic array of QR-RLS with downdating

triangular array. Alternatively, the systolic array of downdating, which is proposed by [3], is employed in this paper. The lower triangular (downdating) section (on the right hand side of dash line) rotates the R^{-II} matrix stored in the ◇ cells and an externally applied vector of zeros. Obviously, both the ICs and the Downdating Cells (DC) execute nearly the same operation. The only difference is that the *forgetting factor* in each DC is equal to $1/\lambda$. The bottom row of Extraction Cells in Figure 1 is employed to extract the error $e(k)$ and weights $w_{i,j}(k)$ by the multiply-accumulate (MAC) operation.

The Double Angle Complex Rotation (DACR) approach [7] is widely applied for the complex Givens rotation based QRD to reduce the input matrix to a triangular form, by applying successive rotations to matrix elements below the main diagonal. This rotation is described by two rotation angles θ_b and θ_1, where θ_b is the phase information of complex value b, and $\theta_1 = \tan(B/A)^{-1}$. The DACR based formula can be summarized as Eq. (2) [7]. Base on Eq. (2), Figure 2 and 3 graphically show the data flows of DACR based BC and IC.

$$\begin{bmatrix} a' \\ b' \end{bmatrix} = \begin{bmatrix} \cos\theta_1 & \sin\theta_1 \\ -\sin\theta_1 & \cos\theta_1 \end{bmatrix} \begin{bmatrix} 1 & 0 \\ 0 & e^{-j\theta_b} \end{bmatrix} \begin{bmatrix} a \\ b \end{bmatrix} = \begin{bmatrix} \cos\theta_1 & \sin\theta_1 e^{j\theta_b} \\ -\sin\theta_1 & \cos\theta_1 e^{j\theta_b} \end{bmatrix} \begin{bmatrix} a \\ b \end{bmatrix} \quad (2)$$

3. PIPELINE-INTERLEAVING COARSE ANGLE CORDIC FOR QR-RLS

According to the circuit implementation of conventional CORDIC, based on Eq. (3), two subcircuits are required for the rotation of vector (x^m, y^m) and a third to keep track of the corresponding angle $\theta = z^m$ for a n iterations CORDIC (where $m = 0, 1... n - 1$). For the QR-RLS, the vectoring mode CORDIC within the BC of systolic

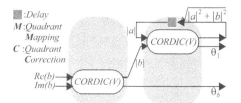

Figure 2. Signal Flow of Simplified DACR Based BC

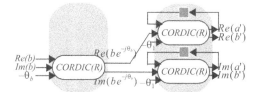

Figure 3. Signal Flow of Simplified DACR Based IC

array computes the angle θ through which the vector is rotated onto the x axis, and the IC and DC uses CORDIC in rotation mode to perform a Givens rotation of the same angle [5].

$$\begin{aligned} x^{m+1} &= x^m - d_m(2^{-m}y^m) \\ y^{m+1} &= y^m + d_m(2^{-m}x^m) \\ z^{m+1} &= z^m - d_m(\text{atan}2^{-m}) \end{aligned} \quad (3)$$

However, the result is scaled by a factor K_n which must be removed at the final stage. The scaling factor K_n (of the value ≈ 1.6467) is derived as:

$$K_n = \prod_{m=0}^{n-1} 1/\cos\theta_m = \prod_{m=0}^{n-1} \sqrt{1 + \tan^2\theta_m} = \prod_{m=0}^{n-1} \sqrt{1 + 2^{(-2m)}}$$

Therefore it is possible for the BCs to instruct the angle of rotation in the ICs and DCs without explicitly computing the angle z, but rather communicating the direction d of the various CORDIC coarse angle values [5]. This leads to hardware resource reduction and produces a more regular array, but without losing the error performance resulted by the original method.

For a typical application with matrix sizes of say 10 or more dimension, the systolic array for a QRD-RLS is too large to be mapped directly to the same number of CORDIC processors. Therefore, a critical stage in designing a chip for such an application is to map this large systolic array to a fixed size array. All the extraction cells in Figure 1 can be easily mapped to a single multiply-accumulate (MAC) arithmetic component, as shown in Figure 4. The way to translate the "rhomboid" (triangularization) part of QR design to a single PE architecture is presented as follows. Firstly, the aforementioned double triangular array in Figure 1 must be transferred to a single row linear array, as shown in Figure 5. Then the next step is 'combining' all the PEs in the linear array by the pipeline-interleaving scheme presented in [5]. This proposed architecture can overcome the high latency (coming from the pipeline stages) of traditional CORDIC. As illustrated in [6], after the initial latency of the circuit, the computation rate of the cell is two new inputs / one output per clock cycle.

4. SCALING-FREE-IN-LOOP

According to Eq. (1), during the QR recursive operation, the new x and d datas are added respectively to the upper triangular matrix R

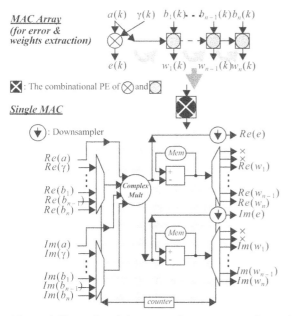

MAC Array
(for error & weights extraction)

⊠ : The combinational PE of ⊗ and ◯

Single MAC

▼ : Downsampler

Figure 4. Error & weights extraction array transformation.

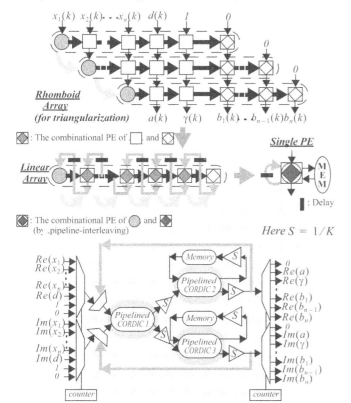

Rhomboid Array
(for triangularization)

◈ : The combinational PE of □ and ◇

Linear Array

Single PE

▮ : Delay

◈ : The combinational PE of ◯ and ◈
(by pipeline-interleaving)

Here $S = 1/K$

Figure 5. Triangularization array transformation

and the column u. The decompositon in Eq. (4) then converts the $\langle R|x \rangle$ matrix to the a new upper triangular matrix by using Given's rotations to zero the elements below the main diagonal. Eq. (4) can be further transformed to Eq. (5). According to Section 3, each CORDIC output must be scaled by a constant $S = 1/K$ to give a true circular rotations. This can be circumvented in our implementation by applying a 1 bit right shift to replace the scaling operation, in order to avoid overflow.

$$\begin{bmatrix} (\cos\theta_1)_{jj} & (\sin\theta_1 e^{j\theta_1})_{ji} & 0 & 0 & 0 \\ (-\sin\theta_1)_{ij} & (\cos\theta_1 e^{j\theta_1})_{ii} & 0 & 0 & 0 \\ 0 & 0 & 1 & 0 & 0 \\ 0 & 0 & 0 & 1 & 0 \\ 0 & 0 & 0 & 0 & 1 \end{bmatrix} \begin{bmatrix} r_{00} & r_{01} & r_{02} & r_{03} & u_0 \\ 0 & r_{11} & r_{12} & r_{13} & u_1 \\ 0 & 0 & r_{22} & r_{23} & u_2 \\ 0 & 0 & 0 & r_{33} & u_3 \\ x_0 & x_1 & x_2 & x_3 & d_0 \end{bmatrix}$$

(G) Givens Rotation $= \begin{bmatrix} r'_{00} & r'_{01} & r'_{02} & r'_{03} & u'_0 \\ 0 & r'_{11} & r'_{12} & r'_{13} & u'_1 \\ 0 & 0 & r'_{22} & r'_{23} & u'_2 \\ 0 & 0 & 0 & r'_{33} & u'_3 \\ 0 & 0 & 0 & 0 & d'_0 \end{bmatrix}$ (4)

$$\begin{bmatrix} (\cos\theta_1)_{jj} & (\sin\theta_1 e^{j\theta_1})_{ji} & 0 & 0 & 0 \\ \left(\dfrac{-\sin\theta_1}{4S^2}\right)_{ij} & \left(\dfrac{\cos\theta_1 e^{j\theta_1}}{4S^2}\right)_{ii} & 0 & 0 & 0 \\ 0 & 0 & 1 & 0 & 0 \\ 0 & 0 & 0 & 1 & 0 \\ 0 & 0 & 0 & 0 & 1 \end{bmatrix} \begin{bmatrix} r_{00} & r_{01} & r_{02} & r_{03} & u_0 \\ 0 & \dfrac{r_{11}}{4S^2} & \dfrac{r_{12}}{4S^2} & \dfrac{r_{13}}{4S^2} & \dfrac{u_1}{4S^2} \\ 0 & 0 & \dfrac{r_{22}}{16S^4} & \dfrac{r_{23}}{16S^4} & \dfrac{u_2}{16S^4} \\ 0 & 0 & 0 & \dfrac{r_{33}}{64S^6} & \dfrac{u_3}{64S^6} \\ x_0 & x_1 & x_2 & x_3 & d_0 \end{bmatrix}$$

(G')

Here $S = 1/K$

$$= \begin{bmatrix} r'_{00} & r'_{01} & r'_{02} & r'_{03} & u'_0 \\ 0 & \dfrac{r'_{11}}{4S^2} & \dfrac{r'_{12}}{4S^2} & \dfrac{r'_{13}}{4S^2} & \dfrac{u'_1}{4S^2} \\ 0 & 0 & \dfrac{r'_{22}}{16S^4} & \dfrac{r'_{23}}{16S^4} & \dfrac{u'_2}{16S^4} \\ 0 & 0 & 0 & \dfrac{r'_{33}}{64S^6} & \dfrac{u'_3}{64S^6} \\ 0 & 0 & 0 & 0 & \dfrac{d'_0}{256S^8} \end{bmatrix}$$ (5)

This new CORDIC can result in the modified Givens rotation - G' in Eq. (5). G' scales the initial values of r and u elements in $\langle R|x \rangle$ and $\langle u|d \rangle$ by an additional factor $(4S^2)^{-1}$ on each Givens updating iteration (i.e $(4S^2)^{-N+1}$ on the $(N-1)$-th iteration, where N is the number of filter weights) to match the initial scaling on the R terms. The initial values of all the r need to be pre-computed and stored in a memory. A final correction operation (scale by $S' = (4S^2)^{N-1}$) is required on the output of channel-interleaving CORDIC. Refering to Eq. (5), we have

$$\frac{d'_0}{(2S)^8} \times K' = \frac{d'_0}{(2S)^8} \times (2S)^8 = d'_0 \quad for\ a\ 4 \times 4\ matrix\ \boldsymbol{R} \quad (6)$$

Both the aforementioned three CORDICs based QR-RLS in Figure 5 and the new presented scaling-free-in-loop one can be further transfered to a two cell based architecture, by time-sharing the $1st$ and $2nd$ CORDIC elements, as shown in Figure 6. As shown in Figure 6, to switch the scaling-in-loop architecture to the new scaling-free-in-loop one, we should replace the ▷ and line → which are highlighted inside the grey ovals with the ⊡ and ▷ block respectively.

The constant multiplication by S and S' can both be efficiently implemented by appropriate binary shifts and adders. There is no cost for the binary shifts which could be hardwired with adders. Rather than the conventional binary representation, the Canonical-Signed Digit (CSD) coding has been widely employed in other publications [8] to produce the constant multiplier. In this paper we use the Reduced Slice Graph (RSG) algorithm [9] which produces a smaller

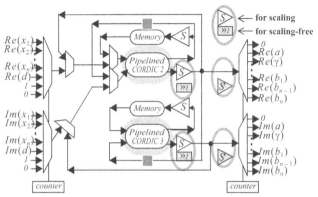

Figure 6. Rolled Scaling Free-In-Loop CORDIC QRD - RLS

FPGA area multiplier block.

Table 1 compares the execution time (for one iteration of QR decomposition) of this section's modified CORDIC based QR-RLS and the original "scaling-in-loop" design in Section 3. CLK represents the maximum clock rate, N is the number of weights, n stands for the total CORDIC iterations and d is the number of clock cycle delays introduced by the CORDIC scaling operations (assuming both the "scaling-in-loop" and "scaling-free-in-loop" designs request the same number of pipelining level), last but not least, the M represented the clock cycle delays introduced by the MAC part and the new "scaling-free-in-loop" architecture accelerates the QR-RLS processor.

Table 1. Execution time of the single PE QR-RLS

Design	Execution time
Scaling-in-loop	$((2n + 2 + d) \times 2N + M) / CLK$
Scaling-free-in-loop	$((2n + 2) \times 2N + d + M) / CLK$

5. PERFORMANCE

Table 2 compares the FPGA ultilization of the 16-iteration 18-bit precision CORDIC based "scaling-free-in-loop" QR-RLS, with the "scaling-in-loop" QR-RLS and the work of [4] which uses backsubstitution for weight extraction. Xilinx ISE 10.1 is used to target a Virtex-4 xc4vsx35-10ff668 device. The size of matrix R can be scalable from 2×2 to $(n - 2) \times (n - 2)$, where n is the number of CORDIC iterations. Based on Table 1, Table 3 provides the timing informations for several configurations of the input data set under the triangularization and MAC parts (backsubstitution part for Table 5) of the QR-RLS processor presented in this paper and [4]. Obviously, the newly proposed architecture can significantly reduce the execution time and while maintaining a low hardware cost.

6. CONCLUSION

This paper has described the design and implementation of the complex number system based single PE QRD-RLS processor. The pipeline-interleaving coarse angle CORDIC based quadrant correction free DACR is employed to combine the low hardware consumption with the benefit of scalability. The scaling-free-in-loop algorithm plays essentially the role of increasing the sampling rate of our proposed QR-RLS processor. The RSG operation speeds up the scaling phase of the CORDIC algorithm with the lowest expense on the ultilization of slices.

Table 2. Synthesis results for CORDIC QR Givens (Size 4×4)

Type	Part	Slice	FF	LUT	DSP48	BRAM
Standard CORDIC Lookup [4] (extra BS stage requ'd)	Triangular'tn	1598	2549	2630	9	5
	BS	1932	2862	3286	4	1
	Total	**3530**	**5411**	**5916**	**13**	**6**
Pipeline-Interleaving Coarse Angle CORDIC (scaling-in-loop)	Triangular'tn	1252	1953	1815	0	4
	MAC	463	392	631	8	0
	Total	**1715**	**2345**	**2446**	**8**	**4**
[This paper] (scaling-free-in-loop)	Triangular'tn	1269	2029	1828	0	4
	MAC	463	392	631	8	0
	Total	**1732**	**2421**	**2459**	**8**	**4**

Note : BS = back-substitution

Table 3. Execution Time Of The QR-RLS for Matrix Sizes

Type	R Size	Cycles for Triangular'tn	Cycles for BS/MAC	Total Cycles	Time (μs) for 250 MHz Clock
Ref [4]	5 x 5	2540	255	2795	11.18
	7 x 7	5656	371	6027	24.11
	9 x 9	10476	495	10971	43.88
Scaling -in-loop	5 x 5	380	9	389	1.556
	7 x 7	532	9	541	2.164
	9 x 9	684	9	693	2.772
[This paper]	5 x 5	344	9	353	1.412
	7 x 7	480	9	489	1.956
	9 x 9	616	9	625	2.5

7. REFERENCES

[1] J G McWhirter, "Systolic Array for Recursive Least-squares Minimisation", *Electronics Letters*, vol. 19, Issue: 18, pp: 729-730, Sept 1. 1983

[2] J E. Volder, "The CORDIC Trigonometric Computing Technique", *IRE Trans. Electronic Computers*, vol. 3, pp. 330-334, Sept. 1959.

[3] Bin Yang, Johann F. Bohme, "Rotation-based RLS algorithm unified derivation, numerical properties, and parallel implementation," *IEEE Trans. on Signal Processing*, vol. 40, no. 5, pp. 1151-1167, May 1992

[4] C Dick, F Harris, M Pajic and D Vuletic, "Real-Time QRD-Based Beamforming on an FPGA Platform". *14th Asilomar Conference on Signals, Systems and Computers*, Oct. 29 - Nov. 1 2006

[5] Q Gao, L Crockett and R Stewart, "Coarse Angle Rotation Mode CORDIC based Single Processing Element QR-RLS Processor", 17th EUSIPCO Conference, Glasgow, Aug 2009

[6] Q Gao and R Stewart, "High Speed Pipeline-Interleaving Coarse Angle CORDIC for QR-RLS Array Processing", *Submitted to IEEE Trans on Circuits and Systems, Sept 2010*.

[7] B Haller, J Gotze, J R Cavallaro, "Efficient implementation of rotation operations for high performance QRD-RLS", *IEEE International Conference on Application-Specific Systems, Architectures and Processors*, pp. 162-174, 14-16 Jul 1997

[8] P. K. Meher, J Valls, T. B. Juang, K Sridharan and K Maharatna, "50 Years of CORDIC: Algorithms, Architectures and Applications", *IEEE Trans on Circuits and Systems - I*, volume 56, issue 9, pp. 1893-1907, 2009

[9] K N. Macpherson, R W. Stewart, "Low FPGA Area Multiplier Blocks for Full Parallel FIR Filters", *Field-Programmable Technology (FPT), IEEE International Conference on Proceedings*, pp. 247-254, Brisbane, Australia, Dec 6-8. 2004

Authenticated Encryption for FPGA Bitstreams

Steve Trimberger, Jason Moore, Weiguang Lu
Xilinx, Inc., 2100 Logic Dr., San Jose, CA 95124 USA
<firstname.lastname>@xilinx.com

ABSTRACT

FPGA bitstream encryption blocks theft of the design in the FPGA bitstream by preventing unauthorized copy and reverse engineering. By itself, encryption does not protect against tampering with the bitstream, so without additional capabilities, bitstream encryption cannot prevent the FPGA from executing an unauthorized bitstream. An unauthorized bitstream might be generated by trial and error to cause the FPGA to leak confidential data, including the decrypted bitstream. Strong authentication detects tampering with the bitstream, providing a root of trust that enables applications that require protection of sensitive data in a hostile environment. This paper describes the SHA HMAC-based bitstream authentication algorithm and protocol in Virtex-6 FPGAs and shows how they are integrated in the bitstream.

Categories and Subject Descriptors

B.7.1 [**Hardware**]: Integrated circuits, FPGA

General Terms

Design, Security

Keywords

FPGA bitstream encryption, authentication, trust, trusted design, self-reconfiguration

1. BACKGROUND

As FPGAs have become more complex, the intellectual property implemented in the bitstream has become more valuable. Bitstream encryption was introduced in Virtex-2 FPGAs to protect the intellectual property of the bitstream. The bitstream is encrypted with a user-selectable key. The same key is pre-loaded in the FPGA. When the FPGA configures, it loads encrypted data and decrypts it internally. During normal operation, neither the key nor the unencrypted bitstream is available outside the FPGA. This mechanism prevents simple bitstream copying because the bitstream can only run in an FPGA that contains the proper decryption key [10]. Privacy provided by encryption safeguards intellectual property of the circuits and algorithms in the design.

Encrypted bitstreams provide two essential features:
1. By restricting the bitstream to only function in a subset of FPGAs (those containing the correct key), encryption prevents unauthorized copy.
2. By providing secrecy of the implementation, encryption prevents reverse-engineering.

The first function, the restriction of the bitstream to a subset of FPGAs, is *not* a property of encryption. This restriction could be provided by a simple password or message authentication code, as is done with computer login or an ATM PIN number. In the FPGA environment, though, an observer can see the entire interaction, so password theft would be trivial. A public-key system with a common key in all FPGAs can prevent reverse-engineering, but is subject to replay attack, admitting unauthorized copy. A straightforward digital signature could perform this same function without requiring encryption. However, an adversary could circumvent the signature by reverse-engineering and re-constructing the bitstream for an FPGA that does not require the signature.

Encryption requires the knowledge of the key without transmitting it. In the bitstream encryption protocol, the key is a shared secret between the encryptor and the FPGA that restricts the pool of FPGAs in which the bitstream can run. Further, by providing privacy, bitstream encryption prevents reverse-engineering. The issue of authorization or authentication remains, however, because contrary to popular belief, encryption does not prevent an adversary from tampering with the encrypted bitstream.

2. TAMPERING WITH ENCRYPTED BITSTREAMS

Xilinx Virtex FPGAs and Spartan-6 FPGAs use 256-bit AES encryption in Cipher Block Chaining (CBC) mode of operation [8]. In CBC decryption, the ciphertext of block n is XORed with the decrypted block n+1 to yield the plaintext of block n+1 (figure 1). CBC causes blocks with identical plaintext (for example, all zero) to decrypt to different cipher text, thereby eliminating a dictionary attack on the data.

However, CBC permits a "bit-flipping" attack on the plaintext, as shown in figure 1. If an adversary inverts a bit in the second encrypted block, the second block will, of course, decrypt to unintelligible nonsense. However, the corresponding bit in the third decrypted block is inverted. Using this technique, an adversary can selectively invert any number of bits in non-consecutive blocks. If the state of the target bit is known, an adversary can set it. For example, if the logic to enable bitstream readback is disabled with a '0' at a specific location, an adversary could re-enable it without reverse-engineering the bitstream by inverting that bit. For this reason, disabling of readback of encrypted FPGA bitstreams in Virtex and Spartan devices is not controlled in the encrypted bitstream, but by hard configuration logic of the FPGA. However, other attacks may attempt to enable the Internal Configuration Access Port, enable I/O blocks or change clock speed in an attempt to gain access to internal data.

Attacks on the bitstream are also possible without knowing the specific bit to attack. In figure 1, the second block of data is scrambled. An adversary does not know the plaintext that results from modifying the ciphertext. However, an adversary with patience may attempt a brute-force attack on part of the bitstream,

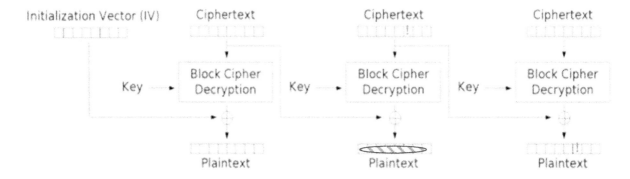

Figure 1. Bit-flipping attack on Cipher Block Chaining mode of operation of cipher (after Wikipedia)

scrambling the bits in an attempt to get the FPGA to reveal sensitive data by, for example, connecting an internal signal to an I/O block. To prevent tampering with the bitstream and to guarantee secure handling of data, authentication is required.

Notice, these attacks do not permit unauthorized copy of the bitstream, or reverse-engineering, so the secrecy of the intellectual property in the bitstream is not compromised. Encryption has not "failed." Encryption still protects the design.

3. AUTHENTICATION

Authentication assures the recipient of a message that the message is exactly the message the sender intended. Virtex-2 through Virtex-5 FPGAs provide authentication using a CRC on the decrypted data. This is termed CRC-then-Encrypt (CtE). CtE detects errors in transmission, defective bits in the external PROM and key mismatch between the FPGA and the bitstream. It also detects the bit-flipping attack. In figure 1, the second block of data is scrambled, so the 32-bit CRC of the decrypted bitstream will succeed with a probability of only 2^{-32}. This detection probability is considered poor by cryptographic standards, where the key is 256 bits, but it is adequate defense against many attacks. Although successfully passing CRC causes the FPGA to accept the bitstream, the adversary still cannot construct a configuration of his choosing. In the bitstream scrambling attack, the probability of success for any one attempt is $2^{\wedge}$-(number of bits required to be controlled). The CRC reduces this by a further factor of 2^{32}. In Virtex devices, it is possible to construct a bitstream where the number of controlled bits required to leak sensitive information is in the hundreds, making the complexity of the attack greater than simple brute-force attack on the key.

However, targeted attacks are still a concern, and for this reason, reconfiguration and access to the Internal Configuration Access Port were restricted in early Virtex devices using decryption. In order to provide secure access to these powerful features and to secure data processed by the FPGA, strong authentication is required.

4. VIRTEX-6 AUTHENTICATION

Authentication of sensitive messages is well-known in the literature and many algorithms exist for authentication alone as

well as for authenticated encryption. Parelkar [8] noted that generic composition of authentication and encryption required more circuit area than authenticated encryption algorithms and recommended CCM mode despite concerns about security. Drimer [2][3] recommended implementing a Cipher Block Chaining (CBC) Message Authentication Code (MAC) which requires an encryptor on the FPGA running in CBC mode along with the decryptor, doubling the size of the security block. Parlour [9] recommended an internal private key and Knapp [6] proposed an internal identifier for authentication. Both these methods require internal non-volatile storage for authentication information.

Table 1 shows the result of our analysis of authenticated encryption methods at the time the decision was made for Vritex-6. We evaluated qualitatively several algorithms against several criteria: **NIST** Approved (**Y**es or **N**o), **Size** in Hardware (**S**mall, **M**edium, **L**arge), throughput **Speed** (**S**low, **M**edium, **F**ast), **Parallelizable** Algorithm (**Y**es or **N**o) and **Patent** Free (**Y**es or **N**o). Following Black [1] and others, we avoided schemes that were encumbered by patents or had been shown to be weak from a cryptanalysis standpoint or unapproved by NIST. We also required a scheme that was parallelizable, because we needed to decrypt and authenticate at our configuration data rate of 800Mbps.

Table 1. Summary of Authenticated Encryption Analysis					
Method	**NIST**	**Size**	**Speed**	**Parallizable**	**Patent**
IAPM	N	S	M	N	N
XECB	N	S	M	N	N
OCB	N	S	M	N	N
CCM	N	M	M	Y	Y
EAX	N	M	M	N	Y
CWC	N	M	M	N	Y
Helix 1	N	M	M	N	Y
Sober	N	M	M	N	Y
GCM	N	M	M	Y	Y
Generic Composition					
G.C. HMAC	Y	L	M	Y	Y
G.C. CMAC	Y	L	S	N	Y

Our choice was a generic composition of a SHA-256 HMAC authentication with AES-256 encryption. SHA-256 [4] produces a 256-bit hash of the message that is computationally intractable to update if the message has been modified. The probability of a successful tamper with the data is 2^{-256}. SHA-256 is implemented in a Keyed Hashed MAC (HMAC) [5]. The HMAC uses a secret key in the hashing algorithm to authenticate the sender as well as the message.

Generic composition with SHA-256-based Keyed HMAC was chosen for several reasons:

- Generic composition is not covered by patents.
- Generic composition of SHA and AES was approved by NIST for commercial applications. A variety of authentication algorithms, including GCM, were proposed at the time, but were not NIST-approved. Some of these algorithms have subsequently been approved. However, the choice of algorithm, once made, was not open to re-evaluation.
- Generic composition is reasonably area-efficient. At first glance, it would seem that a CBC MAC based on AES would be more efficient because it could use the existing AES decryptor. However, AES-CBC MAC uses AES encryption, not decryption. AES encrypt and decrypt use different tables, reducing the amount of sharable logic. Also, since both decryption and authentication must be done simultaneously, little sharing of logic would be possible. Most importantly, though, AES-CBC encrypt is not easily parallelizable. The AES-CBC based MAC would decrease the throughput of configuration.
- Generic composition of SHA256 and AES CBC decryption is easily parallelizable for high-performance configuration.
- Generic composition requires no additional non-volatile memory for storage of the authentication key.

4.1 Integration of Authentication with Bitstream Encryption

Virtex-6 authentication and encryption are composed using Authentication then Encryption (AtE). The MAC is computed on the plaintext, unencrypted bitstream. The configuration data and the MAC result value are then encrypted using 256-bit AES in CBC mode. On the FPGA, the data is first decrypted and the MAC result is re-computed on the decrypted data and compared with the transmitted value in the bitstream. If the two MAC values disagree, the FPGA configuration fails and the FPGA does not become active. The authentication check doubles as a data integrity check.

4.2 Bitstream Structure

Figure 2 shows a Virtex-6 authenticated encrypted bitstream structure. The SYNC word aligns the incoming data to word boundaries. The Security instruction activates device security. CBC IV is the initialization vector for CBC mode of operation and DWC (Decrypt Word Count) is the number of words of encrypted data that follow.

AKEY is the authentication key, and is discussed in more detail below. Header commands and Footer commands initialize on-chip registers. These registers control a variety of functions, including declaring the device type and setting the startup sequence. The available commands and registers are described in the Virtex 6 Configuration User Guide [12]. The Write Data command begins streaming configuration data to the FPGA. After the Footer Commands, ALIGN pads the bitstream to a multiple of 512 bits while the FPGA appends the data length, as required for SHA-256. The bitstream MAC field is the pre-computed MAC from the bitstream which the FPGA compares against the value it computes as it reads the bitstream.

To understand the integration of the HMAC in the bitstream, it is important to understand the structure of the HMAC computation. The HMAC computation is defined algebraically as:

$$MAC(K, text) = SHA256((K \oplus opad) \| H((K \oplus ipad) \| text))$$

K is the authentication key. $\|$ denotes concatentation
ipad is a constant {x'36'} $\oplus$ denotes exclusive-OR
opad is a constant {x'5a'}

The HMAC requires an authentication key in addition to the encryption key. It is important that the two keys are different. When generating an authenticated encrypted bitstream, both keys are specified to the bitstream generation software. However, to save storage space, only the decryption key is stored in the FPGA. The authentication key, AKEY, is transmitted with the encrypted bitstream. The bitstream decryption provides the privacy to keep the authentication key secret. No on-chip key storage is required.

As shown in figure 2, the authentication key AKEY is transmitted to the FPGA twice: at the start of configuration to initialize the MAC computation with *ipad* and again at the end of the computation to be used with *opad*. Thus, the security of authentication depends on the privacy provided by encryption.

5. HARDWARE PROCESS

Figure 3 is a flow diagram of the authenticated decryption process. Encrypted data is first decrypted and passed to the HMAC computation. Decrypted data is also passed to the configuration engine. An unencrypted bitstream merely bypasses the decryption engine. The decryptor and HMAC process data until DWC words have been processed. At that point, the FPGA compares its computed MAC with the pre-computed MAC in the bitstream. If the comparison succeeds, configuration continues normally. After a failed configuration, if "fallback configuration" was enabled, the FPGA will attempt a second configuration from (presumably) a different external configuration data source or address. This fallback reconfiguration only occurs after the configuration memory and state data have been cleared.

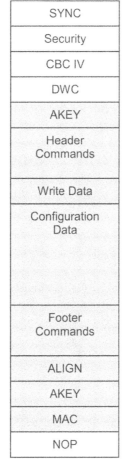

SYNC
Security
CBC IV
DWC
AKEY
Header Commands
Write Data
Configuration Data
Footer Commands
ALIGN
AKEY
MAC
NOP

Figure 2. Virtex-6 authenticated encrypted bitstream. Shaded area is authentication and encrypted.

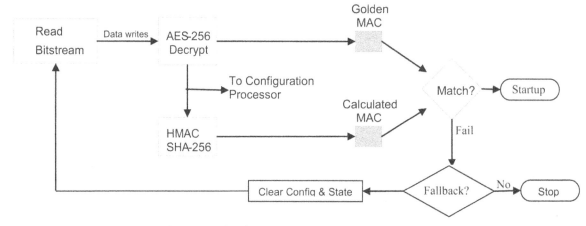

Figure 3: Authenticated Decryption Process in FPGA Silicon

6. NEW FEATURES AND APPLICATIONS

Many security-related configuration restrictions are enforced by dedicated internal hardware in Virtex FPGAs [10]. Among these are:

- No mixing of encrypted and unencrypted configuration.
- No external configuration bitstream readback.
- Key modification clears the FPGA.

Other security restrictions are eased in Virtex-6 because the running bitstream can be trusted. Configuration read and write access are permitted through the Internal Configuration Access Port (ICAP). A running application in the FPGA can use ICAP to implement a secure boot loader. It can implement a custom decryption algorithm, even a public-key algorithm, in FPGA fabric, and self-reconfigure through ICAP. Encryption algorithm implementations in FPGA fabric may be customized to address new side-channel attacks as they appear. A secure boot loader can verify partial configurations or implement pay-per-copy metered IP billing.

Self-reconfiguration can use any number of pins and gigabit transceivers. Using wide internal data paths and high clock rate, decrypted self-reconfiguration can achieve much higher data rate than external configuration. The performance is limited only by the ICAP clock frequency.

An application can read back its own decrypted configuration through ICAP, permitting an operating secure FPGA to self-check to detect random defects or intentional physical tampering with the FPGA. Virtex-6 devices include a bitstream scrubbing option that corrects single-bit errors. Multi-bit error correction cores in fabric can use ICAP to read back configuration data, check and correct more complex error patterns.

Access to ICAP must be used carefully. A design can breach its own security if it, for example, connects the ICAP port directly to I/O pins.

7. CONCLUSION

Authenticated encryption of bitstreams is accomplished by generic composition of keyed HMAC SHA-256 with AES-256 in CBC mode. No additional key storage is required for the authentication key. The bitstream becomes slightly larger to accommodate the authentication information, but configuration data rate is not slowed by authentication.

Authenticated encrypted bitstreams provide a root of trust to enable a broad range of secure applications of the FPGA. These applications open up new areas where FPGAs can supply secure solutions to interesting problems that require secure handling of data, including the ability to supersede the encryption and authentication algorithms provided by the FPGA vendor.

8. REFERENCES

[1] J. Black, "Authenticated Encryption", http://www.cs.colorado.edu/~jrblack/papers/ae.pdf, 2004.

[2] Drimer, S., "Authentication of FPGA Bitstreams, Why and How," in *Applied Reconfigurable Computing*, v 4419 of LNCS, 2007. http://www.cl.cam.ac.uk/~sd410/papers/bsauth.pdf

[3] Drimer 2009] Drimer, S. "Security for Volatile FPGAs", PhD Dissertation, Cambridge University, 2009.

[4] "Secure Hash Standard", FIPS PUB 180-2 + Change Notice to include SHA-224; August 1, 2002, http://csrc.nist.gov/publications/fips/fips180-2/fips180-2withchangenotice.pdf

[5] FIPS, "The Keyed-Hash Message Authentication Code (HMAC)", FIPS PUB 198; March 6, 2002, http://csrc.nist.gov/publications/fips/fips198-1/FIPS-198-1_final.pdf

[6] S. Knapp, "Authentication for Information Provided to an Integrated Circuit", US Patent 7768293

[7] NIST, Recommendation for Block Cipher Modes of Operation, NIST Special Publication 800-38A, 2001, http://csrc.nist.gov/publications/nistpubs/800-38a/sp800-38a.pdf

[8] M. Parlekar, "Authenticated Encryption in Hardware", Master's Thesis, GMU, 2005

[9] D. Parlour, "Intellectual property protection in a programmable logic device", US Patent 6,904,527

[10] S. Trimberger, "Trusted Design in FPGAs," *Design Automation Conference*, 2007, ACM.

[11] J. B. Webb, "Methods for Securing the Integrity of FPGA Configurations", MS Thesis, Virginia Polytechnic Institute and State University, 2006

[12] Xilinx, "Virtex-6 FPGA Configuration User Guide", UG360, July 30, 2010, http://www.xilinx.com/support/documentation/user_guides/ug360.pdf

A 65nm Flash-Based FPGA Fabric Optimized for Low Cost and Power

Jonathan Greene, Sinan Kaptanoglu, Wenyi Feng, Volker Hecht,
Joel Landry, Fei Li, Anton Krouglyanskiy, Mihai Morosan, Val Pevzner

Microsemi Corporation SOC Products Group
2061 Stierlin Court, Mountain View, CA 94043 USA
jonathan.greene@microsemi.com

ABSTRACT

This paper describes a non-volatile reprogrammable FPGA fabric, whose configuration data are provided directly by flash memory. The fabric is optimized for low-cost, low-power applications, leveraging the density of flash and the elimination of conventional configuration SRAM and its attendant static power. After surveying the necessary background on flash and its application to FPGAs, the 1T flash cell is described along with relevant novel aspects of the fabric architecture. The addition of a third level of switching between inter-cluster signals and logic inputs helps to reduce area and raise typical utilization above 95%. Despite the longer signal path, performance is maintained by synergism between the improved routing flexibility and extreme minimization of the fastest LUT input delay. Test cost is reduced by built-in circuits that can test all switches without reprogramming the flash memory. The fabric has been implemented in a 65nm CMOS embedded flash process.

Categories and Subject Descriptors

B.7.1 [**Integrated Circuits**]: Types and Design Style—*gate arrays*

General Terms

Design, Experimentation, Theory.

Keywords

FPGA architecture, flash memory, Clos network, built-in self-test, programmable routing, input interconnection block, IIB, packing

1. INTRODUCTION

The market for integrated circuits with embedded flash memory, principally microcontrollers, is expected to be about $8 billion in 2010 [1]. (This compares to about $4 billion for all types of FPGAs [2].) Embedded flash is clearly serving important market segments.

Flash can also bring significant advantages to FPGAs, especially for low-cost, low-power applications and when security or high reliability is important. Dense blocks of non-volatile memory can be integrated with the programmable logic, and the high-voltage transistors included in the flash process can be leveraged for analog circuitry, providing a multi-faceted system-on-a-chip.

There are two general ways embedded flash memory can be used to store configuration data in an FPGA. One is to integrate a conventional SRAM-based FPGA with a flash memory block from which the configuration can be loaded [3]. The other way is the focus of this paper: using flash memory to provide configuration data directly to the FPGA fabric's logic and interconnect. By replacing the configuration SRAM entirely, these truly flash-based FPGAs eliminate the attendant static power. Flash-based FPGAs are also immune to errors in configuration (firm errors) that may be caused when high-energy particles flip an SRAM bit (single-event upsets).

Flash-based FPGAs have been in the market for many years [4], but their special architectural considerations have not been previously described in the literature. This paper seeks to rectify that, and to describe a new flash FPGA fabric that is more efficient than its predecessors. It has been implemented in 65nm CMOS, and is targeted at low-cost and low-power applications.

Low cost is not simply a matter of raw logic elements per unit die area. By a few architecture changes, we demonstrate a significant increase in the utilization of the logic elements above the level typical of SRAM-based FPGAs. Test cost is another important issue, especially for smaller FPGAs.

SRAM-based FPGAs are generally tested by programming them with a sequence of hundreds of test designs [5][6][7]. Because flash-based FPGAs take longer to program, special care must be taken to limit the number of test designs required. This is not a problem for the simple, flat architectures of previous flash FPGAs [4], but would be for the more complex, clustered architecture described here. We therefore developed a novel built-in test method that eliminates the need for most test designs.

Section 2 covers essential background on flash technology, and its implications for flash FPGA architecture. Section 3 gives an overview of the architecture, focusing on its unique aspects. Section 4 reports some theoretical and experimental results concerning the architecture. Section 5 describes the new test scheme.

2. FLASH MEMORY ESSENTIALS

2.1 Technology

Figure 1 gives a diagram of an embedded flash process. The flash device has a second, floating gate on which charge may be stored. The amount of stored charge determines the threshold voltage Vt of the transistor. An additional deep n-well layer is used to isolate the flash devices, preventing high voltages present on them during programming from damaging the ordinary low-voltage logic. Special spacing rules apply between the floating gate and the ordinary low-voltage logic.

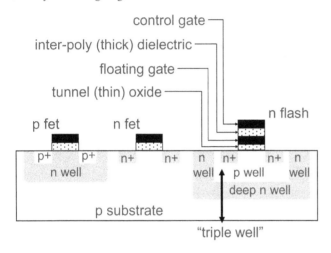

Figure 1: Embedded flash process.

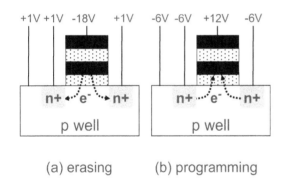

Figure 2: Erasing and programming.

Figure 2 shows how charge is stored or removed from the floating gate. The voltages shown are rough indications only.

During erase, electrons are removed from the floating gate by a mechanism known as Fowler-Nordheim tunneling [8], which lowers Vt and turns the device on. Erasing is typically done in bulk for all devices simultaneously because it takes on the order of seconds.

Once all devices are erased, selected devices are programmed. A device is selected by raising its control gate and lowering its source and/or drain. This adds electrons to the floating gate, again by tunneling. Programming is significantly faster than erase, on the order of milliseconds. Multiple devices may be programmed in parallel as long as they can be properly addressed; however, it is important not to activate any one control gate too many times to avoid disturbing devices that should remain erased. Programming may also be done by hot carrier injection instead of tunneling. Injection takes even less time than tunneling, but requires more current. Hence fewer devices can be programmed simultaneously with a fixed current budget. For details see [8].

Because of the voltages required for programming and erasing, flash processes include special high-voltage transistors with thicker oxides. (As mentioned above, these may also be useful for implementing analog circuitry.)

2.2 Flash Configuration Memory Cells

Figure 3 shows a "1T" flash configuration cell [9]. It replaces the conventional 6T SRAM and NMOS pass device with a single minimum-sized flash transistor (sense device) and a larger flash switch device that share a common floating gate. Programming and erasing is done using the sense device and the word and bit lines to which it is connected. The cell's state can also be read back to verify correct programming in a similar way.

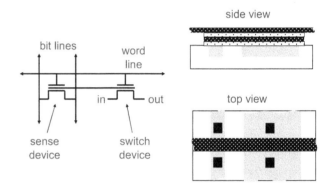

Figure 3: 1T cell schematic and conceptual layout.

During operation, the word line is set to an appropriate bias voltage. In the erased (on) state, the switch's Vt is low enough that the switch will pass full Vdd, eliminating the need for the level-restoring devices sometimes required with NMOS pass devices ([10], p. 107). The Vt in the off state is high enough that typical leakage is on the order of only 10pA.

The 1T cell is able to retain its configuration with zero static power. In addition, it is immune to firm errors caused by high-energy particles [11].

Non-volatile FPGAs have a unique niche in high-radiation environments, notably aerospace applications, so it is important to consider the cell's suitability for such uses. Radiation can cause some loss of charge from the floating gate, raising the on-resistance or lowering the off-resistance [9]. Studies on prior 130nm FPGAs using this cell indicate a performance loss of 10% occurs only after a total ionizing dose (TID) of 22Krad for gamma rays. However it is possible to extend the dose by periodically reprogramming the configuration [12], in a manner conceptually similar to refresh in DRAMs. Configuration errors would not be encountered between properly scheduled refreshes, as would be the case between periodic scrubbings of firm errors in SRAM FPGAs.

If superior radiation tolerance is required, the alternative "2T" cell of Figure 4 may be considered [13]. It includes a pair of n- and p-channel flash devices controlling an NMOS switch device. During normal operation, VSP is at a positive voltage, VSN is at ground, and appropriate biases are applied to VCGP and VCGN. Either one or the other flash device is programmed to conduct, thus turning the switch on or off. Provided that VSP is sufficiently high, the switch can still pass a full Vdd. As the name would imply, the 2T cell is less dense than the 1T, but is highly radiation tolerant.

Because our goal is to support low-cost commercial applications, we employed the 1T cell for this work. However many of our findings would also apply to architectures using the 2T cell.

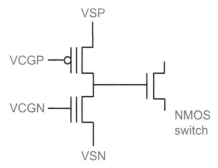

Figure 4: 2T flash configuration cell [13].

2.3 Implications for Architecture

Due to the required well spacings and separation between floating gates and logic, it is most efficient to segregate flash and low-voltage logic into separate stripes in the layout. An appropriate tradeoff must be made between using a few wide stripes to minimize the total separation area versus using many narrow stripes to minimize the length of wires connecting the switches and logic.

Minimizing the capacitance downstream of the switches is important for good performance, especially if the on-resistance of flash switches exceeds that of nmos pass gates. Also, the integration of the sense and switch devices in one cell means that it is very cheap to independently control each switch. These factors tend to favor use of routing muxes having a single level of switches and lower fan-in than is customary in SRAM FPGAs.

This reasoning is exemplified in Figure 5. Part (a) shows a typical 16-input routing mux for an SRAM FPGA, realized as a two-level structure comprised of 20 switches sharing 8 configuration bits. For comparison, part (b) shows two independent flash muxes with a reduced fan-in of 8. These use a total of sixteen 1T flash cells. (The sense devices, not shown, consume negligible area.) With 20% fewer switches and no configuration SRAM, the two flash muxes consume significantly less area. Yet they offer 8x8=64 routing alternatives, instead of only 16 for the SRAM alternative.

During program or erase operations, it is necessary for at least one of the switch device's source/drain terminals be held at Vdd. This is accomplished by replacing the last stage of all routing buffers with a circuit such as that shown in Figure 6. Here NGND is a global switched supply that is at ground during normal operation but raised to Vdd during programming. The pullup ensures that the output is high no matter what the state of the input. The pullup may be

minimum-sized and has no impact on performance (unlike the similarly-situated level-restoring pullups found in some FPGAs).

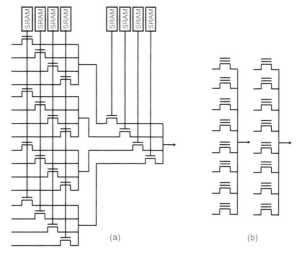

Figure 5: Muxes configured by SRAM vs. flash.

(a) A conventional 16-input mux with 8 SRAM configuration bits. (b) Two 8-input muxes using the 1T flash cell. (The minimum-sized sense device associated with each switch is omitted for clarity.)

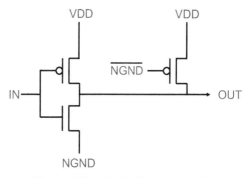

Figure 6: Routing buffer power gating.

3. ARCHITECTURE OVERVIEW

Our goal for the architecture was to make it efficient for flash technology while achieving a balance of area and delay suitable for low-cost applications.

3.1 Logic Cells

The basic logic element (BLE) comprises a 4-input look-up table (LUT) and a dedicated flip-flop, as shown in Figure 7. The LUT size is appropriate for a low-cost, low-power architecture [14]. The flip-flop has control inputs for enable, and synchronous and asynchronous set/reset. Dedicated carry-chain support is also provided.

Each BLE produces a LUT output Y and a flip-flop output Q. (The carry output is connected directly, and only, to the next BLE's carry input.) For efficient packing, the LUT and flip-flop in a BLE can both be used independently, without either one's output having to drive an input of the other. Unlike the standard VPR architecture [15] we do not reduce the Y and Q outputs via an "OUT" mux to a single output. Instead, both Y and Q are made directly accessible to the routing.

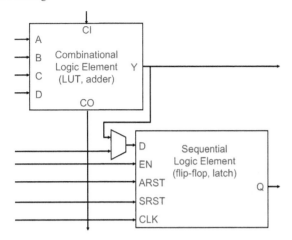

Figure 7: Basic logic element.

The LUT inputs are denoted A, B, C and D, in order of increasing delay. The LUT circuit was optimized to minimize the delay of the A input as much as possible without unduly impacting the average input delay, obtaining a ratio of 4.8 between the delay of the D and A inputs. The speed of the D input is relatively slow in part because a flash configuration mux selecting from among 0, 1, D and $\overline{D}$ is used instead of the traditional two-input mux with D as the select input; this saves area. Figure 8 illustrates this for the first two levels of a LUT.

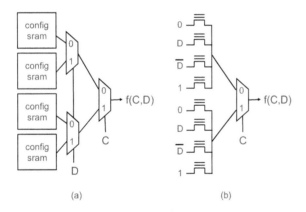

Figure 8: LUT implementations: (a) SRAM; (b) flash.

We found that a cluster size of 11 was optimum for area-delay product, but the curve was fairly flat over a range of 10 to 14. We chose a cluster size of 12 because it is divisible by a variety of factors, which helps maximize layout symmetry when providing routing resources in various appropriate quantities. For example, a resource of which three are required per cluster could be laid out in units of four BLEs, while a resource of which four are required per cluster could be laid out in units of three BLEs.

Most often, a LUT output in the fabric can be inverted and the downstream logic adjusted to compensate. Design software can thus automatically choose LUT output polarities to minimize static power, or to help balance rise and fall delays along a critical path [16]. Compensating at a downstream LUT input is simply a matter of adjusting the LUT function. An inversion at the D input of the flip-flop is handled by propagating the inversion forward to the flip-flop's output and interchanging set and reset options. Finally, all clock and control inputs to the flip-flops may be optionally inverted at the cluster level. This last feature also facilitates support for rising and falling edge flip-flops, and active-high or active-low control signals.

To aid debugging, the state of any two flip-flops may be read continuously at two IOs (analogous to a "peek" in memory terms). The flip-flop addresses are provided via a JTAG interface. In addition, the state of any flip-flop can also be set ("poked"), again via JTAG.

3.2 Routing
Inter-cluster routing tracks of various lengths are provided. Linear tracks of length 1, 2 and 5 clusters are provided in all four directions. A few longer tracks are also provided; their exact quantity and length depend on the size of the FPGA, which may range from less than 1K to over 200K BLEs.

Intra-cluster routing to the LUT inputs was a special challenge, primarily because such routing typically has muxes with high fan-ins that would be suboptimal for a flash implementation. Our solution is described in the next section.

A smaller but analogous intra-cluster routing network drives the flip-flop inputs. These include clock and control signals (enable, set/reset), as well as a separate data input so the flip-flop can be used independently of the LUT. This routing network primarily receives input from a dedicated global signal (e.g., clock) distribution network, but also receives input from a few of the ordinary external signals and muxes used to drive the LUT inputs.

Rows of RAM or math blocks can be embedded in the fabric. Because of the changes to our intra-cluster routing, the larger bandwidth requirements of these embedded blocks are accommodated without any alterations to the pattern of inter-cluster routing (such as providing additional tracks). The external connections of a RAM or math block interface tile exactly match those of an ordinary logic cluster.

With one exception described in the next section, the output of each routing mux is immediately buffered to minimize capacitive load.

3.3 Highlights of Intra-Cluster Routing
This section describes how external (inter-cluster) signals and feedback from BLE outputs reach the LUT inputs.

Initially, we considered a traditional two-level network (like figure 3.1 of [15]), as exemplified in Figure 9. Even with 50% depopulation of the cross bar, fan-in is 20 on the muxes comprising the crossbar, and 24 on the preceding muxes. Such high fan-ins are suboptimal for implementation in flash switches. In addition, the fact that each external signal drives more than one mux in the cluster adds capacitive loading due to the spur wires needed to tie each fan-out to the main inter-cluster trunk carrying the signal. Finally, this scheme permits only 28 external signals to be routed to the LUT inputs. This narrow bandwidth can be limiting, especially for logic using the carry chain or interfaces to RAM or math blocks embedded in the fabric. (Of course more first-level muxes can be added, but this would require more flexibility in the crossbar and additional area).

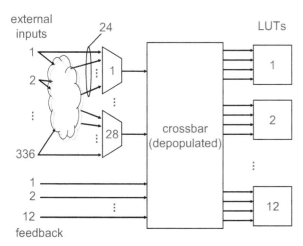

Figure 9: Two-level cluster input routing scheme.

The cloud represents an arbitrary permutation.

A recent paper [17] proposed an alternate architecture, reducing the crossbar population to 25% and the fan-out on external signals to one. It addresses the fan-in, spur, and bandwidth problems. However it allows only 25% of the external and feedback inputs to reach the fast A inputs of the LUTs, which can impact performance.

Instead, we replace the crossbar with a Clos network [10] [18], as shown in Figure 10. Normally a Clos network is built of three levels of (smaller) crossbars, but because the LUT inputs are interchangeable (except for speed differences), the third level is absorbed by the LUTs.[1] The total number of levels of switches between external signals and LUT inputs is thus increased only from two to three.

The efficiency of the Clos network allows a larger number of inputs to the second level than was the case with the single large crossbar. The added inputs were as follows. For improved performance, about 10% of the external signals are allowed to also bypass the first level muxes and drive the second level directly. The number of first level muxes driving the second level is significantly increased, which allows us to reduce their fan-in.

For improved intra-cluster routability, feedbacks from both LUTs and flip-flops are sent to the first level muxes. For improved performance, feedback from each LUT is also sent to the third-level crossbar driving the fastest LUT inputs. We did not provide direct feedback from flip-flops to levels 2 or 3 because flip-flops are less likely to drive only intra-cluster signals.

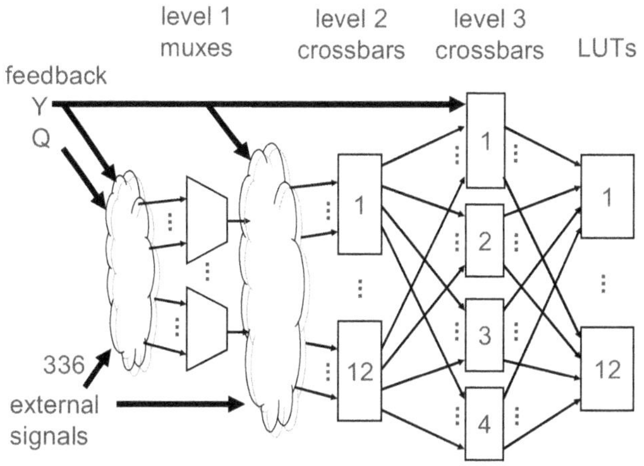

Figure 10: Three-level cluster input routing.

The clouds represent permutations, and the thick lines represent bundles of wires.

The obvious disadvantage of the added level of switching is extra delay. This is mitigated in three ways. First, the spur line capacitance is reduced because most external signals now drive only one load (per cluster). Also, notice that each crossbar in level 2 and the muxes in level 1 driving it can be laid out in a compact unit. This allows us to keep wires short and avoid intermediate buffers. As a result, the additional delay due to the added level of switching is under 100ps. Finally, as we show in Section 4.3 below, the increased flexibility of the three-level scheme helps route the most critical nets to the fastest LUT inputs.

To save area, we limit the number of middle-level crossbars in the Clos network to four, even though this is insufficient to make it rearrangeably non-blocking. Further savings are achieved by depopulating portions of the crossbars. The second-level crossbars are only 78% populated for inputs from the first-level muxes, and 25% for external inputs. The feedback inputs to the third-level crossbar are only 25% populated.

Despite the added routing paths, total switch and buffer area is reduced by about 20% compared with the two-level scheme. The maximum fan-in is reduced to 12 for most muxes in the third level and 15 for those receiving feedback. The fan-in for the first and second-level muxes is reduced to less than 10. Every external and feedback signal can (in the absence of conflicts) be routed to the fastest input of any LUT if it is necessary for speed. The bandwidth limit on incoming external signals is eliminated.

3.4 Low-power Features

A low-leakage process is used to minimize static power while still achieving the desired performance.

As described in Section 0, flash technology requires power gating the routing buffers. It is therefore a simple step to extend the power gating to the logic as well and support a power-down mode to reduce static power. During this mode, the state of the flip-flops is retained in low-power latches. Likewise the block RAMs may be put in a low-power mode that retains their state but reduces static power.

---

[1] Similar networks have been proposed for multi-FPGA emulation systems connected by multiple crossbar ICs where each FPGA, like one of our LUTs, has interchangeable inputs. See, e.g., [19].

It is also possible to power down all but a portion of the fabric. This remaining live portion may be used to implement wakeup logic in soft gates, for example.

Dedicated clock gating circuitry is provided on the global signal distribution networks at the root and at an intermediate point along the H-tree.

The fabric circuitry and layout is designed to be manufactured in either of two versions: a performance version that uses a mixture of standard and high threshold voltage transistors, and a low-power version that uses only high threshold voltage devices.

4. ARCHITECTURE EVALUATION

This section presents a few theoretical and experimental results supporting the noted features of the architecture. (It is not intended as a complete validation of the architecture.)

The benchmark designs used included a variety of industrial circuits, including microprocessors, encoding circuits, etc. In addition, we employed synthetic designs constructed by stitching together smaller designs in a way that satisfied Rent's rule and maintained the statistical properties (e.g. fan-out distribution) of the industrial circuits. Timing-driven placement and routing was rerun for each experimental situation with multiple random seeds and the results averaged. A modified version of our commercial design software was used.

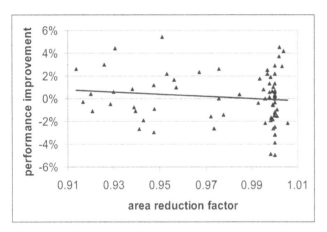

Figure 11: Change in performance and area from allowing up to two I5-packed BLEs per cluster vs. none.

4.1 Impact of Packing on Utilization

As mentioned above, the architecture supports packing an independent LUT and flip-flop in same BLE even when the flip-flop data input and four LUT inputs all come from outside the BLE. We refer to this as I5 packing. This support costs only a small amount of area, about 0.5%, but it is nevertheless interesting to see if it proves worthwhile. A limit on the number of I5-packed BLEs in a cluster is imposed by the clustering software to avoid undue congestion. We evaluated a set of test designs under various values of this limit. Allowing up to two I5 BLEs per cluster reduced the total number of clusters by about 2% on average, with diminishing returns for higher limits.

We compared the area (number of clusters used) and performance of our benchmark designs with an I5 limit of 2 versus a baseline of 0

(no I5 packing allowed). The results are plotted in Figure 11. While most designs were not greatly improved, some saw area reductions of up to 9%. As shown by the least-squares fit line, average performance was maintained.

4.2 Theoretical Comparison of Cluster Input Routability

For purposes of this section, we assume that the four signals driving each LUT may be routed to the LUT inputs in any permutation.

A useful way to quantify routing flexibility is the logarithm of the number of distinct sets of routable connections, or "routing entropy" [17]. For example, the entropy of a cluster's internal interconnect has been shown to correlate with the demands it imposes on usage of inter-cluster resources.

The entropy of the three-level scheme is at least 25.9 bits per LUT. This lower bound is obtained by: giving credit to the second and third level switches only for unicast routes; ignoring the added feedback connections to levels 1 and 3; and ignoring external connections to level 2.

This compares to bounds of 24.6 to 26.2 bits per LUT for the two-level scheme even with a <u>fully</u> populated crossbar (see [17] for details). So the three-level scheme is likely to have routability as good or better despite its lower area.

The next section provides some experimental support for this conclusion.

4.3 Impact of Utilization on Performance

A prior study [20] of a particular two-level architecture found that as utilization is increased, performance declines. In particular, an 18% increase in utilization results in a 5% decrease in performance. We tested whether our architecture escaped this tradeoff by comparing the performance at low and high utilizations. This was accomplished by generating two appropriate-sized virtual FPGAs to test each design, a larger array for lower utilization and a smaller array for higher utilization. Here, utilization is defined as the fraction of BLEs in the chip that are used. The geometric mean utilization of the designs in their respective small arrays is 80%, and the geometric mean utilization of the designs in their respective large arrays is 97%. For each design, the utilization in the smaller array is always at least 1.12 times that in the larger array.

Results are shown in Figure 12. The vertical axis is the ratio of frequency at high utilization to frequency at low utilization. The geometric mean of this ratio across designs is 1.00, showing that performance is not degraded by higher utilization.

4.4 Impact of LUT Input Delay Distribution on Performance

The previous section shows that performance is maintained even for utilizations exceeding 95%. We hypothesize that this is so at least in part because the routing network (and the three-level cluster input network in particular) is able to preferentially route the most critical nets to the fastest LUT inputs. To quantify the magnitude of this effect, we compared the maximum achievable clock frequency using our skewed LUT input delays to that obtained when the LUT input delays are equalized to their average value. The results are shown in Figure 13. The vertical axis is the ratio of frequency with our stated LUT delays to frequency with equalized delays. The geometric mean of this ratio across all test designs is 1.13.

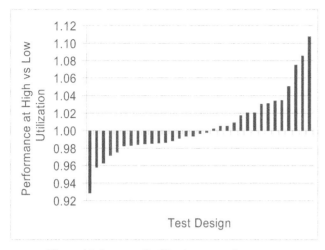

Figure 12: Impact of utilization on performance.

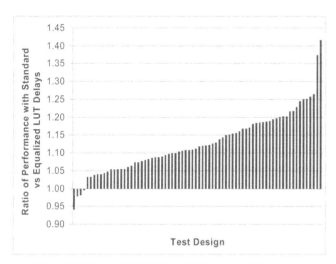

Figure 13: Impact of LUT input delays on performance.

5. TEST COST REDUCTION

Various categories of faults must be covered to ensure correct functionality of a reprogrammable FPGA, including:

- faults in logic cell and routing buffers

- bridging (shorts) between routing tracks

- routing switches that are stuck closed or open, or discontinuities in routing tracks

The third category accounts for the vast majority of the necessary tests in our fabric. (This has also been found to be the case for SRAM FPGAs [7]). In the remainder of this section we describe test circuitry we added to our fabric to cover such faults without needing to program any test designs.

The first requirement is some means to exert control of the switches in the 1T flash configuration cells. Recall that to support programming, the switches are arranged in an array, with a word line connected to the control gates of all switches in a row, as shown in Figure 14. (The sense devices have been omitted for clarity). If all switches are set to the same threshold voltage (e.g. all erased),

selected rows of switches can all be turned on or off by raising or lowering the word lines to appropriate voltages. This addressing capability, though limited, suffices for our purpose.

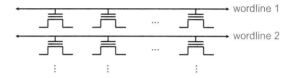

Figure 14: Addressing switches by row.

The next requirement is a means of driving all the routing tracks to a known logic state. Here we take advantage of the pullups and switched ground supply associated with the routing buffers (Figure 6). Finally, we must be able to observe at least one input to each mux. This is done by reusing the bit lines and sense amps already provided for programming. Figure 15 shows a typical test path for two switches in a mux. The word lines for these switches are activated, and TSTEN is raised to reconnect input B to the bit line. If switches A or B are stuck open, or if there is a break in the relevant portion of track 1, the sense amp input will not be pulled high. Most muxes have at least one input that is a constant, and thus is never in the speed path; these are the best choices for the input to be observed via the TSTEN devices. The only additional circuitry required are the devices controlled by TSTEN.

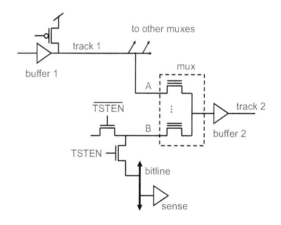

Figure 15: A typical test path.

Some care is required to ensure that all switches can be properly addressed for testing. For instance, no mux can have two of its switches in the same row. Similar techniques can also cover stuck-closed switches. A full explanation is beyond the scope of this paper, but we illustrate below two of the more interesting complications that must be dealt with.

Figure 16 illustrates how parallel paths may arise. When testing switches A and B in mux 1, switches C and D in mux 2 must also be turned on since they share the same word lines. This forms a parallel path from Vdd to A via track 2, C, Y, and D. As a result we may miss a break in track 1 at the indicated location. However this test in combination with a separate test of switches D and E in mux 2 will assure continuity of all parts of track 1.

Another complication arises if there are unbuffered muxes (such as the level 1 muxes in Figure 10). Figure 17(a) represents a wiring tree of unknown topology with input pins A and B, and output pins C and D. Figure 17(b) shows how such a tree may arise when the tree is driven by an unbuffered mux. Suppose we have verified continuity from A to C with one test (c) and from B to D with another test (d). Have we completely verified continuity of the wiring tree? It depends on the layout of the tree. For the layout in Figure 17(e), the answer is yes. For the layout in (f), the answer is no; we might have missed a break at the indicated position in the center of the wiring tree.

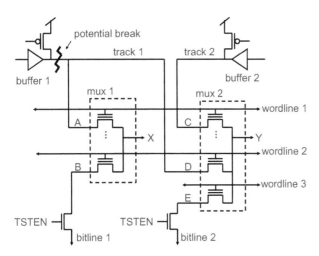

Figure 16: A test path with a loop.

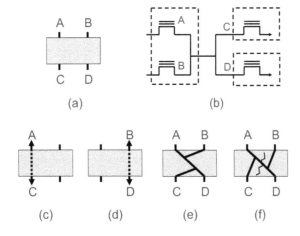

Figure 17: Wiring tree connectivity.

With careful handling of these and other issues, our new test method is able to cover all track discontinuity and stuck-open and stuck-closed switch faults, greatly reducing the number of test designs and reducing test cost.

A common observation is that another type of non-volatile FPGA, using one-time-programmable antifuses, can be tested without programming even once [21]. Why then do we still need any test designs at all for flash FPGAs? The answer is that mux-based routing lacks the regularity of antifuse routing. This makes our mixed approach of mostly built-in testing with a very limited number of conventional test designs less costly than supporting complete built-in testing as in antifuse FPGAs.

6. DISCUSSION

An integrated circuit embodying the fabric has been fabricated in a 65nm CMOS embedded flash process at UMC.

Typical static power per BLE for the high threshold-voltage implementation at 25C is 6 nW in operation, and 0.1 nW in power-down mode.

The design tools (synthesis, placement, and routing) are similar to what would be used for an SRAM-based FPGA. No flash-specific algorithms are required.

Our novel cluster input routing network reduces area while providing improved routability and good performance, at least in the context of our fabric. It may be interesting to reexamine other portions of FPGA routing, such as inter-cluster routing, to see if similar ideas can be applied.

Our testing method substantially reduced the number of test designs required to cover switch and routing track faults. This is vital for flash FPGAs. Similar techniques might be useful for other types of FPGAs, or even in other contexts such as programmable interconnect or switch network ICs.

We also hope that after becoming familiar with the benefits and requirements of non-volatile configuration memory, FPGA researchers may be motivated to invent new architectures that further exploit its advantages.

7. ACKNOWLEDGMENTS

Fethi Dhaoui and John McCollum were instrumental in helping us understand and apply flash technology. Kris Vorwerk and Kai Zhu provided software infrastructure and much useful expertise for architecture experiments. Vidya Bellippady, Marcel Derevlean, Dirk Kannemacher, Victor Nguyen, Bill Plants, and Nicola Telecco made key contributions to the silicon design and implementation. JJ Wang and Sana Rezgui provided references on radiation tolerance. We also thank the reviewers for their helpful suggestions.

8. REFERENCES

[1] Semico Research Corp. 2009. www.semico.com.

[2] Gartner Semiconductor Forecast, Nov. 25, 2009.

[3] Lattice Semiconductor Corp. 2008. *LatticeXP2 Family Data Sheet* (Feb. 2008).

[4] ProASIC Plus and ProASIC3 FPGA families, Actel Corp. www.actel.com.

[5] Huang, W., Meyer, F., Chen, X., Lombardi, F. 1998. Testing configurable LUT-based FPGAs. *IEEE Trans. VLSI Systems*, 6, 2 (June 1998), 276-283. DOI=http://dx.doi.org/10.1109/92.678888.

[6] Tahoori, M., Mitra, S. 2005. Application-independent testing of FPGA interconnects. *IEEE Trans. Computer-Aided Design of Integrated Circuits and Systems*, 24, 11 (Nov. 2005), 1774-1783. DOI=http://dx.doi.org/10.1109/TCAD.2005.852452.

[7] Dhingra, S., Garimella, S., Newalkar, A., and Stroud, C. 2005. Built-in self-test for Virtex and Spartan II FPGAs using partial reconfiguration. *Proc. IEEE North Atlantic Test Workshop*, 7-14.
http://www.eng.auburn.edu/~strouce/class/bist/NATW05fpga.pdf

[8] Brown, W. and Brewer, J. 1998. *Nonvolatile Semiconductor Memory Technology*. IEEE Press.

[9] Wang, J.J., Samiee, S., Chen, H.-S., Huang, C.-K., Cheung, M., Borillo, J., Sun, S.-N., Cronquist, B., and McCollum, J. 2004. Total ionizing dose effects on flash-based field programmable gate array. *IEEE Trans. Nuc. Sci.*, 51, 6 (Dec. 2004), 3759-3766.
DOI=http://dx.doi.org/10.1109/TNS.2004.839255.

[10] Lemieux, G. and Lewis, D. 2004. *Design of Interconnection Networks for Programmable Logic.* Kluwer Academic, Boston, MA.

[11] Rezgui, S., Wang, J., Sun, Y., Cronquist, B., and McCollum, J. 2008. New Reprogrammable and Non-Volatile Radiation Tolerant FPGA: RTA3P. *2008 IEEE Aerospace Conference* (Big Sky, MT, March 1-8, 2008), 1-11.
DOI=http://dx.doi.org/10.1109/AERO.2008.4526472.

[12] Actel Corp. 2010. *Radiation-Tolerant ProASIC3 FPGAs Radiation Effects.* April, 2010.
www.actel.com/documents/RT3P_Rad_Rpt.pdf

[13] Wang, J., Rezgui, S., Sun, Y., Issaq, F., Cronquist, B., McCollum, J., Chan, R., Pan, H., and Kabir, S. 2008. A novel radiation-tolerant floating-gate configuration cell for flash-based FPGA. *2008 IEEE Nuclear and Space Radiation Effects Conf.* (Tucson, AZ, July 14-18, 2008).

[14] Li, F., Chen, D., He, L., Cong, J. 2003. Architecture evaluation of power-efficient FPGAs. In *Proc. 2003 ACM Int'l Symp. on FPGAs* (Monterey, CA, Feb., 2003), 175-184.
DOI=http://doi.acm.org/10.1145/611817.611844.

[15] Betz, V. Rose, J., Marquardt, A. 1999. *Architecture and CAD for Deep-submicron FPGAs.* Kluwer Academic Publishers, Boston.

[16] Zhu, K. 2007. Post-route LUT output polarity selection for timing optimization. In *Proc. 2007 ACM Int'l Symp. FPGAs* (Monterey, CA, Feb. 18-20, 2007). 89-96.
DOI=http://doi.acm.org/10.1145/1216919.1216932.

[17] Feng, W., Kaptanoglu, S., 2008. Designing efficient input interconnect blocks for LUT clusters using counting and entropy, *ACM Transactions on Reconfigurable Technology and Systems*, 1, 1 (March 2008).
DOI=http://doi.acm.org/10.1145/1331897.1331902.

[18] Clos, C. 1953. A study of nonblocking switching networks. *Bell System Tech. J. 32*, 406-424.

[19] Lewis, D., Galloway, D., van Ierssel, M., Rose, J., Chow, P. 1998. The transmogrifier-2: a 1 million gate rapid-prototyping system. *IEEE Trans. VLSI Systems,* 6, 2 (June 1998), 188-198.
DOI=http://dx.doi.org/10.1109/92.678867.

[20] Leventis, P., Chan, M., Lewis, D., Nouban, B., Powell, G., Vest, B., Wong, M., Xia, R., and Costello, J. 2003. Cyclone™: a low-cost, high-performance FPGA. In *Proc. IEEE 2003 Custom Integrated Circuits Conf.* (Sept. 21-24 2003). 49-52.
DOI=http://dx.doi.org/10.1109/CICC.2003.1249357.

[21] Greene, J., Hamdy, E., and Beal, S. 1993. Antifuse field programmable gate arrays. *Proc. IEEE*, 81, 7 (July 1993), 1042-1056. DOI=http://dx.doi.org/10.1109/5.231343.

CoRAM: An In-Fabric Memory Architecture for FPGA-based Computing

Eric S. Chung, James C. Hoe, and Ken Mai

Carnegie Mellon University
5000 Forbes Ave.
Pittsburgh, PA 15213
{echung, jhoe, kenmai}@ece.cmu.edu

ABSTRACT

FPGAs have been used in many applications to achieve orders-of-magnitude improvement in absolute performance and energy efficiency relative to conventional microprocessors. Despite their promise in both processing performance and efficiency, FPGAs have not yet gained widespread acceptance as mainstream computing devices. A fundamental obstacle to FPGA-based computing today is the FPGA's lack of a common, scalable memory architecture. When developing applications for FPGAs, designers are often directly responsible for crafting the application-specific infrastructure logic that manages and transports data to and from the processing kernels. This infrastructure not only increases design time and effort but will frequently lock a design to a particular FPGA product line, hindering scalability and portability. We propose a new FPGA memory architecture called Connected RAM (CoRAM) to serve as a portable bridge between the distributed computation kernels and the external memory interfaces. In addition to improving performance and efficiency, the CoRAM architecture provides a virtualized memory environment as seen by the hardware kernels to simplify development and to improve an application's portability and scalability.

Categories and Subject Descriptors

C.0 [**Computer System Organization**]: [System architectures]

General Terms

Design, standardization

Keywords

FPGA, abstraction, memory, reconfigurable computing

1. INTRODUCTION

With power becoming a first-class architectural constraint, future computing devices will need to look beyond

general-purpose processors. Among the computing alternatives today, Field Programmable Gate Arrays (FPGA) have been applied to many applications to achieve orders-of-magnitude improvement in absolute performance and energy efficiency relative to conventional microprocessors (e.g., [11, 6, 5]). A recent study [6] further showed that FPGA fabrics can be an effective computing substrate for floating-point intensive numerical applications.

While the accumulated VLSI advances have steadily improved the FPGA fabric's processing capability, FPGAs have not yet gained widespread acceptance as mainstream computing devices. A commonly cited obstacle is the difficulty in programming FPGAs using low-level hardware development flows. A fundamental problem lies in the FPGA's lack of a common, scalable memory architecture for application designers. When developing for an FPGA, a designer has to create from bare fabric not only the application kernel itself but also the application-specific infrastructure logic to support and optimize the transfer of data to and from external memory interfaces. Very often, creating or using this infrastructure logic not only increases design time and effort but will frequently lock a design to a particular FPGA product line, hindering scalability and portability. Further, the support mechanisms which users are directly responsible for will be increasingly difficult to manage in the future as: (1) memory resources (both on- and off-chip) increase in number and become more distributed across the fabric, and (2) long-distance interconnect delays become more difficult to tolerate in larger fabric designs.

Current FPGAs lack essential abstractions that one comes to expect in a general purpose computer—i.e., an Instruction Set Architecture (ISA) that defines a standard agreement between hardware and software. From a computing perspective, a common architectural definition is a critical ingredient for programmability and for application portability. To specifically address the challenges related to memory on FPGAs, the central goal of this work is to create a shared, scalable memory architecture suitable for future FPGA-based computing devices. Such a memory architecture would be used in a way that is analogous to how general purpose programs universally access main memory through standard "loads" and "stores" as defined by an ISA—without any knowledge of hierarchy details such as caches, memory controllers, etc. At the same time, the FPGA memory architecture definition cannot simply adopt what exists for general purpose processors and instead, should reflect the spatially distributed nature of today's FPGAs—consisting

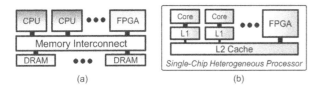

Figure 1: Assumed System Context.

of up to millions of interconnected LUTs and thousands of embedded SRAMs [24]. Working under the above premises, the guiding principles for the desired FPGA memory architecture are:

- *The architecture should present to the user a common, virtualized appearance of the FPGA fabric, which encompasses reconfigurable logic, its external memory interfaces, and the multitude of SRAMs—while freeing designers from details irrelevant to the application itself.*

- *The architecture should provide a standard, easy-to-use mechanism for controlling the transport of data between memory interfaces and the SRAMs used by the application throughout the course of computation.*

- *The abstraction should be amenable to scalable FPGA microarchitectures without affecting the architectural view presented to existing applications.*

Outline. Section 2 presents an overview of the CoRAM memory architecture. Section 3 discusses a possible microarchitectural space for implementing CoRAM. Section 4 demonstrates concrete usage of CoRAM for three example application kernels—Black-Scholes, Matrix-Matrix Multiplication and Sparse Matrix-Vector Multiplication. Section 5 presents an evaluation of various microarchitectural approaches. We discuss related work in Section 6 and offer conclusions in Section 7.

2. CORAM ARCHITECTURE

2.1 System Context

The CoRAM memory architecture assumes the co-existence of FPGA-based computing devices along with general-purpose processors in the context of a shared memory multiprocessor system (see Figure 1). The CoRAM architecture assumes that reconfigurable logic resources will exist either as stand-alone FPGAs on a multiprocessor memory bus or integrated as fabric into a single-chip heterogeneous multicore. Regardless of the configuration, it is assumed that memory interfaces for loading from and storing to a linear address space will exist at the boundaries of the reconfigurable logic (referred to as edge memory in this paper). These implementation-specific edge memory interfaces could be realized as dedicated memory/bus controllers or even coherent cache interfaces. Like commercial systems available today (e.g., Convey Computer [8]), reconfigurable logic devices can directly access the same virtual address space of general purpose processors (e.g., by introducing MMUs at the boundaries of fabric). The combined integration of virtual memory and direct access to the memory bus allows applications to be efficiently and easily partitioned across general-purpose processors and FPGAs, while leveraging the unique strengths of each respective device. A nearby processor is useful for handling tasks not well-suited to FPGAs—e.g., providing the OS environment, executing system calls,

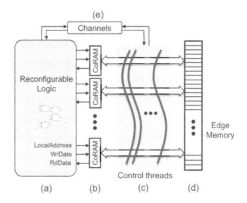

Figure 2: CoRAM Memory Architecture.

and initializing the memory contents of an application prior to its execution on the FPGA.

2.2 Architectural Overview

Within the boundaries of reconfigurable logic, the CoRAM architecture defines a portable application environment that enforces a separation of concerns between computation and on-chip memory management. Figure 2 offers a conceptual view of how applications are decomposed when mapped into reconfigurable logic with CoRAM support. The reconfigurable logic component shown in Figure 2a is a collection of LUT-based resources used to host the algorithmic kernels of a user application. It is important to note that the CoRAM architecture places no restriction on the synthesis language used or the internal complexity of the user application. For portability reasons, the only requirement is that user logic is never permitted to directly interface with off-chip I/O pins, access memory interfaces, or be aware of platform-specific details. Instead, applications can only interact with the external environment through a collection of specialized, distributed SRAMs called CoRAMs that provide on-chip storage for application data (see Figure 2b).

CoRAMs. Much like current FPGA memory architectures, CoRAMs preserve the desirable characteristics of conventional fabric-embedded SRAM [16]—they present a simple, wire-level SRAM interface to the user logic with local address spaces and deterministic access times (see Figure 2b), are spatially distributed, and provide high aggregate on-chip bandwidth. They can be further composed and configured with flexible aspect ratios. CoRAMs, however, deviate drastically from conventional embedded SRAMs in the sense that the data contents of individual CoRAMs are actively managed by finite state machines called "control threads" as shown in Figure 2c.

Control threads. Control threads form a distributed collection of logical, asynchronous finite state machines for mediating data transfers between CoRAMs and the edge memory interface. Each CoRAM is managed by at most a single control thread, although a control thread could manage multiple CoRAMs. Under the CoRAM architectural paradigm, user logic relies solely on control threads to access external main memory over the course of computation. Control threads and user logic are peer entities that interact over predefined, two-way asynchronous channels (see Figure 2e). A control thread maintains local state to facilitate its activities and will typically issue address requests to the edge memory interface on behalf of the application; upon completion, the control thread informs the user logic through channels when the data within specific CoRAMs are ready to be accessed through their locally-addressed SRAM interfaces. Conversely, the user logic can also write its computational results into CoRAMs and issue "commands" to the control threads via channels to write the results to edge memory.

Control actions. To express the memory access requirements of an FPGA application, control threads can only invoke a predefined set of memory and communication primitives called control actions. Control actions describe logical memory transfer commands between specific embedded CoRAMs and the edge memory interface. A control thread at the most basic level comprises a sequence of control actions to be executed over the course of a program. In general, a control thread issues control actions along a dynamic sequence that can include cycles and conditional paths.

Software versus RTL. An important issue that merits early discussion is in determining what the "proper" level of abstraction should be for expressing control threads and control actions. The most straightforward approach to exposing control actions to user logic is to distribute standard, wire-level interfaces throughout the fabric. In this case, the application designer would be directly responsible for constructing hardware control threads (i.e., FSM) that generate memory address requests on behalf of the user logic and issue control actions through the standard interfaces.

In this paper, we make the key observation that from a performance perspective, expressing control threads in a low-level abstraction such as RTL is not a critical requirement. In many cases, the process of generating address requests to main memory is not a limiting factor to FPGA application performance since most time is either spent waiting for memory responses or for computation to progress. For the remainder of this paper, it is assumed that control threads are expressed in a high-level C-based language to facilitate the dynamic sequencing of control actions.

Our selection of a C-based language affords an application developer not only simpler but also more natural expressions of control flow and memory pointer manipulations. The control threads implemented in software would be limited to a subset of the C language and would exclude "software" features such as dynamic memory allocation. Any high-level language used must be synthesizable to finite state machines or even compiled to hard microcontrollers that can execute control thread programs directly if available in an FPGA. Generally, the overall inefficiencies of executing a high-level language would not directly impede the overall computation throughput because the control threads do not "compute" in any usual sense and are used only to generate and sequence the control actions required by an application.

2.3 CoRAM Architecture in Detail

In this section, we describe in detail the standard memory management interface exported by control actions, and how they are invoked within control threads. Figure 3 illustrates the set of control actions available to an application developer. The control actions shown have the appearance of a memory management API, and abstract away the details of the underlying hardware support—similar to the role served by the Instruction Set Architecture (ISA) between software and evolving hardware implementations. As will be demonstrated later in Section 4, the basic set of con-

```
/*** CoRAM handle definition and acquisition ***/
struct {int n; int width; int depth; ...} coh;
coh  get_coram(instance_name, ...);
coh  append_coram(coh coram, bool interleave, ...);

/*** Singleton control actions ***/
void coram_read(coh coram, void *offset,
                void *memaddr, int bytes);
tag  coram_read_nb(coh coram, ...);
void coram_write(coh coram, void *offset,
                 void *memaddr, int bytes);
tag  coram_write_nb(coh coram, ...);
void coram_copy(coh src, coh dst, void *srcoffset,
                void *dstoffset, int bytes);
tag  coram_copy_nb(coh src, coh dst, ...);
bool check_coram_done(coh coram, tag, ...);
void coram_membar();

/*** Collective control actions ***/
void collective_write(coh coram, void *offset,
                      void *memaddr, int bytes);
void collective_read(coh coram, void *offset,
                     void *memaddr, int bytes);

/*** Channel control actions ***/
void fifo_write(fifo f, Data din);
Data fifo_read(fifo f);
void ioreg_write(reg r, Data din);
Data ioreg_read(reg r);
```

Figure 3: Control action definitions.

trol actions defined can be used to compose more sophisticated memory "personalities" such as scratchpads, caches, and FIFOs—each of which are tailored to the memory patterns and desired interfaces of specific applications.

The first argument to a control action is typically a program-level identifier (called co-handle) for an individual CoRAM or for a collection of CoRAMs that are functioning as a single logical structure (in the same way embedded SRAMs can be composed). The co-handle encapsulates both static and runtime information of the basic width and depth of the logical CoRAM structure and the binding to physical CoRAM blocks in the fabric. (A co-handle can also be used to represent a channel resource such as a FIFO or I/O register, although only the appropriate communication control actions are compatible with them.) The CoRAM definitions in Figure 3 comprise basic memory block transfer operations (*coram_read*, *coram_write*) as well as on-chip CoRAM-to-CoRAM data transfers (*coram_copy*). In addition to memory operations, control actions support asynchronous two-way communication between user logic and control threads via FIFOs (e.g., *fifo_write*) and I/O registers (e.g., *ioreg_write*). Although not listed in the definitions, control threads can also communicate to each other through ordered message-passing primitives.

Example. To illustrate how control actions are used, the example in Figure 4 shows how a user would (1) instantiate a CoRAM as a black-box module in their application, and (2) program a corresponding control thread to read a single data word from edge memory into the CoRAM. The control thread program shown in Figure 4 (right) first acquires a co-handle (L2), and passes it into a *coram_write* control action (L3), which performs a 4-byte memory transfer from the edge memory address space to the CoRAM blocks named by the co-handle. To inform the application when the data is ready to be accessed for computation, the control thread

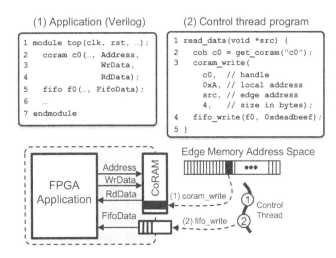

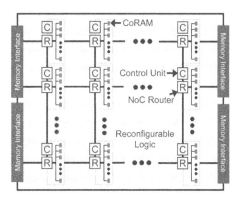

(1) Application (Verilog)

```
1 module top(clk, rst, …);
2   coram c0(…, Address,
3                  WrData,
4                  RdData);
5   fifo f0(…, FifoData);
6   …
7 endmodule
```

(2) Control thread program

```
1 read_data(void *src) {
2   coh c0 = get_coram("c0");
3   coram_write(
       c0,   // handle
       0xA,  // local address
       src,  // edge address
       4,    // size in bytes);
4   fifo_write(f0, 0xdeadbeef);
5 }
```

Figure 4: Example Usage of CoRAMs.

Figure 5: Conceptual Microarchitecture Sketch of Reconfigurable Logic with CoRAM Support.

passes a token to the user logic using the *fifo_write* control action (the acquisition of the channel FIFO's co-handle is omitted for brevity).

Advanced control actions. Control threads can employ more advanced control actions to either increase memory level parallelism or to customize data partitioning. The non-blocking control actions (e.g., *coram_write_nb*) explicitly allow for concurrent memory operations and return a tag that must be monitored using *check_coram_done*. A control thread can also invoke *coram_membar*, which serializes on all previously executed non-blocking control actions by that control thread. For parallel transfers to a large number of CoRAMs, a collective form of read and write control actions is also supported. In the collective form, *append_handle* is a helper function that can be used to compose a static list of CoRAMs. The newly returned co-handle can then be used with collective control actions to perform transfers to the aggregated CoRAMs as a single logical unit. When operating upon the composed handle, sequential data arriving from memory can either be striped across the CoRAMs' local addresses in a concatenated or word-interleaved pattern. Such features allow the user to customize the partitioning of application data across the multiple distributed CoRAMs within the reconfigurable logic.

Future enhancements. It is not difficult to imagine that many variants of the above control actions could be added to support more sophisticated patterns or optimizations (e.g., broadcast from one CoRAM to many, prefetch, strided access, etc.). In a commercial production setting, control actions—like instructions in an ISA—must be carefully defined and preserved to achieve the value of portability and compatibility. Although beyond the scope of this work, compilers could play a significant role in static optimization of control thread programs. Analysis could be used, for example, to identify non-conflicting control actions that are logically executed in sequence but can actually be executed concurrently without affecting correctness.

3. CORAM MICROARCHITECTURE

The CoRAM architecture presented thus far has deliberately omitted the details of how control threads are actually executed and how data is physically transported between the CoRAMs and the edge memory interfaces. The CoRAM architecture definitions (i.e., control actions) form a contractual agreement between applications and hardware implementations. In the ideal case, a good implementation of CoRAM should provide robust hardware performance across a range of applications without affecting correctness and without significant tuning required by the user.

Hardware overview. By construction, the CoRAM architecture naturally lends itself to highly distributed hardware designs. The microarchitectural "sketch" shown in Figure 5 is architected in mind to scale up to thousands of embedded CoRAMs based on current FPGA design trends [24]. CoRAMs, like embedded SRAMs in modern FPGAs, are arranged into vertical columns [26] and organized into localized clusters. Each cluster is managed by an attached Control Unit, which is a physical host responsible for executing the control programs that run within the cluster. Control programs can be realized by direct synthesis into reconfigurable logic (e.g., using high-level synthesis flows) or can be compiled and executed on dedicated multithreaded microcontrollers (e.g., a multithreaded RISC pipeline). Control Units must also maintain internal queues and scoreboarding logic to track multiple outstanding control actions, and to allow querying of internal state (e.g., *check_coram_done*).

Data distribution. An integral component to the Control Unit is the network-on-chip, which is responsible for routing memory address requests on behalf of Control Units to a multitude of distributed memory interfaces and delivering data responses accordingly. Within each cluster, multiple CoRAMs share a single network-on-chip router for communication and data transport. At the macroscale level, multiple routers are arranged in a 2D mesh to provide global connectivity between clusters and memory interfaces. Internal to each cluster, queues and local interconnect provides connectivity between the CoRAMs and the shared router interface. The local interconnect internal to the cluster also contains marshalling logic to break large data transfers from the network into individual words and to steer them accordingly to the constituent CoRAMs based on the data partitioning a user desires (e.g., a *collective_write*).

Soft versus hard logic. To implement the CoRAM architecture, the most convenient approach in the short term would be to layer all the required CoRAM functionality on top of conventional FPGAs. In the long term, FPGAs developed in mind with dedicated CoRAM architectural sup-

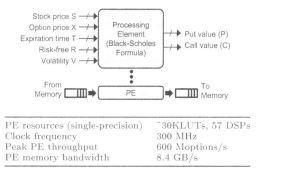

PE resources (single-precision)	~30KLUTs, 57 DSPs
Clock frequency	300 MHz
Peak PE throughput	600 Moptions/s
PE memory bandwidth	8.4 GB/s

Figure 6: Black-Scholes Processing Element.

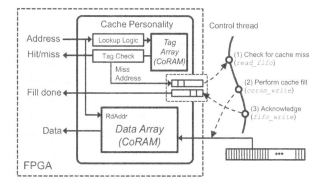

Figure 7: Stream FIFO memory personality.

port can become more economical if certain features become popularly used. From the perspective of a fabric designed to support computing, we contend that a hardwired network-on-chip (NoC) offers significant advantages, especially if it reduces or eliminates the need for long-distance routing tracks in today's fabrics. Under the CoRAM architectural paradigm, global bulk communications are restricted to between CoRAM-to-CoRAM or CoRAM-to-edge. Such a usage model would be better served by the high performance (bandwidth and latency) and the reduced power and energy from a dedicated hardwired NoC that connects the CoRAMs and the edge memory interfaces. With a hardwired NoC, it is also more cost-effective in area and energy to over-provision network bandwidth and latency to deliver robust performance across different applications. Similarly, the control units used to host control threads could also support "hardened" control actions most commonly used by applications. The microarchitecture shown in Figure 5, with its range of parameters, will be the subject of a quantitative evaluation in Section 5. We next present three case studies that demonstrate concrete usage of CoRAM.

4. CoRAM IN USAGE

The CoRAM architecture offers a rich abstraction for expressing the memory access requirements of a broad range of applications while hiding memory system details unrelated to the application itself. This section presents our experiences in developing three non-trivial application kernels using the CoRAM architecture. Below, we explain each kernel's unique memory access pattern requirements and discuss key insights learned during our development efforts. The control thread examples presented in this section are excerpts from actual applications running in our CoRAM

```
1   coh ram = get_coram(...); // handle to FIFO buffer
2   char *src = ...; // initialized to Black-Scholes data
3   int src_word = 0, head = 0, words_left = ...; // size
4   while(words_left > 0) {
5       int tail       = ioreg_read(ram);
6       int free_words = ram->depth - (head - tail);
7       int bsize_words = MIN(free_words, words_left);
8
9       if(bsize_words != 0) {
10          coram_write(ram, head, src +
11                  src_word * ram->wdsize, bsize_words);
12          ioreg_write(ram, head + bsize_words);
13          src_word   += bsize_words;
14          words_left -= bsize_words;
15          head       += bsize_words;
16      }
17  }
```

Figure 8: Control program for Input Stream FIFO.

simulator, which models a microarchitecture based on Figure 5. For our applications, the compute portions of the designs were placed-and-routed on a Virtex-6 LX760 FPGA to determine the peak fabric processing throughput.

4.1 Black-Scholes

The first FPGA application example, Black-Scholes, is widely used in the field of quantitative finance for option pricing [21]. Black-Scholes employs a rich mixture of arithmetic floating-point operators but exhibits a very simple memory access pattern. The fully pipelined processing element (PE) shown in Figure 6 consumes a sequential input data stream from memory and produces its output stream similarly. The application's performance is highly scalable; one could increase performance by instantiating multiple PEs that consume and produce independent input and output data streams. Performance continues to scale until either the reconfigurable logic capacity is exhausted or the available external memory bandwidth is saturated. The characteristics of our Black-Scholes PE are shown in Figure 6 (bottom).

Supporting Streams with CoRAM. To support the sequential memory access requirements of Black-Scholes, we develop the concept of a stream FIFO "memory personality", which presents a simple FIFO interface to user logic (i.e., *data, ready, pop*). The stream FIFO employs CoRAMs and a control thread to bridge a single Black-Scholes pipeline to the edge memory interface. Figure 7 illustrates the stream FIFO module, which instantiates a single CoRAM to be used as a circular buffer, with nearby head and tail registers instantiated within reconfigurable logic to track the buffer occupancy. Unlike a typical FIFO implemented within reconfigurable logic, the producer of the stream FIFO is not an entity hosted in logic but is managed by an associated control thread.

Figure 7 (right) illustrates a simple control thread used to fulfill the FIFO producer role (the corresponding code is shown in Figure 8). The event highlighted in Step 1 of Figure 7 first initializes a source pointer to the location in memory where the Black-Scholes data resides (L2 in Figure 8). In Step 2, the control thread samples the head and tail pointers to compute how much available space is left within the FIFO (L5-L7 in Figure 8). If sufficient space exists, the event in step 3 performs a multi-word byte transfer from the edge memory interface into the CoRAM using the *coram_write* control action (L10 in Figure 8). The event in

```
1  void mmm(Data* A, Data* B, Data *C, int N, int NB) {
2    int j, i, k;
3    for (j = 0; j < N; j += NB) {
4      for (i = 0; i < N; i += NB) {
5        for (k = 0; k < N; k += NB) {
6          block_mmm_kernel(A + i*N + k,
7                           B + k*N + j,
8                           C + i*N + j, N, NB);
9        }
10     }
11   }
12 }
```

Figure 9: Reference C code for Blocked MMM [4].

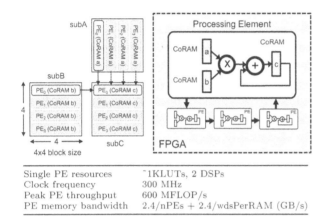

Single PE resources	~1KLUTs, 2 DSPs
Clock frequency	300 MHz
Peak PE throughput	600 MFLOP/s
PE memory bandwidth	2.4/nPEs + 2.4/wdsPerRAM (GB/s)

Figure 10: FPGA design for Blocked MMM.

Step 4 completes the FIFO production by having the control thread update the head pointer using the *ioreg_write* control action to inform the reconfigurable logic within the stream FIFO module when new data has arrived (L12 in Figure 8). Finally, L13-L15 show updates to internal state maintained by the control thread. (Note: we do not show the control thread program for the corresponding output stream FIFO.)

Discussion. The use of CoRAM simplified the overall development efforts for Black-Scholes by allowing us to express the application's memory access pattern at a high level of abstraction relative to conventional RTL flows. Our control thread program described the sequential memory transactions required by Black-Scholes as a sequence of untimed steps using a simple, C-based language. This abstraction was simple to work with and allowed us to iterate on changes quickly and conveniently. An important idea that emerged during our development efforts was the memory personality concept. A memory personality "wraps" CoRAMs and control threads within reconfigurable logic to provide an even higher level of abstraction (i.e., interface and memory semantics) best suited to the application at hand. As will be discussed later, many other kinds of memory personalities can also be constructed and further combined to form a re-usable shared library for CoRAM.

4.2 Matrix-Matrix Multiplication

The next example, Matrix Matrix Multiplication (MMM), is a widely-used computation kernel that multiplies two matrices encoded in dense, row-major format [18]. For multiplications where the input and output matrices are too large to fit in on-chip SRAMs, a commonly used blocked algorithm decomposes the large calculation into repeated multiplica-

```
1.  void mmm_control(Data *A, Data *B, ...) {
2.    coh ramsA = ..; // 'a' CoRAMs, word-interleaved
3.    coh ramsB = ..; // 'b' CoRAMs, concatenated
4.    for (j = 0; j < N; j += NB) {
5.      for (i = 0; i < N; i += NB) {
6.        for (k = 0; k < N; k += NB) {
7.          fifo_read(...);
8.          for (m = 0; m < NB; m++) {
9.            collective_write(ramsA, m*NB, A + i*N+k +
                                m*N, NB*dsz);
10.           collective_write(ramsB, m*NB, B + k*N+j +
                                m*N, NB*dsz);
11.         }
12.         fifo_write(...);
13.       }
14.     }
15.   }
```

Figure 11: MMM control thread code example.

tions of sub-matrices sized to fit within the on-chip SRAMs (see reference C code in Figure 9). This strategy improves the arithmetic intensity of MMM by increasing the average number of floating-point operations performed for each external memory byte transferred.

Figure 10 illustrates a parameterized hardware kernel developed for single-precision blocked MMM. The design employs p identical dot-product processing elements (PE) and assumes that the large input matrices A, B, and the output matrix C are stored in external memory. In each iteration: (1) different sub-matrices $subA$, $subB$, and $subC$ are read in from external memory, and (2) $subA$ and $subB$ are multiplied to produce intermediate sums accumulated to sub-matrix $subC$. The sub-matrices are sized to utilize available SRAM storage. (Square sub-matrices of size 4x4 are assumed in this explanation for the sake of simplicity.) The row slices of $subB$ and $subC$ are divided evenly among the p PEs and held in per-PE local CoRAM buffers. The column slices of $subA$ are also divided evenly and stored similarly. A complete iteration repeats the following steps p times: (1) each PE performs dot-products of its local slices of $subA$ and $subB$ to calculate intermediates sum to be accumulated into $subC$, and (2) each PE passes its local column slice of $subA$ to its right neighbor cyclically (note: as an optimization, step 2 can be overlapped with step 1 in the background).

MMM Control thread. To populate the CoRAM buffers of each PE, a single control thread is used to access all of the necessary per-row and per-column slices of $subA$, $subB$, and $subC$. The pseudo-code of the control thread program used to implement the required memory operations is shown in Figure 11 (for brevity, the reading and writing of $subC$ is omitted). In L2, $ramsA$ is a co-handle that represents an aggregation of all the 'a' CoRAMs belonging to the PEs in word-interleaved order ($ramsA$ can be constructed from multiple CoRAMs using *append_handle*). If passed into a *collective_write* control action, matrix data arriving sequentially from edge memory would be striped and written across multiple 'a' CoRAMs in a word-by-word interleaved fashion. This operation is necessary because the 'a' CoRAMs expect the data slices in column-major format whereas all matrix data is encoded in row-major. The co-handle $ramsB$ expects data in a row-major format and is simply a concatenation of all of the 'b' CoRAMs. Within the body of the inner loop, the control thread first waits for a token from the user logic (L7) before executing the *collective_write* con-

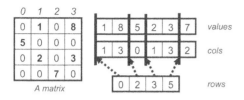

```
1. void spmv_csr (int n_rows, int *cols,
2.                Data *rows, Data *x, Data *y) {
3.   for(int r = 0; r < n_rows; r++) {
4.     int sum = 0;
5.     for(i = rows[r]; i <= rows[r+1]; i++)
6.       sum += vals[i] * x[cols[i]];
7.     y[r] = sum;
8.   }
9. }
```

Figure 12: Sparse Matrix-Vector Multiplication.

trol actions used to populate the CoRAMs (L9-L10). Upon completion, the control thread informs the user logic when the data is ready to be accessed (L12). The control thread terminates after iterating over all the blocks of matrix C.

Discussion. Our overall experience with developing MMM highlights more sophisticated uses of CoRAM. In particular, the collective control actions allowed us to precisely express the data transfers for a large collection of CoRAMs in very few lines of code. Control actions also allowed us to customize the partitioning of data to meet the on-chip memory layout requirements of our MMM design. It is worth noting how the code in Figure 11 appears similar to the C reference code, with the exception that the inner-most loop now consists of memory control actions rather than computation. One insight we developed from this example is that control threads can allow us to easily express the re-assignment of FPGA kernels to different regions of the external memory over the course of a large computation. This feature of the CoRAM architecture could potentially be used to simplify the task of building out-of-core FPGA-based applications that support inputs much larger than the total on-chip memory capacity.

4.3   Sparse Matrix-Vector Multiplication

Our last example, Sparse Matrix-Vector Multiplication (SpMV), is another widely-used scientific kernel that multiplies a sparse matrix A by a dense vector x [18]. Figure 12 (top) gives an example of a sparse matrix A in Compressed Sparse Row (CSR) format. The non-zero values in A are stored in row-order as a linear array of *values* in external memory. The column number of each entry in *values* is stored in a corresponding entry in the column array (*cols*). The i'th entry of another array (*rows*) holds the index to the first entry in *values* (and *cols*) belonging to row i of A. Figure 12 (bottom) gives the reference C code for computing $A \times x$. Of all the kernels we studied, SpMV presented the most difficult design challenge for us due to a large external memory footprint and an irregular memory access pattern.

Figure 13 illustrates an FPGA design for SpMV, where multiple processing elements (PEs) operate concurrently on distinct rows of A. The contents of the *rows* array are streamed in from edge memory to a centralized work scheduler that assigns rows to different PEs. For each assigned row, a PE employs two stream FIFOs to sequentially read in data blocks from the *values* and *cols* arrays, respectively. To

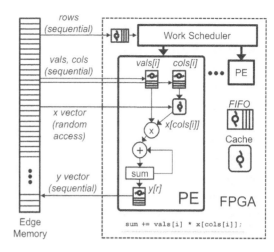

Single PE resources	~2KLUTs
Clock frequency	300 MHz
Peak PE throughput	600 MFLOP/s
PE memory bandwidth	≥3.6GB/s

Figure 13: FPGA design for SpMV.

configure the memory pointers for each of the two stream FIFOs, the PE logic must continously pass row assignment information (via channels) to the control threads belonging to the stream FIFOs. To calculate each term of a dot-product, a PE must make an indirect reference to vector x (L6). This type of memory access poses a particularly difficult challenge because the memory addresses (i.e., *cols*) are not necessarily sequential and could be accessed randomly. Furthermore, x can be a very large data structure that cannot fit into aggregate on-chip memory. Unlike the MMM example from earlier, the performance of SpMV is highly dependent on efficient bandwidth utilization due to its low arithmetic intensity. An optimization to reduce memory bandwidth is to exploit any reuse of the elements of x across different rows through caching.

To implement caching within each PE, Figure 14 illustrates a read-only cache memory personality built using the CoRAM architecture. Within the cache, CoRAMs are composed to form data and tag arrays while conventional reconfigurable logic implements the bulk of the cache controller logic. A single control thread is used to implement cache fills to the CoRAM data arrays. When a miss is detected, the address is enqueued to the control thread through an asynchronous FIFO (step 1 in Figure 14). Upon a pending request, step 2 of the control thread transfers a cache block's worth of data to the data array using the *coram_write* con-

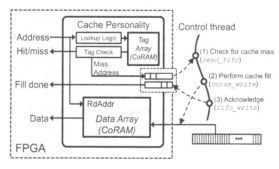

Figure 14: SpMV cache personality.

trol action. In step 3, the control thread acknowledges the cache controller using the *fifo_write* control action.

Discussion. The SpMV example illustrates how different memory personalities built out of CoRAM can be employed in a single design to support multiple memory access patterns. Caches, in particular, were used to support the random access pattern of the x vector, whereas the stream FIFOs from Black-Scholes were re-used for the remaining sequential accesses. In our development efforts of SpMV, the instantiation of CoRAM-based memory personalities along with spatially-distributed PEs allowed us to quickly instantiate "virtual taps" to external memory wherever needed. This level of abstraction was especially convenient as it allowed us to concentrate our efforts on developing only the processing components of SpMV.

4.4 Case Study Remarks

The overall experience in developing applications with CoRAM reveals significant promise in improving the programmability of FPGA-based applications on the whole. While the CoRAM architecture does not eliminate the effort needed to develop optimized stand-alone processing kernels, it does free designers from having to explicitly manage memory and data distribution in a low-level RTL abstraction. Specifically, control threads gave us a general method for dynamically orchestrating the memory management of applications, but did not force us to over-specify the sequencing details at the RTL level. Control threads also did not limit our ability to support fine-grained interactions between processing components and memory. Fundamentally, the high-level abstraction of CoRAM is what would enable portability across multiple hardware implementations.

The memory personalities developed in our examples (stream FIFO, read-only cache) are by no means sufficient for all possible applications and only highlighted a subset of the features possible. For example, for all of the memory personalities described, one could replace the *coram_write* control action with *coram_copy*, which would permit transfers from other CoRAMs within the fabric and not necessarily from the memory edge. Such control actions could, for instance, be used to efficiently compose multi-level cache hierarchies out of CoRAMs (e.g., providing the SpMV PEs with a shared L2 cache) or be used to setup streams between multiple application kernels. It is conceived that in the future, soft libraries consisting of many types of memory personalities would be a valuable addition to the CoRAM architecture. This concept is attractive because hardware vendors supporting the CoRAM abstraction would not have to be aware of all the possible personality interfaces (e.g., caches, FIFOs) but would only be implementing the "low-level" control actions, which would automatically facilitate compatibility with existing, high-level libraries.

5. EVALUATION

This section presents our initial investigations to understand the performance, area, and power implications of introducing the CoRAM architecture to a conventional FPGA fabric. Given the large design space of CoRAM, the goal of this evaluation is to perform an early exploration of design points for future investigations.

Methodology. To model an FPGA with CoRAM support, a cycle-level software simulator was developed in Bluespec

Variables	Selected parameters
FPGA resources	474KLUTs, 720 CoRAMs, 180 threads
Clock rates	User Logic @ 300MHz, CoRAM @ 0.3-1.2GHz
Off-chip DRAM	128GB/sec, 60ns latency
Control Unit	8-thread, 5-stage MIPS core
Network-on-Chip	2D-mesh packet-switched NoC
	3-cycle hop latency, 300MHz-1.2GHz
Topology	{16,32,64} nodes x {8,16} memports
Router datapath	{32,64,128}-bit router datapaths

Table 1: FPGA Model Parameters.

System Verilog [3] to simulate instances of the design illustrated in Figure 5. Table 1 summarizes the key configuration parameters of the simulated fabric design. The simulator assumes a baseline reconfigurable fabric with 474 KLUTs and 720 CoRAMs (4KB each) to reflect the capacity of the Virtex-6 LX760, the largest FPGA from Xilinx today. In the performance simulations, we assume the user logic within the fabric can operate at 300MHz based on placed-and-routed results of the processing kernels from Section 4. For design space exploration, we considered different points based on CoRAMs assumed to operate at 300 MHz to 1.2 GHz to study the relative merits between soft- versus hard-logic implementations.

The simulator models a 2D-mesh packet-switched network-on-chip based on an existing full-system simulator [22]. The NoC simulator models the cycle-by-cycle traffic flow among the CoRAMs and the edge memory traffic resulting from the control actions issued by control threads. The bandwidth available at each network endpoint is shared by a concentrated cluster of locally connected CoRAMs. For design space exploration, we varied the NoC performance along three dimensions: (1) operating frequency between 300MHz to 1.2GHz (in sync with the CoRAM frequency); (2) network link and data width (32, 64, 128 bits per cycle); and (3) number of network end-points (16, 32, 64) and thus the number of CoRAMs sharing an end-point.

To incorporate memory bandwidth constraints, our simulator models an aggressive external memory interface with four GDDR5 controllers, providing an aggregate peak bandwidth of 128GB/sec at 60ns latency. This external memory interface performance is motivated by what can be achieved by GPUs and CPUs today. Even then, the performance simulations of the Sparse Matrix-Vector Multiplication (SpMV) kernels reported in this section are all memory bandwidth bound, never able to completely consume the reconfigurable logic resources available in the fabric.

The Control Unit from Figure 5 is modeled as a multi-threaded microcontroller that executes control thread programs directly. The model assumes that the fabric has 740kB of SRAM (beyond CoRAMs) needed to hold the 180 control thread contexts (code and data). The performance simulator also does not model the multithreaded pipelines explicitly. However, the control threads are compiled and executed concurrently as *Pthreads* within the simulation process and are throttled with synchronization each simulated cycle to mimic execution delay (varied between 300MHz and 1.2GHz for design space exploration).

RTL Synthesis. For each of the design points considered by the performance simulation, the power and area is also estimated by synthesizing RTL-level designs of the CoRAM mechanisms using Synopsys Design Compiler v2009 to target a commercial 65nm standard cell library. The power

C = CoRAMs, T = control threads, N = nodes = clusters, M=mbanks		

C = CoRAMs, T = control threads, N = nodes = clusters, M=mbanks
$K = C/N$ = CoRAMs per cluster, $X = T/N$ = control threads/cluster
P = watts, p = watts/GHz, $freq$ = CoRAM clock frequency

$A_{cluster} = A_{router} + X \times A_{costate} + \frac{X}{8} \times (A_{mips} + A_{other})$
$A_{total} = N \times A_{cluster} + M \times A_{router}$
$P_{cluster} = freq \times (p_{router} + X \times p_{costate} + \frac{X}{8} \times (p_{mips} + p_{other}))$
$P_{total} = N \times P_{cluster} + freq \times M \times p_{router}$

Table 2: Area and Power Overhead Formulas.

Component	mm^2	mW/GHz
MIPS core (8 threads)	.08	59
Per-thread state (SRAM)	.04	8
32-bit router	.07	38
64-bit router	.11	48
128-bit router	.30	64
Other (queues, logic, etc.) (est'd)	.40	-

Table 3: 65nm Synthesis Results.

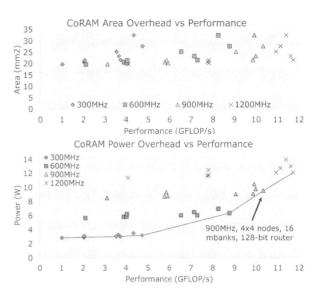

Figure 15: Estimated area and power overhead.

and area of the NoC are estimated by synthesizing an open-sourced router design[1]. The power and area of the Control Unit is estimated by synthesizing an 8-way multithreaded 5-stage MIPS core automatically generated from the T-piper tool [17]. The power and area of the SRAMs for the control thread contexts are estimated using CACTI 4.0 [20]. Table 3 summarizes the resulting area and power characteristics of various components. The total power and area overhead for a particular design point is calculated using the formulas in the bottom of Table 2 by setting the parameters in the top portion of the table.

It is important to keep in mind that, despite the efforts taken, the reported power and area estimates are only approximate. However, by just comparing relative magnitudes, the estimates give an adequate indication that the total cost of adding even an aggressive, pure hard-logic CoRAM implementation is small relative to the inherent cost of a reconfigurable fabric like the Virtex-6 LX760. Our estimates also have a large conservative margin built-in since they are based on a 65nm standard cell library several years old.

5.1 Design Space Exploration Results

From the design explorations, we report results for the Sparse Matrix-Vector Multiplication kernel, which was our most memory-intensive application (results for Matrix Matrix Multiplication and Black-Scholes are discussed qualitatively at the end). We simulated the execution of the SpMV kernel running on design points generated from an exhaustive sweep of parameters given in Table 1. For each design point, we report the SpMV kernel's execution performance averaged over test input matrices from [9]. The graphs in Figure 15 plot the performance (GFLOP/sec) achieved by each design point (on the x-axis) against its area and power overheads (on the y-axis) from adding the CoRAM architecture support. The data points represented by the same markers correspond to design points with CoRAM mechanisms at the same frequency (300MHz, 600MHz, 900MHz or 1.2GHz). All of the design points incur a fixed $18mm^2$ from SRAM storage and the MIPS cores for the required 180 control thread contexts; this can be a very significant portion of the total area overhead for some design points. Nevertheless, the total area overhead is small in comparison to the hundreds of mm^2 typical of even small FPGAs today [1].

In Figure 15 (top), points in the lower-right corner correspond to higher performance and lower area overhead. For all of the frequencies, a nearly minimal area design point achieves almost the best performance possible at a given frequency. This suggests that the operating frequency of the CoRAM mechanisms has a first-order impact on the overall application performance, beyond the impact of microarchitectural choices. This result suggests that it may be difficult for soft implementations of the CoRAM mechanisms to perform comparably well as hard implementations in the future even when reconfigurable logic resources are made plentiful.

The power-overhead-vs-performance plot in Figure 15 (bottom) exhibits a cleaner Pareto front. In this plot, the higher performance design points tend to require a greater power overhead. It should be pointed out that the microarchitecture design point *4x4nodes-16mbanks-128bit* appears consistently on the Pareto front for all frequencies (also optimal in the area-overhead-vs-performance plot). This suggests that it is possible to select this point to achieve minimum area overhead and apply frequency scaling to span the different positions on the power-performance Pareto optimal front. However, this conclusion is based only on the results of the SpMV application kernel. Further study including a much greater range of application kernels is needed. Although performance results were not presented for MMM or BS, our experiments showed that less aggressive designs (e.g., *600MHz-4x4nodes-16mbanks-128bit*) were sufficient for these compute-bound applications to reach peak performance running on the CoRAM architecture.

6. RELATED WORK

A large body of work has explored specialized VLSI designs for reconfigurable computing. GARP [12] is an example that fabricates a MIPS core and cache hierarchy along with a collection of reconfigurable processing elements (PE). The PEs share access to the processor cache but only through a centralized access queue at the boundary of the reconfigurable logic. Tiled architectures (e.g., Tilera [23]) consist of a large array of simple von Neumann processors instead of fine-grained lookup tables. The memory accesses by the cores are supported through per-core private caches

[1] http://nocs.stanford.edu/cgi-bin/trac.cgi/wiki/Resources/Router

interconnected by an on-chip network. Smart Memories [14] on the other hand employs reconfigurable memory tiles that selectively act as caches, scratchpad memory, or FIFOs.

The idea of decoupling memory management from computation in CoRAM has been explored previously for general-purpose processors [19, 7]. Existing work has also examined soft memory hierarchies for FPGAs (e.g., [25, 10, 13, 15]). The most closely related work to CoRAM is LEAP [2], which shares the objective of providing a standard abstraction. LEAP abstracts away the details of memory management by exporting a set of timing-insensitive, request-response interfaces to local client address spaces. Underlying details such as multi-level caching and data movement are hidden from the user. The CoRAM architecture differs from LEAP by allowing explicit user control over the lower-level details of data movement between global memory interfaces and the on-die embedded SRAMs; the CoRAM architecture could itself be used to support the data movement operations required in a LEAP abstraction.

7. CONCLUSIONS

Processing and memory are inseparable aspects of any real-world computing problems. A proper memory architecture is a critical requirement for FPGAs to succeed as a computing technology. In this paper, we investigated a new, portable memory architecture called CoRAM to provide deliberate support for memory accesses from within the fabric of a future FPGA engineered to be a computing device. CoRAM is designed to match the requirements of highly concurrent, spatially distributed processing kernels that consume and produce memory data from within the fabric. The paper demonstrated the ease-of-use in managing the memory access requirements of three non-trivial applications, while allowing the designers to focus exclusively on application development without sacrificing portability or performance. This paper also suggested a possible microarchitecture space for supporting the CoRAM architecture in future reconfigurable fabrics. An investigation of the trade-offs between performance, power, and area suggests that adding support for the CoRAM architecture in future devices only requires a modest overhead in power and area relative to the reconfigurable fabric.

8. ACKNOWLEDGEMENTS

Funding for this work was provided by NSF CCF-1012851. We thank the anonymous reviewers and members of CALCM for their comments and feedback. We thank Xilinx for their FPGA and tool donations. We thank Bluespec for their tool donations and support.

9. REFERENCES

[1] Under the Hood: Intel has company at 65 nm. http://maltiel-consulting.com/Intel_leads_65-nanometer_technology_race_other-Texas_Instruments_Xilinx_AMD_catching_up.htm.

[2] M. Adler, K. E. Fleming, A. Parashar, M. Pellauer, and J. Emer. LEAP Scratchpads: Automatic Memory and Cache Management for Reconfigurable Logic. In *FPGA '11: Proceedings of the 2011 ACM/SIGDA 19th International Symposium on Field Programmable Gate Arrays*, 2011.

[3] Bluespec, Inc. http://www.bluespec.com/products/bsc.htm.

[4] F. Brewer and J. C. Hoe. MEMOCODE 2007 Co-Design Contest. In *Fifth ACM-IEEE International Conference on Formal Methods and Models for Codesign*, 2007.

[5] S. Che, J. Li, J. W. Sheaffer, K. Skadron, and J. Lach. Accelerating Compute-Intensive Applications with GPUs and FPGAs. In *SASP '08: Proceedings of the 2008 Symposium on Application Specific Processors*, pages 101–107, Washington, DC, USA, 2008. IEEE Computer Society.

[6] E. S. Chung, P. A. Milder, J. C. Hoe, and K. Mai. Single-Chip Heterogeneous Computing: Does the Future Include Custom Logic, FPGAs, and GPGPUs? In *MICRO-43: Proceedings of the 43th Annual IEEE/ACM International Symposium on Microarchitecture*, 2010.

[7] E. Cohler and J. Storer. Functionally parallel architecture for array processors. *Computer*, 14:28–36, 1981.

[8] Convey, Inc. http://www.convey.com.

[9] T. A. Davis. University of Florida Sparse Matrix Collection. *NA Digest*, 92, 1994.

[10] H. Devos, J. V. Campenhout, and D. Stroobandt. Building an Application-specific Memory Hierarchy on FPGA. *2nd HiPEAC Workshop on Reconfigurable Computing*, 2008.

[11] T. El-Ghazawi, E. El-Araby, M. Huang, K. Gaj, V. Kindratenko, and D. Buell. The Promise of High-Performance Reconfigurable Computing. *Computer*, 41(2):69 –76, feb. 2008.

[12] J. R. Hauser and J. Wawrzynek. Garp: a MIPS processor with a reconfigurable coprocessor. In *FCCM'97: Proceedings of the 5th IEEE Symposium on FPGA-Based Custom Computing Machines*, page 12, Washington, DC, USA, 1997. IEEE Computer Society.

[13] G. Kalokerinos, V. Papaefstathiou, G. Nikiforos, S. Kavadias, M. Katevenis, D. Pnevmatikatos, and X. Yang. FPGA implementation of a configurable cache/scratchpad memory with virtualized user-level RDMA capability. In *Proceedings of the 9th international conference on Systems, architectures, modeling and simulation*, SAMOS'09, pages 149–156, Piscataway, NJ, USA, 2009. IEEE Press.

[14] K. Mai, T. Paaske, N. Jayasena, R. Ho, W. J. Dally, and M. Horowitz. Smart Memories: A Modular Reconfigurable Architecture. In *ISCA'00: Proceedings of the 27th Annual International Symposium on Computer Architecture*, pages 161–171, New York, NY, USA, 2000. ACM.

[15] P. Nalabalapu and R. Sass. Bandwidth Management with a Reconfigurable Data Cache. In *Proceedings of the 19th IEEE International Parallel and Distributed Processing Symposium (IPDPS'05) - Workshop 3 - Volume 04*, IPDPS '05, pages 159.1–, Washington, DC, USA, 2005. IEEE Computer Society.

[16] T. Ngai, J. Rose, and S. Wilton. An SRAM-programmable field-configurable memory. In *Custom Integrated Circuits Conference, 1995., Proceedings of the IEEE 1995*, May 1995.

[17] E. Nurvitadhi, J. C. Hoe, T. Kam, and S.-L. Lu. Automatic Pipelining from Transactional Datapath Specifications. In *Design, Automation, and Test in Europe (DATE)*, 2010.

[18] W. H. Press, B. P. Flannery, S. A. Teukolsky, and W. T. Vetterling. *Numerical Recipes in C: the Art of Scientific Computing*. Cambridge University Press, 1988.

[19] J. E. Smith. Decoupled access/execute computer architectures. *SIGARCH Comput. Archit. News*, 10:112–119, April 1982.

[20] D. T. S. Thoziyoor, D. Tarjan, and S. Thoziyoor. Cacti 4.0. Technical Report HPL-2006-86, HP Labs, 2006.

[21] Victor Podlozhnyuk. Black-Scholes Option Pricing, 2007.

[22] T. F. Wenisch, R. E. Wunderlich, M. Ferdman, A. Ailamaki, B. Falsafi, and J. C. Hoe. SimFlex: Statistical Sampling of Computer System Simulation. *IEEE Micro*, July 2006.

[23] D. Wentzlaff, P. Griffin, H. Hoffmann, L. Bao, B. Edwards, C. Ramey, M. Mattina, C.-C. Miao, J. F. Brown III, and A. Agarwal. On-Chip Interconnection Architecture of the Tile Processor. *IEEE Micro*, 27(5):15–31, 2007.

[24] Xilinx, Inc. Virtex-7 Series Overview, 2010.

[25] P. Yiannacouras and J. Rose. A parameterized automatic cache generator for FPGAs. In *Proc. Field-Programmable Technology (FPT*, pages 324–327, 2003.

[26] S. P. Young. FPGA architecture having RAM blocks with programmable word length and width and dedicated address and data lines, United States Patent No. 5,933,023. 1996.

Energy-Efficient Specialization of Functional Units in a Coarse-Grained Reconfigurable Array

Brian Van Essen[*‡]   Robin Panda[§]   Aaron Wood[§]

Carl Ebeling[†]   Scott Hauck[§]

[†] Dept. of Computer Science and Engineering and [§] Dept. of Electrical Engineering
University of Washington, Seattle, WA 98195
[†] {vanessen, ebeling}@cs.washington.edu   [§] {robin, arw28, hauck}@ee.washington.edu

[‡] Center for Applied Scientific Computing, Lawrence Livermore National Laboratory, Livermore, CA 94550
[‡] vanessen1@llnl.gov

ABSTRACT

Functional units provide the backbone of any spatial accelerator by providing the computing resources. The desire for having rich and expensive functional units is in tension with producing a regular and energy-efficient computing fabric. This paper explores the design trade-off between complex, universal functional units and simpler, limited functional units.

We show that a modest amount of specialization reduces the area-delay-energy product of an optimized architecture to $0.86\times$ a baseline architecture. Furthermore, we provide a design guideline that allows an architect to customize the contents of the computing fabric just by examining the profile of benchmarks within the application domains.

Categories and Subject Descriptors

B.2.1 [**Arithmetic and Logic Structures**]: Design Styles; C.1.1 [**Processor Architectures**]: Single Data Stream Architectures

General Terms

Design, Performance

Keywords

CGRA, energy-efficiency, functional units, architecture

1. INTRODUCTION

Functional units are the core of compute-intensive spatial accelerators. They perform the computation of interest with support from local storage and communication structures. Ideally, the functional units will provide rich functionality, supporting operations ranging from simple addition, to fused multiply-adds, to advanced transcendental functions and domain specific operations like add-compare-select. However, the total opportunity cost to support the more complex operations is a function of the cost of the hardware,

[*]This work performed under the auspices of the U.S. Department of Energy by Lawrence Livermore National Laboratory under Contract DE-AC52-07NA27344.

the rate of occurrence of the operation in the application domain, and the inefficiency of emulating the operation with simpler operators. Examples of operations that are typically emulated in spatial accelerators are division and trigonometric functions, which can be solved using table-lookup based algorithms [1] and the CORDIC algorithm [2].

One reason to avoid having direct hardware support for complex operations in a tiled architecture like a Coarse-Grained Reconfigurable Array (CGRA) is that the expensive hardware will typically need to be replicated in some or all of the architecture's tiles. Tiled architecture are designed such that their tiles are either homogenous or heterogenous. Homogenous architectures are simpler to design but heterogeneous architectures can be more efficient. Generally, CGRAs try to support a rich set of operations with the smallest possible set of hardware devices.

2. BACKGROUND

This work builds upon the Mosaic research infrastructure and optimized architectures that were designed in [3] and [4]. Furthermore, this work uses the same suite of benchmarks and 65nm process for the architecture's physical models as [4].

2.1 Architecture

The Mosaic CGRA architectures are a class of statically scheduled coarse-grained reconfigurable arrays. They are designed to exploit loop-level parallelism in an application's computationally-intensive inner loops (*i.e.* kernels) in an energy-efficient manner. The architectures are dynamically reconfigured, so that they time-multiplex their functional units and interconnect on a cycle-by-cycle basis. Like many CGRAs ([5], [6], [7]), the Mosaic architecture fits in the design space between FPGAs and VLIW processors, with similarities to a word-wide FPGA and a 2-D VLIW.

The Mosaic CGRA architecture (shown in [4]) is a cluster-based architecture that is arranged as a 2-D grid. To minimize the design complexity, the clusters are homogenous in the set of functional units that are supported. All of the clusters have four 32-bit processing elements. The 32-bit datapath in each cluster also has two large rotating register files for long-term storage, two distributed registers, one or two data memories, and connections to the grid interconnect. The 32-bit data path is complemented by a 1-bit control path that handles predicate generation and evaluation.

2.2 Related Work

Few other research efforts have evaluated the energy advantages and tradeoffs of architectural features in CGRAs. By and large

Benchmark	Category	32-bit Logic & Comparison	Arithmetic Ops.			Arith. & Logical Shifts	1-bit Logic & Comparison
			Simple	Complex	Select		
FIR	Complex	0.7	0.7	47.1	47.1	0.7	3.7
FIR (Banked)	Complex	3.6	23.2	42.9	24.1	0.9	5.4
Convolution	Select	3.4	1.1	27.8	63.4	0.6	3.7
Dense matrix multiply	Select	5.5	0.9	14.6	61.2	14.6	3.2
Motion Estimation	Simple	40.9	18.5	7.2	18.1	3.9	11.5
Smith-Waterman	Simple	39.8	21.0	0.2	36.8	0.0	2.2
K-Means Clustering	Simple	34.5	25.3	0.0	33.5	0.0	6.8
CORDIC	Simple	15.0	26.4	0.0	39.3	7.1	12.1
PET Event Detection	Simple	33.8	8.9	2.9	46.6	5.8	2.0
Matched filter	Balanced	9.5	7.1	21.4	22.2	25.4	14.3
Average		24.4	13.1	11.0	41.0	5.0	5.5

Table 1: Frequency of dynamic operations, reported as percentage, in the benchmark suite.

these efforts have focused on ad-hoc system analysis that examine multiple architecture features simultaneously. Kim et al. [8] looked at the tradeoffs for what they call primitive versus critical functional unit resources in a MorphoSys-style CGRA. Their study found that pipelining and sharing multipliers with other processing elements substantially reduced the area and delay of the architecture. These results align well with the results presented here, although our results started out with a pipelined multiplier and were conducted on a much larger scale. Wilton et al. [9] explore the connectivity requirements for point-to-point interconnects in an ADRES architecture with a heterogenous mix of functional units, when optimizing for area and performance. Others such as [10] were smaller evaluations that confirmed benefits from state of the art design practices, such as clustering multiple functional units together.

3. EVALUATING OPERATOR FREQUENCY

This experiment uses the benchmark suite as detailed in [3] and [4]. Table 1 shows the breakdown of operations within the benchmark suite, as well as an average frequency for each class of operation. Note that simple arithmetic operations are addition, subtraction, and negation, while multiplication and fused multiply-add or multiply-subtract operations are complex operations. Table 1 also shows how applications can be broadly categorized by the dominant type of operations. Note that complex arithmetic was given special priority with a threshold of only 40%, due to its relative importance in the application domain and complexity of the hardware.

- Balanced - relatively even mix of all operation types
- Simple-dominant - $\geq 60\%$ operations are simple arithmetic or logic / comparison operations
- Complex-dominant - $\geq 40\%$ operations are complex arithmetic
- Select-dominant - $\geq 60\%$ operations are select operations

The profile of the benchmark applications shows two key things: select operations are extremely common, while complex multiply or multiply-add operations rarely exceed 25% (and never 50%) of operations in the suite. Select operations provide dynamic data steering within the statically scheduled CGRA, typically staging data for subsequent computation. This makes it attractive to co-locate select hardware with other functional units, such as the ALU.

4. DESIGNING THE FUNCTIONAL UNITS

Tiled spatial accelerators typically eschew embedding the more complex and esoteric functional units, in favor of a simpler repeated tile, focusing on a range that spans simple adders to fused multiply-add units. In this experiment we explore the following primitive and compound functional units for the word-wide datapath. Note that the single-bit datapath uses a 3-input lookup table for its functional units.

- ALU - arithmetic and logic unit, with support for select
- Shifter - logarithmic funnel shifter
- MADD - 2-cycle fused multiply-add
- S-ALU - compound unit with shifter, ALU, and select
- Universal - compound unit with MADD, shifter, ALU, and select

4.1 Compound functional units

The S-ALU and universal compound functional units combine multiple primitive functional units into a single logical group. It is notable that while a compound functional unit could support multiple concurrent operations internally, it lacks the input and output ports necessary to supply and produce multiple sets of operands and results. Sharing the input and output ports mitigates the need to increase the size of the cluster's crossbar as more functionality is added to each functional unit. The cost for adding a port to the crossbar is approximately the same as the hardware for an ALU. In addition to the cost of adding a port to the crossbar, each input and output of the functional unit requires some peripheral hardware in the processing element (PE) to stage operands and results.

By treating compound FUs as one logical device, the placement tool will only map a single operation onto the functional unit per cycle. This ensures that an architecture maintains the same number of concurrent operations per cluster when mixing primitive and compound functional units. Two other advantages of maintaining the same number of concurrent operations per cluster are 1) the external support resources in the cluster do not have to be scaled as capabilities are added to each functional unit, and 2) it is easier to test and make comparisons between two architectural variants.

4.2 Comparison of Functional Units

To evaluate the tradeoff between flexibility and overhead for the functional units we examine several of their characteristics. The area and energy metrics for the each type of processing element (*i.e* functional unit plus word-wide peripheral logic) and their associated crossbar I/O ports are presented in Table 2. Note that the configuration energy includes both the static and dynamic energy of the configuration SRAM and associated logic, since the dynamic energy consumed per clock cycle can be precomputed. The peripheral resources include the local register files, input retiming registers, and multiplexers.

One advantage of using compound functional units instead of a larger number of primitive functional units is that it minimizes the

Processing Element	Area	Static Energy	Config. Energy	Datapath Ports (I/O)
ALU	17754	12.2	519.2	2/1
Shifter	17703	12.3	519.2	2/1
MADD	30754	16.0	631.4	3/1
S-ALU	19177	12.4	531.7	2/1
Universal	38357	19.5	814.4	4/1

Table 2: Characteristics for each type of processing elements (functional unit plus peripheral logic) and crossbar I/O ports. Area is reported in μm^2. Static and configuration energy was computed for a clock period of 1.93ns and are reported for $fJ/cycle$.

number of output ports and peripheral resources required. Since the functional units consume more values than they produce, there are fewer inputs to the crossbar than outputs from it, and thus the crossbar is not square. Therefore, the cost to add an output port to the functional unit (or attaching another device to the crossbar) is significantly more expensive than adding an input port, primarily due to the high number of capacitive loads within the crossbar.

5. EXPERIMENTS

To explore the impact of specializing the functional units in a cluster we test several clusters built with different functional units. The baseline architecture has four universal functional units per cluster and the optimized storage design from [4], with a private rotating register file in each functional unit and one cluster-wide large rotating register file. Each test in this experiment replaced some of those four functional units with a more specialized device. Two design considerations that were followed during this experiment were 1) each cluster could perform all supported operations, and 2) the number of concurrent operations per cluster remained constant.

To specialize the functional units we looked at the frequency of operations in the benchmark suite. The first optimization is to reduce the total number of multipliers within the architecture because they are the most expensive units, require the most input ports, and multiplication and MADD operations only make up ~11% of the dynamic operation mix. As the number of multipliers is reduced, architectures will have a small number of either Universal FUs or MADDs, and the remaining functional units will be either be S-ALUs or ALUs, which are abbreviated as U, M, S, and A, respectively. The set of permutations that we explored in this paper are designated as architectures: A - 4U, B - 3Ux1S, D 2Ux2S, E - 2Ux1Sx1A, F - 2Ux2A, G - 1Ux3S, and K - 1Mx3S.

To test the impact of specializing the functional units, each application in the benchmark suite was mapped to each architectural variant multiple times with different random placement seeds. The target architecture for each application was sized so that the application's critical resource consumed approximately 80% of the architecture's resources. We used 12 placement seeds per application, although FIR and convolution were tested with 20 seeds because they showed a higher variability in quality of placement. After simulating each application to architecture mapping, the area-delay-energy (ADE) product for each tests was calculated and used to select the random seed that produced the best ADE results.

6. RESULTS

Specialization of the functional units involves three key principles: 1) stripping away expensive and underutilized resources, 2) avoiding overly specialized hardware, and 3) creating functional

units with rich functionality when the extra logic is inexpensive (*i.e.* maximizing the utility of fixed resources). The effects of each of these principles is explored in the following three sections as the architecture moves from a general to a specialized fabric design.

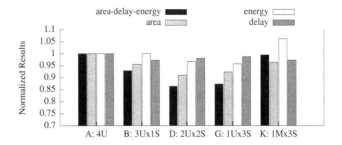

Figure 1: Average area-delay-energy product for architectures that are specialized with a mix of universal, S-ALU, and MADD FUs functional units.

6.1 Paring down underutilized resources

Figure 1 shows the area-delay-energy product, averaged across all benchmarks, for several architecture designs. The delay metric is the execution time averaged across all applications, and the total energy reported includes dynamic, static, configuration, and clock energy. This section focuses on the first four columns, which shows the trends as the MADD units are removed from individual functional units in architectures A, B, D, and G. Specializing the functional units by removing superfluous MADD devices reduces the area-delay-energy product by as much as 0.86× the area-delay-energy of the baseline architecture. The best specialized design, D, has 2 Universal FUs and 2 S-ALU FUs, versus a baseline with 4 Universal FUs.

As the designs go from having 2 to 1 Universal FU per cluster in architectures D and G, the number of clusters required goes up by 6.5%, which gives architecture D its performance advantage. This happens because, as we reduce the number of MADD devices, the complex-dominant (45.0% multiplication) and select-dominant (21.2% multiplication) applications become resource-starved, and require more clusters to have enough multipliers.

6.2 Avoiding excessive specialization

Given the benefits of paring down underutilized resources, it may seem obvious to replace at least one universal functional unit with a dedicated MADD FU, as tested by architecture K. Not only is the MADD functional unit smaller than the Universal FU, it also requires one less crossbar port. It turns out that architecture K is overly specialized with the MADD FU and performs worse, in terms of overall area-delay-energy product and total energy consumed, than all other specialized architectures, and only marginally better than the general design with four Universal FUs as shown in Figure 1. While architecture K required 7% more clusters than G, the 11% increase in energy is partly due to G being able to co-locate instructions on a single functional unit better than K. This allows sequences of operations to stay in the same processing element instead of having to traverse the cluster's crossbar.

6.3 Exploiting fixed resource costs

The third design principle we mentioned earlier is to make functional units as rich as possible when the additional functionality is cheap. Since shift operations are relatively rare in our benchmarks, it might make sense to reduce some or all of the S-ALUs to pure

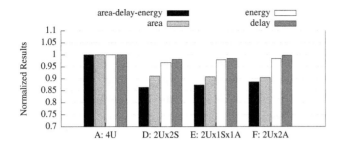

Figure 2: Average area-delay-energy product for architectures with 2 universal FUs and a mix of S-ALU and ALU functional units, with architecture A as reference.

ALUs. However, when we look at Table 2, we see that the shifter is relatively cheap, and that an ALU is only $0.93\times$ smaller than a S-ALU when the peripheral logic and crossbar connections are also factored in.

Figure 2 compares architectures with 2 Universal FUs, and a mix of S-ALUs and ALUs. As can be seen, the differences between the architectures D, E, and F are small, though as we convert from S-ALUs to ALUs we slightly decrease the area, and slightly increase the power and delay. Therefore, it makes sense to use the S-ALU to maximize the utility of both the peripheral logic and crossbar ports. The other advantage of building richer functional units is an increased opportunity for spatial locality when executing a sequence of operations that requires a diverse set of operators.

7. PREDICTING THE MIX OF FUNCTIONAL UNITS

It is valuable to be able to predict a good functional unit mix for different application domains by examining the characteristics of benchmarks in that application domain, instead of using extensive testing. We present a set of guidelines that combines the three principles for specializing the functional units (Section 6), and other constraints discussed in Section 4. Aside from their applicability to the Mosaic CGRA, these guideline can be applied to other CGRAs and tile-based spatial accelerators.

1. Every tile must support all operations.
2. Remove expensive and underutilized hardware: strip away MADD devices where possible.
3. Avoid over specialization, which can lead to under-utilization and poor spatial locality due to a lack of co-location.
4. Make FUs support rich functionality when it is inexpensive to do so: avoid standalone ALUs since a S-ALU is only marginally more expensive and can make better use of peripheral logic and crossbar resources.
5. Provide functional diversity within a tile to allow collocation and simultaneous execution of operations on expensive resources.

Validating the effectiveness of these guidelines is beyond the scope of this paper, but a preliminary evaluation is shown for the simple-dominant application category presented in Table 1. For the simple-dominant applications, our guidelines predict that G is the right architecture, because there is a much smaller percentage of complex operations, only 2.1% on average and a peak of 7.2%. Experimental results (omitted here due to space restrictions) showed that the predicted architecture G was within 2% of the best architecture, which took advantage of the fact that the number of shift operations is significantly smaller (only 3.4%) than for the balanced-dominant and select-dominant categories, and thus had fewer shifters.

8. CONCLUSIONS

Specializing the functional units within a CGRAs tile can improve the architecture's area-delay-energy product by $0.86\times$ just by paring down infrequently used hardware devices. Specifically, multiply and multiply-add operations are expensive and do not dominate all applications within the benchmark suite, thus requiring only one to two out of the four functional units to support them. While shift operations are also infrequent, they are relatively inexpensive to implement. More importantly, they do not require additional ports from the crossbar beyond what is required for an ALU. Therefore, they can be added for minimal cost and improve the opportunities for spatial locality; increased spatial locality reduces crossbar activity and increases the utility of each input port to the functional unit and the peripheral logic that supports the functional unit. Furthermore, maintaining a couple universal functional units within each cluster, rather than a set of FU types without functional overlap, provides better performance for applications within the domains that do not require specialized hardware.

9. REFERENCES

[1] P. Hung, H. Fahmy, O. Mencer, and M. Flynn, "Fast division algorithm with a small lookup table," vol. 2, 1999, pp. 1465 –1468 vol.2.

[2] R. Andraka, "A survey of CORDIC algorithms for FPGA based computers," in *FPGA*. New York, NY, USA: ACM, 1998, pp. 191–200.

[3] B. Van Essen, A. Wood, A. Carroll, S. Friedman, R. Panda, B. Ylvisaker, C. Ebeling, and S. Hauck, "Static versus scheduled interconnect in Coarse-Grained Reconfigurable Arrays," in *FPL*, 31 2009-Sept. 2 2009, pp. 268–275.

[4] B. Van Essen, R. Panda, C. Ebeling, and S. Hauck, "Managing short versus long lived signals in Coarse-Grained Reconfigurable Arrays," in *FPL*. Milano, Italy: IEEE, Aug. 31 - Sept. 2 2010, pp. 380–387.

[5] S. C. Goldstein, H. Schmit, M. Budiu, S. Cadambi, M. Moe, and R. Taylor, "PipeRench: A Reconfigurable Architecture and Compiler," *IEEE Computer*, vol. 33, no. 4, pp. 70–77, 2000.

[6] H. Singh, M.-H. Lee, G. Lu, F. Kurdahi, N. Bagherzadeh, and E. Chaves Filho, "MorphoSys: an integrated reconfigurable system for data-parallel and computation-intensive applications," *IEEE Transactions on Computers*, vol. 49, no. 5, pp. 465–481, 2000.

[7] D. Cronquist, C. Fisher, M. Figueroa, P. Franklin, and C. Ebeling, "Architecture design of reconfigurable pipelined datapaths," in *Advanced Research in VLSI*, Atlanta, 1999, pp. 23–40.

[8] Y. Kim, M. Kiemb, C. Park, J. Jung, and K. Choi, "Resource Sharing and Pipelining in Coarse-Grained Reconfigurable Architecture for Domain-Specific Optimization," in *DATE*. Washington, DC, USA: IEEE Computer Society, 2005, pp. 12–17.

[9] S. Wilton, N. Kafafi, B. Mei, and S. Vernalde, "Interconnect architectures for modulo-scheduled coarse-grained reconfigurable arrays," in *FPT*, 6-8 Dec. 2004, pp. 33–40.

[10] H. Lange and H. Schroder, "Evaluation strategies for coarse grained reconfigurable architectures," in *FPL*, 24-26 Aug. 2005, pp. 586–589.

Thermal and Power Characterization of Field-Programmable Gate Arrays

Abdullah Nazma Nowroz
School of Engineering
Brown University
Providence, RI 02912
Email: abdullah_nowroz@brown.edu

Sherief Reda
School of Engineering
Brown University
Providence, RI 02912
Email: sherief_reda@brown.edu

ABSTRACT

In this paper we propose new techniques for thermal and power characterization of Field Programmable Gate Arrays (FPGAs) using infrared imaging techniques. For thermal characterization, we capture the thermal emissions from the backside of an FPGA chip during operation. We analyze the captured emissions and quantify the extent of thermal gradients and hot spots in FPGAs. Given that FPGAs are fabricated with no knowledge of the potential field designs, we propose soft sensing techniques that can combine the measurements of hard sensors to accurately estimate the temperatures where no sensors are embedded. For power characterization, we propose algorithmic techniques to invert the thermal emissions from FPGAs into spatial power estimates. We demonstrate how this technique can be used to produce spatial power maps of soft processors during operation.

ACM Categories & Subject Descriptors
B.7.1 [Integrated Circuits]: Types and Design Styles.
General Terms: Design, Performance, Algorithms.
Keywords: Thermal characterization, sensors, power mapping.

1. INTRODUCTION

Given that FPGA-based implementations are less area and power efficient than their ASIC counterparts, power characterization for FPGAs is an active topic of research recent literature [11, 4]. The challenges in power characterization of heterogeneous FPGAs pose an interesting problem as these chips host programmable soft or hard processors. The power consumption of these processors is not entirely determined during design time as runtime workloads can impact the exact power consumption. Power consumption leads to heat dissipation which increases junction temperatures. Elevated temperatures and hot spots directly impact all key circuit metrics, including: lifetime and reliability, speed, power, and costs. Thus, it is necessary to conduct comprehensive thermal characterization of FPGAs to reduce the risk of increased temperature operation.

Previous works in FPGA power characterization focused on modeling techniques to estimate the power consumption during design time [11, 4, 10]. Compared to ASICs, the interconnect structure

of FPGAs (especially long routing tracks) consumes a significant amount of dynamic power [10]. A recent work describes a method to track percentage changes in dynamic power by tracking percentage changes in the frequencies of nearby ring oscillators [12]. With respect to thermal characterization, a number of papers attempt to quantify the magnitude of thermal gradients in FPGA chips [5, 12]. Due to the lack of knowledge of hot spot locations in FPGAs, many thermal sensor placement methods spatially allocate the sensors in a uniform way across the die [5, 12]. If the knowledge of a target set of benchmarks is first available, then benchmark-specific sensor insertion techniques can be used [8, 3]. Lopez-Buedo *et al.* propose reconfigurable thermal sensors using ring oscillators [6].

In recent years infrared imaging has received increased attention as a powerful tool for thermal and power characterization of real chips [2, 7, 9]. Despite the research efforts on the application of thermal imagery to processors, there are no reported results in the literature for applying infrared imaging to FPGAs. The objective of this paper is to provide thermal and power characterization techniques for FPGAs from the infrared emissions emitted from the backside of the silicon during operation. The main contributions of this paper are as follows.

- Previously published results on FPGA power and thermal characterization and modeling used either simulations or measurements from a limited number of on-die sensors. This paper complements the research of previous papers by providing thermal and power characterization methods based on infrared emissions emitted from FPGAs. Infrared imaging has not been applied before to FPGAs (at least in the literature), and our paper is the first to make such contribution.

- We quantify the extent of thermal gradients during runtime, and we propose a new technique, *soft sensing*, that can utilize the measurements of hard sensors to accurately estimate the temperatures where no sensors are embedded.

- We propose a power characterization methodology that inverts the spatial thermal emissions from FPGAs into power maps.

- Using a real FPGA chip, we demonstrate the effectiveness of applying our proposed thermal and power characterization methodologies. We estimate the spatial power maps of a soft processor during runtime.

The organization of this paper is as follows. We describe our thermal characterization and sensor allocation techniques in Section 2. Our power characterization technique is described in Section 3. In Section 4 we present our experimental results for both thermal and power characterization. Finally, Section 5 summarizes the main conclusions of this work.

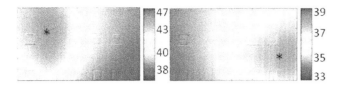

Figure 1: Example of possible thermal gradients in an FPGA.

2. THERMAL CHARACTERIZATION

The fact that FPGA functionality is programmable implies that a diverse range of possible thermal gradients could exist during operation. For thermal characterization, we consider a section of the FPGA die which is approximately 20 mm in width and 10 mm in length. We embed two different designs and capture the thermal emissions as given in Figure 1. The figure demonstrates that the magnitude and location of the maximum temperature, or hot spot, vary significantly among the two traces. For instance, the thermal trace of the first figure shows a maximum temperature of 47°C with a thermal gradient of about 9°C between the hottest and the coldest part of the die's section. The second trace shows a maximum temperature of 39.5°C and a difference of 7°C between the hottest and coldest spots. Furthermore, the hot spot in the right trace is about 14 mm away from the location of the hot spot of the left trace. These variations make the task of allocating thermal sensors particularly challenging.

To enable effective thermal management of FPGAs, it is necessary to insert thermal sensors at potential hot spot locations. All current FPGAs (e.g., Altera's Stratix family or Xilinx's Virtex family) use only one thermal sensor. The possibility of large thermal gradients on the FPGA die as demonstrated in Figure 1 implies that the measurements of one sensor will not necessarily capture the maximum temperature of the FPGA chip.

Because FPGAs are manufactured to accommodate a large number of possible designs, it is not possible to know the locations of hot spots *a priori* during manufacturing time as hot spot locations depend on the design and the design's layout configured into the FPGA. Thus, hot spot locations can only be known after a particular design is programmed into the FPGA. As the locations of hard sensors are fixed into the manufactured FPGA, the locations of these sensors could be far from the true hot spot locations. Increasing the number of sensors is not a feasible idea as digital thermal sensors consume die area because their need to accommodate analog to digital converters, and thus designers limit their numbers. To circumvent this limitation, we propose the idea of *soft sensors* to augment the placed hard sensors measurements and improve thermal tracking by estimating the temperature at locations where no sensor are embedded.

In our proposed technique, a soft sensor measurement is equal to a weighted linear combination of the measurements of the hard sensors. Thus, if $\hat{t}(l)$ denotes the estimated soft sensor temperature at location l then this estimated temperature can be expressed by

$$\hat{t}(l) = \sum_{i=1}^{k} w(l, s_i) \mathbf{t_m}(s_i), \qquad (1)$$

where $\mathbf{t_m}(s_i)$'s are the measurements reported by the k sensors and $w(l, s_1), \ldots, w(l, s_k)$ are the weights corresponding to the k sensors that change depending on the location, l, where the temperature needs to be estimated. To determine the best set of weights for some location l, thermal characterization traces collected from the infrared imaging system or from simulation can be used to learn the optimal way to combine the measurements of the hard sensors. Let the collected thermal traces be donated by $\mathbf{t_m^1}, \ldots, \mathbf{t_m^n}$. Given the n traces, we can construct the following set of equations:

$$
\begin{aligned}
\mathbf{Cw}(l) &= \begin{pmatrix} \mathbf{t_m^1}(s_1) & \cdots & \mathbf{t_m^1}(s_k) \\ \vdots & \vdots & \vdots \\ \mathbf{t_m^n}(s_1) & \cdots & \mathbf{t_m^n}(s_k) \end{pmatrix} \begin{pmatrix} w(l, s_1) \\ \vdots \\ w(l, s_k) \end{pmatrix} \\
&= \begin{pmatrix} \mathbf{t_m^1}(l) \\ \vdots \\ \mathbf{t_m^n}(l) \end{pmatrix} = \mathbf{T}(l), \qquad (2)
\end{aligned}
$$

which can be written succinctly in matrix notation as $\mathbf{Cw}(l) = \mathbf{T}(l)$. The best set of weights $\mathbf{w}(l)$ that minimizes the total least square error can be computed as follows:

$$\mathbf{w}(l) = (\mathbf{C}^T \mathbf{C})^{-1} \mathbf{C}^T \mathbf{T}(l), \qquad (3)$$

where ^{T} indicates the matrix transpose operation. Computing the optimal weights should be carried only once off-line either during (1) design time using the results from thermal modeling and simulation tools, or (2) after fabrication where infrared imaging techniques are typically used to provide the necessary characterization and calibration of the embedded thermal sensors. The computed weights can be then distributed by the FPGA vendor as part of their tool chain. In current FPGA tools, the user must select the exact target device of the tool before synthesizing any design. Thus, storing a set of soft sensor weights for each device fits naturally with existing FPGA tool chain flows. During design time, the FPGA tool can create the necessary soft sensors based on the placement results of the programmed design or at any desired input locations supplied by the user. The physical implementation of a soft sensor requires only one adder-accumulator multiplier to compute the weighted sum as described by Equation (1).

The proposed soft sensing technique has advantages over previously proposed reconfigurable sensors based on ring oscillators [6, 12]. Ring oscillator based sensors are affected by process variability and operating voltages and thus thermal calibration needs to be conducted on every manufactured device independently. On contrast, the weights of the proposed soft sensing technique need to be estimated only once for an entire device family. These weights reflect the thermal conductances between different parts of the die which are not affected by underlying nano-scale electrical variations. Furthermore, these weights can be determined either using infrared measurements (as in our approach) or from the final design layout using thermal modeling tools. Once these weights are determined, they are distributed with the vendor's tools as part of the characteristics of the device family.

3. POWER CHARACTERIZATION

The physical relationship between power and temperature is governed by the heat diffusion equation. In steady state, the heat equation is given by

$$\nabla \cdot (k(x,y) \nabla t(x,y)) - ht(x,y) = -p(x,y), \qquad (4)$$

where $k(x,y)$ is the thermal conductivity at location (x,y), $t(x,y)$ is temperature at location (x,y) relative to the ambient temperature, $p(x,y)$ is the power density at location (x,y), and h is the heat transfer coefficient. The explicit use of location in the thermal conductance $k(x,y)$ is important as different parts of the chip have different material composition which impacts lateral heat diffusion.

In any practical implementation, the heat equation has to be discretized. This discretization comes from the finite memory size of any computer and more importantly from the use of thermal imaging equipment with limited spatial resolution. In a discretized form, the continuous temperature signal $t(x,y)$ is represented by a vector $\mathbf{t}$ that gives the temperatures at a discrete set of die locations, and the continuous power signal $p(x,y)$ is represented by a vector $\mathbf{p}$ that gives the power at the same set of discrete die locations. In such case, Equation (4) is approximated by the following linear matrix formulation

$$\mathbf{R}\mathbf{p} + \mathbf{e} = \mathbf{t} + \mathbf{e} = \mathbf{t_m}, \tag{5}$$

where the matrix $\mathbf{R}$ gives the thermal resistivity between different discrete locations of the die, the vector $\mathbf{e}$ denotes the errors in measurements created by the infrared imaging system, and $\mathbf{t_m}$ denotes the vector of measured temperatures.

The objective of the *thermal to power inversion problem* is to find the vector $\mathbf{p}$ that leads to the temperatures $\mathbf{t}$. Given the thermal measurements $\mathbf{t_m}$ from the infrared camera, the objective is to find the best power pattern $\mathbf{p}$ that minimizes the total squared error between the temperatures as computed using Equation (5) and the measured temperatures; that is,

$$\arg_{\mathbf{p}} \min \parallel \mathbf{R}\mathbf{p} - \mathbf{t_m} \parallel_2^2, \tag{6}$$

where $\parallel \cdot \parallel_2$ indicate the L_2 norm, and under the constraints that the sum of the elements of the power vector is equal to the total power consumption of the chip p_{total} and that the power estimates must be greater than zero; i.e.,

$$\parallel \mathbf{p} \parallel_1 = \sum_i p_i = p_{total} \text{ and } \mathbf{p} \geq \mathbf{0}, \tag{7}$$

where where $\parallel \cdot \parallel_1$ indicate the L_1 norm and p_{total} is the total power consumption of the chip. We use MATLAB's quadric optimization solver (`lsqlin`) to minimize (6) under the constraints of Equations (7). The solver uses the active-set strategy (also known as a projection method) which relies on two step solution. The first step calculates a feasible solution point, and the second phase generates an iterative sequence of feasible solution points that converge to the final solution.

4. EXPERIMENTAL RESULTS

We use a 90 nm Altera Stratix II EP2S180 FPGA with 180,000 logic elements. For our experiments, we only consider a portion the die of dimensions 20 mm × 10 mm. To capture the thermal emissions from the backside of the FPGA, we use a FLIR SC5600 infrared camera with a mid-wave spectral range of 2.5 μm − 5.1 μm. The camera is capable of operating at 100 Hz with a spatial resolution of 30 μm with a 0.5× microscopy kit. The camera's cyrogenic cooled InSb detectors have a sensitivity of about 20 mK noise equivalent temperature difference. We devise a pixel-by-pixel calibration process that translates the captured emissions (as measured by the digital levels of the camera's analog to digial converters) to temperatures to get an accurate thermal imagery. For total power measurement, we externally intercept the current to the FPGA by a 1 mΩ shunt resistor. The voltage (1 mV for every 1 A) across the shunt resistor is measured through an Agilent 34410 digital multimeter. Our setup is illustrated in Figure 2.

The objective of the first experiment is to demonstrate the advantages of using soft sensors to augment hard sensors. For the hard sensors, we consider their locations to be allocated in a regular and uniform way across the die. We first collect tens of thermal traces that arise from different designs embedded in the FPGA. These designs have different spatial power allocations which vary the thermal characteristics. To quantify the error in hot spot tracking, we define the *thermal error* for a thermal trace as the difference between the maximum of the measurements at the locations of the thermal sensors and the maximum temperature in the trace. We report the *worst thermal error* across all traces as a function of the number of sensors in Figure 3 for both hard and soft sensors. The results show that soft sensing can cut the tracking error by 40% bringing the error to within less than 1°C with just three sensors.

In the second experiment we evaluate our spatial power mapping technique by inverting the thermal emissions of the Nios II soft processor, while running the standard Dhrystone 2.1 application, into spatial power estimates. We consider two different configurations of the Nios II processor: the standard model Nios II/s with multipliers implemented in the FPGA's DSP blocks and the full-performance model Nios II/f. We first constrain the logic blocks of the Nios II processor to fit into a 30 × 30 array of logic blocks (about 6.4 mm × 7.0 mm) of the layout as shown in Figure 4.a and then capture the steady-state thermal emissions $\mathbf{t_m}$ from this area as shown in Figure 4.b. The total power consumption of the two configurations are 315 mW (Nios II/s) and 477 mW (Nios II/f).

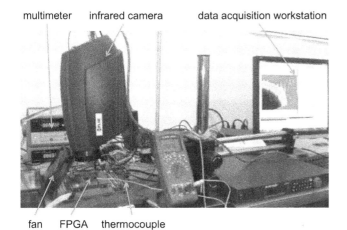

multimeter   infrared camera   data acquisition workstation

fan   FPGA   thermocouple

Figure 2: Experimental setup.

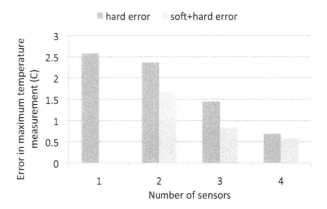

Figure 3: Error in temperature tracking in °C as a function of the number of sensors using soft sensors.

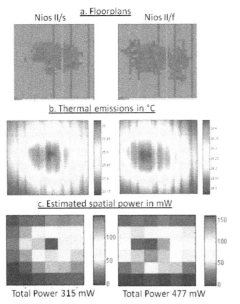

a. Floorplans

Nios II/s   Nios II/f

b. Thermal emissions in °C

c. Estimated spatial power in mW

Total Power 315 mW   Total Power 477 mW

Figure 4: Spatial power estimates of Nios II processors running Dhrystone 2.1 application.

For the purpose of spatial power mapping, we discretize the layout area into 6×6 regions, and thus the $\mathbf{p}$ vector is comprised of 36 elements that need to be estimated.

To compute the power map $\mathbf{p}$ from the thermal emissions $\mathbf{t_m}$, we need to estimate the matrix $\mathbf{R}$ as given by Equation (5). We estimate the matrix $\mathbf{R}$ in a column-by-column basis. We note that the kth column of matrix $\mathbf{R}$ can be obtained by setting the vector $\mathbf{p}$ to be equal to $[0\ 0 \cdots 1 \cdots 0\ 0]^T$, where the "1" is at the kth location of the $\mathbf{p}$ vector, and then use the resultant emissions $\mathbf{t_k}$ directly as the kth column of matrix $\mathbf{R}$. To realize this setting, we utilize the fact that FPGAs are programmable. For each power region k, we embed, and turn on, ring oscillators precisely into the logic array blocks that are available in the region, while the rest of the blocks in the design are inactive. Such precise embedding is possible with Altera's Quartus II tool. The resultant thermal emissions $\mathbf{t_k}$ from such embedding are then normalized by the total power p_k that is measured externally through the digital multimeter. Thus, column k of matrix $\mathbf{R}$ is equal to $\mathbf{t_k}/p_k$. We automate the whole process in order to measure the 36 columns of $\mathbf{R}$ with fast turn-around time. Our earlier work describes the automated embedding procedure in more details [1].

With the estimated matrix $\mathbf{R}$ and thermal emissions from the Nios II processor (Figure 4.b), we compute the spatial power maps using the procedure given in Section 3. The estimated spatial power maps in mW are plotted in Figure 4.c. Our estimated spatial maps augment the floorplan with valuable spatial power density estimates. The revealed detailed power estimation maps can be used to calibrate the estimates from high-level dynamic power modeling tools. Given that the design of the Nios II processor is proprietary, it is not possible for us to match the spatial power consumption estimates to the various functional blocks of the processor.

5. CONCLUSIONS

In this paper we have presented new techniques for thermal and power characterization of FPGAs using infrared emissions. We described experimental techniques to capture the infrared emissions from the backside of FPGAs. Using the thermal images, we elucidated the magnitude of thermal gradients and hot spots in FPGAs.

We have demonstrated that up to 9°C gradients can exist within our tested FPGA. To circumvent the lack of knowledge of hot spots in FPGAs and improve thermal tracking, we proposed a soft sensor technique that combines the measurements of hard sensors to estimate the temperatures at locations where no sensors are embedded. Our technique is capable of reducing the thermal tracking error by 40%. For power characterization, we proposed a new technique for thermal to power inversion for FPGAs using quadratic program optimization. We have proposed experimental techniques to estimate the different parameters required for power mapping. We used our power mapping methodology to estimate the spatial power distribution of an embedded soft processor during operation.

6. REFERENCES

[1] R. Cochran, A. Nowroz, and S. Reda, "Post-Silicon Power Characterization Using Thermal Infrared Emissions," in *International Symposium on Low Power Electronics and Design*, 2010, pp. 331–336.

[2] H. Hamann, A. Weger, J. Lacey, Z. Hu, and P. Bose, "Hotspot-Limited Microprocessors: Direct Temperature and Power Distribution Measurements," *IEEE Journal of Solid-State Circuits*, vol. 42, no. 1, pp. 56–65, 2007.

[3] B. Lee, K. Chung, B. Koo, and N. Eum, "Thermal Sensor Allocation and Placement for Reconfigurable Systems," *Transactions on Design Automation of Electronic Systems*, vol. 4, no. 41, pp. 50:1–23, 2009.

[4] F. Li, Y. Lin, L. He, D. Chen, and J. Cong, "Power Modeling and Characteristics of Field Programmable Gate Arrays," *IEEE Transactions on Computer Aided Design of Integrated Circuits*, vol. 24, no. 11, pp. 1712–1724, 2005.

[5] S. Lopez-Buedo and E. I. Boemo, "Making Visible the Thermal Behaviour of Embedded Microprocessors on FPGAs: A Progress Report," in *International Symposium on Field Programmable Gate Arrays*, 2004, pp. 79–86.

[6] S. Lopez-Buedo, J. Garrido, and E. Boemo, "Dynamically Inserting, Operating, and Eliminating Thermal Sensors of FPGA-Based Systems," *IEEE Transactions on Components and Packaging Technologies*, vol. 25, no. 4, pp. 561–566, 2002.

[7] F. J. Mesa-Martinez, M. Brown, J. Nayfach-Battilana, and J. Renau, "Measuring Performance, Power, and Temperature from Real Processors," in *International Symposium on Computer Architecture*, 2007, pp. 1–10.

[8] R. Mukherjee, S. Mondal, and S. O. Memik, "Thermal Sensor Allocation and Placement for Reconfigurable Systems," in *International Conference on Computer Aided Design*, 2006, pp. 437–442.

[9] A. N. Nowroz, R. Cochran, and S. Reda, "Thermal Monitoring of Real Processors: Techniques for Sensor Allocation and Full Characterization," in *Design Automation Conference*, 2010, pp. 56–61.

[10] K. Poon, S. Wilton, and A. Yan, "A Detailed Power Model for Field-Programmable Gate Arrays," *ACM Transactions on Design Automation of Electronic Systems*, vol. 10, no. 2, pp. 279–302, 2005.

[11] L. Shang, A. Kaviani, and K. Bathala, "Dynamic Power Consumption in Virtex-II FPGA Family," in *International Symposium on Field Programmable Gate Arrays*, 2002, pp. 157–164.

[12] K. Zick and J. Hayes, "On-line Sensing for Healthier FPGA Systems," in *International Symposium on Field Programmable Gate Arrays*, 2010, pp. 239–248.

DEEP: An Iterative FPGA-based Many-Core Emulation System for Chip Verification and Architecture Research

Juergen Ributzka, Yuhei Hayashi,
Guang R. Gao
University of Delaware
140 Evans Hall
Newark, DE 19716
{ributzka,hayashi,ggao}@capsl.udel.edu

Fei Chen
ARM Inc.
3711 S. Mopac Expressway
Building 1, Suite 400
Austin, TX 78746
fei.chen@arm.com

ABSTRACT

This paper introduces the Delaware Enhanced Emulation Platform (DEEP) - a FPGA-based emulation system for hardware/software co-verification of many-core chip architectures. This platform exhibits the following three characteristics: fast compilation of logic designs, debugging support, and affordability. It is based on a novel iterative emulation methodology for hardware design and verification.

We also conducted a logic design and integration of a new architectural feature that provides Full/Empty bit fine-grain synchronization for the IBM Cyclops-64 many-core architecture and evaluated its performance against existing synchronization constructs.

Categories and Subject Descriptors

C.4 [**PERFORMANCE OF SYSTEMS**]: Measurement techniques

General Terms

Design, Verification, Performance

1. INTRODUCTION

Currently, full-system verification still requires an armada of computers or expensive specialized hardware [1, 4] to achieve reasonable emulation speed. A cluster of computers can be made easily available to a larger group of developers, but the overall emulation speed is still limited. On the other hand, specialized hardware is much faster, but it is a scarce resource. Faster and cheaper hardware emulation and verification systems are needed to mitigate this problem.

The need for better and faster verification frameworks is growing even stronger with the introduction of new execution models for massive many-core designs. These models provide feedback to hardware architects about possible advantageous features. This results in a symbiotic relationship,

which requires hardware/software co-development methodologies. These new methodologies have caught the attention of many high profile research institutions, including DARPA, which is funding a project with the main objective to explore these techniques [2]. Development of such techniques would greatly benefit from better, faster and affordable emulation systems.

Among the new many-core designs, we have the IBM Cyclops-64 (C64) many-core architecture. The architecture consists of 160 homogeneous processing elements called Thread Units (TUs). These 160 TUs are connected via a high speed crossbar interconnect and share 4.7 MiB of internal memory. There are no data caches on this architecture - only Instruction-Caches (ICs). Moreover, the architecture has support for hardware based barriers. Finally, all levels of the memory hierarchy are fully software managed and distributed across three different memory spaces: Scratch Pad memory, the Global Interleaved SRAM and the off chip DDR2 memory.

To test the C64 architecture's hardware features and software stack, a custom made FPGA-based emulation system (DEEP) was created. The emulation system for the C64 architecture was specifically designed and built for many-core architecture emulation and verification. Its unique iterative approach allows the emulation of huge many-core systems with a limited set of FPGAs based on a methodology introduced in [6].

The original work behind this paper has covered two distinct topics: many-core emulation methodologies and architectural research. However, due to the space limitation, this short paper will mainly focus on the first topic. For a more complete coverage of both topics please refer to [5].

The remainder of the paper is structured as following: Section 2 explains the emulation system, its emulation methodology, and its debugging features. Section 3 evaluates the implementation of fine-grain synchronization and provides performance results compared to other synchronization constructs. Section 4 gives a overview of related work and Section 5 concludes the paper.

2. DEEP: THE EMULATION SYSTEM

In this section we describe the hardware platform, the emulation methodology and the debugging support of the Delaware Enhanced Emulation Platform (DEEP). DEEP has been developed in order to validate the C64 chip's hardware features and test its software stack. It can be ported to emulate other many-core architectures too. The major ob-

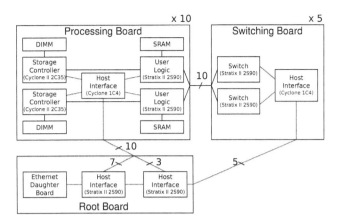

Figure 1: Block Diagram of DEEP: The figure shows the tree-like connections between the FPGAs and the different board types - root board, processing boards, and switching boards.

jectives of DEEP are to support all design and test stages, to realize good turn-around time for the early stages and high emulation speed for the later stages of development, to do the whole chip emulation as well as to provide an efficient debugging environment.

2.1 DEEP Hardware Platform

The DEEP hardware platform is comprised of a host system and a custom made system with a series of highly connected FPGAs. Figure 1 shows the block diagram of DEEP. 16 FPGA boards are plugged into the backplane, which provides not only power, but also the global clock (100 MHz) and interconnection to all FPGA boards. There are three different type of FPGA boards: root board, processing boards, and switching boards. The root board has two Altera Stratix II 2S90 FPGAs and a daughter board for the Ethernet connection to the host system. The Ethernet daughter board has additional logic, which allows the remote programming of all FPGAs in the system via Ethernet. The FPGAs on the root board are used to implement the root node of a tree. The remaining FPGAs in the system are connected in a tree like fashion to the root board. This allows the host system to communicate with all FPGAs. The processing board has five FPGAs. One Cyclone 1C4 FPGA for the tree node, two Stratix II 2S90 FPGAs for the user logic, and two Cyclone II 2C35 FPGAs for interfacing logic to the DIMMs. These additional FPGAs for the memory interface are required to refresh the memory while reprogramming the user logic in the other FPGAs. The switching board has two Stratix II 2S90 FPGAs, which are used to implement the switching logic for the emulation system. The processing boards are connected via the backplane to the switching boards. These connections are used during emulation to pass data between the different processing boards. The tree connection is only used by the host for communication with the FPGAs. Overall, only 20 Stratix II 2S90 FPGAs can be used for emulating user logic.

2.2 DEEP Emulation Methodology

In order to achieve its main objective, DEEP supports two different modes: simulation mode and emulation mode. The simulation mode is a *logic processor* based logic simulation methodology. In this mode, the original logic design

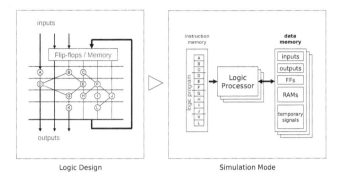

Figure 2: Simulation Mode: User Logic Design to Logic Program mapping. The logic primitives (A-L) shown in the original logic design on the left are translated into instructions for the logic processor shown on the right.

is translated into logic programs. This means the logic design, which usually consists of a netlist of gates and memory cells, is mapped to a series of logic instructions. Therefore, the *logic processors* are able to simulate any logic design. These instructions are executed on a large number of *logic processors* on the processing FPGAs. Figure 2 shows the translation of a logic design into a logic program. DEEP can quickly generate logic programs from an original logic design, because only a simple translation from a netlist to an instruction stream is required. No synthesize is required, because the *logic processors* do not change. For instance, the C64 combinatorial logic design (around 43 million gates) can be translated into logic programs within two minutes. Logic programs generated from an original design are executed on a huge number of *logic processors* (400 in DEEP). Each processing FPGA has 20 *logic processors*. One instruction queue is shared by all *logic processors* in one FPGA. There are only 20 processing FPGAs, therefore at most 20 different submodules in a logic design can be simulated in this system. If one submodule has more than 20 instances, then multiple processing FPGAs are utilized for it. The simulation mode is also available on a general workstation, so logic simulation can be done anywhere without the DEEP hardware, although the simulation speed is much slower. In case of the C64 design the average simulation speed of the whole chip is around 110 cycles/second. We do not have any comparable numbers for the software version on a workstation, because we never simulated the whole chip in software. We only simulated a subset of the C64 chip (only 10 Thread Units), which is just a 16th of the whole design, with approximately 1 cycle/second.

On the other hand, the emulation mode design is based on an iterative emulation methodology [6]. Since the whole many-core architecture design cannot fit into a single FPGA of DEEP (or any current available FPGA on the market), the architectural design is separated into submodules. Even though each submodule fits into one FPGA, a lot of FPGAs would be required to implement the entire chip in the emulation system. In particular, the C64 chip would require 236 FPGAs to emulate the whole chip logic. Instead of mapping each submodule to a different FPGA, the emulation system adopts an iterative emulation approach (see Figure 3). Combinatorial logic equivalent submodules are implemented on only one (or a few FPGAs), and then iteratively utilized to emulate all instances of the submodule.

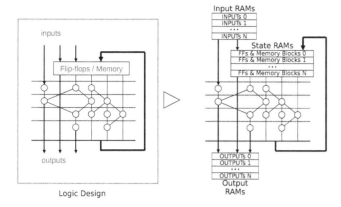

Figure 3: Emulation Mode: User Logic Design to Iterative Emulation mapping. FFs and RAMs are extracted from the original logic design on the left and mapped to instance addressable memory blocks in the FPGA. The combinatorial logic is used iteratively in the FPGA.

This emulation methodology drastically reduces the necessary number of FPGAs. Each submodule's FFs and internal RAM blocks are isolated from the original logic design. The content of the FFs and RAMs are independent of each submodule's instance, so they must be stored separately. The emulation system utilizes internal memories for FFs and external memories for RAM blocks, and only the combinatorial logic is implemented in the FPGA. The flow described above is done by the DEEP software automatically for the C64 architecture. The partitioning of the full logic design is currently done manually and other architectures would require the same manual procedure of partitioning and assigning submodules to FPGAs. Because logic design needs to be synthesized and mapped into FPGAs, it takes much more preparation time than the simulation mode until the logic design is ready to be emulated. Since the submodules can be synthesize in parallel, the whole process takes around 2-3 hours for the C64 chip. However, after the logic design is mapped into the FPGA, it works as real logic on a FPGA, even though it is required to emulate the logic iteratively. In case of the C64 design the average emulation speed of the whole chip is around 80k cycles/second.

2.3 DEEP Debugging Support

At last we discuss the debugging support in DEEP, which is available for simulation mode and emulation mode.

In simulation mode, there are two ways to obtain signals. If inputs, outputs and contents of FFs/RAM blocks of a submodule need to be observed, the DEEP host can directly accesses the external memory, where the target data is stored. For the other signals, additional processing is required, because all intermediate signals are in the local temporary memory of a *logic processor* and may be overwritten. Furthermore, they are also unreachable for the DEEP host. Additional debugging control logic is required to perform the following steps: First, the DEEP host sets a breakpoint in the debugging special-purpose register of the *logic processor*. Second, the *logic processor* starts execution until the program counter reaches the breakpoint. Third, the debugging control unit issues several logic instructions to move the value of the signal to the external memory of the FPGA. Finally, the DEEP host loads the data from the external

memory. For this debugging feature, there are 16 special purpose registers available. If more than 16 signals in one submodule are necessary to be observed at the same time, the DEEP host needs to repeat this process for every set of 16 signals. By utilizing both ways to obtain signals, it is possible to achieve 100% signal debugging coverage. Moreover, not only simple signal tracing is possible, but also program tracing is supported, when a processor is simulated.

In emulation mode debugging support is very useful to locate bugs in long running benchmarks. There are again two ways to obtain signals in emulation mode. The first way is the same as for the simulation mode. Input, outputs, FFs, etc of a submodule can be directly accessed by the DEEP host. Unfortunately, in this mode all combinatorial logic is mapped into the FPGA, so it cannot be observed directly. A software simulator on the DEEP host is used in conjunction with the hardware emulator to obtain signals inside combinatorial logic. All the required content from the inputs, FFs and memory blocks of a submodule is obtained by the DEEP host and the resulting combinatorial signal is calculated by the simulator. Even though it is technically not possible to observe all signals inside the FPGA, the missing signal can still be simulated on the DEEP host to obtain full signal debugging coverage. Of course also program tracing is supported in emulation mode if a processor is emulated.

3. CASE STUDY

We used the DEEP platform to enhance the Cyclops-64 architecture with Full/Empty Bit support. In this section we evaluate the performance benefits of our fine-grain synchronization extension. In particular, we took a closer look at a wavefront computation-style program. We created a micro-benchmark, which resembles the data dependencies of a wavefront computation. Since obeying these dependencies are the critical factor of any wavefront computation, this micro-benchmark should be able to give us an estimate on the performance benefits of Full/Empty Bit support versus traditional synchronization constructs.

Due to the dependence of an element on its previously computed neighbors, parallel versions of the wavefront kernel require synchronization constructs to ensure correctness.

We implemented the wavefront computation kernel in four different versions. The different versions are Serial, Barrier, Full/Empty Bit Busy-Wait, and Full/Empty Bit Sleep-Wakeup. The Full/Empty Bit Busy-Wait version constantly polls the memory location until the value has been written. On the other side, the Full/Empty Bit Sleep-Wakeup version only tries once to read the value and then goes to sleep. The producer will wake up the consumer once the value is available. All kernels were completely hand-coded and optimized in assembly to allow for a fair comparison. We run the benchmark on the emulation system for problem sizes starting at 16x16 at increments of 16 up to the maximum supported problem size of 512x512 elements. For each problem size we run the wavefront benchmark with different numbers of threads. Starting from one thread all the way up to 159 threads[1] at increments of one. The numbers collected were measured only for the kernel part of the application and the speedup was calculated based on the results of the serial version.

---

[1] Only 159 threads can be used, because the OS micro kernel is running on the first thread unit

For the barrier version of the benchmark we achieved a maximal speedup of 24x. Even though the barrier is very efficient, because it has hardware support, the speedup of the application is limited. This is due to the weakest link in the chain, which is the slowest thread. All other threads have to wait for the slowest thread before they can continue doing useful work. Using barriers for these kind of workloads is not necessarily a good choice and dynamic scheduling approaches have achieved better results. We are aware of this, but we chose to demonstrate the barrier implementation for two important reasons. First, the barrier is a hardware supported synchronization construct and we wanted to compare different hardware supported synchronization constructs. Second, from a programing point of view the barriers seems to be an easy and efficient construct, because the work for each thread is the same. We wanted to show that this thinking cannot be applied anymore to many-core architectures and that congestion, bank conflicts, etc can have unpredictable impacts on a threads execution.The Full/Empty bit versions of the benchmarks achieved much better speedups of 60x and 50x respectively. We took a closer look at both benchmarks by using performance counters. In summary we can say both versions of the Full/Empty bit implementation are not memory bound. The busy-wait version has a synchronization failure rate of 150%. That means every synchronizing load operation has to be repeated 1.5 times in average, because the data had not been written yet by the producer. The sleep-wakeup on the other hand had a failure rate of only 1-2%. Nevertheless, the busy-wait approach still achieved better speedups. The second approach generates less memory operations and also saves power, but the price is a longer synchronization delay, which hinders parallelism and therefore performance.

4. RELATED WORK

There have been many logic verification technologies and products developed in both academia and industry [7, 3]. These technologies have been used to address the many challenges in the logic verification processes.

The iterative emulation methodology, which is adopted in the emulation mode of DEEP, was introduced by Dr. Sakane et al. [6] in 2003. Their emulation system was implemented into one Xilinx Virtex-II FPGA, because of the limited size of the verification target. Moreover, there is no debugging support.

ASIC based logic verification environments and emulation systems have been developed from many Electrical Design Automation (EDA) tool vendors. Mentor Graphics Veloce platform and Cadence Palladimu system are good examples. The Veloce platform [4] is an ASIC based logic verification system developed by Mentor Graphics. This hardware accelerated logic simulation platform utilizes a custom designed emulation chip that contains a programmable logic block for the target logic and a fixed functional block. This fixed functional block handles signal tracing and interconnecting operations. The Palladium platforms [1] from Cadence provide simulation acceleration and in-circuit emulation in a single system.

The RAMP [7] system developed at Berkeley is a FPGA-based many-core emulation platform. This system deploys Xilinx Virtex-II Pro FPGAs on 16-21 BEE2 boards to implement a many-core system composed of 1000 plus cores. The purpose of this project is to explore the architectural design space for future many-core computer architectures and enable early software development and debugging.

A more detailed collection and comparison of related work is presented in [5].

5. CONCLUSIONS

This short paper presented our emulation platform DEEP with its simulation mode, emulation mode, and debugging features. A more detailed explanation of the emulation methodologies and a full coverage of the fine-grain synchronization architecture research can be found in [5].

We also presented a study on how to enhance a many-core chip design with a novel architecture feature using the DEEP framework. In this study, we used the frameworks extensive debugging capabilities to isolate and fix several bugs in our design. Finally, we found that by adding fine-grain synchronization to the C64 design, we can get substantial performance improvements (60x speedup versus 24x speedup) in wavefront like applications.

We also observed a shortcoming of DEEP in the connection between the DEEP host system and the DEEP emulation platform. The current connection uses gigabit Ethernet, which it is unsuitable for tracing hundreds of cores. This requires more research in compact parallel tracing formats and better interconnects.

6. ACKNOWLEDGMENTS

Our utmost respect goes to Monty Denneau for creating such a great architecture. This work would have not been possible without the support by NSF (CNS-0509332, CSR-0720531, CCF-0833166, CCF-0702244), and other government sponsors.

7. REFERENCES

[1] Cadence. Incisive Palladium Series. http://www.cadence.com.

[2] DARPA. Ubiquitous High Performance Computing. https://www.fbo.gov/spg/ODA/DARPA/CMO/DARPA-BAA-10-37/listing.html.

[3] J. Darringer, E. Davidson, D. J. Hathaway, B. Koenemann, M. Lavin, J. K. Morrell, K. Rahmat, W. Roesner, E. Schanzenbach, G. Tellez, and L. Trevillyan. EDA in IBM: Past, Present, and Future. *IEEE Transactions on Computer Aided Design of Integrated Circuits and Systems*, 22:1476–1497, 2000.

[4] M. Graphics. Veloce SoC Verification System. http://www.mentor.com.

[5] J. Ributzka, Y. Hayashi, F. Chen, and G. Gao. CAPSL Technical Memo 103: DEEP: An Iterative FPGA-based Many-Core Emulation System for Chip Verification and Architecture Research, December 2010.

[6] H. Sakane, L. Yakay, V. Karna, C. Leung, and G. Gao. DIMES: An Iterative Emulation Platform for Multiprocessor-System-on-Chip Designs. In *2003 IEEE International Conference on Field-Programmable Technology (FPT), 2003. Proceedings*, pages 244–251, 2003.

[7] J. Wawrzynek, D. Patterson, M. Oskin, S. Lu, C. Kozyrakis, J. Hoe, D. Chiou, and K. Asanovic. RAMP: Research Accelerator for Multiple Processors. *IEEE Micro*, 27:46–57, 2007.

Bridging the GPGPU-FPGA Efficiency Gap

Christopher W. Fletcher†‡, Ilia Lebedev‡, Narges B. Asadi◊, Daniel R. Burke‡, John Wawrzynek‡

† CSAIL, Massachusetts Institute of Technology; Cambridge, MA, USA
‡ EECS Dept., University of California, Berkeley; Berkeley, CA, USA
◊ EE Dept., Stanford University; Stanford, CA, USA
cwfletcher@csail.mit.edu, {ilial,drburke,johnw}@berkeley.edu, nargesb@stanford.edu

ABSTRACT

This paper compares an implementation of a Bayesian inference algorithm across several FPGAs and GPGPUs, while embracing both the execution model and high-level architecture of a GPGPU. Our study is motivated by recent work in template-based programming and architectural models for FPGA computing. The comparison we present is meant to demonstrate the FPGA's potential, while constraining the design to follow the microarchitectural template of more programmable devices such as GPGPUs.

The FPGA implementation proves capable of matching the performance of a high-end Nvidia Fermi-based GPU— the most advanced GPGPU available to us at the time of this study. Further investigation shows that each FPGA core outperforms workstation GPGPU cores by a factor of $\sim 3.14\times$, and mobile GPGPU cores by $\sim 4.25\times$ despite a $\sim 4\times$ reduction in core clock frequency. Using these observations, we discuss the efficiency gap between these two platforms, and the challenges associated with template-based programming models.

Categories and Subject Descriptors

C.3 [**Computer Systems Organization**]: Special-Purpose and Application-Based Systems

General Terms

Design, Performance, Algorithms

Keywords

FPGA, GPGPU, OpenCL, Reconfigurable Computing, Bayesian Networks

1. INTRODUCTION

FPGA designs are often highly specialized for their application, employing custom architectures and a variety of execution models [6, 8, 9, 12]. Conversely, GPGPU (general-purpose graphics processing unit) approaches follow well-defined programming models such as CUDA and OpenCL [13, 14]. The GPGPU's execution model is rigid, causing applications that do not map well to the GPGPU architecture to perform relatively poorly. FPGAs, on the other hand, can adapt to the natural, optimal, and sometimes arbitrary computation and architectures required by specific applications. For this reason, FPGAs make a compelling platform for targeting classes of applications that do not easily map to standard GPGPU methods of execution.

It is less clear whether FPGAs have value as targets for applications that *do* match a GPGPU in execution model and map well to a GPGPU architecture. This paper considers one such application, Bayesian inference, and characterizes it on an FPGA using computation patterns akin to OpenCL. To this end, we present a custom FPGA implementation that naturally resembles an application-specific GPGPU at a high level, but differs in its implementation of the arithmetic modules ("cores") and memory access scheduling. Specifically, this paper first contributes a new approach to Bayesian inference on FPGAs and GPGPUs which allows us to characterize both implementations using an OpenCL-like execution model. Secondly, we perform a study examining algorithm kernel performance on FPGA and GPGPU platforms, and normalize core performance across devices to help explain differences in their observed efficiency.

We have conducted this research alongside related work in developing microarchitectural template-based programming models for FPGA computing [11]. Both the GPGPU and FPGA designs used in this work follow the same execution model and feature similar many core-based architectures. The FPGA implementation, however, was designed manually at the RTL level, while the GPGPU implementation was described at a high level with OpenCL. Related work proposes automatic mappings from CUDA and OpenCL flows to the FPGA [7, 10]. We intentionally avoided automatic hardware generation in this work to (a) evaluate the FPGA as an implementation target for microarchitectural template-based programming models, and (b) establish and upper-bound on template-based FPGA performance.

1.1 Bayesian Inference

Bayesian networks (BNs) are graph-based models that have numerous applications in bioinformatics, finance, signal processing, and computer vision. Bayesian inference is the process by which a BN's graph structure is learned from a set of quantitative data, or "evidence," that the BN seeks to model. Once a BN's structure (a set of nodes $\{V_1, \ldots, V_{\mathcal{N}}\}$) is determined, and the conditional dependence of each node V_i on its parent set Π_i is tabulated, the joint distribution over the nodes can be expressed as:

$$P(V_1, \ldots, V_{\mathcal{N}}) = \prod_{i=1}^{\mathcal{N}} P(V_i | \Pi_i)$$

Despite significant recent algorithmic advances, BN inference from evidence is an NP-hard problem and remains infeasible except for cases with only a small number of variables [3, 5].

The algorithm surveyed in this paper is the union of two BN inference kernels, the order[1] and graph samplers (jointly called the *order-graph sampler*). The order sampler takes a BN's prior evidence ($\mathcal{D}$ or *data*), along with an initial order to use as a starting point, and produces a set of "high-scoring" BN orders (orders that best explain the evidence). The graph sampler takes this set of high-scoring orders and produces a single "highest-scoring" graph for each order.

We generate the prior evidence $\mathcal{D}$, which consists of $\mathcal{N}$ sets of $\mathcal{P}$ local score/parent set pairs, prior to invoking the order-graph sampler. Following [4, 5, 12], the order-graph sampler itself uses Markov chain Monte Carlo (MCMC) sampling to perform an iterative random walk in the space of BN orders—until the order score has converged. Each step in the random walk (1) breaks the current order into $\mathcal{N}$ disjoint "local orders," and (2) iterates over each node's parent sets, accumulating each local score whose parent set is *compatible* with the node's local order. To decrease time to convergence and to increase confidence in the results, $\mathcal{O}$ distinct orders can be dispatched though a technique known as parallel tempering, coupled with random restarts.

Computationally, the order-graph sampler is a compute intensive set of nested loops (Algorithm 1) with an innermost kernel called the *score* function, given between lines 8 and 19. To put the number of loop iterations into perspective, typical parameter values for $\{\mathcal{I}, \mathcal{O}, \mathcal{N}\}$ are $\{10000, 512, 37\}$, where $\mathcal{I}$ is the number of MCMC iterations. Furthermore, $\mathcal{P} = \sum_{i=0}^{4} \binom{\mathcal{N}-1}{i}$ and $|\mathcal{D}| = \mathcal{N} * \mathcal{P}$.

Different degrees of parallelism and data locality can be exploited in the loops within Algorithm 1. Traditionally, the loop over $\mathcal{O}$ was placed outside the loop over $\mathcal{I}$ as $\mathcal{O}$ contributed course-grained and dependency-free parallelism [12, 14]. In this work, we have re-ordered the loops, moving the $\mathcal{O}$ dispatches to within the loop over $\mathcal{N}$, reducing the communication requirement of the algorithm, and relaxing loop dependencies. We classify the reformulated loop nest as compute-intensive because of the relatively small amount of input (a local order) needed for the inner-loop arithmetic to compute per-node results.

1.2 The OpenCL Execution Model

OpenCL [1] is a programming and execution model for heterogeneous systems (containing GPPs (general-purpose processors), GPGPUs, FPGAs [10] and other accelerators) designed to explicitly capture data and task parallelism in an application. The OpenCL model distinguishes control thread(s) (to be executed on a GPP host) from kernel threads (data parallel loops to be executed on a GPGPU, or similar accelerator). The user specifies how the kernels map to

---

Algorithm 1 The order-graph sampler loop nest. *ps*, *ls*, and *o*[*n*] are parent set, local score, and local order, respectively.

```
     for i in I do
         Setup (partition O orders into O * N local orders)
         for n in N do
             for o in O do
5:               s_o, s_g ← −∞
                 g ← NULL
                 for p in P do
                     if compatible(D[n][p].ps, o[n]) then
                         d ← D[n][p].ls − s_o
10:                      if d ≥ HIGH_THRESHOLD then
                             s_o ← D[n][p].ls
                         else if d > LOW_THRESHOLD then
                             s_o ← s_o + log(1 + exp(d))
                         end if
15:                      if D[n][p].ls > s_g then
                             s_g ← D[n][p].ls
                             g ← D[n][p].ps
                         end if
                     end if
20:              end for
                 Teardown (post-process s_o, s_g, and g)
             end for
         end for
     end for
```

an n-dimensional dataset, given a set of arguments (such as constants or pointers to device/host memory). The runtime then distributes the resulting workload across available compute resources on the device. Communication between control and kernel threads is provided by shared memory and OpenCL system calls such as barriers and bulk memory copy operations. With underlying SIMD principles, OpenCL is well-suited for data-parallel problems, and maps well to the parallel thread dispatch architecture found in GPGPUs.

2. IMPLEMENTATION

The order-graph samplers on both the FPGA and GPGPU are many core-based systems that map instances of the *score* function over a two-dimensional space (given by $\mathcal{O} \times \mathcal{N}$) according to the OpenCL model. In this work, GPGPU cores correspond to Nvidia CUDA cores while FPGA cores are custom datapaths implementing the BN scoring kernel.

2.1 FPGA

The FPGA implementation is composed of compute cores that are paired with block RAMs (BRAMs). Each core iterates over a disjoint subset of the *score* calls, while the BRAMs are responsible for caching and streaming the data needed by those *score* calls. All *score* function arithmetic is built directly into the FPGA fabric to eliminate resource contention. We implemented the $log(1 + exp(d))$ function (Algorithm 1) as a table lookup, given that it is non-linear over the narrow range of d that it is called. To maximize the read bandwidth and throughput achievable by the BRAMs, cores are replicated to the highest extent possible and fine-grain multi-threaded across multiple iterations of the *score* function.

To balance logic and BRAM utilization, each node's *score* operation is mapped onto multiple cores which run in parallel and accumulate results upon completion. This technique

---

[1] An order is a graph whose nodes have been topologically sorted (each node is placed after its parents).

reduces parallel completion time, yet requires increased complexity to accumulate partial node scores at the end of the *score* loop. To maximally hide this overhead, we chain cores together, using a dedicated interconnect, and interleave the cross-core partial result accumulation process with the next local order's scoring period. To simplify the accumulation logic, we linearly reduce all threads across a core, and then accumulate linearly across cores.

To better understand FPGA performance, the following analytic model can be used to estimate the number of FPGA core cycles needed to score $\mathcal{O} * \mathcal{N}$ local orders over subset S of the data (where S is scored for each of the $\mathcal{N}$ nodes):

$$\mathcal{N} * \left[\mathcal{O} * \left(\frac{|S|}{C} + (T+1)\right) + (T^2 + T*C) + \text{Cycles}_{\text{DRAM}}\right]$$

$\text{Cycles}_{\text{DRAM}}$ is the number of cycles (normalized to the core clock) required to page S into the cores' BRAMs, C is the number of cores assigned to subset S, and T is the number of hardware threads per core. The $T+1$ and $T^2 + T*C$ overheads are due to cross-thread and cross-core accumulations, respectively.

2.2 GPGPU

The primary strategies used to implement the GPGPU's *score* function were to optimize data placement in memory and to minimize the latency of a single kernel thread. Upon dispatching work to the GPGPU, we compacted the input to the *score* function by order and then by node ([$\mathcal{N}$][$\mathcal{O}$]), based on the relatively large number of orders that are to be processed per node. When possible, we aligned data in memory—rounding both $\mathcal{O}$ and $\mathcal{P}$ to the next power of two, to avoid false sharing in wide word memory operations, and to improve data alignment. In the *score* loop, we found that a direct implementation of the $log(1+exp(d))$ operation performed better than a table lookup, most likely due to the algorithm's limited use of floating point arithmetic. Broadly speaking, many of the strategies guiding our *score* function optimization effort are outlined in [2].

3. RESULTS AND ANALYSIS

We evaluate the FPGA fabric's efficiency relative to the GPGPU by normalizing the *score* function's performance to device core count, for each device shown in Table 1.

Device	BW$_i$ (Gb/s)	BW$_o$ (Gb/s)	M$_c$ (Kb)	Cores	f_{core} (MHz)
gt-330m	n/a	204.8	128.0	48	1265
gtx-480	n/a	1419.2	512,6144	480	1401
v5-155t	3731	51.2	1640,7632		
v6-240t	7322	51.2	3650,14976		

Table 1: FPGA and GPGPU devices employed in each study. BW$_i$ and BW$_o$ describe on-chip and off-chip memory bandwidths, respectively. M$_c$ describes the on-chip memory capacity ({distributed, block} RAM on FPGA and {local, global L2$} on the GPGPU). "Core" denotes an Nvidia CUDA core.

We have chosen to map to both the Virtex-5 LX155T (v5-155t) and Virtex-6 LX240T (v6-240t) to show FPGA core count scalability given additional fabric. The GT 330m (gt-330m—a mobile GPGPU platform) is used because its power envelope is known to be comparable to the FPGAs'. The GTX 480 (gtx-480—a workstation GPGPU based on

the Nvidia Fermi architecture) allows us to compare the highest-performing GPGPU available to us with the highest performing FPGA parameterization. All studies assume single-socket systems (one FPGA/GPGPU paired with one GPP for system initialization).

3.1 Methodology

The FPGA implementation (whose best-effort parameterizations are shown in Table 2) was written in Verilog HDL and mapped to the device using Synplify Pro (Synopsys) and the Xilinx ISE 12.1 flow for placement and routing (PAR). We measured performance through cycle-accurate traces taken from post-PAR simulation, after verifying that the post-PAR netlist met timing closure and was functionally correct. To measure the GPGPU total iteration time, we ran the application for 1000 iterations without profiling code in the loop. We then calculated the percent time spent in the *score* function through measuring (a) the *score* time using timers placed around the inner loop, and (b) the total time across 1000 iterations, with the timers from (a) enabled.

Name	$\mathcal{N}$	f_{core} (MHz)	LUT (%)	FF (%)	BRAM (%)	Cores
v5-155t	32	250	66	79	95	48
v5-155t	37	250	70	83	95	48
v6-240t	32	300	80	64	99	120
v6-240t	37	300	83	67	99	120

Table 2: Best-effort FPGA configurations used.

3.2 Core Normalization Study

This study compares the absolute (T_{Sc}) and percent time spent (% Sc) in the *score* function across both GPGPU and FPGA. All sample points assume $\mathcal{O} = 512$. The results for experimental 32-node and synthetic 37-node networks are given in Table 3. We chose these datasets for their significant increase in complexity—previously surveyed networks [6, 12] did not offer enough work per iteration to saturate a GPGPU system. We focus on the *score* function and not the outer-loop control logic (shown as *Setup* and *Teardown* in Algorithm 1) because execution time is dominated by the *score* function (as shown by the % Sc columns in Table 3).

Device	T_{Sc} (s)	T_i (s)	% Sc	T_{Sc} (s)	T_i (s)	% Sc
v5-155t	0.051	0.051	99.0	0.110	0.110	99.3
v6-240t	0.018	0.018	97.7	0.036	0.037	98.4
gt-330m	0.180	0.217	82.6	0.394	0.458	86.1
gtx-480	0.014	0.020	71.4	0.027	0.037	73.5

Table 3: Absolute time (T_{Sc}) and percent time spent (% Sc) in the *score* function, relative to the latency of a single iteration (T_i). Results are given for the 32 node network (left) and the 37 node network (right), over $\mathcal{O} = 512$ orders.

Network	FPGA	T_{Sc} Speedup		T_i Speedup	
		gt-330m	gtx-480	gt-330m	gtx-480
32 Nodes	v5-155t	3.55	.275	4.26	.392
	v6-240t	10.0	.777	12.1	1.11
37 Nodes	v5-155t	3.58	.250	4.16	.336
	v6-240t	10.9	.750	12.4	1.00

Table 4: Speedup achieved by FPGA systems relative to GPGPU systems. T_{Sc} and T_i time is detailed in Table 3.

To gain insight into the performance discrepancies between the FPGA and GPGPU, we normalize performance to the number of compute cores available on each device. The resulting metric, shown in Table 5, is given by $\text{Sc} * \frac{C_g}{C_f}$ where Sc corresponds to a T_{Sc} speedup from Table 4, and $\{C_g, C_f\}$ refers to the number of {GPGPU, FPGA} cores available on the device. We also scale the Virtex-5 FPGA performance (by $\frac{300}{250}$) to compensate for its lower obtainable frequency (in comparison with the Virtex-6 FPGA), in order to show how normalized performance is consistent across all FPGA sample points.

	gt-330m	gtx-480
v5-155t	$4.26 - 4.30$	$3.00 - 3.30$
v6-240t	$4.00 - 4.36$	$3.00 - 3.11$

Table 5: FPGA relative to GPGPU T_{Sc} speedup, normalized to the number of compute cores available and to the FPGA compute core frequency.

The algorithm is compute bound on both the FPGA and the GPGPU platforms, which is underlined by the consistent speedups in Table 5. We believe that the discrepancy in normalized performance between GPGPUs is a function of GPGPU architecture (g80 for the gt-330m and Fermi for the gtx-480) and GPGPU datapath clock frequency (1265 MHz for the gt-330m and 1401 MHz for the gtx-480).

4. DISCUSSION AND CONCLUSIONS

Notably, the application surveyed in this study does not make significant use of floating point or off-chip memory bandwidth, which are well-known strengths of the GPGPU platform. Nevertheless, it is important to account for the discrepancy in normalized performance (Table 5) between the FPGA and GPGPU platforms, especially given the relatively high GPGPU core clock frequencies. Tables 1 and 2 show that the FPGA core clocks fall between 250 and 300 MHz[2] while GPGPU core clocks reach as high as 1265 and 1401 MHz. In the case of the mobile GPGPU, we must rationalize why normalized performance falls in the FPGA's favor by a factor of $\sim 4.18\times$, while the core clock frequency of the FPGA design is $4.21\times$ less than that of the GPGPU. Similarly in the case of the Nvidia Fermi GTX480, we must account for the FPGA's $\sim 3.05\times$ gain in performance despite a $4.67\times$ loss in clock frequency.

We believe the performance gap predominantly results from (a) the performance delta between programmable cores and custom hardware datapaths, and, to a lesser extent (b) the effect of optimizing the memory access pattern between each FPGA core and its BRAM. Each FPGA core is built with replicated arithmetic units and an application-specific local memory system—which allows each FPGA core to commit one *score* inner loop iteration per cycle in the steady state. To better understand the *score* inner loop on the GPGPU, we compiled the GPGPU OpenCL kernel to a variety of GPP architectures using GCC. Using full optimization, the compiler produces kernels with loops averaging 39 RISC-like instructions.[3] This, coupled with the fact that

not all inner loop iterations will pass the *compatible*() check in Algorithm 1, helps explain FPGA core performance.

One metric by which FPGA devices continue to lag, in the area of computing, is the time and expertise required to design, verify, and "compile" to an FPGA platform. Related work in high-level tools for productive FPGA design, using MIMD and SIMT many-core templates [11], has begun to address this challenge. Perhaps this approach can be extended to take advantage of a hierarchical tool flow, significantly reducing tool time. Looking forward, this approach could allow rapid prototyping of high-performance FPGA implementations with a design time and expertise requirement similar to the GPGPU programming environment.

5. ACKNOWLEDGMENTS

This project was supported by the NIH, grant no. 130826-02, the DoE*, award no. DE-SC0003624, and the Berkeley Wireless Research Center. We would also like to thank the members of the Berkeley Reconfigurable Computing group, for contributing ideas and discussions surrounding this work, and the Stanford Nolan Lab for providing data for the 32 and 37 node networks. *: Support from the DoE does not constitute the DoE's endorsement of the views expressed in this paper.

6. REFERENCES

[1] Khronos Group - OpenCL. http://www.khronos.org/opencl/

[2] Nvidia OpenCL Best Practices Guide.

[3] D. M. Chickering. Learning bayesian networks is np-complete. *Learning from Data: Artificial Intelligence and Statistics.* V. Springer Verlag, 1996.

[4] M. Teyssier and D. Koller. Ordering-based search: A simple and effective algorithm for learning bayesian networks. *Proc. of the Twenty-first Conference on Uncertainty in AI (UAI)*, pages 584–590, Edinburgh, Scotland, UK, July 2005.

[5] B. Ellis and W. H. Wong. Learning causal bayesian network structures from experimental data. *Journal of the American Statistical Association*, 103(482), 2008.

[6] N. B. Asadi, T. H. Meng, and W. H. Wong. Reconfigurable computing for learning bayesian networks. *Proc. of the 16th Intl. Symposium on FPGAs*, 2008.

[7] A. Papakonstantinou, K. Gururaj, J. A. Stratton, D. Chen, J. Cong and W. m. Hwu. FCUDA: Enabling Efficient Compilation of CUDA Kernels onto FPGAs *Proc. of the Symposium on Application Specific Processors*, 2009.

[8] K. Server, B. Khaled, and L. Ying. A high performance fpga-based implementation of position specific iterated blast. *Proc. of the 17th Intl. Symposium on FPGAs*, 2009.

[9] M. Lin, I. Lebedev, J. Wawrzynek. High-throughput bayesian computing machine with reconfigurable hardware. *Proc. of the 18th Intl. Symposium on FPGAs*, 2010.

[10] M. Lin, I. Lebedev, J. Wawrzynek. OpenRCL: low-power high-performance computing with reconfigurable devices. *Proc. of the 20th Intl. Conference on Field Programmable Logic and Applications*, 2010.

[11] I. Lebedev, S. Cheng, A. Doupnik, J. Martin, C. Fletcher, D. Burke, M. Lin, J. Wawrzynek. MARC: A Many-Core Approach to Reconfigurable Computing. *Proc. of the 6th international conference on reconfigurable computing and FPGAs*, 2010.

[12] N. B. Asadi, C. W. Fletcher, G. Gibeling, E. N. Glass, K. Sachs, D. Burke, Z. Zhou, J. Wawrzynek, W. H. Wong, and G. P. Nolan. *Paralearn: a massively parallel, scalable system for learning interaction networks on fpgas. Proc. of the 24th Intl. Conference on Supercomputing*, 2010.

[13] D. Kumar, M. A. Qadeer. Fast heterogeneous computing with CUDA compatible Tesla GPU computing processor. *Proc. of the International Conference and Workshop on Emerging Trends in Technology*, 2010.

[14] M. D. Linderman, R. Bruggner, V. Athalye, T. H. Meng, N. B. Asadi, and G. P. Nolan. High-throughput bayesian network inference using heterogeneous multicore computers. *Proc. of the 24th Intl. Conference on Supercomputing*, 2010.

---

[2] We normalize to 300 MHz for the rest of this discussion.

[3] These instruction counts are estimates as we are unable to directly examine the output of the OpenCL compiler.

A CAD Framework for MALIBU: An FPGA with Time-multiplexed Coarse-Grained Elements

David Grant   Chris Wang   Guy G.F. Lemieux

Department of Electrical and Computer Engineering
University of British Columbia, Vancouver
{davidg,chrisw,lemieux}@ece.ubc.ca

ABSTRACT

Modern FPGAs are used to implement a wide range of circuits, many of which have coarse-grained and fine-grained components. The ever-increasing size of these circuits places great demand on CAD tools to synthesize circuits faster and without loss in quality. Synthesizing coarse-grained components onto fine-grained FPGA resources is inefficient, and past attempts to optimize FPGAs for word-oriented datapaths have met with limited success. This paper presents a CAD flow to fully compile Verilog into a configuration bitstream for a new type of FPGA with time-multiplexed coarse-grained resources. We demonstrate two approaches with gains of 61x and 42x in synthesis time on average compared to QuartusII, but due to time-multiplexing and current synthesis limitations we achieve circuit speeds of 14x and 8.5x slower on average. We show the tools can also trade density for maximum clock frequency.

Categories and Subject Descriptors

B.6.3 [**Design Aids**]: Automatic Synthesis; B.7.2 [**Design Aids**]: Placement and routing

General Terms

Algorithms, Design, Performance

1. INTRODUCTION

Modern FPGA devices contain over 1 million LUTs, over 1000 hard memory or multiplier blocks, and about 300 wires per row or column. In addition, they are continuing to grow with Moore's law. As a result, great demand is placed on synthesis tools to compile ever-larger netlists without degrading result quality or increasing run-time. Given already long FPGA CAD run-times, vendors are turning to parallel compilation. While this may help when powerful compute systems are available, light-weight approaches would be preferred.

One reason for slow CAD is that FPGAs are still bit-oriented. This partly reflects their past when they were used for glue logic, but modern usage has expanded to implementing a wide range of circuits. Increasingly popular are generators like SOPCBuilder,

EDK, and C-to-gates flows that generate large hardware datapaths. These new circuits are mostly word-oriented, but they may also have many fine-grained control signals.

Past attempts to optimize FPGAs for word-oriented datapaths have met limited success. By organizing wires and logic into words, the number of configuration bits can be reduced by sharing them among a word, and multiplexer sizes can be reduced. However, only a small overall savings of roughly 10% [34] has been realized.

One feature not attempted in prior datapath-FPGA research is time-multiplexing. By time-multiplexing the coarse-grained elements and coarse-grained interconnect, the area-cost of these large components can be amortized over many clock cycles. The improved density also allows larger circuits to be mapped into smaller architectures by trading off the maximum clock frequency. Moreover, it reduces the placement and routing problem size, which reduces synthesis time. Time-multiplexing has been applied to fine-grain logic research [31, 14, 7], commercially by Tabula[12], and to CGRAs[9, 22]. However, time-multiplexed coarse-grain elements like ALUs as a logic resource for compiled HDL in an FPGA is relatively unexplored.

What is needed for these word-oriented circuits is a heterogeneous time-multiplexed architecture that combines features from FPGAs and CGRAs, and a set of CAD tools to synthesize circuits to such an architecture. This research is focused on the CAD, and specifically on the steps after logic synthesis, that is, the placement, routing, and scheduling.

This paper presents a complete CAD flow that can compile the full synthesizable subset of Verilog2005 into a configuration bitstream for this new type of FPGA. Common tools such as VPR [1], ABC [2], OdinII [13], and Verilator [29] are used within the tool flow, but new tools have been created for placing, routing, and scheduling the time-multiplexed coarse-grain logic along with the (not time-multiplexed) fine-grained logic. In Section 4 these tools are compared to standard flows with QuartusII and VPR, demonstrating that significant gains in compile-time and logic density are possible. In Section 4.4 we demonstrate that the tools can trade density for circuit speed, mapping large circuits to run slowly on a small device, or run faster on a larger device. Also in Section 4.4, we demonstrate that the tools can improve circuit speed at the cost of compile-time by altering the bit-width (W_f) of signals considered "fine-grained" and pushing more (or less) logic to the fine-grained LUTs and interconnect. While the current results do not achieve the same F_{max} performance of standard flows, there are many opportunities for significant performance gains in the future.

Our new FPGA architecture is called "Malibu" and is presented in Section 2. Our proposal is to add coarse-grained ALU-like elements (CGs) to the FPGA's CLB. The CG is time-multiplexed,

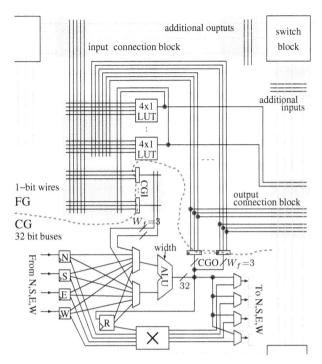

input connection block

additional ouptuts

switch block

4x1 LUT

4x1 LUT

CGI

additional inputs

1–bit wires

FG

CG

32 bit buses

W_f=3

output connection block

From N,S,E,W

N

S

E

W

R

width

ALU

CGO / W_f=3

32

To N,S,E,W

×

Figure 1: The Malibu Architecture CLB with the fine-grained (FG) and coarse-grained (CG) parts.

Table 1: Malibu Units and Detailed Operations

Units	Operators	Area (T)
Multiply	*[1]	35,000
Arithmetic	+,−,<[1],≤[1],=,≠,>,≥[1]	1,995
Logic	bitwise(&, |, ∧, ∼), ternary(?:), extend[1], reductions(&, |, ∧, !)	3,208
Interconnect	4x4 32b Xbar, CGI/Os, CG muxes	5,482
BarrelShift	≪, ≫, concat	1,791
FG	16 4-LUTs, LUT I/O	19,455
	Connection and Switch Blocks	17,519
	Combined, incl. Multiply	82,739
	Combined, no Multiply	47,739

[1]: Operators with both Signed and Unsigned modes

whereas the original CLB (now a portion of the CLB, called FG) and the FPGA routing fabric is not. The CG also has dedicated word-wide interconnect to the CG in the neighbouring CLBs. The ALU we propose is Verilog-specific and supports Verilog operators not found in typical ALUs, like bit concatenation (ab[7:0] = {a,b}) and unary logic reductions (parity[0] = ^a).

2. MALIBU ARCHITECTURE

For Malibu, the most important thing is to extract plenty of word-wide operations from the source Verilog. These are mapped to the time-multiplexed ALUs in the architecture. As well, the fine-grained logic "leftovers" must also be extracted and mapped to the LUTs in the architecture. However, before we can present the details of the CAD flow, we must first present a target architecture and explain the coarse-grain/fine-grain interface.

The architecture (Figure 1) starts with a standard fine-grained (FG) FPGA, and adds a time-multiplexed coarse-grained processing element (CG) to the CLB. The CG connects to the fine-grained CLB through coarse-grained inputs (CGI) and outputs (CGO). There are N_{cgi} CGIs, where each one aggregates a bundle of W_f signals from the fine-grained (FG) resources as an input to the ALU, zero-extended to 32-bits. There are N_{cgo} CGOs, where each

CGO latches the W_f least significant bits produced by a specific instruction, providing them to the LUTs or FPGA routing resources. When $W_f = 0$, the fine-grained resources (*all* traditional LUTs and interconnect) are removed, leaving only the new CG.

Each CG is time-multiplexed; it always executes one instruction per cycle, and all communication is explicitly pipelined and scheduled. It operates on a system clock that is different than the user clock cycle; we anticipate a 1 GHz system clock in 65nm technology using custom layout techniques can be readily achieved. Each CG contains a schedule with exactly SL instructions (the schedule length). On the active user clock edge, the instructions start executing, one per system clock cycle. At the end of the SL instructions, the CG pauses for the next user clock edge before starting over. One complete pass of the SL is required for each user clock cycle, so this limits the F_{max} to $\frac{1}{SL} \cdot 1$ GHz.

All common Verilog operations can be easily mapped onto the ALUs in the CG. For example, adding two 4-bit values in Verilog, written as o = a + b, can be expressed using 32-bit ALU operations in C language as o = ((a&0xf) + (b&0xf))&0xf. However, the ALUs we propose are Verilog-specific; they automatically truncate output results to the desired width by forcing all upper bits to zero. The width is encoded in the instruction, and is a separate input to the ALU as shown in Figure 1. For some operations the width has a special meaning, for example for concat it is used to specify the number of bits to concatenate from the LSB input (the remaining $32 - width$ bits are taken from the MSB input), and the output is not truncated. Each input operand width is left unspecified and the CAD ensures the correct width is provided by inserting zero-extend or sign-extend operations where necessary.

A complete list of all operations in Malibu are shown in groups in Table 1, including the estimated area using VPR's units of minimum-width transistor area (T). The area estimate is from a manual gate-level design of each part except the multiplier [5], counting the number of basic components (gates, muxes, etc.) required for each, and then converting those into minimum-width transistors. E.g., an OR gate requires 3 NMOS and 3 PMOS transistors, and a PMOS requires 1.5x the area of an NMOS, so the OR gate requires 7.5 T.

The combined area for the blocks is slightly less than the sum of individual unit areas due to redundancy removal when combined. The acronym MALIBU, an extension of ALU, originates from the name of these groups or units. The ALU itself comprises a total of 30 operations. Multiply and comparisons have signed and unsigned variations. Each CG operation also requires a 5-bit width parameter for the output width in bits. Exceptions are sign extension, Verilog unary logic reduction, and concatenation which use the width an input because the output width is implied. To save area, only one in five columns of CLBs contain a multiplier.

The result of a CG operation can potentially be written to any address in the R memory, to any of the CGOs, and to any address in each of the N, S, E, W (NSEW) memories concurrently. Each of these memories operate synchronously using a single write port and three read ports. So far, our CAD results indicate each NSEW memory should have up to 16 entries, and the R memory should have up to 64 entries.

To simplify the tools, the FG does not contain any flip-flops. Instead, the flip-flop state is stored in either an R or NSEW memory. The value is transferred to a CGO latch at the beginning of each user clock cycle so the value is stable for the duration of the cycle.

To avoid introducing another memory block in the CG to implement user-circuit memory, we have a novel feature where user-circuit memory blocks are packed into a contiguous block of space in R. Special load/store operations are used and require one extra

Table 2: Malibu Memory Area Estimates

	Specifications	SRAM μm^2	eDRAM μm^2	Flash μm^2
NSEW	32x16, 3R1W	1,229 – 3,521	—	—
R	32x128, 3R1W	4,669 – 28,160	—	—
Instr.	90x256, 1RW	11,290 – 30,849	6,682	1,579
Instr.	90x1024, 1RW	45,158 – 96,840	26,726	6,318

system cycle to perform the required indexing. The largest user memory block in our benchmarks is 2kbit, for which we add 64 more entries to R (total 128).

Figure 1 also shows a 4x4 routing crossbar. It writes values to the NSEW memories located in the four cardinal neighbours by taking values from the local NSEW and R memories. Although there are 5 sources, a 4:1 mux is sufficient because the W crossbar output never requires the W crossbar input, for example. The crossbar routes coarse-grained signals concurrently with computation, and keeps CG communication off the FG routing resources. The ALU cannot write to the same NSEW memory as the crossbar in the same clock cycle. The CAD detects this condition and writes to R instead, then schedules a transfer from R to the target NSEW in the next available cycle. We found the ability for the ALU to write to NSEW directly is important for performance.

We have encoded each CG instruction, including all of the source and destination addresses and crossbar control, into 90 bits. In contrast, there are well over 1,000 configuration bits in a traditional VPR-style CLB (ten 6-LUTs require 640 bits, the 60 LUT inputs require at least 5 bits each, plus bits needed to configure flip-flops and all of the interconnect). However, after time-multiplexing, the CG requires $SL \times 90$ bits. If the user extensively time-multiplexes a large circuit onto very few CLBs, upwards of 1024 instructions per CLB might be required. However, our current tools show 256 is sufficient. The long-term goal of the CAD is to significantly reduce this value.

The CG makes extensive use of memories. We estimated the area of these memories, but found results can vary as shown in Table 2. The NSEW and R memories need very fast read and write access, so they should be implemented as SRAM. The instruction memory is primarily read-only and accessed sequentially, allowing it to be pipelined. It may be implementable in SRAM, eDRAM, or flash. An upper bound on SRAM area was obtained using the Artisan Memory Compiler. However, it is not optimized for small memories and includes overhead like redundancy. Using technology parameters for SRAM [24, 28], eDRAM [15] and flash [17], we computed lower bounds on area as follows. Using transistor counting, we estimate control logic overhead (decoders, sense amps, drivers) as 50% area per bit, which correlates with data in [15]. Each extra port is modelled as 100% area per bit. For example, a 3-port, 32b memory implemented in $0.25\mu m^2$/bit technology would require $0.25 \times 32 \times 3 \times 1.5 = 36\mu m^2$ area. To convert to VPR transistor-area (T) metrics, the iFAR repository assumes the area of $1T \approx 0.5\mu m^2$ in 65nm. Using the SRAM lower bounds, each MALIBU CLB requires $17,188\mu m^2$ for memory, compared with $15,110\mu m^2$ for the FG and CG logic (no multiplier), and $8,760\mu m^2$ for the FG interconnect.

One limitation of this architecture is the assumption of a single user clock domain. We believe this greatly simplifies the types of circuits created by C-to-gates flows, which we hope would naturally target this type of architecture. Nevertheless, it is important to address multiple clock domains in our future work.

For the details presented in this section, please keep in mind this architecture is intended to be a starting point for many optimizations which we have not yet performed. The emphasis in this paper is about producing a flexible CAD system that can allow us to model many variations in the architecture. We assume fully-populated C blocks and IOBs, and all FG and CG interconnect wires are directional but span only a single CLB in length. As well, we usually run the tools in an "exploratory mode", where the number of resources float, allowing us to find the natural demand rather than trying to fit to a fixed limit.

3. MALIBU TOOLFLOW

The Malibu CAD tools use a CDFG (Control and Data Flow Graph) representation of the circuit where graph nodes are circuit operations and graph edges are communication. Each node has an operation type, a set of ordered sources, a set of sinks, and an output bit-width. Each edge has a delay (number of system cycles) and a bit-width equal to that of the driving node. The value W_f is the fine-grained width threshold; all nodes and edges wider than W_f are implemented on the CG resources only, placing the nodes and edges W_f or smaller in the FG resources only.

The objective of the tool flow is to assign each coarse-grained node to a <CG, timeslot>-tuple, each fine-grained node to a LUT, and to route all edges. The tools are divided into several steps for fine-grained synthesis and FPGA mapping, placement, routing, and a step called scheduling to order the time-multiplexed operations over time. All steps are timing-driven, which means minimizing the schedule length.

The academic FPGA CAD flow is shown in Figure 2a. It uses T-VPack and VPR[20], which have become the *de facto* standards for academic FPGA clustering, placement, and routing. Synthesis from Verilog to technology-mapped LUTs is done with QuartusII since OdinII only implements a subset of Verilog. This toolflow is used as a baseline comparison for results in Section 4.

This section describes two approaches for mapping a circuit to the Malibu architecture: Malibu-CAD (M-CAD) and Malibu-HOT (M-HOT). Both approaches extend the academic FPGA CAD flow to add support for coarse-grained time-multiplexed entities. Figure 2b shows the M-CAD approach, which follows the same order of operations as the traditional CAD flow. Figure 2c shows the height-oriented tool (M-HOT) approach which performs placement, routing, and scheduling simultaneously. These two approaches are identical up to the clustering step. Generally, M-CAD runs faster but produces slower circuits than M-HOT.

Prior work [11] details RVETool, which is the coarse-grained part of the M-CAD approach. Therefore, in this paper we only include the details required for the fine-grained integration and for the new M-HOT approach. We refer the reader to [11] for the details of the M-CAD coarse-grained synthesis.

The input Verilog is parsed, elaborated, then split into fine-grained and coarse-grained parts. The fine-grained part is synthesized to LUTs and then merged with the coarse-grained operations for clustering, placement, routing, and scheduling. The parse step outputs the fine-grained circuit parts using a subset of Verilog compatible with OdinII and ABC for synthesis to LUTs.

Not shown in Figure 2 is an architecture file input used to specify the number of PEs, the width of buses, the size of each memory, and the resources in each PE (e.g., if the PE can perform I/O). These parameters act as constraints in the tool flow and are available at all steps.

3.1 Parse and Coarse-Grained Synthesis

The first step in both the M-CAD and M-HOT flow is to construct a CDFG representation of the circuit. A modified version of Verilator [29] parses the input and performs several simple optimizations like module elaboration, dead code elimination, and constant fold-

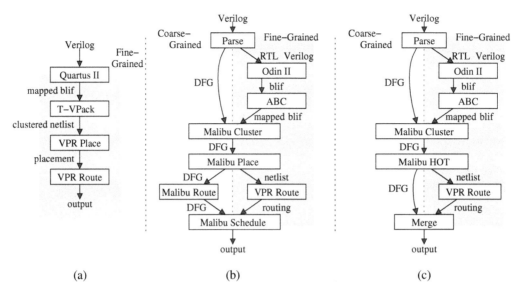

(a)   (b)   (c)

Figure 2: Three CAD flows: (a) Academic (traditional), (b) M-CAD, (c) M-HOT. M-CAD follows the traditional place-then-route flow. M-HOT performs placement, routing, and scheduling simultaneously.

ing. Verilator is not a full-scale commercial-quality synthesis tool, it is designed to output a sequential C++ program, not perform full synthesis of parallel logic. We use Verilator because it is easy to extract a CDFG before it begins to serialize the graph, and because it generates high-quality output for many circuits. However, it appears to perform poorly in some cases (see Section 5).

The Verilator output requires further processing for the Malibu architecture. Signals and operations (CDFG edges and nodes) less than or equal to a specified width ($W_f = 3$ in Figure 1), are considered fine-grained and marked to use the FG resources. Coarse-grained operations that compute FG signals (like a comparison) are mapped to CGOs, while CG operations that depend on FG signals are mapped to CGIs. The remaining operations are considered coarse-grained, and most map trivially onto the supported CG operations. However some require more complicated graph transformations [11] to legalize the CDFG for the architecture.

Before producing the final CDFG, the FG logic is separated from the CG logic and written to a distinct RTL Verilog file for OdinII synthesis.

3.2 Fine-Grained Synthesis

The fine-grained parts of the circuit are synthesized to LUTs using OdinII and ABC, then merged back into the coarse-grained CDFG for clustering. Using RTL Verilog simplifies the description when $W_f > 1$: OdinII elaborates the design to single-bit operations, then ABC cleans up any dangling logic (e.g. from an add operation where the carry bit is discarded), and tech-maps to LUTs.

LUT packing into CLBs is integrated with the placement tool and done with the CG placement. The number of CGI and CGO interfaces needed in a CLB will change while performing CG placement, so LUT packing is done as part of placement.

3.3 Malibu Cluster

The clustering tool collects CG operations into CLB clusters for each CLB. It also groups the LUTs which source or sink CG values into the same CLBs as the CG operation. The overall goal is to reduce the amount of communication by the CG logic.

The tool can cluster code to varying degrees to target any number of CLBs, allowing a tradeoff between area (number of CLBs) and performance (F_{max}). This is demonstrated in Section 4.4.

For the M-CAD approach, the clustering tool uses hMETIS [16] to partition the graph using recursive bisection. To guide hMETIS, all nodes are assigned a weight of 1, except constants which are replicated as needed and assigned a weight of 0 so they can be placed in any CLB for free. Load and store operations from user memory, and CGI/CGO interface operations, are connected with very high edge weights to ensure they will not be separated.

The M-HOT approach keeps CG instructions independent (cluster size of one) because it favours a "move-and-compute" model where computation is done while values are being routed through the current CLB en route to a final CLB instead of being computed in a CLB, stored locally, and then routed later. Other than keeping together the load/store and CGI/CGO interface operations, no clustering is done for M-HOT.

3.4 M-CAD Flow

The M-CAD tool flow performs placement, routing, and scheduling in distinct steps as in traditional CAD. Information is only passed forward so the routing result, for example, cannot be used to go back and generate a better placement. This section briefly describes each step and how the coarse-grained and fine-grained resources are handled. Prior work [11] details just the CG aspects, but the FG aspects presented here are new.

3.4.1 Malibu Place

The Place tool assigns the code clusters to CGs and LUTs into FGs. The goal is to keep the critical path small.

The tool uses VPR's [20] timing-driven annealing placement algorithm with two changes to the cost function. First, a different definition of "delay" is used in the cost function computation to handle both the fine-grained and coarse-grained operations being placed. Second, a parameter $penalty$ discourages illegal placements.

To simplify placer delay estimates, all delays are expressed as integers. Each hop of a coarse-grained communication path has a delay of one, with the total delay being the number of hops. We pre-computed Elmore delays with VPR to estimate how far (in CLBs) a fine-grained signal travels in one system clock cycle. The placer can thus estimate FG delays quite easily. The Schedule tool ultimately determines the order of execution of instructions using the

126

actual delays from VPR routing, so an estimate at this point is sufficient.

The time-multiplexed network introduces an additional level of complexity not found in regular FPGAs: two nodes within the same CG may be scheduled in timeslots far apart, causing additional delay not modeled by the number of hops. Unfortunately this delay is not known until scheduling is complete, so at this stage we assume it is zero.

The delay computation is used with a slack and criticality computation to calculate the $timing\_cost$, which is part of the placement cost function. The slack, criticality, and $timing\_cost$ computations are the same as in VPR.

The placer allows illegal placements to be considered. The $penalty$ parameter adds a fixed cost each time memory size is exceeded, unavailable CG or FG resources are used, too many CGI/CGO registers are used, or too few/many CLBs, are used.

At the end of placement, if required, the Place tool also packs multiple small user memories into each CG, ensuring they do not overlap. However, the problem of splitting a large user memory across multiple CG is left for future work.

3.4.2 *Malibu Route*

After placement, VPR's PathFinder router is used to route the fine-grained logic. The schedule tool reads the delay information from VPR and records the delay of each fine-grained link in the DFG.

The coarse-grained routing problem is different from conventional CAD flows because the routing network is time-multiplexed, so temporal as well as spatial decisions must be made. The spatial routing is done using a simple horizontal-then-vertical routing strategy. The router follows existing routes from the same source as far as possible before branching the route towards the new destination CG.

The temporal routing decisions are made during scheduling. When the endpoint of a route is to be scheduled, the scheduler follows each hop of the route, checking that the necessary CG resources are available. If a conflict arises, the route is held in place for as many timeslots as necessary until the resources are available at the next hop. For the F_{max} results in Section 4.1 it was never necessary to hold a value to avoid a routing conflict for any circuit. In practise over all our experiments we have never seen a value held more than two cycles, meaning the architecture has an abundance of CG routing resources.

3.4.3 *Malibu Schedule*

The Schedule tool orchestrates the overall execution of code and movement of data to reproduce the behaviour of the original circuit. It assigns each instruction to a timeslot in a CG, it assigns each coarse-grained route-hop to a timeslot resolving all routing collisions along the way, and it ensures all values are produced/consumed at the appropriate times on the fine-grained resources.

The scheduling algorithm is variation of list scheduling. It begins at $timeslot = 0$ and assigns as many operations as it can across all CGs in that timeslot. It iterates over the sinks of the scheduled operations and uses the routing delay information to compute the minimum timeslot in which those sinks may be scheduled. It then moves on to the second timeslot, and so on. This timeslot-oriented approach ensures the scheduler is fast and is always making forward progress. NOP instructions are inserted in all timeslots that do not contain a circuit node after scheduling.

An operation may be scheduled in $timeslot$ if:

- The $timeslot$ is empty in the CG's ALU.

- All source signals have arrived in time.

- All internal CG resources required by the operation are available.

- All routing resources required by the output of the operation (fine-grained and coarse-grained) are available for the first-hop of the route.

At each timeslot, nodes are considered in order of criticality as computed during placement. This simple ordering reduces the final SL and thus increases the F_{max} by $\approx$10%.

At the end of scheduling, accesses to the NSEW and R memories are assigned specific offsets using a greedy approach. At this point, the CG operations and FG LUTs for each CLB are packed into a single output bitstream.

3.5 M-HOT Flow

The Malibu height-oriented tool flow (M-HOT) is shown in Figure 2c. M-HOT is based a modulo graph embedding scheduler [25], which was tested on a CGRA up to 4x4 PEs. There are several distinctions from the work presented here which are elaborated upon in the following sections.

- Support was added to place, route, and schedule fine-grained operations in parallel with the coarse-grained operations. VPR is called to obtain the FG routing delays.

- Support was added for registers. M-HOT ensures that expected flip-flop behaviour is reproduced.

- M-HOT uses a variable-length schedule that is increased as needed. This is sub-optimal, but it avoids searching for the lowest schedule length through multiple invocations of the tool. M-HOT also supports a fixed schedule length.

- The placement cost function was modified to encourage nodes at each height to spread out to many CLBs, and also modified so that multiple CDFG paths that end at the same user register (logic reconvergence) will tend towards the CLB which holds the register state.

The M-HOT approach makes better decisions because integrated placement, routing, and scheduling has greater information about resource usage than approximate cost functions in segregated flows like M-CAD. However, it does increase runtime over M-CAD.

The top-level code of the algorithm is shown in Figure 3. The algorithm accepts a CDFG and computes an as-late-as-possible (ALAP) height for each node (operation). At the bottom at height 0 are the CDFG outputs. It processes each height, starting at the largest (which are always CDFG inputs), because those nodes have the longest path to the outputs at the bottom, so they are the most critical.

At each height, it computes an affinity matrix and performs a low-temperature anneal to assign each node to a CLB and the earliest timeslot that gives it the lowest cost. When annealing is complete, all nodes at the current height are locked so they cannot be moved, and the next height is annealed.

3.5.1 *Annealing*

At each height, the annealer assigns coarse-grained operations to CGs and fine-grained operations to LUTs in the FGs. The coarse-grained and fine-grained nodes are annealed together, so either can be a move candidate. After choosing a move, the annealer invokes

```
1: Compute ALAP height of each node
2: for height = maxheight to 0 do
3:    nodes ← all nodes at height=height
4:    aff ← compute_affinity(nodes)
5:    anneal(aff, nodes)
6: end for
7: Finalize modulo routes
```

Figure 3: M-HOT Top-Level Code

the router to determine the earliest timeslot for the current operation in the chosen CLB. Coarse- and fine-grained routing delays are computed the same as the M-CAD approach.

If the operation is registered, it requires special handling. Not only are the routes computed from the source operations to this register, but unlike traditional operations the destination sinks will already have known locations and timeslots. Hence, the paths to them can be computed as well. They are known because a registered operation is always the terminus of a path, so it is always at height 0 in the ALAP tree. However, the sinks of a register are placed as some of the earliest operations. These routes are "modulo routes", wrapping around the schedule back to timeslot 0. The M-HOT approach does not target a fixed SL. Instead, it lengthens SL as needed. As a result, the links on these modulo routes may become broken as additional timeslots are added. The last step of the main loop in Figure 3 completes and reconnects these dangling routes.

At the heart of the annealer is a cost function. The annealing schedule is from VPR but with a lower initial temperature. The annealing cost function is from [25], but modified for the Malibu architecture to achieve better results for mapping circuits. The cost function for a node is:

$$cost = producer\_cost + affinity\_cost + parallel\_cost$$
$$+ register\_cost + penalty$$

3.5.2 Producer Cost

The *producer_cost* is the cost of placing a CG operation in a certain CLB at a certain timeslot, or a LUT in a certain CLB. It uses actual routing information to compute the real cost (something the M-CAD approach can only approximate by using the Manhattan distance). The cost is the sum of the timeslot differences from each source to the current node.

This is the same cost as in [25], except as follows. When the CG operation has a register as a source, that source will not be placed until height 0 is processed. Yet, a placement is needed to compute this cost. In this case, to avoid spreading out the siblings of that source register and incurring lengthy fanout delays when the register is finally placed, the producer cost is the total Manhattan distance from the candidate CLB location to each of the already-placed siblings of the register.

3.5.3 Affinity Cost

The affinity cost keeps nodes with common descendants close together to reduce future routing costs. It is computed among all nodes at each height, and is calculated as described in [25]. Briefly, it weights the Manhattan distance between a pair of nodes at this height by the affinity weight between them. The affinity weight counts the common sinks between the nodes in future graph levels which are not yet placed. It looks up to 3 levels deep, with the common sink count being counted 4 times at level 1, twice at level 2, and once at level 3. Thus, two nodes with many common sinks in the very next level of the graph will be penalized by a higher affinity cost if they are placed too far apart.

3.5.4 Parallel Cost

This cost attempts to spread out nodes from the same level so they are placed in *different* CLBs. This cost simply counts the number of node-pairs placed into the same CLB. Without this cost, they tend to bunch up in the same CLB, requiring more timeslots to schedule. The implementation in [25] prefers to place nodes "on the left" of the array, since this is where I/O is located. For Malibu, it is better to force the nodes to spread out.

3.5.5 Register Cost

In a circuit with registers, two sinks of a register may be placed far apart since there is no cost to tie them together, in turn creating unnecessarily long routes and artificially inflating the SL. [25] avoids this problem by pre-placing all inputs, outputs, registers, and memories. If the circuit has a specific pin mapping this would be a reasonable approach for M-HOT too, however it is not always desirable to impose this restriction so two costs are added to the cost function: a cost to keep sinks of registers together, this was shown previously as the *producer_cost*, and a cost for register path reconvergence.

To encourage reconvergence, a *register_cost* is computed to be the sum of the Manhattan distances between each node in the current height and the sinks of any registers in the node's respective fanout cone. This encourages the operation to be placed along the straight-line path between the source and eventual register location. While the registers themselves have not yet been placed, the sinks of those registers have been placed, so the Manhattan distance can be computed. The cost for sinks is exponentially weighted by powers of 2 based on depth in the same way as the affinity calculation.

3.5.6 Penalty Cost

The *penalty* cost discourages invalid/illegal placements. It is computed the same way as the M-CAD approach.

3.5.7 Routing

Because placement, routing, and scheduling are done together with the M-HOT tool, there is no opportunity to incorporate the actual FG routing delays into the flow without of invoking VPR in the inner loop of the annealer.

Instead, the M-HOT tool estimates the FG routing delay based on Manhattan distance and Elmore delay, and calls VPR at the end of scheduling to compute the actual delay for each route. In all our benchmark trials we have found that even when the routing delay is underestimated (e.g. a route has to go around some CLBs to avoid congestion), it is close enough to the actual delay that the value will still arrive before it is needed. M-HOT flags any routes with timing violations and reports an error.

4. EXPERIMENTAL RESULTS

In the following sections, the M-CAD and M-HOT tools are evaluated on the Malibu architecture. For baseline comparison, the benchmarks were synthesized with QuartusII 10.0 for a StratixIII (EP3SL340F1760I4L) FPGA, and with VPR 5.0 using 65nm iFAR [33] architecture parameters (n10k04l04.fc15.area1delay1.cmos65nm). For VPR, the ten 4-LUT architecture was selected for area efficiency. The length-four wires in the architecture were changed to length-one wires without changing the delay characteristics to over-compensate for the CG area being added to each of the FG CLBs. The architecture was also modified to place the CLB pins only on the top or right of the CLB to mimic overhead routing.

In Section 4.1 the maximum user clock speed (F_{max}) is compared. In Section 4.2 synthesis time is compared to QuartusII. Sec-

Table 3: Benchmark Circuit Information

Circuit	QuartusII ALM	QuartusII 18×	VPR 4LUT	Malibu Nodes	Malibu Nets	Malibu %r	Malibu %1b
ethernet	6868	0	19626	9693	13686	15	61
fft16	6412	84	17006	2120	2236	29	0
wb_conmax	5349	0	16098	17917	23558	2	40
fft8	2075	28	5248	800	836	29	0
dma	1714	0	5071	18514	23650	6	41
ac97_ctrl	1254	0	3538	4911	6097	8	47
aes_core	1154	0	5021	3380	3970	1	8
tv80	850	0	2330	12186	16027	2	44
jpeg_enc	791	64	2836	4486	5882	11	13
systemcaes	716	0	2181	3043	3799	0	23
spi	488	0	987	664	856	6	37
des	298	0	865	4114	5497	0	34
systemcdes	237	0	650	1688	2131	0	24
pci_master	137	0	325	957	1342	8	71
me	5148	0	14388	5954	7020	14	0
chem	3526	175	36143	568	714	0	0
honda	1216	52	3795	249	293	0	0
dir	1150	8	6620	884	1190	6	22
mcm	1057	56	3067	232	288	0	0
wang	797	24	2275	134	152	0	0
pr	646	18	1893	176	194	0	0

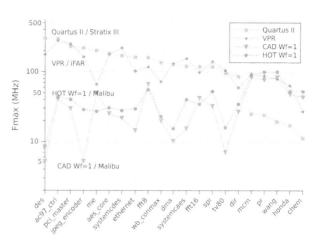

Figure 4: F_{max} **results (ordered by QuartusII** F_{max}**.**

Table 4: Synthesis Time Speedup vs. Quartus

Tool	All Circuits $W_f=0$	Circuits with fine-grained signals $W_f=0$	$W_f=1$	$W_f=2$	$W_f=4$
M-CAD	61.1x	20.1x	8.5x	8.6x	8.7x
M-HOT	42.0x	4.9x	12.1x	11.8x	12.1x

tion Section 4.3 looks at the minimum-transistor-area required for each benchmark. And finally in Section 4.4 we show the tools can make tradeoffs among F_{max}, compile time, and density.

To evaluate these metrics, a variety of Verilog benchmarks are used, summarized in Table 3. The **chem**, **dir**, **honda**, **mcm**, **pr**, and **wang** benchmarks [30] are dataflow– and DSP-style non-pipelined computational circuits described in behavioural Verilog; **me** is our own motion estimation design; **fft8** and **fft16** are our own deeply pipelined 8- and 16-point complex FFTs implemented using a radix-2, decimation-in-time decomposition; **jpeg_encoder** is from [32]. The other benchmarks are the 11 largest (in ALM count) from the IWLS 2005 benchmark set[6], excluding the ones with names of the form sXXXXX which appear to be the output of another synthesis tool since they are composed entirely of 1-bit logic gates with mangled names.

Table 3 shows the synthesized size of each benchmark using QuartusII for a StratixIII, VPR for the modified iFAR architecture, and Malibu. The 18× column is the number of 18×18 multipliers used. We were unable to use QuartusII to produce BLIF with hard multipliers, and OdinII's limited Verilog support would require a massive rewrite of our benchmarks, so the VPR results use LUTs exclusively. The %r column is the percent of nodes which are registered, and is important in the HOT approach where these nodes are all at height=0. The %1b column is the percent of nodes which output a single-bit value. These nodes are implemented on the fine-grained resources when $W_f \geq 1$. For some circuits, like **dma** and **tv80**, much fewer QuartusII ALMs than Malibu nodes are needed. This highlights the strong need for us to examine and improve the front-end logic synthesis in our flow. Since that is a major undertaking, we leave that for future work.

4.1 Maximum Frequency (F_{max})

Figure 4 graphs the F_{max} across all circuits for the baseline Quartus and VPR test, and for the M-CAD and M-HOT tools with $W_f = 1$. The data is fastest result of 10 trials, and for the Malibu results is the fastest result for all architecture sizes. The data, sorted by the Quartus F_{max}, allows us to highlight three trends. First, the QuartusII F_{max} is 10x higher on average than M-CAD with $W_f = 1$. Changing to $W_f = 4$ (not shown), M-CAD improves to an 8.4x gap. Alternatively, if we eliminate the FG LUTs completely ($W_f = 0$), the M-CAD F_{max} is 14x lower. We consider this a fairly good result for time-multiplexing.

Second, the F_{max} results for the M-HOT tool are, on average, 45% higher than M-CAD across all values of W_f. Compared to Quartus the M-HOT tool F_{max} is 8.5x, 6.3x, and 4.8x lower for $W_f=0$, 1, 4 respectively. For time-multiplexed architectures, this indicates that this may be a better way to map circuits than following traditional CAD.

Third, the benchmarks towards the left of Figure 4 have a large percentage of fine-grained wires. FPGAs implement these very well, but the time-multiplexed Malibu architecture does not, averaging 15x slower (M-CAD, $W_f = 1$). However, on the right of the graph where the FPGA performs poorly are the coarse-grained benchmarks. These are the types of circuits the Malibu architecture is targeted for, and they show a 3x higher F_{max} over the Stratix III result.

4.2 Compile Time

Table 4 shows speedup, compared to Quartus, of the complete Verilog-to-bitstream compile time for the Malibu M-CAD and M-HOT toolflows.

Both Malibu CAD approaches show a significant speedup compared to Quartus ranging from 249x faster (chem) down to 1.3x faster (dma) for M-CAD. Malibu compile-time is designed to be fastest with coarse-grained-only circuits (fft16, me, chem, fft8, honda, mcm, wang, and pr). When removed, the overall speedup decreases as expected. Since these circuits have no fine-grained signals, setting $W_f > 0$ has no effect on results as the fine-grained handling code is never invoked.

For the remaining circuits, on average, there is still a speedup when fine-grained signals are implemented on the FG resources. However, the speedup range changes from 42x faster (spi) to almost 50x slower (wb_conmax). We consider wb_conmax to be anomalous because a traditional VPR route of wb_conmax takes 14 minutes, whereas VPR called by the Malibu to route the FG resources takes 5 hours. This further highlights the need for improvements to our front-end synthesis: the traditional VPR route uses Quartus-generated BLIF, whereas Malibu is extracting nearly the same number of FG nodes as the entire Quartus-optimized circuit.

For both the M-CAD and M-HOT flows, the compile-time

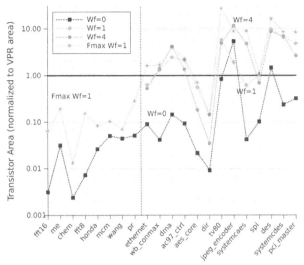

Figure 5: Area savings for the minimum-required-area compared to the F_{max} area. Normalized to the VPR area results.

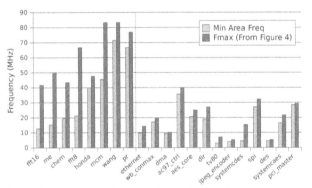

Figure 6: Frequency lost to achieve the minimum-area compared to the F_{max} for $W_f = 1$.

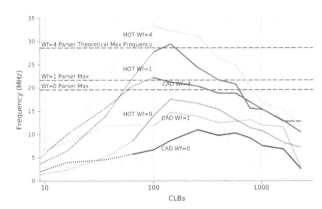

Figure 7: Frequency versus area tradeoff for the ethernet benchmark. M-HOT produces faster results than M-CAD. Increasing W_f also improves the frequency.

changes little as W_f increases. Once the fine-grained resources are invoked they require approximately the same time to process even though the quantity of FG logic increases. Also, M-CAD gets slower but M-HOT gets faster with $W_f > 0$ because M-HOT anneals fewer objects at each height as W_f increases.

4.3 Area

Figure 5 shows the transistor area, normalized to the VPR area result, of the smallest Malibu architecture size required to successfully synthesize each benchmark. It also shows the area required for the F_{max} results presented in Figure 4 for each benchmark. The Malibu area is the sum of the tile area (Tables 1 and 2) and the FG routing area as reported by VPR. In many cases, particularly for $W_f = 0$, the minimum area is achieved by time-multiplexing the circuit on just a few CLBs. However the tools are enforcing resource constraints so this is not possible for all circuits. The mapping is constrained by the instruction memory (256 instructions), R (64 plus 64 user data-memory entries), NSEW (16 entries), CGIs (4 per CLB), CGOs (16 per CLB), LUTs (16 per CLB), and circuit I/Os (one CG input and one CG output per CLB).

The benchmarks to the left of the vertical divider have no fine-grained elements so the result for $W_f = 1, 2, 4$ is the same as $W_f = 0$. For $W_f = 0$, on average, the required architecture is 15.5x smaller, with an average user clock speed of 20.1 MHz. This is expected because the smallest area is most often a 3x3 or 4x4

array of CLBs, and the Malibu CAD tools fold the operations in time to fill the instruction memory which is the limiting constraint.

For $W_f = 1, 2, 4$ (circuits to the right of the vertical divider), the minimum required area is, on average, 1.8x, 1.5x (not shown), and 1.8x larger than the VPR area results. The limiting constraint in these cases was the number of LUTs per CLB, which was set to 16. More FG resources per CLB would help in this case, so would a heterogeneous architecture where some CLBs do not have the CG component, and so would a better CG/FG partitioning strategy and better front-end logic synthesis. The Malibu CAD tools will enable such architecture and tool exploration in future work.

For comparison, Figure 5 also shows the area for the F_{max} results presented in Figure 4 for $W_f = 1$. This architecture size is always larger than the minimum size. On average, the maximum frequency is 1.4x higher, but uses 3.1x the area of the minimum architecture size. This demonstrates the tool's ability to trade area for performance, this is further explored in the next section.

Figure 6 shows the F_{max} from Figure 4 compared to the minimum-area frequency for $W_f = 1$. The F_{max} is, on average, 1.4x larger. Again, to the left of the divide are benchmarks with no fine-grained elements, so W_f is actually zero. There is a larger frequency difference for these circuits because the CGI, CGO, and LUT constraints are removed, and the tools can time-multiplex more aggressively at the expense of speed (only really constrained by instruction memory). When the FG resources are used (to the right of the divider) the additional constraints (CGIs, CGOs, and LUTs) increase minimum area required to synthesize. This pushes the area closer to the architecture size where the F_{max} is achieved, resulting in the higher frequency. For future work we plan to investigate the ratio of CG and FG resources in each CLB, as this result indicates more FG resources may be beneficial in some cases.

4.4 Feature Evaluation

This section examines some unique features of the Malibu tool flow. Figure 7 shows the user frequency of the **ethernet** benchmark for the M-CAD and M-HOT approach for $W_f = 0,1,4$ over a range of architecture sizes from 3x3 CLBs to 45x45 CLBs. For each size, the tools are forced to use all available CLBs, hence the decrease in performance on larger architectures once communication delay dominates the schedule. The tools would not normally be run in this mode unless fitting a large circuit on a small architecture. Usually the tools would be allowed to find the best architecture size by allowing some CLBs to remain empty. The dotted line represents the range of architectures where constraints were violated in the final result, so the synthesized circuit is not viable given our architectural settings.

This graph shows the Malibu tools can trade density (number of CLBs) for speed by targeting any sized architecture and time-multiplexing more code (or less) on the CGs. This is useful for fitting a large design in a small architecture.

The graph also shows the tradeoff involving W_f. Increasing W_f from 0 to 1 for both the M-CAD and M-HOT flows, causes the frequency to also increase. It also causes the peak F_{max} to require slightly fewer CLBs, meaning density is increased. This result is expected, because the fine-grained control logic is moved to the FG resources where it can be computed and distributed more quickly.

It is possible to estimate a theoretical maximum frequency of a circuit using the graph-depth of the CDFG after parsing by assuming each node in the CDFG takes one system clock cycle and that communication is free. These maximums are shown on Figure 7 for the ethernet benchmark for each value of W_f. For $W_f = 0$ M-CAD is achieves 56% of the maximum and M-HOT 89%. M-HOT exceeds the maximums at $W_f = 1$ and 4 because of chains of fine-grained operations are being optimized and synthesized by OdinII and ABC into LUTs, reducing the number of operations along the critical path after parsing. Because of this, the important metric is the $W_f = 0$ value where no optimizations are applied. Averaging across all circuits, M-CAD achieves 35% of the post-parsing maximum frequency, and M-HOT 52%. Therefore, the performance of M-HOT could be, at most, doubled without using optimizations or a better parsing/CDFG construction tool.

5. LIMITATIONS AND FUTURE WORK

Moving forward, we plan to remove limitations of the Malibu tool flow like the restriction of a single clock domain. There are also promising scheduling approaches like the edge-centric modulo scheduler proposed by Park et al. [27] that could further improve circuit speed or density and keep compile time low.

VPR takes several hours to route the fine-grained parts of the wb_conmax, fft16, and tv80 benchmarks from within the Malibu framework. All other benchmarks route within a few seconds from within the framework. By itself, VPR can place and route those benchmarks in under 14 minute with input generated by Quartus (see Figure 2a). Despite this long runtime, VPR still produces a high-quality result. This is something that requires investigation and could result in improvements to VPR or the fine-grained netlist generator in the Malibu tools.

There are two avenues for future work to improve the quality of the results. Figure 7 shows that M-HOT achieves 89% of the theoretical maximum frequency based on the parser output graph depth. Overall, the M-HOT approach is 52% of this maximum, so better placement, routing, and scheduling algorithms can only close this gap. Adding optimizations is one way to reduce the graph depth and increase the frequency. The other option is to replace Verilator with a commercial-quality front-end synthesis tool. Verilator was chosen because it is easy to extract a coarse-grain CDFG from parsed and elaborated Verilog. These hooks need to be added to other synthesis software.

Having a CAD flow is essential to enable architecture exploration. We also plan to test various architectural parameters like the size of the memories, the number of LUTs per CLB, and heterogeneous architectures involving multipliers, CLBs with no CGs, and CLBs with large memories, to try and reduce the required transistor area while still maintaining a high-quality synthesis result and a fast compile time. Also, the limitations of our front-end logic synthesis needs to be investigated, as we are producing graphs with significantly more nodes (and larger depth) than is likely needed.

6. RELATED WORK

Synthesizing a circuit for an FPGA is a well researched and understood problem. In this work we make use of academic tools T-VPack+VPR [1], ABC [2], and ODIN II [13], as well as QuartusII, a commercial tool.

Mapping to a CGRA also has many academic solutions, e.g. [18, 35]. These tools are designed to map software loop "kernels" from sequential *programs* into the CGRA, not HDLs. CGRA architectures are usually controlled by a host processor, and have access to global memory. When mapping *circuits* to an FPGA with coarse-grained resources, there is no host processor or global memory. Other novel CGRA scheduling solutions include reconvergent scheduling [19], DRESC [21], SPR [9], and modulo graph embedding [26]. These solutions all use iterative algorithms to achieve a high-quality mapping solution. Malibu seeks very fast compiles with some loss of quality, so iterative approaches are incompatible with our runtime objective.

Many CGRA architectures exist which time-multiplex coarse-grained resources (e.g. ADRES [22], PipeRench [10], Tartan [23], RaPiD [8], SCORE [3]). In contrast, this work offers an approach for implementing *circuits*, not programs. Unlike other work, we integrate LUTs into the architecture to implement fine-grained signals. No resources are used to implement a C or C-like programming model (e.g., no branch instructions or global memory). There is ALU support for HDL operations like bit concatenation, unary logic reduction, and automatic truncation of results.

The tradeoff between density and circuit speed in time-multiplexed architectures was first demonstrated for fine-grained FPGAs with VEGA [14] and later with TSFPGA [7]. TSFPGA also added a modulo scheduling refinement, which we do not yet implement. However, in this work we time-multiplex the coarse-grained resources, not the fine-grained resources.

Datapath-oriented FPGA research has investigated logic configuration bit-sharing [4], as well as interconnect configuration-bit sharing and bus-based multiplexers [34]. However, this research has not looked at time-multiplexing.

7. CONCLUSIONS

Modern FPGAs implement a wide range of circuits which have both coarse-grained and fine-grained elements. Great demand is on CAD tools to synthesize these ever-larger circuits faster, and without loss in quality. To address these issues, we have proposed adding coarse-grained time-multiplexed resources to the FPGA CLB to create Malibu, a new FPGA architecture.

To study the tradeoffs of new architecture, we have developed a full CAD flow which fully compiles Verilog2005 into a configuration bitstream. Two physical mapping approaches were demonstrated: M-CAD is based on the traditional FPGA CAD tool flow with scheduling at the end, and M-HOT is based on a CGRA scheduler for simultaneous placement, routing, and scheduling.

For M-CAD we demonstrate compile-time speedups of up to 249x (61x average) compared to QuartusII synthesizing for a StratixIII FPGA. However, due to time-multiplexing and current synthesis limitations we achieve a circuit speed 14x slower on average. The M-HOT synthesis takes longer, only 42x faster than Quartus on average, but the final circuit speed is improved to only 8.5x slower. Enabling the fine-grained resources improves the final circuit speed, and this slows compile-time for M-CAD but speeds it up for M-HOT.

Finally, we demonstrate up to 15.5x savings in transistor area utilizing the tool's ability to trade density for the final circuit speed, and time-folding the circuit as much as possible onto a small target architecture.

It is difficult to compare tools such as this with more mature work such as VPR and Quartus, but the architecture and tools show promising results. Most importantly, they show it is possible to achieve fast synthesis and good performance on the Malibu architecture. This is really the starting point for significant additional future work, where various algorithms, heuristics, and architectural features can be optimized and improved. In particular, we believe significant gains in F_{max}, runtime, and density can all be obtained.

8. ACKNOWLEDGMENTS

This research is supported by the Natural Sciences and Engineering Research Council of Canada (NSERC). Equipment donations by CMC Microsystems are gratefully acknowledged. The authors would also like to thank Deming Chen, Russell Tessier, and Graeme Smecher for providing several benchmark circuits, as well as the authors and the many additional contributors to the various open-source tools used in this research. Verilator: Wilson Snyder, Duane Galbi, and Paul Wasson. OdinII: Peter Jamieson, Kenneth B. Kent, Farnaz Gharibian, and Lesley Shannon. VPR: Vaughn Betz, Jonathan Rose, and Alexander Marquardt. ABC: Alan Mishchenko.

9. REFERENCES

[1] V. Betz and J. Rose. VPR: A new packing, placement and routing tool for FPGA research. In *Proc. FPL*, pages 213–222, 1997.

[2] R. Brayton and A. Mishchenko. ABC: An Academic Industrial-Strength Verification Tool. In *Computer Aided Verification*, volume 6174 of *Lecture Notes in Computer Science*, pages 24–40. 2010.

[3] E. Caspi, M. Chu, R. Huang, J. Yeh, J. Wawrzynek, and A. DeHon. Stream Computations Organized for Reconfigurable Execution (SCORE). In *FPL*, pages 605–614, 2000.

[4] D. Cherepacha and D. Lewis. DP-FPGA: An FPGA architecture optimized for datapaths. *VLSI Design*, 4(4):329–343, 1996.

[5] K. Choi and M. Song. Design of a high performance 32x32-bit multiplier with a novel sign select booth encoder. In *Proc. International Symposium on Circuits and Systems*, pages 701–704, May 2001.

[6] Christoph Albrecht. IWLS 2005 Benchmarks. [Online]. Available: http://www.iwls.org/iwls2005/benchmarks.html, 2005.

[7] A. DeHon. *Reconfigurable architectures for general-purpose computing*. PhD thesis, Massachusetts Institute of Technology, 1996.

[8] C. Ebeling, D. C. Cronquist, and P. Franklin. RaPiD - reconfigurable pipelined datapath. In *Proc. FPL*, pages 126–135, 1996.

[9] S. Friedman, A. Carroll, B. Van Essen, B. Ylvisaker, C. Ebeling, and S. Hauck. SPR: an architecture-adaptive CGRA mapping tool. In *Proc. FPGA*, pages 191–200, 2009.

[10] S. C. Goldstein, H. Schmit, M. Moe, M. Budiu, S. Cadambi, R. R. Taylor, and R. Laufer. PipeRench: A coprocessor for streaming multimedia acceleration. In *ISCA*, pages 28–39, 1999.

[11] D. Grant, G. Smecher, G. G. Lemieux, and R. Francis. Rapid synthesis and simulation of computational circuits in an MPPA. In *Proc. FPT*, pages 151–158, Dec. 2009.

[12] T. R. Halfhill. Tabula's time machine. *Microprocessor Report*, Mar. 2010.

[13] P. Jamieson, K. B. Kent, F. Gharibian, and L. Shannon. Odin II - An Open-source Verilog HDL Synthesis tool for CAD Research. In *Proc. FCCM*, pages 149–156, 2010.

[14] D. Jones and D. Lewis. A time-multiplexed FPGA architecture for logic emulation. In *Proc. Custom Integrated Circuits*, pages 495–498, 1995.

[15] M.-E. Jones. 1T-SRAM-Q quad-density technology reins in spiraling memory requirements. http://csserver.evansville.edu/˜mr56/cs838/Paper16.pdf, retrieved Sept 2010.

[16] G. Karypis, R. Aggarwal, V. Kumar, and S. Shekhar. Multilevel hypergraph partitioning: applications in VLSI domain. *IEEE Trans. VLSI*, 7(1):69–79, Mar 1999.

[17] S. K. Lai. Flash memories: Successes and challenges. In *IBM Journal of Research and Development*, volume 52, pages 529 –535, Jul. 2008.

[18] J.-e. Lee, K. Choi, and N. D. Dutt. Compilation approach for coarse-grained reconfigurable architectures. *IEEE Des. Test*, 20(1):26–33, 2003.

[19] W. Lee, D. Puppin, S. Swenson, and S. Amarasinghe. Convergent scheduling. In *Proc. MICRO*, pages 111–122, 2002.

[20] A. Marquardt, V. Betz, and J. Rose. Timing-driven placement for FPGAs. In *Proc. Field Programmable Gate Arrays*, pages 203–213, 2000.

[21] B. Mei, S. Vernalde, D. Verkest, H. D. Man, and R. Lauwereins. DRESC: a retargetable compiler for coarse-grained reconfigurable architectures. *Proc. FPT*, pages 166–173, 2002.

[22] B. Mei, S. Vernalde, D. Verkest, H. D. Man, and R. Lauwereins. ADRES: An architecture with tightly coupled VLIW processor and coarse-grained reconfigurable matrix. In *Proc. FPL*, pages 61–70, 2003.

[23] S. C. Mishra, Mahim; Goldstein. Virtualization on the Tartan reconfigurable architecture. In *FPL*, pages 323–330, 2007.

[24] K. Nii *et al.* A 65 nm ultra-high-density dual-port SRAM with 0.71um2 8T-cell for SoC. In *VLSI Circuits*, pages 130 –131, 2006.

[25] H. Park. *Polymorphic Pipeline Array: A Flexible Multicore Accelerator for Mobile Multimedia Applications*. PhD thesis, The University of Michigan, 2009.

[26] H. Park, K. Fan, M. Kudlur, and S. Mahlke. Modulo graph embedding: mapping applications onto coarse-grained reconfigurable architectures. In *Proc. CASES*, pages 136–146, 2006.

[27] H. Park, K. Fan, S. A. Mahlke, T. Oh, H. Kim, and H.-s. Kim. Edge-centric modulo scheduling for coarse-grained reconfigurable architectures. In *Proc. PACT*, pages 166–176, 2008.

[28] J. Singh, D. Aswar, S. Mohanty, and D. Pradhan. A 2-port 6T SRAM bitcell design with multi-port capabilities at reduced area overhead. In *ISQED*, pages 131 –138, Mar. 2010.

[29] W. Snyder. Verilator-3.652, June 2007.

[30] M. B. Srivastava and M. Potkonjak. Optimum and heuristic transformation techniques for simultaneous optimization of latency and throughput. *IEEE Trans. VLSI*, 3(1):2–19, 1995.

[31] S. Trimberger, D. Carberry, A. Johnson, and J. Wong. A time-multiplexed fpga. In *Proc. FCCM*, pages 22–28, 1997.

[32] University of Massachusetts. UMass RCG HDL Benchmark Collection. [Online]. Available: http://www.ecs.umass.edu/ece/tessier/rcg/benchmarks, 2006.

[33] University of Toronto. iFAR - intelligent FPGA Architecture Repository. [Online]. Available: http://www.eecg.utoronto.ca/vpr/architectures, 2008.

[34] A. Ye and J. Rose. Using bus-based connections to improve field-programmable gate array density for implementing datapath circuits. In *IEEE Trans. VLSI*, pages 3–13, 2005.

[35] J. W. Yoon, A. Shrivastava, S. Park, M. Ahn, R. Jeyapaul, and Y. Paek. SPKM: a novel graph drawing based algorithm for application mapping onto coarse-grained reconfigurable architectures. In *Proc. ASP-DAC*, pages 776–782, 2008.

Line-Level Incremental reSynthesis Techniques for FPGAs

Doris Chen and Deshanand Singh
Altera Corporation
151 Bloor Street West, Toronto, Canada
dochen|dsingh@altera.com

ABSTRACT

FPGA logic density is roughly doubling at every process generation. Consequently, it is becoming increasingly challenging for FPGA CAD tools to keep up with the growing complexities of high-speed designs while keeping CAD runtimes reasonable. In this paper, we present a novel incremental resynthesis tool called Line-Level Incremental reSynthesis (LLIS), integrated within an industrial tool suite, that addresses the problems of timing closure as well as CAD runtime (patent pending). We describe a general framework that can incrementally reuse results from a previous compile based on automatic differencing of HDL changes. We show that it is possible to reduce synthesis runtime by 6.5x for common HDL changes. As compared with complete resynthesis, we preserve known good timing solutions more than 82% of the time. This represents a 3X improvement vs. non-incremental techniques.

Categories and Subject Descriptors

B.6.3 [**Hardware**]: Logic Design—*Design Aids*

General Terms

Algorithms

1. INTRODUCTION

Advancements in process technology continue to drive the evolution of modern devices. Because of the ever increasing needs of designers, the size and complexity of FPGAs are growing at a tremendous rate. These improvements have made FPGAs a much more attractive option for a larger class of designs where entire systems can now be implemented on a single device. These systems typically have throughput and/or operating speed requirements that constantly increase as next-generation standards evolve. As these large, high-speed designs become more prevalent, it is essential that we develop new, more scalable CAD tools to deal with the challenges that these designs bring.

One important aspect of the design development process is the amount of time needed to implement the initial design such that it satisfies the system specifications. This design development time can be broken down into two components. First, in order to use the FPGA as the implementation platform, the designer must use the CAD tool provided by the FPGA vendor to convert the design description into a design that can be programmed to function on the target device. Next, if this implemented design does not meet system requirements, the designer must then make changes to his/her design before compiling the design again using the FPGA CAD tool. This iterative approach is often referred to as the **Timing Closure Cycle**, which is depicted in Figure 1.

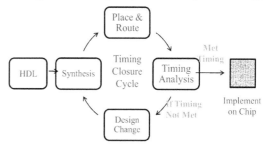

Figure 1: Timing Closure Cycle.

Unfortunately, as designs grow larger and more complex, the design development time is increasing rapidly. First, the algorithms employed by FPGA CAD tools work to solve a computationally intensive problem. These algorithms, often superlinear with respect to the design size, can lead to long compile times. It is not uncommon to have runtimes on the order of hours for a single compilation. Furthermore, because the design may not meet system requirements, the user may need to do some manual work to improve their design. This can range from turning on advanced CAD features [17] to making changes to their HDL. Since the designer often needs to iterate on design changes in order to meet timing, the long compile times can add up, and can result in lowered designer productivity.

A second side effect with FPGA CAD tools is the variability of the final placed-and-routed result. To cope with the computational difficulty while maintaining reasonable runtimes, CAD algorithms typically employ complex heuristics. While these heuristics guide us to a good solution, they do not necessarily guarantee that the achieved solution is the optimal answer. Thus, there will be some amount of variability in the quality of solution from compile to compile. In some cases, it is this variability that causes a design to fail to meet its timing constraints, adding to designer frustration.

In order to improve FPGA designer productivity, it is clear that both compile time and timing variation must be addressed. We need to reduce design compilation time in order to shorten each iteration through the Timing Closure Cycle. At the same time, we also need to reduce the variability of the CAD tool so that fewer iterations are required.

Numerous approaches, such as parallelizing FPGA CAD algorithms using multi-CPU systems [12] or GPUs [4, 5] have been documented to tackle the compile time challenge. While these methods are able to reduce compile time by using more computational resources, the timing variability issue remains. Similar CAD enhancements have been suggested [16, 19, 20] to improve runtimes. However, these techniques often sacrifice some quality to obtain speedups and are ineffective at reducing the overall time spent by the designer as they attempt to close timing. In this paper, we argue that a radically different methodology is required, and that we can address both of these issues without requiring extra computational resources.

By inspecting the Timing Closure Cycle, we can anticipate the most common user scenarios and work to address timing variability and compile time for these cases. We note that often a designer only makes a small change to their HDL, intended to correct a bug or add some small amount of new functionality, before compiling again. In this case, most of the design remain unchanged. Thus, if we can preserve the placed-and-routed result from the previous compile, we may be able to shorten compile time and reuse these unchanged portions of the design. By reusing previous results, we are also effectively reducing timing variability of the entire design since only the changed portion of the logic will be subject to timing variability inherent in the tool.

In this paper, we describe a high-quality *incremental* CAD tool, built into Altera's Quartus II [1], which can automatically identify small changes to the designer's HDL and produce an incremental solution based on the previous compile. This incremental CAD flow not only reduces the runtime of a single design compilation, it also can preserve timing in such a way that the designer is less affected by variability.

To accomplish this goal, all major parts of the CAD flow were made incremental. In this paper, we focus only on incremental resynthesis algorithms; however, we describe how it is integrated with our incremental P&R technology. The remainder of this paper is organized as follows: We first describe related work in this area and contrast these approaches to our approach. We then present our Line-Level Incremental reSynthesis (LLIS) algorithm, which we believe to be the first of its kind to be published. Results are then presented to show that we can dramatically reduce runtime and significantly improve timing preservation of a large suite of industrial designs. Finally, we present concluding remarks and provide directions for future work in this area.

2. SYNTHESIS BACKGROUND

Logic Synthesis is the process of translating the user's design description into a netlist of logical building blocks present on the FPGA. These include Logic Elements (LEs), which consist of lookup-tables (LUTs) and registers. In addition, the netlist may contain more complex elements such as RAMs, DSPs, and hard-IP blocks. Synthesis can be subdivided into the following phases:

Extraction parses a user's HDL design and creates a gate-level description that implements the functionality.

RTL-Level Optimizations (RTL) perform transformations of high-level constructs in the design. It operates on state-machines, multiplexers, multipliers, and adder trees to find coarse-grained optimizations that can improve circuit quality. The RTL stage creates an optimized gate-level representation for each of these high-level structures.

Multi-Level Synthesis (MLS) operates on the gate-level representation. It attempts to reduce the total number of gates in the design to improve area and the number of logic levels to improve timing.

Technology Mapping is the final step of the synthesis flow. Its goal is to transform the optimized gate-level netlist into a netlist of LEs that are present on the device. Technology mapping attempts to minimize the number of LUTs created and the number of logic levels.

As noted previously, these algorithms are computationally complex and somewhat variable in the quality of the final achieved solution. For example, consider the situation depicted in Figure 2. Here we show two compiles for identical regions of logic. Logic synthesis may produce different structures that are functionally equivalent, but have different structures. Even if the structure changes slightly, it becomes almost impossible to preserve a previous P&R solution that is known to meet timing.

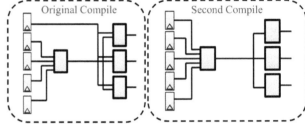

Figure 2: Incremental Resynthesis Motivation.

The optimizations in RTL, MLS and Technology Mapping take the vast majority of synthesis runtime. We believe that incremental CAD is an intriguing method of handling the runtime and variability issues. For example, consider the design change depicted in Figure 3. On the left, we show

Original	Design Change
| ```
// Registers
always @ (posedge CLK)
begin
    sumreg1 <= sum1;
    sumreg2 <= sum2;
end

// 3-bit additions
assign sum1 = A + B + C;
assign sum2 = sumreg1 + D + E;

assign OUT = sumreg2;
``` | ```
// Registers
always @ (posedge CLK)
begin
    sumreg1 <= sum1;
    sumreg2 <= sum2;
end

// 3-bit additions
assign sum1 = A + B + C;
assign sum2 = sumreg1 + X + Y;

assign OUT = sumreg2;
``` |

Figure 3: Simple Design Change.

a Verilog implementation for the original design and on the right we show a simple change. This design consists of two ternary adder trees. Discounting register retiming for simplicity, we note that the tree that involves $A + B + C$ is completely independent of $sumreg1 + X + Y$. An ideal tool could perform intelligent reuse from the results of the original compile as illustrated in Figure 4. Notice that we can simply reuse all of the synthesized logic for the portions of the design that have not changed. Only the newly modified ternary adder tree needs to be resynthesized from scratch. For typical design changes to large circuits, we find that

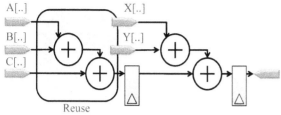

Figure 4: Design Reuse.

an extremely large fraction of the circuit can be reused exactly from the previous full compilation. In the case where the design change involves logic that is not timing critical, this strategy will lead to critical logic having exactly the same implementation as a previously good solution. For cases where we do change critical logic, we can now afford to spend more CAD runtime to find a high quality solution for the design change.

Several algorithms for incremental resynthesis have been previously published [3, 6, 7, 8, 9, 10, 11, 13, 14, 15, 18]. Several of these works [6, 13, 14] only handle specific types of incremental changes such as gate replacements and missing/extra gates. We do not consider techniques that target restricted subsets of changes due to their lack of generality.

The earliest related work on incremental resynthesis was proposed by Shinsha et. al [15]. The main concern of this work is to reuse gates that have been optimized for physical implementation used in a layout system. This layout system is a technology mapping step that picks the best physical implementation of a gate. This is illustrated in Figure 5. Logic functions are optimized using logic synthesis and physical implementations of these functions are chosen by the layout system. Given a design change, this paper describes a method by which we can reuse physical implementations from the original compilation. This is accomplished using an $O(N^2)$ algorithm that uses structural metrics to help select physical realizations that can be reused. However, it assumes that the logic synthesis step is mostly the same. In our experience, this assumption is not true for modern logic synthesis systems due to the use of heuristics. While these

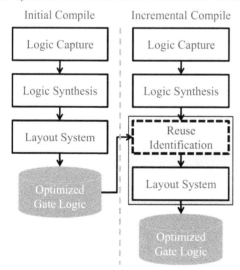

Figure 5: Shinsha Approach DAC-1986

techniques form the basis for any incremental resynthesis approach in that we need methods to determine reusable

portions of the initial results, the methods described are not applicable to our problem. These methods are not scalable for any circuit of modern size and do not deal with the complexities of reusing the logic synthesis step itself.

A more recently published paper [11] describes the use of boolean satisfiability (SAT) as a method for incrementally resynthesizing circuits. SAT solvers are tools that evaluate whether there is an assignment of variables that cause a boolean expression to evaluate to *true*. For expressions with large numbers of variables, the SAT solver has a worst case complexity that approaches exponential time. The basic method of operation is illustrated in Figure 6. Two netlists are assumed to exist. The first is the *model* netlist, a gate-level representation of the changed circuit and denoted as y_s. The second is a technology mapped netlist of LUTs that implements the original circuit. The LUTs in the orginal netlist are denoted $g_1, g_2 \ldots g_n$. A new LUT, F_c, is added to the original netlist and connected to a subset of the LUTs in the original LUT-mapped netlist. Boolean satisfiability is used to determine if there exists a function, F_c, which is able to implement the same functionality as the model netlist:

$$\exists F_c, \forall_{w,u,v,x,y,z} \; y_s = y_c \qquad (1)$$

Finding the subset of existing LUTs that should connect to F_c is done using random simulation to quickly prune away sets of LUTs which cannot possibly be used to compute F_c. However, the process of finding the correct subset of existing LUTs may be difficult and may require iterations. The

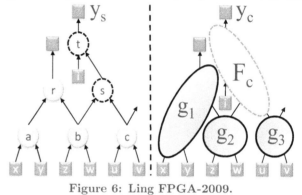

Figure 6: Ling FPGA-2009.

authors note that their solution can be used for any design change that does not include register retiming. In fact, their solution is not applicable to any design change where registers change at all. While the approach of using a SAT solver is interesting, it may not scale to extremely large industrial circuits. Since this technique cannot handle common design changes involving sequential elements and its scalability issues, we have not pursued this type of implementation.

The most practical published approach to this problem is described by a work from Intel [7]. The goal of this paper is to use external synthesis and formal verification tools to create an incremental resynthesis flow. This flow attempts to find the maximum amount of reuse, but does not target reduction in runtime. Maximum reuse is just as important in ASIC flows due to the complexity and variability of CAD algorithms. The high-level idea is shown in Figure 7. Given a logic cone, they attempt to find boundary points which can be exactly reused from a previous compilation. These cones of logic can then be stitched together with changed logic to form a hybrid cone that reuses as much logic as possible as illustrated in Figure 8. The general approach to finding the

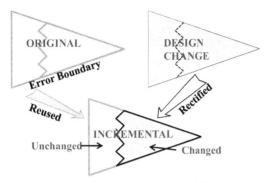

Figure 7: Intel Approach DAC-2009.

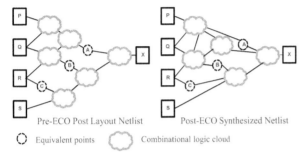

Pre-ECO Post Layout Netlist   Post-ECO Synthesized Netlist

◯ Equivalent points   ☁ Combinational logic cloud

Figure 8: Intel Approach DAC-2009.

maximum amount of reuse relies on using a formal verification tool to find points in the netlist which are exactly the same between the previous result and the changed netlist. Formal verification tools use techniques such as BDDs, SAT, and simulation to *prove* that cones of logic implement the same functionality regardless of its structure. Few formal verification tools are able to robustly deal with the complexities of sequential transformations such as retiming, register merging, duplication and state encoding.

Given that Intel was constrained to use external 3rd party tools, the flow of using a formal verifier to identify equivalent points is sensible; however, it is possible to do far better. In this paper, we propose a method in which the synthesis tool itself keeps track of equivalent points. This allows us to handle sequential optimizations and in addition, we can completely eliminate the runtime penalty of using formal verification techniques. Our technique can find large amounts of reuse, while simultaneously providing a dramatic reduction in runtime.

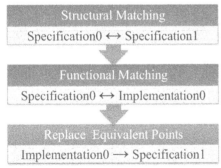

Figure 9: IBM Resynthesis Approach

The approach proposed by Brand et. al [3] is somewhat similar to our proposed method with one key difference. Their high-level algorithm is shown in Figure 9. Four netlists are assumed to exist:

- **Specification0** and **Specification1** correspond to structural representations to be synthesized for the original compile and the incremental compile, respectively.

- **Implementation0** and **Implementation1** are synthesized and technology mapped versions of the two corresponding specifications.

The goal is to reuse as much of Implementation0 as possible in the creation of Implementation1 from Specification1 by performing a structural difference of Specification1 and Specification0 to determine reusable parts of the netlist. Once the common parts of the two Specifications are identified, the next step is to stitch in parts of Implementation0 into parts of Specification1 that are identical to Specification0. Thus a matching algorithm between Specification0 and Implementation0 is needed. Simple structural methods cannot be used to find the matching as the two netlists are functionally identical but can have vastly different structural properties. Hence boolean methods are used to prove the equivalence of points between the Specification and Implementation. The authors propose an $O(N^2)$ algorithm for this step which is based on test pattern generation. We argue that it is possible to perform the matching of Specification0 and Implementation0 in **constant time** by allowing logic synthesis itself to keep track of the equivalence points.

Related methods which make heavy use of boolean and functional proof methods can be found in [8, 9, 18]. These techniques usually reach a point where runtime becomes expensive and cannot offer the savings that we target.

3. LLIS OVERVIEW

All previous approaches treat logic synthesis as a complex black box that inputs a gate-level specification and outputs a technology mapped netlist. Complex boolean or formal techniques are then necessary to reverse engineer the operation of synthesis and find equivalences between netlists. We propose a new approach, **Line-Level Incremental reSynthesis (LLIS)**, that tightly integrates equivalence tracking within the synthesis step itself, thereby alleviating the need for computationally expensive post-synthesis equivalence checking.

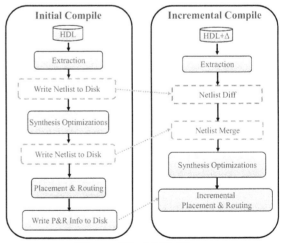

Figure 10: LLIS Flow.

The overall flow of LLIS can be seen in Figure 10. Incremental resynthesis typically begins with two consecutive compiles: the initial compile, and the incremental compile.

The initial compile is non-incremental, and provides a basis for comparison for the subsequent incremental compile. In the initial compile, we take two snapshots of the netlist, once before and once after logic synthesis optimizations steps of RTL, MLS and Technology Mapping. Theoretically, these netlist snapshots can be taken at any two points in the flow. We chose these two points to provide the maximum amount of netlist reuse for synthesis.

In the incremental compile, we take a snapshot of the netlist before synthesis optimization, and we compare it to the equivalent netlist from the initial compile. The purpose of this comparison is to determine what parts of the netlist remain unchanged from the initial compile. A key point to emphasize is that we use a structural netlist difference technique to identify portions of the netlist that are the same. Structural differencing is extremely fast in that it only flags portions of the netlist that are identical if the structure of the logic is identical. This is far less complex than functional or formal methods; however, it is unnecessary to use formal methods as the netlists are differenced after the Extraction step of the synthesis CAD flow. Netlist Extraction is simply a parser that is well-behaved. Since it produces identical logic structures for identical regions of HDL, there is no variability between compiles.

Once we have identified the unchanged portions, we perform a Netlist Merge to replace the unchanged portions of the *pre-synthesis* netlist with the equivalent *post-synthesis* result. The challenge here is that we know which parts of the extracted netlist are identical to the previous compile; however, we need a method of extracting the portions of the *post-synthesis* netlist which can be used as replacements for the identical logic. This is accomplished using a tracking mechanism, known as the Functionally Invariant Boundary (FIB), which is discussed in the next subsection.

At the end of Netlist Merge, the resulting netlist is a hybridized netlist consisting of both pre- and post-synthesis blocks. We can then run synthesis on this hybridized netlist. We mark post-synthesis blocks so that synthesis will not be performed on these blocks, thus saving compile time and ensuring preservation. There are three main parts of our approach: The establishment of Functionally-Invariant Boundaries, the Netlist Diff, and the Netlist Merge. Next, we will discuss each of these components in greater detail.

3.1 Functionally-Invariant Boundaries (FIBs)

The fundamental building block of our approach is the concept of Functionally-Invariant Boundaries (FIBs). Establishing FIBs gives us the means to determine whether or not nodes can be reused in the incremental compile. We define FIBs as follows:

- A FIB can be any arbitrary type of node in the netlist.

- A FIB is functionally invariant. This indicates that no optimizations have changed the functionality of this node. For example, if a node is transformed from an XOR to an OR gate due to some don't care optimizations, it has been functionally changed. However, if its structure changes such as becoming a LUT with the same function, then it is still considered to be a FIB.

At the beginning of logic synthesis, we mark all nodes in the netlist as FIBs. As synthesis optimizations occur, nodes may be collapsed and/or decomposed as we attempt

to satisfy QoR requirements and design constraints such as minimizing delay, power, or area. When FIBs nodes are affected by optimizations, they are no longer guaranteed to be be functionally-invariant. As a result, we remove optimized nodes from the list of FIB nodes. We keep track of changes to all FIBs throughout synthesis. At the end of synthesis, typically only a subset of the nodes in the netlist can be considered as FIBs. These remaining nodes in the FIB list are the **true** boundaries we have found in the netlist. By definition of the FIB node, these remaining nodes should be identical both before and after synthesis.

Once FIBs are established, we can then identify the FIB-to-FIB cones of logic as shown in Figure 11. The FIBs al-

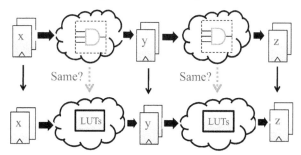

Figure 11: Isolating Changes.

low us the ability to fragment the netlist into independent parts. We can then match portions of the *post-synthesis* netlist to their functionally equivalent structure in the *pre-synthesis* netlist. Design changes made to one fragment of the netlist will have no effect on other independent portions of the netlist. Thus, the FIB effectively *filters out* design changes, and enables the isolation of design changes.

These fragments are guaranteed to have equivalents in the *post-synthesis* netlist because we have explicitly kept track of whenever optimizations change the functionality of any FIB. We can then easily replace unchanged FIB-to-FIB cones with their post-synthesis equivalents.

As an example, consider a netlist from the initial compile shown in Figure 12. At first, each node is considered to be

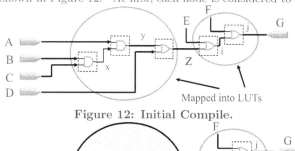

Figure 12: Initial Compile.

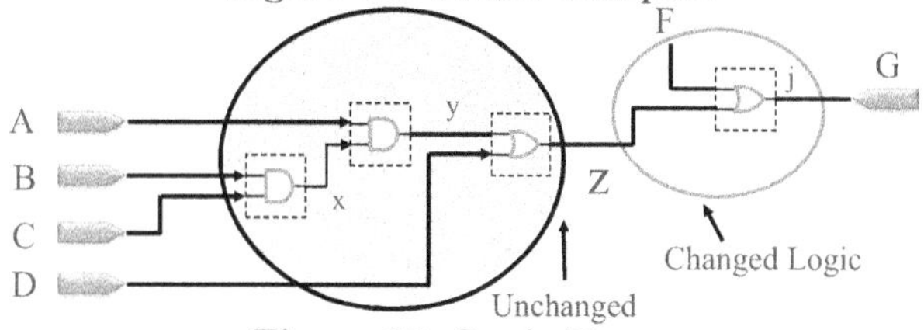

Figure 13: Logic Reuse.

a FIB (x, y, Z, i, j and the pins as well). However, after technology mapping we might find that some nodes have been completely covered by LUTs (x, y, i.) These nodes that have internal outputs covered by LUTs are invalidated as FIBs because their functionality is no longer observable. In the case of a design change shown in Figure 13, it is now possible to reuse Z. Because the functionality of Z is identical

Listing 1: Netlist Diff Pseudocode

```
1  bool diff_fib( FIB old, FIB new ) {
2    identical = node_is_same(old, new);
3    if (!is_a_fib(new)){
4      for ( i=0; i<fanins(new); i++ ) {
5        identical = identical &&
6          diff_fib( fanin( old, i ),
7                    fanin( new, i ) );
8      }
9    }
10   return identical;
11 }
```

in both compiles, the synthesized logic can replace the cone of logic that generates Z.

3.2 Netlist Differ

The objective of the Netlist Differ is to identify portions of the netlist that have remained unchanged from the previous compile. We compare the structure of the *pre-synthesis* netlist of the previous compile with structure of the *pre-synthesis* netlist of the current compile. The algorithm of the Netlist Differ can be found in Listing 1. We first identify all FIBs in the two netlists. Then, we traverse backwards from all FIB nodes. At every node encountered, we check to see if the node is functionally equivalent between the two compiles. If they are, we continue to traverse backwards on this node to ensure that the inputs of this node are also functionally equivalent. We terminate the recursion if we encounter a difference in the netlist, or if FIBs are reached. If we traverse all the way back to the FIB inputs, and found no changes, then we can conclude that this FIB-to-FIB cone of logic has remained unchanged between the previous compile and the current compile. However, if at any point we found a difference in the netlist, then we conclude that any nodes between the changed node and the FIB we started with have been changed. As a result, we can no longer reuse the nodes in this FIB-to-FIB cone as illustrated in Figure 14. We tra-

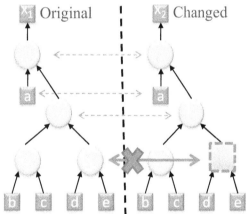

Figure 14: A Netlist Difference.

verse backwards from the FIBs x_1 and x_2 to check that these nodes have identical structure. Once a difference is encountered, the entire FIB-to-FIB cone is flagged as *different* and cannot be reused from the previous compile.

To make this algorithm efficient, we *speculatively* assume that FIBs with the same *identifier* between the original and

incremental compile are structurally identical. We then use the recursive algorithm described above to *prove* that these FIBs are indeed identical. The *identifier* is a combination of the name assigned by the HDL parser and a number of hash values that allow us to incorporate netlist structure as well. If we did not use this technique, the process of finding maximal amounts of reuse becomes far more complicated as each FIB in the incremental compile may need to be compared with all FIBs in the original compile. Clearly, such super-linear algorithms would not allow us to achieve runtime savings.

3.3 Netlist Merge

In the Netlist Merge step, the objective is to replace unchanged FIB-to-FIB cones of the *pre-synthesis* netlist with the equivalent FIB-to-FIB cone from the *post-synthesis* netlist of the previous compile. It is best described through an example. Consider a pictorial representation of the original *pre-synthesis* netlist shown in Figure 15a. For simplicity, we will assume that the only FIBs here are the input and output pins of the design. The corresponding *post-synthesis* netlist

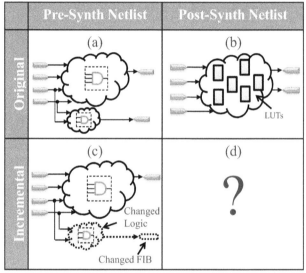

Figure 15: Netlist Merge Example.

for this design is shown in Figure 15b, where the gate-level netlist has been transformed into an implementable netlist of LUTs. On the incremental compile, we may encounter a design change to a relatively small portion of logic. This is indicated by the dotted region of Figure 15c.

The first step of our Netlist Merge routine is to create a single netlist consisting of the changed *pre-synthesis* netlist with the previous *post-synthesis* netlist as illustrated in Figure 16. We also attach the input pin FIBs to the corresponding FIBs in the synthesized netlist.

Next the most essential step occurs. We connect the input of FIBs that are the same as identified by the Netlist Diff to the input of the equivalent FIB in the *post-synthesis* netlist. As shown in Figure 17, the unchanged portion of the netlist can simply reuse the functionality of *post-synthesis* netlist from the previous compile.

Finally, we remove unused pins and sweep away unconnected logic as shown in Figure 18. Since the changed logic cannot reuse the outputs from the previous compile, we simply remove the unneccessary output pin and then sweep away all logic that is not needed. This will result in por-

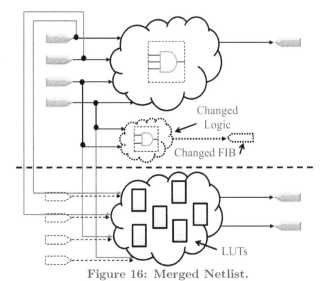

Figure 16: Merged Netlist.

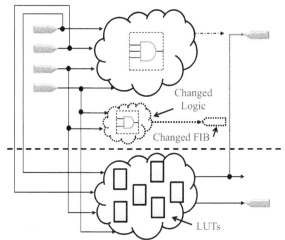

Figure 17: Connecting the Outputs.

tions of the *pre-synthesis* netlist being removed since it has been replaced by equivalent logic. Parts of the *post-synthesis* netlist that are not needed are also removed. We note that

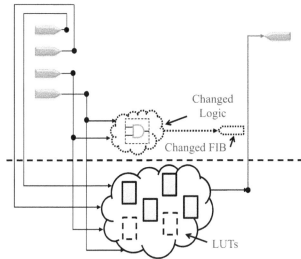

Figure 18: Sweep Logic.

both the Netlist Differ and Netlist Merge are $O(N)$ algorithms that take insignificant amounts of runtime.

3.4 Register Optimizations

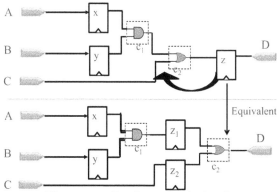

Figure 19: Register Optimizations.

The techniques described thus far have the additional benefit of being able to handle circuits that have undergone sequential synthesis optimizations such as register retiming. This situation is illustrated in Figure 19. Consider the register z. Suppose that it is retimed backwards to increase the core operating speed of this circuit. A simple way to handle this transformation would be to invalidate z as a FIB since there is no longer a FIB with an identifier related to the original register z. However, this conservative scheme reduces the amount of reuse in the presence of sequential transformations. A better method is to note that the combinational gate c_2 and the register z implement the same functionality. This transformation can be implemented by adding a small amount of extra tracking information to the FIB data structures to allow us to keep track of alternative *functionally-equivalent choices*. This allows for handling of register retiming, duplication and merging.

3.5 Additional Compile Time Optimizations

The ability to isolate design changes yields many possible methods to save compile time. First, we can now place design changes into a partition, and only perform synthesis on this partition. This way, we avoid the overhead of iterating through many synthesized nodes while performing no useful operations. We can also analyze the nodes to synthesize, and customize our many synthesis scripts to specifically target these nodes. For example, if no multipliers were changed, optimizations targeting these types of nodes need not be run. This can yield additional compile time savings. Conceptually, this can be implemented using custom synthesis scripts on each FIB-to-FIB region as illustrated in Figure 20.

4. EXPERIMENTAL RESULTS

In this section, we describe the experimental results obtained by applying these techniques to a set of industrial designs. We begin by describing the methodology used for evaluating the effectiveness of incremental CAD. We then discuss our results in detail.

4.1 Experimental Methodology

The Rapid Recompile feature of Altera's Quartus II CAD tool is a way to improve the user experience and maximize user productivity through incremental compilation. The

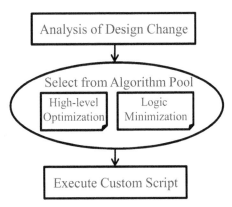

Figure 20: Synthesis Scripts.

goals of this feature include: To preserve timing in the presence of non timing critical design changes, and to reduce compile time when only a small portion of the netlist is changed. This reduction in compile time and improvement to timing preservation aid in reducing the number of iterations the designer will need during development.

In Quartus II V 9.1, the P&R step was made incremental. It performs a structural diff, similar to our method described in Section 3.2, and tries to preserve as much of the placement and routing information from the previous compile. Although the incremental P&R tool was able to reduce compile time significantly, maximum preservation of the previous compile could not be achieved due to non-incremental synthesis. Because non-incremental synthesis can make substantially different netlist structures with small design changes, some reusable P&R information were discarded. Therefore, in Quartus II v10.1, synthesis was made fully incremental by using techniques detailed in this paper.

To measure the effectiveness of our algorithms, we established a set of benchmarks of approximately 40 industrial designs. Small design changes were created by hand for each design. These changes can include simple rewiring, changes to state machines, constants and parameters. We can also add or remove non-critical logic or pipelining stages. We then run full compiles on these designs. First, we constrain every clock in the designs to 1GHz to obtain the maximum achievable operating frequency (F_{max}) to simulate a situation where the design is pushing the absolute maximum boundaries of operating speed on every clock domain. This is our *initial compile*. We then apply a small design change to each circuit and run our LLIS algorithm in conjunction with incremental P&R. This *incremental compile* is run with each clock set to a constraint equal to 99% of achievable F_{max} of the same clock in the initial compile. These constraints are difficult to meet but provides some timing slack to accomodate logic changes. As described previously, there is some variability in the solution returned by FPGA CAD tools. Even an excellent tool may only meet a relatively aggressive timing constraint 85% of the time; however, a common circuit may have 8 distinct clock domains. In this case, the probability of passing **all** clock domains is $(0.85)^8 = 27\%$. Our metric of success is to see if we can satisfy timing constraints on all clock domains in the circuit given this challenging setup. Even if a single domain fails to meet its constraint, then the designer must make at least one further iteration through the CAD flow to satisfy their timing requirements.

4.2 Optimization Results

Table 1 demonstrates the effectiveness of our incremental synthesis techniques on large industrial circuits, ranging in size from 20K-400K LEs targeted to the Stratix IV [2] device family. This table highlights two significant results. First, the 3rd column shows the ratio of the incremental LLIS compile time in relation to the runtime of the original compile. This displays a dramatic reduction of runtime, with ratios ranging from 3% to 77% of the original compile. On average, LLIS shows an impressive runtime reduction as the incremental compile is 15% of the original runtime.

There are two reasons for the non-uniform nature of our compile time savings. First, each circuit differs in terms of the design change applied. Therefore, the relative size of the design change is not uniform across all designs. Generally, design changes such as adding a pipeline stage are typically easier to incorporate than a random change to combinational logic which may invalidate a more significant FIB-to-FIB cone. Secondly, we find that runtime savings is also correlated the size of the FIB-to-FIB cloud to be resynthesized. For example, a small design change involving a state machine may require some complex encoding optimizations whereas a similarly sized design change involving only a tree of simple AND-gates may require far less CAD optimizations.

The second significant result from Table 1 is the ability of LLIS to improve timing preservation as shown in Columns 4, 5 and 6. Column 4 shows the *worst-case* slack after P&R is complete using constraints that are set to 99% of the F_{max} of each clock as described previously. Notice that 32 of the 39 circuits shown meet all timing contraints. Contrast this result with the same experiment using our default non-incremental synthesis flow as shown in Column 6. Only 11 of the same 39 circuits pass using the same methodology. In this case, the only difference is that synthesis starts from scratch on the incremental compile. We conclude that LLIS increased the ability to meet these difficult timing constraints from a rate of approximately 28% to 82%. The main reason for the improved pass rate is that LLIS enabled incremental P&R to reuse constraints from the original compile for unchanged portions of the circuit. Column 5 shows a measure of the P&R preservation for each circuit. In most cases, the P&R preservation exceeds 99% and falls in line with designer expectations.

There are some types of small HDL design changes where the reduction in compile time is not as substantial. For example, if a design change is made to a huge cloud of combinational logic that has undergone heavy optimizations, we cannot preserve any of post-synthesis logic since most of the FIBs would be invalidated, creating a large FIB-to-FIB cone. In these cases, the user will most likely benefit from complete resynthesis of this logic cone. Also, if the design change affects the structure and connectivity of many nodes in the netlist, reusability of the previous result may be low. For example, a parameter change in Verilog may only affect a single constant, but may change the structure of the entire circuit. The benchmark suite has three such circuits, evidenced by their high runtime ratios, where the design change cannot be easily isolated with our current implementation.

Even though small HDL changes may result in large affected portions of the circuit, our algorithm is robust in these circumstances. To demonstrate this, we took a number of circuits and simulated design changes of $x\%$ by randomly selecting FIBs from the netlist and injecting an artificial

Table 1: Optimization Results

1	2	3	4	5	6	7
Circuit	Area (LEs)	Runtime Ratio	LLIS WC Slack (ns)	LLIS P&R Preservation	NO LLIS WC Slack (ns)	NO LLIS P&R Preservation
cct1	401986	9.9%	0.03	100.0%	-0.36	88.7%
cct2	283462	21.5%	-0.27	98.7%	0.01	98.7%
cct3	270397	7.3%	-0.03	99.9%	-0.65	93.5%
cct4	278606	7.2%	0.04	100.0%	0.07	73.4%
cct5	256703	8.1%	0.02	100.0%	-0.30	93.6%
cct6	232960	76.9%	0.02	100.0%	0.02	100.0%
cct7	164090	9.1%	0.01	100.0%	-0.87	99.2%
cct8	164982	6.0%	0.03	100.0%	-0.30	97.7%
cct9	153940	17.8%	0.01	100.0%	-0.92	98.1%
cct10	127676	22.1%	0.03	100.0%	-0.21	94.9%
cct11	133328	15.5%	0.02	99.8%	-0.48	99.9%
cct12	136727	17.8%	0.05	99.9%	0.14	98.5%
cct13	131441	12.4%	0.15	89.8%	-0.22	78.9%
cct14	116686	20.6%	0.02	97.6%	-0.28	95.0%
cct15	121936	6.1%	0.10	100.0%	-0.27	97.9%
cct16	127188	3.4%	0.03	100.0%	-0.09	95.7%
cct17	134802	9.6%	-0.38	100.0%	-0.89	90.9%
cct18	131027	14.0%	0.07	99.8%	0.06	99.7%
cct19	94769	17.1%	0.02	99.1%	-0.48	98.6%
cct20	102206	26.1%	-1.38	99.5%	0.02	100.0%
cct21	101316	31.8%	0.03	99.4%	-1.21	98.8%
cct22	106152	15.6%	0.02	100.0%	-0.26	99.7%
cct23	98772	26.8%	0.03	99.8%	0.03	97.2%
cct24	84643	26.7%	0.02	100.0%	-0.23	94.5%
cct25	80466	14.5%	-0.07	99.5%	-0.86	97.8%
cct26	92941	22.2%	0.02	99.1%	-0.39	94.7%
cct27	85427	13.1%	-0.05	99.1%	-0.45	96.4%
cct28	84851	47.5%	0.02	99.9%	0.02	95.9%
cct29	78657	20.1%	0.02	99.9%	0.09	94.5%
cct30	82815	19.0%	0.05	99.3%	-0.51	98.4%
cct31	79181	46.3%	0.02	100.0%	-1.22	97.3%
cct32	78412	11.1%	0.02	100.0%	-1.77	96.9%
cct33	73398	13.6%	0.02	100.0%	-1.12	99.7%
cct34	68778	9.4%	0.03	99.3%	0.07	97.6%
cct35	67830	7.6%	0.02	100.0%	-0.50	99.7%
cct36	53221	15.6%	0.01	99.9%	-0.39	98.9%
cct37	53646	20.4%	0.06	99.7%	-0.90	99.7%
cct38	45796	18.2%	0.03	100.0%	-0.10	97.6%
cct39	23180	23.3%	-0.06	99.4%	0.03	100.0%
Geomean	110021	15.4%	32/39 Passing		11/39 Passing	

difference. This method allows us to sweep the value of x along many points up to 100% netlist difference. The results are shown in Figure 21. There is generally a small constant time incurred regardless of the design change size. This is because we must always parse and extract the gate-level representation of the HDL files. After accounting for the constant time, the runtime ratio is relatively linear with the size of the design change. This result is very encouraging because it shows that our LLIS algorithm can be applied by default since there are *no* adverse effects on compile time regardless of the change size.

There are cases where the LLIS approach can slightly increase area of the design. Consider the design change shown in Figure 22. If we can only use the input and output pins as FIBs, then we will obtain a poor optimization result as shown in Figure 23. In this example, *out* is reused by dropping in its LUT implementation. The signal *out2* is synthesized from scratch; however, the shared logic between the reused LUT and the identical multiplexer is not captured. The resulting netlist will contain two LUTs that implement the *same* multiplexer $(d[s])$. This can potentially increase the area of the incrementally synthesized circuit. However,

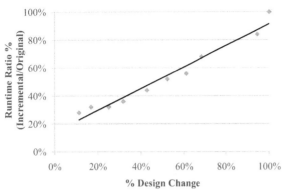

Figure 21: Rutime vs Design Change.

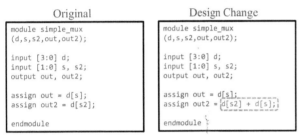

Figure 22: Duplication Design Example.

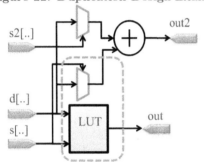

Figure 23: Unnecessary duplication.

we found that area duplication was not an issue with LLIS. In our benchmark set, the average size of design changes is 3.6% of the full netlist. In the incremental compile, we see an average area increase of 0.1%, which is negligible. This indicates that our established FIBs are very good in isolating design changes. We note that cct20 and cct39 are the only cases where LLIS is adversely affected by this scenario.

5. CONCLUSIONS & FUTURE WORK

In this paper, we have described a practical approach to incrementally resynthesize designs. We have shown that a design flow based on incremental reuse can be an effective strategy to cope with the runtime complexities of the large, high-speed designs common in the latest FPGAs. We show that it is possible to reduce synthesis runtime by 6.5x for common HDL changes. When compared with complete resynthesis, we preserve known good timing solutions more than 82% of the time. This represents a 3X improvement vs. non-incremental techniques.

We believe that this is the first work on incremental resynthesis that can address general design changes with a method that has scalable runtime for large circuits. Through experimental results on a suite of industrial circuits, we demonstrated the viability of the proposed approach.

One interesting area of research would be the judicious application of SAT-based techniques for design changes that are truly small. For example, if a single AND-gate is transformed into an OR-gate, there are situations where a multi-LUT cone cannot be reused. Since we have already partitioned the netlist into small clouds, we could easily apply SAT-based techniques to change the lutmask (LUT truth table) to reflect this design change.

6. REFERENCES

[1] Altera. *Quartus II Handbook v9.0*, 2009.
[2] Altera. *Stratix IV Device Handbook*. v3.3, Jun. 2009.
[3] D. Brand, A. Drumm, S. Kundu, P. Narain, *Incremental synthesis*, Proceedings of the 1994 IEEE/ACM international conference on Computer-aided design, p.14-18, November 1994.
[4] D. Chen, D. Singh, *Parallelizing FPGA Technology Mapping using Graphics Processing Units (GPUs)*, Proceedings of the international conference on Field Programmable Logic and Applications, September 2010.
[5] A. Choong, R. Beidas, J. Zhu, *Parallelizing Simulated Annealing-Based Placement Using GPGPU*, Proceedings of the international conference on Field Programmable Logic and Applications, September 2010.
[6] P. Chung, I. Hajj, *ACCORD Automatic Catching and CORrection of Logic Design Errors in Combinational Circuits*, Proc. of International Test Conference, September 1992.
[7] A. Jayalakshmi, *Auto ECO Flow Development for Functional ECO Using Efficient Error Rectification Method Based on FV Tool*, Proceedings of the 38th ACM/IEEE conference on Design automation, 2009.
[8] S. Krishnaswamy, H. Ren, N. Modi, R. Puri, *DeltaSyn: An Efficient Logic Difference Optimizer for ECO Synthesis*, Proceedings of the International Conference on Computer Aided Design, November 2009.
[9] Y. Kukimoto , M. Fujita, *Rectification method for lookup-table type FPGA's*, Proceedings of the 1992 IEEE/ACM international conference on Computer-aided design, p.54-61, November 1992.
[10] C. Lin , Y. Huang, S. Chang , W. Jone, *Design and design automation of rectification logic for engineering change*, Proceedings of the 2005 conference on Asia South Pacific design automation, January 18-21, 2005.
[11] A. Ling, S. Brown, J. Zhu, S. Safarpour, *Towards automated ECOs in FPGAs*, Proceeding of the ACM/SIGDA international symposium on Field programmable gate arrays, February 2009.
[12] A. Ludwin, V. Betz, K. Padalia, *High-quality, deterministic parallel placement for FPGAs on commodity hardware*, Proceedings of the international ACM/SIGDA symposium on Field programmable gate arrays, February 2008.
[13] J. Madre, O. Coudert, J. Billon, *Automating the Diagnosis and the Rectification of Design Errors with PRIAM£¡*, Proc. of ICCAD, November 1989, pp. 30-33.
[14] I. Pomeranz, S. Reddy, *On Diagnosis and Correction of Design Errors*, Proc. of ICCAD, November 1993.
[15] T. Shinsha, T. Kubo, Y. Sakataya, J. Koshishita, K. Ishihara, *Incremental logic synthesis through gate logic structure identification*, Proceedings of the 23rd ACM/IEEE conference on Design automation, p.391-397, July 1986.
[16] Y. Sankar, J. Rose, *Trading quality for compile time: ultra-fast placement for FPGAs*, Proceedings of the 1999 ACM/SIGDA seventh international symposium on Field programmable gate arrays, p.157-166, February 1999.
[17] D. Singh, V. Manohararajah, S. D. Brown, *Two-Stage Physical Synthesis for FPGAs*, Proceedings of the IEEE Custom Integrated Circuits Conference, p.171-178, Sept 2005.
[18] G. Swamy, S. Rajamani, C. Lennard, R. Brayton, *Minimal logic re-synthesis for engineering change*, International Symposium on Circuits and Systems, 1997.
[19] J. Swartz , V. Betz , J. Rose, *A fast routability-driven router for FPGAs*, Proceedings of the 1998 ACM/SIGDA sixth international symposium on Field programmable gate arrays, p.140-149, February 1998.
[20] R. Tessier, *Fast placement approaches for FPGAs*, ACM Transactions on Design Automation of Electronic Systems (TODAES), v.7 n.2, p.284-305, April 2002.

Towards Scalable FPGA CAD Through Architecture

Scott Y.L. Chin and Steven J.E. Wilton
Department of Electrical and Computer Engineering
University of British Columbia
Vancouver, British Columbia, Canada
scottc@ece.ubc.ca, stevew@ece.ubc.ca

ABSTRACT

Long FPGA CAD runtime has emerged as a limitation to the future scaling of FPGA densities. Already, compile times on the order of a day are common, and the situation will only get worse as FPGAs get larger. Without a concerted effort to reduce compile times, further scaling of FPGAs will eventually become impractical.

Previous works have presented fast CAD tools that trade-off quality of result for compile time. In this paper, we take a different but complementary approach. We show that the architecture of the FPGA itself can be designed to be amenable to fast-compile. If not done carefully, this can lead to lower-quality mapping results, so a careful tradeoff between area, delay, power, and compile run-time is essential. We investigate the extent to which run-time can be reduced by employing high-capacity logic blocks. We extend previous studies on logic block architectures by quantifying the area, delay and CAD runtime trade-offs for large capacity blocks, and also investigate some multi-level logic block architectures. In addition, we present an analytically derived equation to guide the design of logic block I/O requirements.

Categories and Subject Descriptors

B.7.1 [**Integrated Circuits**]: Types and Design Styles—
Gate Arrays

General Terms

Design

Keywords

Field-Programmable Gate Arrays, FPGAs, Architecture, CAD
Run-time

1. INTRODUCTION

Since their introduction, Field-Programmable Gate Arrays (FPGAs) have grown substantially in capacity due to

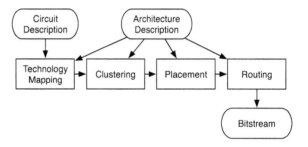

Figure 1: Typical FPGA CAD Flow

the continued scaling of transistor sizes. This has opened up new markets for FPGAs since they can now implement more complex digital systems. However, this scaling also means that the FPGA CAD tools need to perform an increasing number of operations to complete the mapping process. For modern FPGAs, place and route for even a moderate-sized design can take an entire workday. As FPGA capacity continues to scale, the problem will become worse. To exacerbate the problem, the computer processors used to run the CAD tools are no longer scaling in speed with transistor size and parallel CAD implementations provide sub-linear speedups. This is not sustainable. Left unaddressed, further scaling of FPGA capacity will eventually become impractical due to CAD runtime.

To combat this problem, significant advances have been made to improve the efficiency of FPGA CAD algorithms. However, tackling this issue should not be left solely to CAD developers. Since architecture and CAD are tightly connected, it is conceivable that architecture designers can design architectures that are amenable to fast CAD runtimes, balanced against the more traditional optimization goals of power, delay, and density. This approach is a large unexplored area of research and the techniques from this approach may be orthogonal, and hence complementary, with existing and future algorithmic research.

We can identify two general approaches for designing such architectures:

1. *Architectures with features to recoup degraded mapping quality of fast CAD algorithms.* Most fast CAD techniques lead to degraded mapping quality (i.e. density, delay, and or power) [18]. It is conceivable to over-design or optimize the architecture to compensate for this degradation. The end goal would be to achieve equivalent mapping quality and faster CAD at the ex-

pense of absolute area. The Plasma architecture is one example of this approach [3].

2. *Architectures that lead to a reduced problem size in the computationally expensive stages of the FPGA CAD flow.* The FPGA CAD flow contains a number of stages. The more prominent stages are shown in Figure 1. Some stages, such as placement and routing, take much longer than others. It may be possible to modify the architecture so that the problem size presented to the computationally expensive stage(s) is reduced, thus directly reducing the runtime of these stages. This may come at the expense of increasing the problem size for other (less computationally intense) stages, or require the introduction of whole new stages to the CAD flow.

In this paper, we focus on the second approach, and *investigate to what extent it is possible to architect high-capacity logic blocks to reduce CAD runtime.* More specifically, we consider two approaches for building high-capacity logic blocks: directly scaling traditional architectures, and using a multi-level architecture. We explore logic block sizes beyond the range looked at in previous studies and approach this study from the new perspective of CAD runtime. In addition, we present a new analytical relationship for determining the number of inputs per logic block which accounts for interconnect demand.

The paper is organized as follows: Section 2 discusses background the related work. Section 3 describes the logic block architectures explored in this paper. Section 4 presents the experimental methodology Section 5 discusses the results of our experiments. And Section 6 concludes the paper.

2. BACKGROUND

2.1 Related Studies in CAD Runtime

Reducing the time needed to map a circuit to the FPGA architecture has garnered much research interest. Most of these studies aim to improve the efficiency of the underlying CAD algorithms [4, 23, 5]. More recently, there has been interest in parallelizing the CAD algorithms [14] to take advantage of the increasing number of processor cores on a single CPU.

Some methods impact the FPGA user's design flow. Incremental compilation [21] allows the FPGA user to re-map only the portion of the circuit that has been changed as opposed to remapping the entire circuit. Floorplanning leverages the fact that large-scale designs are often developed using pre-defined macroblocks or using hierarchical hardware design languages [22]. This may allow the mapping of each macroblock to occur independently, or provide additional locality information to help the mapping process converge faster.

These previous techniques focus on *algorithmic* modifications; in this paper, we investigate *architectural* modifications that may be orthogonal to these CAD approaches.

2.2 Logic Block Architecture Terminology

Logic blocks (LB) in modern FPGAs are implemented as clusters of lookup tables (LUTs) and registers, and include additional specialized circuitry to perform clock distribution, control (register set and reset), and fast arithmetic operations. For simplicity, we assume the commonly used view

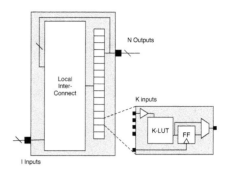

Figure 2: Logic Block and Basic Logic Element (BLE)

shown in Figure 2. Each LB consists of a fast local interconnect network and a group of basic logic elements (BLEs). Each BLE contains a LUT, a register, and a programmable multiplexer (MUX), and each BLE output can drive signals outside of the LB. This architectural model can be used to describe a family of architectures using the following three parameters:

- K denotes the size of each LUT

- N denotes the number of BLEs within a logic block

- I denotes the number of unique inputs that can be supplied to the logic block

2.3 Previous Studies on Logic Block Size

Architecture studies have been performed to investigate the impact of LB size on area, delay, and power. When optimizing the architecture for area [4, 17, 1] or power efficiency [20], an LB size in the range of $N = 4$ to 9 is shown to be best. Three competing trends lead to this optimal range. As LB size increases, the area and power dissipation of each LB increases. However, the total number of LBs needed to implement a circuit decrease. The amount of global routing resources is also reduced as more nets are completely absorbed and implemented by the local interconnect.

The critical path delay of a circuit is also affected in a similar way. Delay through a single LB increases, but the total number of LBs along the critical path decreases and more nets are implemented using the faster local interconnect. Unlike area and power, the studies showed that the latter trend dominates. Thus, critical path delay decreases monotonically for increasing cluster size.

Due to the area and power results, there has never been a compelling reason to investigate large LB sizes (commercial devices use a LB size in the range of $N = 8$ to 16). Now that CAD runtime is becoming a major concern (its relative importance to area, delay, and power is still debatable) we have a reason to revisit these topics.

Although [17] observed that logic block size affects CAD runtime, none of these studies directly investigate the CAD runtime versus quality (area, delay, power) trade-offs afforded by logic block size. In addition, none of these studies investigate an LB size greater than $N = 20$ [1].

---

[1] [1, 20] looked at sizes up to $N = 10$ for a 180um process, [4] and [17] looked at sizes up to $N = 16$ and $N = 20$, respectively, for a 350um process.

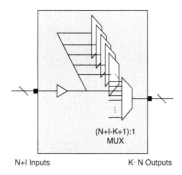

Figure 3: Logic block local interconnect

2.4 Why Logic Block Size Affects Runtime

Intuitively, as the logic block size increases, the logic capacity of each LB is increased. This has two major effects on CAD runtime:

1. The number of logic blocks needed to implement the user circuit is reduced, thus directly reducing the placement problem size and runtime.

2. The number of nets that need to be routed outside of the logic blocks is reduced, thus directly reducing the routing problem size and runtime.

These effects have been observed experimentally [17] and expressed analytically [6].

Of course, increasing logic block size will increase the run-time of the CAD stages that map logic to these blocks. However, the run-time of these stages is much smaller than the run-time of the placement and routing stages.

3. HIGH-CAPACITY LOGIC BLOCK ARCHITECTURES

In this paper, we consider two methods to architect large logic blocks. The first approach is to directly increase N in the logic block architecture that we have discussed so far. We will refer to this approach as *flat*. The second approach will use a partly hierarchical construction with two levels of hierarchy. We will refer to this as *multi-level*. This is similar to the APEX logic block architecture [2]. We do not consider fully hierarchical architectures or any further levels of hierarchy within this paper.

3.1 Flat Logic Block

Section 2.2 has already described this architecture. In our study, we consider sizes up to $N = 50$. We assume a depopulated LB local interconnect using the technique from [24] that maintains full logical connectivity, but reduces the number of transistors needed to implement the network. This scheme guarantees that at least one of the K BLE inputs can be connected to any of the I logic block inputs, and is possible due to the logical equivalence of the LUT input pins. The effect is a reduction in width of the $N \cdot K$ local routing MUX's (one for each BLE input pin in the logic block) from $(N + I) : 1$ to $(I + N - K + 1) : 1$. The local interconnect is illustrated in Figure 3.

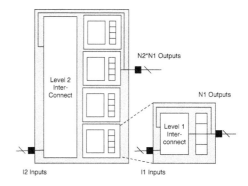

Figure 4: Multi-Level Logic Block

3.2 Multi-Level Logic Block

This architecture consists of two levels. The first level is the same as the flat architecture from the previous section. We use K, $N1$, and $I1$ to denote the architecture parameters of the first level. The second level of hierarchy consists of a second level of interconnect and $N2$ first-level blocks. The number of inputs available at the second level is parameterized as $I2$. Figure 4 shows this architecture.

We chose this architecture because it fits easily into an island-style FPGAs and does not require any major changes to the global routing architecture or CAD tools. Investigating more radical alternative architectures is an interesting area of future research.

3.3 Logic Block I/O and Interconnect Demand

Determining the appropriate number of inputs (I, $I1$, and $I2$) for the LB is critical to the area and packing efficiency of the architecture. Too few inputs force BLEs to go unused and too many lead to an unnecessarily large silicon area due to the size of the local interconnect.

The total number of BLE inputs within a LB is $K \cdot N$. But, due to shared and feedback connections (which are implemented by connections already inside the LB) in the circuits being implemented, LBs typically do not need the $K \cdot N$ maximum number of unique inputs.

Betz [4] found that the relationship shown in Equation 1 allowed 98% of BLEs to be used on average. This relationship was determined empirically when investigating architectures of $K = 4$ and N in the range of 1 to 16. It was later generalized by Ahmed [1] based on experimental data using architectures of $K = 2$ to 7 and $N = 1$ to 10. This equation has since become a well-accepted rule of thumb.

$$I = \frac{K}{2}(N + 1) \tag{1}$$

We found that this relationship becomes less appropriate when scaling to very large LB sizes. The main shortcoming is that it does not directly account for the the interconnect demand of circuits being implemented on the FPGA. The end result is a higher than necessary number of input pins per LB. Using analytical methods from [12], we derive a more accurate relationship that accounts for interconnect demand of the circuits being implemented on the FPGA.

Starting with the same goal of the traditional equation, we aim to determine a value I such that 98% of the BLEs are utilized on average. Let us denote the number of K-LUTs

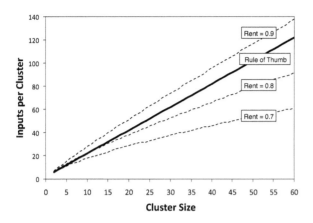

Figure 5: Equations for determining number of inputs per logic block

required to cover a circuit as n_k. We then denote the number of LBs needed to cover these K-LUTs as n_c. Each LB contains N K-LUTs so the total number of programmable K-LUTs available across all LBs is $n_c \cdot N$. If only 98% of the available K-LUTs are used, we can then form the following equality:

$$n_k = 0.98 \cdot n_c \cdot N \qquad (2)$$

We then use Equation 3 directly from [12] [2]. This equation models the number of clusters (logic blocks) required, denoted as n_c, to implement a circuit that has been technology mapped to n_k LUTs. Note that this equation accounts for the interconnect demand of the circuit being implemented; p and f denote the Rent parameter and average fanout of the circuit, respectively. γ is a model parameter that describes the average number of unused LUT input pins. The full derivation can be found in [12], and its accuracy has been validated against experimental results.

$$n_c = n_k \cdot \sqrt[p]{\frac{K + 1 - \gamma}{I \cdot \left(1 + \frac{1}{f}\right)}} \qquad (3)$$

Substituting Equation 3 into Equation 2 and solving for I yields Equation 4.

$$I = (0.98 \cdot N)^p \cdot \frac{K + 1 - \gamma}{1 + \frac{1}{f}} \qquad (4)$$

We can interpret the Rent parameter p in Equation 4 as the Rent parameter of the architecture. In other words, it describes the architecture's *interconnect supply*. Figure 5 compares the traditional rule-of-thumb equation (shown in the solid line) to the new analytical equation (shown in dashed line for three values of interconnect supply. Note that we used a fanout value of of $f = 3.4$ based on the

---

[2]The model in [12] contains two equations for n_c depending on whether the logic architecture leads to N-Limited, or I-Limited packing. In our scenario, we state that only 98% of BLEs are used because I is chosen in a way to limit full occupancy. Therefore, we use the I-Limited equation

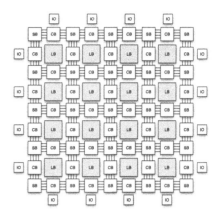

Figure 6: FPGA Overview

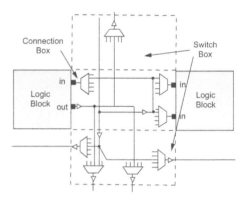

Figure 7: FPGA Routing Architecture Overview

average fanout of our benchmark suite presented later in Section 4). From this figure, we can see that beyond $N = 15$, the traditional equation produces architectures with an intrinsically high amount of interconnect supply.

As a reference point, previous studies have quantified the architecture Rent exponent of the Altera Cyclone architecture and Altera Apex architecture to be 0.7256 [19], and 0.78 [11], respectively. Those studies also quantified the interconnect demand of 77 industrial circuits and found the Rent parameter to range from 0.5-0.8 with an average of 0.6.

For the remainder of this paper, we will use this relationship to determine the number of input pins per logic block. For the multi-level architecture, we determine $I1$ by substituting $N1$ into the equation, and we determine $I2$ by substituting in the *effective* cluster size $N2 \cdot N1$.

4. EXPERIMENTAL METHODOLOGY

In the next section, we will experimentally quantify the area, delay, and CAD run-time trade-offs for the architectures described in Section 3. This section will describe the experimental methodology including architectural assumptions, area and delay models, CAD tools and benchmarks.

4.1 Architectural Assumptions

We assume a homogeneous FPGA consisting only of logic block tiles with a single clock domain. The routing archi-

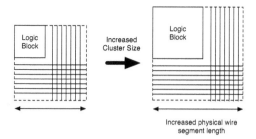

Figure 8: Effects of Cluster Size on Physical Wire Segment Length

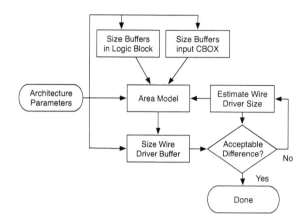

Figure 9: Buffer Sizing Flow

tecture is based on single-driver directional routing which is consistent with VPR 5.0. Figure 6 and 7 show an overview.

Each LB output pin drives an isolation buffer which then drives $Fcout \cdot W$ routing MUXes, where W is the number of routing tracks per channel and $Fcout$ is the percentage of W tracks to which the the the output pin can connect. Wire segments connect to LB inputs through an isolation buffer which then drives $Fcin \cdot (2 \cdot I/4)$ input pins, where $Fcin$ is the fraction of wire segments in the routing channel that can drive a given input pin. We assume that LB pins are evenly distributed along all four sides of the LB. Therefore, there are $I/4$ input pins on each side, and two LBs surrounding each channel. Wire segments entering a Switch Box can connect to Fs outgoing wire segments.

In our experiments, we set $Fcout = 0.1$, $Fcin = 0.15$, $Fs = 3$ and assume that wire segments span a single LB. The channel width W is set to the minimum width that still enables the circuit to be routed. This is determined independently for each circuit and each set of logic block parameter values. Similarly, the FPGA grid size is set just large enough to accommodate all of the required LBs for each circuit. Inputs per LB is chosen based on a Rent parameter of $p = 0.8$. We performed our experiments for $p = 0.7$ and $p = 0.9$ as well but have omitted the results since the trends and conclusions were similar.

I/O blocks are found on the periphery of the FPGA. Each I/O block contains a number of pads that allow for off-chip communication. To maintain a similar I/O Pad to I/O Block density across all our architectures, we set the number of pads per block according to Equation 5 [17].

$$PadsPerIOBlock = \lceil 2 \cdot \sqrt{N_{eff}} \rceil \qquad (5)$$

For the flat architecture, $N_{eff} = N$ and for the multi-level architecture, $N_{eff} = N2 \cdot N1$.

4.2 Area Model, Delay Model, and Circuit Design

We use an area model based on counting the number of minimum-width transistor areas (MWTA) needed to implement the architecture [4]. In the model, SRAM cells are implemented with six minimum-size transistors. LUTs are implemented as full binary trees of NMOS pass-transistors and all pass transistors are minimum width. Multiplexers (MUX) are implemented as two-stage pass transistor trees, which is consistent with VPR's assumptions. Routing SBOX drivers are implemented as three stage buffers similar to [13]. All other buffers are two-stage. Buffers are sized to minimize

delay using HSPICE automatic-sizing. We use circuit-level designs similar to those described in [10]. We assume a 45nm process througout and use the Predictive Technology Model [25] to acquire process information for HSPICE.

As the size of a LB increases, the physical distance between clusters also increases. This directly affects the physical length (as shown in Figure 8) of the routing wire segments which in turn affects the SBOX driver sizes. To account for this effect, we use the iterative flow show in Figure 9. We first size all buffers except for the wire driver. These sizings, along with an estimate of the SBOX driver size, are then supplied into the area model to obtain a MTWA count for a single tile in the FPGA. We then convert this count to a physical area (and wire length) assuming a 60% layout density [4] and size the SBOX drivers. This repeats until the estimate for the SBOX driver size becomes acceptable.

4.3 CAD and Benchmarks

We use a CAD flow similar to [17, 1]. First, benchmark circuits are technology mapped to LUTs using Flowmap [7]. We then use a timing-driven packing algorithm T-VPack [17] to pack LUTs and registers into logic blocks. Placement and routing is performed using VPR 5.0 [15].

In our experiments with multi-level cluster architectures, we apply two iterations of the T-VPack algorithm to pack a circuit. Although specialized multi-level packing algorithms have been proposed [8, 9], we focus on the trade-offs in the architecture by keeping the same algorithm across both the flat and multi-level packing. To perform timing analysis during place and route for the multi-level LBs, we have made straight-forward extensions to the timing-graph construction in VPR's code. The core timing analysis algorithms are unchanged.

Runtime measurements are performed on Xeon 2.6GHz processors. When quantifying the routing runtime, we only measure the time needed to route to the minimum channel-width architecture (as opposed to measuring the entire binary-search routing process needed to determine the minimum channel width).

We use the synthetic benchmarks listed in Table 1 for most of the experiments. We chose to use synthetic circuits because the circuits in the traditional MCNC benchmark suite are too small for this study. The synthetic benchmarks mimic modern system-level designs and were generated us-

Table 1: Synthetic Benchmark Circuits

Circuit	4-LUTs	Nets	Rent	Avg. Fanout
synth01	15818	38047	0.654	3.3023
synth02	8831	21288	0.658	3.3745
synth03	10906	26598	0.641	3.5053
synth04	20007	48460	0.631	3.4597
synth05	18115	42917	0.609	3.3955
synth06	11786	28300	0.657	3.4675
synth07	26461	63934	0.648	3.4377
synth08	20961	50008	0.646	3.4388
synth09	12085	29020	0.659	3.3614
synth10	10009	24014	0.648	3.3776
synth11	16867	38661	0.605	3.4438
synth12	13131	31161	0.692	3.3252
synth13	3160	7973	0.648	3.3799
synth14	12405	31085	0.689	3.1425

Table 2: MCNC Benchmark Circuits

Circuit	4-LUTs	Nets	Rent	Fanout
alu4	1522	1536	0.630	3.362
apex2	1878	1917	0.640	3.442
apex4	1262	1271	0.683	3.307
bigkey	1707	2194	0.626	3.910
clma	8381	8797	0.537	3.336
des	1591	1847	0.699	2.939
diffeq	1494	1935	0.574	3.064
dsip	1370	1823	0.673	2.820
elliptic	3602	4855	0.643	2.944
ex1010	4598	4608	0.618	3.344
ex5p	1064	1072	0.700	3.480
frisc	3539	4445	0.638	3.395
misex3	1397	1411	0.642	3.437
pdc	4575	4591	0.674	3.759
s298	1930	1942	0.542	3.851
s38417	6096	7588	0.603	2.914
s38584	6281	7580	0.612	2.889
seq	1750	1791	0.662	3.417
spla	3690	3706	0.639	3.704
tseng	1046	1483	0.603	3.123

ing the tool published in [16]. We use the entire MCNC suite of circuits to form the IP library needed by the circuit generation tool. All generated circuits are sequential.

We repeat some of the experiments using the smaller MCNC20 suite shown in Table 2 to highlight the effects of circuit size on some experimental conclusions.

5. EXPERIMENTAL RESULTS

5.1 Directly Scaling N

Figure 10 shows the effects of LB size on area, delay, and CAD runtime using the synthetic benchmark suite. Each data point is the averaged over the entire suite. For area and delay, both logic and routing components are shown along with the total. For CAD runtime, both placement and routing runtime are shown along with the total runtime.

5.1.1 Area

The impact on area agrees with previous studies. Logic area increases as the area of each LB grows. The routing area decreases until approximately $N = 25$ as more and more nets are completely absorbed into the LB. Beyond this point, the routing area increases for two reasons. First the number of pins on an LB increases which means that an increasing number of nets need to connect to each LB. This makes it challenging for the placement algorithm to minimize wirelength since moving a single block perturbs many nets. The routing also becomes more challenging as congestion density increases, leading to the need for more routing tracks per channel.

One difference from previous studies is the optimal range for LB size. In this study, $N = 14$ to 18 leads to minimum area. We repeated the experiment using the smaller MCNC20 benchmark suite and the area results are shown in Figure 11a. The results with the smaller circuits gives an optimal range closer to previous studies of $N = 5$ to 12. As circuit size increases, the average post-placement wirelength also increases. This leads to the need for more wire tracks per channel and hence more routing area per tile.

5.1.2 Delay

Figure 10b and Figure 11b show that critical path delay decreases as logic block size increases. This occurs as more

nets are implemented using the fast local LB interconnect. Although, the delay through an LB also increases, it does so at a much slower rate. For the range of LB sizes that we investigate, there is no optimal range. Delay continues to decrease as LB size is increased.

5.1.3 CAD Runtime

Logic block size has a significant impact on placement and routing runtime as shown in Figure 10c and 11c. When the packing efficiency of the architecture is not constrained by the number of inputs available to logic blocks, the number of LBs required to implement a circuit is proportional to $1/N$. Since the placement problem size is proportional to the number of LBs to place, we see a $1/N$ trend in placement time. Routing time is also reduced as fewer nets need to be routed on the global routing network.

5.2 Multi-Level Logic Blocks

In this set of experiments, we construct LBs with an effective size ranging from $N_{eff} = N2 \cdot N1 = 2$ to 50. We considered three values for the second level hierarchy size ($N2=2,4,6$) and vary $N1$ accordingly. Inputs at each level were chosen based on Equation 4 using a Rent parameter of p=0.8. We found that the results did not vary significantly across the different values of $N2$. In the following we discuss only the case of $N2 = 4$. The experiments are performed using the Synthetic benchmark suite.

5.2.1 Area

The solid lines in Figure 12 show the logic, routing, and total area results. The dashed lines are the flat architecture results from Figure 10a. This comparison shows that the multi-level architecture is more area-efficient beyond $N_{eff} = 20$. The are two reasons for this. First, since the overall multi-level local interconnect network is implemented as two stages (second-stage local interconnect and first-stage local interconnect), the MUXes are narrower than in the

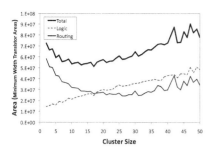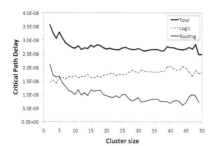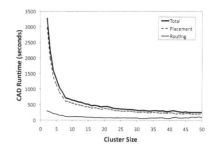

Figure 10: Effect of Flat Cluster Size (using synthetic circuits) on a) Area b) Delay c) CAD Runtime

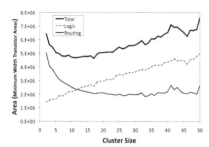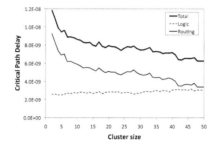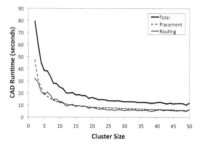

Figure 11: Effect of Flat Cluster Size (using MCNC circuits) on a) Area b) Delay c) CAD Runtime

flat architecture. Thus they need fewer transistors overall to implement.

The second factor is packing efficiency. Both the flat architecture and the multi-level architecture require almost identical number of LBs to implement each circuit. However, we found that the flat architecture was able to absorb more nets, thus requiring the use of fewer LB pins which in turn reduces the routing channel width and routing area. The reason for this is that the multi-level architecture has a physical I/O constraint that must be met at the first-level which in turn limits the size of nets that can be completely absorbed at the second level. This is why the flat architecture uses less routing area up to $N = 30$. Beyond this point, the flat architecture's required channel width begins to increase again which leads to high routing area.

5.2.2 Delay

In Figure 12b, the solid lines show the logic, routing and total critical path delay in the multi-level architecture. We only show the *total* delay from the flat architecture for comparison. The difference in delay is significant. For the same reasons in the area results, we found that packing efficiency played a large role in this gap. Since the multi-level architecture requires more global routing, more of the critical path is implemented using the slower global routing resources.

There is also a secondary factor that leads to a delay overhead in the logic delay of the multi-level architecture compared to the flat architecture. To uncover this, we repeated the experiments on the flat architecture using the same packing and placement solutions from the multi-level experiments. Converting the packing solutions was done by simply *flattening* the netlists produced by the multi-level packing tool. The dashed lines show the results from this approach.

Routing delay remains the same because the sources and

sinks of all nets remain at their original locations. Logic delay is slightly worse for the multi-level LBs. In the multi-level architecture, an LB input pin connecting to a BLE input pin must traverse through two levels of local interconnect. Since each level is implemented as 2-stage MUXes, the signal must propagate through a total of four pass transistors compared to only two in the flat architecture. We investigated different MUX implementation schemes (such as one-hot) but found that 2-stage MUXes were still optimal.

5.2.3 CAD Runtime

The behaviour in CAD runtime is the same as that of the flat architecture since the number of LBs, and hence place and route problem sizes, is being varied on the same scale but through a different architecture. We therefore omit the data for brevity.

5.3 Quality versus CAD Runtime Trade-off

Figure 13a and b show the area versus P&R runtime trade-off, and the delay versus P&R runtime trade-off for the flat architecture, respectively. The data points have been normalized to the values for the smallest LB size of $N = 2$. The solid line represents the data for the synthetic benchmark suite and dashed line represents the data for the MCNC20 suite. These figures summarize the CAD runtime trade-offs that can be achieved through logic block architecture size.

In general, there is an asymptote for the amount of CAD runtime reduction that can be achieved. However, it is important to observe that this asymptote is not static. As FPGAs grow in capacity and user circuits become larger, the total runtime increases but the room for improvement through the techniques in the paper also increase. This is highlighted by the gap between the solid line representing

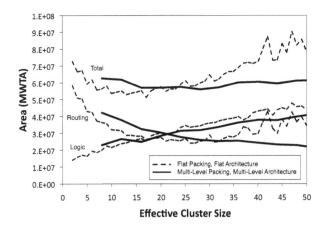 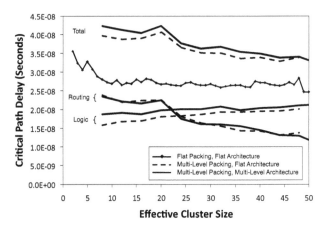

Figure 12: Effect of Multi-Level Cluster Size on a) Area b) Delay

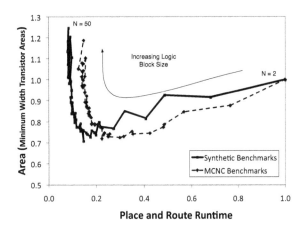 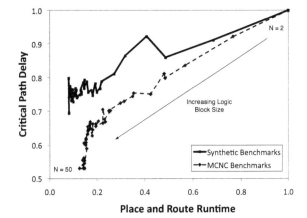

Figure 13: Flat Total Runtime a) Area-Runtime Tradeoff b) Delay - Runtime Tradeoff

the larger synthetic circuits, and the dashed line representing the much smaller MCNC circuits.

These figures also show that the main trade-off for reducing CAD runtime is an increase in area. While we do not see an increase in delay, it is expected that delay would eventually increase at some point (imagine the extreme case, the entire FPGA as a single LB).

Figure 14 shows a similar area and delay versus CAD runtime trade-off for the multi-level architectures. While the trade-off for area is not as steep, the critical path delay that can be achieved by these architectures is worse than the flat architecture.

Overall, there is a clear trade-off between mapping quality (area and delay) and CAD runtime when modifying the logic block architecture.

6. CONCLUSION AND FUTURE WORK

Long runtimes is a growing problem for FPGA CAD. In this paper, we have argued that it is possible to design the architecture of an FPGA while balancing CAD run-time with the more traditional optimization metrics of area, delay, and power. We investigated the use of high-capacity logic blocks to reduce the placement and routing problem sizes directly.

We focused on two ways to architect these blocks: direct scaling of a flat logic block and a multi-level approach. We first derived an equation to determine the amount of I/O needed for both types of logic blocks. Then, using an experimental methodology, we quantified the area, delay and place and route runtime trade-offs of these architectures.

We found that the multi-level architecture is slightly more area efficient but slightly less delay efficient when compared to the flat architecture. Using specialized multi-level packing algorithms may help close the quality gap that we observed when using iterative T-VPack. We also found that the I/O constraints of the first hierarchy affects the overall packing efficiency.

Overall, we showed a clear trade-off between mapping quality (area and delay) and CAD runtime that was affected by architecture design. The architectures explored in this paper are relatively straight-forward and interesting solutions may lie in more radical approaches. Runtime-aware architecture design is a very large unexplored area of research. Some interesting directions include:

- Revisit past architecture optimization studies when using only fast CAD tools. Do the architectural conclusions change when only fast CAD tools are used?

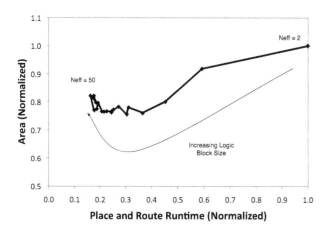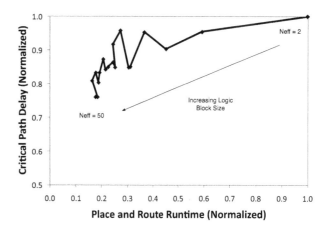

Figure 14: Multi-Level a) Area-Runtime Tradeoff b) Delay - Runtime Tradeoff

- Improving routability is a major goal in all CAD stages prior to routing. Routing itself is also a very timing consuming step in the CAD flow. This paper has focused on logic block architecture. More opportunities for affecting CAD runtime likely exist in the FPGA interconnect design.

- Developing parallel CAD algorithms will no doubt play an important role in the future as desktop CPUs continue to move deeper into the use of multicore architectures. How does the FPGA architecture affect the amount of parallelism that can be employed in the CAD algorithms? Can new architectures be developed that are more amenable to parallel CAD?

Acknowledgment

This research was funded by Altera and the Natural Sciences and Engineering Research Council of Canada.

7. REFERENCES

[1] E. Ahmed and J. Rose. The effect of lut and cluster size on deep-submicron fpga performance and density. *IEEE Trans. on VLSI*, 12(3):288–298, March 2004.

[2] Altera. Apex20 family data sheets.

[3] R. Amerson, R. Carter, W. Culbertson, P. Kuekes, G. Snider, and L. Albertson. Plasma: an fpga for million gate systems. In *Procs. of the Int'l Symp. on Field Programmable Gate Arrays*, pages 10–16, 1996.

[4] V. Betz, J. Rose, and A. Marquardt. Architecture and cad for deep-submicron fpgas. *Springer*, pages ISBN 0–7923–8460–1, 1999.

[5] H. Bian, A. C. Ling, A. Choong, and J. Zhu. Towards scalable placement for fpgas. In *Procs. of the Int'l Symp. on Field Programmable Gate Arrays*, pages 147–156, 2010.

[6] S. Chin and S. Wilton. An analytical model relating fpga architecture and place and route runtime. In *Procs. of the Int'l Conf. on Field-Programmable Logic and Applications*, pages 146–153, Aug. 2009.

[7] J. Cong and Y. Ding. An optimal technology mapping algorithm for delay optimization in lookup-table based fpga designs. In *Proc. of Int'l conf. on Computer-aided design*, pages 48–53, 1992.

[8] J. Cong and M. Romesis. Performance-driven multi-level clustering with application to hierarchical fpga mapping. In *Procs. of the Design Automation Conference*, pages 389–394, 2001.

[9] M. Dehkordi and S. Brown. Performance-driven recursive multi-level clustering. In *Int'l Conf. on Field-Programmable Tech.*, pages 262–269, Dec. 2003.

[10] E. Hung, S. J. E. Wilton, H. Yu, T. C. P. Chau, and P. H. W. Leong. A detailed delay path model for fpgas. In *Procs. of the Int'l Conf. on Field-Programmable Technology*, pages 96–103, Dec. 2009.

[11] M. Hutton. Interconnect prediction for programmable logic devices. In *Int'l workshop on System-level interconnect prediction*, pages 125–131, 2001.

[12] A. Lam, S. Wilton, P. Leong, and W. Luk. An analytical model describing the relationships between logic architecture and fpga density. In *Int'l Conf. on Field-Programmable Logic and Applications*, 2008.

[13] G. Lemieux, E. Lee, M. Tom, and A. Yu. Directional and single-driver wires in fpga interconnect. In *Int'l conf. on Field-Programmable Tech.*, pages 41–48, 2004.

[14] A. Ludwin, V. Betz, and K. Padalia. High-quality, deterministic parallel placement for fpgas on commodity hardware. In *Procs. Int'l Symp. on Field programmable gate arrays*, pages 14–23, 2008.

[15] J. Luu, I. Kuon, P. Jamieson, T. Campbell, A. Ye, W. M. Fang, and J. Rose. Vpr 5.0: Fpga cad and architecture exploration tools with single-driver routing, heterogeneity and process scaling. In *Proc. of Int'l Symp. on FPGA*, pages 133–142, 2009.

[16] C. Mark, A. Shui, and S. Wilton. A system-level stochastic circuit generator for fpga architecture evaluation. In *Procs. of the Int'l Conf. on Field-Programmable Technology*, 2008.

[17] A. Marquardt, V. Betz, and J. Rose. Speed and area tradeoffs in cluster-based fpga architectures. *IEEE Trans. V. Large Scale Integr. Syst.*, 8(1):84–93, 2000.

[18] C. Mulpuri and S. Hauck. Runtime and quality tradeoffs in fpga placement and routing. In *Int'l Symp on Field programmable gate arrays*, pages 29–36, 2001.

[19] J. Pistorius and M. Hutton. Placement rent exponent calculation methods, temporal behaviour and fpga architecture evaluation. In *workshop on System-level interconnect prediction*, pages 31–38, 2003.

[20] K. K. W. Poon, S. J. E. Wilton, and A. Yan. A detailed power model for field-programmable gate arrays. *ACM Trans. Design Automation of Electronic Systems*, 10(2):279–302, 2005.

[21] D. P. Singh and S. D. Brown. Incremental placement for layout driven optimizations on fpgas. In *Int'l Conf. on Computer-aided design*, pages 752–759, 2002.

[22] R. Tessier. Fast placement approaches for fpgas. *ACM Trans. Design Automation of Electronic Systems*, 7(2):284–305, 2002.

[23] K. Vorwerk, A. Kennings, and J. W. Greene. Improving simulated annealing-based fpga placement with directed moves. *Trans. Computer-Aided Design of Integrated Circuits and Systems*, 28(2):179–192, 2009.

[24] A. G. Ye. Using the minimum set of input combinations to minimize the area of local routing networks in logic clusters containing logically equivalent i/os in fpgas. *IEEE Trans. Very Large Scale Integr. Syst.*, 18(1):95–107, 2010.

[25] W. Zhao and Y. Cao. New generation of predictive technology model for sub-45nm early design exploration. *IEEE Trans. Electron Devices*, 53(11):2816–2823, 2006.

Scalable and Deterministic Timing-Driven Parallel Placement for FPGAs

Chris Wang
Dept. of ECE
University of British Columbia
Vancouver, BC, Canada
chrisw@ece.ubc.ca

Guy G.F. Lemieux
Dept. of ECE
University of British Columbia
Vancouver, BC, Canada
lemieux@ece.ubc.ca

ABSTRACT

This paper describes a parallel implementation of the timing-driven VPR 5.0 simulated annealing engine. By restricting the move distance to a confined neighborhood, it is possible to consider a large number of non-conflicting moves in parallel and achieve a deterministic result. The full timing-driven algorithm is parallelized, including the detailed timing analysis updates done periodically while placement progresses. The limited move slightly degrades the placement quality, but this is necessary to expose greater degrees of parallelism. The overall bounding box metric degrades about 11% and critical path delay metric degrades about 8% compared to VPR's original algorithm, but we show the amount of degradation is independent of the number of threads. Overall, the parallel implementation scales to a speedup of 123x using 25 threads compared to VPR. With additional tuning effort, we believe the algorithm can be scaled to a larger number of threads, perhaps even run on a GPU, with little additional quality degradation.

Categories and Subject Descriptors

B.7.2 [**Integrated Circuits**]: Design Aids—*Placement and routing*; D.1.3 [**Programming Techniques**]: Concurrent Programming—*Parallel Programming*

General Terms

Algorithms, Design, Performance

Keywords

Parallel placement, FPGA, Timing-driven placement

1. INTRODUCTION

As FPGA logic capacity steadily increases at the rate provided by Moore's Law, FPGA CAD must synthesize, place and route more logic blocks and more nets every generation. Keeping runtime and quality of results (QoR) constant while the number of objects continues to grow is a demanding task because uniprocessor performance improvements do not track FPGA capacity growth. To keep

runtime in check, Altera and Xilinx have been continuously optimizing their tools. While this has helped, it is unlikely that such algorithm engineering efforts can be sustained at the rate required by several more generations of Moore's Law. As a result, continuous technology scaling without comparable scaling of FPGA synthesis runtime will lead to a runtime crisis. The runtime crisis manifests itself as a reduction in productivity and an increase in engineering costs. A promising solution to the runtime crisis is to employ parallel CAD algorithms so the number of working processor cores and FPGA capacity can both scale at similar rates. However, in addition to the raw numbers scaling, the algorithms must also demonstrate good scaling results in terms of QoR and runtime. With multicore processors now common, Altera[1] and Xilinx[2] have both started to implement parallel algorithms that offer some runtime improvement.

One of the most time-consuming steps in the FPGA CAD flow is placement. A good quality placement is essential to reduce interconnect delay, localized congestion, wirelength and power. Simulated annealing, the placement engine used in VPR and Altera's Quartus II tools, is widely regarded as producing very good QoR and being able to handle complex legalization constraints. A comparison between a simulated annealing based algorithm, namely VPR, and a few best-in-class academic placers based on other techniques was recently presented in [3]. The conclusion was that "simulated annealing based placement would still be in dominant use for a few more device generations." In VPR, the number of moves needed to find an optimized solution grows as $O(N^{4/3})$ [4], where N is the number of CLBs being placed. As more objects must be placed, the VPR placement algorithm slows down due to nonlinear scaling.

In recent work, Altera described a parallel timing-driven annealing-based algorithm in Quartus II [5] which evaluates many moves in parallel, but serially commits the moves to achieve a deterministic placement. A speedup of 2.2x was demonstrated on 4 processors, and QoR is equivalent to the serial version. However, this algorithm may not runtime-scale to a large number of cores because multiple cores increases the probability of both *hard* and *soft* conflicts[1] between moves. A conflict of any type requires a speculated move to be abandoned, or its cost to be recomputed serially at commit time.

In contrast, this paper parallelizes the full timing-driven annealing-based algorithm in VPR5. However, unlike the Altera work, we show that our approach can scale to a larger number of processors. We do this by allowing moves and commits to occur in parallel. The key is to avoid generating moves that have *hard conflicts* by greatly restricting the range of motion of CLBs for each move. By using stale (or imprecise) placement information for dis-

---

[1]Conflicts are defined in Section 2.

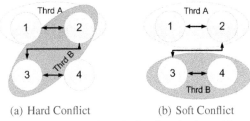

(a) Hard Conflict   (b) Soft Conflict

Figure 1: Illustration of a hard and soft conflict

tant CLBs handled by other threads, the overhead of fine-grained synchronization between threads can be avoided. Although threads lack fine-grained synchronization, they still achieve a deterministic (reproducible) result that depends only upon the number of threads and does not depend on the number of processors nor race conditions. While Altera emphasizes serial equivalence for easier regression testing and customer support, we believe that an algorithm that is deterministic is sufficient.[2] These changes introduce about 11% and 8% lost QoR on bounding box cost and critical path delay, respectively. However, the QoR does not degrade as the number of threads is increased, and the algorithm exhibits good self-speedup up to 25 threads. The algorithm achieves a speedup of 123x with 25 threads compared to the original sequential VPR algorithm. With additional tuning, we believe that it is possible to achieve additional speedup with no further lost QoR if more threads are used. Finally, we think it may be possible to implement a GPU-hosted version of this parallel placement algorithm as well.

2. PREVIOUS WORKS

Parallel placement research has been underway for more than two decades. To the best of our knowledge, all published work with the exception of [5] have targeted wirelength only. Furthermore, determinism, an extremely important feature for bug reproducibility and testing [5], has not been considered except in [5, 6]. Our work addresses both of these issues, and is the first academic parallel placer that produces a timing-driven and deterministic result with significant speedup.

Before we review placement algorithms, we must first define two types of conflicts. A simple circuit with four CLBs is shown in Figure 1, where arrows represent nets that connect CLBs. A *hard conflict* arises when the same CLB is considered by more than one thread concurrently. In the first example, threads A and B both consider block 2 for a move, producing a hard conflict. A *soft conflict* arises when different CLBs that are connected by the same net are considered concurrently. In the second example, thread B now considers block 3 and 4 to resolve the hard conflict, but a soft conflict remains since blocks 2 and 3 are connected by the same net. The soft conflict arises because each thread makes cost-based decisions that depend on these shared nets, but the parallel movement of CLBs attached to these shared nets may invalidate the decision.

Parallel simulated annealing placement algorithms can be loosely categorized into two groups: the shared and partitioned region.

- The first group of algorithms allows all processors to work within the same region (often the entire grid), but restricts swaps that are being evaluated in parallel to be from independent sets [7, 8, 9]. Speculative move proposal was employed to further accelerate the algorithm [5], and a dependency

checker, executed serially, is used to ensure no hard-conflict has occurred. The algorithm as reported in [5] achieved a speed up of 2.2x on four cores. However, it likely suffers in terms of scalability beyond four cores. The main reason is that the probability of a soft or hard conflict increases with the number of processors, making it more difficult to find moves that do not conflict.

- The second group of algorithms allocate a specific region to each processor with no or minimal overlap and different methods are employed to allow blocks to migrate from one region to the other [6, 10]. Sun and Sechen [10] employed an algorithm based on dynamic region generation by dividing the chip vertically and horizontally on alternating iterations. It was implemented on multiple machines connected by LAN. During each iteration, each machine would receive an independent region to work on, and is terminated by the first machine that completes a pre-determined number of moves. In order to minimize communication, all machines would only update cells changes at the end of each iteration and move evaluation is based on the cell locations from the previous iteration. It achieved a speedup of 5.3x using six machines and yielded comparable results against the best serial algorithm known at the time. While the dynamic region generation may have helped with cell movement, it greatly hinders the amount of parallelism the algorithm can achieve and thereby limits the overall speedup. In addition, this algorithm and all of the other ones in this group considers bounding box cost only and are non-deterministic, making them unsuitable to be implemented in commercial tools.

Interested readers are encouraged to consult [4] and [5] for more detailed summaries and other parallelization methods.

Work by Wrighton and DeHon [11] presented a distributed annealing algorithm for a systolic architecture. While the architecture was prototyped on an FPGA, it was only capable of computing placement for a much smaller array size than the "host" FPGA. Still, it demonstrated that hardware acceleration could obtain significant speedups from 500x to 2500x. The algorithm worked by restricting the swap range of each block to its 4 immediate neighbors only. This allowed purely local placement decisions to be made between adjacent elements, thus exposing vast amounts of parallelism. One notable characteristic of this work was the use of stale (old) placement information when making local decisions – this was done deliberately to avoid the overhead of broadcasting updates after every move. Instead, placement information was updated infrequently using a daisy-chain. Overall, this approach suffers from 36% quality degradation in the final placed circuit. The QoR did not depend upon information staleness.

More recently, work by Smecher, Wilton and Lemieux [12] demonstrated that the algorithm used in [11] could be applied to placement of communicating tasks for massively parallel processor arrays (MPPAs). Since MPPAs contain reasonably powerful CPUs, they can "self-host" or place themselves. The paper further shows that expanding the neighbor region to 8 cells (ie, includes diagonals) or 12 cells (within Manhattan distance of 2) improves QoR to within 5% of traditional simulated annealing while still offering significant speedups.

One limitation with both [11] and [12] is that only bounding box cost is considered. Another limitation is that specialized hardware such as a very large FPGA or an MPPA is required. In this work, we apply techniques from [11] and [12] to the full timing-driven placement algorithm from VPR5 using pthreads so it runs on readily available shared-memory multicore computers.

---

[2]In our work, the algorithm is deterministic because T threads, where T is fixed, can be run on any number of processors (even $< T$) and produce the same result.

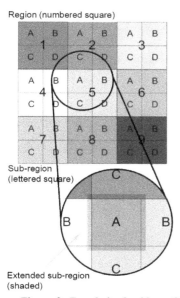

Region (numbered square)

Sub-region
(lettered square)

Extended sub-region
(shaded)

Figure 2: Equal-sized grid partition

For our experiments, we ran our parallelized VPR on an 8-core (64-thread) Sun Niagara 2 system, an Intel quad-core Nehalem and dual quad-core Clovertown, and an AMD quad hex-core Istanbul system. We report only Sun results due to the larger available parallelism, but Intel/AMD results were similar. Based on our results, we expect it is possible to develop an OpenCL or CUDA implementation that can also achieve good speedup. *The parallel placement code is freely available from the authors.*[3]

3. ALGORITHM DESCRIPTION

3.1 Algorithm Overview

Our parallel placement algorithm is based on partitioned regions, namely the second group of algorithms described in Section 2. The entire grid is first partitioned into approximately equal-sized private regions and assigned to a unique thread. An example is shown in Figure 2 with regions 1 through 9. The increased capacity (number of cells) in IOs around the peripheral of the chip can be ignored as the sparse IO cell occupancy balances this out. Therefore it can be estimated that each block, whether CLB or IO, contains approximately one cell. When the number of rows/columns in the grid cannot be evenly divided, the non-peripheral (not first, nor last) rows/columns will receive the extra rows/columns first. The number of columns and rows does not need to be same, *i.e.*, each region can be rectangular. Each thread will iterate sequentially through all CLB locations in its private region and considers the block at each position for a swap. To achieve a good quality versus runtime result, not every block is considered for the swap: a randomly generated number determines whether a particular block should be considered. If selected, this block will be paired with another randomly selected block within its legal swap region (defined below).

Placement data about blocks inside a thread's private region is precise, but placement data about blocks being managed by other threads is allowed to grow stale and updated only periodically. By further dividing each private region into sub-regions A through D (Figure 2), and placing only one sub-region at a time, we can ensure the resulting placement is deterministic. When placing a sub-region, blocks that reside inside will have the chance of swapping with blocks located near the edge of the adjacent sub-regions, a

---

[3] http://www.ece.ubc.ca/ lemieux/download/

window we call the extended sub-region (Figure 2), to allow blocks to migrate. An adaptive schedule is used to guide the simulated annealing process.

To summarize, Figure 1 shows 9 *private regions*, numbered 1 through 9 and 4 *sub-regions* for each *private region*, lettered A through D. The zoomed figure at the bottom shows the *extended sub-region* for *sub-region* 5A.

3.2 Pseudo-code

The following is the thread-level pseudo code:

```
1:  while !exit_condition do
2:    for iteration = 1 to region_place_count do
3:      barrier()
4:      timing_update_parallel()
5:      for n = 1 to num_of_subregion do
6:        barrier()
7:        global_to_local_data_update()
8:        for each block position in subregion do
9:          if rand[0, 100) ≥ PROB_SKIPPED then
10:            try_swap()
11:          end if
12:        end for
13:        local_to_global_data_update()
14:        barrier()
15:      end for
16:      bounding_box_update_parallel()
17:    end for
18:    update_anneal_schedule()
19:    barrier()
20: end while
```

In this algorithm, `PROB_SKIPPED` is used to randomly determine whether the selected block will be considered for a swap. We experimentally determined a good value to be 10 (Section 3.3.3), implying there is a 90% probability that each block is considered for a swap or simply, 90% of the blocks will be considered.

Additionally, barriers are needed to enforce synchronization between the threads. Barriers help ensure deterministic behaviour; very little data structure locking is necessary, and of the locks we used, none of them lead to race conditions or non-deterministic behavior.

3.3 Implementation Details

We implemented our changes directly into VPR 5.0.2 [13], which is based on the original VPR first published in [14], by parallelizing the *try_place()* function. We did not make major changes to the existing data structure in the software. To alleviate the demand on communication cost and create a deterministic program, we created local copies of global variables used to keep track of block location, timing cost and bounding box cost data. These data are updated frequently enough that they do not risk becoming too stale. For example, prior to evaluating each sub-region, all threads retrieve the latest data from global memory to local memory. Conversely, after evaluating each sub-region, all threads update the global memory to reflect the changes made to their extended sub-region.

POSIX threads (pthreads) were used. However, the POSIX barriers may suspend and resume the thread, which can introduce process scheduling overheads. In our program, the overhead to suspend and resume is not justifiable because most threads have approximately equal work and hence similar execution time. Instead, we implemented tree-based polling barriers using shared global memory based on [15]. Our custom barriers performed much better than the POSIX barriers.

155

Prior to this shared-memory implementation, we initially wrote a message-passing implementation using MPI. This provided us with a great understanding of how to replicate local copies of the data structures without inadvertently sharing global structures. Ultimately, we discarded the MPI implementation because it did not achieve good speedups.

Except where noted, data presented in this paper are geometric means of all circuits normalized against values obtained from VPR.

3.3.1 Determinism Enforcement

We first subdivide each private region into four (2×2) approximately equal *sub-regions*. Each sub-region then is extended by two rows or columns along its boundaries to allow blocks to migrate between sub-regions, we name this combined region (sub-region and the two rows/columns) the *extended sub-region*. To achieve determinism, we must make sure all active extended sub-regions *do not* overlap with each other, thereby avoiding hard conflicts.

As shown in Figure 2, each of the sub-regions is labelled A through D. All threads start by placing in sub-region A, and barriers are used to ensure no thread can proceed to sub-region B before every thread finishes with sub-region A. During this time, each thread updates placement data for its own extended sub-region, but allows placement data about all other threads grow stale. At the end of the sub-region placement, all threads broadcast their placement updates, giving a single consistent view of all placements. Using this synchronization as a new starting point, all threads proceed to the next sub-region. This allows each thread to work in its private region independently without costly fine-grain synchronization. As we will show in Section 5.3, stale data does not deteriorate the quality of the placed result.

Calculations of timing, delay, and bounding box costs are parallelized by dividing the netlist across multiple threads. Each thread returns a partial result which needs a final summation. These functions use floating point values, which are not associative and can produce different results due to round-off if the order of addition changes. We maintain a constant order for the final addition by allocating an array with one entry for each thread. A master thread performs the summation in sequential order only after all worker threads complete, producing a deterministic sum. Since the work division scheme (more details in Section 3.3.5) depends only on the connectivity of the nets, which is constant for a given circuit, the work allocated to each thread is also deterministic. This ensures partial results will also be the same. Thus, cost results are all deterministic.

Finally, to keep the program deterministic, each thread tracks its own random number state. Thus, random numbers generated in one thread do not disturb the sequence of those made by other threads.

To help verify determinism, we ran each circuit at least 1000 times on different computer systems (eg, Intel and AMD) using the same binary executable. For a given number of threads, we observed the same bounding box, critical path delay, and placement CRC values across all the runs.

3.3.2 Legal Swap Region

The legal swap region is the neighborhood from which each block finds its swap candidate. To allow blocks to migrate between private regions, our algorithm allows each thread to consider blocks within its extended sub-region as swap candidates, provided they also fall within the legal swap region window. Therefore, the minimum dimension for each sub-region is 4×4, so that even if two neighboring threads decide to swap with blocks two blocks beyond its boundary, hard conflicts will always be avoided.

We first implemented the legal swap region as all blocks within

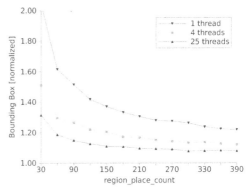

(a) with no restriction on size

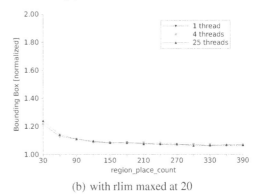

(b) with rlim maxed at 20

Figure 3: Legal swap region quality variation

a Manhattan distance of two as described in [12], however, it produced no significant advantage in the quality versus runtime graph when compared against VPR. Next, we extended the legal swap region to the entire extended sub-region and realized the result was even worse for certain number of threads and the result varied as depicted in Figure 3(a). Then we added the parameter *rlim* as used in VPR to limit the legal swap region as the placer begins to consider timing path delay. This dramatically improved the QoR. Finally, we experimentally determined that limiting the *rlim* value to 20 produces better QoR. The result is shown in Figure 3(b), and it is clear that we have successfully minimized the quality variation using an *rlim* value maxed at 20.

3.3.3 PROB_SKIPPED Characterization

The PROB_SKIPPED value adds an extra degree of freedom to tweak the program for quality and runtime trade-offs. It controls the inner most loop of the algorithm which makes it a standalone parameter that can be varied with only minimal disturbance to the behavior of the other parameters. It dictates the probability each block will *not* be considered for a swap. A value of 100 is equivalent to not making any swaps, resulting in the initial placement. Figure 4 shows the runtime versus quality trade-off sweeping PROB_SKIPPED from 0 to 100 with 4 threads and an *region_place_count* value of 90. The experiment uses the *rlim* value maxed at 20 (Section 3.3.2) and the sequential block selection scheme (Section 3.3.4). The leftmost point (greatest runtime) is obtained with PROB_SKIPPED of 0, since every block is considered. As PROB_SKIPPED increases, fewer blocks are considered, resulting in shortened runtime and reduced quality.

The purpose of this experiment is to determine whether it is possible to not consider every block and still maintain a good result. We see from Figure 4 that the quality of both parameters degrades rather slowly for small PROB_SKIPPED values. We selected a

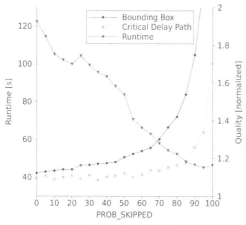

Figure 4: PROB_SKIPPED sweep

PROB_SKIPPED value of 10 as it gave us an approximately 14% runtime reduction for approximately 1% quality loss.

3.3.4 Sequential vs Random Block Selection

Unlike VPR, our algorithm sequentially iterates through each block position in the grid. To reach this conclusion, we ran an experiment with a controlled number of swaps per temperature range and compared the result from the sequential vs random block selection scheme using 1 thread and 25 threads. The program also incorporates *rlim* maxed at 20 (Section 3.3.2) and PROB_SKIPPED value of 10 (Section 3.3.3). The result is shown in Figure 5.

It can be seen that the quality of bounding box was clearly better in the case of sequential block selection. In the critical path delay graph, the quality is somewhat indistinguishable between the two block selection methods. Therefore, we adopted the sequential block selection scheme as it performed no worse than the alternative method.

3.3.5 Parallel Timing Analysis

Periodically, after a significant number of moves, it becomes necessary to perform a timing analysis to identify critical paths. This time-consuming task quickly became a bottleneck, so we had to be careful not to invoke it too frequently, and we had to update it in parallel using multiple threads. The function *timing_update_parallel()* in the pseudo-code indicates this task.

This function first calculates the *edge delay* for each connection in the circuit based on the current placement and uses this to compute the *slack values*. The slack values are then used to calculate the *criticality values*, which are used in the calculation of *timing* and *delay cost*. Barriers were used to enforce data dependencies between the aforementioned functions, as well as further enforce precedence in the calculations.

The parallelization of edge delay, timing and delay cost calculation are straight forward. As these functions loop through all the nets in the circuit, we could simply allocate an equal number of nets to each thread. Each thread stores its partial result in pre-allocated location in an array, which is later summed by the master thread as described in Section 3.3.1.

Parallel slack and criticality computation requires more synchronization because it traverses the tree to perform breath-first modifications twice. As there are no data dependencies within each level, we can process each level at a time and safely distribute the work of each level among the threads.

We made a slight data structure change to assist with parallelizing the tree traversal process. In the original VPR code, only children of each node were stored, which was adequate since the arrival

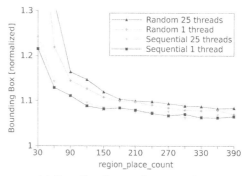

(a) Bounding Box quality comparison

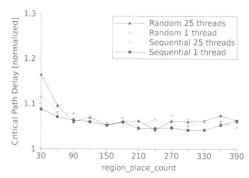

(b) Critical Path Delay quality comparison

Figure 5: Sequential vs random block selection comparison

time for each node was calculated passively. Each parent calculates the earliest arrival time of the child with respect to itself and compares with the arrival value stored in the child node, which may have been computed earlier by another parent of the child. While this approach works for a single threaded program, we run into issues in the parallel version if two different parents are evaluating the same child concurrently. To resolve this, we decided to store the parent of each node, so that each node can determine its own latest arrival time by traversing through all of its parents. This is parallelizable and ensures there are no data dependencies between nodes at the same level. It also load balances a bit better, since fan-ins are more balanced/limited than fan-outs.

In many cases, the amount of work depends on an attribute of the inner loop, which is not directly visible to the outer loop. For example, loading the net delay matrix requires looping through all sinks of each net. Simply distributing an equal number of nets does not yield a good load balance, as some nets have only 1 sink, whereas some others may contain hundreds or even thousands of sinks. We use a dynamic workload distribution system where each thread keeps track of the amount of work (ie, the number of sinks visited in this case) that was done, and returns that value when it has finished. We then compare the workload of two neighboring partitions, and shift the boundaries to even out the workload if there is significant imbalance. The initial partition is simply an even distribution of nets; however, it will be dynamically rebalanced out as more calls to the function are done.

3.3.6 Parallel Move Evaluation

Each parallel worker thread must consider moves or swaps within its region (one sub-region at a time). The *try_swap()* function is executed by each thread with their respective local data or unchanged global data. Therefore, inter-thread interference is not possible in this function call. For each block that is considered, we randomly select a neighbor from the legal swap region to be con-

Table 1: Adaptive simulated annealing schedule

Success Rate	Change in parameter	
	temperature	region_place_count
> 0.96	old_t * 0.5	input_region_place_count
> 0.80	old_t * 0.9	input_region_place_count
> 0.15 or rlim > 1	old_t * 0.9	input_region_place_count/4
otherwise	old_t * 0.6	input_region_place_count/20

sidered for a swap. In the case where the randomly selected spot is invalid, (eg, swap a CLB with an I/O pad) another neighbor is selected. These 2 blocks will be assessed based on the difference in timing cost and bounding box cost and evaluated for a swap using identical functions as implemented in VPR.

3.3.7 Bounding Box Update

In the serial VPR program, bounding box update is done incrementally (except when needed to eliminate round-off error) as part of the swap cost evaluation function. However, in the parallel program, each thread calculates its incremental bounding box cost based on stale data which contains imprecise data about all blocks that are not located within its private region. Therefore, a fresh bounding-box calculation using non-stale data is needed at the end of every iteration to ensure correctness and determinism (Line 16 in Section 3.2). This is extra work that the serial VPR program does not need to execute. The bounding box calculation is parallelzed using the dynamic distribution scheme described in Section 3.3.5, and the final result calculation employs the method described in Section 3.3.1 to ensure determinism.

3.3.8 Adaptive Annealing Schedule

A slight modification from the annealing schedule of VPR is used in order to cope with the different move behavior of this new parallel placement algorithm. It allows for more iterations during high success rate phases, or equivalently, the high temperature phases. This alleviates the effect of restricted block movement. At high temperature, traditional VPR is capable of swapping two arbitrary blocks with only the *rlim* restriction on the distance between them. Initially, *rlim* encompasses the entire grid, and it gradually shrinks as the success rate drops below a certain value. To achieve the same effect while only using smaller sub-regions in our parallel VPR, the algorithm must consider more iterations so all blocks can have a chance of migrating toward any location on the grid. This inevitably leads to more iterations and hence more work than the original VPR algorithm. However, the ability to use more threads has enabled us to overcome this overhead and achieve a speedup as shown in the result section. Using this intuition, we experimentally determined the annealing schedule parameters as shown in Table 1.

3.3.9 Summary

Our parallel algorithm is based on the simulated annealing algorithm in VPR with the following modifications:

- Partitioning each private region into four sub-regions and enforcing all threads to work on the same sub-region in its respective partition, thereby avoiding hard conflicts and enforcing determinism.

- Avoiding fine-grain synchronization by assessing moves using locally stored data, which may be stale.

- Limiting the range of swaps to all blocks with *rlim* capped at 20 or the sub-region boundaries to improve quality versus runtime trade-off result.

- Sequentially iterating through the grid instead of randomly selecting blocks to be swapped.

- In order to improve runtime for negligible quality loss, we modified the algorithm and only select 90% of the blocks to swap.

- More iterations are needed at higher temperature in order to allow blocks to migrate across the entire grid.

4. BENCHMARKING METHODOLOGY

This section describes the circuits used for benchmarking and the experimental process.

4.1 Benchmarking Circuits

The traditional Toronto20 MCNC benchmark circuits are too small to use for parallel placement experiments and large FPGA circuits are rare. Therefore, we used the benchmarks provided with the Un/DoPack flow which are fully described in [16]. These large synthetic circuits are built using the GNL tool in hierarchical mode, using 20 subcircuits which are based on the Toronto20 MCNC circuits. For each of 7 synthetic circuits generated, the overall average Rent exponent is 0.62, but the Rent exponent in the inner subcircuits is varied to produce a standard deviation in Rent values from 0.00 to 0.12 in 0.02 increments. As a result, the synthetic circuit with the smallest standard deviation is easiest to route and has the most uniform packing of interconnect wires, while the largest standard deviation is hardest to route due to hotspots which need a much wider channel to route. Using GNL in this way is a bit better than simply stitching the 20 MCNC circuits at the I/O pins; the latter approach is more likely to have large independent subcircuits which are more amenable to parallel placement. The circuits were clustered using T-VPack 5.0.2 with 6-input lookup tables, a cluster size of 10, and a maximum of 35 inputs per cluster.

The architecture file used is obtained from the iFar repository[17], which models realistic FPGA architectures. We selected the file that matched our clustering specifications using 65nm CMOS technology.[4]

4.2 Hardware Environment

We evaluated the performance of our program using an Ultra-SPARC T2 (Niagara 2) machine from Sun Microsystems. It contains 8 SPARC cores, threaded 8 ways, to support a total of 64 threads, running at 1.2 GHz [18]. The system has 32GB of memory and the operating system is Sun Solaris 5.10. We also performed a number of experiments on Intel quad-core Nehalem and dual quad-core Clovertown, and AMD quad hex-core Istanbul systems. Except for Section 5.2, we only report the Sun results here to demonstrate scaling to a larger number of threads that should soon be available in future Intel/AMD systems.

4.3 Experimental Methodology

Our work is compared against VPR running with the flag '-place_only'. There is a '-fast' flag in VPR that is faster (9.7x) than the default and achieves only 2.4% loss in bounding box metric and 1.2% loss in critical path delay metric on average for our circuits. Our quality values in this section are compared against default VPR and not VPR '-fast'.

The runtime reported in the results (Section 5) includes placement time only, which is primarily the pseudo-code shown in Section 3.2. Time excluded from measured time, including netlist loading and precomputation of delay tables used for costing, is the same between VPR and our parallel placer. This initialization overhead

---

[4] n10k06l04.fc15.area1delay1.cmos65nm.bptm taken from iFAR version 0.3-296.

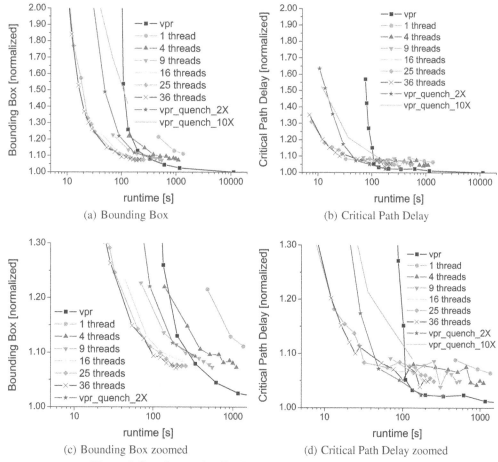

(a) Bounding Box

(b) Critical Path Delay

(c) Bounding Box zoomed

(d) Critical Path Delay zoomed

Figure 6: Runtime vs Quality (geomean of 7 benchmark circuits)

is considerable, but we were able to dramatically reduce it with a few very small changes. It can be further optimized, perhaps even parallelized, to avoid it from becoming a bottleneck. This common initialization runtime is not part of our measurement.

5. RESULTS/DISCUSSION

In this section, we compare the quality and runtime of our parallel placement algorithm against VPR. Also, we present the self-speedup of the parallel algorithm versus a single-thread implementation of the same parallel algorithm and discuss its runtime scaling limitations. Then, we show that the quality of placed circuits is preserved while scaling.

All quality values are geometric means of values which are normalized against VPR. For example, a value of 1.06 implies 6% quality degradation while 0.97 corresponds to a 3% quality improvement.

5.1 Quality vs Runtime

We compare the final post-placement bounding box cost and critical path delay between the two programs. These should correlate with the quality of routed result. We had insufficient time to generate and compare post-routing quality metrics in this paper.

We ran all the circuits and obtained a quality/runtime trade-off curve by varying the *region_place_count* values and the number of threads. Figure 6 shows the quality vs runtime comparison for our parallel program versus VPR. The runtime is plotted on x axis in log scale, the normalized quality result is shown on the y axis, and a separate graph is shown for bounding box and critical path delay.

The datapoints for VPR are obtained by starting with default VPR (slowest runtime, quality = 1.0). We then improve VPR runtime, first by adding '-fast' flag, then by further decreasing *inner_num* to values less than 1.

5.1.1 Comparison Trends

Figure 6 shows the runtime versus quality comparison between VPR and our placer. The black line with solid square is VPR's runtime curve; the right-most data point (at ~10,000s) is VPR and the 2nd data point from the right (at ~1,000s) is VPR '-fast'.

It can be seen that the single-threaded version of the parallel algorithm is slower than VPR '-fast'. This is mainly due to the associated overheads needed to make the algorithm parallelizable. As more threads are used, our program begins to outperform VPR. The 25 threaded version is able to achieve better bounding box and critical path delay results faster than VPR.

Figures 6(c) and 6(d) shows the same graph as Figures 6(a) and 6(b) with re-adjusted x and y axes to focus on the interesting portion of the graphs. It can be seen that VPR's QoR degrades sharply at approximately 100s; our algorithm is still able to sustain a decent QoR as runtime shrinks. We improved VPR's QoR in this extremely fast runtime region by using a technique known as quenching, where the temperature is decreased rapidly so the program spends more time making good moves greedily. *vpr_quench_2x* and *vpr_quench_10x* is achieved by multiplying the temperature by 0.5 and 0.1 respectively at every temperature update, achieving a 2X and 10X speedup in cooling speed. As seen on the graph, in the extremely fast runtime region, this produced a QoR superior to standard VPR in both bounding box and critical delay quality

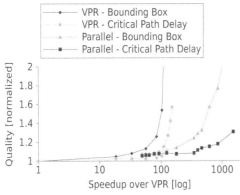

Figure 7: Quality from speeding up VPR and Parallel (25 threads)

Table 2: Parallel (25 threads) compared to VPR

	# luts	# clbs	bb cost	crit. delay	speedup
stdev000	40013	5036	1.09	1.11	133
stdev002	40013	5051	1.10	1.04	130
stdev004	40013	5037	1.13	1.08	121
stdev006	40013	5023	1.09	1.05	124
stdev008	40013	5041	1.11	1.06	114
stdev010	40013	5043	1.18	1.14	124
stdev012	40013	5060	1.07	1.12	116
25 threads	Geo. Mean		1.11	1.08	123
VPR-superfast	Geo. Mean		2.09	1.15	110

metrics, however, it is still inferior to our parallel program using 25 threads. This makes our algorithm an attractive candidate for users that are willing to trade some quality for extremely fast run-time. It can also be noted while the QoR for our parallel program converges, it is still unable to match the quality of VPR '-fast'. The QoR gap is approximately 3-4% on average and minimizing this gap would be an interesting future work.

5.1.2 Comparison with 25 Threads

To compare VPR and the parallel algorithm at a single data point, we need a strategy for selecting a point of comparison. Moving right-to-left along the quality/runtime curves in Figure 6, we selected the first point where our parallel version with 25 threads outperforms VPR in *both* bounding box cost and critical path delay; this occurs around 85 seconds. We describe this point along the VPR curve as '-superfast', obtained by setting the *inner_num* to 0.015625. In comparison, at this point our parallel version with 25 threads uses a *region_place_count* value of 90. To be fair, we did not compare VPR_quench against our parallel algorithm in this section, as quenching could potentially affect the performance of our parallel algorithm as well.

At this selected point in the runtime/quality space, the parallel placer and VPR '-superfast' have similar speedups, but the parallel version beats VPR in quality. Table 2 shows the actual quality and speedups obtained of the 25 threads on each benchmark, as well as the geometric mean. In comparison, VPR '-superfast' is slightly outmatched in critical path delay (1.15 vs 1.08), and already vastly outmatched in bounding box quality (2.09 vs 1.11) by the parallel version.

A more general quality vs speedup trade-off comparison is plotted in Figure 7. It can be seen that VPR's speedup plateaus at approximately 100X, but our parallel algorithm can achieve speedups around 1000X for similar sacrifices in quality.

5.2 Runtime Scaling

Figure 8 shows the self-speedup obtained using up to 64 threads relative to the single-threaded version of the parallel algorithm with *region_place_count* value of 90. The Niagara system scales well

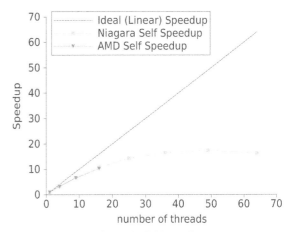

Figure 8: Self speedup

up to 25 threads, beyond which only a minor additional speedup is observed. In this figure, we also show the self speedup up to 16 threads using a quad hex-core AMD system running at 2.4 GHz with 64 GB of system memory. It can be seen that the self speedup obtained on the AMD machine tracks Niagara curve quite well up to 16 threads. We were unable to run with more than 16 threads on the AMD system due to sharing of the machine with other users. However, this result gives us confidence to believe that speedup obtained on Niagara can also be obtained on AMD or Intel machines when the hardware becomes available.

We attribute the scalable nature of our algorithm to the highly parallelizable inner loop. The inner loop, which iterates through the CLBs within each thread's private region, operates independently from all other threads with minimal (at most 4 barriers) interference and little inter-thread communication (broadcast updates at each barrier). This enables good scaling for a well load-balanced workload distribution, since all threads will progress at similar rates and they'll all arrive at the barrier at approximately the same time. These aspects of the algorithm lend themselves well to a GPU-based implementation. The other parts of our algorithm include the parallelized timing and bounding box updates. These require more barriers to enforce precedence, which may limit speedups and cause GPUs some trouble (it may have to remain on a multicore host processor). Finally, the total amount of data copied between global and local data updates is constant regardless of the number of threads, but this part may become a bottleneck due to contention.

5.2.1 Runtime Breakdown

Table 3 shows the runtime breakdown using *stdev000* circuit with *region_place_count* = 90. The initialization column includes memory allocation and data initialization for the parallel algorithm. The inner loop column measures time spent identifying swap candidates and the associated cost calculations needed for incremental swap evaluation. Incremental bounding box calculation time is included in the inner loop as well. However, a separate bounding box calculation must be done for the parallel program to ensure correctness, and is displayed in the bounding box update column (details in Section 3.3.7). The global to local data copy is time spent making local copies of global data structures, such as the timing information, needed for swap evaluation. The data broadcast column on the other hand measures the time consumed doing data broadcasts at the end of each sub-region evaluation (Line 7 and 13 in Section 3.2). Finally, the barrier column shows the average time each thread spent idling at the barrier on Line 6 in Section 3.2. This quantifies load imbalance in our approach.

It is interesting to note that the single-threaded version of the

Table 3: Runtime breakdown

# thread	initialization [s]	%	timing update [s]	%	bounding box update [s]	%	global to local data copy [s]	%	inner loop [s]	%	data broadcast [s]	%	barrier (line 6) [s]	%	total [s]	self speedup
VPR	–	–	73.4	1	–	-	–	-	11045	99	–	–	–	–	11183	-
VPR-fast	–	-	55.0	5	–	-	-	-	1120	94	–	–	–	–	1190	-
1	0.2	0	290.5	20	62.8	4.4	3.3	0	1067	75	8	1	0	0	1431	1
4	0.2	0	78.1	18	18.3	4.2	3.6	1	317	73	6	1	9	2	432	3
9	0.2	0	37.5	17	8.5	3.8	3.8	2	155	69	7	3	12	5	224	6
16	0.2	0	17.7	16	3.8	3.4	3.1	3	73	66	5	4	8	8	111	13
25	0.4	0	13.7	16	2.8	3.3	3.9	5	53	62	4	5	8	9	85	17
36	0.7	1	11.8	16	2.2	3.0	6.0	8	41	55	4	5	8	11	73	20
49	1.1	2	12.5	18	2.2	3.2	7.9	12	33	49	10	15	8	12	68	21
64	1.4	2	14.3	19	2.4	3.1	7.0	9	31	40	3	4	13	17	77	19

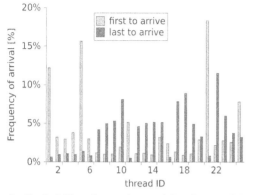

Figure 9: Probability of a region arriving first and last at a barrier due to workload imbalance

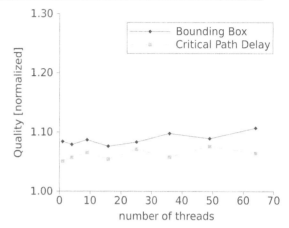

Figure 10: QoR by varying the number of threads

parallel algorithm considered more swaps (about 20% more) than VPR '-fast', but its inner loop's runtime actually shorter than VPR. Nevertheless, after adding the parallelization overhead, the single-threaded version is slower than VPR '-fast'.

As seen in the self-speedup curves in Figure 8, the program scales quite well up to 25 threads. However, efficiency drops when scaling beyond that point. We believe the following factors contribute to this performance degradation.

First, to paraphrase Amdahl's law, the speedup is limited by the non-scalable portions of the program. The non-scalable portions consist of initialization, global to local data copy, and data broadcast. These three components make up minimal runtime (<1%) at 1 thread. However, at 25 threads, their total runtime makes up approximately 10%. Furthermore, timing update has limited scalability due to the strong data dependencies discussed in Section 3.3.5; its speedup plateaus at just 16 threads. As the number of threads increase, the size of each private region decreases, leading to less parallel work assigned to each processor. As a result, the inner loop work after being parallelized with 25 threads makes up only 62% of the runtime at this point.

Second, barriers, one of the most important mechanisms employed by our program to ensure determinism, can also be utilized to measure the amount of workload imbalance. We instrumented only the barrier on Line 6 of the pseudocode and measured the average barrier time loss due to load imbalance. Each thread ID is assigned a unique number in ascending order, starting from top left corner to the right bottom corner. We measure the frequency that each thread (a) arrives first at the barrier, meaning it takes the shortest time to complete its assigned work, and (b) arrives last at the barrier, meaning it is slowest to complete its assigned work. The 25-threaded version was measured with *stdev000* circuit and the result is shown in Figure 9. It can be seen that corner regions with thread IDs 1, 5, 21 and 25 are often the first to arrive, while thread IDs in centre rows or columns are often the last to arrive. Although we attempted to assign similar work to each thread, execution time

can still vary. For example, whitespace collects in the corners and requires fewer swap evaluations, while high-fanout nets may collect in the centre and need extra computation time. Although we clearly need better load balancing, we have not yet been able to improve it.

The inner loop continues to scale, though minimally, beyond 25 threads. However, since it no longer dominates the overall runtime, significant speedup is no longer achieved. We believe that increasing the amount of work allocated to each thread is necessary to obtain better speedups. Simply using bigger circuits may add more useful work to each thread, resulting in better speedups with more threads.

5.3 Quality Scaling

Figure 10 shows the quality compared to VPR using up to 64 threads for the parallel algorithm with a *region_place_count* value of 90. We can see the result is relatively constant, with a very mild upward trend towards 64 threads. All quality values are within 3% of each other. This suggests that the QoR is relatively unaffected by increasing the number of threads.

Another interpretation of these flat curves is that it is unaffected by (the amount of) stale data. Most importantly, the single-threaded version contains no stale data at all, yet it does not perform significantly better than the 49-threaded version which does contain stale data. As the number of threads increases, each thread uses more stale data (since the region owned by a thread, which is perfect and not stale, shrinks in size). However, by the same logic, the use of more threads will also refresh the stale data more frequently, limiting the staleness.

One explanation for the good behaviour with stale data is due to the restricted local swap region size. Since a CLB is unlikely to move a great distance in just one iteration, its previous location (the location assumed by all other threads) becomes a rather good estimate for its new location. Even assuming a bad move has been made, due to the limited range of movements the amount of degradation to the placement is limited as well.

In addition, the way we divide work into sub-regions also contributes to QoR and mitigates the impact of staleness. In particular, the limited range of movement within a sub-region keeps changes small relative to the length of long nets, thus mitigating the impact of stale data. Although very small nets have highest sensitivity, they often fall entirely within the current sub-region and are not subject to staleness. Slightly longer nets which extend just beyond the extended sub-region might also be sensitive to staleness. However, this is mitigated by 'buffer zone' gap of CLBs (located in between all sub-regions named A, for example) where the algorithm is not actively trying to move CLBs. This means that very short nets, where stale data has a large impact on cost, likely does not have stale data. On the other hand, medium length nets are unlikely to have their CLBs moved, and very long-length nets will have their CLBs move only a short distance.

6. FUTURE WORK

It can be seen in Figure 6(b) and the zoomed version Figure 6(d) that the QoR curve is somewhat 'twitchy', in another words, more runtime does not necessarily lead to better quality. One possible cause of the problem as explained in [19] is due to stale data information and the infrequent execution of timing analysis. More analysis could be done and implementing the incremental timing analysis update in [19] could be helpful.

Our algorithm was shown to scale up to 25 threads, but further scaling requires careful study to alleviate the bottlenecks. New data structures to support fully parallelizable timing update and efficient barrier designs could be part of the future work. A dynamic region allocation scheme where the net connectivity is considered in addition to number of CLBs would be useful to remove load imbalance issues. More characterization could be done to elicit a better understanding of various tuning parameters that govern the trade-off between runtime and quality. It would also be helpful to analyze the algorithm using designs of various sizes to obtain the relationship between speedup and circuit size. Furthermore, it would be preferable to route our circuits to obtain the final quality metrics.

7. CONCLUSIONS

We presented a parallel placement algorithm that is both deterministic and timing-driven. VPR's simulated annealing can be accelerated by performing fewer moves per temperature, but quality of result degrades severely past 100X speedup. In contrast, at the point where the parallel algorithm beats VPR in quality, we achieved a speedup of 123X using 25 threads, with bounding box and critical path delay degraded by 11% and 8% respectively. While VPR cannot accelerate much beyond 100X, our parallel algorithm scales up to 1000X.

Varying the number of threads and using stale data does not have a dramatic effect on the quality of result. This is encouraging as it shows the algorithm can potentially scale to more threads without any further loss of quality. Our scaling bottleneck beyond 25 threads appears to be load balancing, but timing updates and other parallel overheads are also significant at this point. Our inner loop calculations may be suitable for GPU implementation, but timing update calculations are difficult and may need to remain on a multicore host CPU.

8. ACKNOWLEDGMENTS

This research is supported by the Natural Sciences and Engineering Research Council of Canada (NSERC), the Institute for Computing, Information and Cognitive Systems (ICICS) at UBC, and WestGrid computing resources. The authors would also like to thank Tor Aamodt for interesting discussions regarding GPUs, Mark Greenstreet for allowing us to use the Niagara machine, Graeme Smecher for early advice, and Valavan Manohararajah for preliminary performance testing.

9. REFERENCES

[1] Altera Corporation, "Quartus II 10.0 Handbook," http://www.altera.com/literature/hb/qts/qts_qii51008.pdf, 2010.

[2] M. Santarini, "Xilinx Tailors Four Tool Flows to Customer Design Disciplines in ISE Design Suite 11.1," http://www.xilinx.com/support/documentation/white_papers/wp307.pdf, 2009.

[3] H. Bian et al., "Towards scalable placement for FPGAs," in FPGA, 2010, pp. 147–156.

[4] W. Swartz and C. Sechen, "New algorithms for the placement and routing of macro cells," in ICCAD, Nov. 1990, pp. 336 –339.

[5] A. Ludwin et al., "High-quality, deterministic parallel placement for FPGAs on commodity hardware," in FPGA, 2008, pp. 14–23.

[6] M. Haldar et al., "Parallel algorithms for FPGA placement," in GLSVLSI, 2000, pp. 86–94.

[7] S. Kravitz and R. Rutenbar, "Placement by simulated annealing on a multiprocessor," IEEE TCAD, vol. 6, no. 4, pp. 534 – 549, Jul. 1987.

[8] P. Banerjee et al., "Parallel simulated annealing algorithms for cell placement on hypercube multiprocessors," IEEE Trans. Parallel Distrib. Syst., vol. 1, no. 1, pp. 91–106, 1990.

[9] A. Choong et al., "Parallelizing simulated annealing-based placement using GPGPU," in FPL, Aug. 2010, pp. 31–34.

[10] W.-J. Sun and C. Sechen, "A loosely coupled parallel algorithm for standard cell placement," in ICCAD, 1994, pp. 137–144.

[11] M. G. Wrighton and A. M. DeHon, "Hardware-assisted simulated annealing with application for fast FPGA placement," in FPGA, 2003, pp. 33–42.

[12] G. Smecher et al., "Self-hosted placement for massively parallel processor arrays," in FPT, Dec. 2009, pp. 159 –166.

[13] J. Luu et al., "VPR 5.0: FPGA CAD and architecture exploration tools with single-driver routing, heterogeneity and process scaling," in FPGA, 2009, pp. 133–142.

[14] V. Betz and J. Rose, "VPR: a new packing, placement and routing tool for FPGA research," in FPL, 1997, pp. 213–222.

[15] M. L. Scott and J. M. Mellor-Crummey, "Fast, contention-free combining tree barriers for shared-memory multiprocessors," in International Journal of Parallel Programming, 1994, 22(4), pp. 449–481.

[16] M. Tom et al., "Un/DoPack: re-clustering of large system-on-chip designs with interconnect variation for low-cost FPGAs," in ICCAD, Nov. 2006, pp. 680 –687.

[17] I. Kuon and J. Rose, "Area and delay trade-offs in the circuit and architecture design of FPGAs," in FPGA, 2008, pp. 149–158.

[18] Sun Microsystems, "UltraSPARC T2 Processor System On a Chip," http://wikis.sun.com/download/attachments/31400118/N2_Announce_Breakout_final.pdf?version=1&modification-Date=1212688201000,2007.

[19] K. Eguro and S. Hauck, "Enhancing timing-driven FPGA placement for pipelined netlists," in DAC, 2008, pp. 34–37.

Improved Delay Measurement Method in FPGA based on Transition Probability

Justin S. J. Wong and Peter Y. K. Cheung *

Department of Electrical and Electronic Engineering, Imperial College, London, UK

{justin.s.wong02, p.cheung}@imperial.ac.uk

ABSTRACT

The ability to measure delay of arbitrary circuits on FPGA offers many opportunities for on-chip characterisation and optimisation. This paper describes an improved delay measurement method by monitoring the transition probability at the output nodes as the operating frequency is swept.

The new method uses optimised test vector generation to improve the accuracy of the test method. It is effectively demonstrated on a 4th order IIR filter circuit implemented on an Altera Cyclone III FPGA.

Categories and Subject Descriptors

B.8.1 [**Performance and Reliability**]: Reliability, Testing, and Fault-Tolerance

General Terms

Measurement, Performance

Keywords

FPGA, Transition Probability, Timing, Self Test

1. INTRODUCTION

Reconfigurability of FPGA, whether at power-up or during run-time, can be exploited effectively for self-testing and self-characterisation. Since the test hardware can subsequently be reconfigured to perform operational functions, the costs of including such test circuits are limited to a small overhead in memory storage for the test configuration and the extra configuration time, either during power-up or during operation. Recently a number of techniques have been proposed to provide not just "go" or "no-go" test results, but to measure the speed of either combinatorial circuit paths [12, 17, 10, 4, 11, 8] or even complete circuit modules with sequential circuits [16]. The ability to measure delay in specific circuits opens up many new possibilities. For example,

* The authors would like to acknowledge the support of Altera Corporation, Terasic and the EPSRC under the grants: EP/H013784/1 and EP/I012036/1.

these techniques can be employed to measure delay variability [17] and timing degradation [14] in the latest generation of FPGAs. These test methods concerning the unique delay mapping of circuits in FPGAs are also essential to hardware security schemes such as *Physical Unclonable Function* (PUF) [7], as well as delay-aware placement and routing methods [5, 3, 9, 13] that provide promising solutions against process variability in FPGAs to improve reliability.

Among all the proposed technique, the one based on transition probability (TP) [16] is the most promising because: 1) it is capable of measuring delays in both combinatorial and sequential circuits; 2) it is essentially a black-box approach, not requiring detail knowledge of the internal circuitry; 3) it can be implemented on existing FPGAs as built-in self-test (BIST); 4) it is time and resources efficient. While earlier results demonstrate the potential of this technique, the previously published work by the authors left a number of important fundamental questions unanswered relating to the accuracy of the measurements, the sensitivity of the technique to different types of timing errors, and the optimality of the test stimuli beyond using a test vector set that is uniformly distributed. Within this context, the new contributions of this work are: 1) a detailed analysis of the behaviour of transition probability in complex multi-path circuits; 2) an in-depth study of the timing error sensitivity of the TP technique in digital circuits; 3) a novel method to optimise the sensitivity by controlling the probability distribution of the test stimuli to provide high measurement accuracy; 4) the improved technique is applied and demonstrated on both complex combinatorial and sequential circuits on an Altera Cyclone III EP3C25 FPGA.

2. BACKGROUND

2.1 The Transition Probability Test Method

An indirect timing measurement method based on transition probability (TP) was proposed in [16]. It has three key features: (a) It is able to measure the delay of components such as interconnects, LUTs and registers involved in typical user circuits. (b) The test circuit itself is robust against timing failure, measurement accuracy is largely independent from process variation and degradation of the test circuitries. (c) No structural change or internal signals probing of the circuit-under-test (CUT) is required, delay can be measured by pure observation of the output.

The test method estimates the propagation delay of a specific circuit path indirectly by measuring the transition probabilities of the output node. The transition probability at a signal node is defined as the probability that the node will

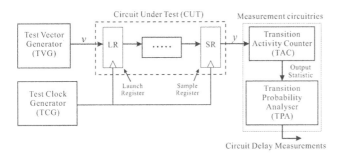

Figure 1: Basic principle of the delay measurement method.

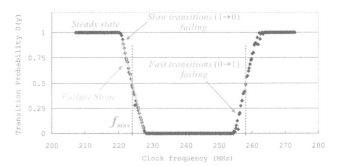

Figure 2: Example of a typical output transition probability $D(y)$ against frequency from [14].

change state when the next input stimuli is applied to the circuit. For a sequence of output samples $y(k)$, $k = 1, \ldots$, the transition probability $D(y)$ is defined in [16] as:

$$P\{y(k+1) = \overline{y(k)}\} = P\{y(k) = 0\}P\{y(k+1) = 1\} + P\{y(k) = 1\}P\{y(k+1) = 0\} \quad (1)$$

The test measures the transition probabilities at the output signal node while ramping the clock frequency up. By detecting changes in the transition probability, it is possible to indirectly derive the frequency at which the circuit starts to fail and hence its propagation delay.

Consider a functional combinatorial circuit with one input and one output z. It can be seen that any transition at the output must be the result of a transition at the input. Therefore if the input is driven by a source with stationary transition probability, the output will also exhibits a stationary transition probability (unchanging).

For our test method, we capture the output of the Circuit-Under-Test (CUT) with a register at a certain clock frequency f_{clk}. The register captures a sample $y(k)$ of the output z at time T after applying the input $v(k)$. If the clock frequency is low enough, then the CUT operates without fault: $y(k) = z(k)$ and so $D(y) = D(z)$. However, because of propagation delays in the CUT, the output z will only change some time after the input is applied. If the test clock frequency is increased, at some point the CUT will begin to fail, and y will begin to sample the value of z from the previous cycle, such that $y(k) = z(k-1)$ some of the time. This changes the output transition probability $D(y)$. Therefore, finding the frequency where the $D(y)$ begins to deviate from its stationary value will yield an accurate measure of its maximum operating frequency f_{max}. This statement holds true as long as the CUT has only a single input to output path and the input is driven by a stationary process, such as a signal that toggles every clock cycle.

Fig. 1 shows the general structure of the test circuit. The circuit-under-test (CUT) input is driven by a Test Vector Generator (TVG). The CUT contains two registers (LR and SR) for launching the input and sampling the output of the combinatorial circuit between them. The registers are controlled by a common clock from the Test Clock Generator (TCG). The TCG contains runtime reconfigurable PLLs, allowing the clock frequency to be changed during a test. The timing resolution of the test is given by $\Delta t \approx \frac{\Delta f}{f^2}$ in [16], which depends on the clock frequency (f) and the size of frequency steps (Δf) during the frequency sweep. Using $\Delta f = 0.25\text{MHz}$ at 500MHz would yield a considerably good timing resolution of 1ps. The output from the sam-

ple register is processed by the Transition Activity Counter (TAC) which is essentially a simple asynchronous counter that counts the number of transition in y over a certain period of time. Transition probability can be derived from the transition count using:

$$D(y) = \frac{\text{signal transition count}}{K} \quad (2)$$

where K is the number of output samples or the number of clock cycles elapsed in the counting period. The calculation of $D(y)$ is carried out by the Transition Probability Analyser (TPA) using (2) and then organised into a detailed Transition Probability profile (TP profile) of the CUT over the range of test frequencies. An example of a TP profile is shown in Fig. 2 taken from a CUT containing 9 LUTs on a Cyclone III EP3C25 [14]. As can be seen, the profile begins with a stationary plot at low frequency but declined steeply when timing failure began at approximately 220MHz. This change corresponds to the failure of slower signal transitions. In this case, the $1 \rightarrow 0$ transitions. The gradient and shape of the failure slope is related to the clock jitter and characteristics of the registers respectively. The second failure slope shows the failure of the faster $0 \rightarrow 1$ signal transitions and the transition probability returns to its initial stationary level after both types of transitions have completely failed.

The beauty of the TP method is that it gives more than just the worst-case delay for each CUT — it is able to measure the two types of transition separately. This can potentially be useful for design level timing optimisation where signals are deliberately inverted between combinatorial nodes to even out and reduce the impact of the slow transitions on the overall worst-case propagation delay. The versatility of test results, non-invasive nature and the high measurement precision makes it an ideal candidate for delay measurement of a wide range of arbitrary circuits on FPGAs.

3. MEASURING COMPLEX MULTI-PATH CIRCUITS

The general TP measurement circuitry shown earlier in Fig. 1 can be adapted to test complex multi-path circuits by using a pseudo random test vector generator. Since the vector generation process is stationary, the statistics of the resultant random test vectors are also stationary. Apart from transition probability $D(y)$, the random vectors' statistics can also be quantified by the probability of a logical *high* occurring, which we termed the *High Probability* (HP) or

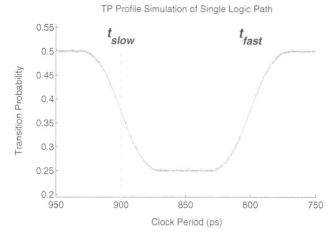

Figure 3: An example of basic TP profile of a single logic path failing at t_{slow} and t_{fast} for falling and rising transitions respectively.

$H(y)$ of signal y. It has a range of 0 to 1, where 0 and 1 implies a stuck at *low* or *high* respectively. In the case of random bit sequences, the values of TP and HP are linked by a simple quadratic relationship:

$$D(y) \approx 2 \times H(y) \times (1 - H(y)) \qquad (3)$$

When defining or quantifying the statistic of random input sequences, the use of HP is preferred, because it represents a unique random bit pattern. TP values, on the other hand, could result in two different HP solutions according to (3) with opposite bit patterns, causing unnecessary confusions. The only exception where TP points to a unique random bit pattern is when it is at its maximum — $D(y) = 0.5$.

3.1 Characteristics of Transition Probability

3.1.1 Basic TP Model

Fig. 3 depicts a simulated TP profile of a single logic path with uniformly distributed random input sequence. The falling and rising transitions are assigned different propagation delay values t_{slow} and t_{fast}. The gradual failure slopes are caused mainly by the stochastic behaviour of clock jitter [16], where it can be describe by a random variable τ in terms of the relative time from the expected clock edge, with a specific probability density function $PDF_{Jitter}(\tau)$. By assuming each clock edge has independent random jitter and consistent $PDF_{Jitter}(\tau)$ throughout the test frequency range, the behaviour of the TP profile as a function of clock period (T) can be approximated from the cumulative distribution of the PDFs centered at t_{slow} and t_{fast}:

$$TP_{indep}(T) \approx \frac{1}{2}\left[\frac{3}{4} + \left(\frac{1}{2} - \int_{-\infty}^{t_{fast}-T} PDF_{Jitter}(\tau)\, d\tau\right)\right.$$
$$\left.\times \left(\frac{1}{2} - \int_{-\infty}^{t_{slow}-T} PDF_{Jitter}(\tau)\, d\tau\right)\right] \quad (4)$$

where $t_{fast} \leq t_{slow}$.

The behaviour of the resultant TP profile also depends on the degree of jitter correlation between consecutive clock edges, which affects the timing failure interaction between the rising and falling transitions through the CUT. According to [6], most PLL generated clock signals are likely to

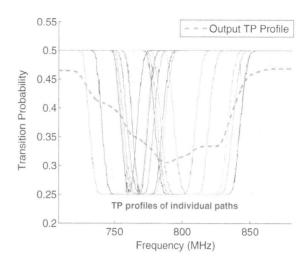

Figure 4: A TP profile measurement of the 2nd LSB output of a 9x9 embedded multiplier on the Cyclone III EP3C25. The unusual shape of the TP profile is the result of individual paths failing at different times. The corresponding paths are isolated and tested separately to obtain their basic TP profile components for reference.

exhibit multi-cycle jitter, which introduces edge-to-edge jitter correlation. Therefore, it is important for the model to also cover such correlated case. The TP behaviour with complete correlation is given by:

$$TP_{corr}(T) \approx \frac{1}{2}\left[1 - \frac{1}{2}\left(\int_{-\infty}^{t_{slow}-T} PDF_{Jitter}(\tau)\, d\tau\right.\right.$$
$$\left.\left. - \int_{-\infty}^{t_{fast}-T} PDF_{Jitter}(\tau)\, d\tau\right)\right] \quad (5)$$

where $t_{fast} \leq t_{slow}$.

Note that both TP_{indep} and TP_{corr} gives identical results in normal cases when the failure caused by t_{fast} and t_{slow} do not overlap (Fig. 3). Yet, when the two types of failure do overlap, the jitter correlation causes their respective change of TP to cancel each other out, reducing the magnitude of change in the TP profile.

Clock signals in real systems are likely to exhibits both independent and correlated jitter. Therefore, a combination of TP_{indep} and TP_{corr} can be used:

$$TP(T) = (1 - k) \times TP_{indep} + k \times TP_{corr} \qquad (6)$$

where k defines the correlation factor ranging from 0 to 1. In reality, it is highly unlikely to have perfect edge-to-edge correlation $(k = 1)$. Therefore, the TP profile should always show a measurable amount of change, even if t_{fast} and t_{slow} are exactly identical.

3.1.2 Analysis of Multi-Path TP Profile

The previously described single path models are useful for predicting the TP profile of a failing path. Yet, the problem with them is that they are not scalable to more complex multi paths circuits. Fig. 4 depicts the TP profile of the 2nd LSB output of a 9x9 embedded multiplier on the Cyclone III EP3C25. As can be seen, the observed output TP profile is related to all the basic TP profiles of each individual path. While the TP profile may appear to be a direct combination

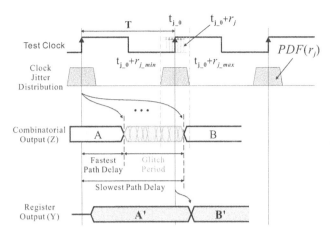

Figure 5: Timing diagram showing the activity of the output bit (Z) and registered output (Y) in a multi input paths to single output circuit. A certain _glitch period_ occurs after each clock edge due to variations between propagation delay of different paths. The position of clock edge is governed by the jitter distribution $PDF(r_j)$, and the probability of the register capturing the correct value in B$'$ depends on both the glitch pattern and the overlapping jitter region.

of the basic TP profile components of the paths, it is actually not possible to recreate the exact TP profile using the basic single path components alone. The main reason for this is that the failure process of the paths are interrelated with each other in a difficult to predict manner.

Consider the timing illustration in Fig. 5, where a circuit with multiple internal paths is stimulated by random vectors. The probability that an input transition through a particular path is observable at the output depends on the input pattern and the state of the other paths, which means each path could contribute differently to the observed TP profile. Such behaviour is only predictable if the exact circuit implementation, structure and layout are known.

Although each active path may produces a signal transition some time after the clock edge, their different arrival time result in a "glitch period" containing a series of unwanted transition activities. These glitch activities are unpredictable especially when random input vectors are used. When the glitch period coincides with the next clock edge, where the clock edge position itself is unpredictable due to clock jitter, the actual value captured by the register (B$'$) is not deterministic, and hence the resultant transition probability cannot be determined with certainty. Also, the rapid transitions in the glitch period could cause undesirable metastability problem in the output register [2], further increasing the unpredictability of the output value.

For these reasons, the direct approach of modelling the TP profile based on specific path quickly becomes impractical with complexity. For FPGA designs, a mere change of placement and routing could produce a layout with completely different TP profile. The only way that a precise model of the TP profile can be obtained is if a perfect physical model of the circuit is available with precise information on signal propagations, interactions, and clock jitter behaviour, so that the exact glitch pattern is known and

the registered output value is predictable. Though, if such perfect physical model exists, a delay measurement method would not be necessary in the first place. A better strategy would be to consider the timing error sensitivity of TP rather than its exact profile, and deduce an effective way to control its sensitivity to timing errors in complex circuits, such that good measurement accuracy is achieved.

3.1.3 Controlling Sensitivity of TP to Timing failure

Timing error Sensitivity of TP for a circuit is defined as the difference between the normal operating level of output TP and the level of TP after the slowest type of signal transitions through the worst-case path has failed. The higher the difference, the more likely errors are detected and hence provide better sensitivity to timing failure. The ability to control the sensitivity of TP against timing failure allows the test method to produce more reliable results, avoiding inaccuracy caused by sensitivity loss. There are three typical cases where sensitivity could be affected:

(i) Sensitivity dilution – a logic block with large number of inputs converging to one output suffers from reduced observable TP failure response. This problem can be easily observed in an N-input AND gate where errors can only propagate through when all inputs are _high_ and the TP sensitivity decreases as N increases.

(ii) Sensitivity blocking – in a circuit with multiple combinatorial stages separated by pipeline registers, the changes in TP profile due to timing failure of one stage could be blocked by its following stage(s) under certain conditions, causing it to be invisible at the output.

(iii) Failure blind spot – when a logic block with N inputs is supplied with inputs S_N with certain $H(S_N)$, the failure of specific internal paths may not cause any observable change at the output TP profile.

The problem of diluted sensitivity (i) is unavoidable in most cases, especially with random test vectors. Yet, the sensitivity is only reduced and never completely lost, meaning that it can be improved by taking a higher number of transition count samples to form a TP profile with less residue noise from the random inputs and hence higher relative sensitivity (see (2)). This approach, however, increases the total test time and it does not solve the problems in cases (ii) and (iii) where complete loss of sensitivity is possible.

To provide a general solution for the three cases while maintaining short test time, we propose a method that can improve TP sensitivity by controlling the statistic of the random input vector in terms of high probability (HP).

In Fig. 6, the sensitivity of rising or falling transition failure in a single path can be improved by adjusting the HP of input vector V. The usual choice of uniformly distributed random test vectors, where $H(V) = 0.5$, do not actually provide the best sensitivity to errors. Instead, a maximum sensitivity can be achieved when $H(V)$ is 0.33 or 0.67 depending on whether the rising or falling transitions fail first.

This unusual asymmetrical phenomenon can be explained and modelled probabilistically through the following cases. Consider 3 cycles of input vector sequences $V(k), k = 1, 2, 3$. If the falling transitions fail to propagate within 1 cycle, a transition is only detected at the output register on the 4th cycle when V has a sequence of $0 \rightarrow 0 \rightarrow 1$ or $1 \rightarrow 0 \rightarrow 0$.

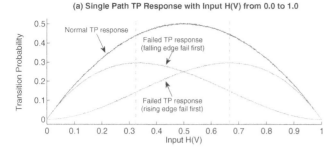

(a) Single Path TP Response with Input H(V) from 0.0 to 1.0

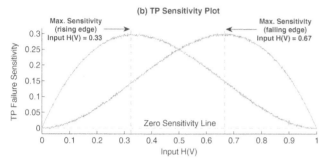

(b) TP Sensitivity Plot

Figure 6: Plots evaluating the sensitivity of TP to timing failure in a circuit path. Maximum sensitivity is achieved when the input vector V has high probability $H(V) = 0.67$ when falling transitions fail first, or $H(V) = 0.33$ when rising transitions fail first.

Therefore, the output TP of the failed path in terms of V is given by the probability of the two sequences occurring:

$$
\begin{aligned}
TP_{\text{fall\_failed}} &= 2 \times P(V=1) \times P(V=0) \times P(V=0) \\
&= 2 \times P(V=1) \times (1 - P(V=1))^2 \\
&= 2H(V)(1 - H(V))^2 \qquad (7)
\end{aligned}
$$

In the same way, when the rising transitions fail, a transition is only detected when V is $0 \rightarrow 1 \rightarrow 1$ or $1 \rightarrow 1 \rightarrow 0$. This produce a similar probability expression:

$$
\begin{aligned}
TP_{\text{rise\_failed}} &= 2 \times P(V=1) \times P(V=1) \times P(V=0) \\
&= 2 \times P(V=1)^2 \times (1 - P(V=1)) \\
&= 2H(V)^2 (1 - H(V)) \qquad (8)
\end{aligned}
$$

By subtracting these failed TP responses from the normal TP response (TP_{normal}) which is given earlier by (3), the TP sensitivity of both falling and rising transitions can be derived:

$$
\begin{aligned}
\text{Sensitivity}_{\text{fall}} &= TP_{\text{normal}} - TP_{\text{fall\_failed}} \\
&= 2H(V)^2 (1 - H(V)) \qquad (9)
\end{aligned}
$$

$$
\text{Sensitivity}_{\text{rise}} = 2H(V)(1 - H(V))^2 \qquad (10)
$$

These expressions describe exactly the sensitivity behaviour observed in Fig. 6 and the HPs corresponding to their maximums (peaks) computed through solving their derivatives, giving exactly the observed optimal HP values: 0.33 (1/3) and 0.67 (2/3) for rising and falling transitions respectively.

This asymmetrical sensitivity to different transition types means that uniformly distributed random vectors is not necessary the optimal choice, given the CUT is known to have one type of transitions failing at a significantly lower clock

frequency than the other. Such behaviour is common in CMOS circuits where the pull-up and pull-down transistors are sized differently or when extra pull-up or down transistors are added to improve signal strength. The only advantage of uniformly distributed random vectors is when the CUT has exactly matched rising and falling transition delay or their failure order is not known in advance.

3.1.4 TP Response and Sensitivity Mapping of Logic Circuits

To further understand how varying the input HP can improve the cases with potential sensitivity loss – sensitivity blocking and failure blind spot, we carried out a series of sensitivity simulation on a 2-input logic block. The layout of the block is depicted in Fig. 7, where it has two internal paths, each with its corresponding rising and falling transitions delays ($t_{\text{A-fall}}$, $t_{\text{A-rise}}$ and $t_{\text{B-fall}}$, $t_{\text{B-rise}}$). The idea is to stimulate both inputs of the circuit with random vectors A and B of varying $H(A)$ and $H(B)$ to create extensive two-dimensional mappings of TP response and sensitivity, and identify possible sensitivity issues.

The first issue we encountered is sensitivity blocking, which occurs in circuits with multiple pipeline stages. Fig. 8 demonstrates how certain failure response from the preceding logic stage could be blocked by simple logic functions. For a circuit with multiple pipeline stages, it is important to have the TP response caused by failure of early stages to propagate all the way through to the output, so that it can be detected. This process can, however, be blocked by logic stages, if the input statistics $H(A)$ and $H(B)$ change in a specific way that follow the contour lines in the TP response maps. Each of the lines represents a constant level of output TP. Thus, $H(A)$ and $H(B)$ changing along these lines would yield no output TP change, effectively blocking any timing failure response from reaching the output. In this case an XOR gate posses the most problem, because it has a large flat region at the centre where variation of $H(A)$ and $H(B)$ would not produce any change at the output. The obvious solution against this problem is to adjust the input HPs such that the observed TP response blocking does not happen.

Another serious issue with TP sensitivity is when a timing failure in a circuit leads to no change of TP with specific input HPs – the failure blind spot. Such cases could be demonstrated in 2-input functions and they are depicted in Fig. 9. In the three cases of 2-input functions: AND, OR and XOR, the falling transition delay from input A is set to have the worst-case delay and hence it fails first in the simulation. The deviation of TP caused by A failing is recorded for all possible input HPs of A and B to form a sensitivity map for each case. The level where sensitivity is zero is marked by contour lines. Therefore, any $H(A)$ and $H(B)$ values that fall on or near these lines will result in undetectable TP response. Clearly, for AND and OR function, the blind spots with zero sensitivity are rare and can be avoided relatively easily. On the other hand, XOR has a wide spread region across the middle where $H(A) = 0.5$. Such region should be avoided by using different values for $H(A)$ and $H(B)$. For linked input HP values where $H(A) = H(B)$, $H(A) = H(B) = 0.87$ gives approximately the best sensitivity. It can also be seen from the sensitivity maps that when $H(A)$ is 1, 0, and 1 or 0 for the AND, OR and XOR cases respectively, the optimal sensitivity is achieved at $H(B)$ predicted by (9) where falling transitions are assumed to be slower.

167

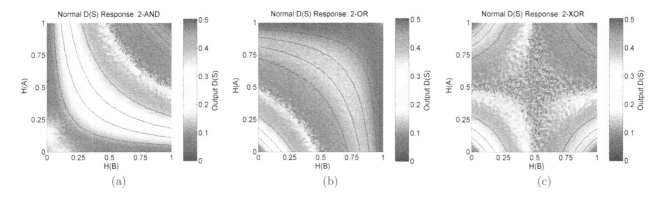

Normal D(S) Response: 2-AND   Normal D(S) Response: 2-OR   Normal D(S) Response: 2-XOR

(a)   (b)   (c)

Figure 8: The output TP response mapping of all possible input HPs for (a) AND gate, (b) OR gate and (c) XOR gate. The contour lines on the maps represent levels of the same output TP, hence any change of input $H(A)$ and $H(B)$ along the contour lines leads to an unchanging output $D(S)$, possibly blocking failure responses from the previous logic stages.

The effect of the XOR's blind spot is demonstrated in Fig. 10 and Fig. 11 in terms TP profile, where cases with different path delay order is shown. In Fig. 10, the error sensitivity is completely lost, due to the uniform input HPs. Whereas in Fig. 11, the TP profile showed a certain change when $t_{\text{B-fall}}$ is violated, but still missed the failure of the worst-case path ($t_{\text{A-fall}}$). In both case, the sensitivity is restored and improved dramatically when $H(A) = H(B) = 0.87$ is used.

3.2 Self-Optimising Complex Circuit Test Platform

The complete complex circuit test platform is depicted by Fig. 12. The test circuit automatically optimise its random input vectors with specific probability weights to improve the TP's sensitivity against timing errors in the CUT.

3.2.1 Adaptive Input Probability Weighting

The *circuit response tester* (CRT) stimulates the CUT by toggling one input bit at a time while cycling the remaining bits with a counter every two clock cycles. Each count would form a pair of input patterns differ only by the single toggle bit. This forms a set of exhaustive *single input change* (SIC) test vectors. This approach effectively exercise every path in the combinatorial logic blocks in the CUT with full input access. The Output pattern is analysed by the *circuit response checker* (CRC). Input pattern pairs from the CRT that leads to actual activities at specific output bit are recorded and marked as "effective". Since a significant number of input patterns are likely to produce no output transitions, the refined "effective" input patterns would form a vector series with distinctive average HP values for each input bit when applied in sequence. Such HP values are then applied to the *probability weighting circuit* as HP weights to generate weighted random sequences with specific HP. The HP optimised random vectors are likely to exercise the internal paths of the CUT more thoroughly than the uniformly distributed random vectors, because it is probabilistically similar to the "effective" input patterns that exercised every paths in the exposed combinatorial parts of the CUT.

For the earlier 2-input XOR example, the effective input vectors are: $*0$, $0*$, $*1$ and $1*$, where $*$ represents the input bit being toggled by the CRT. Assuming a toggling bit is

Arbitrary 2-Input Function

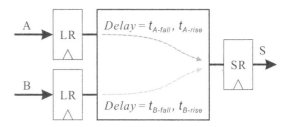

Figure 7: A simple two input arbitrary functional block for testing the sensitivity of transition probability to timing failure with multiple signal paths.

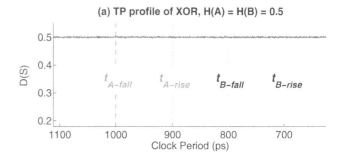

(a) TP profile of XOR, H(A) = H(B) = 0.5

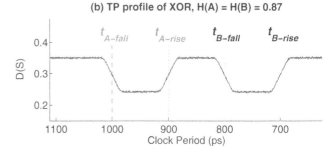

(b) TP profile of XOR, H(A) = H(B) = 0.87

Figure 10: Simulated TP profile of an XOR gate showing (a) sensitivity loss to timing failure in all paths when using uniformly distributed random inputs, and (b) sensitivity restored using $H(A) = H(B) = 0.87$.

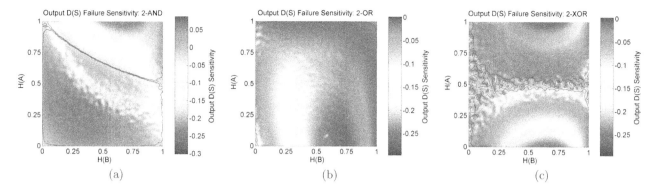

Figure 9: The TP failure sensitivity mapping of all possible input HP for (a) AND gate, (b) OR gate and (c) XOR gate. The contour lines represents the level at which sensitivity is zero. Both positive and negative sensitivity values represent a measurable change of TP, but in different directions.

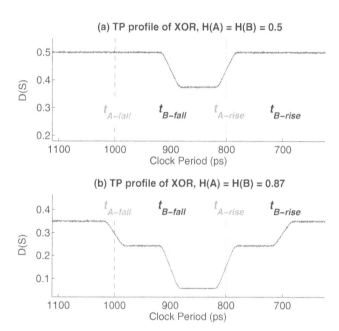

Figure 11: (a) shows the sensitivity loss to failure of the slowest type of transitions in the XOR and regain sensitivity when both type of transitions have failed. (b) shows the regained sensitivity using $H(A) = H(B) = 0.87$.

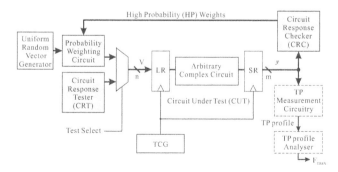

Figure 12: Block diagram of the self-optimising complex circuit test platform.

assigned an HP of 0.5, one could argue that the average HP of the four vector pairs equates to 0.5 for both input bits, which is shown to give zero sensitivity. However, due to the asymmetrical sensitivity of delay paths described earlier by (9) and (10), the overall average of the effective vectors may not form appropriate HP weights. Instead, the vectors should be divided into groups according to the pattern of the non-toggling bits and compute their average HP weights separately. In this case, they form two groups: $\{*0, 0*\}$ and $\{*1, 1*\}$. Assuming falling transitions are slower, optimal sensitivity is achieved when the $*$ bits are assigned an HP of 0.66, and the resultant HP weight of both input bits for the 1st and 2nd group are $(0.66 + 0)/2 = 0.33$ and $(0.66 + 1)/2 = 0.83$ respectively. Given that HP weights greater than 0.5 favour higher failure sensitivity of the slower falling transitions in this case, the HP weight from the 2nd group (0.83) closest to the optimal HP weights of 0.87 shown earlier should be used. For circuits with unknown internal structure, the HP weight pattern from each vectors group can be applied and tested separately for maximum accuracy. The test time would increase but not in multiples of a single test, because the test clock frequency range would be reduced considerably after the first few HP weight patterns.

While this approach may appear to neglect sequential feedbacks in circuits, where combinatorial blocks with feedback inputs may not be directly controllable from the proposed input sequences; it is the very nature of feedback in sequential circuits that allows the TP test method to maintain high timing error sensitivity, where errors are accumulated through the feedback paths and cause a significant change in the output TP response.

3.2.2 Generating Weighted Probability Test Vectors

Weighted random sequences can be generated easily by combining several independent uniformly distributed random bit streams together with simple boolean logic [15]. Table 1 shows an example of 9 levels HP weighting using three independent random bit streams: $R0$, $R1$ and $R2$. For FPGAs with dynamic LUT mask reconfigurability, the HP weight can be modified easily through changing the LUT's function on the fly. Otherwise, the same controllable HP can be implemented with several LUTs at the expense of slightly more area. For the Cyclone III EP3C25 without dynamic reconfigurable LUTs, a weighted random bit stream with 17 HP levels requires three 4-input LUTs to implement.

Table 1: Example of weighted random generation logics with different high probability (HP).

Weights	HP	Logic Expression
1	0	GND
2	0.125	$R2 \cdot R1 \cdot R0$
3	0.25	$R2 \cdot R1$
4	0.375	$R2 \cdot (R1 + R0)$
5	0.5	$R2$
6	0.625	$R2 + R1 \cdot R0$
7	0.75	$R2 + R1$
8	0.875	$R2 + R1 + R0$
9	1.0	VCC

4. TEST PLATFORM IMPLEMENTATION AND EVALUATION ON FPGA

The proposed complex circuit test platform is implemented on the Cyclone III EP3C25 FPGA to evaluate its accuracy and efficiency. Fig. 13 depicts the hardware layout of the test circuit on the FPGA. In this particular case, the TP measurement circuitries and CRC are placed next to the CUT for a more compact representation. However, there are no limitation on where these circuitries should be placed, because they are completely asynchronous from the CUT and do not suffer from timing issues if placed at a remote location. The random vector generator is implemented as an LFSR and is followed by a 17 levels HP weighting circuit.

The test procedure contains two phases. First the circuit's response is analysed by the CRT and CRC to generate the optimised HP weights, then they are used to conduct the TP test to obtain its maximum operating frequency or worst-case delay measurements. The response analysis phase is only required once for each design. In some cases, it can be skipped completely if the optimised HP weights can be obtained through analysis or simulation of the CUT during the design process. Results consistency are ensured through repeated tests until the FPGA's temperature stabilises.

The test platform is evaluated by two types of CUTs: A 4x4 LUT based multiplier and a Butterworth IIR Filter. The layout in Fig. 13 is taken from the Butterworth Filter case. The test candidates were chosen such that both combinatorial and sequential circuits are evaluated. Since practical FPGA applications in general contain mostly LUT based functions, the LUT based multiplier test would give us a clear guideline on how well the test method performs in general.

4.1 Multiplier Test Case

The LUT based multiplier is tested with both the proposed TP method and a full exhaustive test method proposed in [17] to give an absolute measurement reference for accuracy comparison. For the TP test, the random inputs with and without optimised HP weighting are tested to identify their effectiveness. The placement and routing of the CUT are kept exactly identical between both tests.

4.1.1 Results

The measured maximum operating frequencies of the multiplier are shown in Fig. 14. The results with optimised input HP tracks the exhaustive test results very closely and is accurate within 1% of the results. The apparent accuracy difference between the normal and optimised HP results are not very high in this case because the test using uniformly

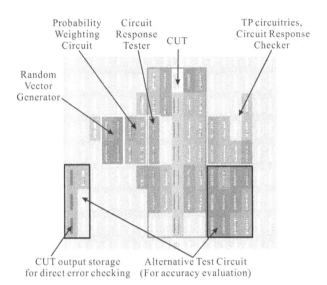

Figure 13: Layout of the hardware test platform on a Cyclone III EP3C25 for complex CUT. An alternative test circuit is included for accuracy evaluation of the TP test platform.

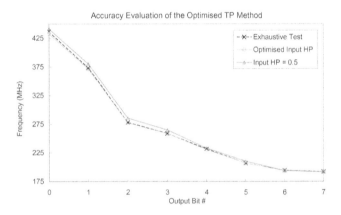

Figure 14: Accuracy evaluation of the TP method on a 4x4 LUT based multiplier with optimised input HP against an exhaustive test method proposed in [17].

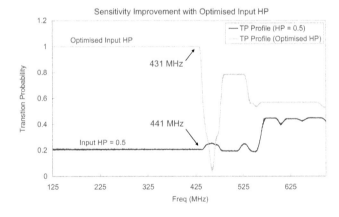

Figure 15: Plot showing the error sensitivity improvement of the TP profile of a single multiplier output bit using optimised input HP.

170

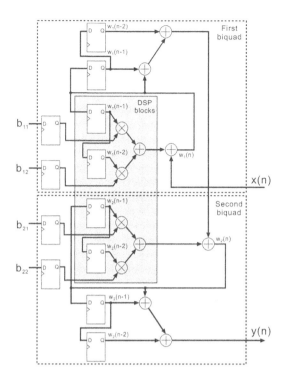

Figure 16: A 4th order Butterworth IIR filter design from Altera [1], where x(n) is the input and y(n) is the output.

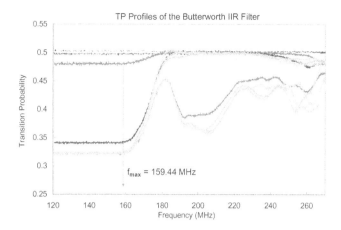

Figure 17: The TP profiles of all 21 output bits of the Butterworth IIR filter.

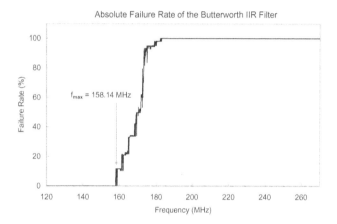

Figure 18: The absolute failure rate of the Butterworth IIR Filter between 120 and 270MHz.

distributed random inputs is already very close to the exhaustive test references. Nonetheless, a clear improvement can still be seen between the two. We suspect that the good accuracy from the uniform random inputs is due to a high degree of glitch acitivity at the combinatorial output of the multiplier. Referring back to Section 3.1.2 and Fig. 5, it can be seen that when the glitch period is violated by the clock edge and jitter region, the registered output becomes highly unpredictable. Although it is not possible to predict the exact TP response, the increased uncertainty may have caused a more distinctive TP deviation from its normal value and thus increased the TP sensitivity.

In Fig. 15, the TP profiles taken from the same output bit using uniform HP and optimised HP are compared. The TP profile with optimised HP shows a significantly higher timing error sensitivity – a larger deviation in TP response and more accurate measurement using simple TP thresholds.

The optimised TP method may produce slightly more conservative results than the exhaustive test because it is not possible to take the effect of clock jitter into account with the complex TP behaviour produced by multiple paths failing. Whereas the exhaustive test method examine each path individually and is able to produce a nominal f_{max} according to the expected clock edge position at the centre of the jitter distribution. Please refer to [17] for more information.

The test time of the multiplier is under 3 seconds, assuming the optimal input HP weights are extracted in advance or pre-computed from the functional model of the multiplier.

4.2 Butterworth IIR Filter Test Case

The Butterworth IIR Filter (Fig. 16) is implemented with multiple 18x18 embedded multipliers, adders, feedback paths and register stages on the Cyclone III. Such complexity of the CUT resembles most practical designs in FPGAs and it would give a good representation of the TP test platform performance in terms of accuracy in realistic situation.

To evaluate the measurement accuracy, an absolute comparison based test method that basically gathers the filter outputs at a series of finely spaced clock frequencies steps and compare them against a set of pre-calculated reference results to identify any timing errors. The layout of the extra test circuit is depicted in Fig. 13 as "Alternative Test Circuit". Note that this alternative test circuit is built purely for the purpose of accuracy evaluation, its area overhead and test time are far too high for practical use.

4.2.1 Results

Results from the optimised TP test platform in the form of TP profiles (Fig. 17) gave a maximum operating frequency (f_{max}) measurement of 159.44MHz, which is within 1% of the absolute f_{max} obtained from the comparison based method (Fig. 18). This reference f_{max} is derived from the point where error starts to occur in the failure rate plot.

The test time in this case is similar to the previous multiplier test case, where a test takes approximately 3 seconds to complete. This is mainly because the test time is linked to the range of frequency sweep and a relatively short frequency range was needed to obtain the results in both cases.

171

5. CONCLUSIONS

In this paper, we have shown that the proposed optimised TP test method could provide a highly accurate delay and frequency measurements in both complex combinatorial and sequential circuits. Providing accuracy within 1% of the absolute measurements from the much more time consuming and area expensive full exhaustive and direct comparison reference methods. Effects of environmental variations were minimised by placing the test circuits together and repeating the test process until temperature stabilises. The proposed technique to optimise random input test vectors in terms of high probability weights has enabled a large variety of complex circuits to benefit from the elegant TP test method with highly accurate and reliable timing results. Moreover, the test circuit is highly area efficient, where overhead is not directly proportional to the CUT's complexity but the number of input and output bits, and it is contributed mainly to input vectors generation. The TP circuitries can also be shared among different outputs or circuits to achieve further area reduction at the cost of longer test time. Otherwise, multiple TP counters could be used in parallel for very short test time.

The main limitation of the test method is that the actual response in a TP profile cannot be reliably predicted for complex circuits due to glitches and clock jitter uncertainties. That means there could be a certain degree of unpredictability in the measurement's accuracy. However, given the achieved accuracy in the test cases, such unpredictability could be easily guarded using a relatively small guard band and have minimal impact on the results optimality. Also, as future work, memory oriented designs as well as a wider variety of circuits should be tested to explored and improve the effectiveness and accuracy of the measurement method to further reinforce its general usability.

The generalised test modules and the flexibility on placement location of the TP measurement circuitries allow FPGA users to easily apply the test platform to their circuit designs for accurate and efficient physical delay measurements. Such test platform could potentially be integrated into conventional FPGA design flow, to give users an immediate knowledge of their circuit's timing performance under the actual FPGA hardware and physical conditions. Timing models in existing FPGA design tools are usually made to be highly conservative to account for process, temperature and voltage variations (PVT) as well as possible delay degradation over the FPGA's life. This often leads user to under rate their designs' operating speed and wastes a significant amount of potential performance. With the proposed test platform as a quick physical timing analysis tool, such problems could be mitigated and greatly increase the productivity of FPGAs.

6. REFERENCES

[1] Altera Corp. *Implementing High Performance DSP Functions in Stratix & Stratix GX Devices*, 2004.

[2] Altera Corp. *Understanding Metastability in FPGAs*, 2009.

[3] L. Cheng, J. Xiong, L. He, and M. Hutton. FPGA performance optimization via chipwise placement considering process variations. In *Proc. International Conference on Field Programmable Logic and Applications (FPL)*, pages 44 – 49, Aug. 2006.

[4] K. Katoh, T. Tanabe, H. Zahidul, K. Namba, and H. Ito. A delay measurement technique using signature registers. In *Proc. 18th Asian Test Symposium (ATS 2009)*, pages 157 – 162, Nov. 2009.

[5] K. Katsuki, M. Kotani, K. Kobayashi, and H. Onodera. A yield and speed enhancement scheme under within-die variations on 90nm LUT array. In *Proc. IEEE Custom Integrated Circuits Conference*, pages 601 – 604, Sept. 2005.

[6] K. Kundert. *Predicting the Phase Noise and Jitter of PLL-Based Frequency Synthesizers*. Designer's Guide Consulting Inc., 4g edition, Aug. 2006.

[7] A. Maiti and P. Schaumont. Improving the quality of a physical unclonable function using configurable ring oscillators. In *Proc. 19th International Conference on Field Programmable Logic and Applications (FPL)*, pages 703 – 707, Aug. 2009.

[8] T. Matsumoto. High-resolution on-chip propagation delay detector for measuring within-chip variation. In *International Conference on Integrated Circuit Design and Technology*, pages 217 – 220, May 2005.

[9] Y. Matsumoto, M. Hioki, T. Kawanami, T. Tsutsumi, T. Nakagawa, T. Sekigawa, and H. Koike. Performance and yield enhancement of FPGAs with within-die variation using multiple configurations. In *Proc. ACM/SIGDA International Symposium on Field Programmable Gate Arrays - FPGA*, pages 169 – 177, Feb. 2007.

[10] S. Pei, H. Li, and X. Li. A low overhead on-chip path delay measurement circuit. In *Proc. 18th Asian Test Symposium (ATS 2009)*, pages 145 – 150, Nov. 2009.

[11] A. Raychowdhury, S. Ghosh, and K. Roy. A novel on-chip delay measurement hardware for efficient speed-binning. In *Proceedings - 11th IEEE International On-Line Testing Symposium, IOLTS 2005*, pages 287 – 292, Jul. 2005.

[12] M. Ruffoni and A. Bogliolo. Direct measures of path delays on commercial FPGA chips. In *Proceedings - 6th IEEE Workshop on Signal Propagation on Interconnects, SPI*, pages 157 – 159, May 2002.

[13] P. Sedcole and P. Y. K. Cheung. Parametric yield modelling and simulations of FPGA circuits considering within-die delay variations. *ACM Transactions on Reconfigurable Technology and Systems*, 1(2), 2008.

[14] E. A. Stott, J. S. J. Wong, P. Sedcole, and P. Y. Cheung. Degradation in FPGAs: Measurement and modelling. In *Proc. ACM/SIGDA International Symposium on Field Programmable Gate Arrays - FPGA*, pages 229 – 238, Feb. 2010.

[15] L.-T. Wang, C.-W. Wu, C.-W. Wu, and X. Wen. *VLSI test principles and architectures: design for testability*. The Morgan Kaufmann series in systems on silicon. Academic Press, 2006.

[16] J. S. J. Wong, P. Sedcole, and P. Y. K. Cheung. A Transition Probability based delay measurement method for arbitrary circuits on FPGAs. In *Proc. IEEE International Conference on Field-Programmable Technology*, pages 105 – 112, Dec. 2008.

[17] J. S. J. Wong, P. Sedcole, and P. Y. K. Cheung. Self-measurement of combinatorial circuit delays in FPGAs. *ACM Transactions on Reconfigurable Technology and Systems (TRETS)*, 2(2):1 – 22, 2009.

Timing-Driven Pathfinder Pathology and Remediation: Quantifying and Reducing Delay Noise in VPR-Pathfinder

Raphael Rubin
Computer and Information Systems
University of Pennsylvania
3330 Walnut Street
Philadelphia, PA 19104
rafi@seas.upenn.edu

André DeHon
Electrical and Systems Engineering
University of Pennsylvania
200 S. 33rd Street
Philadelphia, PA 19104
andre@acm.org

ABSTRACT

We show that, with the VPR implementation of Pathfinder, perturbations of initial conditions may cause critical paths to vary over ranges of 17–110%. We further show that it is not uncommon for VPR/Pathfinder to settle for solutions that are >33% slower than necessary. These results suggest there is room for additional innovation and improvement in FPGA routing. As one step in this direction, we show how delay-targeted routing can reduce delay noise to 13% for our worst-case design and below 1% for most designs. Anyone who uses VPR as part of architecture or CAD research should be aware of this noise phenomena and the techniques available to reduce its impact.

Categories and Subject Descriptors

B.7.2 [**Integrated Circuits**]: Design Aides—*placement and routing*; B.6.1 [**Logic Design**]: Design Styles—*logic arrays*

General Terms

Algorithms, Measurement

Keywords

Timing-Driven Routing, VPR, Pathfinder, Noise, Sensivity

1. INTRODUCTION

While exploring techniques to tolerate variation [9], using VPR [1, 2], our efforts were severely hampered by results that contradicted intuition. As we added controls to check for and prevent systematic errors, it became increasingly apparent that the results were not self consistent; they were erratic and *noisy*. After seeking advice and tuning VPR, we devised a simple test to asses the stability of the delay results from the router: adding tiny variations to the resource graph several orders of magnitude smaller than the nominal delays. The result—a critical path delay spread greater than

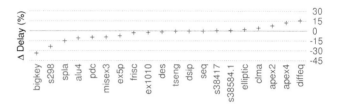

Figure 1: Percent delay improvement for faster-wire architecture over uniform architecture for the Toronto 20 benchmarks

50% of the average—was so shocking and initially unbelievable that we devised several more approaches to evaluate the sensitivity of the router. We also tried randomly breaking ties during routing and randomly shuffling the order of nets in the netlist file (this does not effect the structure, but does alter the routing order). For each of these tests, one would expect to see little or no change in the critical path delay across the samples; however, in every case not only did we get spreads in the 20–100% range, the distributions were similar to the initial approach.

We hope to raise awareness of the current state of the published and publicly available versions of the Pathfinder [6] algorithm. VPR is the defacto standard router for academic FPGA architecture and CAD research, and anyone who uses it should be aware of noise inherent in its operation as well as steps one can take to reduce the noise. We review and quantify the effects of tuning with the pressure factor multiplier to reduce delay noise (Section 4) and present a small modifications to VPR/Pathfinder to target a particular delay that can further reduce delay noise (Section 5). These results suggest that, while VPR/Pathfinder is very good, FPGA routing is not a solved problem and, deeper analysis and refinement of the Pathfinder algorithm is well warranted.

2. TRY THIS AT HOME

Our observations may be surprising. We encourage readers to see these effects for themselves. Input files, external tools (*e.g.* our netlist shuffler), scripts, and patches to VPR 4.3 [1] and 5.0.2 [7] to reproduce most of the techniques and results presented in this paper are available at: http://www.seas.upenn.edu/~icgroup/publications/pf_fpga_2011

We start with a simple example comparing two architectures. We use the architecture k4-n4.xml from the VPR 5.0.2 distribution where all wires have the same character-

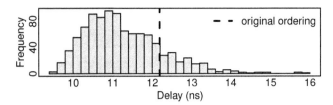

Figure 2: Distribution of Delay from VPR when routing 1000 Netlist Shuffles of alu4 at Channel Width 28

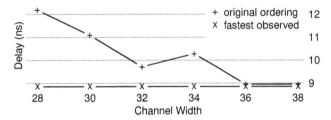

Figure 3: VPR routed and feasible delays as a function of channel width for alu4. Maximum iterations is set to 1000 to ensure success at all widths routed.

istics for the first; in the second architecture, half the wires are slightly faster such that if all bottleneck signals utilize the faster resources we scale the critical path delay by 0.995. We route each netlist on both architectures with the same placement and channel width target, determined by running VPR with defaults and the `-verify_binary_search` option, to get the results in Figure 1. This graph is surprising for two reasons: (1) the second architecture is slower than the first on one quarter of the designs, (2) while the improvement should only have a 0.5% impact on delay, we see delay changes from -34% to +15%. This magnitude of effect cannot be a result of the architectural change compared.

Next, we keep the architecture (k4-n4), placement, and channel width the same but alter the ordering of the CLBs within the input netlist file. This *netlist shuffling* transformation does not alter the structure of the problem, only the order in which VPR routes signals. Figure 2 shows the results of routing with 1000 unique permutations of alu4 along with the routed delay from the original netlist ordering. This shows that VPR/Pathfinder is highly sensitive to the order in which nets are routed, with some net orderings being 67% worse than others. The result VPR produces with the original ordering is 29% worse than the best result in this range.

A common architectural parameter to vary during experiments is the channel width. Channel width may affect delay when there are insufficient resources to allocate least delay paths for all nets, forcing some nets to take non-minimal paths to avoid congestion. Adding tracks to each channel allows more critical signals to take shorter paths, at least until the critical signals all utilize the least delay routes. However, it is not uncommon for VPR to produce graphs like Figure 3 where the delay descent is not monotonic in channel width. We define the feasible delay, $T_{feasible}$, as the smallest delay found by any of our routing attempts; this delay is known to be achievable and is an upper bound on the true minimum delay, T_{true}, for the routing task. Note that the feasible delay line is flat, suggesting that the decrease in

delay is **not** because the architecture cannot be routed at minimum delay for low channel widths, but that the router is doing an increasingly poor job of finding low delay paths.

3. IMPLICATIONS

These results suggest that the critical path delay that the VPR/Pathfinder router will find for any netlist, placement, and architecture includes a large, random component in addition to the true delay, T_{true}, the architecture supports.

$$T_{vpr\_rt}(\text{net,place,arch}) = T_{true}(\text{net,place,arch}) + Noise \quad (1)$$

We observe *Noise* that ranges from 0–67% with a median of 17% (Figure 2) compared to $T_{feasible}$, our upper bound estimate on T_{true} ($T_{feasible} \geq T_{true}$).

Graphs like Figure 1 are common ways of showing the varying effects of an architecture or CAD optimization across a benchmark set. Prior to seeing results like Figure 2, we thought these graphs were primarily capturing the fact that some netlists could benefit more from the optimization than others. It is now clear that at least part of the difference in benefits among the netlists is this random *Noise* component.

Anyone using VPR/Pathfinder in the CAD flow to analyze architectures or pre-routing CAD optimizations should be aware of this noise level. Changes that have an impact below this noise level will be difficult to quantify reliably and will demand more work than simply reporting the mean speedup on 20 benchmarks. Larger changes can be measured, but the precision of the result is limited by the noise effects.

These results suggest both a need to better understand Pathfinder behavior to be able to interpret its results and a need to continue to improve our routing techniques to reduce this noise effect.

4. PRESSURE FACTOR MULTIPLIER

Lemieux previously reported that the VPR router would produce results across a large delay range and demonstrated how tuning `pres_fac_mult` (*pfm*) can shrink that range in a trade off with runtime [5]. *pfm* controls the rate at which the Pathfinder edge cost function shifts priority to congestion minimization instead of delay minimization. The edge cost for net $i \rightarrow j$ to use node n is:

$$C(n,i,j) = \alpha_{ij} * d_n + (1 - \alpha_{ij}) * (b_n + h_{n,t}) * p_n \quad (2)$$
$$p_n = 1 + \max\left(0, (1 + occupancy - capacity)\right) pf_t$$
$$pf_t = pf_1 \times (pfm)^{t-1} \quad (3)$$
$$\alpha_{ij} = \min\left(\frac{T_{ij}}{T_{crit}}, max\_crit\right) \quad (4)$$

Where d_n is the delay of the node, b_n is a base cost for using the node, $h_{n,t}$ is the congestion history term for the node, T_{ij} is the longest unregistered path containing the 2-point net $i \rightarrow j$, pf_1 is the initial pressure factor, and *pfm* is the pressure factor multiplier. To quantify this effect, we compare the normal VPR router run with two different values *pfm* values: 1.3 (the default for VPR 5.0.2) and 1.1. For each of these cases, we routed 1000 different permutations of each of the Toronto 20 benchmarks [3]. A single placement and channel width, is used for all routing trials. The results in Table 1 confirm that reducing *pfm* does improve delay and shrink the range of values observed. However, the noise is still significant ($\geq 25\%$) and uncontrolled for most designs (14 of 20).

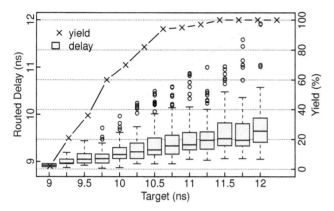

Figure 4: Routed Delay versus Specified Delay Target for 100 Netlist Shuffles of Delay-Targeted Routing of alu4 at Channel Width 28

5. DELAY TARGETED ROUTING

So [8] demonstrated that routing with a delay target and pruning paths that did not meet that target could often achieve the congestion-oblivious lower bound route—the delay achievable when all nets are allowed to take the minimum delay path ignoring congestion. So used a sophisticated scheme for slack allocation. We exploit the same basic idea of delay targets but use a simpler strategy that trivially integrates with VPR/Pathfinder and works with any target bound. Rather than allow the critical path delay in VPR to float, we target a fixed delay goal, T_{target}. This is achieved by replacing the critical delay (T_{crit}) in the VPR/Pathfinder criticality computations (Equation 4) by T_{target}, giving us:

$$\alpha_{ij} = \min\left(\frac{T_{ij}}{T_{target}}, max\_crit\right) \qquad (5)$$

VPR's imposed upper bound (max_crit) on allowed criticality prevents the criticality term from exceeding 1.0 on super critical paths. The VPR 5.0.2 default for max_crit is 0.99. We also add delay target satisfaction to the termination conditions of the main Pathfinder loop. This approach avoids the arduous task of slack budgeting and, like Pathfinder's congestion negotiation, permits potentially valuable super critical intermediate states.

Figure 4 shows that delay-targeted routing can consistently achieve the requested target, T_{target}, when the target is slighly above $T_{feasible}$. When the target is not close to the $T_{feasible}$, it will often return routes faster than requested.

We can perform a single route for a particular T_{target} in time comparable to a timing-driven VPR route at a fixed channel width, whereas So's technique takes an order of magnitude more time per target.

A single delay target does not address the delay minimization problem; for that we use the search in Algorithm 1. In the initial route, congestion is disabled, allowing each path to takes its delay minimizing path, thus computing the congestion-oblivious lower bound on delay. We determine an upper bound by exponentially increasing our target until one succeeds—the same technique used by VPR when searching for a minimum channel width. The reduction is a binary search with two modifications. Upon a successful route trial we pivot on the resulting delay instead of the input target since Figure 4 showed that the delay-target search often find

Algorithm 1: Delay Target Search

$T_{current}$=CongestionObliviousRoute
$max = min = T_{current}$ /* Initial lower bound */
repeat   /* Find initial upper bound */
  | max *= 2
until $try\_route(max)$
$stage$=0
repeat   /* Refine */
  | $retry = 0$
  | $stage$++
  | $success$=false
  | **repeat**
  | | $T_{target} = (max + min)/2$
  | | **if** $((T_{current} = try\_route(T_{target}))!=FAIL)$ **then**
  | | | T_{target}+ = $(max - T_{target})/1000$
  | | | $success$=true
  | **until** $retry$++ >= $retries$ or $success$
  | **if** $success$ **then**
  | | $max = T_{current}$
  | **else**
  | | $min = T_{target}$
until $max <= min * (1 + target\ precision)$
    or $stage >= max\_stages$

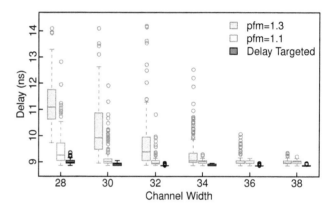

Figure 5: Spread of Routed Delays vs. Channel width for *pfm* Tuning and Delay-Targeted Routing for 200 netlist shuffles of alu4

delays well below its target. In practice this provides a significant acceleration in the reduction of the search window. Secondly: we are still limited by the heuristic nature of the router and cannot trust a negative result (Figure 5). To compensate we slightly shift the target to perturb the route and sample again from the noise distribution.

One consequence of using the delay target in Equation 5 is that T_{target} also limits criticality when T_{target} is even slightly larger than T_{true}. This allows delay-targeted routing to run with larger max_crit values that do not necessarily converge in default VPR.

To test the efficacy of this technique, we performed the same netlist shuffle delay experiment we performed for *pfm* (Section 4) for the delay-targeted router (with *pfm* = 1.1 and $max\_crit = 0.999$) and included the results in Table 1. Delay targeted-routing, though not perfect, reduces the noise to a tolerable level for all but a few designs (four designs with ranges around 10%).

175

Design	W	VPR 5.0.2 pfm = 1.3 CDF	med.	%	pfm = 1.1 med.	%	Delay Targeted med.	%
alu4	28		11.0	67	9.3	45	9.0	7.3
apex2	34		12.0	65	12.0	32	12.0	0.0
apex4	36		12.0	79	9.7	84	9.3	13.0
bigkey	20		6.0	74	5.6	58	5.6	0.9
clma	42		28.0	57	28.0	11	28.0	0.1
des	20		12.0	40	12.0	5	12.0	3.2
diffeq	22		8.0	110	7.4	59	7.4	0.0
dsip	20		7.3	30	7.3	6	7.3	0.0
elliptic	34		15.0	59	14.0	32	14.0	0.0
ex1010	36		20.0	17	20.0	3	20.0	1.9
ex5p	36		11.0	66	10.0	25	10.0	0.0
frisc	38		15.0	58	15.0	28	15.0	0.0
misex3	30		12.0	83	9.5	72	9.1	10.0
pdc	50		20.0	60	17.0	63	17.0	9.3
s298	22		19.0	88	15.0	50	14.0	4.0
s38417	30		16.0	39	16.0	2	16.0	0.0
s38584.1	28		12.0	38	12.0	2	11.0	0.0
seq	34		12.0	63	11.0	31	11.0	0.0
spla	44		16.0	61	14.0	43	14.0	2.0
tseng	20		7.5	72	7.4	39	7.3	0.9

Table 1: Comparison of Routed Delay Range for VPR *pfm* Tuning and Delay-Targeted Routing. Each result is based on 1000 netlist shuffles. W is the target channel width. The dots mark the result found by VPR (original ordering). Vertical lines in Cumulative Distribution Function (CDF) column mark the median.

Figure 5 revisits the channel width noise in Figure 3. To provide perspective, the boxplots represent the distributions for delay-targeted routing and unmodified VPR routing at each channel width. By including the distributions, we expose the non-monotonicity of the curve not as a meaningful effect, but as set of random points selected from the *Noise* distribution at each channel width. The distributions better fit our expectations, the range shrinks and shifts downward with each additional pair of tracks. The delay-targeted results are also a distribution, just one that is much tighter than the *pfm*=1.1 case. Even at 28 tracks per channel the range is just 7.3%, showing that delay-targeted routing significantly reduces the anomalies we saw in Figure 3.

We see the improvements in routing quality offered by our delay-targeted routing not as a final solution to the quality and noise problems raised but more as further demonstration of the opportunity to improve Pathfinder-based routing. Future work is needed to better characterize or guarantee quality and noise bounds and to reduce the additional runtime required to achieve high quality.

6. RELATED WORK

Yan [10] explored the sensitivity of architecture results to CAD tools. The changes that result from different pre-routing tool flows (logic mapping, placement) also present different tasks into routing, but Yan only presents a few distinct cases into routing for each benchmark and makes no attempt to differentiate the impact of *systematic* improvement from better placements or mappings from the *random* impacts of routing. In that sense, our experiments more

cleanly characterize just the sensitivity of routing to changes that should **not** change the results. Nonetheless, the highest level intent is the same—to alert users to the potential pitfalls and suggest approaches to mitigate these effects.

Our work is also related to the known optimums and lower bound work from Cong (*e.g.* [4]). We demonstrate that our most popular tools (VPR/Pathfinder) are not finding the best solutions and quantify how far from optimum they are. As with Cong's work, this highlights the need for future work in algorithms and implementations to close the gap.

Acknowledgments Benjamin Gojman helped create the tables and graphs. This research was funded in part by National Science Foundation grant CCF-0904577. Any opinions, findings, and conclusions or recommendations expressed in this material are those of the authors and do not necessarily reflect the views of the National Science Foundation.

7. REFERENCES

[1] V. Betz. VPR and T-VPack: Versatile Packing, Placement and Routing for FPGAs. <http://www.eecg.toronto.edu/~vaughn/vpr/vpr.html>, March 27 1999. Version 4.30.

[2] V. Betz and J. Rose. VPR: A new packing, placement, and routing tool for FPGA research. In W. Luk, P. Y. K. Cheung, and M. Glesner, editors, *Proceedings of the International Conference on Field-Programmable Logic and Applications*, number 1304 in LNCS, pages 213–222. Springer, August 1997.

[3] V. Betz and J. Rose. FPGA Place-and-Route Challenge. <http://www.eecg.toronto.edu/~vaughn/challenge/challenge.html>, 1999.

[4] J. Cong and K. Minkovich. Optimality study of logic synthesis for LUT-based FPGAs. *IEEE Transactions on Computer-Aided Design of Integrated Circuits and Systems*, 26(2):230–239, February 2007.

[5] G. Lemieux and D. Lewis. Using sparse crossbars within LUT clusters. In *Proceedings of the International Symposium on Field-Programmable Gate Arrays*, pages 59–68, 2001.

[6] L. McMurchie and C. Ebeling. PathFinder: A Negotiation-Based Performance-Driven Router for FPGAs. In *Proceedings of the International Symposium on Field-Programmable Gate Arrays*, pages 111–117, 1995.

[7] J. Rose et al. VPR and T-VPack: Versatile Packing, Placement and Routing for FPGAs. <http://www.eecg.utoronto.ca/vpr/>, 2008.

[8] K. So. Enforcing long-path timing closure for FPGA routing with path searches on clamped lexicographic spirals. In *Proceedings of the International Symposium on Field-Programmable Gate Arrays*, pages 24–33, 2008.

[9] J. S. J. Wong, P. Sedcole, and P. Y. K. Cheung. Self-measurement of combinatorial circuit delays in FPGAs. *Transactions on Reconfigurable Technology and Systems*, 2(2):1–22, 2009.

[10] A. Yan, R. Cheng, and S. J. E. Wilton. On the sensitivity of FPGA architectural conclusions to experimental assumptions, tools, and techniques. In *Proceedings of the International Symposium on Field-Programmable Gate Arrays*, pages 147–156, 2002.

Performance Estimation Framework for Automated Exploration of CPU-Accelerator Architectures

Tobias Kenter
Paderborn Center for Parallel Computing
University of Paderborn, Germany
kenter@upb.de

Marco Platzner
Computer Engineering Group
University of Paderborn, Germany
platzner@upb.de

Christian Plessl
Paderborn Center for Parallel Computing
University of Paderborn, Germany
christian.plessl@upb.de

Michael Kauschke
Intel Microprocessor Technology Lab
Braunschweig, Germany
michael.kauschke@intel.com

ABSTRACT

In this paper we present a fast and fully automated approach for studying the design space when interfacing reconfigurable accelerators with a CPU. Our challenge is, that a reasonable evaluation of architecture parameters requires a hardware/software partitioning that makes best use of each given architecture configuration. Therefore we developed a framework based on the LLVM infrastructure that performs this partitioning with high-level estimation of the runtime on the target architecture utilizing profiling information and code analysis. By making use of program characteristics also during the partitioning process, we improve previous results for various benchmarks and especially for growing interface latencies between CPU and accelerator.

Categories and Subject Descriptors

B.8.2 [**Performance and Reliability**]: Performance Analysis and Design Aids; I.6.m [**Simulation and Modeling**]: Miscellaneous

General Terms

Performance, Design, Algorithms

1. INTRODUCTION

Reconfigurable hardware accelerators promise to improve performance and energy efficiency over conventional CPUs for a wide range of applications. The integration of CPU and accelerator is an essential design decision since the characteristics of the chosen interface have a major impact on the granularity of functions that can be offloaded to the accelerator, on feasible execution models, and on the achievable performance or performance/power benefits. Related work has proposed numerous approaches for this interface [1], such

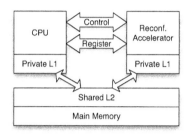

Figure 1: Architecture with shared L2 and two private L1 caches

as accelerators integrated as functional units into a CPU's data-path or attached to a CPU via the co-processor interface, the multi-processor interconnect, the memory subsystem, or an IO bus. In this work we focus on a subclass of CPU-accelerator architectures, where the accelerator is embedded into the compute system through two interfaces as illustrated in Figure 1. First a direct low latency interface to an adjacent general purpose CPU allows fine grained interaction mainly on the control level like activating a particular configuration of the accelerator, triggering its execution and synchronizing with its results. The second interface gives the accelerator access to the memory hierarchy independently from the CPU.

Performance estimation and design space exploration for this and other classes of CPU-accelerator architectures are challenging problems. Simulation is the most common approach to evaluate the architectural integration of reconfigurable accelerators before prototyping. The time-consuming design process of simulation or co-simulation often limits it to assume a specific interface and a hardware/software partitioning that is hand tailored to the characteristics of this interface. The challenge for an automated design space exploration is that the specifications of the interface affect what parts of the application can be mapped to the accelerator during hardware/software partitioning.

The contribution of this paper is a new approach for fast and fully automated performance estimation of CPU-accelerator architectures. By combining high-level analytical performance modeling, code analysis and profiling and automated hardware/software partitioning we can estimate the achievable speedup for arbitrary applications executing on a

Table 1: Data computed by the framework

Execution count of instruction I_k	$n(I_k)$
Count of control flow from B_l to B_m	$n(B_l, B_m)$
Mapping of basic block or instruction	$p(B_l), p(I_k)$
Cache level that executes a load/store	$v(I_k^j)$
Register value used or produced by B_l	$R_u(B_l), R_w(B_l)$

wide range of CPU-accelerator architectures. The intended use of our method is to quickly identify the most promising areas of the large CPU-accelerator design space for subsequent in-depth analysis and design studies. Consequently, we emphasize modeling flexibility and speed of exploration rather than a high accuracy of the estimation method. The main benefit of our method is that it needs only the application source code or LLVM binary and does not require the user to extract any application-specific performance parameters by hand.

We have introduced the basic performance estimation approach underlying this work in [3]. This preliminary work however showed limitations in the greedy block based hardware/software partitioning strategy that was susceptible to get stuck in local minimal. Here, we present an improved multi level partitioning algorithm that uses loop and function information gained with code analysis which yields significantly better results for some benchmarks and increases the overall robustness in the presence of longer communication latencies. Further, we provide a more comprehensive presentation of our method and evaluate it with a broader range of benchmarks. Among known high level estimation methods, the approach of Spacey et al. [5] is most closely related to our work. There are, however, three differences. First, in contrast to the estimation method of Spacey et al. which models the memory subsystem with a single bandwidth parameter, our framework includes cache models and thus more realistically mimics relevant architectures. Second, their partitioning approach is limited to the block level while we show our new multi level partitioning technique to be clearly inferior. Finally, whereas the system of Spacey et al. is x86 assembly based and can therefore be applied to x86 binary code, our framework leverages the LLVM infrastructure [4] which will allow us to extend the framework towards automated code generation for various targets.

2. ESTIMATION METHOD

In this section, we present the basic terms and definitions of our model and how they are combined into the total runtime estimation. We furthermore describe how the analysis framework gathers data of the execution characteristics of a program as shown in Table 1. The architecture parameters of our model are also introduced here. They are summarized along with their default values in Table 2.

Our estimation framework is based on the LLVM compiler infrastructure [4]. The investigated software is compiled into LLVM assembly language, which is the intermediate code representation on which LLVM's analysis and optimization passes work. We model a program as a set of instructions $I = \{I_1, I_2, \ldots, I_{\texttt{nins}}\}$, and classify the instructions into memory dependent operations (e.g., load/store) and independent operations: $I_k \in \{\texttt{ld/st}, \texttt{op}\}$. The program structure groups the instructions into a set of basic blocks $B = \{B_1, B_2, \ldots, B_{\texttt{nblks}}\}$. The basic blocks form a

control flow graph where an edge $B_l \rightarrow B_m$ denotes that block B_m might be executed directly after block B_l. The instructions of B_l use a set of register values $R_u(B_l)$ and produce a set of register values $R_w(B_l)$.

The architecture comprises two processing units, the CPU and the accelerator (ACC), and a memory hierarchy consisting of L1, L2 and optional L3 caches, and main memory (MEM). The caches can be private for each core like the L1 cache in Figure 1 or shared between both units like the L2 cache in the same figure. We model the execution efficiencies $\epsilon(\texttt{CPU})$ and $\epsilon(\texttt{ACC})$ of the cores through the average number of clock cycles spent per instruction. The efficiency reflects on the one hand raw execution times of instructions and on the other hand parallel execution units and pipelining effects, which increase the throughput. The efficiencies can vary for different instruction classes, but lacking more accurate data for both cores, in this work we use identical efficiency for all instructions except for two instruction classes. First, we assume that LLVM typecast instructions are implemented on the accelerator through wiring and thus are executed in zero execution time. Second, load/store instructions are also considered in a different way, because their execution time depends on the level in the memory hierarchy that they access. We describe the corresponding access latencies with $\lambda_m(\texttt{L1})$, $\lambda_m(\texttt{L2})$ and $\lambda_m(\texttt{MEM})$, expressed in clock cycles. When a core requires data resident in the private cache of the other core we include a latency penalty for writing back the data to the shared cache.

For communication between the CPU and the accelerator, we define λ_c as latency for transferring control between the cores. This control latency also covers the efficiency losses that may occur, when the pipelining of instructions is reduced by control changes. Furthermore, we denote λ_r as latency for transferring a register value. Refining the register value transfer model, we foresee a push method with a low latency of $\lambda_{r,\texttt{push}}$ for actively sending a register value from one location to the other and a somewhat slower pull method with latency $\lambda_{r,\texttt{pull}}$ for requesting a register value from the other location and receiving it. Since the analysis of register dependencies is based on the code in LLVM intermediate representation, no register allocation has taken place, so all values are treated as available in an infinite register file after their first occurrence.

The partitioning process maps each basic block to either the CPU or the accelerator. We denote the mapping of block B_l as $p(B_l)$ with the two possible values $p(B_l) = \texttt{CPU}$ or $p(B_l) = \texttt{ACC}$. Obviously, the partitioning of basic blocks also implies a partitioning $p(I_k)$ of instructions I_k into $p(I_k) = \texttt{CPU}$ or $p(I_k) = \texttt{ACC}$, since $\forall k, l : I_k \in B_l \rightarrow p(I_k) = p(B_l)$. At this time we do not assume a concurrent execution on both CPU and accelerator, so the execution order of the program remains unchanged regardless of the mapping. Our model limits the total number of instructions mapped to the accelerator and accounts for a unit area for each such instruction. The use of an averaged area value is most reasonable when the internal architecture of the accelerator is a coarse grained array of homogenous functional units.

Using the LLVM infrastructure to profile program executions, we determine the execution count for an instruction I_k as $n(I_k)$, for a basic block B_l as $n(B_l)$, and the number of control flows over an edge $B_l \rightarrow B_m$ of the control flow graph as $n(B_l, B_m)$. Furthermore, we denote the jth execution of instruction I_k as I_k^j and use this separation to determine the level accessed in the memory hierarchy for each load/store instruction as $v(I_k^j)$, with the possible values L1, L2 and MEM. To determine these values $v(I_k^j)$, we add a memory profiling pass to LLVM and perform a simulation of an inclusive, direct mapped cache hierarchy. These characteristics of the cache enables us, together with a data dependency analysis, to compute the memory access time for each partitioning step without a repeated cache simulation, which would otherwise slowdown the partitioning process significantly. At this point we also profit from the missing register allocation in that no register spills occur, which would change the memory access patterns for different mappings.

We estimate the total program runtime as the sum of four components: the **execution time** t_e of instructions with only register operands, the **memory access time** t_m for load and store instructions, the **control transfer time** t_c for switching control between successive basic blocks mapped to different cores, and the time **register value transfer time** t_r:

$$t = t_e + t_m + t_c + t_r$$

$$t_e = \sum_{k:I_k=\text{op}} n(I_k) \cdot \epsilon(p(I_k))$$

$$t_m = \sum_{k:I_k=\text{ld/st}} \sum_{j=1}^{n(I_k)} \lambda_m(v(I_k^j))$$

$$t_c = \sum_{(l,m)} n(B_l, B_m) \cdot \lambda_c$$

$$\forall (l,m): (B_l \to B_m) \land p(B_l) \neq p(B_m)$$

$$t_r = \sum_R \min\left(n(B_l) \cdot \lambda_{r,\text{push}}, n(B_m) \cdot \lambda_{r,\text{pull}}\right)$$

$$\forall R: R \in R_w(B_l) \land R \in R_u(B_m) \land p(B_l) \neq p(B_m)$$

3. PARTITIONING APPROACH

We utilize a greedy partitioning algorithm that starts with all blocks at the CPU and iteratively moves partitioning objects *po* to the accelerator, as long as the cumulative area of all moved blocks fits the size of the accelerator. An overview of the partitioner is given in Algorithm 1. At each step, the partitioning object with the highest attractiveness, which is the ratio of estimated speedup to area requirements, is chosen in the function *getBestPartitionObject*. We compare two versions of the partitioning approach, which differ by the definition of their partitioning objects. For the basic block level partitioning, we utilize all single basic blocks as partitioning objects. For the improved multi level partitioning, we use not only all single basic blocks as partitioning objects but additionally all loops (inner as well as nested loops) and all functions. Furthermore, whenever the partitioner moves part of a loop or function to the accelerator, the remaining basic blocks of the loop or function form another new partitioning object. This definition of partitioning objects is a heuristic covering the most promising objects of the total space of potential partitioning objects which grows exponentially with the number of basic blocks.

By this extension of the simple block level partitioning method which we have used in our earlier work, we were able to achieve significantly better results in cases when moving a single basic block lead to a local maximum in the cost function preventing detection of a minimum only reachable

Input: Resources of Accelerator, All BasicBlocks mapped to CPU
Output: Partitioned BasicBlocks
Next ← getBestPartitionObject(Resources);
while *Next ≠ null* **do**
  moveToAccelerator(Next);
  Resources ← Resources - computeArea(Next);
  Next ← getBestPartitionObject(Resources);
end
Algorithm 1: Algorithm of our Partitioning Approach

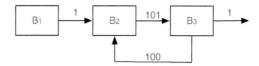

Figure 2: Example of a control flow graph where the basic blocks forming a loop might not be moved to the accelerator with block level partitioning (edges labeled with execution frequency)

by moving a collection of basic blocks like those representing a loop. Figure 2 illustrates an example where this may occur. Let's assume that every single execution of each individual basic block B_1 to B_3 can save one clock cycle when it is executed on the accelerator instead of the CPU. Let furthermore each control flow between two blocks that are assigned to different processing units lead to a communication overhead of also one clock cycle. Now neither B_2 nor B_3 will provide a speedup when individually moved to the accelerator, which is what will be tried by the block level partitioning method. Since the two basic blocks B_1 and B_2 form a loop the new multi level partitioning will also attempt to move both loop blocks at once to the accelerator, which yields a speedup in the example.

4. RESULTS

We evaluate our performance estimation framework with 13 benchmarks, most taken from the MiBench suite [2] and selected to represent a wide range of application classes. The architecture parameters for the tests are summarized in Table 2. They allow a speedup of up to factor 2 in execution times, but offers at best identical memory access times compared to a CPU only solution.

In Figure 3, we give an overview of the expected speedups for each individual benchmark with both partitioning approaches. It comes as no surprise, that speedup potential varies a lot depending on the application characteristics. According to the multi level partitioning results, it ranges

Table 2: Default model parameters

Execution efficiencies		Cache sizes	
ϵ(CPU)	1.0 cycles	L1	32KB
ϵ(ACC)	0.5 cycles	L2	4MB
Communication latencies		Cache latencies	
λ_c	2 cycles	λ(L1)	3 cycles
$\lambda_{r,push}$	1 cycles	λ(L2)	15 cycles
$\lambda_{r,pull}$	3 cycles	λ(MEM)	200 cycles
Accelerator size: 2048 units			

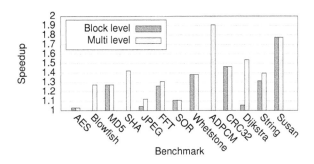

Figure 3: Speedups for 13 benchmarks at accelerator size 2048 for both partitioning approaches

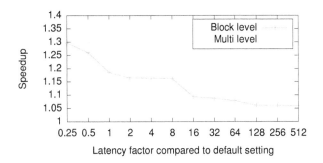

Figure 4: Speedups for different interface latencies, averaged over 13 benchmarks, with block level and multi level partitioning

from 1.03 to 1.91, with the median at 1.38. When studying the effect of multi level partitioning compared to our previously utilized block level partitioning, the new approach performs consistently better or identical to the older one. The differences of individual results reflect to which degree the benchmarks contain loops that are responsible for a large percentage of the total execution time and have large communication requirements if split between CPU and accelerator. For example we observe that for ADPCM with default parameters, a loop with seven basic blocks is moved to the accelerator as first partitioning object.

Most remarkable are the effects of multi level partitioning when regarding the robustness for growing interface latencies in Figure 4. With a hypothetical minimal latency, the block level partitioning performs actually better, because here the multi level partitioning gets stuck in a local optimum for the FFT benchmark, whereas all other benchmarks show almost identical results between both approaches. But then the block level partitioning rapidly looses lots of performance, whereas the multi level partitioning can retain around 85% of its maximum speedups. This observation underlines that longer interface latencies increase the need to place basic blocks with relevant communication requirements together at one component, for which the multi level partitioning method is better suited.

Similarly to changing the interface latencies, we can vary the other specified architecture parameters individually or in groups and also investigate different configurations for the architectural integration of the accelerator into the memory hierarchy, enabling design space exploration. Due to space limitations we can not present details here, for early results

with the block level partitioning algorithm refer to [3]. A central result of the former work has been confirmed with the new partitioning algorithm and the 13 benchmarks presented here. It indicates, that a sharing a L1 cache between CPU and accelerator is the best way to integrate the two cores, if there is no penalty for the increased complexity of a shared cache over a private one. However, once we assume an increased latency of only 1 cycle in order to reflect this increased complexity, the picture changes. Under this premise, a shared L2 cache with private L1 caches for both CPU and accelerator turns out as the best memory hierarchy after a penalty for the shared cache is applied.

5. CONCLUSION AND FUTURE WORK

This paper presents our estimation and hardware/software partitioning framework, which yields significantly better partitioning results than our previous work. The capability of our framework to provide fully automated estimation and partitioning results can be used for a systematic design space exploration that was previously hard to undertake for new architectures.

For assessing the absolute quality of the partitioning results found with our multi level partitioning, we plan to compare them to optimal results that we hope to obtain by formulating the design space exploration as an integer linear programming problem which can be solved exactly with appropriate solvers. We also intend to cover the register allocation and to refine the latency based communication and memory latency models, and to evaluate the refined models by applying them to existing CPU-accelerator architectures.

Acknowledgment

This work is supported by Intel Corporation through a grant for the project "A multimode reconfigurable processing unit (MM-RPU)".

6. REFERENCES

[1] K. Compton and S. Hauck. Reconfigurable computing: A survey of systems and software. *ACM Computing Surveys*, 34(2):171–210, June 2002.

[2] M. R. Guthaus, J. S. Ringenberg, D. Ernst, T. M. Austin, T. Mudge, and R. B. Brown. Mibench: A free, commercially representative embedded benchmark suite. In *WWC '01: Proceedings of the Workload Characterization, 2001. WWC-4. 2001 IEEE International Workshop*, pages 3–14, Washington, DC, USA, 2001. IEEE Computer Society.

[3] T. Kenter, M. Platzner, C. Plessl, and M. Kauschke. Performance estimation for the exploration of CPU-accelerator architectures. In O. Hammami and S. Larrabee, editors, *Proc. Workshop on Architectural Research Prototyping (WARP)*, June 2010.

[4] C. Lattner and V. Adve. LLVM: A compilation framework for lifelong program analysis & transformation. In *Proc. Int. Symp. on Code Generation and Optimization (CGO)*, pages 75–86. IEEE Computer Society, Mar 2004.

[5] S. A. Spacey, W. Luk, P. H. J. Kelly, and D. Kuhn. Rapid design space visualization through hardware/software partitioning. In *Proc. Southern Programmable Logic Conference (SPL)*, pages 159–164. IEEE, Apr. 2009.

An Analytical Model Relating FPGA Architecture Parameters to Routability

Joydip Das, Steven J. E. Wilton
University of British Columbia
Vancouver, BC, Canada
{dasj, stevew}@ece.ubc.ca

ABSTRACT

We present an analytical model relating FPGA architectural parameters to the routability of the FPGA. The inputs to the model include the channel width and connection and switch block flexibilities, and the output is an estimate of the proportion of nets in a large circuit that can be expected to be routed on the FPGA. We assume that the circuit is routed to the FPGA using a single-step combined global/detailed router. Together with the earlier works on analytical modeling, our model can be used to predict the routability without going through an expensive CAD flow. We show that the model correctly predicts routability trends.

Categories and Subject Descriptors

B.7.1 [**Types and Design Styles**]: Gate arrays

General Terms

Design, Peformance, Measurement

Keywords

FPGA, Analytical Model, Architecture Development, Routability

1. INTRODUCTION

FPGA vendors invest significant resources in developing new logic, routing and embedded block architectures, and this activity shows no signs of diminishing. Traditionally, FPGA architectures have been designed and tuned using an experimental approach, in which designers perform numerous iterations of experiments, where benchmark circuits are mapped using representative computer-aided design (CAD) tools, and the effectiveness of potential architectures are validated using detailed area, power, and delay models [1, 2, 13]. Recent works have shown that this experimental approach can be supplemented by *analytical models* which relate the effectiveness of an FPGA to parameters describing the architecture of the FPGA [6, 7, 9, 10, 19, 18]. These models may accelerate the FPGA development process, allowing vendors to explore a much wider range of architectures, potentially leading to better devices. The models also provide important insight into what makes

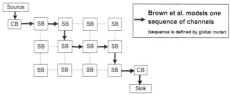

a) Work of [3]: Routing of a net with length=6 for a detailed router

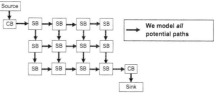

b) Our work: Routing of the same net for a single-stage combined router

Figure 1: The work of Brown et al. [3] and our work

a good FPGA, and it has been suggested that they will be an important design tool for the rapid development of application-specific FPGAs [20].

A key part of any FPGA is the routing fabric. As new embedded blocks are added to an existing device, or as new logic blocks are designed, it is critical to ensure that the routing fabric provides sufficient routability and speed. Ensuring this can be helped by an analytical model that relates the overall routability of an FPGA to the architecture of that FPGA. Such a model would provide a fast way of estimating the routability impact of proposed architectural changes, allowing FPGA architects to focus only on potential architectures that are likely to be successful in routing the circuits.

Several techniques have been proposed to investigate the routability for FPGAs, such as, fGREP [11], RISA [4], Lou's method [12] and Rent's Rule Derivatives [17]. These works, however, do not relate routability directly to FPGA architecture parameters.

A model to predict the routability as a function of architecture parameters was described by Brown et al. [3]. However, that model makes the assumption that nets are routed using a two-stage *global/detailed* router, as shown in Figure 1(a). With such a router, the set of channels that will be used by each net are determined using a global router, which does not consider the detailed routing architecture parameters. The detailed router then only considers routes that follow this sequence of channels. For example, in Figure 1(a), there are many potential paths connecting the source and the sink logic blocks. However, only *a single* set of channels will be selected by the global router and the detailed router will consider paths within these pre-selected channels. In Figure 1(a), the work of [3] models the routability using only one such sequence of channels, such as the channels on the 'dark-solid' path, and will ignore the other potential channels, such as the 'light-dotted' paths.

In contrast, modern FPGA CAD suites usually employ a single-step *combined* global/detailed router [2]. Such a router considers all possible paths for each net, while simultaneously respecting the constraints imposed by the detailed routing architecture. Thus, we would expect that the routability predicted by the model in [3] may be quite different than that experienced by the modern routers. We present results that show that this is indeed the case. Our results further show that, for a combined router, the model of [3] can not properly capture the trend of the changes in routability values with respect to the changes in routing architecture.

We present a routability model that better captures the behavior of a modern FPGA combined router. Our model considers all potential paths between the source and the sink nodes, as shown by the 'dark-solid' lines in Figure 1(b). The model contains a set of simple closed-form expressions that relate the FPGA architectural parameters to routability. More specifically, the output of our model is an estimate of the routability of the routing fabric, in terms of *the expected proportion of the nets in a large circuit that can be successfully routed*. The inputs to our model are the FPGA architectural parameters: channel width W; connection block flexibilities $F_{c_{in}}$ and $F_{c_{out}}$; and switch box flexibility F_s. The input parameters also include a small number of circuit parameters (minimum grid-size to implement a circuit N_{xy}, total number of nets $|\Psi|$, post-placement average wirelength l_{avg} and post-placement maximum wirelength l_{max}). The circuit dependent input parameters can be obtained from the earlier works on analytical modeling [6, 14, 19]. Combined with these earlier works, our model can predict routability without going through the expensive stages of a CAD flow.

We observe that our problem is related to the problem of estimating the reliability of a stochastic network with given network constraints. Numerous publications have attempted to determine the reliability of a connection between the source terminal and the sink terminal of such stochastic networks [5, 8, 16, 15]. Out of these works, Shanthikumar uses the consecutive minimal cutsets of a stochastic network for bounding the reliability of systems [15, 16]. We apply the techniques from Shanthikumar to our problem.

We show that our model can successfully predict the routability for a combined router. We also show that our model performs better than the previous model [3] when a combined router is used. We further demonstrate that our model can correctly predict the routability trends with respect to the changes in the routing architecture. The latter suggests that our model will be a valuable tool for FPGA architects in the early stage architecture evaluation.

The rest of the paper is organized as follows. Section 2 presents the model formulation. Section 3 validates our model and explains the results. Finally, conclusions are presented in Section 4.

2. MODEL FORMULATION

In our derivation, we make two important simplifications. First, we assume that each net has only one sink. As we will later show, even with this simplification, we get acceptable results. The second simplification is that all nets are routed using their shortest path.

The formulation of our model consists of three stages, as briefly described below. Due to space, we do not present the equations that we derive in each stage, however an implementation of the model can be downloaded from *http://www.ece.ubc.ca/~dasj*.

2.1 Stage I: Formation of the Graph

Stage I of the model formulation consists of two phases. First, we assume the use of a combined router and construct a graph

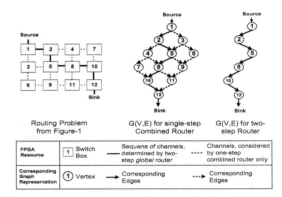

Figure 2: Graph G(V,E) for the routing problem in Figure 1

$G(V, E)$ to represent the possible routing paths *for a single net with a given length*. Each vertex V represents a switch box (SB) or a connection box (CB) along the path of this net. A directed edge E represents a channel connecting two vertexes.

For the example routing problem of Figure 1, Figure 2 shows the graph $G(V, E)$. We omit the CB nodes for clarity. For completeness, we also show the graph $G(V, E)$ that would be obtained if a two-step detailed router was employed.

After forming the graph $G(V, E)$, we assign weights to the edges of $G(V, E)$. The weight of an edge (channel) corresponds to the routability of the net across this channel, as a function of FPGA architectural parameters. This weight depends on the distance of the channel from the source node (CB) along the path of the corresponding net. Brown et al. [3] models the probability of successful routing across the SBs along the path of a net with given length. We use this model to assign weight to a channel. We make necessary modifications to the equations of [3] to make them more suitable for the later stages of our model.

Without loss of generality, as shown in Figure 2, we assume that all connections enter a SB from left or top, and exit the SB from right or bottom. In our model, we divide the SBs into two types. All SBs on the top and the left side of the grid will be referred as *Type 1* SBs, and the other SBs will be referred to as *Type 2* SBs. Type 1 SBs have the property that if they are used in the path of the net, the net will only enter this SB from one side. On the other hand, the Type 2 SBs have the property that the net may enter from one of *two* sides. Our weight assignment differentiates between these two types. In Figure 2, example nodes for Type 1 SBs are 1, 2, 3; and example nodes for Type 2 SBs are 5, 8 and 9.

We make an important approximation in assigning weights to the *Type 2* SBs. We assume that if a tracks are incident from either side, they will combinedly attempt to connect to $max(2a, W)$ number of tracks on the outgoing side. In other words, two sets of incident tracks will connect to separate sets of outgoing tracks. This may not be the case since some incident tracks from the horizontal and the vertical directions may be connected to the same outgoing track of the SB. Thus, our model may provide optimistic values for routability. The other approximation that we make is that the conditional events of success for the channels incident to a SB are independent. The relaxation of these approximations may be an interesting topic for future research.

The output of stage I is the graph $G(V, E)$ that captures all possible paths for a net in a combined router; and the weigths associated with the edges. Our work can be extended to remove the shortest path constraints. Compared to the $G(V, E)$ for shortest-path routing, the extended graph will have more vertices and edges.

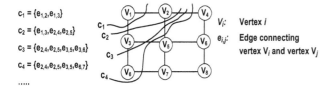

$c_1 = \{e_{1,2}, e_{1,3}\}$

$c_2 = \{e_{1,3}, e_{2,4}, e_{2,5}\}$

$c_3 = \{e_{2,4}, e_{2,5}, e_{3,5}, e_{3,6}\}$

$c_4 = \{e_{2,4}, e_{2,5}, e_{3,5}, e_{6,7}\}$

.....

V_i: Vertex i

$e_{i,j}$:   Edge connecting vertex V_i and vertex V_j

Figure 3: Examples of consecutive cutsets

2.2 Stage II: Overall Routability of a Net

The next step is to use the graph $G(V, E)$ from Stage I to estimate the overall routability of one net in the circuit with a given length. In doing so, we model the routability of the net on a *two-dimensional* grid. We are interested in computing the probability that *at least one* potential path is available to route the net.

We use methods from network reliability theory. Several studies in the reliability domain consider methods to bound (upper and/or lower) the reliability of a multipath network. These studies perform this task by finding the probability of having at least one successful path between the source terminal and the sink terminal, given the failure rate of each link [5, 8, 15]. Our problem is similar, we consider a "failed link" along a potential routing path to consist of at least one channel that is too congested to route the net.

We use the technique proposed by Shanthikumar [16, 15] to bound the routability of a net with given length. Shantikumar uses the consecutive cutsets to *upper*-bound the reliability of a network. To use this technique, we first determine the ordered set of r number of consecutive minimal cutsets C, where $C \equiv c_1, c_2, \cdots, c_r$. In Figure 3, we present example consecutive cutsets for a graph. A net is unroutable only when all the edges (FPGA channels) on at least one consecutive minimal cutset fail. For example, the net in Figure 3 will be unroutable if each of the edges of the cutset c_2 (such as, $e_{1,3}$, $e_{2,4}$ and $e_{2,5}$) fails.

We use the edge-weights from Stage I to model the probability of such failure events. This consequently gives us the probability of successful routing of a single net with given wirelength, while considering all possible routing paths between the source terminal and the sink terminal. For the $\Psi_i{}^{th}$ net with length l, we denote this probability as $Pr[R_{\Psi_i|l}]$. Due to space, we omit the detailed analysis and the mathematical expressions related to this stage.

2.3 Stage III: Routability of a Net with Any Probable Length

We next model the routability of a single net that may assume any length within the range $(1, l_{max})$ with l_{max} being the maximum wirelength. Assuming the geometric wirelength distribution [3], we express the routability of a net Ψ_i by:

$$Pr[R_{\Psi_i}] = \sum_{l=0}^{l_{max}} Pr[\Psi_i|l] \cdot Pr[R_{\Psi_i|l}] \qquad (1)$$

where, $Pr[\Psi_i|l] = p_\Psi \cdot q_\Psi^{l-1}$, with $p_\Psi = 1/l_{avg}$ and $q_\Psi = 1 - p_\Psi$. l_{avg} is the average wirelength of two-terminal nets for the circuit being modeled. We can substitue $Pr[R_{\Psi_i|l}]$ from Stage II to determine the routability of a net, that does not have any length constraint.

We find that, due to the geometric nature of the wirelength distribution, the probability term $Pr[\Psi_i|l]$ in Equation 1 diminishes with the increasing value of length l. In other words, ignoring the higher values of l in Equation 1 will only weakly affect the overall routability of the net. This observation allows designers to use a lower value of l_{max} to speed up the estimation process.

Finally, the routability of a circuit with total $|\Psi|$ number of two-

terminal nets (Ψ_i's) can be expressed by the following equation:

$$Pr[R_{ckt|comb}] = \frac{1}{|\Psi|} \cdot \sum_{i=1}^{|\Psi|} Pr[R_{\Psi_i}] \qquad (2)$$

3. MODEL VALIDATION

In this section, we compare our model predictions with experimental results, obtained using VPR [2]. We also compare our predictions with the predictions from the model by Brown et al. [3]. We investigate the effects of varying routing architecture parameters, such as W, $F_{c_{in}}$, $F_{c_{out}}$ and F_s.

3.1 Methodology for collecting model results

To model the routability of a circuit, our equations require the grid-size needed to implement the circuit N_{xy}, the average post-placement wirelength l_{avg}, and the maximum post-placement wirelength l_{max}. These parameters are modeled using earlier works. N_{xy} can be approximated as $\sqrt{n_c}$, where the number of clusters n_c is obtained from the model in [6]. Similarly, l_{avg} and l_{max} can be modeled respectively from the works in [19] and [14]. We use these input parameters in our model and find the routability values by sweeping the routing architecture parameters. To obtain the results for the earlier model [3], we directly use their equations.

3.2 Methodology for collecting VPR results

We first attempt to route a circuit in VPR using 50 iterations [2]. We approximate the minimum-path constraint by setting the *bb* flag to 0. If after 50 iterations, some nets can not be routed, we break down the multi-terminal nets into two-terminal nets. We then iterate through these two-terminal nets to investigate the resources that they use. For a net, if the capacity of any used resource is lower than the occupancy of the same resource, we mark the corresponding net as unroutable. For all resources that this net uses, we decrement the occupancy values by one. After iterating through all two-terminal nets, we calculate the percentage of the nets that are routable for the corresponding set of architectural parameters.

3.3 Validation Results

Figure 4 presents the results. As we can see from the Figure 4, our model is more accurate than the earlier model of [3] in most cases, especially for the highly constrained architectures. We also find that the earlier model can not properly capture the trend of the experimental results with respect to the changes in routing architecture. Thus, when a combined router is used, the designers can not use this model to investigate the effects of routing architecture parameters on routability. These observations justify the extension that we present in this paper for a combined router.

We find that our model predictions follow the routability trends with respect to the architectural parameters quite closely. We believe that this characteristic makes our model a valuable tool in modeling routability in the early stage architecture evaluation.

From Figure 4, it is clear that our model overestimates the experimental results, especially for the resource constrained architectures. From our earlier discussion, we identify three reasons for such over-estimation. First, since we use the upper bounds of the routing graph $G(V, E)$ to estimate the routability, the model is expected to over-estimate the experimental results. Secondly, we assume that the switch box construction is such that two sets of incident tracks will connect to the separate sets of tracks on the outgoing side of the switch block. Finally, the methodology that we follow in collecting experimental results contributes to the over-estimation of the model results.

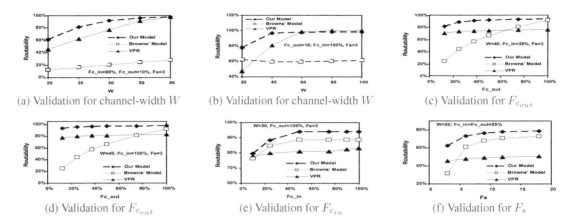

(a) Validation for channel-width W (b) Validation for channel-width W (c) Validation for $F_{c_{out}}$

(d) Validation for $F_{c_{out}}$ (e) Validation for $F_{c_{in}}$ (f) Validation for F_s

Figure 4: Validation for 10 MCNC benchmark circuits (geometric average)

4. CONCLUSIONS

In this paper, we have presented an analytical model relating FPGA architectural parameters to the routability of an FPGA. We assume that the circuit is routed on an FPGA using a single-step combined global/detailed router. Through comparisons to VPR, we have shown that the model correctly predicts routability trends.

We envisage that this model will be useful during early stage architecture investigation, when architectures are being evaluated without the luxury of having a complete experimental CAD flow. We believe that in combination with previously published models [7, 14, 19], our model can provide useful insight into routability during these early stages of architecture investigation, allowing FPGA architects to quickly rule out "bad" architectures, and identify "interesting" architectures for more detailed evaluation.

There are a number of limitations to our model. First, we consider two-terminal nets for modeling routability. Second, we approximate a switch box construction in which we assumed that incoming tracks from different directions can connect to separate set of outgoing tracks. We also assumed that the events describing the number of available tracks to each channel incident to a switch block are statistically independent. Future work should address each of these limitations, and evaluate how much of an impact they have on the overall accuracy of the model. Follow up work may also target the improvement of CAD tools utilizing the routability information, obtained from this work. An executable version of our model can be downloaded from *http://www.ece.ubc.ca/~dasj.*

5. ACKNOWLEDGMENTS

This work has been funded by Altera Corporation and NSERC of Canada.

6. REFERENCES

[1] J. H. Anderson and F. N. Najm. Power estimation techniques for FPGAs. *VLSI, IEEE Trans. on*, 12(10):1015–1027, 2004.

[2] V. Betz, J. Rose, and A. Marquardt. *Architecture and CAD for Deep-submicron FPGAs*. Kluwer Academic Publishers, 1999.

[3] S. D. Brown, J. Rose, and Z. Vranesic. A stochastic model to predict the routability of field-programmable gate arrays. *CAD of Circuits and Systems, IEEE Trans. on*, 12(12):1827–1838, Dec. 1993.

[4] C. E. Cheng. RISA: Accurate and efficient placement routability modeling. In *ICCAD '94*.

[5] C. J. Colbourn. Combinatorial aspects of network reliability. *Annals of Operations Research*, 33(1):1 – 15, January 1991.

[6] J. Das, A. Lam, S. Wilton, P. Leong, and W. Luk. An analytical model relating FPGA architecture to logic density and depth. *Very Large Scale Integration (VLSI) Systems, IEEE Trans. on*, accepted/to appear.

[7] J. Das, S. J. E. Wilton, P. Leong, and W. Luk. Modeling post-techmapping and post-clustering FPGA circuit depth. In *FPL '09*.

[8] E. Elmallah and H. AboElFotoh. Circular layout cutsets: An approach for improving consecutive cutset bounds for network reliability. *Reliability, IEEE Trans. on*, Dec. 2006.

[9] W. M. Fang and J. Rose. Modeling routing demand for early-stage FPGA architecture development. In *FPGA '08*.

[10] E. Hung, S. J. E. Wilton, H. Yu, T. C. P. Chau, and P. H. W. Leong. An analytical FPGA delay path model. In *FPT '09*.

[11] P. Kannan, S. Balachandran, and D. Bhatia. fGREP - fast generic routing demand estimation for placed FPGA circuits. In *FPL '01*.

[12] J. Lou, S. Krishnamoorthy, and H. S. Sheng. Estimating routing congestion using probabilistic analysis. In *ISPD '01*.

[13] K. K. W. Poon, S. J. E. Wilton, and A. Yan. A detailed power model for field-programmable gate arrays. *Design Automation of Electronic Systems, ACM Trans. on*, 10(2):279–302, 2005.

[14] A. Rahman, A. Fan, and R. Reif. Wire-length distribution of three-dimensional integrated circuit. In *SLIP '99*.

[15] J. Shanthikumar. Bounding network-reliability using consecutive minimal cutsets. *Reliability, IEEE Trans.*, 37(1):45–49, Apr 1988.

[16] J. G. Shanthikumar. Reliability of systems with consecutive minimal cutsets. *Reliability, IEEE Trans.*, Dec. 1987.

[17] A. Singh, G. Parthasarathy, and M. Marek-Sadowska. Interconnect resource-aware placement for hierarchical FPGAs. In *ICCAD '01*.

[18] A. M. Smith, G. A. Constantinides, S. J. E. Wilton, and P. Y. K. Cheung. Concurrently optimizing FPGA architecture parameters and transistor sizing: Implications for FPGA design. In *FPT '09*.

[19] A. M. Smith, J. Das, and S. J. Wilton. Wirelength modeling for homogeneous and heterogeneous FPGA architectural development. In *FPGA '09*.

[20] S. Wilton. Keynote talk: Towards Analytical Methods for FPGA Architectural Investigation. In *ARC 2010*, Mar. 2010.

The RLOC is Dead – Long Live the RLOC

Satnam Singh

Microsoft Research, Cambridge, UK

satnams@microsoft.com

ABSTRACT

Are user specified layout constraints of significant value anymore? Certainly in the past the use of the RLOC layout constraint for Xilinx FPGAs was essential for achieving the best possible performance for many kinds of highly structured designs. However, have CAD tools evolved to the point where they can always compute layouts as good as (if not better than) humans? Or has the introduction of on-chip hard cores, which create an irregular 2D surface for layouts, made layout specification impractical? Or has the varying pitch and types of combinational logic blocks (CLBs) made it intractable to produce layout descriptions that are portable across architectures? We show that the use of layout constraints still delivers a large performance gain for Xilinx's recent Virtex-6 family of FPGAs. The performance gain is sometime large enough to accommodate a reduction of two speed grades.

Categories and Subject Descriptors

C.0. [Computer Systems Organization]: Types and Design Style - General

General Terms Design, Performance

Keywords circuit layout

1. INTRODUCTION

Does a good place lead to a good route? Is user specified circuit layout still of value for improving the performance or layout footprint of FPGA circuits? There are several reasons to doubt that layout specification is relevant to Xilinx's more recent FPGA architectures. Questions we should consider include:

- Have fundamental changes in more recent FPGA architectures rendered user specified layout information of little or infrequent value?

- Have FPGA CAD tools evolved to a level of sophisticated that rarely requires user specified layout information [1] ?

The Xilinx vendor implementation tools have supported the specification of 'relative placement macros' (RPMs) for many years. The relative placement of one component (e.g. LUT) can be specified relative to another component. The absolute placement on the FPGA is then still determined by the place and route tools.

The RPMs act like a "stencil" which ensures that the relative layout relationships between components are maintained. It is also possible to specify the absolute location of a component on the FPGA although we do not use this capability for the experiments in this paper.

The two types of circuits we use as experimental subjects are very representative of a wide class of structured designs. The adder tree example captures a map-reduce [13][10] style pattern which is commonly used for the pipelined parallel composition of repeated operations applied in parallel. The butterfly-style sorting network is representative of designs which have a non-trivial recursive structure in which it is beneficial to have intra-column only wiring for maximum performance and such circuits are of value in FPGA accelerated database style operations [7][8] and applications like the frequent item problem [12].

This paper presents an updated version of a previously published description of how circuit components can be laid out on FPGAs without resorting to complicated expressions involving Cartesian coordinates [11]. This paper also presents experimental evidence drawn from a high structured circuit with a parameterized layout specification which shows that there is still a significant advantage for user guided layout information. This includes a demonstration that layout information can allow a design to achieve the same performance on an FPGA two speed graders higher.

We do not advocate the layout of all kinds of circuits – finite state machines (FSMs) are probably best left to vendor tools for mapping, placement and routing. However, for critical kernels like the adder reduction tree his is a large advantage to be gained through layout specification. In these cases layout specification is often enough to map a design to a part that is two speed grades slower which in turn reduces cost. There may be other advantages to careful layout specification, such as reduced power consumption. However, we do not explore these potential advantages in this paper.

2. EXPERIMENTAL METHODOLOGY

2.1 SYNTHESIS AND IMPLEMENTATION TOOLS

All FPGA synthesis and implementation experiments in this paper were performed using the Xilinx ISE2.2 tools running on a 64-bit Windows 7 Enterprise machine. The synthesis tool used was XST which is a part of ISE. However the designs we use do not involve any non-trivial synthesis because we generate structural netlists which directly instantiate UNISIM Xilinx FPGA primitives.

The synthesis and implementation tools were run with a high level of effort corresponding the "Timing Performance" Design Goals and Strategies effort level in the ISE tools. To be absolutely clear about how the implementation tools were used we list the exact set of flags used for each.

For the mapping phase we use the following options:

- **-logic_opt off**: do not perform post-placement physical synthesis combinational logic optimizations during trimming driven packing.
- **-ol high**: effort level (choices are standard or high).
- **-xe n**: extra effort level for timing-driving packing using additional algorithms to meet timing.
- **-t 1**: timing-driven cost table entry.
- **-xt 0**: extra cost table entry.
- **-register_duplication off**: do not duplicate registers/LUTs during timing-driven packing
- **-global_opt off**: do not perform global optimizations before mapping.
- **-mt 2**: use multithreading with 2 cores.
- **-ir off**: use RLOC constraints to generate RPMs.
- **-pr b**: pack internal flops and latches into input and output IOBs.
- **-lc off**: do not use LUT combining.
- **-power off**: do not use power optimizations.

For the place and route tools we use the following options:

- **-ol high**: use high overall effort level.
- **-xe n**: extra effort level but do not carry on for impossible placements.
- **-mt 4**: use multithreading with 4 cores.

To drive the implementation flow we initially used the XFLOW command line tool. However, we abandoned this tool because there was a mismatch between the high effort settings used by XFLOW and the actual settings required by the map and place and route tools (especially for the Virtex-6 architecture). We also investigated the SmartXplorer script that Xilinx provides to try out a variety of implementation strategies for getting the best timing and for also farming out jobs to multiple processors and machines. However, for the type of circuits that we analyze in this paper, SmartXplorer never produced an implementation which was any better than running the regular ISE tools with the timing performance goal. We instead developed our own tool (IMPLEMENT) that executes the implementation tools with the options described in this section.

When conducting the experiments, we tried to follow the best practices outlined by Drimer [1] on the meaning and reproducibility of FPGA implementation results. In particular, Drimer recommends using all 100 seeds for place and route runs because he observed that there is a deviation of about 5% to 10% from the median speed when one considers all the seed values. The mapping process uses cost tables although we always run with the same cost table entry because our input designs are already effectively mapped.

Drimer emphasizes the need to provide the complete source of design examples to allow others to reproduce experimental results. The entire source code for each of the example circuits used in the paper appears in full within the paper and these descriptions can be compiled to generate VHDL implementations using a freely available Lava compiler (which also available in source form).

When we present a performance result which states that a netlist with user specified layout operates at a higher frequency that the same netlist with the layout information removed we also claim the monotonicity property that for all lower target frequencies there is never a situation when the circuit without layout performs better than the circuit with layout information.

3. ADDER REDUCTION TREE TEST

The structured design with parameterized layout used for experimental evaluation in this paper is an adder tree. The adder tree is an example of a common class of reduction operations which are used in many digital designs. Our experiments use the Lava [3] system for producing layouts which is based on a model that exploits the properties of functional geometry [5] to describe sophisticated layouts without resorting to Cartesian coordinates. We have also performed experiments with structured designs with layouts that could not have been easily specified using RLOCs e.g. for recursively structured butterfly sorting networks.

The adder tree layout experiments we performed tried to find a layout for an adder reduction tree which performs faster with a user specified layout than the corresponding network with the layout RLOC attributes removed. An example of an adder tree reduction network for adding eight numbers is shown in Figure 1. We do not grow the bit size at each level of the reduction tree i.e. the carry out of each addition is discarded.

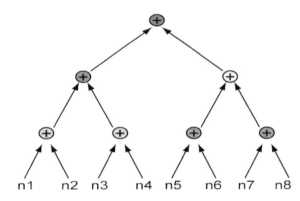

Figure 1. Adder tree (reduction network)

The user-specified layout scheme we use to lay out the adder tree is illustrated in Figure 2. The objective is to try and minimize the length of the longest wire. This scheme works by simply "sliding down" the operator elements shown in Figure 1 until they form a horizontal arrangement. Now the longest wires are from the outputs of the two sub-adder trees to the adder in the middle (which computes the final sum).

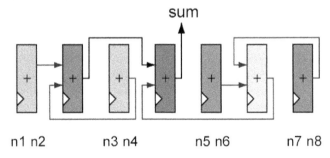

Figure 2. Layout scheme for the adder tree

This description was instantiated for an adder tree of 106 64-bit integers. The generated layout is shown in Figure 3.

The adder tree which is laid out with the middle scheme achieve a speed of **at least** 362MHz on the XV6VLX75T part with speed grade -3 and package FF784. Removing the layout information produces a design that operates at around 280MHz with a floorplan produced by the automatic placement tools show in Figure 4. This significant difference in performance is greater than two speed grades. Using the slower -2 package the laid out adder tree can run at 320MHz.

The best results we could achieve for the adder tree with and without layout, for all three speeds grades of the XC6VLX75T-FF784 FPGA are shown in 0.

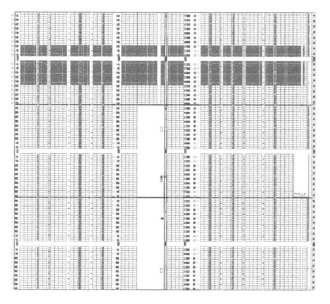

Figure 3. An adder tree for 106 64-bit integers on an XC6VLX75T-3FF784 FPGA using RLOCs.

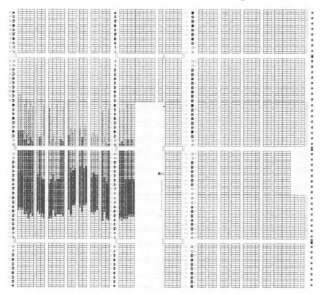

Figure 4. The same adder tree 106 64-bit input netlist with layout information removed

Table 1. Performance Comparison for the Adder Tree

Speed Grade	-1	-2	-3
With Layout	270MHz	320MHz	362MHz
Without Layout	210MHz	260MHz	280MHz

In addition to showing a significant performance advantage for using layout constraints this table also shows that the use of layout can help to reduce cost by allowing one to map to a cheaper lower speed grade part. For example, if one required the adder tree design above to operate at 270MHz, and layout constraints are not used then for this part and package, the highest speed and most expensive speed grade -3 is required. However, if exactly the same netlist is subject to layout constraints, it is possible to map the same design to a -1 part (two speed grades lower).

Reduction operations like adder trees are an important class of highly structured circuits and we conclude that our observations about the value of user specified layout also apply to manner similar kinds of circuits.

4. LAYOUT OVER GAPS

To allow for designs that can avoid obstacles in the middle of the FPGA we have modified the layout mechanism in the Lava system to allow the specification of conditional translations which are expressed using a predicate and a lambda expression for each dimension. Now any set of obstacles or areas to avoid can be specified and the generated layout is adjusted accordingly. For example, the top-level description of a Batchers bitonic sorter sorter contains a conditional layout combinator condShift which allows the sorter blocks to cross over the middle portion of the FPGA that does not have CLBs. The layout is shown in Figure 5 and could not have been feasibly achieved through Cartesian-based RLOC specifications.

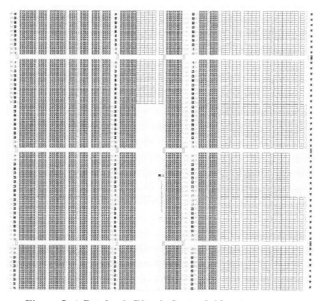

Figure 5. A Batcher's Bitonic Sorter laid out over a gap

5. FUTURE WORK

In future work we will analyze the power consumption implications of layout specification (if any). Other uses for layout include the ability to lay out symmetric function blocks which make it harder to decode secret information on FPGAs. We also hope to study the gap between designs with and without layout across the various generations of Xilinx FPGAs to see if there is a trend e.g. of diminishing returns for using layout specification.

In the future we may have FPGAs in a 3D form which introduces extra challenges for automatic placement and routing systems. The techniques we describe in this paper are readily extensible to 3D volumes by adapting the functional geometry system systematically for the extra dimension.

6. CONCLUSIONS

Xilinx's Core Generator IP cores have all but given up on the use of layout constraints. However, we have carefully produced experimental results that show the continuing value of user specified layout for highly structured designs which are often representative of functions found in IP libraries. We speculate that one of the reasons why user guided layout has fallen out of favor is the difficulty of specifying parameterized circuit layouts which can map to multiple architectures. We believe the functional geometry system used for the circuit designs in the paper provides a technique which could make layout specification tractable for sophisticated designs without having to resort to complicated and error prone formulas involving Cartesian coordinates.

As FPGAs see a wider adoption for the emulation of architecture research [6] there is an increasing need to have components that are well optimized and well behaved which do not have a negative effect on implementation runtime. This is another area where layout specification can make a useful contribution.

Although we have demonstrated the continuing value of layout constraints we at times encountered difficulties with the design tools when we submitted very large flat designs (i.e. no module hierarchy) which contain thousands of LUTs and flip-flops all with layout constraints. In particular, the synthesis tool XST can take a long time to process the RLOC constraints on some kids of designs (but not others) however this seems odd since the attachment of a constraint to a primitive component should be a very fast operation (and the design is flattened anyway early on in the implementation process). We overcome this problem by generating EDIF netlists from Lava for very large networks which are consumed without issues by the Xilinx NGDBUILD tool.

Another arbitrary restriction in the ISE tools which introduces unnecessary complexity is the lack of support of layout attributes on primitive gates (defined in the UNISIM library) e.g. one cannot attach a functioning layout attribute to the and3 component but must instead use a LUT3 component. This restriction seems very arbitrary and we argue for Xilinx to remove it and thus making layout specification a little easier.

Not all circuits are suitable for user guided layout and the increasing use of synthesis and higher level languages like Blusepec [9] makes it harder to specify layout. However, for specific important classes of circuits that are likely to form the critical path of an application it is useful to have the option of user guided layout to help reach timing closure. Another advantage of user provided layout specification is that it is much easier to get reproducible able results. One important advantage of providing layout information is that the runtime of the place and route tools can be considerably shorter for RLOC-ed designs. For many of the experiments in this paper the place and route time for the unconstrained designs was an order of magnitude longer than the RLOC-ed designs.

For achieving the best performance for some kinds of structured designs or for reducing cost by targeting lower speed grade parts we have demonstrated that the RLOC is still king.

7. REFERENCES

[1] Hannah Bian, Andrew Ling, Jianwen Zhu, Alexander Choong, "Towards Scalable Placement for FPGAs", IEEE Symposium on FPGAs. 2010.

[2] K.E. Batcher, "Sorting networks and their applications," In AFIPS Spring Joint Computing Conference, volume 32, 1969.

[3] Per Bjesse, Koen Claessen, Mary Sheeran, Satnam Singh, "Lava: Hardware Design in Haskell," ICFP'98. Springer-Verlag LNCS, 1998.

[4] Saar Drimer, "The Meaning and Reproducibility of FPGA Results", Chapter 5, PhD Thesis, "Security for Volatile FPGAs." The University of Cambridge. November, 2009.

[5] Peter Henderson, "Functional Geometry", Higher Order and Symbolic Computation, 15(4), 2002.

[6] Jason Lee and Lesley Shannon, "Predicting the Performance of Application-Specific NoCs Implemented on FPGAs", IEEE Symposium on FPGAs. 2010.

[7] René Müller, Jens Teubner, Gustavo Alonso, "Streams on Wires: A Query Compiler for FPGAs", In Proceedings of the VLDB Endowment, Vol 2, No. 1--2, 2009. (VLDB 2009), Lyon, France.

[8] René Müller, Jens Teubner, Gustavo Alonso, "Data Processingon FPGAs", In Proceedings of the VLDB Endowment, Vol 2, No. 1--2, 2009. (VLDB 2009), Lyon, France.

[9] Rishiyur Nikhil, "Bluespec SystemVerilog: Efficient, correct RTL from high-level specifications," Formal Methods and Models for Co-Design (MEMOCODE), 2004.

[10] Yi Shan, Bo Wang, Jing Yan, Yu Wang, Ningyi Xu2, Huazhong Yang, "FPMR : MapReduce Framework on FPGA - a Case Study of RankBoost Acceleration", IEEE Symposium on FPGAs. 2010.

[11] Satnam Singh, "Death of the RLOC?" IEEE Symposium on FPGAs for Custom Computing Machines (FCCM), April 2000.

[12] Jens Teubner, René Müller, Gustavo Alonso, "FPGA Acceleration for the Frequent Item Problem", In Proceedings of the 26th Int'l Conference on Data Engineering (ICDE), Long Beach, CA, USA March 2010

[13] Jackson H.C. Yeung, C.C. Tsang, K.H. Tsoi, Bill S.H. Kwan, Chris C.C. Cheung, Anthony P.C. Chan and Philip H.W. Leong, "Map-reduce as a Programming Model for Custom Computing Machins", IEEE Symposium on FPGAs for Custom Computing Machines (FCCM), April 2008.

Building a Multi-FPGA Virtualized Restricted Boltzmann Machine Architecture Using Embedded MPI

Charles Lo and Paul Chow
Department of Electrical and Computer Engineering
University of Toronto
Toronto, ON, Canada M5S 3G4
{locharl1, pc}@eecg.toronto.edu

ABSTRACT

Several FPGA architectures exist for accelerating Restricted Boltzmann Machines (RBMs). However, the network size for most is limited by the amount of available on-chip memory. Therefore, many FPGAs are required to implement very large networks for use in real-world applications. A virtualized design is able to time-multiplex the hardware resources and handle much larger networks but suffers a performance penalty due to the context switch. In this paper, we present a number of improvements to a virtualized FPGA architecture for RBMs. First, we take advantage of 16-bit arithmetic to pack larger networks onto a chip. Second, a custom DMA engine is designed to reduce the performance impact of the large amount of memory transactions. Finally, the architecture is scaled to multiple FPGAs to gain additional performance through coarse grain parallelism. The design effort required to implement these changes is minimized through the use of an embedded MPI framework. The architecture, tested on a Berkeley Emulation Engine 3 platform running at 100 Mhz, achieves a speed of 12.563 GCUPS on a 8192x8192 network.

Categories and Subject Descriptors

C.3 [**Computer Systems Organization**]: Special-Purpose and Application-Based Systems; I.5.5 [**Computer Methodologies**]: Pattern Recognition—*Implementation*

General Terms

Design, Performance

Keywords

Restricted Boltzmann Machines, Neural Network Hardware, FPGA, High Performance Computing

1. INTRODUCTION

A Restricted Boltzmann Machine (RBM) is a type of Artificial Neural Network that has garnered interest in the Machine Learning community recently due to its role as a fundamental building block of Deep Belief Networks (DBNs). DBNs have been successfully applied to a number of machine learning problems including semantic hashing of text documents [1] and recognition of handwritten digits [2]. However, a serious impediment to applying RBMs in real world applications is the quadratic increase in computation time with network size. Training of large DBNs can take days on general purpose computers [2].

Fortunately, the structure of the RBM is very amenable to parallel hardware architectures and several FPGA implementations have been proposed to accelerate operations on the network [3, 4, 5]. These architectures are able to achieve a very large speed-up relative to software implementations by utilizing the FPGA multiplier and RAM resources to perform the RBM operations in linear time. However, the size of network is limited by the amount of available on-chip memory. In follow-up works, Ly and Chow developed two methods to handle larger networks. First, one could distribute the network onto multiple FPGAs [6]. This method has the advantage of achieving additional speed-up due to the parallelism afforded by the extra FPGAs, but it does not scale well since the number of required FPGAs increases quadratically with network size. Second, one could virtualize the hardware of a single FPGA to compute the different portions of the network sequentially as they are loaded from external memory [7]. This method is more practically viable, but memory bandwidth and latency become the limiting factors for performance. Kim et al. also proposed loading the network from off-chip [3, 4], but have not yet demonstrated such a system. In comparison to software implementations, a multi-FPGA implementation by Kim et al. [4] achieved a speed-up of 76.67 fold over a MATLAB implementation and a 32 fold speed-up was observed with the virtualized architecture by Ly and Chow [7] relative to an optimized C implementation.

In this paper, we present a number of improvements to the virtualized system in [7]. First, to increase the network size operable on a single FPGA as well as simplify logic, the fixed-point representation of the RBM parameters was reduced from 32-bits to 16-bits. This allowed for a doubling of network size that could fit on-chip. Second, a new Direct Memory Access (DMA) engine was designed to increase the throughput to the external memory as well as minimize processor interaction. Finally, the virtualized design was ex-

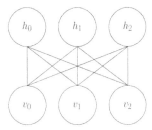

Figure 1: Structure of a 3×3 Restricted Boltzmann Machine. Each line between nodes is a weighted connection.

tended to multiple FPGAs to gain additional performance through coarse grain parallelism.

The architecture in [7] was developed using an embedded Message Passing Interface (MPI) programming model. MPI is popular in the High Performance Computing (HPC) community for implementing parallel distributed memory systems. In embedded systems, MPI allows for the abstraction of hardware engines, streamlining the design flow as well as providing a simple method of interaction between hardware and software components. However, due to the differences between HPC and embedded system environments, MPI implementations in the embedded domain are still maturing. This work presents an opportunity to study the use of embedded MPI. In particular, we examine how the MPI programming model facilitates the modification and extension of embedded FPGA applications.

The rest of the paper is organized as follows: Section 2 provides some background on the operation of Restricted Boltzmann Machines as well as an overview of the basis virtualized architecture. Section 3 describes the modifications made to the hardware due to the 16-bit fixed point representation. Section 4 describes some of the communication challenges involved in implementing the virtualized system as well as the custom DMA engine. In Section 5 the extension to multiple FPGAs is presented. Section 6 examines the use of embedded MPI in this project. Results are presented in Section 7 and conclusions are given in Section 8.

2. BACKGROUND

A Restricted Boltzmann Machine (RBM) consists of two layers of binary-valued neurons or *nodes*; a *visible* layer as well as a *hidden* layer. The network is a bipartite graph, where each node of one layer is connected to all of the nodes of the opposite layer by a weighted connection with no connections between nodes of the same layer. We will denote the weight connecting visible node i to hidden node j by $w_{i,j}$. A graphical representation of this topology is shown in Fig. 1.

If we partition the visible and hidden nodes into subsequences, the weights can be represented as a block matrix as shown in Eqns. 1-3

$$\mathbf{W} = \begin{bmatrix} W_{0,0} & \cdots & W_{0,M-1} \\ \vdots & \ddots & \vdots \\ W_{N-1,0} & \cdots & W_{N-1,M-1} \end{bmatrix} \quad (1)$$

$$\mathbf{V} = [V_0 \cdots V_{N-1}] \quad (2)$$

$$\mathbf{H} = [H_0 \cdots H_{M-1}] \quad (3)$$

Each weight block and related visible and hidden sub-sequences have the same structure as the overall weight matrix and node layers. Thus, operations performed on the overall network can be divided into similar operations on the smaller partitions of the network. This method of partitioning is important for time-multiplexing the RBM hardware. Eqns. 4-6 show the individual components of partition (n, m) assuming the sub-sequences are of equal length K.

$$W_{n,m} = \begin{bmatrix} w_{nK,mK} & \cdots & w_{nK,(m+1)K-1} \\ \vdots & \ddots & \vdots \\ w_{(n+1)K-1,mK} & \cdots & w_{(n+1)K-1,(m+1)K-1} \end{bmatrix} \quad (4)$$

$$V_n = [v_{nK} \cdots v_{(n+1)K-1}] \quad (5)$$

$$H_m = [h_{mK} \cdots h_{(m+1)K-1}] \quad (6)$$

The state of each node is a function of the sum of its weighted connections, which can be interpreted as an *energy*. Eqns. 7 and 8 show the energy for the visible node i and hidden node j respectively. For the partitioned block weights and nodes, *partial energies* may be computed that must be accumulated to then form the final energy.

$$E_{V_i} = \sum_{j=0}^{MK-1} h_j w_{i,j} = \sum_{m=0}^{M-1} \left(\sum_{k=0}^{K-1} h_{mK+k} w_{i,mK+k} \right) \quad (7)$$

$$E_{H_j} = \sum_{i=0}^{NK-1} v_i w_{i,j} = \sum_{n=0}^{N-1} \left(\sum_{k=0}^{K-1} v_{nK+k} w_{nK+k,j} \right) \quad (8)$$

The energy calculation may also be expressed in vector form:

$$\mathbf{E_V} = H \cdot W^T = \begin{bmatrix} \mathbf{E_{V_0}} \\ \vdots \\ \mathbf{E_{V_{N-1}}} \end{bmatrix} = \begin{bmatrix} \sum_{m=0}^{M-1} H_m W_{0,m}^T \\ \vdots \\ \sum_{m=0}^{M-1} H_m W_{N-1,m}^T \end{bmatrix} \quad (9)$$

$$\mathbf{E_H} = V \cdot W = \begin{bmatrix} \mathbf{E_{H_0}} \\ \vdots \\ \mathbf{E_{H_{M-1}}} \end{bmatrix} = \begin{bmatrix} \sum_{n=0}^{N-1} V_n W_{n,0} \\ \vdots \\ \sum_{n=0}^{N-1} V_n W_{n,M-1} \end{bmatrix} \quad (10)$$

Given the energy, node states are determined stochastically using the *sigmoid* function shown in Eqns. 11 and 12.

$$P(v_i = 1) = \frac{1}{1 + e^{-E_{V_i}}} \quad (11)$$

$$P(h_j = 1) = \frac{1}{1 + e^{-E_{H_j}}} \quad (12)$$

RBM training consists of two main stages: a node state calculation stage called Alternating Gibbs Sampling (AGS) and a weight update stage. AGS consists of a number of phases. In the first AGS phase, the visible layer is initialized with a training example or test data and the hidden layer is *generated* using the equations above. In the next

AGS phase, the visible layer is similarly *reconstructed*. This node selection continues in an alternating fashion until some S'th AGS phase. The AGS phase will be denoted by a superscript so that v_i^1 is the state of the i'th visible node in the first AGS phase. The energy calculation during the AGS phases is an $O(n^2)$ operation in a sequential processor and the sigmoid function involves costly division and exponentiation operations.

The weight update stage involves taking the nodes from the first and S'th AGS phases and applying the learning rule shown in Eqn. 13 where ϵ is the *learning rate*. The most precise weight update is calculated when $S = \infty$. However, learning has been shown to perform well when $S = 3$ [8] . Notice that the weight updates may be performed independently for each partition of the network.

$$\Delta w_{i,j} = \epsilon((v_i h_j)^0 - (v_i h_j)^S) \tag{13}$$

To have weight updates that represent the entire set of training data, it would be best to calculate the average weight update for all training examples before committing the change; this is called *batch learning*. However for large training sets, this method of weight update could result in long computation times between updates. To address this problem, we can reduce the number of training examples by splitting them into *mini-batches* and thus increase the update rate at the expense of precision. The number of training examples used per weight update is called the *mini-batch size*. More details on RBM operation can be found in [9].

This work extends upon the single FPGA virtualized architecture in [7]. That system consisted of four major components connected via an embedded MPI network: A Restricted Boltzmann Machine Core (RBMC), an Energy Accumulator Core (EAC), a Node Select Core (NSC) and a PowerPC processor. The RBMC performed Eqns. 7 and 8 in $O(n)$ time by operating on a row or column of the weight matrix in parallel. To facilitate this kind of access pattern, many Block RAMs (BRAMs) were required to store components of the weight matrix, thus the size of RBM was limited by the number of BRAMs available on the FPGA. Partial energy accumulation was handled by the EAC that then passed the energy to the NSC to perform stochastic node selection (Eqns. 11 and 12) using a look up table and piecewise linear interpolator. The PowerPC was used to arbitrate the hardware engines as well as stream data to and from external memory.

3. FIXED-POINT REPRESENTATION

The virtualized Restricted Boltzmann Machine architecture in [7] represented weight and energy values as 32-bit fixed-point numbers. This data width was a convenient design choice since the on-chip network operated with 32-bit data widths and the configurable dual-ported Block RAMs (BRAMs) supported up to 36-bit widths. However, significant performance improvements can be realized with a reduction in bit widths. In particular, by reducing the width to 18-bits or less, two weights can be stored on the same BRAM. This is significant since it doubles the amount of weight data the RBMC can process at once.

Reducing the fixed-point precision can introduce some serious problems that must be weighed against the performance advantages. Depending on the RBM application, there exists the possibility of overflow or underflow. This

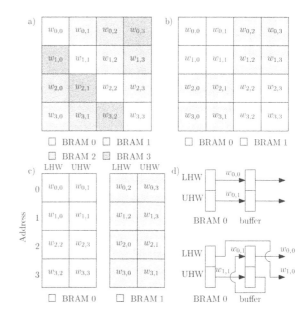

Figure 2: Arrangement of a 4×4 weight matrix in BRAM. a) Original BRAM structure with one weight at each address. b) Block diagonal structure where each BRAM is responsible for two adjacent elements of every row and column. c) Layout of the weights in the BRAMs. One set of weights occupies the Lower Half Word (LHW) at each address while the other occupies the Upper Half World (UHW). d) The two phases of weight re-ordering during a column read. This pipeline stage allows one column to be read out each cycle. The weights shown illustrate reading the first two columns of the weight matrix from BRAM 0.

could lead to problems finding a set of values in weight space to accurately represent the given training set. Based on software simulations, a width of 16-bits for weights and energies was found to be adequate for training images from the MNIST data set of handwritten digits. In addition, the RBM implementation by Kim et al. uses 16-bit weight representation [3] and previous studies support the use of 16-bit weights in neural networks [10].

The RBMC was able to to access rows or columns of the weight matrix in parallel by storing the diagonals of the matrix in separate BRAMs such that each was only responsible for one element in every row and column. A special addressing scheme was used to ensure the correct elements were accessed during the row or column reads.

By halving the fixed-point precision, the same BRAM can store two sets of weights but the access pattern becomes more complicated since two weights, not necessarily at the same address, must be accessed in parallel on the same BRAM. FPGA RAM primitives are typically dual-ported, so a simple way of accessing two weights simultaneously is to take advantage of the independent read ports. However, there are advantages to using a single read port. For instance, the 18 Kbit Xilinx Virtex-5 BRAMs can be configured in simple dual-ported mode in which case the port width doubles from 18-bits to 36-bits, with a corresponding decrease in depth, but with one dedicated read port and one dedicated write port. To take advantage of this type of

RAM, we would like a method of addressing using only one read port. This can be achieved by storing block diagonals of the weight matrix in each RAM as shown in Fig. 2b.

This method of weight distribution in BRAM allows for any two sequential rows or columns of the weight matrix to be read every two cycles. When reading rows of the matrix, the elements of any row may be accessed in parallel by simply setting the address of all of the BRAMs to the appropriate row number. However, when reading columns, the weights must be reordered as they exit the BRAMs before they can enter the energy calculation hardware. This step requires one buffer and can be pipelined so that effectively one column is read per cycle. Fig. 2d shows an example of how this buffer works to re-order the weights during column reads.

4. COMMUNICATIONS

Communications can easily become the bottleneck in hardware systems. This is especially true in virtualized systems where it is important to minimize the time spent moving new data and synchronizing components during a context switch relative to the time spent in computation. In this section we will examine the data flow to and from memory required to virtualize the hardware engines, the capabilities of the MPI network on chip and describe a new DMA Engine that helps reduce the cost of communication and thus increase the relative time spent in computation.

4.1 Context Switch

The memory structure in the RBMC works well when weights are loaded in BRAMs with individual read ports. However, the access patterns are not well suited to streaming portions of weights from external memory since noncontiguous addresses must be read and thus burst reads may not be used. Instead of streaming, the virtualized design in [7] used full context switches; loading entire weight blocks into the BRAMs before any computation. This allowed for the use of bursts, but created a very large amount of idle time for the RBMC while data was being read and written back to external memory.

To examine the data flow in the virtualized system, we can break the computation into three main parts for each network partition. First, in the energy computation phase, weights and node states are sent to the RBMC after which partial energy is calculated and written back for each node layer in the mini-batch. During the node selection phase, the partial energies calculated for a row or column are accumulated in the EAC which forwards the result to the NSC. The NSC then calculates the node states and the result is written back to memory. Note that node selection occurs once for each block row or column of the weight matrix consisting of P partitions and thus only occurs for a fraction of the total partitions. Finally, in the weight update phase, weights are sent once more to the RBMC along with the node states calculated during the AGS phases and the updated weights are written back to memory. Fig. 3 shows the data flow between hardware components and Table 1 summarizes the types and amount of data that must be sent for each phase.

Of primary concern in terms of performance is the $O(n^2)$ amount of weights that must be transferred during energy computation and weight update. The system achieves speedup by performing the RBM operations in $O(n)$ time, thus if

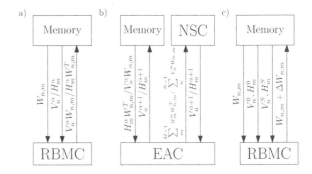

Figure 3: Data flow between memory and the hardware components for a network partition (n,m). a) Energy computation for AGS phase α. b) Node selection for AGS phase α. c) Weight update phase

Energy Computation		
Data Type	Complexity	Size [bits]
weights	$O(n^2)$	$16n^2$
energy	$O(n)$	$16n * L$
nodes	$O(n)$	$n * L$
Node Selection		
Data Type	Complexity	Size [bits]
energy	$O(n)$	$16n * L * P$
nodes	$O(n)$	$n * L$
Weight Update		
Data Type	Complexity	Size [bits]
weights	$O(n^2)$	$2 * 16n^2$
nodes	$O(n)$	$4 * n * L$

Table 1: Summary of major memory transfers for each network partition during a batch update where n is the number of nodes in the layers of the network partition, L is the batch size and P is the number of partitions in a row or column assuming the network is symmetric

the majority of the time is spent in weight transfers, we lose a dramatic amount of performance. One way of reducing the impact of the context switches is by using large batch sizes. Once the weights are loaded into the RBMC BRAMs, computing energies and weight updates only require the transfer of node states and energy. These transfers are much smaller in size and grow linearly with network and batch size. Thus, we can amortize the cost of the weight transfers by using sufficiently large batch sizes such that the operating time becomes dominated by the $O(n)$ operations. Fig. 5 in the results section shows the effect of batch size on performance.

4.2 Network on Chip

The communication layer is provided by ArchES-MPI[1] [11], an embedded implementation of the Message Passing Interface (MPI). Processors and hardware engines are abstracted by the concept of *ranks* and a maximum throughput of 128 bits/cycle is available between each rank via point-to-point links. Hardware engines interact with the network via a message passing engine (MPE) that handles the details of the network protocol. To initiate a transfer, one

---

[1] ArchES-MPI is derived from TMD-MPI

72-bit command is written to the MPE. Thus, the layer is low overhead while providing high bandwidth. ArchES-MPI supports both rendezvous and ready sends. The former incurs additional latency due to the synchronization of the transmitting and receiving MPEs but is safer and avoids network congestion.

The 128-bit data path allows for the transfer of eight 16-bit weights or energies per cycle or 128 node states per cycle. To take advantage of the wide datapath, the EAC and NSC were modified to perform parallel energy accumulation and node selection on the eight incoming energies per cycle. This required the use of eight parallel uniform random number generators for node selection. During the development of this system, multiple Tausworthe-88 generators [12] were instantiated with arbitrarily chosen seeds to facilitate testing. This is not satisfactory in practice, since generated subsequences could overlap and are not necessarily uncorrelated [13]. The other FPGA RBM architectures [4, 6] also used parallel node selection but also have not addressed the problem of parallel random number generation. This is left as a topic for future work.

4.3 DMA Engine

In [7], the processor was responsible for queuing MPI data transfers between the compute cores and the external memory. A Direct Memory Access (DMA) engine connected via the Processor Local Bus (PLB), called the PLB_MPE, was used to interface the processor with the MPI network. The PLB_MPE allowed for the use of burst transactions from a Multi-Port Memory Controller (MPMC) [14] over the PLB as well as nonblocking sends and recieves. However, the PLB has significant overhead and relatively low throughput. In addition, the PowerPC incurred function call overheads when beginning MPI transactions.

Instead of using a PLB connected interface, a new Memory Access Core (MAC) was designed to use the Native Port Interface of the MPMC. The MAC operates using a simple set of instructions identifying the MPI operation (Ready Send, Synchronous Send or Receive), the memory location to access, the message tag and the size of the message. These instructions are stored on a simple FIFO and can be loaded either from another rank or read directly from external memory. Thus, once loaded in the FIFO, only one cycle is required to fetch the next instruction and begin the next MPI transaction. By operating the core at the memory frequency, twice that of the hardware cores, the MAC is able to saturate its MPI link with 128-bits per cycle during bursts. The MAC handles all memory accesses and essentially replaces the processor during computation. A processor is only required as an interface to load data from a host computer and to send the first instruction to the MAC. In the future, the on-chip processor could be completely replaced with a MPI link directly to an external X86 processor.

5. EXTENSION TO MULTIPLE FPGAS

The goal in extending the virtualized architecture to multiple FPGAs is to use the coarse grain parallelism to provide extra speed-up. Two primary challenges arise when distributing the RBM across chips. First, the amount of work should be balanced such that the available hardware is being fully utilized at all times. Second, since communication costs can be very high in off-chip interconnects, inter-FPGA communication should be minimized.

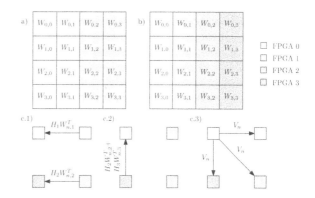

Figure 4: Distribution of 4×4 partitions of weights among multiple FPGAs. a) Two FPGAs: Each FPGA can calculate two blocks of hidden nodes independently but synchronization is required between both FPGAs during selection of visible nodes. b) With four FPGAs, each is responsible for one block of hidden nodes and synchronization is required for visible node selection. c) Visualization of energy summation and node selection for a block of visible nodes V_n in the four-FPGA system shown in (b).

The partitioning method described for virtualizing a RBM on a single FPGA can be easily applied to distribute the work across multiple FPGAs. Partitions of the weight matrix and the corresponding nodes are distributed across the FPGAs by grouping the partitions into larger contiguous blocks as shown in Fig. 4a and 4b. The system operates very similarly to the single FPGA version. The phases of energy computation and weight update only require data local to each partition, so they can be performed independently on each FPGA. During node selection, energies are first summed locally and if required, accumulated across FPGAs before the final node calculation. For instance, when calculating visible node states in the two FPGA system shown in Fig. 4a, two partial energies would be accumulated locally on each FPGA before being summed on one FPGA. The selected nodes are then broadcast to the participating FPGAs. Notice that if the partitions on an FPGA span an entire row or column of the weight matrix, no inter-FPGA communications are required to calculate the corresponding node states.

The synchronization step involved in node selection represents a major bottleneck in terms of the scalability of the system. To facilitate the transfer of partial energies between many FPGAs, the EACs were modified to support a large scale tree-adder style summation. This helps reduce network congestion by limiting the number of energy transmissions at any one time to $log_2(N)$ where N is the number of FPGAs. Fig. 4c shows the steps in node selection for a four-FPGA system. The node states are only n bits, where n is the number of nodes per layer in the RBM partition, so the broadcast is acceptable. However, the number of node transmissions increases linearly with the number of FPGAs, thus the overall cost of synchronization increases as $O(N)$ with the number of FPGAs.

6. MPI PROGRAMMING MODEL

As FPGAs increase in size, they become more and more viable as platforms for reconfigurable hardware accelerators such as the RBM architecture presented in this paper. However, as the systems become more complex, they also become more difficult to design and manage. The Message Passing Interface (MPI) programming model provides one method of partitioning embedded systems and simplifying their design.

In an MPI design flow, the application is first explicitly partitioned into a number of tasks. These tasks are performed by compute engines divided into *ranks*. Through the abstraction provided by the concept of ranks, the implementation details of compute engines are hidden from other components in an MPI system. This abstraction can be provided in a reconfigurable hardware design by embedded MPI implementations such as ArchES-MPI. In ArchES-MPI, hardware engines interact with an on-chip point-to-point network via a Message Passing Engine (MPE). The MPE hides the details of the communication layer and thus isolates the engine from other parts of the system.

The use of ArchES-MPI has several benefits from a design and maintainability standpoint. First, since the hardware components are encapsulated into ranks, the design becomes portable and scalable over platform changes. Designs may take advantage of larger FPGAs by simply instantiating more engines on the same chip. Since each instantiation is an independent rank, the control required to utilize the additional hardware is just the appropriate MPI messages. Likewise, additional FPGAs may be added to the system by connecting them to the MPI network. No significant redesign is required to take advantage of additional resources.

ArchES-MPI also provides an abstraction between hardware and software components. This enables the seamless interaction of software and hardware though a standard interface. Since the implementation details of each rank are hidden, systems may be easily prototyped in software and very intensive tasks can be independently moved to hardware without affecting the operation of the remaining software components. In addition, hardware changes can be made very easily without affecting the operation of the rest of the system. This is imperative for incremental improvements in large designs.

Finally, from a system design perspective, ArchES-MPI allows for a flexible data flow. Since data is routed through a point-to-point network on chip, the data path can be easily reconfigured via messages. This creates flexibility in the way hardware engines are used in different situations.

During the design of the multi-FPGA RBM architecture in this paper, we took advantage of several of the features provided by ArchES-MPI. First, the architecture was ported from the Berkeley Emulation Engine 2 (BEE2) [15] platform to the Berkeley Emulation Engine 3 (BEE3) [16]. The BEE2 consisted of five Virtex-II Pro FPGAs with hard PowerPC processors connected in a mesh whereas the BEE3 contained four Virtex-5 FPGAs connected in a ring without any hard processor. In the absence of the PowerPCs, MicroBlaze soft-processors were instantiated and integrated seamlessly into the MPI network. Since the hardware engines were behind the MPI layer, only an update in the netlist was required during the transition. In addition, the details of the inter-FPGA links were abstracted by the network on chip. Since the data ports between FPGAs on the BEE3 were only 72-bits wide, the width of the MPI network had to be reduced to 32-bits to facilitate synchronous communication between the FPGAs. A packet width converter was used to split the 128-bit MPI data into four 32-bit parts before being sent over the interconnection. This change in data width was also transparent to the hardware components. Second, the MAC took over many of the responsibilities of the processor. Originally, the processor was used to feed the compute engines since the PLB interface was a simple way to access external memory. However, when additional performance was desired, the MAC was designed. No modifications to the rest of the hardware cores were required to accommodate this change. Finally, the programmable nature of the MPI network allowed the EACs to be configured to act as a large scale tree adder across chip boundaries as well as simple summation units.

ArchES-MPI may not be appropriate for all scenarios. First, not all designs may be amenable to an MPI based dataflow. In particular, the design must be carefully partitioned such that portions requiring very high throughput and specific control such as pipelined datapaths do not transfer data through the network. In addition, some overhead is incurred during data transfer, especially during synchronous sends where handshaking is required between the sender and receiver. Finally, to make the most of the on-chip links, the data width of the hardware engines should be matched to the width of the network. Designs should be evaluated to determine whether or not they fit the MPI framework.

7. RESULTS AND ANALYSIS

The design was tested on the Berkeley Emulation Engine 3 (BEE3) hardware platform [16]. The BEE3 contained four Xilinx Virtex-5 XC5VLX155T FPGAs connected in a ring via 72-bit wide interconnects. Each FPGA was also configured with a 2GB RDIMM. The XC5VLX155T has 24,320 logic slices (each slice contains four 6-input LUTS) and 424 18 Kbit BRAMs for 7,632 Kbits of embedded RAM. Based on the number of BRAMs available, a maximum RBMC size of 256x256 was instantiated on each FPGA. A MicroBlaze soft processor was also instantiated on every FPGA to initialize the system. The compute engines, MicroBlaze and MPI network ran at 100 MHz while the DDR2 memory controller and MAC ran at 200 MHz. The clock frequency was limited by long wire delays on this platform. Future work will include the investigation of these critical paths to achieve timing closure at higher clock frequencies. Computation time was measured by calling the MPI function *MPI_TIME()* on the MicroBlaze after each mini-batch.

7.1 Metrics

One popular method of measuring neural network performance is Connection Updates per Second (CUPS). This is defined as the number of weight updates per second or:

$$CUPS = \frac{n^2}{T} \qquad (14)$$

Where n is the size of the node layers and T is the amount of time for all of the weights to be updated. One problem with CUPS when measuring hardware performance is it does not take into account mini-batch size; as mini-batch size increases, CUPS will decrease although the number of weight update calculations increases.

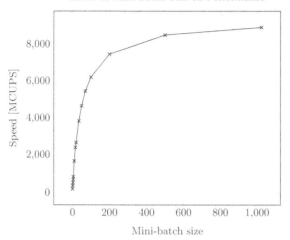

Figure 5: Relationship between mini-batch size and performance for a 1024x1024 network running on a four-FPGA virtualized system.

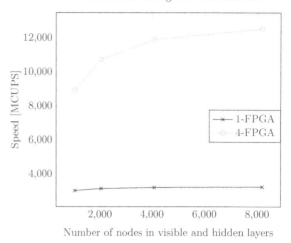

Figure 6: Performance of the single-FPGA and four-FPGA virtualized systems for different network sizes. The mini-batch size was fixed at 1024.

We will use a slightly modified version of CUPS in this paper:

$$CUPS = \frac{n^2}{T}L \qquad (15)$$

Where L is the mini-batch size. This definition of CUPS is the effective number of weight changes per second.

In [4], Kim et al. described a performance measure called mult/s which measured the major vector multiplication operations involved in RBM training. For three AGS phases, this results in:

$$1 \text{ CUPS} = 5 \text{ mult/s} \qquad (16)$$

We will use CUPS as defined in Eqn. 15 as the metric for the rest of this paper.

7.2 Context Switch Penalty

As mentioned in Section 4, the transfer of weights during context switches represents a very large performance penalty. Fig. 5 shows the speed of the four-FPGA 1024x1024 system for different mini-batch sizes. Performance increases dramatically with mini-batch size. For small mini-batch sizes, the majority of time is spent transferring the weights to and from the RBMC during the energy computation and weight update phases. Once the weights are loaded into the RBMC, the remaining operations of transferring node states and energies as well as the computations take a relatively small percentage of time. Thus, performance scales linearly at low mini-batch sizes with diminishing returns once batch operations begin to dominate at large mini-batch sizes.

It is clear from these results that large mini-batches should be used to maximize the performance of the virtualized system. From an RBM training perspective, this is acceptable since the precision of weight updates increases with mini-batch size for stationary data. The trade-off for mini-batch size has traditionally been computation time. However, since the virtualized system is bottlenecked by the weight transfers for small mini-batches, there is very little penalty in performance for increasing mini-batch size in this system.

7.3 Scalability

The scalability of the system to additional FPGAs is limited by the energy accumulation and node broadcast steps during the node selection phase. Although node selection only takes place for a fraction of the total compute time and involves relatively few operations, the cost of this step is exacerbated by the limited bandwidth available and latency in the FPGA interconnects. In the BEE3 platform, the links are direct PCB connections and thus relatively low latency, but MPI data must be converted to 32-bit words when crossing FPGA boundaries because of the limited number of connections. In addition, during node broadcast, the node states must cross two inter-FPGA links to reach a diagonal FPGA due to the ring topology of the platform. Depending on the distribution of the network partitions, a good topology would have connections between FPGAs which share rows and columns of the weight matrix. In the performance tests, a distribution similar to Fig. 4b was used, so a fully connected network would be desired since all FPGAs must interact to reconstruct visible nodes. These costs cause the scalability of the system to be limited when working with smaller networks.

As the network size increases, the proportion of time spent carrying out inter-FPGA synchronization decreases relative to the amount of work performed independently on each FPGA. Therefore, the synchronization penalty decreases as network size increases and almost linear speed-up can be achieved. Fig. 6 shows the speed of the virtualized system running on the single and four-FPGA systems for different network sizes. At a network size of 1024x1024, the four-FPGA system achieves a speed of 9.0 GCUPS or about a three-fold improvement over the single FPGA performance of 3.1 GCUPS. However, at a network size of 8192x8192, the four-FPGA system demonstrates an almost linear speed-up of 12.6 GCUPS relative to the 3.3 GCUPS of the single FPGA.

This architecture performs best when a small number of FPGAs are working on a large network. This type of application is the focus of the virtualized RBM design, and thus the limits on scalability will not affect the majority of use cases. However, the application should be kept in mind when using this architecture.

7.4 Hardware Architecture Comparison

Table 2 shows a performance comparison of the different FPGA architectures. First, in comparison with the previous virtualized RBM architecture in [7], the improvements made to this system allow it to achieve much greater performance. The architecture in [7] was implemented on a Virtex-II Pro XC2VP70 FPGA with 328 18 Kbit configurable BRAMs. That platform allowed for a maximum 32-bit RBMC of size 128x128 to be instantiated at 100 MHz. On a single FPGA, virtualized systems do not gain much extra performance from increasing RBM size since the number of partitions grows as $O(n^2)$. This can be seen in Fig. 6 where the single-FPGA implementation remains at around 3 GCUPS over a large range of network sizes although the four-FPGA implementation gets extra performance by amortizing the inter-FPGA communication. Therefore, we can roughly compare the raw performance of the single-FPGA virtualized systems and see that the modifications made in this architecture allow for an over four-fold improvement in performance compared to the design in [7].

The virtualized architecture in this paper allows for large networks to be accelerated, but at the cost of performance limitations. First, to achieve maximum performance, the application of this design is limited to large mini-batch sizes and large RBM sizes relative to the number of FPGAs. These conditions are necessary to amortize the cost of the context switch as well as the inter-FPGA communication. Next, even for large mini-batches, the performance of this system is limited by the memory latency and bandwidth. In the best case, the system would achieve maximum performance by keeping the RBMC constantly performing vector and matrix operations. However, since frequent memory accesses are required during node selection, the RBMC must wait for that stage to complete before it can continue processing new data. The latency of external memory access is an additional performance penalty relative to on-chip RAM access.

It is interesting to compare this architecture to the ones proposed by Kim et al. [3, 4]. In their designs, an array of multipliers was used to perform the vector-matrix multiplications. This allowed them to use real valued visible nodes instead of binary valued ones. A key decision in their design was the use of the same memory access pattern for accessing weights from BRAM at the cost of having different sets of accumulator logic for row and column operations. By storing their weights and batch data on-chip, they were able to keep the multiplier array almost constantly busy and thus achieved very high performance. Their architecture also did not require very large batch or RBM sizes to maintain high performance since they did not have external memory access costs to amortize. A disadvantage of this method is that the network and mini-batch sizes are limited by the amount of on-chip resources. However, they may take less of a performance hit if weight streaming is implemented, since the regular weight addressing allows for the use of burst reads and writes from external memory and thus higher bandwidth.

The multi-FPGA architecture presented by Kim et al. [4] also scales better at smaller network sizes. They achieve very high scalability by requiring only nearest neighbour

transactions and thus reduce the overhead associated with inter-FPGA communication. In contrast, the architecture presented in this paper only scales well once the cost of inter-FPGA synchronization is accounted for by using large RBM sizes. However, the topology of FPGAs in their architecture is restricted to a ring structure, whereas the multi-FPGA implementation presented in this paper may be used in many different network topologies due to the flexibility provided by ArchES-MPI.

Kim et al. implemented their architecture on four Stratix III EPSL340 FPGAs with the RBM modules running at 150 MHz. The FPGAs were connected in a ring via LVDS pairs with a datarate of 4.8 Gbps in each direction. An EPSL340 FPGA contains 130,000 Adaptive Logic Modules, each acting as two combined 6-input LUTs, for a total of 260,000 6-input LUTs. In addition, the chip contains 288 18x18 multipliers and 16,272 Kbits of embedded RAM. The number of multipliers limits the number of compute elements on each FPGA to 256, thus each FPGA was able to perform 256 multiplications per cycle during the vector operations. This is equivalent to the RBMC size on the BEE3 since a 256x256 RBMC can also operate on 256 vector elements per cycle.

Note that the XC5VLX155T FPGAs in the BEE3, with 97,280 6-input LUTS and 7,632 Kbits of embedded RAM, have about half the logic and RAM capacity as the EPSL340. Given FPGAs with a greater amount of embedded RAM, additional RBMCs could be instantiated to increase computational throughput of this system. The difference in clock frequency also plays an important part in relative performance of the two architectures. The implementation by Kim et at. has inherently 50% greater performance due to the higher clock frequency. Clock frequency was limited by long wire delays on the BEE3 platform; further investigation will be performed to address the critical paths and achieve timing closure at greater frequencies.

As seen in Table 2, performance of the four-FPGA virtualized design is dramatically worse than the multi-FPGA architecture by Kim et al. when compared at the same network size of 1024x1024 and mini-batch size of 16. The low mini-batch size causes the RBMC to be idle for a large portion of the running time while weights are being transferred during the context switch. This is discussed in Section 7.2, and the effect of mini-batch size on performance is shown in Fig. 5. The performance of the architecture by Kim et al. was reported as being invariant to mini-batch size provided the multiplier pipelines were kept fed [4], thus a comparison is still valid at larger mini-batch sizes. Unfortunately, no comparison may be made for larger network sizes, but it can be noted that at 1024x1024 nodes, the inter-FPGA communication costs are not yet amortized and thus the virtualized four-FPGA system performs sub-optimally. If performance is compared at a network size of 8192x8192 and a mini-batch size of 1024, the performance gap partially closes. The remaining difference exists due to the greater clock speed as well as the limited memory bandwidth and latency issues as described earlier. Although the architecture by Kim et al. achieves very high performance in its custom pipeline, the flexibility of MPI makes the design presented in this paper very portable and extensible.

Finally, a number of implementations using Graphics Processing Units (GPUs) have been designed to accelerate RBM training [4], [17]. Since the RBM operations are very heavy

Implementation	Network Size	mBatch Size	Absolute Performance
Virtualized 1-FPGA	1024x1024	16	1051 MCUPS
Virtualized 4-FPGA	1024x1024	16	2433 MCUPS
Virtualized 1-FPGA	1024x1024	1024	3070 MCUPS
Virtualized 4-FPGA	1024x1024	1024	8958 MCUPS
Virtualized 1-FPGA	8192x8192	1024	3286 MCUPS
Virtualized 4-FPGA	8192x8192	1024	12563 MCUPS
Virtualized 1-FPGA [7]	256x256	1024	725 MCUPS
Kim et al. 4-FPGA [4]	1024x1024	16	30666 MCUPS

Table 2: Absolute performance comparison between different FPGA implementations. Here, mBatch size is the mini-batch size. Virtualized FPGA designs were run with a clock speed of 100 MHz and the architecture by Kim et al. used a clock speed of 150 MHz.

in terms of vector and matrix operations, GPUs perform well with respect to general purpose computers and competitively with FPGAs. Comparisons between FPGAs and GPUs may be found in [7] and [4].

8. CONCLUSION

This paper presents several methods of improving the performance of a virtualized Restricted Boltzmann Machine architecture within an embedded MPI framework. Core modifications were made to improve the operable network size and reduce the impact of swapping data to and from external memory. In addition, extra performance was gained through the extension of the architecture to multiple FPGAs. The design effort was greatly reduced through the abstraction provided by ArchES-MPI. Performance of 12.6 GCUPS was achieved on a 8192x8192 RBM with a four-FPGA platform. Very large RBM networks can be realized using this virtualized approach, but due to the inherent performance penalties incurred during memory access, this architecture should be used for applications with large networks and batch sizes to achieve the most speed-up.

Avenues of future work include removing the MicroBlaze processor and replacing it with a PCIe connection to a host processor. This would free up LUTs and BRAMs on the FPGAs as well as improve the speed of initializing the DRAM with test data relative to the JTAG connection currently used. In addition, given more resources, a second MAC could be instantiated to perform node selection in parallel with energy computation. This would reduce the amount of idle time for the RBMC and thus further improve performance. Many neural networks share a similar structure and thus require similar operations. Given the flexibility of the MPI framework, the acceleration of other types of neural networks could also be investigated with this architecture. Finally, the application of this system to Deep Belief Network problems such as the classification of handwritten digits in [2] is currently being investigated.

9. ACKNOWLEDGMENTS

We gratefully acknowledge Daniel Ly for his advice and feedback, NSERC and Xilinx for providing funding and CMC/SOCRN for the hardware and tools used in this project. We also thank the anonymous reviewers for their helpful comments.

10. REFERENCES

[1] Ruslan Salakhutdinov and Geoffrey Hinton. Semantic Hashing. *International Journal of Approximate Reasoning*, 50(7):969–978, July 2009.

[2] Geoffrey Hinton and Simon Osindero. A Fast Learning Algorithm for Deep Belief Nets. *Neural Computation*, 18(7):1527–1554, July 2006.

[3] Sang Kyun Kim, Lawrence MacAfee, Peter Leonard McMahon, and Kunle Olukoton. A Highly Scalable Restricted Boltzmann Machine FPGA Implementation. In *Proceedings of the 19th International Conference on Field Programmable Logic and Applications*, pages 367–372, August 2009.

[4] Sang Kyun Kim, Peter Leonard McMahon, and Kunle Olukotun. A Large-Scale Architecture for Restricted Boltzmann Machines. In *Proceedings of the 2010 18th IEEE International Symposium on Field-Programmable Custom Computing Machines*, pages 201–208, May 2010.

[5] Daniel Le Ly and Paul Chow. A High-Performance FPGA Architecture for Restricted Boltzmann Machines. In *Proceedings of the ACM/SIGDA International Symposium on Field Programmable Gate Arrays*, pages 73–82, February 2009.

[6] Daniel Le Ly and Paul Chow. A Multi-FPGA Architecture for Stochastic Restricted Boltzmann Machines. In *Proceedings of the 19th International Conference on Field Programmable Logic and Applications*, pages 168–173, August 2009.

[7] Daniel Le Ly and Paul Chow. High-Performance Reconfigurable Hardware Architecture for Restricted Boltzmann Machines. *IEEE Transactions on Neural Networks*, 21(11):1780–1792, November 2010.

[8] Guy Mayraz and Geoffrey E. Hinton. Recognizing Handwritten Digits Using Hierarchical Products of Experts. *IEEE Transactions on Pattern Analysis and*, 24(2):189–197, February 2002.

[9] Yoav Freund and David Haussler. Unsupervised learning of distributions on binary vectors using 2-layer networks. In *Advances in Neural Information Processing Systems 4*, pages 912–919, 1991.

[10] Perry D. Moerland and Emile Fiesler. Neural Network Adaptations to Hardware Implementations. In *Handbook of Neural Computation*, chapter E1.2. Oxford University Press, 1997.

[11] Manuel Saldaña, Arun Patel, Christopher Madill, Daniel Nunes, Danyao Wang, Henry Styles, Andrew Putnam, Ralph Wittig, and Paul Chow. MPI as an Abstraction for Software-Hardware Interaction for HPRCs. *Proceedings of the Second International Workshop on High-Performance Reconfigurable Computing Technology and Applications*, pages 1–10, November 2008.

[12] Pierre L'Ecuyer. Maximally Equidistributed Combined Tausworthe Generators. *Mathematics of Computation*, 65(213):203–213, January 1996.

[13] Ashok Srinivasan, Michael Mascagni, and David Ceperley. Testing parallel random number generators. *Parallel Computing*, 29(1):69–94, January 2003.

[14] Xilinx. Multi-Port Memory Controller (MPMC) Data Sheet v4.02.a, June 2008.

[15] Chen Chang, John Wawrzynek, and Robert W. Brodersen. BEE2: A High-End Reconfigurable Computing System. *IEEE Design & Test of Computers*, 22(2):114–125, March-April 2005.

[16] John D Davis, Charles P Thacker, and Chen Chang. BEE3: Revitalizing computer architecture research. Technical report, Microsoft Research, April 2009.

[17] Rajat Raina, Anand Madhavan, and Andrew Y. Ng. Large-scale Deep Unsupervised Learning using Graphics Processors. In *Proceedings of the 26th Annual International Conference on Machine Learning*, pages 873–880, 2009.

A Monte-Carlo Floating-Point Unit for Self-Validating Arithmetic

Jackson H. C. Yeung
Department of Computer
Science and Engineering
The Chinese University of
Hong Kong
hcyeung@cse.cuhk.edu.hk

Evangeline F. Y. Young
Department of Computer
Science and Engineering
The Chinese University of
Hong Kong
fyyoung@cse.cuhk.edu.hk

Philip H. W. Leong
School of Electrical and
Information Engineering
The University of Sydney

philip.leong@sydney.edu.au

ABSTRACT

Monte-Carlo arithmetic is a form of self-validating arithmetic that accounts for the effect of rounding errors. We have implemented a floating point unit that can perform either IEEE 754 or Monte-Carlo floating point computation, allowing hardware accelerated validation of results during execution. Experiments show that our approach has a modest hardware overhead and allows the propagation of rounding error to be accurately estimated.

Categories and Subject Descriptors

B.2.0 [**Arithmetic and Logic Structures**]: General

General Terms

Design

Keywords

FPGA, Floating-Point, FPU, Monte Carlo Arithmetic

1. INTRODUCTION

Rounding error is inevitable for all finite precision computations. The most common solution is to perform each arithmetic operation at sufficiently high precision so the accumulation of error in the result is within an acceptable limit. Static analysis using affine arithmetic can also be used to estimate the propagation of rounding error in fixed point computations [3, 9] and this technique is widely used in bit-width optimization of digital circuits.

Unfortunately, analysis of rounding error propagation in floating point computations is not as straightforward. Unlike fixed point operations, the error is not bounded in a fixed interval and depends on the magnitude of the operands. A method for static analysis of floating point error based on affine arithmetic is proposed in references [4] and [5]. These methods depend on input range information and can produce overly pessimistic error bounds unless the range is bound to a small interval. In a general computing problem, the range of possible input values can either be large, or simply unavailable before runtime. Moreover, associativity of mathematical operations does not hold in floating point computations and the analysis of rounding error is highly dependent on the sequence of operations. In practice, to produce correct results, numerical computing applications implemented in software often rely on the inherent stability of the algorithm rather than careful error analysis. When such an algorithm is implemented in reconfigurable hardware, any change to the floating point implementation and sequence of operations can compromise its stability.

A different, complementary approach for dealing with rounding errors is to track their propagation at runtime. Such self-validating numerical methods can produce not only the required result, but also an error bound. A traditional approach is interval arithmetic [8] which produces strict upper and lower bounds by operating on an interval instead of a point. Unfortunately, the bound is overly pessimistic in most cases, a major reason being that this technique does not take correlations into account. Affine arithmetic [14] overcomes this problem, however, the length of the error term grows as the computation proceeds, and estimating the propagation of rounding errors at runtime is very expensive. Another approach suitable for runtime implementation is the CESTAC method [16] in which the computation is repeated using three different rounding modes and the part of the result that is the same for all rounding modes are assumed to be the significant digits.

Monte Carlo Arithmetic (MCA) [11] can track rounding errors at runtime by applying randomization to make rounding errors behave like random variables. Over a number of trials, a normal computation is turned into a Monte Carlo simulation and hence statistics on the effect of rounding errors can be obtained. Apart from floating point, MCA has also been applied to logarithmic number systems [17]. In this paper we focus on applying MCA to detect catastrophic cancellation which is the major cause of loss of significant digits in a computation.

While self-validating numerical methods produce valuable information on how rounding error affects the accuracy of the result, their implementation to date has mainly been in software which suffers from poor performance compared with hardware. This is especially problematic since applications that require high accuracy often require high performance.

In a field-programmable computing device, the flexibility to use custom floating point units to improve performance is present. A limited number of hardware implementations of interval arithmetic can be found in the literature [1, 12, 13]. A hardware implementation of the CESTAC method has also been published [2]. We are not aware of any hardware implementations of affine or Monte Carlo floating point arithmetic.

In this paper we describe a novel self-validating floating point unit (FPU) which uses MCA to track rounding error propagation. We also show that the area and performance overheads are modest compared to a standard FPU. We believe that self-validating numerical methods are important in reconfigurable computing for the follow reasons:

- The ability to produce an error estimate at runtime allows more aggressive optimizations to be used.

- For applications where the accuracy of the result is critical, a hardware generated error bound on the result is very useful.

- The ability to analyze rounding error at runtime enables the construction of computer systems that can dynamically tune themselves according to the input data. Such an ability would fully capitalize on the strength of reconfigurable hardware.

The remainder of the paper is organised as follows. In Section 2, we provide background on floating point numbers and MCA. A modified hardware algorithm for MCA addition and multiplication is described in Section 3. The implementation of the MCA arithmetic unit is described in Section 4. Results are shown in Section 5 and conclusions drawn in Section 6.

2. BACKGROUND

2.1 Floating Point Numbers

A binary floating point number x_{fp} can be represented as a 3-tuple $< n, f, e >$, where $n \in \{0, 1\}$ is the sign, f is an unsigned fraction referred to as the significand, and e is the integer exponent. Such a floating point number represents the real value:

$$x = -1^n \cdot f \cdot 2^e.$$

The significand of a normalized floating point number has a range of $1 \leq f < 2$. It has an implicit most significant bit of 1, called the hidden bit and so the actual value stored in the binary representation of the significand is $f - 1$. e is represented as a signed binary integer in excess format.

We define machine precision, p, to be the number of bits in the significand, excluding the hidden bit. For an IEEE 754 single precision floating point number, $p = 23$.

The IEEE-754 floating point standard also supports denormalized floating point numbers which represent those below the range representable by normalized numbers. For these numbers, the exponent is set to its smallest value and no hidden bit is assumed. In this case, assuming single precision, $< n, f, e >$ represents the real value:

$$x = -1^n \cdot (f - 1) \cdot 2^{-126}.$$

Our implementation is fully IEEE 754 compliant and hence supports denormalized numbers. Without loss of generality, normalized floating point numbers are assumed in the rest of this paper unless otherwise specified.

2.2 MCA

MCA, proposed by Parker [10], is a way to detect catastrophic cancellation and overcome several arithmetic anomalies in floating point calculations. Parker employs a high precision floating point unit to perform low precision Monte Carlo floating point computation. In his experiments, a double precision floating point unit is used to perform single precision Monte Carlo floating point computations.

Exact values are real numbers that can be represented exactly within the floating point precision whereas *inexact values* are rounded due to finite precision or real values that are not completely known. In MCA, an inexact value x is modeled with a random variable that agrees with x to s digits:

$$\tilde{x} = inexact(x, s, \xi) = x + 2^{e-s+1}\xi$$

where e is the base 2 exponent of x, s is a positive integer, and ξ is a random variable in the interval $(-\frac{1}{2}, \frac{1}{2})$, representing the uncertainty. Exact values are represented as their floating point value and are not random variables.

A full MCA floating point operation is computed as:

$$op(x, y) = round(inexact(op($$
$$inexact(x, t, \xi), inexact(y, t, \xi))), t, \xi)$$

where t is the virtual precision, emulating a precision less than the actual machine precision ($t \leq p$), and ξ is a random variable uniformly distributed in the interval $(-\frac{1}{2}, \frac{1}{2})$. The function $round()$ is any floating point rounding function. In this paper, we assume round to the nearest.

In a full MCA floating point operation, the function $inexact()$ is applied: (1) once to each of the operands, and (2) also to the result of the floating point operation before rounding. The former is called *precision bounding* and can be used for detection of catastrophic cancellation. The latter is *random rounding*, which improves the statistical properties of floating point rounding and can be used to address anomalies in floating point arithmetic such as non-associativity and bias of round-off errors. This is because, if random rounding is applied, the expected value of the result converges to the correct value.

Precision bounding and random rounding can be used independently. In this work, we only consider the precision bounding operation since our objective is to estimate the propagation of rounding error. The techniques described in this paper could also be applied to random rounding,

In MCA, a computation is performed n times with the same input, forming a Monte Carlo simulation. The output is an n-tuple $X = < x_1, x_2, \ldots, x_n >$. The arithmetic mean of X is used as the result, while the distribution of X can be used to estimate the rounding error. Instability in rounding is reflected by an X with large variance.

3. MCA ARITHMETIC UNIT

In Parker's work, double precision floating point arithmetic was used to perform single precision MCA so that finite precision effects were negligible. This approach is obviously very inefficient for hardware implementations. In this section, we propose a modified algorithm for MCA floating point that uses lower precision arithmetic.

The key idea is to use a random perturbation of operands and operator result to model rounding error. For a round to nearest scheme, the rounding error is at most $\frac{1}{2} \cdot 2^{e-p}$, where

e is the exponent of the number. This is approximately half the difference of the two adjacent floating point numbers. Therefore, the rounding error can be modeled as a random variable:

$$round(x_{real}) = x_{real} + \epsilon$$

where ϵ is a random number distributed in $[-2^{e-p-1}, 2^{e-p-1}]$. If ϵ is assumed to be uniformly distributed, the forward error, δ, for a floating point operation can be computed as:

$$fop(x,y) + \delta = fop(x + \xi_x, y + \xi_y)$$

where ξ_x and ξ_y are random numbers uniformly distributed in the interval $[-2^{e_x-p-1}, 2^{e_x-p-1}]$ and $[-2^{e_y-p-1}, 2^{e_y-p-1}]$. Since ξ_x and ξ_y are less than $\frac{1}{2}$ a unit in the last place (ulp), computing $fop(x,y) + \delta$ requires extending the precision of the arithmetic unit. Our algorithm avoids this by computing a result that matches the statistical distribution of $fop(x,y) + \delta$ without directly evaluating the expression. Since our objective is estimating the propagation of rounding error in IEEE floating point computation, we do not apply random rounding.

3.1 MCA Addition

We define a function *unround* as the hardware equivalent of the precision bounding operation:

$$unround(<n, f, e>) = <n, f + 2^{-p} \cdot \Xi, e>$$

where Ξ is a uniformly distributed random variable with a probability density function

$$f_\Xi(x) = \begin{cases} 1, & \text{if } -\frac{1}{2} \leq x < \frac{1}{2} \\ 0, & \text{otherwise} \end{cases}$$

For implementation purposes, we use the equivalent function:

$$unround(<n, f, e>) = <n, f + 2^{-p} \cdot \Phi - 2^{-p-1}, e> \quad (1)$$

where Φ is a random variable uniformly distributed in the interval $[0, 1)$. The probability density function for Φ is:

$$f_\Phi(x) = \begin{cases} 1, & \text{if } 0 \leq x < 1 \\ 0, & \text{otherwise} \end{cases}$$

Let a, b, c be 3 floating point numbers such that

$$\begin{aligned} a &= -1^{n_a} \cdot f_a \cdot 2^{e_a} \\ b &= -1^{n_b} \cdot f_b \cdot 2^{e_b} \\ c &= -1^{n_c} \cdot f_c \cdot 2^{e_c} \\ a &> b. \end{aligned}$$

MCA addition can be defined as

$$mc\_add(a,b) = c = unround(a) + unround(b).$$

This function is realized in hardware by making some changes to the standard floating point addition algorithm. In the standard algorithm, operand significands are aligned by shifting the smaller operand to the right by an amount equal to the difference of the exponents. The aligned operands are then added together. If the normalization step is not considered, this step can be represented by the following equation:

$$f_c = f_a + f_b \cdot 2^{e_b - e_a} + \phi_a \cdot 2^{-p} + \phi_b \cdot 2^{-p} \cdot 2^{e_b - e_a}$$

Our goal is to compute this expression without extending the precision of the adder. In a floating point adder, the adder is $p + 4$ bits wide, where $p + 1$ is the width of the significand, and an additional 3 bits are used for rounding. We will compute f_c under this bit-width constraint. During normalization, the rightmost $e_b - e_a - 3$ bits of f_b are shifted out. In normal floating point addition, rounding of these lost bits is tracked via the sticky bit. Since there are an infinite sequence of random bits to the right of the least significant bit, the sticky bit is not necessary. We denote those bits shifted out f_{b0} and the remaining ones f_{b1}. Hence, $f_b = f_{b0} + f_{b1}$, and f_c can be computed as:

$$f_c = f_a + f_{b1} \cdot 2^{e_b - e_a} + \varepsilon$$
$$\varepsilon = f_{b0} \cdot 2^{e_b - e_a} + \phi_a \cdot 2^{-p} + \phi_b \cdot 2^{-p} \cdot 2^{e_b - e_a}$$

Computing ε exactly would require enlarging the adder to a width of $2p - 3$ bits. Instead, we approximate f_{b0} using a uniform random number. This approximation only produces a small error (as confirmed experimentally later in the paper) since the bits shifted out consist of the lower order bits of the number, which are roughly randomly distributed. Under this assumption, we can compute ε using the expression:

$$\varepsilon = \phi_a \cdot 2^{-p} + \phi_x \cdot 2^{-p}$$

where ϕ_x is a random number taken from the distribution Φ, representing all lower order bits of f_b that are not visible. The lower order bits are the sum of two random numbers distributed in the interval $[0, 1]$. Since the lower order bits are not recorded, we only need to know how the sum of the random numbers affect rounding. If A, B are independently distributed uniform random variables $U[0, 1]$, $P(A + B \geq 1) = \frac{1}{2}$ and the uncomputed part of the addition generates a carry $\frac{1}{2}$ of the time, during rounding a carry input is added to the least significant place with probability $\frac{1}{2}$. After taking the carry operation into account, the unrecorded bits are uniformly distributed and its value is simply rounded to the nearest floating point number.

3.2 MCA Multiplication

Let a, b, c be 3 floating point numbers such that $a = -1^{n_a} \cdot f_a \cdot 2^{e_a}$, $b = -1^{n_b} \cdot f_b \cdot 2^{e_b}$, and $c = -1^{n_c} \cdot f_c \cdot 2^{e_c}$. Using the function $unround()$ defined in Equation 1, MCA multiplication can be defined as

$$mc\_mult(a, b) = c = unround(a) \times unround(b).$$

This function is realized in hardware by making some changes to the standard floating point multiplication algorithm. The first step is to compute the product of the significand. Ignoring the normalization step, the significand of c can be computed by the following equation:

$$f_c = (f_a + \phi_a \cdot 2^{-p}) \cdot (f_b + \phi_b \cdot 2^{-p})$$

A random error is injected to both operands. Since a floating point multiplier does not use any guard bit in the multiplication stage, the multiplier width must be increased to accommodate the error injected. The number of extra bits added affects how precise the error is propagated after the multiplication. The absolute error of a multiplication is $(f_a \phi_b + f_b \cdot \phi_a) \cdot 2^{-p} + \phi_a \phi_b 2^{-2p}$. Since $\phi_a \phi_b 2^{-2p}$ is a very small value, it is ignored. Taking normalization into account, the relative error can be represented by the equation:

$$\frac{(f_a + f_b) \cdot 2^{-p}}{\lfloor f_a \cdot f_b \rfloor}$$

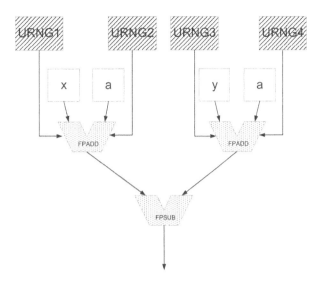

Figure 1: Example showing how correlated error is handled for the expression $(x + a) - (y + a)$. URNG2 and URNG4 are initialized with the same seed and hence have identical sequences.

Since both f_a and f_b are both normalized, $f_a \in [1, 2)$ and $f_b \in [1, 2)$. The maximum relative error is $2(2^{-p})$, and this translates to an error of at most 2 ulp in the result. Since the final result is rounded to 1 ulp, the error cannot be represented in high precision in the result, so there is little advantage to computing the error propagated in high precision. The multiplier width is increased by 1 bit to accommodate the injected error. Zero error is injected with a probability of $\frac{1}{2}$, an error of -1 and $+1$ is injected with a probability of $\frac{1}{4}$.

Rounding is unchanged except that the extra 2 bits from the multiplier output are included the calculation of sticky bit.

3.3 Handling correlated rounding error

In a datapath circuit, when a intermediate result becomes the input of more then one subsequent operation, the rounding error of the input is necessarily correlated. In such a case, our scheme can partially account for the correlation between rounding errors by arranging for all PRNGs corresponding to the same variable to be initialized with the same random seed. This causes all operations using the same intermediate result to perturb the input using the same random number. Figures 3 and 5 show the modifications made to the adder and the multiplier for handling correlated error.

Figure 1 shows an example of how correlation can be handled. In this example, the expression $(x + a) - (y + a)$ is computed, where a is the result from some previous computation. URNG2 and URNG4 are initialized with the same random seed so that the same random sequence is used in the all unround operations associated with the variable a.

4. IMPLEMENTATION

A floating point adder/subtractor and multiplier incorporating the MCA algorithm described in the previous section is implemented. The floating point unit can operate in either MCA mode or IEEE 754 single precision mode. Our test design is based the floating point unit used in refer-

ence [6], which itself is derived from an open source floating point unit [15]. The floating point unit is a IEEE 754 compliant single precision one, supporting all IEEE 754 rounding modes and denormalized numbers. Four pipeline stages are employed, this being optimized for latency rather than maximum clock frequency. It would be possible to add additional pipeline stages to operate at a higher clock frequency. We will highlight the major changes made to support MCA operation.

The architecture for the adder is shown in Figure 2. A 32-bit combined Tausworthe pseudo-random number generator [7] is used to generate the random numbers, and is described in Listing 1. A 32-bit random number is produced each clock cycle by combining the output of 3 Tausworthe generators s1, s2 and s3.

The floating point adder is composed from 4 major modules: the prenormalization unit, the fixed point adder/subtractor, the post-normalization unit and the rounding unit. The parts that are modified for MCA are highlighted in Figure 2. Here we list the modifications made to each of the modules.

- In the prenormalization unit, 3 bits from the URNG are appended to the significand of each operand. A binary value '100' is then subtracted from the significand of each operand.

- In the fixed point adder/subtractor, 1 is added to the sum with a probability $\frac{1}{2}$ for addition. For subtraction, 1 is subtracted from the sum with a probability $\frac{1}{2}$. This is implemented by feeding a random bit to the carry in so no additional adder is required.

- In the normalization left shift, random digits are filled into the least significant bit (LSB) instead of zero.

- In Monte Carlo mode, the sticky bit is ignored, the result is rounded up if and only if the round bit is 1.

Figure 3 shows the modifications made to the adder to account for rounding error correlation. Different PRNGs are used for each operand. The PRNG corresponding to each variable is initialized with a different random seed so the same pseudo-random sequence is used by each fan-out of a variable, as shown in Figure 1.

A diagram for a floating point multiplier using the proposed algorithm is shown in Figure 4. A 32-bit combined

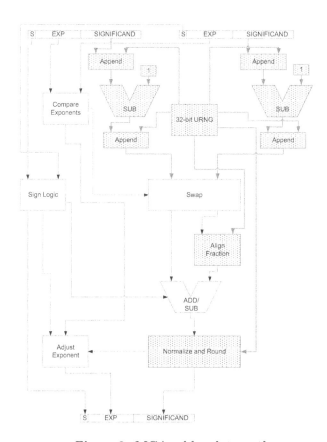

Figure 2: MCA adder data-path.

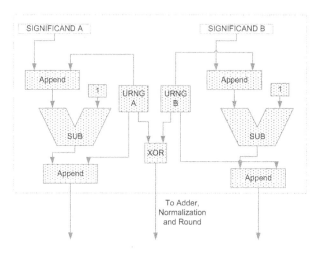

Figure 3: Modification made to adder to account for correlation of rounding error.

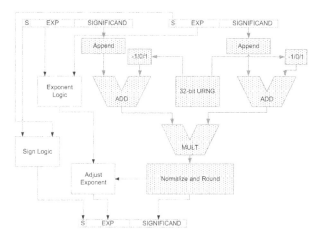

Figure 4: MCA multiplier data-path.

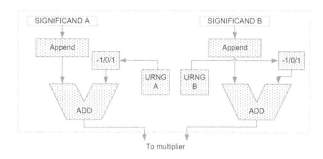

Figure 5: Modification made to multiplier to account for correlation of rounding error.

Tausworthe pseudo-random number generator is used and only 4 bits of the output are used. The modifications for MCA are highlighted in Figure 2. For clarity, only relevant signals are shown. Here we list the modifications made.

- Both operands are extend by 1 bit by appending a zero. Then 1 is either subtracted from or added to the least significant bit with a probability of $\frac{1}{4}$ for addition and $\frac{1}{4}$ for subtraction.

- The multiplier is extended by one bit to 25×25.

- During rounding, the addition output bits from the multiplier is included in the calculation of the sticky bit.

Figure 5 shows the modifications made to the multiplier to account for rounding error correlation. Different PRNGs are used for each operand. The PRNG corresponding to each variable is initialized with a random seed so that the same pseudo-random sequence is used by each fan-out of a variable.

The adder and multiplier are synthesized on a Xilinx Virtex 5 XC5VLX50T FPGA using ISE 11.1 using the default settings of optimising for timing performance with IOB packing. In the current implementation, a single Monte Carlo floating point adder occupied 460 slices and runs at 86 MHz while the unmodified adder occupied 304 slices and runs at 110 MHz. The Monte Carlo multiplier occupies 419 slices, and runs at 90 MHz, while the unmodified multiplier occupies 284 slices, and runs at 86 MHz. Note that the adder uses only 26 of the 32 output bits of the URNG while the multiplier uses only 4 of the 32 bits. If both the adder and multiplier are implemented, the URNG can be shared, eliminating a URNG.

5. RESULTS

5.1 Logarithmically Distributed Inputs

To test the effectiveness of the algorithm, pairs of double precision floating point numbers are drawn by independently generating the significand and exponent from uniform distributions in the required range. The resulting floating point numbers are logarithmically distributed. The numbers are then rounded to single precision and fed to the MCA floating point unit. A total of 64 Monte Carlo iterations are performed for each pair and the standard deviation of the output computed. The floating point unit is also run in non-MCA mode for 1 iteration to obtain an IEEE 754 single precision result. The results are compared by performing the same operation in double precision using the original pair of double precision floating point number. The rounding error is the difference between the MCA result and the double precision calculation.

Figure 6 shows the results from the MCA floating point adder. A total of 5000 pairs of numbers distributed in the full range of single precision floating point number are tested and the rounding error is plotted against the standard deviation. Here we test how the standard deviation of the MCA simulation can be used to estimate the distribution of the rounding error. If the result of the Monte Carlo iterations are approximately normally distributed, we will expect that most of the values will lie within 3 standard deviation of the population. The dotted line indicates the point where the rounding error is equal to 3 standard deviations. It can be seen that, as expected, the data-points lie below the 3 standard deviation line. Figure 7 shows the same test with the MCA multiplier and similar results are observed.

5.2 Inputs in the range $[1.0, 2.0]$

Figures 8 and 9 show the results of a similar test with the generated range limited to $[1.0, 2.0]$. The exponent is equal to 0 and the significand is uniformly distributed over its full valid range. A total of 100000 pairs of number are tested for the MCA adder and 10000 for the multiplier. The ratio of the rounding error and standard deviation is plotted against the result and a range between 0 and 3 observed. This shows that the standard deviation of the Monte Carlo iterations give a good indication of the distribution of rounding error.

5.3 Comparison with Double Precision Simulation

The addition of pairs of single precision random numbers using MCA is compared to a double precision MCA simulation using a virtual precision of 23 bits. An example of the output distribution for $-1.0 + 1.0009765625$ is shown in Figure 10. The values were chosen to have a large relative error. The output distribution closely matches the double precision simulation. Figure 11 shows the result of a similar test for the MCA multiplier calculating 1.5×1.5, with the x-axis plotted in ulp. The sparse distribution is due to the fact that the error propagation is small compared to 1 ulp.

5.4 Catastrophic Cancellation

Catastrophic cancellation occurs when two inexact floating point values, similar in magnitude, are subtracted. Consider the example $a = 1.10000000000000000000000_2 \times 2^0$, $b = 1.10000000000000000000001_2 \times 2^0$, $c = a - b$. When computed in single precision, the value of c is $1.00000000000000000000000_2 \times 2^{-23} \approx 1.19209 \times 10^{-7}$. This would be the exact result if a and b are exact values. However, when a and b are result of some previous floating point operations, they are subjected to rounding errors. In this case, the value of c contains no more then 1 binary significant digit, the other digits being rounding errors from previous operations. When the same computation is run on our floating point unit in MCA mode over 1024 iterations, we obtain a mean of $1.18244651 \times 10^{-7}$, and standard deviation of 4.913304×10^{-8}. These values clearly indicate that the result contains large rounding errors.

6. CONCLUSION

Based on Monte Carlo Arithmetic, an hardware algorithm for randomising rounding errors was devised and an IEEE 754 compliant single precision floating point unit incorporating the algorithm implemented. Experiments show that the floating point unit gives an accurate estimation of the propagation of rounding error. In our implementation using 4 pipeline stages, the multiplier has no speed penalty and occupies 51% more area than a standard one. The adder has a 22% increase in delay and 47% increase in area. We did not make any attempt to optimize the speed and area of the implementation. Speed could be improved by better balancing of pipeline stages and area can be reduced by sharing of the PRNGs between the adder and multiplier.

This work shows our approach can effectively estimate the propagation of rounding error with a minimal impact on performance. Future work will involve applying this approach at a system level and exploring aggressive floating point optimizations that reduce hardware resources while tracking rounding errors at runtime.

7. REFERENCES

[1] A. Amaricai, M. Vladutiu, and O. Boncalo. Design of floating point units for interval arithmetic. In *Research in Microelectronics and Electronics, 2009. PRIME 2009. Ph.D.*, pages 12 –15, july 2009.

[2] R. Chotin and H. Mehrez. A floating-point unit using stochastic arithmetic compliant with the IEEE-754 standard. In *Electronics, Circuits and Systems, 2002. 9th International Conference on*, volume 2, pages 603 – 606 vol.2, 2002.

[3] J. Cong, K. Gururaj, B. Liu, C. Liu, Z. Zhang, S. Zhou, and Y. Zou. Evaluation of static analysis techniques for fixed-point precision optimization. In *FCCM '09: Proceedings of the 2009 17th IEEE Symposium on Field Programmable Custom Computing Machines*, pages 231–234, Washington, DC, USA, 2009. IEEE Computer Society.

[4] C. Fang, T. Chen, and R. Rutenbar. Floating-point error analysis based on affine arithmetic. In *Proceedings of the 2003 IEEE International Conference on Acoustics, Speech, and Signal Processing*. IEEE Computer Society, 2003.

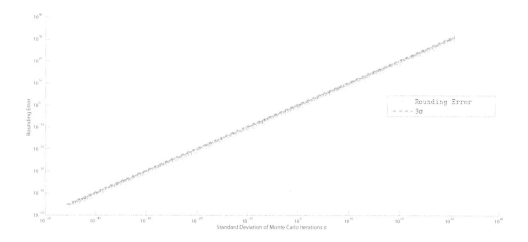

Figure 6: MCA adder - comparison of rounding error to standard deviation of Monte Carlo iterations.

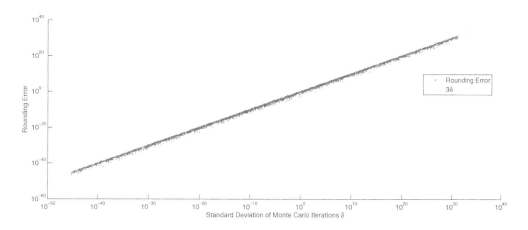

Figure 7: MCA multiplier - comparison of rounding error to standard deviation of Monte Carlo iterations.

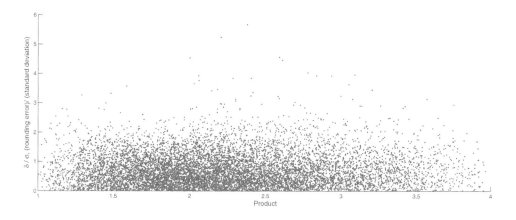

Figure 8: MCA multiplier - rounding error vs standard deviation.

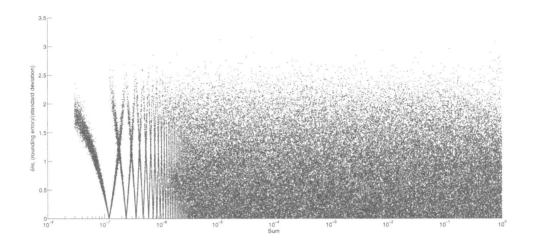

Figure 9: MCA adder - rounding error vs standard deviation.

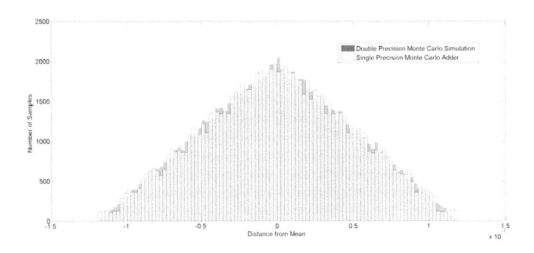

Figure 10: Comparison between hardware MCA addition and double precision MCA simulation.

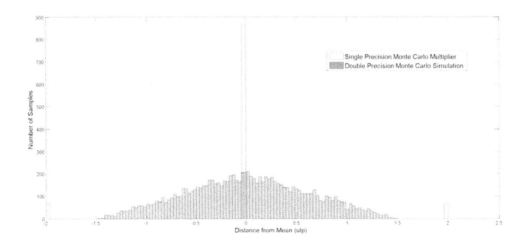

Figure 11: Comparison between hardware MCA multiplication and double precision MCA simulation.

[5] C. F. Fang, R. A. Rutenbar, M. Püschel, and T. Chen. Toward efficient static analysis of finite-precision effects in DSP applications via affine arithmetic modeling. In *Design Automation Conference (DAC 2003*, pages 496–501, 2003.

[6] C. H. Ho, C. W. Yu, P. Leong, W. Luk, and S. J. E. Wilton. Floating-point FPGA: architecture and modeling. *IEEE Trans. Very Large Scale Integr. Syst.*, 17(12):1709–1718, 2009.

[7] P. L'Ecuyer. Maximally equidistributed combined tausworthe generators. In *Math. Computation*, volume 65, pages 203 –213, 1996.

[8] R. E. Moore. *Interval Analysis*. Prentice-Hall, 1966.

[9] W. Osborne, R. Cheung, J. Coutinho, W. Luk, and O. Mencer. Automatic accuracy-guaranteed bit-width optimization for fixed and floating-point systems. In *Proc. International Conference on Field Programmable Logic and Applications (FPL)*, pages 617–620, 2007.

[10] D. S. Parker. Monte carlo arithmetic: exploiting randomness in floating-point arithmetic. 1997. http://www.cs.ucla.edu/~stott/mca/CSD-970002.ps.gz.

[11] D. S. Parker, B. Pierce, and P. R. Eggert. Monte carlo arithmetic: How to gamble with floating point and win. *Computing in Science and Engineering*, 2(4):58–68, 2000.

[12] M. Schulte and J. Swartzlander, E.E. A family of variable-precision interval arithmetic processors. *Computers, IEEE Transactions on*, 49(5):387 –397, may 2000.

[13] J. Stine and M. Schulte. A combined interval and floating point multiplier. In *VLSI, 1998. Proceedings of the 8th Great Lakes Symposium on*, pages 208 –215, feb 1998.

[14] J. Stolfi and L. H. de Figueiredo. *Self-validated numerical methods and applications*. Brazilian Mathematics Colloquium Monograph, IMPA, Rio De Janeiro, Brazil, 1997.

[15] R. Usselmann. Floating point unit, 2009. http://opencores.org/project,fpu.

[16] J. Vignes. A stochastic arithmetic for reliable scientific computation. *Math. Comput. Simul.*, 35(3):233–261, 1993.

[17] P. Vouzis, M. Arnold, S. Collange, and M. Kothare. Monte Carlo logarithmic number system for model predictive control. In *Proc. International Conference on Field Programmable Logic and Applications (FPL)*, pages 453–458, 2007.

An FPGA Implementation of a Sparse Quadratic Programming Solver for Constrained Predictive Control

Juan L. Jerez
Department of Electrical and
Electronic Engineering
Imperial College London
SW7 2AZ, United Kingdom
juan.jerez-
fullana@ic.ac.uk

George A.
Constantinides
Department of Electrical and
Electronic Engineering
Imperial College London
SW7 2AZ, United Kingdom
gac1@ic.ac.uk

Eric C. Kerrigan
Department of Electrical and
Electronic Engineering
Department of Aeronautics
Imperial College London
SW7 2AZ, United Kingdom
e.kerrigan@ic.ac.uk

ABSTRACT

Model predictive control (MPC) is an advanced industrial control technique that relies on the solution of a quadratic programming (QP) problem at every sampling instant to determine the input action required to control the current and future behaviour of a physical system. Its ability in handling large multiple input multiple output (MIMO) systems with physical constraints has led to very successful applications in slow processes, where there is sufficient time for solving the optimization problem between sampling instants. The application of MPC to faster systems, which adds the requirement of greater sampling frequencies, relies on new ways of finding faster solutions to QP problems. Field-programmable gate arrays (FPGAs) are specially well suited for this application due to the large amount of computation for a small amount of I/O. In addition, unlike a software implementation, an FPGA can provide the precise timing guarantees required for interfacing the controller to the physical system. We present a high-throughput floating-point FPGA implementation that exploits the parallelism inherent in interior-point optimization methods. It is shown that by considering that the QPs come from a control formulation, it is possible to make heavy use of the sparsity in the problem to save computations and reduce memory requirements by 75%. The implementation yields a 6.5x improvement in latency and a 51x improvement in throughput for large problems over a software implementation running on a general purpose microprocessor.

Categories and Subject Descriptors

B.5 [**Register Transfer Level Implementation**]: Design—*Control design, Datapath design, Memory design, Styles*

General Terms

Design, Algorithms, Performance

1. INTRODUCTION

A control system tries to maintain the stable operation of a physical system, known as the plant, over time in the presence of uncertainties by means of feedback. Initially, a mathematical model of the dynamical system is used to assess the effect of a sequence of input moves on the evolving state of the outputs in the future. In linear sampled-data control the state-space representation of a system is given by

$$
\begin{aligned}
x_{k+1} &= Ax_k + Bu_k, & \text{(1a)} \\
y_k &= Cx_k, & \text{(1b)}
\end{aligned}
$$

where $A \in \mathbf{R}^{n \times n}$, $B \in \mathbf{R}^{n \times m}$, $C \in \mathbf{R}^{p \times n}$, $x_k \in \mathbf{R}^n$ is the state vector at sample instant k, $u_k \in \mathbf{R}^m$ is the input vector and $y_k \in \mathbf{R}^p$ is the output vector. As an example, consider the classical problem of stabilising an inverted pendulum on a moving cart. In this case, the system dynamics are linearized around the upright position to obtain a representation such as (1), where the states are the pendulum's angle displacement and velocity, and the cart's displacement and velocity. The single input is a horizontal force acting on the cart, whereas the system's output could be the pendulum's angle displacement, which we want to maintain close to zero.

In optimal control, the goal of the controller is to minimize a cost function. This cost function typically penalizes deviations of the predicted output trajectory from the ideal behaviour, as well as the magnitude of the inputs required to achieve a given performance, balancing the input effort and the quality of the control. For instance, an optimal controller on an aeroplane could have the objective of steering the aircraft along a safe trajectory while minimizing fuel consumption.

Unlike conventional control techniques, MPC explicitly considers operation on the constraints (saturation) by incorporating the physical limitations of the system into the problem formulation, delivering extra performance gains [17]. As an example, the amount of fluid that can flow through a valve providing an input for a chemical process is limited by some quantity determined by the physical construction of the valve and cannot be exceeded. However, due to the presence of constraints it is not possible to obtain an analytic expression for the optimum solution and we have to solve an optimization problem at every sample instant, resulting in very high computational demands.

In linear MPC, we have a linear model of the plant (1), linear constraints, and a positive definite quadratic cost function, hence the resulting optimization problem is a convex quadratic program [6]. Without loss of generality, the time-invariant problem can be described by the following equations:

$$\min_{\theta} \left[\frac{1}{2} x_T' \widetilde{Q} x_T + \sum_{k=0}^{T-1} (\frac{1}{2} x_k' Q x_k + \frac{1}{2} u_k' R u_k + x_k' S u_k) \right] \quad (2)$$

subject to:

$$x_0 = \widehat{x} \quad (3a)$$
$$x_{k+1} = A x_k + B u_k \qquad \text{for } k = 0, 1, 2, ..., T-1 \quad (3b)$$
$$J x_k + E u_k \leq d \qquad \text{for } k = 0, 1, 2, ..., T-1 \quad (3c)$$
$$J_T x_T \leq d_T \quad (3d)$$

where

$$\theta := [x_0', u_0', x_1', u_1', \ldots, x_{T-1}', u_{T-1}', x_T']', \quad (4)$$

$\widehat{x}$ is the current estimate of the state of the plant, T is the control horizon length, $Q \in \mathbf{R}^{n \times n}$ is symmetric positive semi-definite (SPSD), $R \in \mathbf{R}^{m \times m}$ is symmetric positive definite (SPD) to guarantee uniqueness of the solution, $S \in \mathbf{R}^{n \times m}$ is such that (2) is convex, $\widetilde{Q} \in \mathbf{R}^{n \times n}$ is an approximation of the cost from $k = T$ to infinity and is SPSD, x' denotes transposition, and $\leq$ denotes componentwise inequality. $J \in \mathbf{R}^{l \times n}$, $E \in \mathbf{R}^{l \times m}$ and $d \in \mathbf{R}^l$ describe the physical constraints of the system. For instance, upper and lower bounds on the inputs and outputs could be expressed as

$$J := \begin{bmatrix} C \\ -C \\ 0 \\ 0 \end{bmatrix}, E := \begin{bmatrix} 0 \\ 0 \\ I_m \\ -I_m \end{bmatrix}, d := \begin{bmatrix} y_{max} \\ -y_{min} \\ u_{max} \\ -u_{min} \end{bmatrix},$$

$$J_T := \begin{bmatrix} C \\ -C \end{bmatrix}, d_T := \begin{bmatrix} y_{max} \\ -y_{min} \end{bmatrix}.$$

At every sampling instant a measurement of the system's output is taken, from which the current state of the plant is inferred [17]. The optimization problem (2)–(3) is then solved but only the first part of the solution (u_0) is implemented. Due to disturbances, model uncertainties and measurement noise, there will be a mismatch between the next output measurement and what the controller had predicted based on (1), hence the whole process has to be repeated again at every sample instant to provide closed-loop stability and robustness.

In conventional MPC the sampling interval has to be greater than the time taken to solve the optimization problem. This task is very computationally intensive, which is why, until recently, MPC has only been a feasible option for systems with very slow dynamics. Examples of such systems arise in the chemical process industries [17], where the required sampling intervals can be of the order of seconds or minutes.

Intuitively, the state of a plant with fast dynamics will respond faster to a disturbance, hence a faster reaction is needed in order to control the system effectively. As a result, there is a growing need to accelerate the solution of quadratic programs so that the success of MPC can be extended to faster systems, such as those encountered in the aerospace [9], robotics, electrical power, or automotive industries. The work described in this paper takes a first step towards this objective by proposing a highly efficient parameterizable FPGA architecture for solving QP problems arising in MPC, which is capable of delivering substantial acceleration compared to a sequential general purpose microprocessor implementation. The emphasis is on a high throughput design that exploits the abundant structure in the problem and becomes more efficient as the size of the optimization problem grows.

This paper is organized as follows. In Section 2 we justify our choice of optimization algorithm over other alternatives for solving QPs. Previous attempts at implementing optimization solvers in hardware are examined and compared with our approach in Section 3. A brief description of the primal-dual method is given in Section 4 and its main characteristics are highlighted. In Section 5 we present the details of our implementation and the different blocks inside it, before presenting the results for the parametric design in Section 6 and demonstrating the performance improvement with an example in Section 7. The paper concludes in Section 8.

2. OPTIMIZATION ALGORITHMS

Modern methods for solving QPs can be classified into interior-point or active-set [19] methods, each exhibiting different properties, making them suitable for different purposes. The worst-case complexity of active-set methods increases exponentially with the problem size. In control applications there is a need for guarantees on real-time computation, hence the polynomial complexity exhibited by interior-point methods is a more attractive feature. In addition, the size of the linear systems that need to be solved at each iteration in an active-set method changes depending on which constraints are active at any given time. In a hardware implementation, this is problematic since all iterations need to be executed on the same fixed architecture. Interior-point methods are a better option for our needs because they maintain a constant predictable structure, which is easily exploited.

Logarithmic-barrier [6] and primal-dual [22] are two competing interior-point methods. From the implementation point of view, a difference to consider is that the logarithmic-barrier method requires an initial feasible point and fails if an intermediate solution falls outside of the region enclosed by the inequality constraints (3c)–(3d). In infinite precision this is not a problem, since both methods stay inside the feasible region provided they start inside it. In a real implementation, finite precision effects may lead to infeasible iterates, so in that sense the primal-dual method is more robust. Moreover, with primal-dual there is no need to implement a special method [6] to initialize the algorithm with a feasible point.

Mehrotra's primal-dual algorithm [18] has proven very efficient in software implementations. The algorithm solves two systems of linear equations with the same coefficient matrix in each iteration, thereby reducing the overall number of iterations. However, the benefits can only be attained by using factorization-based methods for solving linear systems, since the factorization is only computed once for both systems. Previous work [4, 16] suggests that iterative methods might be preferable in an FPGA implementation, due to the small number of division operations, which are very expensive in hardware, and because they allow one to trade off accuracy for computation time. In addition, these methods are easy to parallelize since they mostly consist of large matrix-vector multiplications. As a consequence, simple primal-dual methods, where a single system of equations is solved, could be more suited to the FPGA fabric.

3. RELATED WORK

Existing work on hardware implementation of optimization solvers can be grouped into those that use interior-point methods [11, 13–15, 20] and those that use active-set methods [3, 10]. The suitability of each method for FPGA implementation was studied in [12] with a sequential implementation, highlighting the advantages of interior-point methods for larger problems. Occasional numerical instability was also reported, having a greater effect on active-set methods.

An ASIC implementation of explicit MPC, based on parametric programming, was described in [8]. The scheme works by dividing the state-space into non-overlapping regions and pre-computing a parametric piecewise linear solution for each region. The online implementation is reduced to identifying the region to which $\hat{x}$ belongs and implementing a simple linear control law, i.e. $u_0 = K\hat{x}$. Explicit MPC is naturally less vulnerable to finite precision effects, and can achieve high performance for small problems, with sampling intervals on the order of μseconds being reported in [8]. However, the memory and computational requirements typically grow exponentially with the problem size, making the scheme unattractive for handling large problems. For instance, a problem with six states, two inputs, and two steps in the horizon required 63MBytes of on-chip memory, whereas our implementation requires less than 1MByte. In this paper we will only consider online numerical optimization, thereby addressing relatively large problems.

The challenge of accelerating linear programs (LPs) on FPGAs was addressed in [3] and [13]. [3] proposed a heavily pipelined architecture based on the Simplex method. Speed-ups of around 20x were reported over state-of-the-art LP software solvers, although the method suffers from active-set pathologies when operating on large problems. Acceleration of collision detection in graphics processing was targeted in [13] with an interior-point implementation based on Mehrotra's algorithm [18] using single-precision floating point arithmetic. The resulting optimization problems were small; the implementation in [13] solves linear systems of order five at each iteration.

In terms of hardware QP solver implementations, as far as the authors are aware, all previous work has also targeted MPC applications. Table 2 summarizes the characteristics of each implementation. The feasibility of implementing QP solvers for MPC applications on FPGAs was demonstrated in [15] with a sequential Handel-C implementation. The design was revised in [14] with a fixed-area design that exploits modest levels of parallelism in the interior-point method to approximately halve the clock cycle count. The implementation was shown to be able to respond to disturbances and achieve sampling periods comparable to stand-alone Matlab executables for a constrained aircraft example with four states, three outputs, one input, and three steps in the horizon. A comparison of the reported performance with the performance achieved by our design on a problem of the same size is given in Table 1. In terms of scalability, the performance becomes significantly worse than the Matlab implementation as the size of the optimization problem grows. This could be a consequence of solving systems of linear equations using Gaussian elimination, which is inefficient for handling large matrices. In contrast, our circuit becomes more efficient (refer to Section 5) as the size of the optimization problem grows, hence the performance is better for large-scale optimization problems.

A design consisting of a soft-core processor attached to a co-processor used to accelerate computations that allowed data reuse was presented in [11], addressing the implementation of MPC on very resource-constrained embedded systems. The emphasis was on minimizing the resource usage and power consumption. Similarly, [20] proposed a mixed software/hardware implementation where the core matrix computations are carried out in parallel custom hardware, whereas the remaining operations are implemented in a general purpose microprocessor. The emphasis was on a small area design and the custom hardware accelerator does not scale with the size of the problem, hence the performance with respect to our design will reduce further for large problems. The computational bottlenecks in implementing a barrier method for solving an unstructured QP were identified for determining which computations should be carried out in which unit. However, we will show that if the structure of the QPs arising in MPC is taken into account, we can reach different conclusions as to the location of the computational bottleneck and its relative complexity with respect to other operations. The implementation was applied to a rotating antenna example with two states, one input, and three steps, and to a glucose regulation example with one input, two states and two steps in the horizon. The reported performance is compared with our implementation in Table 1.

The hardware implementation of MPC for non-linear systems was addressed in [10] with a sequential QP solver. The architecture contained general parallel computational blocks that could be scaled depending on performance requirements. The target system was an inverted pendulum with four states, one input and 60 time steps, however, there were no reported performance results. The trade-off between data word-length, computational speed and quality of the applied control was explored in an experimental manner.

In this work, we present a QP solver implementation based on the primal-dual interior-point algorithm that takes advantage of the possibility of formulating the optimization problem as a sparse QP to reduce memory and computa-

Table 1: Performance comparison for several examples. The values shown represent computational time per interior-point iteration. The throughput values assume that there are many independent problems available to be processed simultaneously (refer to Section 5).

Ref.	Example	Original Implementation	Our Implementation Latency	Throughput
[14]	Citation Aircraft	$330\mu s$	$185\mu s$	$8.4\mu s$
[20]	Rotating Antenna	$450\mu s$	$85\mu s$	$2.5\mu s$
[20]	Glucose Regulation	$172\mu s$	$60\mu s$	$1.4\mu s$

Table 2: Characteristics of existing QP solver implementations. n_v and m_c denote the number of decision variables and number of inequality constraints respectively. Their values correspond to the largest reported example in each case. '-' indicates data not reported in publication.

Year	Ref.	Number Format	Method	QP Form.	Target Technology	Design Entry	Operating Frequency	QP size n_v	m_c
2006	[15]	float	Primal-Dual IP	Dense	FPGA	Handel-C	25MHz	3	60
2007	[8]	32/16-bit fixed-point	Explicit	N/A	ASIC	C>Verilog	20MHz	-	-
2008	[14]	float	Primal-Dual IP	Dense	FPGA	Handel-C	25MHz	3	52
2009	[12]	float	Active Set	Dense	FPGA	Handel-C	25MHz	3	52
2009	[11]	float	Primal-Dual IP	Dense	FPGA	C/VHDL	100MHz	-	-
2009	[10]	float	Active Set	Dense	ASIC/FPGA	-	-	-	-
2009	[20]	16-bit LNS	Barrier method	Dense	FPGA	C/Verilog	50MHz	3	6
2010	this paper	float	Primal-Dual IP	Sparse	FPGA	VHDL	150MHz	704	544

tional requirements. The design is entered in VHDL and employs deep pipelining to achieve a higher clock frequency than previous implementations. The parametric design is able to efficiently process problems that are several orders of magnitude larger than the ones considered in previous implementations.

4. PRIMAL-DUAL INTERIOR-POINT ALGORITHM

The optimal control problem (2)–(3) can be written as a sparse QP of the following form:

$$\min_{\theta} \frac{1}{2}\theta^T H\theta$$

$$\text{subject to} \quad F\theta = f$$
$$G\theta \leq g$$

where θ is given by (4),

$$H := \begin{bmatrix} \begin{bmatrix} Q & S \\ S' & R \end{bmatrix} \otimes I_T & 0 \\ 0 & \tilde{Q} \end{bmatrix},$$

$$F := \begin{bmatrix} -I_n \\ A & B & -I_n \\ & & \ddots \\ & & A & B & -I_n \end{bmatrix}, \quad f := \begin{bmatrix} -\hat{x} \\ 0 \\ \vdots \\ 0 \end{bmatrix},$$

$$G := \begin{bmatrix} \begin{bmatrix} J & E \end{bmatrix} \otimes I_T & 0 \\ 0 & J_T \end{bmatrix}, \quad g := \begin{bmatrix} d \\ \vdots \\ d \\ d_T \end{bmatrix},$$

where $\otimes$ denotes a Kronecker product, I is the identity matrix, and 0 denotes a matrix or vector of zeros.

The primal-dual algorithm uses Newton's method [6] for solving a nonlinear system of equations, known as the Karush-Kuhn-Tucker (KKT) optimality conditions. The method solves a sequence of related linear problems. At each iteration, three tasks need to be performed: linearization around the current point, solving the resulting linear system to obtain a search direction, and performing a line search to update the solution to a new point.

The algorithm is described in Algorithm 1, where ν and λ are known as Lagrange multipliers, s are known as slack variables, W_k is a diagonal matrix, and I_{IP} is the number of interior-point iterations (refer to the Appendix and [21] for more details).

Algorithm 1 QP pseudo-code

Choose initial point $(\theta_0, \nu_0, \lambda_0, s_0)$ with $[\lambda_0', s_0']' > 0$
for $k = 0$ to $I_{IP} - 1$ **do**

1. $\mathcal{A}_k := \begin{bmatrix} H + G'W_kG & F' \\ F & 0 \end{bmatrix}$

2. $b_k := \begin{bmatrix} r_k^\theta \\ r_k^\nu \end{bmatrix}$

3. Solve $\mathcal{A}_k z_k = b_k$ for $z_k =: \begin{bmatrix} \Delta\theta_k \\ \Delta\nu_k \end{bmatrix}$

4. Compute $\Delta\lambda_k$

5. Compute Δs_k

6. Find $\alpha_k := \max_{(0,1]} \alpha : \begin{bmatrix} \lambda_k + \alpha\Delta\lambda_k \\ s_k + \alpha\Delta s_k \end{bmatrix} > 0$.

7. $(\theta_{k+1}, \nu_{k+1}, \lambda_{k+1}, s_{k+1}) :=$
$(\theta_k, \nu_k, \lambda_k, s_k) + \alpha_k(\Delta\theta_k, \Delta\nu_k, \Delta\lambda_k, \Delta s_k)$

---
end for
---

5. FPGA IMPLEMENTATION

5.1 Linear Solver

Most of the computational complexity in each iteration of the interior-point method is associated with solving the system of linear equations $\mathcal{A}_k z_k = b_k$. After appropriate row re-ordering, matrix $\mathcal{A}_k$ becomes banded (refer to Figure 4) and symmetric but indefinite, hence has both positive and negative eigenvalues. The size and half-bandwidth of $\mathcal{A}_k$ in terms of the control problem parameters are given respectively by

$$N := T(2n + m) + 2n, \quad (5a)$$
$$M := 2n + m. \quad (5b)$$

Notice that the number of outputs p and the number of constraints l does not affect the size of $\mathcal{A}_k$, which we will show

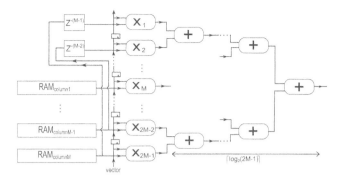

Figure 1: Hardware architecture for computing dot-products. It consists of an array of $2M - 1$ parallel multipliers followed by an adder reduction tree of depth $\lceil \log_2(2M-1) \rceil$. The rest of the operations in a MINRES iteration use dedicated components. Independent memories are used to hold columns of the stored matrix $\mathcal{A}_k$ (refer to Section 5.6 for more details). z^{-M} denotes a delay of M cycles.

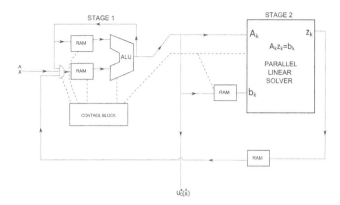

Figure 2: Proposed two-stage hardware architecture. Solid lines represent data flow and dashed lines represent control signals. Stage 1 performs all computations apart from solving the linear system. The input is the current state measurement $\widehat{x}$ and the output is the next optimal control move $u_0^*(\widehat{x})$.

to determine the total runtime. This is another important difference between our design and previous MPC implementations.

The minimum residual (MINRES) method is a suitable iterative algorithm for solving linear systems with indefinite symmetric matrices [7]. At each MINRES iteration, a matrix-vector multiplication accounts for the majority of the computations. This kind of operation is easy to parallelize and consists of multiply-accumulate instructions, which are known to map efficiently into hardware in terms of resources.

In [4] the authors propose an FPGA implementation for solving this type of linear systems using the MINRES method, reporting speed-ups of around one order of magnitude over software implementations. Most of the acceleration is achieved through a deeply pipelined dedicated hardware block (shown in Figure 1) that parallelizes dot-product operations for computing the matrix-vector multiplication in a row-by-row fashion. We use this architecture in our design with a few modifications to customize it to the special characteristics of the matrices that arise in MPC. Notice that the size of the dot-products that are computed in parallel is independent of the control horizon length T (refer to (5b)), thus computational resource usage does not scale with T.

The remaining operations in the interior-point iteration are undertaken by a separate hardware block, which we call Stage 1. The resulting two-stage architecture is shown in Figure 2.

5.2 Pipelining

Since the linear solver will provide most of the acceleration by consuming most resources it is vital that it remains busy at all times. Hence, the parallelism in Stage 1 is chosen to be the smallest possible such that the linear solver is always active.

Notice that if both blocks are to be doing useful work at all times, while the linear system for a specific problem is being solved, Stage 1 has to be updating the solution and linearizing for another independent problem. In addition, the architecture described in [4] has to process P independent problems simultaneously to match latency with throughput and make sure the dot product hardware is active at all

times to achieve maximum efficiency. Hence, our design can process $2P$ independent QP problems simultaneously.

The expression for P in terms of the matrix dimensions and the control problem parameters is given by

$$P := \left\lceil \frac{3N + 24\lceil \log_2(2M-1) \rceil + 154}{N} \right\rceil \quad (6a)$$

$$= \left\lceil \frac{6(T+1)n + 3Tm + 24\lceil \log_2(4n+2m-1) \rceil + 154}{2(T+1)n + Tm} \right\rceil . (6b)$$

For details on the derivation of (6a), refer to [4]; (6b) results from the formulation given in Section 4. The linear term results from the row by row processing for the matrix-vector multiplication (N dot-products) and serial-to-parallel conversions, whereas the log term comes from the depth of the adder reduction tree in the dot-product block. The constant term comes from the other operations in the MINRES iteration. It is important to note that P converges to a small number ($P = 4$) as the size of $\mathcal{A}_k$ increases, thus for large problems only $2P = 8$ independent threads are required to fully utilize the hardware.

5.3 Sequential Block

When computing the coefficient matrix $\mathcal{A}_k$, only the diagonal matrix W_k, defined in the Appendix, changes from one iteration to the next, thus the complexity of this calculation is relatively small. If the structure of the problem is taken into account, we find that the remaining calculations in an interior-point iteration are all sparse and very simple compared to solving the linear system. Comparing the computational count of all the operations to be carried out in Stage 1 with the latency of the linear solver implementation, we come to the conclusion that for most control problems of interest (large problems with large horizon lengths), the optimum implementation of Stage 1 is sequential, as this will be enough to keep the linear solver busy at all times. This is a consequence of the latency of the linear solver being $\Theta(T^2)$ [4], whereas the number of operations in Stage 1 is only $\Theta(T)$.

As a consequence, Stage 1 will be idle most of the time for large problems. This is indeed the situation observed in Figure 3, where we have defined the floating point unit

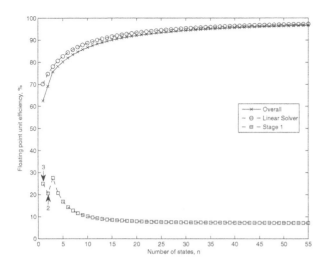

Figure 3: Floating point unit efficiency of the different blocks in the design and overall circuit efficiency with $m = 3$, $p = 3$, $T = 20$, and 20 line search iterations. Numbers on the plot represent the number of parallel instances of Stage 1 required to keep the linear solver active when more than one instance is required.

efficiency as

$$\frac{\text{floating point computations per iteration}}{\#\text{floating point units} \times \text{cycles per iteration}}.$$

For very small problems it is possible that Stage 1 will take longer than solving the linear system. In this cases, in order to avoid having the linear solver idle, another instance of Stage 1 is synthesized to operate in parallel with the original instance and share the same control block. For large problems, only one instance of Stage 1 is required. The efficiency of the circuit increases as the problems become larger as a result of the dot-product block, which is always active by design, consuming a greater portion of the overall resources.

5.3.1 Datapath

The computational block performs any of the main arithmetic operations: addition/subtraction, multiplication and division. Xilinx Core Generator [1] was used to generate highly optimized single-precision floating point units with maximum latency to achieve a high clock frequency. Extra registers were added after the multiplier to match the latency of the adder for synchronization, as these are the most common operations. The latency of the divider is much larger (27 cycles) than the adder (12 cycles) and the multiplier (8 cycles), therefore it was decided not to mach the delay of the divider path, as it would reduce our flexibility for ordering computations. NOPs were inserted whenever division operations were needed, namely only when calculating W_k and s_k^{-1}.

Comparison operations are also required for the line search method (Line 6 of Algorithm 1), however this is implemented by repeated comparison with zero, so only the sign bit needs to be checked and a full floating-point comparator is not needed.

The total number of floating point units in the circuit is given by

$$\text{Number of Floating Point Units} = 8n + 4m + 27, \quad (7)$$

where only three units belong to Stage 1, which explains the behaviour observed in Figure 3.

5.3.2 Control Block

Since the same computational units are being reused to perform many different operations, the necessary control is rather complex. The control block needs to provide the correct sequence of read and write addresses for the data RAMs, as well as other control signals, such as computation selection. An option would be to store the values for all control signals at every cycle in a program memory and have a counter iterating through them. However, this would take a large amount of memory. For this reason it was decided to trade a small increase in computational resources for a much larger decrease in memory requirements.

Frequently occurring memory access patterns have been identified and a dedicated address generator hardware block has been built to generate them from minimum storage. Each pattern is associated with a control instruction. Examples of these patterns are: simple increments $a, a+1, ..., a+b$ and the more complicated read patterns needed for matrix vector multiplication (standard and transposed). This approach allows storing only one instruction for a whole matrix-vector multiplication or for an arbitrary long sequence of additions. Control instructions to perform line search and linearization for one problem were stored. When the last instruction is reached, the counter goes back to instruction 0 and iterates again for the next problem with the necessary offsets being added to the control signals.

5.3.3 Memory Subsystem

Separate memory blocks were used for data and control instructions, allowing simultaneous access and different word-lengths in a similar way to a Harvard microprocessor architecture. However, in our circuit there are no cache misses and a useful result can be produced almost every cycle. The data memories are divided in two blocks, each one feeding one input of the computational block. The intermediate results can be stored in any of these simple dual-port RAMs for flexibility in ordering computations. The memory to store the control instructions is divided into four single port ROMs corresponding to read and write addresses of each of the data RAMs. The responsibility for generating the remaining control signals is spread out over the four blocks.

5.4 Latency and Throughput

Since the FPGA has completely predictable timing, we can calculate the latency and throughput of our system. For large problems, where the linear solver is busy at all times, the overall latency of the circuit will be given by

$$\text{Latency} = \frac{2I_{IP}(PN + P)I_{MINRES}}{\text{FPGA}_{freq}} \text{ seconds}, \quad (8)$$

where I_{MINRES} is the number of iterations the MINRES method takes to solve the linear system to the required accuracy, I_{IP} is the number of outer iterations in the interior-point method (Algorithm 1), FPGA_{freq} is the FPGA's clock frequency, $(PN + P)$ is the latency of one MINRES iteration [4], and P is given by (6a). In that time the controller will be able to output the result to $2P$ problems.

5.5 Input/Output

Stage 1 is responsible for handling the chip I/O. It reads the current state measurement $\widehat{x}$ as n 32-bit floating point values sequentially through a 32-bit parallel input data port. Outputting the m 32-bit values for the optimal control move $u_0^*(\widehat{x})$ is handled in a similar fashion. When processing $2P$ problems, the average I/O requirements are given by

$$\frac{2P(32(n+m))}{\text{Latency given by (8)}} \text{ bits/second.}$$

For the example problems that we have considered in Section 6, the I/O requirements range from 0.2 to 10 kbits/second, which is well within any standard FPGA platform interface, such as PCI Express. The combination of a very computationally intensive task with very low I/O requirements, highlights the affinity of the FPGA for MPC computation.

5.6 Coefficient Matrix Storage

When implementing an algorithm in software, a large amount of memory is available for storing intermediate results. In FPGAs, there is a very limited amount of fast on-chip memory, around 4.5MBytes for high-end memory-dense Xilinx Virtex-6 devices [2]. If a particular design requires more memory than available on chip, there are two negative consequences. Firstly, if the size of the problems we can process is limited by memory, it means that the computational capabilities of the device are not being fully exploited, since there will be unutilized slices and DSP blocks. Secondly, if we were to try to overcome this problem by using off-chip memory, the performance of the circuit is likely to suffer since off-chip memory accesses are slow compared to the on-chip clock frequency. By taking into account the special structure of the matrices that are fed to the linear solver in the context of MPC, we substantially reduce memory requirements so that this issue affects a smaller subset of problems.

The matrix $\mathcal{A}_k$ is banded and symmetric (after re-ordering). On-chip buffering of these type of matrices using compressed diagonal storage (CDS) can achieve substantial memory savings with minimum control overhead in an FPGA implementation of the MINRES method [5]. The memory reductions are achieved by only storing the non-zero diagonals of the original matrix as columns of the new compressed matrix. Since the matrix is also symmetric, only the right hand side of the CDS matrix needs to be stored, as the left-hand columns are just delayed versions of the stored columns. In order to achieve the same result when multiplying by a vector, the vector has to be aligned with its corresponding matrix components. It turns out that this is simply achieved by shifting the vector by one position at every clock cycle, which is implemented by a serial-in parallel-out shift register (refer to Figure 1).

The method described in [5] assumes a dense band; however, it is possible to achieve further memory savings by exploiting the structure of the MPC problem even further. The structure of the original matrix and corresponding CDS matrix for a small MPC problem are shown in Figure 4, showing variables (elements that can vary from iteration to iteration of the interior-point method) and constants.

The first observation is that non-zero blocks are separated by layers of zeros in the CDS matrix. It is possible to only

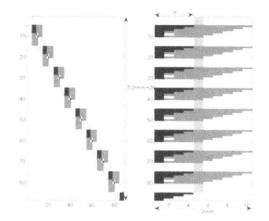

Figure 4: Structure of original and CDS matrices showing variables (black), constants (dark grey), zeros (white) and ones (light grey) for $m = 2, n = 4$, and $T = 8$.

store one of these zeros per column and add common circuitry to generate appropriate sequences of read addresses, *i.e.*

$$0, 0, ..., 0, 1, 2, ..., m+n, 0, 0, ..., 0, m+n+1, m+n+2, ..., 2(m+n)$$

The second observation is that only a few diagonals adjacent to the main diagonal vary from iteration to iteration, while the rest remain constant at all times. This means that only a few columns in the CDS matrix contain varying elements. This has important implications, since in the MINRES implementation [4], matrices for the P problems that are being processed simultaneously have to be buffered on-chip. These memory blocks have to be double in size to allow writing the data for the next problems while reading the data for the current problems. Constant columns in the CDS matrix are common for all problems, hence the memories used to store them can be much smaller. Finally, constant columns mainly consist of repeated blocks of size $2n + m$ (where n values are zeros or ones), hence further memory savings can be attained by only storing one of those blocks per column.

A memory controller for the variable columns and another memory controller for the constant columns were created in order to be able to generate the necessary access patterns. The impact on the overall performance is negligible, since these controllers consume few resources compared with floating point units and they do not slow down the circuit.

If we consider a dense band, storing the coefficient matrix using CDS would require $2P(T(2n+m)+2n)(2n+m)$ elements. By taking into account the sparsity of matrices arising in MPC, it is possible to only store $2P(1 + T(m + n) + n)n + (1+m+n)(m+n)$ elements. Figure 5 compares the memory requirements for storing the coefficient matrices on-chip when considering: a dense matrix, a banded symmetric matrix and an MPC matrix (all in single-precision floating-point). Memory savings of approximately 75% can be incurred by considering the in-band structure of the MPC problem compared to the standard CDS implementation. In practice, columns are stored in BlockRAMs of discrete sizes, therefore actual savings vary in the FPGA implementation.

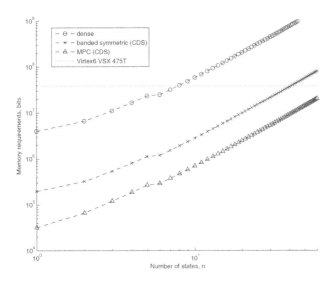

Figure 5: Memory requirements for storing the coefficient matrices under different schemes. Problem parameters are $m = 3$ and $T = 20$. p and l do not affect the memory requirements of $\mathcal{A}_k$. The horizontal line represents the memory available in a memory-dense Virtex 6 device [2].

6. RESULTS

6.1 Resource Usage

The design was synthesized using Xilinx XST and placed and routed using Xilinx ISE 12 targeting a Virtex 6 VSX 475T [2]. Figure 6 shows how the different resources scale with the problem size. For m and T fixed, the number of floating point units is $\Theta(n)$, hence the linear growth in registers, look-up tables and embedded DSP blocks. The memory requirements are $\Theta(n^2)$, which explain the quadratic asymptotic growth observed in Figure 6. The jumps occur when the number of elements to be stored in the RAMs for variable columns exceeds the size of Xilinx BlockRAMs. If the number of QP problems being processed simultaneously is chosen smaller than the value given by (6a), the BlockRAM usage will decrease, whereas the other resources will remain unaffected.

6.2 Performance

Post place-and-route results showed that a clock frequency above 150MHz is achievable with very small variations for different problem sizes, since the critical path is inside the control block in Stage 1. Figure 7 shows the latency and throughput performance of the FPGA and latency results for a microprocessor implementation. For the software benchmark, we have used a direct C sequential implementation, compiled using GCC -O4 optimizations running on a Intel Core2 Q8300 with 3GB of RAM, 4MB L2 cache, and a clock frequency of 2.5GHz running Linux. Note that for matrix operations of this size, this approach produces better performance software than using libraries such as Intel MKL.

As expected, the microprocessor performance is far from its peak for smaller problems, since the algorithm involves lots of movements of small blocks of data to exploit structure, specially for the operations outside the linear solver. Figure 7 shows how the performance gap between the CPU

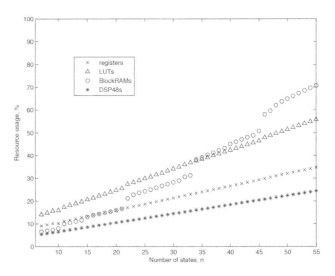

Figure 6: Resource utilization on a Virtex 6 VSX 475T ($m = 3, T = 20, P$ given by (6a)).

and FPGA widens as the size of the problem increases as a result of increased parallelism in the linear solver. Approximately a 6.5x improvement in latency and a 51x improvement in throughput are possible for the largest problem considered. However, notice that even for large problems there is a large portion of unutilized resources, which could be used to extract more parallelism in the interior-point method and achieve even greater speed-ups.

7. CASE STUDY

To illustrate the performance improvement that can be achieved with the sampling frequency upgrade enabled by our FPGA implementation, we apply our MPC controller to an example system under different sampling intervals. The example system consists of 16 masses connected by equal springs (shown in Figure 8). Mass number three is eight times lighter than the other masses, which results in an oscillatory mode at 0.66Hz. There are two states per mass, its position and velocity, hence the system has 32 states. Each mass can be actuated by a horizontal force ($m = 16$) and the reference for the outputs to track is the zero position for all masses ($p = 16$).

The control horizon length (T_h) for a specific system is specified in seconds, therefore, sampling faster leads to more steps in the horizon (T) and larger optimization problems to solve at each sampling instant. For the example system we found that this quantity was approximately $T_h = 3.1$ seconds. Table 3 shows the sampling interval and computational delays for the CPU and FPGA implementations for different number of steps in the horizon. For each implementation, the operating sampling interval is chosen the smallest possible such that the computational delay allows solving the optimization problem before the next sample needs to be taken. Figure 9 presents the simulation results, which highlight the better tracking achievable with the FPGA implementation, leading to lower control cost. Notice the terrible response of the CPU implementation after the disturbance takes place, whereas the FPGA response is oscillation absent.

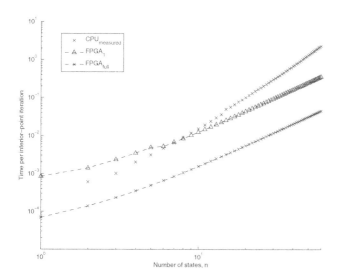

Figure 7: Performance comparison showing measured performance of the CPU, and FPGA performance when solving one problem and $2P$ problems given by (6a). Problem parameters are $m = 3$, $T = 20$, $p = 3$, and **FPGA**$_{freq} = 150$**MHz.**

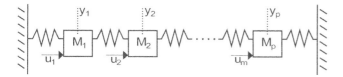

Figure 8: Spring-mass system.

8. CONCLUSION

This paper has described a parameterizable FPGA architecture for solving QP optimization problems in linear MPC. Various design decisions have been justified based on the significant exploitable structure in the problem. The main source of acceleration is a parallel linear solver block, which reduces the latency of the main computational bottleneck in the optimization method. Results show that a significant reduction in latency is possible compared to a sequential software implementation, which translates to high sampling frequencies and better quality control. The potential for industrial take-up of this technology is currently being explored with our partners.

We are currently working on completely automating the design flow with the objective of choosing the data representation and level of parallelism that makes the most efficient use of all resources available in any given target FPGA platform, avoiding the situation observed in Figure 6, where for a large number of states, memory resources are exhausted well before logic resources.

9. ACKNOWLEDGMENTS

The authors would like to acknowledge the support of the EPSRC (Grant EP/G031576/1), discussions with Prof. Jan Maciejowski, Prof. Ling Keck Voon, Mr. David Boland and Mr. Amir Shazhad, and industrial support from Xilinx, the Mathworks, and the European Space Agency.

Table 3: Computational delay for each implementation when $I_{IP} = 14$. In MPC, the computational delay has to be smaller than the sampling interval. The grey region represents cases where the computational delay is larger than the sampling interval, hence the implementation is infeasible. The smallest sampling interval that the FPGA can handle is 0.388 seconds (2.58Hz), whereas the CPU samples every 0.775 seconds (1.29Hz). The relationship $Ts = \frac{T_h}{T}$ holds.

T	FPGA	CPU	Sampling interval, T_s
4	0.110	0.503	**0.775**
5	0.161	0.721	0.620
6	0.221	0.995	0.517
7	0.291	1.291	0.442
8	0.371	1.641	**0.388**
9	0.460	2.023	0.344

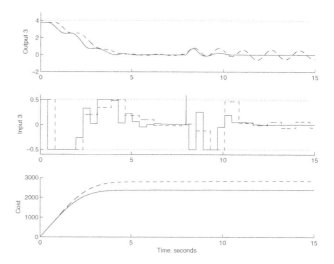

Figure 9: Comparison of the closed-loop performance of the FPGA (solid) and the CPU (dashed). The dotted lines represent the physical constraints of the system. The simulation includes a disturbance on the inputs between 7 and 8 seconds.

10. REFERENCES

[1] Core Generator guide, 2010
http://www.xilinx.com/itp/xilinx6/books/docs/cgn/cgn.pdf.

[2] Virtex-6 family overview, 2010
http://www.xilinx.com/support/documentation/data_sheets/ds150.pdf.

[3] S. Bayliss, C. S. Bouganis, and G. A. Constantinides. An FPGA implementation of the Simplex algorithm. In *Proc. Int. Conf. on Field Programmable Technology*, pages 49–55, Bangkok, Thailand, Dec 2006.

[4] D. Boland and G. A. Constantinides. An FPGA-based implementation of the MINRES algorithm. In *Proc. Int. Conf. on Field Programmable Logic and Applications*, pages 379–384, Heidelberg, Germany, Sep 2008.

[5] D. Boland and G. A. Constantinides. Optimising memory bandwidth use for matrix-vector multiplication in iterative methods. In *Proc. Int. Symp. on Applied Reconfigurable Computing*, pages 169–181, Bangkok, Thailand, Mar 2010.

[6] S. P. Boyd and L. Vandenberghe. *Convex Optimization*. Cambridge University Press, Cambridge, UK, 2004.

[7] B. Fisher. *Polynomial based iteration methods for symmetric linear systems*. Wiley, Baltimore, MD, USA, 1996.

[8] T. A. Johansen, W. Jackson, and P. T. Robert Schreiber. Hardware synthesis of explicit model predictive controllers. *IEEE Transactions on Control Systems Technolog*, 15(1):191–197, Jan 2007.

[9] T. Keviczky and G. J. Balas. Receding horizon control of an F-16 aircraft: A comparative study. *Control Engineering Practice*, 14(9):1023–1033, Sep 2006.

[10] G. Knagge, A. Wills, A. Mills, and B. Ninnes. ASIC and FPGA implementation strategies for model predictive control. In *Proc. European Control Conference*, Budapest, Hungary, Aug 2009.

[11] S. L. Koh. Solving interior point method on a FPGA. Master's thesis, Nanyang Technological University, Singapore, 2009.

[12] M. S. Lau, S. P. Yue, K.-V. Ling, and J. M. Maciejowski. A comparison of interior point and active set methods for FPGA implementation of model predictive control. In *Proc. European Control Conference*, pages 156–160, Budapest, Hungary, Aug 2009.

[13] B. Leung, C.-H. Wu, S. O. Memik, and S. Mehrotra. An interior point optimization solver for real time inter-frame collision detection: Exploring resource-accuracy-platform tradeoffs. In *Proc. Int. Conf. on Field Programmable Logic and Applications*, pages 113–118, Milano, Italy, Sep 2010.

[14] K.-V. Ling, B. F. Wu, and J. M. Maciejowski. Embedded model predictive control (MPC) using a FPGA. In *Proc. 17th IFAC World Congress*, pages 15250–15255, Seoul, Korea, Jul 2008.

[15] K.-V. Ling, S. P. Yue, and J. M. Maciejowski. An FPGA implementation of model predictive control. In *Proc. American Control Conference*, page 6 pp., Minneapolis, USA, Jun 2006.

[16] A. R. Lopes and G. A. Constantinides. A high throughput FPGA-based floating-point conjugate gradient implementation for dense matrices. In *Proc. 4th Int. Workshop on Applied Reconfigurable Computing*, pages 75–86, London, UK, Mar 2008.

[17] J. Maciejowski. *Predictive Control with Constraints*. Pearson Education, Harlow, UK, 2001.

[18] S. Mehrotra. On the implementation of a primal-dual interior point method. *SIAM Journal on Optimization*, 2(4):575–601, Nov 1992.

[19] J. Nocedal and S. J. Wright. *Numerical Optimization*. Springer, New York, USA, 2006.

[20] P. D. Vouzis, L. G. Bleris, M. G. Arnold, and M. V. Kothare. A system-on-a-chip implementation for embedded real-time model predictive control. *IEEE Transactions on Control Systems Technology*, 17(5):1006–1017, Sep 2009.

[21] S. J. Wright. Applying new optimization algorithms to model predictive control. In *Proc. Int. Conf. Chemical Process Control*, pages 147–155. CACHE Publications, 1997.

[22] S. J. Wright. *Primal-Dual Interior-Point Methods*. SIAM, Philadelphia, USA, 1997.

APPENDIX

This appendix provides the remaining details of the QP algorithm, removed from the pseudo-code in Algorithm 1 for readability. In the following, σ is a scalar between zero and one known as the centrality parameter [21], and Λ_k and S_k are diagonal matrices containing the elements of λ_k and s_k respectively.

$$W_k := \Lambda_k S_k^{-1}$$

$$\mu_k := \frac{\lambda_k' s_k}{Tl + 2p}$$

$$r_k^\theta := -(H + G'W_kG)\theta_k - F'\nu_k - G'(\lambda_k - W_kg + \sigma\mu_k s_k^{-1})$$

$$r_k^\nu := -F\theta_k + f$$

$$\Delta\lambda_k := W_k(G(\theta_k + \Delta\theta_k) - g) + \sigma\mu_k s_k^{-1}$$

$$\Delta s_k := -s_k - (G(\theta_k + \Delta\theta_k) - g)$$

Exploration of FPGA Interconnect for the Design of Unconventional Antennas

Abhay Tavaragiri
abhay@vt.edu

Jacob Couch
jacouch@vt.edu

Peter Athanas
athanas@vt.edu

Bradley Department of Electrical and Computer Engineering
Virginia Polytechnic Institute and State University
Blacksburg, VA 24061-0111 USA

ABSTRACT

The programmable interconnection resources are one aspect that distinguishes FPGAs from other devices. The abundance of these resources in modern devices almost always assures us that the most complex design can be routed. This underutilized resource can be used for other unintended purposes. One such use, explored here, is to concatenate large networks together to form pseudo-equipotential geometric shapes. These shapes can then be evaluated in terms of their ability to radiate (modulated) energy off the chip to a nearby receiver. In this paper, an unconventional method of building such transmitters on an FPGA is proposed. Arbitrary shaped antennas are created using a unique flow involving an experimental router and binary images. An experiment setup is used to measure the performance of the antennas created.

Categories and Subject Descriptors

B.4.1 [**Input/Output and Data Communications**]: Data Communications Devices— *Transmitters*

General Terms

Design, Experimentation, Measurement, Performance

Keywords

Antenna Design, Geometric Routing, Embedded Transceivers, Hidden Transmitter

1. Introduction

Traditionally, circuits constructed on FPGAs are designed using Hardware Description Languages (HDL) like Verilog or VHDL. Digital and analog signals are presented to the FPGA at the boundary of the FPGA fabric. All signals are then converted to digital signals for use within the FPGA. This practice leads to the logical conclusion that the target circuits on an FPGA are typically digital in nature.

Modern FPGAs have highly complex, programmable, interconnection structures, fabricated using many metal layers. For example, the Virtex-4 FPGA is fabricated utilizing an 11-metal-layer process [14]. Typically, 80% of the configuration bits in a given bitstream control the wire segments and programmable switches that make up the programmable interconnect network [5]. This network is made up of long segment routing, dedicated routing, local routing, and switch matrices, which are in turn made of wire segments and programmable interconnect points (PIPs). There are instances where the programmable interconnect can be used for other things beyond connecting two or more wires. Such a process would not involve the CLBs in the FPGA; clearing the path for a non-digital circuit.

The creation of non-digital circuits on an FPGA is an interesting concept with the potential for extending the opportunities for FPGAs. It does, however, seem improbable since non-traditional circuits are neither supported by HDLs nor the FPGA primitives.

One non-traditional use of FPGAs is the creation of geometric shapes and filled patterns, by using the programmable interconnect as a pallet. A *shape* is defined here as a single two-dimensional curve that consists of a long network of interconnected wire segments forming a single net that completely fills the interior of the curve. Such structures serve no obvious function in a typical digital circuit, yet can provide other auxiliary unintended functionality such as the ability to create various shaped antennas. For the purposes of this paper, an antenna is defined as a structure that radiates energy in a controlled manner. This energy could then be used to transmit a digital signal. One theory investigated here is that these antennas in turn act as conventional antennas, by resonating at various frequencies depending upon the shape, and radiating energy when properly excited. Due to the abundance of the programmable interconnect, these geometric structures can reside *transparently* on top of a normal (digital) design without interfering or changing the functionality of the digital circuit. A signal or a set of signals from the digital circuit can be used to modulate a *carrier signal* whose frequency is selected based upon the resonant frequency of the geometric structure. The end result is an on-chip circuit capable of radiating selective information off-chip.

Xilinx FPGAs are used in this study since the underlying configuration bitstream can be readily modified at abstraction levels lower than HDL (XDL in this case). These low-level manipulations, which are not readily available on other FPGA platforms, allow the creation of these unconventional

Figure 1: A sample binary bitmap file in Microsoft Paint

routing designs. This use-case utilizes the programmable interconnect as something that was never intended: as a medium for radiating energy off a device.

Section 2 of this paper describes the process of creating 2D shapes, or geometric structures using the programmable interconnect and a special router. The resulting shapes can serve a useful function. Section 3 outlines the process of transforming the shapes into antenna, and the experiments used to measure the effectiveness of the antenna. Section 4 presents applications of these techniques. And finally, Section 5 concludes the paper.

2. Creating Geometric Shapes

This section presents a way of creating 2D structures using the abundance of underutilized wires within the FPGA fabric. In the tool flow presented here, shapes are initially described as a simple binary bitmap image that can be created using any drawing tool (Figure 1). FPGAs contain many resources that are arranged on a grid where each cell is known as a *tile*. The crucial aspect is that the dimensions of the bitmap file provide a one-to-one mapping to the tile resources of the FPGA being targeted. With the use of some software manipulations, the bitmap file is mapped into a new structure of '0's and '1's with '0's representing the white portion of the image and '1's representing the black portion of the image. Therefore, a '1' in the mapping selects a tile in which all of its free routing resources are merged with all adjacent '1' tiles, and the '0's map to tiles that are left alone.

It should be noted that only the routing resources of the FPGA are being utilized in this application. There are many other resources on the FPGA that do not allow routing such as SLICEL, SLICEM, DSP, BRAM, and IOB sites. With the exception of a few special resource columns in the FPGA, every other row contains an interconnect on the switch matrix that allows for precise structured routing. Although non-switch matrix resources are represented in the bitmap, the enablement of these resources allows for the inputs of the resource to be saturated while the resource itself is not utilized. This prevents any horizontal or vertical routing expansion through these non-routing resources [10].

The process of creating geometric structures on a FPGA is divided into two major phases: a static design phase, and a geometric shape design phase. The static design phase is the normal process of creating a digital circuit for an FPGA. There are no restrictions on placement or resources used in this design. The second phase is the creation of the geometric shape using the routing resources. These phases are then merged together. An electrical connection between the two phases is accomplished through the use of a "dummy" bus-macro. This is similar to how a partial region is connected to a static region in partially re-configurable designs per the Xilinx Partial Reconfiguration toolchain [2]. This single connection provides a means of actively driving the single-net geometric structure.

2.1 Design Merging

As stated above, once the static design is defined, it must provide a mechanism to be connected to the geometric structure. This is accomplished by placing a "dummy" bus-macro on the net which excites the geometric structure. Bus-macros are merely slices on the FPGA that pass a signal through the LUT and only buffer the logic value while not changing the logic value. Any pass-through logic element would work for the interconnection between the two phases, and is used only for its anchoring abilities. It also provides a new source which regenerates the signal for the geometric structure net. The bus-macro, and the interconnect tile directly to the west of the bus-macro slice, must be within the black region in the bitmap. If this does not occur, then the driving line for the geometric structure cannot be brought from the bus-macro to the actual routed geometric structure. Once the bus-macro is placed and added to the proper nets, the net is re-routed utilizing the standard Xilinx router [2].

After the static design is created and the bus-macro is placed on the FPGA, all wire segments on the FPGA that are utilized by the static design must be found and marked as used. This prevents the geometric structure design from interfering with the static design. With the Xilinx FPGA routing schema, routing conflicts are not always detectable based on PIP names. The router must assure that it does not attempt to place two nets on the same indivisible segment on the FPGA.

ADB is a connectivity database originally created at Virginia Tech that provides wiring data for most modern Xilinx FPGAs [6]. Within ADB, a concept known as wire segments provides a unique hash value for each possible indivisible wire grouping. By utilizing the ADB as a tool to identify the segment membership of each PIP, wire segment conflicts can be identified and removed from the design.

2.2 Fill Router

Typically, routers use algorithms such as Pathfinder that go through several routing iterations to determine the best possible routing for two or more nodes on a given network [4]. However, for the given application, an unconventional router is used. This router is agnostic with respect to critical paths and, its goal is to saturate the geometric structure within a specified region. This special router that saturates regions with routes, called the *Fill Router*, has been created specifically for this task [8].

The Fill Router works by having a collection of wire segments that is initially seeded with a known allowable wire segment. For the static design, the wire segment that is the output from the bus-macro is adequate to seed the Fill Router. From these wire segments, all possible fan-out paths

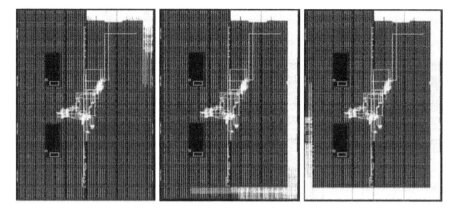

Figure 2: Fill Router coverage after six, eleven and fifteen wavefronts using the seed image in Figure 1.

are discovered by querying ADB. Each PIP that is found through the fan-out process is then evaluated to determine if it satisfies the following constraints:

- The newly merged segment does not conflict with the static design.

- The newly merged segment is currently not being utilized in the existing geometric structure.

- The newly merged segment is in a location that is within an allowable region based on the bitmap image.

Each new wire segment that is discovered and approved is then placed into a collection for the next round. Furthermore, each PIP that passes the constraint evaluation is added to the geometric structure net.

An iteration is completed after all PIPs discovered from the wire segment collection are evaluated, and the PIP is either added to the geometric structure net or discarded. This process continues until there are no additional PIPs added in a round. The iterative process is captured at multiple stages in the FPGA_Editor screen shots shown in Figure 2. Although this process does not have a control parameter to determine how much to grow each round, because the goal is to saturate the region and the region is bounded, the process will eventually complete after all available and allowable resources on the FPGA are exhausted. Figure 3 depicts the final design where the loop structure of Figure 1 is iteratively filled, and then layered onto a simple existing design.

The resulting design has the characteristic of being a single long trunk with many short branches. This structure should provide an almost uniform propagation path along the design by preventing multiple paths from the beginning to the end of the geometric structure path. Furthermore, the net retains its tree like parameters and is unlike a directed graph in which there can be a convergence of multiple paths.

2.3 Integration into Xilinx Toolchain

All manipulations of the design are conducted at the XDL level [11]. XDL is an intermediate data format that Xilinx provides that allows for the manipulation of modules, instances, and nets within a FPGA design. To get a design into the XDL format, the output file after the static place and route process is captured as a NCD file. The NCD file is

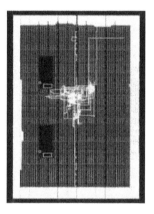

Figure 3: The consolidated geometric structure

Figure 4: Another geometric structure implemented on a XCV5LX110T

221

then converted to a XDL file utilizing the XDL2NCD utility [11]. The XDL file is first evaluated and the custom bus-macro and geometric structure net are then inserted into the XDL representation of the design. Although the NCD file could be captured before the static translating, mapping, placing and routing, a risk remains that the static design could then not be inserted into the design if the geometric structure net is inserted first. Once all manipulations are added to the XDL file, the XDL can be converted back to a NCD file and re-inserted into the Xilinx toolchain to generate a bitstream.

3. Shapes as Antennas

In this paper, the sole purpose of creating the geometric structures is to evaluate their ability to resonate and radiate energy off-chip. Unlike a traditional radio transmitter process, there are no readily available amplifiers, pulse shapers, or analog filters. One must make-do with the limited digital circuitry available within the FPGA. In the experiments performed here, the output of a numerically-controlled oscillator is directly connected to the geometric shape through the dummy bus macro. Various shapes were created and tested, and radiated energy was measured. The theory tested here is that the shape of the antenna effects the radiated energy. It is possible that some other phenomenon is influencing the observed behavior, yet the experiments conducted appear to support the initial hypothesis. Control experiments were created where no geometric shapes were deployed to verify the effectiveness of the antenna structures.

The performance of the antenna structures created is measured by an experimental setup. Using a spectrum analyzer, connected to a signal detection coil placed under the target FPGA board, radiated energy can be measured.

It should be emphasized that the usage of the term "antenna" may not directly correspond to antennas in conventional radios. The transmission characteristics are quite different and the power efficiencies are worse than a conventional "antenna". The geometric structures created in this flow may indeed be driven in-phase by a single driver, yet is not necessarily an equipotential region. Note that there is no explicit knowledge of the underlying VLSI design beyond what is exposed in FPGA_Editor [10]. For typical antenna designs, designers are interested in the geometric shape and characteristic impedance of all segments. This design is unable to evaluate these characteristics because the physical characteristics are not released by Xilinx, thus there is no knowledge of which physical metal layers are being utilized for each net [16]. It is likely that the geometric structure net is passing through many metal layers of the FPGA, some of which may be entirely shielded. Because these nets are designed as digital networks, it is not only likely, but probable that the antenna net passes through resources such as digital switches, MUXes, keepers, terminators, and buffers. Interestingly, the antenna structures on the FPGAs have enough portions of the net that possess good radiating characteristics such that a corresponding receiver outside the FPGA can detect the radiation from the FPGA.

3.1 Signal Detection

The radiated energy transmitted by the antenna on the FPGA is captured using a signal detection coil. The coil is constructed to be a square of six turns with dimensions of $2cm \times 2cm$. The trivial nature of the detection circuitry

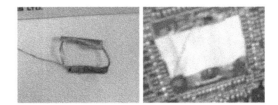

Figure 5: The detection coil taped to the FPGA board

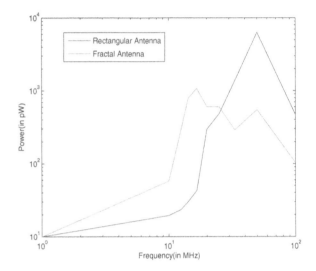

Figure 6: The antenna energy radiation graph

implies that the energy captured might be slightly lesser than what is actually being radiated. A more sophisticated system for detecting the radiation might lead to a better radiation efficiency.

The FPGA board used to conduct the initial experiments is the Xilinx ML410 (Revision E) which has an on-board Virtex-4 FPGA with the part number XC4VFX60-CES4S-FFG1152-11. The ML410 board is equipped with two crystal oscillator sockets (X6 and X10) each wired for standard LVTTL-type oscillators [15]. The X6 is populated with a 100MHz oscillator that provides the system clock which is used as an input to the user controlled excitation source previously described.

The Virtex-4 FPGA has a metal casing on top, which is in direct contact with a metal heat sink. This combination is likely quite effective in blocking radiated energy. Further, the Virtex-4 is packaged in a Flip-Chip BGA. Unlike traditional packaging in which the die is attached to the substrate face up and the connection is made by using wire, the solder bumped die in flip-chip BGA is flipped over and placed face down, with the conductive bumps connecting directly to the matching metal pads on the laminate substrate [13]. Thus, the maximum expected radiation would be if the detection is done below the FPGA chip rather than above it. In the experiments performed, the coil is attached to the board right beneath the FPGA chip (Figure 5) to capture the radiation from the FPGA through the PCB (also likely to have ground and power planes).

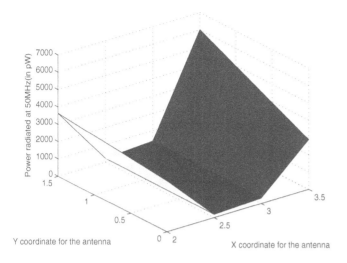

Figure 7: Effect of detection coil position on energy radiation

3.2 Methodology

The FPGA is initially powered on and the response of the signal detection coil is noted on a spectrum analyzer. The on-chip programmable oscillator is then turned on using Xilinx's ChipScope [12] software to the desired frequency and the response is measured again. As the frequency is swept, the peaks are observed for a given geometric shape. The frequency at which the highest peak is observed is assumed to be the resonant frequency of the geometric shape. When the oscillator is turned off, the peak reduces back to its original value, indicating that the energy dissipation is indeed caused by the excitation of the antenna in the FPGA. The energy radiation graph of the rectangular antenna is compared with that of a fractal antenna (discussed in Section 3.5) in Figure 6.

3.3 Sensing the Radiated Energy

An important aspect to be considered is the position of the detection coil under the FPGA chip. The detection coil is approximately $2cm \times 2cm$ whereas the FPGA chip is a square of approximately $3.5cm \times 3.5cm$. It is observed that the best performances are achieved when two of the sides of the square coil coincide with those of the FPGA. In contrast, the worst performance is when the coil is placed in the middle of the chip dimensions with no edges coinciding (Figure 7).

3.4 Antenna's Contribution to Radiation

An experiment was performed to verify that the antenna was actually contributing to the radiated energy. This was verified by making a slight change to the design. Instead of connecting the oscillator output to the antenna structure, it was connected to a slice just outside of the antenna net (Figure 8) and the procedure detailed in Section 3.2 was repeated. The radiated energy in this case was nearly zero confirming that it was indeed the antenna structure causing the radiation.

3.5 The Fractal Antenna

In order to illustrate the robustness and the system in-

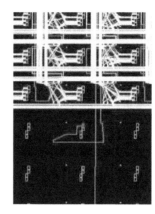

Figure 8: Oscillator connected just outside of the antenna net

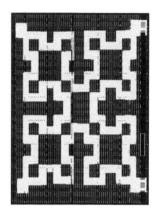

Figure 9: The fractal antenna

dependence of the above mentioned approach, a wideband fractal antenna is also implemented. The fractal antenna structure used in this experiment has a maximum number of corners in addition to a maximal path length [1].

The XUPV5 (Revision A) board, consisting of the Virtex-5 FPGA XC5LX110T-FF1136-1, is used for this experiment. The experiment setup and the mechanism for measuring the radiated energy are the same as the ML410 experiment, except the XUPV5 is the FPGA under test. The energy radiation graph of the fractal antenna confirms that radiation is emanating from the FPGA in this experiment. An FPGA_Editor snapshot of the fractal antenna (Figure 9) is shown. As illustrated in Figure 6, although the total power radiated is less than the rectangular antenna, the frequency peak is much wider in comparison to the rectangular antenna.

3.6 Hidden Transmitter

An interesting application of the structures created is that of a hidden transmitter. The transmitter antenna designed can be embedded onto a dense logic design covering almost the entire FPGA. As mentioned before, these structures can be merged with a dense design while remaining electrically isolated and without impacting the operation of the intended circuit, all due to the abundance of programmable interconnect. The design of such a system would make it nearly impossible to detect the transmitter through visual inspection or by netlist extraction. To the untrained observer, the

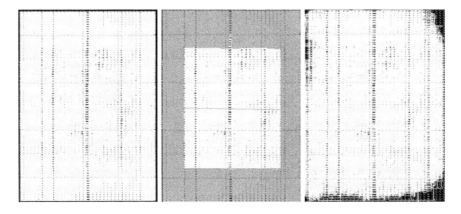

Figure 10: Dense design illustration in FPGA_Editor (a) design with antenna overlayed, (b) antenna net highlighted, (c) design without antenna

FPGA provides the intended digital operation, yet behind the scene, a hidden transmitter is actively producing a signal. The transmitter could also be further hidden by running the signal through bus-macros and route-throughs throughout the design. Figure 10 clearly illustrates this concept. The FPGA_Editor snapshot on the left shows the original dense design with the non-discernible embedded antenna structure. The middle snapshot shows the actual antenna structure when highlighted using FPGA_Editor. The snapshot on the right shows the untampered design without the antenna structure.

It is important to distinguish the concept of a hidden transmitter from that of side-channel power analysis attacks. A broad family of statistical power analysis techniques can be used to infer data from within a device. These can be further sub-categorized into Simple Power Analysis (SPA), Differential Power Analysis (DPA) and Correlation Power Analysis (CPA) [7]. SPA and DPA attacks directly use the power consumption information of a signal to break a cryptographic algorithm by monitoring the voltage and current fluctuations of a circuit [3]. CPA, on the other hand, is a technique of withdrawing the correct key using correlation coefficient of statistics [9].

Both the hidden transmitter and the power analysis techniques retrieve non-exposed data from a FPGA. However, the hidden transmitter uses it for radiating energy rather than capturing information about the underlying circuit.

4. Future Research

The results obtained from the experiments have been encouraging; however, there is still room for enhancement in certain aspects of the design. The initial experiments were performed on the ML410 (Revision E) board with a Virtex-4 FPGA and a XUPV5 board with a Virtex-5 FPGA. Both of these FPGAs have a metal cap as well as a heat sink on the chip. Although a radiated signal can be detected below the FPGA, much of the radiated energy is being absorbed into the metal cap and the heatsink. This may be affecting the radiation being captured by the spectrum analyzer. The PCB power planes are also an effective means of shielding which may further affect the energy captured. Preliminary experiments were performed on a Spartan 3E FPGA, which has a plastic cap. After initial observations this has resulted in higher power numbers.

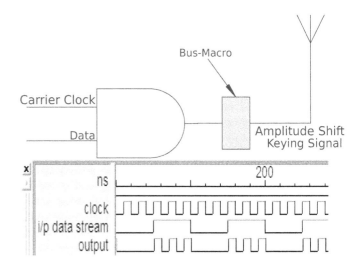

Figure 11: Amplitude shift keying setup

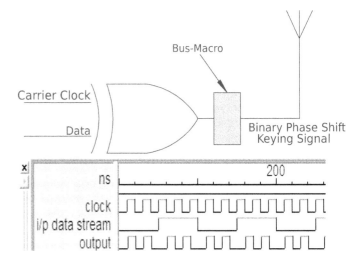

Figure 12: Binary phase shift keying setup

Another potential application for this work is the creation of a complete transmitter system. There are many possible modulation techniques that could be applied here. Two common modulation techniques, Amplitude Shift Keying (ASK) and Binary Phase Shift Keying (BPSK), are outlined below. These techniques can be easily implemented on an FPGA using basic logic gates.

ASK is a modulation technique where a carrier frequency is either present or absent indicating a '1' or a '0' for the transmitted data. A logical AND gate can be used to implement ASK. The clock signal is connected to one input of the AND gate with the other input connected to the input data stream. The ASK setup as well as a waveform illustrating the operation of the circuit are shown in Figure 11.

Phase-shift keying (PSK) is another modulation technique in which the carrier frequency's phase is altered to indicate the transmitted data. The simplest form of this technique is BPSK. BPSK works by locking onto a carrier frequency and then monitoring when it becomes inverted. There are multiple coding techniques for placing the data into this modulation technique, but a simple 0 for in-phase and 1 for out-of-phase could be implemented utilizing a XOR gate. The clock signal is connected to one input of the gate while the input data stream is connected to the other gate. The BPSK setup and the corresponding waveform are shown in Figure 12. This modulation scheme has the advantage in that it has a nearly flat power signature.

The modulated signals generated can then be transmitted using the antenna structures created to implement a comprehensive transmitter system.

5. Conclusion

A technique for the construction of transmitters on FPGAs has been discussed. The transmitter antenna demonstrated good energy radiation characteristics and responded well to slight variations. Since the structures generated on programmable interconnect are in no way similar to classical antennas, some ambiguity remains as to the exact mechanisms behind the radiated energy. But as long as there is radiation being detected outside the FPGA, it is plausible that with a modified design, data could be radiated off a net and decoded by antennas outside the FPGA. A more detailed study of the results could help understand the usefulness of the approach in the bigger scheme of things and the road ahead. It was also discussed that this technique is distinct from and is in no way related to the side-channel attacks involving power monitoring.

6. Acknowledgments

The authors would like to thank USC-ISI East and the Harris Corporation for supporting this research and for providing insight into the antenna structures. The authors would also like to thank the Brigham Young University Configurable Computing Lab for their assistance and insightful conversations. The authors would like to convey a special thanks to Neil Steiner and Aaron Wood from ISI for providing excellent tools for the routing and segment identification.

7. REFERENCES

[1] S. R. Best. A comparision of the resonant properties of small space-filling fractal antennas. In *IEEE Antennas and Wireless Propagation Letters*, 2003.

[2] C. Claus, B. Zhang, M. HÃijbner, C. Schmutzler, J. Becker, and W. Stechele. An xdl-based busmacro generator for customizable communication interfaces for dynamically and partially reconfigurable systems. 2007.

[3] J. Jaffe, P. Kocher, and B. Jun. Differential power analysis. In *Proc. 19th International Advances in Cryptology Conference CRYPTO99*, 1999.

[4] L.McMurchie and C.Ebeling. Pathfinder: a negotiation-based performance-driven router for fpgas. In *Proc. of the 1995 ACM Third Int. Symp. on Field Programmable Gate Arrays*, 1995.

[5] L.Wang, C.Stroud, and N.Touba. *System On Chip Test Architectures: Nanometer Design for Testability*. Morgan Kaufmann, 2007.

[6] N.Steiner. A standalone wire database for routing and tracing in xilinx virtex, virtex-e, and virtex-ii fpgas. Master's thesis, Virginia Polytechnic Institute and State University, 2002.

[7] M. Z. Rahaman and M. A. Hossain. Side channel attack prevention for aes smartcard. In *Proc. 11th International Conference on Computer and Information Technology ICCIT2008*, 2008.

[8] A. Sohanghpurwala. A preview of the openpr open-source partial reconfiguration toolkit for xilinx fpgas. 2010.

[9] K. Wu, H. Li, B. Peng, and F. Yu. Correlation power analysis attack against synchronous stream ciphers. In *Proc. 19th International Conference for Young Computer Scientists ICYCS2008*, 2008.

[10] Xilinx Inc. *FPGA Editor Guide 3.1i*, 2000.

[11] Xilinx Inc. *Xilinx Integrated Software Enviroment 4.2i Documentation*, 2001.

[12] Xilinx Inc. *Chipscope VIO, Datasheet DS 284*, 2004.

[13] Xilinx Inc. *XAPP426: Implementing Xilinx Flip-Chip BGA Packages*, 2006.

[14] Xilinx Inc. *Virtex4 Family Overview, Datasheet DS112*, 2007.

[15] Xilinx Inc. *ML410 Embedded Development Platform, User Guide*, 2008.

[16] Xilinx Inc. *PlanAhead User Guide 11.4*, 2009.

Architecture Description and Packing for Logic Blocks with Hierarchy, Modes and Complex Interconnect

Jason Luu, Jason Anderson, and Jonathan Rose
The Edward S. Rogers Sr. Department of Electrical and Computer Engineering
University of Toronto, Toronto, ON, Canada
jluu|janders|jayar@eecg.utoronto.ca

ABSTRACT

The development of future FPGA fabrics with more sophisticated and complex logic blocks requires a new CAD flow that permits the expression of that complexity and the ability to synthesize to it. In this paper, we present a new logic block description language that can depict complex intra-block interconnect, hierarchy and modes of operation. These features are necessary to support modern and future FPGA complex soft logic blocks, memory and hard blocks. The key part of the CAD flow associated with this complexity is the packer, which takes the logical atomic pieces of the complex blocks and groups them into whole physical entities. We present an area-driven generic packing tool that can pack the logical atoms into any heterogeneous FPGA described in the new language, including many different kinds of soft and hard logic blocks. We gauge its area quality by comparing the results achieved with a lower bound on the number of blocks required, and then illustrate its explorative capability in two ways: on fracturable LUT soft logic architectures, and on hard block memory architectures. The new infrastructure attaches to a flow that begins with a Verilog front-end, permitting the use of benchmarks that are significantly larger than the usual ones, and can target heterogenous FPGAs.

Categories and Subject Descriptors

B.6.3 [**Design Aids**]: Hardware description languages, Optimization

General Terms

Algorithms, Design, Languages, Measurement, Performance

1. INTRODUCTION

As the semiconductor industry evolves and accounts for the prohibitive cost of custom chip design and fabrication, together with the continued exponential growth in logic capacity per die, there is a need to make pre-fabricated and programmable chips more capable. That enhanced capability may in part be expressed through more complex programmable logic blocks. These logic blocks may perform cer-

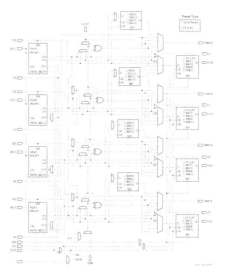

Figure 1: Commercial Virtex-6 logic block

tain computations more efficiently, or store data, or perhaps contain novel soft logic structures.

Today's publicly available FPGA CAD tools lack the ability to target the complexity present in modern commercial architectures - the Altera Stratix IV [1] and Xilinx Virtex 6 [2] FPGAs contain highly complex soft logic blocks, hard memories and mulitpliers. For example, it simply isn't possible to represent the details of the Virtex-6 logic block, illustrated in Fig. 1 [3], in the architecture description language provided in VPR 5.0 [20]. While commercial tools can be used to synthesize to this exact architecture, there is no capability for researchers to explore new issues (such as process variability) for that device, or to modify important aspects of the architecture.

Furthermore, the MCNC benchmark circuits [33] often used in research are no longer representative of modern or future FPGA applications because they are no larger than a few thousand 4-LUTs while commercial FPGAs today can target applications that contain hundreds of thousands and soon millions or more 4-LUT-equivalents. There is a need, then, for modern, public benchmarks and CAD tools that can deal with the heterogeneity inherent in those benchmarks in order to do relevant, scientific research on FPGA architecture and CAD.

In this paper, we describe two key new capabilities for an FPGA CAD flow that provide the ability to describe and synthesize for the necessary complexity: first, we present a new logic block description language that can express far more complex logic blocks than is currently possible with any publicly available toolset. It can describe complex logic blocks with arbitrary internal routing structures (such as all the small muxes in Fig. 1), it permits arbitrary levels of hierarchy within the logic block and it can give blocks different *modes* that represent significantly different functionality and interconnect of portions of the block. Modern commercial FPGAs have different modes in their memory blocks, for example, they can be configured as say 4Kx8, or 8Kx4, or 16Kx2 memories and so on. The new language permits the description of an FPGA with many different kinds of blocks, each of which can have the above features. The new language also allows the specification of timing for the atoms and their interconnect.

Secondly, we present a new area-driven packing framework and algorithm that takes as input a user design as well as an architectural description in the language mentioned above, and then determines area-efficient legal groupings of the atoms in the design into the logic blocks specified in the language. This problem is far more complex than the traditional LUT-packing problem [5] because of the non-simple interconnects, hierarchy and modes. Indeed, this kind of packing problem contains within it a combined placement and routing problem. Fortunately, the packing context permits some efficiencies which we describe in the paper.

We illustrate these new capabilities through two architectural experiments: one that explores different fracturable LUTs, now commonly used in industry, and one that explores different aspects of hard block memory architectures. In each of these experiments, we use a new set of large-scale Verilog circuits that contain both memory and multipliers.

This paper is organized as follows: the next section provides relevant background; Section 3 describes the new language with examples, and Section 4 gives the generic packing algorithm. The new features are integrated into an existing FPGA CAD system. Section 5 gives the illustrative architecture explorations. Section 6 concludes.

2. BACKGROUND AND TERMINOLOGY

The architecture of an FPGA consists of the set of blocks that perform internal computing, the input/output blocks that communicate with the extra-chip environment, and the programmable routing structure that connects them. As FPGAs have evolved, they have employed increasingly more complex logic blocks that consist of a larger number of small components, which we will call *primitives*, grouped together. One purpose of this grouping, often called *clusters*, is to leverage the locality typically found in circuits. This section describes the prior work on languages that describe such complex blocks and algorithms that pack a user circuit into complex blocks.

2.1 Complex Block Architecture Description Languages

In order to explore the large space of complex block architectures, a language that can precisely specify those complex blocks is needed. Over the years, several languages have been developed that target different trade-offs between expressiveness and conciseness for complex blocks.

Some languages gain conciseness by limiting the complex block architectures that they can describe to a restricted subset and then employ parameters to select between different instances of that subset. These languages include those used in VPR 4.30 [6] and VPR 5.0 [20] which tar-

get a simple block consisting of a cluster of fully-connected basic logic elements and Ho's language [13] which describes more sophisticated floating-point cores as blocks.

Other languages focus more on expressiveness. Cronquist's Emerald [10], Filho's CGADL [12], Ebeling's language for RaPiD [11], and the languages described in [26], use a netlist representation which, though very expressive, is cumbersome and verbose when expressing simple soft logic complex blocks. Paladino proposed a general complex block description language called CARCH in [29] which employs properties and rules to gain expressiveness, but was focussed on more microscopic attributes of common soft logic blocks.

2.2 Packing Algorithms

There is large body of prior work on the packing problem for FPGAs. Most of it focuses on the optimization of area, delay, and/or power for the basic (LUT-based) soft logic complex blocks. These algorithms include T-VPack [21], T-RPack [7], IRAC [30], HDPack [9], and others [17] [18]. Lemieux [16] and Wang [32] investigated packing to a basic soft logic complex block that contains a depopulated crossbar.

There has also been work on packing for complex blocks that are significantly different from the basic complex block. Ni proposed an algorithm that packs together netlist blocks for clusters with arbitrary interconnect and an arbitrary number of heterogeneous primitives [28]. The algorithm does not scale and it is intractable to use it to model all but the smallest soft logic clusters. Ahmed described packing DSP blocks to make use of regularity in placement and routing [4]. Paladino proposed a design rule check (DRC) based packer called DC that can pack to the soft logic of two different Altera FPGA families [29]. Limitations with the tool prevent it from exploring non-trivial complex blocks such as memories and fracturable LUTs.

3. A NEW COMPLEX BLOCK ARCHITECTURE DESCRIPTION LANGUAGE

A key goal of this work is to enable architecture exploration and CAD tool research for FPGAs with far more complex logic and interconnect than has been possible with prior public tools. In this section, we describe a new modeling language that permits the description of logic blocks with an arbitrary amount of hierarchy, that permits complex specification of the interconnection between logical elements, and that allows the specification of different modes of operation. To be as easy to use as possible, we seek to have the language be:

- Expressive: The language should be capable of describing a wide range of complex blocks.

- Simple: The language constructs should match closely with an FPGA architect's existing knowledge and intuition.

- Concise: The language should permit complex blocks to be described as concisely as possible.

In the following sections, we provide an introduction to the new language that shows how these goals are met. Due to space limitations, the full language itself, with detailed examples, is presented at http://www.eecg.utoronto.ca/vpr/arch_language.html. This language will be supported in the next release of VPR.

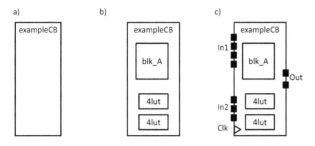

Figure 2: Example physical blocks

3.1 Overview

The new language uses XML syntax; readers unfamiliar with XML should review [31]. It also incorporates constructs that directly correspond to the hardware structures that most commonly occur in FPGA complex blocks – such as muxes and LUTs.

At the highest-level, the language contains two categories of construct: 1) physical blocks, and 2) interconnect. Physical blocks are used to represent the core logic, computational, and memory elements within the FPGA. This includes LUTs, flip-flops and memories. Interconnect constructs represent connectivitiy within and between physical blocks, including wiring, programmable switches, and multiplexers. We begin by describing the physical block construct.

3.1.1 Physical Blocks

The basic physical block type in the language is specified using the XML element *pb_type* which has a name attribute to identify it. To obtain the ability to describe arbitrary hierarchy, any *pb_type* start-end block can contain other *pb_type* specifications. For example, consider the empty complex block shown in Fig. 2 a). It is specified by the following code:

```
<pb_type name="exampleCB">
</pb_type>
```

A more complex block is shown in Fig. 2 b), which has three child blocks in it, two of the same type (labelled 4lut) and one different block (labelled blk_A). The language construct *num_pb* can be used to specify the number of instances of a child physical block that are contained in its parent physical block. The full specification of the example complex block in Fig. 2 b) is as follows:

```
<pb_type name="exampleCB">
  <pb_type name="blk_A" num_pb="1">
  </pb_type>
  <pb_type name="4lut" num_pb="2">
  </pb_type>
</pb_type>
```

Physical blocks must communicate with one another, and also with other blocks at the same level, as well as the external inter-block routing. A physical block will have a combination of input, output, and/or clock ports. A port comprises of one or more pins. The input, output, and clock ports are described using XML tags *input*, *output*, and *clock*, respectively. Each tag is declared as a child element of the *pb_type* on which the ports reside. Each port tag must be given an identifier with the *name* attribute. The number of pins associated with a port is specified with the *num_pins* attribute. For example, the block shown in Fig. 2 c) adds

four ports to the complex block of part b), and its language specification is given below. Notice that the In1 port has four pins; the In2 port has three pins; the Out port has 2 pins; and, the Clk port has a single pin.

```
<pb_type name="exampleCB">
  <input name="In1" num_pins="4"/>
  <input name="In2" num_pins="3"/>
  <output name="Out" num_pins="2"/>
  <clock name="Clk" num_pins="1"/>
  <pb_type name="blk_A" num_pb="1">
  </pb_type>
  <pb_type name="4lut" num_pb="2">
  </pb_type>
</pb_type>
```

3.1.2 Modeling Primitives

Primitives are physical blocks at the bottom level of hierarchy – they do not contain other physical blocks. A primitive corresponds to the elements present in the technology-mapped user netlist, prior to the packing phase. The language attribute, *blif_model* must be included in the primitive *pb_type* element, and it specifies the type of input user netlist block that the primitive implements. The packer, described below, uses BLIF as the netlist format. The value of the *blif_model* attribute for a primitive pb_type is a string that should exactly match the string in BLIF used for the netlist block that can reside in the primitive.

The new language incorporates special handling for three of the most common types of primitives found in FPGAs: flip-flops, LUTs, and memory. We chose to do this to make it easier to deal with specific features of these primitives. The language *class* attribute is used to identify these primitives. Consider again the example in Fig. 2 b): we make the *4lut* a LUT primitive type by adding the *blif_model* and *class* attributes as follows:

```
<pb_type name="exampleCB">
  <input name="In1" num_pins="4"/>
  <input name="In2" num_pins="3"/>
  <output name="Out" num_pins="2"/>
  <clock name="Clk" num_pins="1"/>
  <pb_type name="blk_A" num_pb="1">
  </pb_type>
  <pb_type name="4lut" num_pb="2"
          blif_model=".names" class="lut">
  </pb_type>
</pb_type>
```

In processing the input user netlist, the BLIF construct *.names* is assumed to map into a LUT.

In addition to the *class* attribute, the ports on these primitives must be declared with a special attribute called *port_class* which provides necessary information about the pins on these special types of primitives, as described below:

1. *lut*: The LUT primitive has one port class for its inputs (called *lut_in*) and one for its output called *lut_out*. This is useful for example, so that downstream tools can take advantage of input pin *swapability*: signals on LUT inputs can be permuted and the LUT's truth table re-programmed accordingly. Note that more complex LUTs, such as fracturable LUTs, are described as clusters; basic LUTs within the more complex LUT are described using this LUT primitive.

2. *flipflop*: A flip-flop has three port classes: input (D), output (Q), and clock (*clock*), which have exactly one pin each. The library could be extended to support more ports for flip-flops (such as asynchronous clear).

3. *memory*: Single-port memories have three input port classes: *address*, *data_in*, and *write_en* and one output port class: *data_out*, which represent the related functionality of memories. Dual-port memories have six input port classes: *address1*, *data_in1*, *write_en1*, *address2*, *data_in2*, and *write_en2* and two output port classes: *data_out1* and *data_out2*. Both single and dual-port memories have one optional clock port class: *clock* (for synchronous memories). The library can be extended to support more ports for memories.

The following example describes a single-port memory primitive type to illustrate the usage of the *class* and *port_class* attributes:

```
<pb_type name="mem_1024x2"
        blif_model=".subckt single_port_ram"
        class="memory" num_pb="1">
 <input name="addr" num_pins="10" port_class="address"/>
 <input name="data" num_pins="2" port_class="data_in"/>
 <input name="we" num_pins="1" port_class="write_en"/>
 <output name="out" num_pins="2" port_class="data_out"/>
 <clock name="clk" num_pins="1" port_class="clock"/>
</pb_type>
```

It may occur to the reader that an alternative to introducing the *class* and *port_class* attributes would be to require that the architect give specific pre-defined names to pb_types and ports. We considered that approach, however, we deemed it overly restrictive. With the proposed class and port class scheme, the architect is free to name pb_types and ports any way he/she likes, which enhances readability and may ease integration with other tools that use different naming conventions.

3.2 Intra-Block Interconnect

The ports and pins on physical blocks are connected to one another using an *interconnect* element that is declared *within* a parent physical block type. There are three kinds of interconnect:

1. *complete*: This represents a complete crossbar switch from a set of inputs pins to a set of output pins. It is assumed that the particular input pin that is matched with a particular output pin is controlled by signals internal to the FPGA whose values are set during device configuration.

2. *direct*: This is a direct connection from one set of pins to another set of pins. This is used to model single metal wires or buses that have no programmability or switching.

3. *mux*: This is a multiplexed connection of single or multi-bit (bus) signals. As in the case of *complete*, it is assumed that signals internal to the FPGA (likely driven by configuration bits) control the select inputs of the multiplexer. That is, this construct represents a bus-based multiplexer whose input-to-output path is set during FPGA configuration.

The input and output pins of interconnect elements are specified by one *input* attribute and one *output* attribute declared within the interconnect element. The *complete* element has one set of pins for its input and one set of pins for its output. The *direct* element has one set of pins for its inputs and another set of pins for its outputs. The *mux* element has multiple sets of pins for its input and one set of

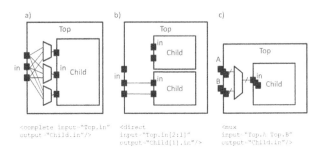

Figure 3: Examples interconnect types: a) complete b) direct c) mux

pins at its output. Each set of input pins is delimited by a space.

A set of pins to be connected is specified by first selecting physical blocks that are to be connected, and then specifying the desired pins on those blocks: In the case of there being multiple instances of a physical block, the following syntax is used:

```
<pb_type name>[<start index of physical block>:
  <end index of physical block>]
```

Physical blocks are indexed from 0 to *num_pb* - *1*. If only one physical block is selected, then the colon and ending index may be eliminated. If there is only one physical block, then the entire *[* to *]* specification is not needed.

The pins on the block are specified in the following way:

```
<physical block port name>[<start index of pins>:
  <end index of pins>]
```

Pin indices start from 0 and end at *num_pins* - *1*. There is one shortcut for pin selection: if the architect wishes to select all the pins of a port, then he can skip the section from *[* to *]*.

Fig. 3 gives examples of the three interconnect constructs. Underneath each figure is the code that produces the corresponding interconnect. The examples assume that interconnect connectivity is *from* pins on a physical block called *Top* to pins on one of Top's child physical blocks. For the *complete* interconnect case (in Fig. 3 a)), there is one physical block for each *pb_type* so only the *pb_type* is specified when selecting the blocks. All pins of the ports are used, so only the names of the ports are specified.

For the *direct* interconnect example (in Fig. 3 b)), only the last two of the three *Top.in* pins are used so the corresponding code specifies the range of pins using *[2:1]*. There are two physical blocks of type *Child* and only the one with index 1 is used, so the code includes a *[1]* in *Child[1]* to identify that block. This specification creates a one-to-one mapping between two input pins of *Top* and two input pins of *Child[1]*.

The *mux* interconnect example specifies a 3-bit 2-to-1 mux (in Fig. 3 c)). The input attribute to the mux has two 3-bit pin sets. The first pin set is *Top.A* and the second pin set is *Top.B*. The two pin sets are separated by a space. The output of the mux is one 3-bit pin set of *Child.in*.

For ease-of-use, the language provides a mechanism to concatenate sets of pins together. It follows a similar syntax to the concatenate construct in Verilog [8].

A "scope" question naturally arises with the use of the interconnect element: in an arbitrary multi-level hierarchy of physical blocks, which ports/pins can be used within an interconnect element that is declared within a physical block

230

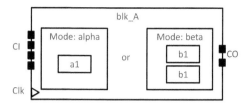

Figure 4: Example of a physical block with multiple modes of operation

at some specific level of the hierarchy? We take a straightforward approach to interconnect scope – the interconnect element can use pins of its parent physical block, or can use pins of any physical block declared in the same level of the hierarchy.

3.3 Modes

A physical block in an FPGA may have multiple modes of operation and such modes are normally mutually exclusive. For example, consider an FPGA memory block that can be configured with different aspect ratios such as 512x8 and 1024x4 [27]. Each of these different configurations needs to be represented by a unique mode of operation. To represent the mode concept, the language allows the definition of one or more *mode* elements within the *pb_type*. Multiple modes of operation are represented by multiple sibling *mode* elements declared within a parent *pb_type*. If a mode is declared, child physical blocks and interconnect can be declared *inside* the mode element, representing blocks (and connectivity) that is specific to the particular mode. In general, modes represent different ways of using a given piece of underlying FPGA hardware. A mode has one attribute *name* that serves as an identifier. Fig. 4 shows a physical block with multiple modes of operation. The first mode is called *alpha* and it contains one physical block *a1* and the second mode is called *beta* and contains two physical blocks of type *b1*. The corresponding code is:

```
<pb_type name="blk_A">
  <input name="CI" num_pins="4"/>
  <output name="CO" num_pins="2"/>
  <clock name="Clk" num_pins="1"/>
  <mode name="alpha">
    <pb_type name="a1" num_pb="1">
    </pb_type>
  </mode>
  <mode name="beta">
    <pb_type name="b1" num_pb="2">
    </pb_type>
  </mode>
</pb_type>
```

Different modes can each have their own unique interconnect by declaring one or more *interconnect* elements as children of a *mode* element.

Using these language constructs, we can model complex logic structures, including the one shown in Fig. 1. Due to space limitations, examples of how to model this and other logic structures are found in the website provided earlier.

4. PACKING ALGORITHM

In this section, we introduce our architecture-aware packing algorithm, *AAPack*. We begin with a top-level overview of the algorithm, and then elaborate on each step.

```
1: while (unpacked_netlist_blocks_exist())
2:     s = seed_netlist_block()
3:     B = new_complex_block(s)
4:     while (attempt_more_packs(B))
5:         c = candidate_netlist_block(B)
6:         attempt_pack(c,B)
7:     add B to output packed netlist
```

Figure 5: Generic iterative packing algorithm.

4.1 Overview

The input to the packer is a technology mapped netlist of unpacked netlist blocks, as well as a description of an FPGA architecture (specified in our language). The output is a netlist of *packed* complex blocks that implements the same functionality as the input netlist. Fig. 5 gives pseudocode for a generic iterative packing algorithm closely resembling those in published literature. The outer `while` loop at line 1 continues until all input netlist blocks are packed into complex blocks. At line 2, a seed netlist block, *s*, is selected for a new complex block. Line 3 creates a new complex block, *B*, containing the seed block. The algorithm then proceeds to pack additional netlist blocks into *B* (inner loop on lines 4-6). The loop on line 4 continues until no further packs into *B* should be attempted. Line 5 identifies a netlist block, *c*, that is a candidate for packing into *B*. Line 6 attempts to pack *c* into *B*, which presents unique challenges owing to the range of complex block architectures that can be described in our language. The process of finding additional netlist blocks to pack into *B* continues iteratively until either: 1) *B* is full, or 2) no such primitives are found. *B* is then added to the output packed netlist (line 7) and control returns to the outer loop.

The algorithm in Fig. 5 represents a core packer engine that calls several functions for which a variety of implementations are possible. We elaborate on our initial implementation choices below.

4.2 Selecting Netlist Blocks and Complex Blocks

To choose the seed netlist block, *s*, for a new complex block (line 2 in Fig. 5), we borrow the approach of [5] and choose *s* to be the unpacked block with the largest number of nets attached.

Having initialized a new complex block with a seed netlist block, we use an affinity metric to select additional netlist blocks to pack into the complex block (line 5 of Fig. 5). Consider a netlist block *p* and a partially filled complex block *B*. The affinity between *p* and *B* is defined as:

$$Aff = \frac{(1-\alpha) \cdot nets(p,B) + \alpha \cdot connections(p,B)}{num\_pins(p)} \quad (1)$$

where $nets(p,B)$ is the number of shared nets between *p* and *B*, and $connections(p,B)$ is tied to the number of pins on *p*'s attached nets that lie outside of *B*:

$$connections(p,B) = \frac{1}{ext(p,B) + packed(p) + 1} \quad (2)$$

where $ext(p,B)$ represents the sum total of pins on *p*'s nets that reside on netlist blocks *not* packed into *B*, and $packed(p)$ represents the total number of pins on *p*'s nets that attach to netlist blocks already packed into *other* complex blocks (aside from *B*). Connections between *p* and netlist blocks that are already packed are guaranteed to be inter-block connections in the packing solution, and thus, they are penalized in (2). Observe that $connections(p,B)$ is a pin-based count, whereas $nets(p,B)$ is a net-based count. The $num\_pins(p)$

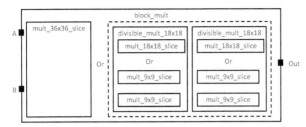

Figure 6: Reconfigurable multiplier example.

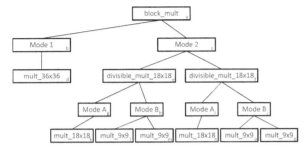

Figure 7: Tree representation of a complex block.

in the denominator of (1) is the number of used pins on p and it serves to normalize affinities across netlist blocks with different numbers of used pins. Parameter α in (1) is a scalar weight that we set to 0.9 for our experiments.

We use the affinity metric (1) to choose packing candidates in the `candidate_netlist_block` function in Fig. 5, preferring to pack together netlist blocks with high affinity for one another. Blocks that, based on their type, cannot be accommodated in the current complex block being packed are automatically filtered out from consideration by the `candidate_netlist_block` function. For example, we never consider packing a LUT into a multiplier-based complex block.

4.3 Legality Checking in Packing

Our packer must be able to handle arbitrary hierarchy and arbitrary interconnect – requirements that ultimately impact the `attempt_pack(c,B)` function in Fig. 5. The function performs two key tasks: 1) it finds a candidate primitive (location) for a netlist block c within a hierarchical complex block B; and, 2) for the chosen location, it ensures that the packing is *legal* from the perspective of routing c's nets through B's interconnect. These steps are analogous to placing and routing the netlist blocks within a complex block.

4.3.1 *Location Assignment*

For the purposes of packing, we represent a hierarchical complex block as an ordered tree. Nodes in the tree correspond to physical blocks or modes. Edges between nodes represent the parent/child relationships between physical blocks and/or modes. The root node of the tree corresponds to an entire complex block. Leaf nodes correspond to primitives within a complex block. Fig. 7 gives the tree representation for the multiplier-based complex block illustrated in Fig. 6. Observe that the tree is ordered: fine-grained physical blocks are on the right; coarse-grained physical blocks are on the left. The ordering allows us to traverse the tree according to non-decreasing physical block size. In general, it is desirable to pack a netlist block into the smallest primitive that can accomodate it (doing otherwise would likely

result in poor utilization) – the tree ordering assists us in meeting this objective.

Given a candidate netlist block, c, and the tree representation of a complex block, we use a depth-first search to identify a location for c. Our search prioritizes exploring right children before left children. That is, we explore fine-grained physical blocks before coarse-grained blocks. As an example, consider a technology mapped netlist containing two multiplier blocks: a 16x16 multiplier and an 8x8 multiplier. We wish to pack the netlist into the complex block shown in Fig. 7, starting with the 16x16 multiplier block. Referring to the labels on each node, the search traverses downwards from the root, visiting nodes a, c, f and j. Since mode B at node j cannot accommodate the 16x16 block, the search backtracks to node f and continues until a feasible location is discovered, eventually packing the multiplier into node n. At this point, a routability check must be performed (described below). If the check is unsuccessful, the depth-first search continues for an alternative location. If the check is successful, we move onto the task of packing the next block, the 8x8 multiplier.

When a netlist block is successfully packed into a tree node, the depth-first search *pops up* to the node's parent, which corresponds to a sub-tree of the complex block hierarchy. We then look for netlist blocks that can pack into that sub-tree (using depth-first search). We try to fill up the sub-tree before proceeding to explore other parts of the hierarchy. Note that the `candidate_netlist_block` function filters blocks according to the current sub-tree being packed. For example, if we packed a LUT into a sub-tree comprising a LUT/flip-flop pair, our algorithm would attempt to find a flip-flop that can be packed together with the LUT. We attempt up to 30 packs on a sub-tree before the depth-first search pops up to explore other sub-trees.

4.3.2 *Ensuring Routability*

Simply finding a primitive for a netlist block within a complex block is not a sufficient condition for feasible packing. Our language allows the description of arbitrary interconnect within a complex block, and therefore, we must check that the netlist block's nets can be routed, both in the context of the interconnect specified for the complex block, and also in the context of other netlist blocks that are already packed into the same complex block. Each netlist block packed into a complex block may have connections to other netlist blocks packed into the same block and we must ensure there is sufficient intra-block interconnect for such connections. Likewise, a netlist block may have connections to netlist blocks packed in other complex blocks. Such connections will be routed through the general FPGA interconnect fabric. We must ensure that for such connections, there is a path to a top-level complex block pin (a "way out" of the complex block).

To assess routing feasibility, we first execute a basic check regarding whether packing the candidate netlist block into the current placement within the complex block causes the pin demand to exceed the available pins of any parent blocks. If this check fails, the candidate block is disqualified from packing into the complex block. Otherwise, we move onto a more rigorous routing assessment.

We model the complex block interconnect using a routing graph. A node in the routing graph represents a pin on a physical block in the complex block hierarchy. Directed edges between nodes correspond to paths through complex block interconnect. For the set of nodes corresponding to the top-level complex block output pins, we create directed edges to the nodes corresponding to the top-level complex block input pins. In so doing, we model the ability for a primitive to connect to another primitive in the same complex block through the general FPGA interconnect fabric. We assume that the general FPGA interconnect is rich enough to allow any output pin on a complex block to connect to any other input pin on a complex block (as is generally the case for commercial FPGAs). This assumption eases the routing problem, as it means that external connections to (from) a primitive can be routed from (to) any top-level output (input) pin node of the complex block.

Having formulated the routing problem using a routing graph and a set of required pin-to-pin connections to route, we directly apply the PathFinder negotiated congestion routing algorithm [22] to determine if a feasible routing solution can be found. The maze router used within our PathFinder implementation is undirected (breadth-first), as packing does not incorporate a notion of geographical proximity

4.4 Handling Memories

Memories present a unique challenge for packing. The user's design may contain memories that are wider and/or deeper than the size of a physical memory block in the target FPGA. In such cases, multiple memory blocks in the FPGA are needed to implement the user's memory. The AAPack algorithm requires that memories in the input netlist be specified as one-bit-wide memories of depth not exceeding the depth of the largest physical memory in the FPGA[1]. For example, if the user's design contains a 256 x 8 memory, the packer's input will contain eight 256 x 1 memories that, ultimately, may be packed together in a single RAM primitive. In other words, for a memory instance in the user design, the total number of netlist blocks to represent that memory is equal to the word width of that memory instance. Memory primitives are thus handled differently than all other types of primitives in the sense that more than one memory netlist block in AAPack's input netlist may pack into a single memory primitive.

For memory blocks in the input netlist to be packed together into one physical memory primitive, two requirements must be met: 1) the memory blocks in the netlist must have the same address bus width, and 2) the signals on corresponding bits of the address bus and control signals must be identical.

4.5 Limitations of the Packing Algorithm

As is apparent from the discussion above, in our initial release, we have focused on area-driven packing. An implementation of timing-driven packing requires a detailed delay model for complex block interconnect and logic. Work is underway on this front and timing-driven packing will be included in a future tool release (the packer currently reads in timing and capactitance information but does not act on this information).

While the intent of AAPack is to provide good quality results for *any* complex block architecture, it is difficult to demonstrate this capability for the universe of architectures that can be modeled in our language. In this study, we have limited the types of complex blocks investigated to the following: 1) LUT-based complex blocks (including blocks with fracturable LUTs), 2) fracturable multipliers, and 3) memories with reconfigurable aspect ratios. Such types of complex

blocks are pervasive in commercial FPGAs, yet they are unsupported by any public-domain packer.

We have also placed an architectural constraint that different complex block types cannot legally accomodate the same netlist block. For example, we do not investigate architectures where flip-flops can be packed into either a LUT-based complex block or a multiplier-based complex block. This constraint makes the choice of complex block type based on a netlist block straightforward – there can be only one complex block type that can accomodate a particular netlist block. We acknowledge that commercial FPGA packing does not have this limitation and we plan to remove this limitation in the future.

5. EXPERIMENTS

In this section, we describe the methodology and experiments to illustrate the new FPGA architecture language's ability to model and enable exploration of more complex blocks than in the past. This is done first by modelling and exploring soft logic blocks containing fracturable LUTs, and then block RAMs of different sizes with different configurable aspect ratios. We also evaluate the quality of the new generic packing algorithm, against a lower bound computation. We also compared our packing algorithm against a previous algorithm on a legacy architecture [19]; however, the results are omitted here due to a lack of space.

The complete CAD flow consists entirely of publicly-accessible source tools. We use ODIN II [14] for front-end HDL parsing, elaboration and partial synthesis. The ABC framework [25] is used for technology-independent optimization (using the resyn2 script) and technology mapping. Circuits are mapped to minimize area using WireMap [15], implemented within ABC's priority cuts-based mapper [24]. Technology mapping is executed with *choices* [23] – an approach for reducing structural bias whereby mapping is done concurrently on multiple functionally equivalent circuit representations and the best mapping result is selected. Large circuit blocks (e.g. block RAMs and multipliers) are passed through ABC as black box modules. Note that the description of the complex blocks themselves are not used by ABC during logic synthesis but rather used afterwards during packing. Packing is performed by the algorithm described in Section 4. We use a modified version of VPR 5.0 [20] for non-timing-driven placement and routing. The packer is integrated into the VPR source code. The routing architecture is held constant for all experiments, and consists of single-driver length-4 wire segments, $F_s = 3$, and $F_c(in) = 0.15$ and $F_c(out)=0.125$, as per the usual nomenclature. Around the chip perhiphery, we assume there to be 7 I/O tiles per complex block column/row.

We employ a new set of benchmark circuits, as described in Table 1. This new suite of circuits contain block RAMs and multipliers of various sizes and were collected from a variety of sources. They include soft processors, video image processors, and range in size from 256 to 24,587 6-input LUTs. The columns in this table describe the name of the circuit, followed by the physical resources demanded by each circuit after technology mapping, including: the number of flip-flops, the total number of 6-input (or less) LUTs, the total number of memory bits, the number of logical memories, the maximum depth and width across those memories, and the number of multipliers.

---

[1]The upstream RTL synthesis tool, ODIN II [14], splits memories to ensure that this requirement is met.

Table 1: New Benchmarks and statistics.

Circuit	FFs	LUTs	Bits	#Mem	Max Depth	Max Width	#Mult
boundtop	1620	2779	32768	1	1024	32	0
ch_intrinsics	233	402	256	1	32	8	0
mkDelayWorker	2440	5046	532916	9	1024	313	0
mkPktMerge	36	256	7344	3	16	153	0
mkSMAdapter	952	1706	4456	3	64	61	0
or1200	611	2369	2048	2	32	32	1
raygentop	1185	1938	5376	1	256	21	18
reed_solomon	1591	3096	30720	15	256	8	0
stereovision0	12628	12318	33554432	1	524288	64	0
stereovision1	9558	10563	33554432	1	524288	64	152
stereovision2	13670	24587	33554432	1	524288	64	564

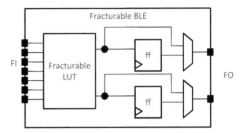

Figure 9: A fracturable BLE with 7 inputs, 2 outputs, and optional output registers

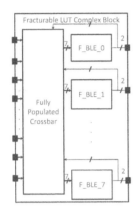

Figure 8: Global Structure of Fracturable Complex Block

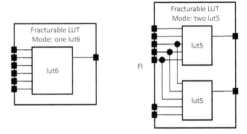

Figure 10: Two modes of a fracturable 6-LUT with 7 inputs.

5.1 Fracturable LUT Experiments

We demonstrate the utility of the new language and packer by using them to model complex blocks that contain *fracturable* LUTs. A fracturable LUT can be broken into two smaller LUTs that share input pins. Modern commercial FPGAs incorporate fracturable LUTs for the purpose of improving logic density, because many circuits synthesized by tools contain small LUTs that can be paired together and implemented in a single fracturable LUT.

Fig. 8 shows the global structure of a complex block based on fracturable LUTs, which looks similar to a classical cluster, except that each BLE has two outputs. A fracturable BLE contains a fracturable (dual-output) LUT and two bypassable registers – one register for each LUT output. Fig. 9 shows a fracturable BLE with 7 inputs and bypassable registers. A fracturable LUT has two modes of operation: 1) as a single K-input LUT, or 2) as two LUTs that together use at most FI inputs. In the dual-LUT mode, parameter FI determines the amount of pin sharing that is required between the pair of LUTs that are implemented in the fracturable LUT. Fig. 10 shows an example of a fracturable LUT. This fracturable LUT can operate as either one 6-LUT ($K = 6$) or two 5-LUTs that share 3 inputs ($FI = 7$).

A key architectural question for fracturable LUT architectures concerns the selection of the value for FI. Larger values for FI will permit more packing flexibility at the cost of more pins, whereas lower values of FI will reduce packing flexibility. We explore this question for a base architecture with $K = 6$ (the LUTs have 6-inputs when used in single-output mode) and $N = 8$ (there are 8 fracturable BLEs per complex block). We vary FI from 5 to 10, covering all possible pin sharing amounts from all to none. The meaning of $K = 6$ and $FI = 5$ requires elaboration: when the LUT

is used in dual-output mode, the two LUTs are allowed to use no more than 5 distinct input signals (as is the case for Virtex 6 [3]). We also note that the number of inputs to the full complex block itself, I, is set equal to $FI \times N$, which implies that no pin sharing requirements are imposed *between* BLEs within the complex block. This architectural choice creates some architectural side-effects as described in the results below.

We evaluate the effectiveness of various fracturable LUT architectures by comparing the number of complex blocks in packing solutions, and with a lower bound on the optimal number of complex blocks needed. The lower bound is computed as follows:

```
# CB lower bound = ceiling((
    (# 5-LUTs or smaller + # unabsorbable FFs) / 16)
    + (# 6-LUTs / 8))
```

The "# 5-LUTs or smaller" count is the number of LUTs in the input to the packer that use 5 or fewer inputs. The "# unabsorbable FFs" is the number of flip-flops that structurally cannot be packed with a LUT (such as flip-flops fed by memories). The # 6-LUTs is the number of LUTs that use *exactly* 6 inputs. The bound was developed through a counting argument: There are 8 fracturable BLEs in a complex block. Each fracturable BLE can implement one 6-LUT, so the number of 6-LUTs in a design increases the complex block count by 1/8. Each fracturable BLE can alternatively implement (*at most*) two 5-LUTs, so each LUT in a benchmark circuit that uses 5 or fewer inputs increases the complex block count by 1/16. Flip-flops that cannot structurally be packed into a LUT prohibit a 5-LUT from being used so they increase the complex block count by 1/16. With this lower bound we can define the *logic efficiency* for fracturable LUT-based complex blocks packing as follows:

```
efficiency = # CB Achieved / # CB lower bound
```

Fig. 11 illustrates the result of packing the circuits in Table 1 into different fracturable LUT architectures with the parameters cluster size $N = 8$, and LUT size $K = 6$, with

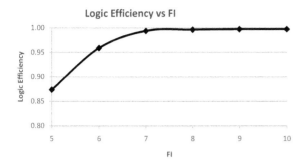

Figure 11: Logic efficiency vs. Number of Inputs to Fracturable LUT (FI).

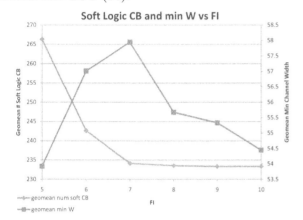

Figure 12: Number of Soft Logic CB and Min W vs. Number of Inputs to Fracturable LUT (FI).

FI varied from 5 to 10. The Y-axis in the figure gives the logic efficiency as defined above. Each point is the geometric average across the 11 new benchmarks. We can observe several things from this figure: First, for some values of FI, the packer achieves 100% efficiency against the lower bound, giving us some confidence that it is working well. Second, there is a significant leap in efficiency when the value of FI moves from 6 to 7, suggesting that there are many situations in which there are smaller LUTs to pack in with larger LUTs. It is clear, from this data, that a value of 7 or possibly 6 for the number of inputs (FI) is sufficient for these circuits and architectures.

Fig. 12 illustrates the impact of varying FI on the number of soft logic complex blocks and the minimum achievable channel width after placement and routing. As expected, the number of logic blocks declines with increasing FI, as the block gains flexibility. The effect of FI on channel width is more complex, in part due to an architectural artifact described above: on the left hand side of the figure, channel width increases with FI as there are more pins being routed into the logic blocks. However, after FI = 7, the number of pins saturates at the maximum (as shown in Fig. 11). A this point, the fact that we continue to provide extra routing pins on the outer complex block only serves to make the routing problem easier, increasing flexibility and therefore lowering channel width.

5.2 Memory Architectures

The purpose of the second experiment we ran is to illustrate the new language and packer's ability to describe and explore different physical block memory architectures. The complete target FPGA architecture contains traditional

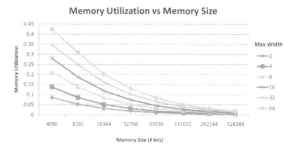

Figure 13: Memory utilization of architectures with varying physical memory sizes.

$N = 8/K = 6$ non-fracturable LUT soft logic blocks, fracturable 36x36 hard multipliers, and configurable hard memory blocks. The memories have a configurable aspect ratio, in which the width and depth can be traded-off, as is now common in commercial FPGAs. These are represented as different modes of the memory, as discussed above. The memories can also be configured to be either single-port or dual-port mode, with the maximum number of total data pins across each mode kept constant. This means that when the memory operates in dual-port mode, it can be at most half as wide as the widest single-port memory.

We vary two parameters of the physical memories: first, the number of bits contained in each hard memory. This is also the maximum depth of the memory when it is configured to have single-bit data width. Clearly fewer blocks would be needed as the size of the memory grows larger, but more of the bits will be wasted when those larger blocks are used to implement smaller memories. At the same time, smaller physical memories in the FPGA may require more soft logic multiplexers to glue together smaller memories into larger logical memories. The second parameter is the maximum data width of the configurable memory. For example, a 1024-bit memory with a maximum width of 8 can implement all powers of 2 width up to the maximum: a 1024x1, 512x2, 256x4, or 128x8 memory. If this number is too small, the memory architecture won't be flexible enough to efficiently use the memory bits. We again use the 11 benchmark circuits described in Table 1 in the flow described above.

Fig. 13 gives a plot of memory utilization (defined as the number of used memory bits divided by the total number bits in used memory blocks after packing) versus the size of the physical memory block in bits, for six values of maximum width, ranging from 2 to 64. This figure shows the expected trends, with utilization increasing as the physical memory size decreases. Also, as the maximum width increases, utilization gets better.

Fig. 14 gives the geometric mean of the number of soft logic complex blocks used (across all 11 circuits) as the physical memory size is varied. Clearly, for the smaller physical memories, the amount of soft logic needed to implement the multiplexers begins to grow significantly for memories less than 4K bits, at least for the logical memories demanded by our benchmarks. Although we show the count for only the case of max width = 64, these results are the same for all values of max width.

Taken together, Fig. 13 and Fig. 14 suggests the need for actually having at least two physical memory sizes - a small one to achieve good utilization on small memories and a larger one to prevent the inefficiencies of gluing together many small blocks.

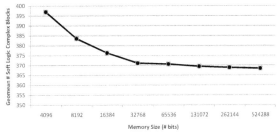

Figure 14: Soft logic complex block count with varying physical memory sizes.

6. CONCLUSIONS

We have presented a new FPGA logic block architecture description language that permits the modelling of far more complex soft logic blocks and hard logic blocks than was previously possible. The key features of the language are its ability to describe hierarchy, modes and arbitrary interconnect between atomic elements in the block. We have also presented a packing algorithm that begins to address the complexities of the FPGAs that use the new language, and shown it can be applied to explore block architectures that weren't previously explorable with public software - fracturable LUT-based architectures, and memory architectures. These are but a few of the blocks that can be studied with the new capabilities. We have demonstrated these capabilities with a new infrastructure capable of synthesizing circuits from Verilog, and with circuits that use memory and multipliers that are significantly larger than the previous standard benchmarks.

There is much more research and development remaining to flesh out the new capabilities: the packer must become timing-driven, and be enhanced to deal with the heterogenous case when one logical atom can be packed into two or more different complex physical blocks. We also need to explore more widely varying architectures and enhance the speed of the packer and quality of the packer for these architectures. Ultimately, we will employ this infrastructure to explore far more widely varying FPGA architectures from the area, speed and power perspectives.

7. REFERENCES

[1] Stratix IV Device Family Overview. http://www.altera.com/literature/hb/stratix-iv/stx4_siv51001.pdf, 2009.
[2] Xilinx Virtex-6 Family Overview. http://www.xilinx.com/support/documentation/data_sheets/ds150.pdf, 2009.
[3] Xilinx Virtex-6 FPGA Configurable Logic Block User Guide. http://www.xilinx.com/support/documentation/user_guides/ug364.pdf, September 2009.
[4] T. Ahmed, P. Kundarewich, J. Anderson, B. Taylor, and R. Aggarwal. Architecture-Specific Packing for Virtex-5 FPGAs. In *ACM Int'l Symp. on FPGAs*, pages 5–13, 2008.
[5] V. Betz and J. Rose. Cluster-Based Logic Blocks for FPGAs: Area-Efficiency vs. Input Sharing and Size. *IEEE Custom Integrated Circuits Conf.*, pages 551–554, 1997.
[6] V. Betz, J. Rose, and A. Marquardt. *Architecture and CAD for Deep-Submicron FPGAs*. Kluwer Academic Publishers, Norwell, Massachusetts, 1999.
[7] E. Bozorgzadeh, S. Memik, X. Yang, and M. Sarrafzadeh. Routability-driven Packing: Metrics and Algorithms for Cluster-Based FPGAs. *Journal of Circuits Systems and Computers*, 13:77–100, 2004.
[8] S. Brown and Z. Vranesic. *Fundamentals of Digital Logic with Verilog Design*. Tata McGraw-Hill, 2007.
[9] D. Chen, K. Vorwerk, and A. Kennings. Improving Timing-Driven FPGA Packing with Physical Information. *Int'l Conf. on Field Programmable Logic and Applications*, pages 117–123, 2007.
[10] D. Cronquist and L. McMurchie. Emerald: An Architecture-Driven Tool Compiler for FPGAs. In *ACM Int'l Symp. on FPGAs*, pages 144–150, 1996.
[11] C. Ebeling, D. Cronquist, and P. Franklin. RaPiD Reconfigurable Pipelined Datapath. *Field-Programmable Logic Smart Applications, New Paradigms and Compilers*, pages 126–135, 1996.
[12] J. Filho, S. Masekowsky, T. Schweizer, and W. Rosenstiel. CGADL: An Architecture Description Language for Coarse-Grained Reconfigurable Arrays. *IEEE Trans. on VLSI*, 17(9):1247–1259, 2009.
[13] C. Ho, C. Yu, P. Leong, W. Luk, and S. Wilton. Floating-point FPGA: Architecture and Modeling. *IEEE Trans. on VLSI*, 17(12):1709–1718, 2009.
[14] P. Jamieson, K. Kent, F. Gharibian, and L. Shannon. Odin II-An Open-Source Verilog HDL Synthesis Tool for CAD Research. In *IEEE Annual Int'l Symp. on Field-Programmable Custom Computing Machines*, pages 149–156. IEEE, 2010.
[15] S. Jang, B. Chan, K. Chung, and A. Mishchenko. WireMap: FPGA Technology Mapping for Improved Routability. In *ACM Int'l Symp. on FPGAs*, pages 47–55. ACM, 2008.
[16] G. Lemieux and D. Lewis. *Design of Interconnection Networks for Programmable Logic*. Kluwer Academic Publishers, Norwell, Massachusetts, 2004.
[17] J. Lin, D. Chen, and J. Cong. Optimal Simultaneous Mapping and Clustering for FPGA Delay Optimization. In *ACM/IEEE Design Automation Conf.*, pages 472–477, 2006.
[18] A. Ling, J. Zhu, and S. Brown. Scalable Synthesis and Clustering Techniques Using Decision Diagrams. *IEEE Trans. on CAD*, 27(3):423, 2008.
[19] J. Luu. A Hierarchical Description Language and Packing Algorithm for Heterogeneous FPGAs. Master's thesis, University of Toronto, Toronto, Ontario, Canada, 2010.
[20] J. Luu, I. Kuon, P. Jamieson, T. Campbell, A. Ye, W. M. Fang, and J. Rose. VPR 5.0: FPGA CAD and Architecture Exploration Tools with Single-Driver Routing, Heterogeneity and Process Scaling. In *ACM Int'l Symp. on FPGAs*, pages 133–142, 2009.
[21] A. Marquardt, V. Betz, and J. Rose. Using Cluster-Based Logic Blocks and Timing-Driven Packing to Improve FPGA Speed and Density. *ACM Int'l Symp. on FPGAs*, pages 37–46, 1999.
[22] L. McMurchie and C. Ebeling. PathFinder: A Negotiation-Based Performance-Driven Router for FPGAs. In *ACM Int'l Symp. on FPGAs*, pages 111–117, 1995.
[23] A. Mishchenko, S. Chatterjee, and R. Brayton. Improvements to Technology Mapping for LUT-Based FPGAs. In *ACM Int'l Symp. on FPGAs*, pages 41–49, 2006.
[24] A. Mishchenko, S. Cho, S. Chatterjee, and R. Brayton. Combinational and sequential mapping with priority cuts. In *IEEE/ACM Int'l Conf. on CAD*, pages 354–361, 2007.
[25] A. Mishchenko et al. ABC: A System for Sequential Synthesis and Verification. http://www.eecs.berkeley.edu/alanmi/abc, 2009.
[26] P. Mishra and N. Dutt. Architecture Description Languages for Programmable Embedded Systems. *IEEE Proc. on Computers and Digital Techniques*, 152(3):285–297, 2005.
[27] T. Ngai, J. Rose, and S. Wilton. An SRAM-programmable field-configurable memory. *IEEE Custom Integrated Circuits Conf.*, pages 499–502, 1995.
[28] G. Ni, J. Tong, and J. Lai. A new FPGA packing algorithm based on the modeling method for logic block. In *IEEE Int'l Conf. on ASICs*, volume 2, pages 877–880, Oct. 2005.
[29] D. Paladino. Academic Clustering and Placement Tools for Modern Field-Programmable Gate Array Architectures. Master's thesis, University of Toronto, Toronto, Ontario, Canada, 2008.
[30] A. Singh, G. Parthasarathy, and M. Marek-Sadowksa. Efficient Circuit Clustering for Area and Power Reduction in FPGAs. *ACM Trans. on Design Automation of Electronic Systems*, 7(4):643–663, Nov 2002.
[31] W3C. Extensible Markup Language (XML). http://www.w3.org/XML/, 2003.
[32] K. Wang, M. Yang, L. Wang, X. Zhou, and J. Tong. A novel packing algorithm for sparse crossbar FPGA architectures. In *Int'l Conf. on Solid-State and Integrated-Circuit Technology*, pages 2345–2348, 2008.
[33] S. Yang. Logic Synthesis and Optimization Benchmarks User Guide Version 3.0. *MCNC*, Jan, 1991.

Reducing the Pressure on Routing Resources of FPGAs with Generic Logic Chains

Hadi Parandeh-Afshar[†]
hadi.parandehafshar@epfl.ch

Grace Zgheib[‡]
grace.zgheib@lau.edu.lb

Philip Brisk[§]
philip@cs.ucr.edu

Paolo Ienne[†]
paolo.ienne@epfl.ch

[†]Ecole Polytechnique Fédérale de Lausanne (EPFL)
School of Computer and Communication Sciences, 1015 Lausanne, Switzerland

[‡]Department of Electrical and Computer Engineering
Lebanese American University, Byblos, Lebanon

[§]Department of Computer Science and Engineering
University of California Riverside, 900 University Ave., Riverside CA92521, U.S.A.

ABSTRACT

Routing resources in modern FPGAs use 50% of the silicon real estate and are significant contributors to critical path delay and power consumption; the situation gets worse with each successive process generation, as transistors scale more effectively than wires. To cope with these challenges, FPGA architects have divided wires into local and global categories and introduced fast dedicated carry chains between adjacent logic cells, which reduce routing resource usage for certain arithmetic circuits (primarily adders and subtractors).

Inspired by the carry chains, we generalize the idea to connect lookup tables (LUTs) in adjacent logic cells. By exploiting the fracturable structure of LUTs in current FPGA generations, we increase the utilization of the existing LUTs in the logic cell by providing new inputs along the logic chain, but without increasing the I/O bandwidth from the programmable interconnect. This allows us to increase the logic density of the configurable logic cells while reducing demand for routing resources, as long as the mapping tools are able to exploit the logic chains. Our experiments using the combinational MCNC benchmarks and comparing against an Altera Stratix-III FPGA show that the introduction of logic chains reduce the average usage of local routing wires by 37%, with a 12% reduction in total wiring (local and global); this translates to improvements in dynamic power consumption of 18% in the routing network and 10% overall, while utilizing 4% fewer logic cells, on average.

Categories and Subject Descriptors

B.6.1 [**LOGIC DESIGN**]: Design Styles—*Logic arrays, Combinational logic*; B.7.1 [**INTEGRATED CIRCUITS**]: Types and Design Styles—*Gate arrays*

General Terms

Design, Performance

Keywords

FPGA, Logic Chain, Routing Wire, Dedicated Connection, Generic Synthesis

1. INTRODUCTION

The programmable interconnect fabric dominates silicon area in modern high-performance FPGAs. The fraction of silicon dedicated to programmable routing increases with each successive technology generation, because transistors scale more effectively than wires. This trend directly impacts the performance and power consumption of FPGAs. Moreover, the feasibility of synthesizing a circuit onto an FPGA can be limited by the availability of routing resources, rather than programmable logic.

To reduce the negative impact of routing resources, a number of architectural innovations have been proposed in recent years. One approach, was to divide the routing network into global and local components [4, 22]. This enabled to have fast local routing within clusters of logic (e.g., *Logic Array Blocks, or LABs* in Altera's FPGAs) and reduced the demand for global routing resources between the clusters. The introduction of carry chains within logic clusters allowed for the efficient propagation of arithmetic carries along a fixed wire, native to the carry chain; consequently, these wires were completely moved out of the programmable interconnect.

This paper introduces a new logic cell architecture that reduces the demand for programmable routing resources when utilized effectively by the mapper. The key idea is to establish dedicated connection wires between adjacent logic

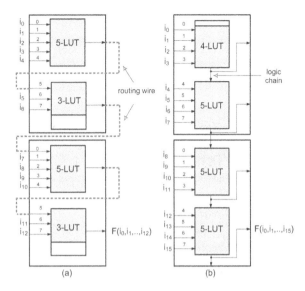

(a)   (b)

Figure 1: Key idea. (a) Two logic cells, each has 8 inputs and two base 5-LUTs. Many 13-input logic functions can be mapped to a linear cascade of the base LUTs; routing resources are required to connect adjacent LUTs in the cascade. (b) A dedicated logic chain between adjacent LUTs eliminates the overhead due to routing resources and increases the input bandwidth of logic cell. Many 16-input logic functions can be mapped with the same number of available LUTs.

cells; this so-called *Logic Chain* is similar in principle to a carry-chain, but connects programmable logic resources rather than fixed-function gates that can only perform carry-propagate addition. Through effective decomposition and mapping algorithms, it is possible to map logic functions of non-trivial size onto the dedicated logic chains, rather than using programmable interconnect. This reduces pressure on the routing network, as nets from the technology-mapped circuit are moved onto dedicated wires in the logic chain.

The other benefit of the logic chain is that it increases the utilization of LUTs in the logic cell by providing more bandwidth, but without increasing the I/O bandwidth of the cell in terms of connections to the programmable routing network. This allows us to improve the logic density of the logic cells by making better usage of the available resources. The logic chain is implemented to reuse as many of the circuit elements within the logic cell as possible; a small number of additional multiplexers and configuration bits must be added to augment the logic cell with the new logic chain.

The following section begins with a simple example to illustrate the main idea.

1.1 Key Idea

The motivation behind logic chains comes from the observation that many technology mapped circuits contain linear chains of LUTs after mapping. Based on our experiments, on average, 85% of the LUTs are chainable. Suppose that a circuit has been synthesized in such a manner that four LUTs are cascaded linearly and form a chain. Figure 1 il-

lustrates how this circuit is differently implemented on two different FPGAs, one with a conventional logic cell and the other with the new logic cell that has the dedicated logic chain.

In Figure 1 (a), there are two FPGA logic cells, each having 8 inputs and a fracturable LUT structure. In this fracturable LUT structure, each logic cell has two base 5-LUTs and a bigger 6-LUT is formed using the two sub-LUTs followed by a multiplexer, which is not shown in this figure.

One drawback of this particular architecture is that the routing resources must be used to connect one sub-LUT to its successor in the cascade. The other drawback is that the second sub-LUT in each logic cell is under utilized due to the logic cell input bandwidth constraint. The first 5 inputs are used by the first sub-LUT and the remaining 3 inputs are used by the second sub-LUT. This means that a 5-LUT is used to implement a 3-input function.

Figure 1 (b) has the dedicated logic chains within the cluster so that the output of each sub-LUT connects directly to the input of the subsequent sub-LUT along the chain; in principal, this is similar to the interconnection structure of arithmetic carry chains in commercial FPGAs today. The introduction of these direct connections eliminates the need to use the global routing network to synthesize the cascade. This has several advantages: reduced pressure on the routing network, reduced critical path delay and reduced power consumption. Moreover, the logic chain provides a way that the available sub-LUTs are utilized more efficiently, since the input bandwidth of the logic cell is increased by the logic chain without any change in the local routing network of the logic array block.

Comparing these two figures, we see that with the new logic cell we can map bigger functions to the same number of logic cells. The logic cells in Figure 1 (a) can implement many functions with 13 inputs, while the logic cells in Figure 1 (b) can implement many 16-input functions.

2. RELATED WORK

Different and restricted types of LUT chains exist in some FPGA devices from both *Altera* and *Xilinx* families. Logic Cells (LC) in *Stratix* and *Cyclone* devices from *Altera*, have a local connection which connects the output of one LC's LUT to the input of the adjacent LC [4]. These connections allow LUTs within the same LAB to cascade together for wide input functions. Conceptually our proposed logic chain is similar to the mentioned local chains, but there are some fundamental differences. The main difference is that in contrast to the above FPGAs, we do not use the available input bandwidth of the LC to connect the logic output of the adjacent LC. This will increase the available bandwidth and hence wider functions can be implemented without any need to change the LC interface. The other difference is that the LC in current FPGA devices has a *fracturable* LUT structure and this allows to use the available LUT resources in a LC to implement larger functions considering our logic chain as the extra input.

Xilinx FPGAs also have a kind of local connections between the adjacent LCs, which goes through a number of multiplexers in each LC [22]. This local connection is mainly used for implementing carry look-ahead adders, but it can also be exploited for mapping of a limited number of generic functions. In its most general case, it can be used to implement the AND cascade of functions. For instance, a wide input AND function can be partitioned into some parts that are mapped to the LUTs and cascaded through the local connection. In contrast to such FPGAs, our logic chain is more general. The proposed logic chain goes through a LUT and forms the last input of the LUT; therefore, no specific logic constraint exist for cascading different functions.

Constructing bigger LUTs by cascading smaller ones is also possible in *Virtex-5 Xilinx* FPGAs. There are some multiplexers in the *Virtex-5* LC for this purpose and by using such multiplexers, we can build up to 8-input LUTs. However, the routing wires are required to connect smaller LUTs and also there is a concern about the feasibility and usefulness of synthesizing a circuit onto such big LUTs. Prior research [2] indicates that a LUT size of 4 to 6 provides the best area-delay product for an FPGA.

In [9], an FPGA chip was developed with the logic blocks that are comprised of cascaded LUTs. In this work, each logic block has three 4-input LUTs hard-wired together for high performance. In contrast to our design, the hard-wired connection is exclusively limited to the logic blocks internal and does not cross the logic blocks boundaries.

Other relevant ideas consist in introducing carry chains into modern high-performance FPGAs and developing advanced technology mapping algorithms that attempt to exploit carry chains.

The vast majority of carry chains that have been proposed are for different types of adders [8, 14, 17, 18, 19]; the carry chains on commercial FPGAs available from Xilinx and Altera also fall into this category. One interesting alternative is a carry chain that allows an Altera-style logic cell to be configured as a 7:2 compressor, which is used for multi-operand addition [20].

Similar to our work, one recent paper has presented a non-arithmetic carry chain in which two 2-LUTs are combined to form a 3-LUT [15]; however, it was based on a carry-select structure used in Altera's Stratix, which has since been deprecated. Starting with the Stratix II, Altera's carry chains have employed a ripple-carry structure.

There have been a handful of papers that have successfully mapped operations other than 2- or 3-input addition (or subtraction) onto the carry chains of commercial FPGAs. In a previous contribution [21], we mapped generalized parallel counters, also used for multi-operand addition, onto the carry chains used by Altera's Stratix III series FPGAs, which are still in use today. This approach target a limited set of logic functions (multi-operand addition) and cannot map general logic functions onto carry chains.

The ChainMap algorithm attempts to map arbitrary logic functions onto the carry chain of the Altera Stratix and Cyclone FPGAs [16]; as mentioned above, this carry chain has been deprecated and the authors readily admit that their algorithm is not applicable to newer Altera FPGAs or Xilinx FPGAs. Our chaining heuristic does share some principle similarities with ChainMap, but targets the logic chain that we have proposed rather than carry chains.

Traditional formulations of the technology mapping problem focus on converting a structural HDL implementation of a circuit into a network of K-cuts, where each K-cut can be mapped onto a single K-LUT. These formulations assume that the programmable routing network is used to connect the LUTs; it does not attempt to use carry chains, fracturable LUTs, embedded multipliers, or DSP blocks; likewise, these formulations could not account for the fixed

wiring structure in the logic chain proposed here. Cong and Ding proved that minimizing the number of LUTs on the longest path can be done in polynomial time [10]; several others have proven that the decision problems corresponding to minimizing the total number of LUTs used in the covering and minimizing power consumption are NP-complete [12, 13]. Many heuristics to solve different variations of the technology mapping problem have been presented over the years; there are far too many to enumerate here.

Additionally, several papers have tried to perform logical decompositions to optimize the structural circuit description in conjunction with technology mapping [7][11]; as logical optimization is NP-complete in the general case, this formulation of the problem is NP-complete as well, although the use of decomposition can significantly improve the quality of the technology mapping that can be achieved. In principle, this type of decomposition and of technology mapping approach would be appropriate for use with the logic chains proposed here; the decomposition could exploit the specific fixed interconnect structure between adjacent LUTs on the logic chain; this approach is likely to be more effective than what we have done here: searching for chainable candidates in a technology mapping solution that was produced by a more general technology mapping algorithm that was unaware of the presence of the logic chains.

3. NEW LOGIC CHAIN

Figure 2 (a) illustrates the structure of *Altera*'s *Stratix-III Adaptive Logic Module (ALM)* configured as two independent 5-LUTs, which have two shared inputs; the two shared inputs are necessary because the ALM has an input bandwidth constraint of 8. Consequently, if the user wishes to map two logic functions without shared inputs onto an ALM, the only possibilities are to use two 4-LUTs or a 5-LUT and a 3-LUT.

Figure 2 (b) illustrates a way that an ALM can realize a limited subset of 7-input logic functions: the 5-LUT is cascaded with the 3-LUT, however, the interconnection between the two requires the usage of the routing network. On the other hand, if the user wants to cascade two 5-LUTs with one another, then two ALMs are required, as shown in Figure 2 (c), once again using the routing network; if the two ALMs are placed within the same *Logic Array Block (LAB)*, then the fast local routing network could be used instead of the global routing network.

Altera's ALM is fracturable, meaning that several small LUTs (sub-LUTs) exist natively in the ALM and can be concatenated together, via multiplexers, to form larger LUTs. This paper uses this approach to build larger LUTs out of the sub-LUTs along the dedicated vertical connection that we call a *logic chain*. The basic idea is to re-use the current LUTs in the ALM and add a few multiplexer to provide a way to form larger LUTs with a fixed interconnection pattern. Figure 2 (d) illustrates the main idea. The modified logic cell now contains two 5-LUTs that are cascaded; one input of each of the 5-LUTs comes from the preceding 5-LUT in the logic chain; thus, only 8 input signals are provided from the routing network, keeping the design within the bandwidth constraints of the ALM. This allows the new logic cell to implement a subset of 9-input logic functions, without requiring the routing network and assuming that one of the inputs comes from the preceding logic cell along the logic chain; if the vertical input is unavailable, then it

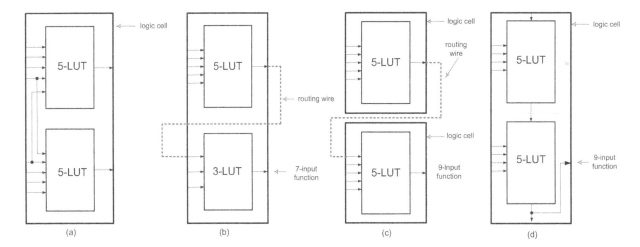

Figure 2: (a) Altera's ALM configured to implement two 5-input logic functions; the ALM imposes the constraint that the two functions must share two inputs. (b) Using fracturable LUTs, a subset of 7-input logic functions can be synthesized on an ALM, but this requires routing a signal from one sub-LUT to the next. (c) To implement two cascaded 5-input functions with no common inputs, two ALMs are required. (d) All three of the preceding logic functions can be synthezed on the proposed logic cell using the logic chain and without using the global routing network; moreover, the proposed cell can implement a subset of 9-input logic functions.

can still implement a subset of 8-input logic functions without using the routing network. This is significantly more powerful than the ALM, which can implement any 6-input logic function and limited 7-input crossbar switch without using the routing network.

The logic chain borrows many ideas from arithmetic carry chains, that also employ vertical connections between adjacent logic cells. The goal of carry chains, however, is to improve the resource usage and critical path delay of addition/subtraction operations, which are common, but limited. One of the key benefits of these carry chains was that carry propagation was performed along the vertical connections and therefore did not enter the routing network. This reduced contention for routing resources and also reduced critical path delay and power consumption, as the wires in the vertical connection are shorter and do not have additional delays caused by configuration elements placed periodically along them. By integrating LUTs into the vertical connections instead, it is possible to synthesize a wide variety of operations, including addition/subtraction, onto the logic chains.

Figure 3 shows how the fracturable structure of ALMs is used to embed the logic chain and form bigger LUTs along the logic chain. Each half-ALM contains two 4-LUTs which can form a 5-LUT using a multiplexer controlled by a fifth input; all inputs between the two 4-LUTs are shared. This design is effectively a Shannon decomposition. The shaded area of the figure illustrates the logic chain. Using a similar idea, we instantiate a vertical multiplexer, which is controlled by the logic chain, at the outputs of each pair of 4-LUTs; this forms a new 5-LUT along the logic chain. This provides us with the option to form either a horizontal or a vertical 5-LUT in each half-ALM. The output of the vertical 5-LUT propagates along the logic chain.

In Figure 3 there is no way to access the output of the LUTs that are placed in the logic chain; this severely limits the ability to use the logic chain when a LUT placed in the chain has a fanout that exceeds one. The FPGA already contains several multiplexers on its output: one to select between the LUT and carry chain outputs; another to optionally select the flip-flop's output, allowing for sequential circuits. We add an additional multiplexer, as shown in Figure 4 to select between the carry chain output and the logic chain output. The shaded area in the figure indicates the additional logic that we add to the half-ALM to support the logic chains. The additional multiplexer that we have added will not increase the critical path delay of the non-arithmetic modes of the ALM, since it does not lie along those paths.

To estimate the area overhead of the new logic, we count the number of transistors in the logic that we added and compare it coarsely with the number of transistors in a simplified ALM. We have added four multiplexers and two configuration bits (SRAMs); based on the components that are known to exist already in the Stratix-III ALM architecture [4], we are confident that the area overhead is less than 3%.

4. CHAINING HEURISTIC

The objective of the mapping heuristic is to identify chains of logic having the maximum possible lengths. The input is a *Direct Acyclic Graph(DAG)*, where each node represents a logic function and each edge represents the input and output dependencies among the functions. The DAG is generated after technology mapping, so each node is a prospective function that can map onto the LUTs. The number of inputs (K) of each node in the DAG cannot exceed the number of LUT inputs; each node has K child nodes and one or more parents based on the fanout of the node output.

The mapping heuristic visits the DAG nodes in *Depth First Search (DFS)* order, starting from the outputs and

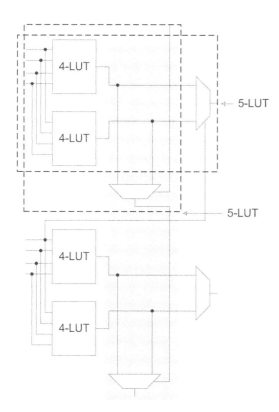

Figure 3: Integrating the logic chain into the structure of an ALM. The shaded area indicates the logic chain. Existing 4-LUTs are used to form vertical 5-LUT on the logic chain using a multiplexer. The fifth input is the vertical logic chain. This figure also shows how a 5-LUT is built in an ALM using smaller LUTs. The key point is that the ALM input bandwidth remains the same, therefore two cascaded 5-LUT with no shared inputs can be mapped to the new cell.

working back toward the inputs. The heuristic recursively assigns a depth to each node in the DAG.

DEFINITION 4.1. *A node is **chainable**, if it has at most K inputs and is not part of another chain.*

DEFINITION 4.2. *The **depth** of a node is the number of chainable nodes that can be accessed consecutively through that node; the **depth** of an internal node is the maximum depth among all input nodes from which it is reachable.*

Once a depth has been assigned to all nodes, then we can select specific nodes to map onto the logic chain. In particular, we search for the longest chain of nodes in the DAG, which is a chain whose head node has the maximum depth. This chain is then mapped onto a logic chain in the FPGA; the head of the chain can be either a DAG output or a child of a node that is not chainable.

Figure 5 (a) provides a simple example. In this figure, there are two chain candidates, each having a length of 5; the chains intersect at node $N2$. Since each node can be part of one chain, $N2$ is arbitrarily chosen for one of the chains.

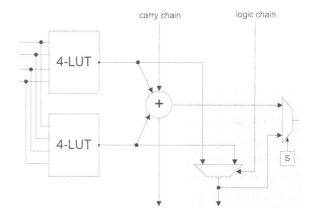

Figure 4: The logic chain integrated with the carry chain. In addition to the vertical multiplexer, a horizontal multiplexer selects between the output of the full adder and the logic chain fanout; this multiplexer is required when the logic chain has fanout.

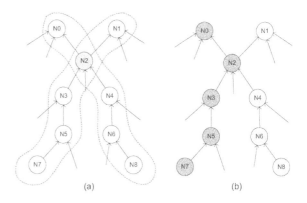

Figure 5: (a) Two chains intersecting at a shared node. (b) The shared node is assigned to one of the chains, breaking the other chain into two smaller sub-chains.

As shown in Figure 5 (b), the second chain is then broken into a chain of 3 nodes and a singleton node, which itself is not part of a chain

Figure 6 presents the chaining algorithm. The loop in the main function recursively traverses the DAG using the DFS, starting from the outputs, and computes the depth of each node. In this approach, first the depths of each node's inputs are computed and then the maximum depth value is increased by one and assigned as the node depth. For the nodes that are either primary inputs or non-chainable, zero is considered as the depth. Figure 7 illustrates an example, in which each node is marked by its depth. The shaded nodes are not chainable, since they are already assigned to other chains.

The depth information then allows the heuristic to identify the logic chains using the *sort_chains* function. The head node of a chian is the one that has the highest depth. All of the nodes in the selected chain are marked as *CHAINED*, to avoid placing a node in more than one chain. This process

```
1: Chaining_Heuristic(pDAG) {
2:    while(!termination_condition) {
3:      for(i=0 to nDAGOutputs) {
4:        Find_Node_Depth_Rec(pDAG->out[i])
5:      sort_chains();
6:      mark_nodes_in_longest_chain();
7:    }
8: }
//------------------------------------------------
1: int Find_Node_Depth_Rec(pNode) {
2:    for(i = 0 to nLeaves-1) {
3:      if(pNode->Leaves[i] == DAGInput) {
4:        pNode->depth[i] = 0;
5:        break; // go to the next leaf
6:      }
7:      else
8:        pTmpNode = pNode->Leaves[i];
9:
10:       depth = Find_Node_Depth_Rec (pTmpNode );
11:       if(pNode->chainable)
12:         pNode.depth[i] = depth + 1;
13:       else
14:         pNode.depth[i] = 0;
15:    } // end of for loop
16:    pNode->max_depth = pNode->Find_Max_Depth();
17:    return  pNode->max_depth;
18: }
```

Figure 6: Pseudo-code of the Chaining Heuristic.

repeats until the maximum length of all remaining chains is less than some threshold value. The time complexity of the heuristic is $O(nh)$, where n is the number of nodes in the DAG and h is the depth of the DAG.

5. TOOL CHAIN FLOW

Figure 8 presents the tool chain flow that we use for our experiments. First, we synthesize each benchmark using *Quartus-II*, a commercial tool provided by Altera; Quartus-II generates a *Verilog Quartus Mapping (VQM)* file netlist; parsing the VQM file yields a DAG-based circuit representation that is fed to the chaining heuristic. Next, the *Verilog* writer routine is called to generate an atom-level netlist for the new mapped circuit. In terms of logic, the Verilog netlist is equivalent to the original VQM netlist; however, the mapping of some cells have bee changed. Lastly, the new netlist is placed and routed by Quartus-II targeting an Altera Stratix-III FPGA. The number of resources that are utilized are obtained for each benchmark. Additionally, the timing revision tool analyzes the timing report produced by Quartus-II and delay numbers are extracted. The *Power-Play Early Power Estimator* tool is employed to extract the power consumption. Details of the key steps are presented in the following subsections.

5.1 DAG Generator

Quartus-II synthesizes the benchmarks and maps them onto LUTs. Quartus-II's synthesizer generates the VQM file in ASCII text, which contains a node-level (or atom-level) netlist. Since our proposed logic cell is a modified version of the Stratix-III ALM, we felt that Quartus-II was the most appropriate mapper to use. We also considered the possibility of using Berkeley's ABC synthesis tool [1]; however, ABC

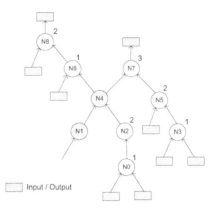

Figure 7: The depths of different nodes in a sample DAG. The shaded nodes are part of other chains and hence not chainable.

is a more general technology mapper and does not consider many ALM-specific features, such as fracturable LUTs.

We implemented a VQM parser in C++, which produces a DAG corresponding to the netlist. Each node in the DAG corresponds to an FPGA cell in the VQM netlist and the edges between nodes in the DAG represent data dependencies. Each DAG node is a C++ class object. Some of the class members are initialized when the VQM file is parsed and others are initialized by the chaining heuristic: the depth of a node; whether a node has been assigned to a chain; the id of the chain to which a node has been assigned; and the order of the node in the chain.

5.2 Placement and Routing

Once the circuits have been mapped to the new FPGA logic cells using the logic chain, we need to place-and-route the mapped circuit to obtain accurate estimates of the area, critical path delay and power consumption. Our area metric includes the number of logic blocks that are used and also the amount of local and global routing resources required to realize the circuit.

We considered the possibility of modifying VPR [5][6] as our experimental platform; however, two problems caused us to look for other alternatives. Firstly, VPR's architectural model does not include carry chains and its packing, placement and routing algorithms would be unable to handle their presence if they were supported architecturally; secondly, a comparison between VPR and Quartus-II is not meaningful, as these are two completely different frameworks; it is difficult to say whether a disparity in favor of either the baseline FPGA or our modified FPGA would be due to architectural superiority or differences between Quartus-II and VPR.

Fortunately, we discovered a way to let Quartus-II model our new FPGAa logic cell; this allowed us to use Quartus-II's placement and routing algorithms, rather than developing our own algorithms to better exploit the modified ALM architecture that we propose. The basic idea is to leave the ALM structure alone and to simply "pretend" that existing carry chains represent the logic chains that we want to introduce. This is possible because the carry output of the adder is a function of the carry input and four ALM inputs, which is similar in principle to our proposed logic chain in terms of connectivity. Therefore, we can assume that the output

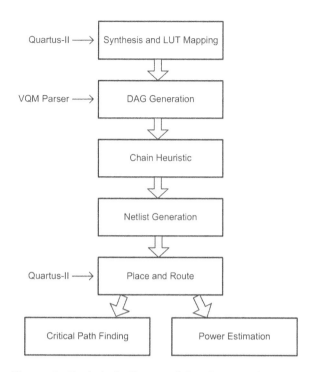

Figure 8: Tool chain flow used for the experiments.

of the vertical 5-LUT in Figure 3 is the carry output of the adder; when we have a fanout that exceeds one, we can take the sum output of the adder as the fanout connection.

Consequently, it is necessary to configure the ALM in a way that the nodes on the logic chain are mapped to the carry chain in a corresponding fashion. To do so, we instantiate the ALM cells and provide the connections and configurations as explained previously; for the other nodes that are not on any chain, we write back the original cell description that was obtained after synthesis to the final netlist. The output, therefore, is a netlist of ALM cells, similar to the original VQM file; nodes that use the logic chain are configured in arithmetic mode, while others are mapped using the ALM's normal mode. Quartus-II then proceeds to place and route the resulting netlist. This gives precise estimates of the usage of logic blocks and routing resources; however, some additional work is required in order to accurate model the critical path delay. To obtain the most dense implementation, we lock the logic in rectangular regions and shrink the region size to the extent that the tool is not able to fit the logic. This guarantees that we have the most packed implementation for both original netlist and the modified one.

5.3 Timing Analysis

As described in the preceding section, we effectively use the carry chains that are present in the Stratix-III FPGA to mimic the logic chains we have proposed for the purposes of placement and routing; however, the critical path delays that are obtained from Quartus-II are based on the delays of the full adders on the carry chains, rather than the multiplexers that we introduced in the logic chain. Therefore, the delay of each adder in the carry chain should be replaced

with the delay of the multiplexer instead. Our experiments revealed that the delay between the ALM inputs and the outputs of the adder are significantly greater than the delay of a 5-LUT in the same ALM. Consequently, we take the delay of the normal 5-LUT in the ALM to be the delay of the 5-LUT that is realized in the logic chain; as the result, this reduces the overall delay compared to the timing report produced by Quartus-II.

This analysis has to be performed on a path-by-path basis. The critical path, as identified by Quartus-II's timing report, may no longer be critical once the delays of the logic chain have been properly accounted for. To solve this problem, we repeatedly adjust the delays of subsequent critical paths until we identify a path that includes no nodes mapped onto the logic chains. We wrote a script to perform this task for a specific number of critical paths; the termination condition is to stop when the first path that does not include an adder on the carry chain is found. The paths are then sorted based on their adjusted critical path delays and the maximum is returned as the critical path delay of the circuit synthesized on an Stratix-III style FPGA that has been modified to include our proposed logic chain.

5.4 Power Estimation

To estimate the dynamic power consumption of the mapped circuits, we use *PowerPlay Early Power Estimator* [3] provided by *Altera*. This tool obtains the amount of resources used by each benchmark, the clock frequency after synthesis, the average fanout, the device type and the toggle rate of the wires and estimates the dynamic power consumption of the circuit. The power that is reported is broken down into routing power, logic block power and total power. Here we assume that the dynamic power of the new logic block is approximately equal to the dynamic power of the standard ALM. One potential source of error could be the difference between the toggle rate of the adder output that we use for modeling compared to the toggle rate of the logic in our carry chain. To observe the difference, we modeled the real cell and the ALM in VHDL and applied several stimulause vectors to each and computed the average toggle rates. Our results validated our assumption that toggle rates are approximately equal, on average.

6. EXPERIMENTAL RESULTS

We evaluate the modified ALM-style logic cell with the new logic chain; we consider several factors, including critical path delay, ALM usage, routing resource usage and dynamic power consumption. We used the MCNC benchmarks for our experiments and selected the combinatorial benchmarks exclusively; to synthesize the sequential circuit benchmarks, it is necessary to separate the combinational cones of logic that are placed between the registers and apply the chaining heuristic to each cone; this is left open for future work.

The Stratix-III ALM can be configured with logic functions having up to 7-inputs; any 6-input logic function can be mapped onto the ALM, along with a subset of 7-input logic functions. Table 1 shows the distribution of functions in terms of the number of inputs for the different benchmarks. The majority of the functions have 5 inputs; we have selected logic functions having at most 5 inputs for mapping onto the chains; on average, 85% of logic functions are chainable.

Table 1: LUT mapping and chaining heuristic statistics.

Benchmark	3-LUT	4-LUT	5-LUT	6-LUT	7-LUT	Chainable	Chained	Max Chain	Ave Chain
alu4	163	89	413	32	6	94%	39%	12	5.2
pdc	431	214	538	139	5	89%	53%	9	5.8
misex3	179	99	376	43	1	93%	42%	9	5.1
ex1010	166	148	336	419	1	60%	47%	8	5.3
ex5p	149	89	234	60	0	88%	46%	7	5.2
des	134	89	159	110	0	77%	20%	4	3.1
apex2	206	101	284	108	2	84%	39%	8	4.9
apex4	127	74	354	119	1	82%	59%	8	4.3
spla	258	229	719	114	2	91%	46%	11	5.3
seq	205	150	356	96	2	88%	43%	6	4.9
Average	201	128	376	124	2	85%	44%	8.2	4.9

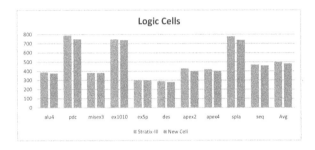

Figure 9: Number of logic cells (ALMs) that are used in each method. On average, the introduction of our logic chain reduces ALM usage by 4%.

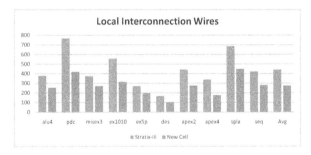

Figure 10: The number of local interconnection wires (i.e., within a LAB) used for each benchmark. On average, the introduction of the logic chain reduces the number of local wires used by 37%.

The last three columns in Table 1 summarize the chaining heuristic. The column labeled "Chained" reports the percentage of eligible functions that are placed onto the logic chain, which is 44%, on average; we set the minimum length chain to 4 for all benchmarks, except for *apex4* and *sec*, where we allowed minimum chain lengths of 3. The last two columns of the table report the maximum and average chain lengths for each benchmark.

Quartus-II is used to place-and-route each circuit. To evaluate the new logic cell, we compare against the Stratix-III FPGA as a baseline; as described earlier, we take a netlist that has been mapped onto the Stratix-III, identify logic chains and re-map them onto our new logic cell that includes vertical logic chains.

Figure 9 reports the number of logic cells that are used; our chaining heuristic was able to reduce the number of logic cells used for all benchmarks other than *ex5p* and *misex3*; on average, our approach uses 4% fewer logic cells than the Stratix-III. It is important to note that the Stratix-III ALM is used most effectively when it is configured to implement two 5-input logic functions with shared inputs, as shown in Figure 2 (a); in such cases, which are actually quite common, the introduction of our logic cell with the chaining heuristic cannot offer a significant improvement in terms of logic density.

The real benefit of using our logic block is its ability to reduce the usage of routing resources, as reported in Figures 10 and 11. On average, our logic cell and chaining heuristic reduces the usage of local wires by 37%, with a maximum savings of 45%. On average, we reduce the usage of global and local wires by 12%, with the local wires con-

tributing a reduction in 3%. The minimum saving on total wiring was 7% (*apex2*) and the maximum was 22% (*seq*). To account for different horizontal and vertical wires with different lengths, we have scaled the wires based on their length and we reported their sum in Figure 11.

Reducing the usage of interconnect noticeably improves dynamic power consumption. A large fraction of dynamic power is consumed in the routing network; therefore, replacing a net that is routed on programmable interconnect with a direct connection using the logic chain can help to reduce dynamic power consumption. Figure 12 compares estimates of the dynamic power consumption of the Stratix-III to our proposed FPGA that includes logic chains. On average, we reduce dynamic power consumption in the routing network by 18%. The most dramatic improvement was observed for *seq*, which had the greatest savings in total interconnect as reported in Figure 11.

Figure 13 reports the dynamic power consumption for each benchmark, which includes power consumption of logic resources; on average, the introduction of the logic chain reduces dynamic power consumption by 10%. It is important here to note that the power estimation methodology used here is far from precise; however, our circuits are too large to use a much more accurate methodology such as SPICE simulation. Although we do not trust the exact numbers reported in Figures 12 and 13, we consider them a good indication of the type of savings that is possible using our logic cell.

Lastly, we measure the logic chain's impact on critical

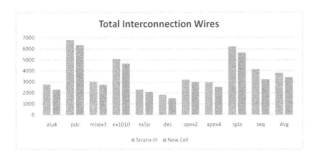

Figure 11: The number of global and local interconnection wires used for each benchmark, scaled by the length of the wires. On average, the introduction of the logic chain reduces the total number of wires used by 12%.

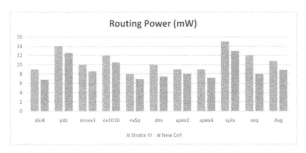

Figure 12: Dynamic power consumption estimates for the routing network; as the logic chain reduces the number of programmable wires used, an average savings of 24% is obtained.

path delay; an improvement is observed for all benchmarks other than *apex2* and *apex4*. The overall improvement in delay is minimal; however, the logic chain was introduced primarily to reduce interconnect and logic block usage, not to improve delay. We do believe that there is potential to further improve the critical path delay, which would require much more aggressive synthesis algorithms that are specific to the new logic chain. In particular, this would require a new logic decomposition algorithm that recognizes the cascaded structure of the logic chain; such an algorithm could be integrated with a technology mapper to make better use of the logic chains than the relatively naive and greedy chaining heuristic described here; this is an important research direction that is currently left open for future work.

7. CONCLUSION

This paper has introduced the concept of logic chains as a way to improve routing resource utilization in modern high-performance FPGAs. The dedicated wires between logic cells in the chain reduce pressure on the routing network. The key idea is based on the observation that many technology mapped circuits contain linear chains of LUTs after mapping; the basic idea is to add a direct connection between LUTs in a cluster that provide a natural mapping target for these chains. Having the fracturable structure of LUTs in modern FPGAs, we form larger LUTs by adding a multiplexer which is controlled by the direct output of a preceding LUT along the chain. This enables us to in-

Figure 13: Total (logic plus routing network) power consumption estimates; the logic chain reduces total power consumption by 10%, on average.

Figure 14: Critical path delay of each benchmark; the introduction of the logic chain marginally improves the critical path delay of most benchmarks.

crease the input bandwidth and logic density of the logic cells without adding any additional inputs. Our experimental results have shown that the proposed logic cell with logic chains can reduce the total number of routing resources required by 12%. This reduction saves 10% of the total dynamic power consumption. Moreover, the number of logic cells used is reduced by 4% and the critical path delay is improved marginally as well.

In this paper, we simply searched for logic chain candidates in a netlist that was produced by a technology mapper that was unaware of the logic chains. We believe that more chains can be found and that pressure on the routing network can be reduced further through the development of logic decomposition and technology mapping algorithms that are aware of and can exploit the logic chains. We intend to pursue the development of these algorithms as future work.

8. REFERENCES

[1] Berkeley Logic Synthesis and Verification Group. ABC: A system for sequential synthesis and verification. In *http://www.eecs.berkeley.edu/~alanmi/abc/*.

[2] E. Ahmed and J. Rose. The effect of LUT and cluster size on deep-submicron FPGA performance and density. In *IEEE Transactions on VLSI Systems*, volume 12, pages 288–298, 2004.

[3] Altera Inc. *PowerPlay Early Power Estimator User Guide*. Available online: http://www.altera.com/literature/ug/ug_epe.pdf.

[4] Altera Inc. *Stratix, Cyclone, Stratix II, III, and IV*

device handbooks. Available online: http://www.altera.com/.

[5] V. Betz and J. Rose. VPR: a new packing, placement, and routing tool for FPGA research. In *Proceedings of the 7th International Workshop on Field-Programmable Logic and Applications (FPL)*, pages 213–222, Sept. 1999.

[6] V. Betz, J. Rose, and A. Marquardt. *Architecture and CAD for Deep Submicron FPGAs*. Kluwer Academic Publishers, Feb. 1999.

[7] G. Chen and J. Cong. Simultaneous logic decomposition with technology mapping in FPGA designs. In *Internation Symposium on Field-Programmable Gate Arrays (FPGA)*, pages 48–55, Feb. 2001.

[8] D. Cherepacha and D. Lewis. DP-FPGA: an FPGA architecture optimized for datapaths. In *VLSI Design*, volume 4, pages 329–343, 1996.

[9] P. Chow, S. Seo, D. Au, B. Fallah, C. Li, and J.Rose. A 1.2um cmos fpga using cascaded logic blocks and segmented routing. In *Workshop on Field Programmable Logic and Applications*, pages 91–102, Sept. 1991.

[10] J. Cong and Y. Ding. FlowMap: an optimal technology mapping algorithm for delay optimization in lookup-table based FPGA designs. In *IEEE Transactions on Computer-Aided Design of Integrated Circuits and Systems*, volume 13, pages 1–12, Jan. 1994.

[11] T. S. Czajkowski and S. D. Brown. Functionally linear decomposition and synthesis of logic circuits for FPGAs. In *IEEE Transactions on Computer-Aided Design of Integrated Circuits and Systems*, volume 12, pages 2236–2249, Dec. 2008.

[12] A. H. Farrahi and M. Sarrafzadeh. Complexity of the lookup-tale minimization problem for FPGA technology mapping. In *IEEE Transactions on Computer-Aided Design of Integrated Circuits and Systems*, volume 13, pages 1319–1332, Nov. 1994.

[13] A. H. Farrahi and M. Sarrafzadeh. FPGA technology mapping for power minimization. In *4th International Workshop on Field-Prog. Logic and Applications*, pages 66–67, Sept. 1994.

[14] M. T. Frederick and A. K. Somani. Multi-bit carry chains for high-performance reconfigurable fabrics. In *International Conference on Field-Programmable Logic and Applications (FPL)*, pages 1–6, Aug. 2006.

[15] M. T. Frederick and A. K. Somani. Non-arithmetic carry chains for reconfigurable fabrics. In *International Conference Computer Design (ICCD)*, pages 137–143, Oct. 2007.

[16] M. T. Frederick and A. K. Somani. Beyond the arithmetic constraint: depth-optimal mapping of logic chains in LUT-based FPGAs. In *Internation Symposium on Field-Programmable Gate Arrays (FPGA)*, pages 37–46, Feb. 2008.

[17] S. Hauck, M. M. Hosler, and T. W. Fry. High-performance carry chains for FPGAs. In *IEEE Transactions on VLSI Systems*, volume 2, pages 138–147, 2000.

[18] A. Kaviani, D. Vranseic, and S. Brown. Computational field programmable architecture. In *IEEE Custom Integrated Circuits*, pages 261–264, May 1998.

[19] K. Leijten-Nowak and J. L. van Meerbergen. An FPGA architecture with enhanced datapath functionality. In *Internation Symposium on Field-Programmable Gate Arrays (FPGA)*, pages 195–204, Feb. 2003.

[20] H. Parandeh-Afshar, P. Brisk, and P. Ienne. A novel FPGA logic block for improved arithmetic performance. In *Internation Symposium on Field-Programmable Gate Arrays (FPGA)*, pages 171–180, Feb. 2008.

[21] H. Parandeh-Afshar, P. Brisk, and P. Ienne. Exploiting fast carry-chains of FPGAs for designing compressor trees. In *Proceedings of the 19th International Conference on Field-Programmable Logic and Applications*, pages 242–49, Prague, Aug. 2009.

[22] Xilinx Inc. *Virtex-5 User Guide*. http://www.xilinx.com/.

Co-synthesis of FPGA-Based Application-Specific Floating Point SIMD Accelerators

Andrei Hagiescu and Weng-Fai Wong
School of Computing
National University of Singapore
Singapore
{hagiescu,wongwf}@comp.nus.edu.sg

ABSTRACT

The constant push for feature richness in mobile and embedded devices has significantly increased computational demand. However, stringent energy constraints typically remain in place. Embedding processor cores in FPGAs offers a path to having customized instruction processors that can meet the performance and energy demands. Ideally, the customization process should be automated to reduce the design effort, and indirectly the time to market. However, the automatic generation of custom extensions for *floating point* computation remains a challenge in FPGA co-design. We propose an approach for accelerating such computation via application-specific SIMD extensions. We describe an automated co-design toolchain that generates code and application-specific platform extensions that implement SIMD instructions with a parameterizable number of vector elements. The parallelism exposed by encapsulating computation in vector instructions is matched to an adjustable pool of execution units. Experiments on actual hardware show significant performance improvements. Our framework provides an important extension to the capabilities of embedded processor FPGAs which traditionally dealt with bit, integer, and low intensity floating point code, to now being able to handle vectorizable floating point computation.

Categories and Subject Descriptors

C.1.3 [**PROCESSOR ARCHITECTURES**]: Other Architecture Styles—*Adaptable architectures*

General Terms

Algorithms, Design, Experimentation, Performance

Keywords

Co-synthesis, Custom instructions, SIMD

1. INTRODUCTION

Embedded applications vary widely in their code structure and profile. As they are often subjected to serious power and resource constraints, specialized hardware extensions are added very conservatively in embedded processors.

Designers of such applications often use reconfigurable extensions to supplement their silicon processor [8, 22]. These extensions are particularly effective when there is a large amount of bit- or word-level parallelism. Although floating point applications often come with even higher amount of parallelism, they are generally not common in reconfigurable computing. They are deemed to consume too much resources, and the desired performance can only be obtained by hand-tuning the application, including conversion to fixed point and then tackling the precision issue. Yet, floating point computation is often the most straight-forward means of expressing an algorithm, especially when fractions and accuracy are involved. In this paper, we aim to show how parallelism in floating point code can be exploited *automatically* using a flexible co-designed approach that includes support for vector operations in a reconfigurable SIMD architecture.

A standard architecture for effective reconfigurable computing consists of processor cores coupled with reconfigurable hardware fabric that often resembles field programmable gate arrays (FPGA) [1, 19]. The reconfigurable fabric offers flexibility, but one cannot possibly hope to match the speed and efficiency of a silicon processor core. On the other hand, a silicon processor core with full vector capabilities like those found in desktop- and server-class processors would mean committing silicon without consideration for the applications' requirements. A dual approach requires a dedicated interconnect, and the combined performance is affected by the partitioning strategy and the data transfer overhead. Finer grain partitioning proves beneficial only when a fast interconnect is available (i.e. when both the processor core and the reconfigurable fabric are placed on the same die).

Embedded processors are getting faster. However, they seldom offer the complete set of support for parallel instruction decoding and issue, as well as enough arithmetic units to satisfy compute intensive applications. In particular, floating point units with long pipelines and separate register file are often not found in the embedded cores, and have only been recently introduced as specialized coprocessors [14]. This deficiency goes beyond compute intensive applications because many algorithms, such as DSP filters, are often designed first in a tool like Matlab before being implemented in an embedded setting [6]. To avoid slow software floating point emulation, designers have to carefully tune their applications to use fixed point computing instead. However, the complexity or certain characteristics of the applications may prevent the scaling of this approach. When input or key parts of the algorithm are changed, the application has to be re-analyzed, often manually, for changes in precision and error propagation. In this paper, we examine the alternative of using the reconfiguration fabric to implement floating point units when the need arises [7]. In particular, we propose an automated design flow that takes advantage of existing auto-vectorization capabilities in compilers, and co-synthesizes code and customized floating point SIMD extensions in reconfigurable hardware. We also propose an algorithm that determines the optimal configurations for our SIMD architecture under the given resource constraints.

SIMD vector instructions are a natural candidate for hardware extensions [2] because they yield an efficient encoding of short instructions that capture a large number of operations and data transfers. Their regular structures also express large amounts of data parallelism. They are also flexible and allow for customization by varying the number of elements in the vector. Custom vector lengths can be used for the register set, operands and operators. We designed a novel architecture that supports the *concurrent* execution of SIMD instructions with different vector lengths. In particular, our architecture supports the concurrent execution of a mix of single precision 4-, 8-, and 16-float long vector instructions[1]. The exact mix used is determined by how the required processing throughput can be matched to the available reconfigurable resources. We achieve the optimal matching by *folding* the execution of larger vectors when resource is scarce. In essence, we expose a *set* of virtual instruction set architectures (determined by instruction level parallelism and other program characteristics) that is implemented by a shared pool of floating point execution units (determined by the reconfigurable resources available). Our framework inherits from the advantages of both traditional custom instructions and loop accelerators. We offer an alternative at an abstraction level where it is easier to find acceleration as well as resource sharing opportunities. On top of that, this approach offers a tighter integration in the design compilation flow. In summary, the major contributions of this paper are as follows.

- We present the design of a customizable SIMD floating point extension on hybrid architectures that have both embedded processor cores and a FPGA-like reconfigurable fabric.

- We implemented a co-design flow for this extension in which both the executable and the hardware for the selected configuration are automatically generated in a single pass.

- We propose a technique for further improving resource usage and energy efficiency by the independent folding of each kind of execution units in the final design.

2. MOTIVATION

In silicon-based processors, the vector instruction set and the vector length of the SIMD extension have to be chosen to suit a broad spectrum of computation patterns and instruction level parallelism exposed across all the application domains. However, if the SIMD extension is reconfigurable, then one may choose to only implement a particular set of vector instructions that best benefit the application at hand,

[1]For brevity, in the rest of the paper, we shall call these 'x4', 'x8', and 'x16', respectively.

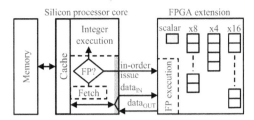

Figure 1: Our target architecture.

and have the system reconfigured to something altogether different when the demand changes. The overall system architecture we target is abstracted in Figure 1. Scalar and vector floating-point (FP) instructions are executed outside the *processor core*, in the attached FPGA *extension*. These instructions are issued in program order on a dedicated interface. One of the key insights behind our work is that unlike general integer computation, many floating point applications have the proper granularity to overcome the inherent penalty of issuing instructions outside the processor cores.

In our target system, load and store instructions have to transfer data through the processor core to the memory. Most instructions are autonomously executed by the FPGA with the exception of vector stores which require data computed in the extension to be written back to memory. The latter entails blocking the subsequent instruction issue until the data transfer is complete. Otherwise, for most other types of instructions, new instructions can be issued in consecutive clock cycles.

The following are some of the considerations that affect the selection of the vector extension to be implemented.

- The use of longer vectors will decrease the number of instructions issued to the extension, each instruction encoding computation of larger granularities.

- As the overall number of issued instructions decreases, the performance bottleneck will shift from the instruction issue to execution. There is an opportunity here to reorganize the individual operations encapsulated by each instruction, and determine a compact hardware implementation according to the exposed data dependencies.

- Larger grain computation requires more data to be transferred before computation can begin. This may cause delays especially in systems where the memory latency is large. In other words, the use of longer vectors may prevent the effective overlapping of memory transfers with computation.

- The kind of data movement is often limited by what the instructions can do. This can degrade the performance of certain operations, such as data transpositions, or the epilogue of vector reductions.

The following example shows the impact of the selected vector length on the execution time of a loop. Figure 2a shows a simple loop expressed in a C-like language based on the Altivec instruction set. The vectorization process identifies computation patterns across multiple loop iterations and coalesces them into vector operations. SIMD architectures available today mostly use vector length of four [5]. Our pseudo-compiled code example uses vector registers `vr`

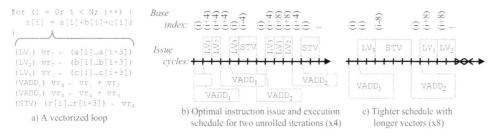

a) A vectorized loop

b) Optimal instruction issue and execution schedule for two unrolled iterations (x4)

c) Tighter schedule with longer vectors (x8)

Figure 2: Executing a loop using x4 and x8 vector instructions.

that can store four single precision floating point numbers. The LV instructions bring the operands from memory into the registers. VADD instructions perform the parallel additions of the corresponding four vector elements, while the STV instructions store data back to memory. Because the loop is vectorized, each iteration corresponds to four scalar loop iterations.

We first analyze the issue and execution schedule of this vectorized loop as it would be handled by our target architecture with a vector length of four (i.e., x4). Figure 2b shows the issue and execution of instructions corresponding to two consecutive vector iterations processing elements with base index i and $i + 4$ respectively. The compiler unrolled the loop twice and software pipelined the LV and STV instructions, placing them in adjacent cycles. Loop unrolling increases register pressure, but can partially hide the latency of the memory transfer operations and subsequently run the pipelines of the execution units more efficient. Each instruction requires a distinct issue cycle which corresponds to the data transfer between the core processor and the vector extension. Once issued, most instructions execute autonomously, spending one or more clock cycles in the pipeline of a hardware execution unit. The exception is the vector store (STV) instruction which occupies the issue bus for several cycles until it returnsdata from the vr to the processor core for subsequent stores to memory. In this example the critical path consists of the two dependent additions, VADD$_1$ and VADD$_2$. LV instructions are software pipelined in the available issue cycles before the start of the current iteration, while STV instructions are issued after the end of the current iteration.

However, due to the sequential data exchange between the core processor and the extension, repeated issuing of vector operations to the vector extension is costly. This can be detrimental to the overall performance because it limits the issue rate of compute instructions. Alternatively, the same vector loop can be compiled for a vector length of eight (x8), as shown in Figure 2c. However, in this architecture, the processor core remains unchanged, and thus all memory transfers, which are routed through the core processor, are split into chunks of four elements. Accordingly, LV instructions now require two issue cycles, while STV instructions require four cycles to transfer the operands. In this configuration, a single x8 loop iteration can handle the computation previously handled by both x4 loop iterations. The schedule becomes shorter, because less VADD instructions are issued.

We can compare the execution time of N iterations of an unrolled vector loop to a single equivalent iteration of a vector loop where vectors were lengthened N times. We assume that once the instructions are issued, they will execute autonomously. Ideally, performance is maximized if there is an

execution schedule where, once instructions are issued, they can execute without delay caused by operand dependencies. Let t_M and t_I be the number of issue cycles used by memory transfer and non-memory transfer instructions in one iteration of the vectorized loop body, respectively. In this model, the unrolled version takes $N \cdot (t_M + t_I)$ cycles to complete, while a single iteration of the loop with longer vectors takes $N \cdot t_M + t_I$ cycles. Thus, the latter approach will improve performance by $\frac{(N-1)t_I}{N(t_M+t_I)}$. For example, if $t_I = t_M$ and $N = 4$, this translates to 37.5% improvement. In practice, this speedup is generally higher for longer vectors, because the compiler generated schedule may not be able to completely hide the instruction dependencies. However, irregular data movement patterns can make it harder to use longer vectors as additional data movement instructions will be required to correctly marshal data into the vector registers. In the final analysis, which vector length yields better performance depends on the computation pattern and available instructions.

Operations of a vector instruction may be mapped onto a reduced set of execution units by means of multiplexing, thereby trading off performance for lower resource demands. By doing so, the overall execution time may increase if the affected instructions are on the critical path. In our proposed framework, we evaluate the profitability of each vector length during compilation, and select the best based on a static model. In the resulting platform, multiple versions of the same instruction corresponding to different vector lengths may coexist. The proposed architecture allows these versions to share the execution units. Due to the sizable resources involved, the alternative of switching via runtime reconfiguration between platforms each implementing a single vector length introduces significant delays, potentially eliminating most of the performance benefits of SIMDization.

3. THE PROPOSED CO-DESIGN FLOW

An established approach for getting good performance in compute intensive applications is the use of mathematical libraries such as ATLAS [20]. The granularity and semantics of the data structures are key factors in achieving optimal results over large portions of the application. Hence, the trend to capture computation at a higher level of abstraction such as vectors or matrices. Libraries rely internally on compiler auto-vectorization of carefully written code to deliver the best performance. For our purpose, we further require support for the new vector instructions that we introduce at the hardware level.

Our choice is Eigen [9], a C++ template library for linear algebra, achieving comparable performance to ATLAS. It includes the data structures for vectors and matrices, as well

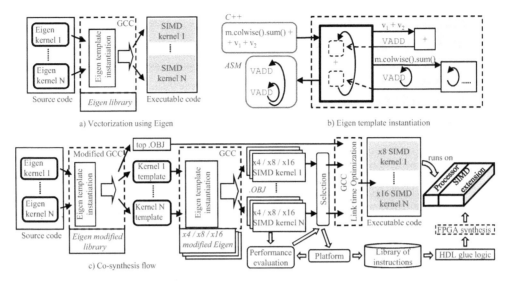

a) Vectorization using Eigen   b) Eigen template instantiation

c) Co-synthesis flow

Figure 3: Our proposed vectorization flow.

as their related algorithms. Eigen uses code inlining extensively to automatically rewrite and lower the code representation, applying vectorization where possible. Its recursive template inlining and instantiation also removes unnecessary temporaries, thereby building loops with large bodies. Multiple instances of the same function template are generated and inlined in different code fragments. We shall use the term *kernel* to refer to a section of the code that has dependencies that are satisfied using (virtual) vector registers. Each kernel may consist of one or more loop nests and the code in between. What is important is that kernels are independent of each other and can be implemented using different vector lengths. The original Eigen compilation flow is presented in Figure 3a. For each computation kernel, the C++ preprocessor uses Eigen library templates and proceeds to recursive inlining which lowers the computation down to built-in functions mapping directly to assembler instructions. Internally, Eigen uses a layered instantiation and its lowest level relies on a set of primitive function templates that correspond to the actual vector instructions supported by the target architecture. The resulting executable code contains all the properly vectorized code inlined into the original functions.

The recursive template instantiation mechanism is shown in Figure 3b. The C++ computation is expressed in terms of vectors v and matrices m. The C++ code in this example sums each of the columns of m, adding the resulting vector to v_1 and v_2. The template library breaks up this sequence of operations hierarchically into a vector addition, which expects to add the result of $v_1 + v_2$ with *m.colwise().sum()*. At this point the addition is expressed in terms of abstract packets which will later be transformed to fit the length of the hardware vectors. The inlining process continues by mapping the addition of packets from v_1 and v_2 to a VADD instruction, while the matrix column summation is mapped to a loop that sums packets of elements from different rows. This loop and the previous VADD are combined in a loop nest in the final assembly code. It is only during the final mapping that the hardware vector length gets used. The packet length is propagated as a constant throughout the kernel. The compiler backend then optimises the resulting code. Recursive template instantiation and inlining are

merely techniques for code rewriting. Therefore, despite the heavy use of template instantiation and inlining, the final executable does not suffer from code explosion.

In our single-pass co-synthesis flow shown in Figure 3c we have modified the library to cease automatic instantiation at the level of kernels, so that we can control and fine-tune the compilation of each template. Because kernels do not share code, we can compile each kernel independently. We pass each of these kernels to the compiler for explicit instantiation. We repeat the explicit instantiation steps so that we get all the different vector length versions of all the kernels. We project the performance of each kernel version as a function of the parameters of our SIMD extension configurations (Section 5). We also collect the list of instructions used by all versions of all the kernels. This information is used in a global selection step (Section 6) that determines the versions of each kernel to be used in the final executable, as well as the extension to be synthesized in order to execute the selected kernels. This is done in a single pass and does not require repeated hardware synthesis. We use the *link-time optimization* feature of GCC [12] to derive all versions of the kernels as well as inline the selected kernel versions for the final executable.

Eigen includes an ISA specific set of primitive template functions that corresponds to vector instructions and their GCC built-ins. We have added templates for other vector lengths in Eigen, and modified GCC by adding new built-ins and machine descriptions. It is important to note that while our choice of Eigen minimized our engineering effort, our approach can be adapted to any vectorizer that is capable of handling multiple vector lengths. This includes the GCC vectorizer, Fortran 95 vector operations, SUIF and other vectorizing compilers.

4. A CUSTOMIZED SIMD EXTENSION

In this section, we shall describe the details of the novel SIMD hardware extension that executes the vector instructions generated by our design flow. Our implementation uses the Xilinx Virtex-5 chip with its embedded PPC440 processor core. We therefore had to be compatible with the IBM AltiVec instruction set architecture [5]. However, with some

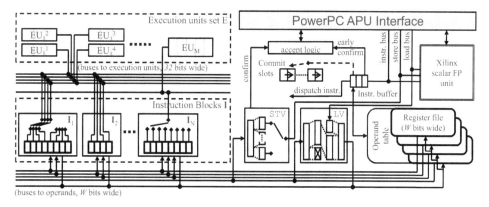

Figure 4: The architecture of the SIMD hardware extension.

amount of re-engineering, it should be possible to port this work to other similar architectures of which several alternatives are commercially available [1, 8].

The instructions for longer vector lengths are semantically simple extensions of the standard AltiVec instructions. Parallel vector operators are extended by increasing the range of their vector indexes. Several of the data movement instructions that do not use operands with absolute element indexing can also be extended in the same manner. For the instructions where an index is given as an immediate operand (i.e. VSLDOI, a left shift instruction), or where such indexes are included in one of the vector registers (i.e. VPERM, a generic permutation instruction that receives an index-based permutation pattern in a vector register) we need to cope with bit-width limitations in the index encoding. When possible, we used previously unused bits in the operand field to encode the larger index. Otherwise, we increase the granularity of the indexes, which by default is a byte. As we implement only the vector FP operations, we can increase this granularity four-fold.

The custom SIMD extension is implemented in the FPGA reconfigurable area and attaches to the Auxiliary Processor Unit (APU) interface of the embedded PowerPC processor. The overall architecture of the extension and its connections to the APU interface are presented in Figure 4. Scalar FP instructions use an IP library module provided by Xilinx, also attached to the same APU interface. The PowerPC core *issues* floating point instructions to the extention via the APU interface. Our SIMD extension includes a collection of vector FP instruction *control blocks*, a unified vector register file and a set of scalar FP pipelined execution units. An instruction control block implements one or more related vector instructions. For example, a single control block implements both the vector add and subtract instructions. The execution units are shared by the vector instructions. Instructions and execution units are connected together with minimal glue logic. We have maintained clear design boundaries between the execution units, instruction control blocks and the SIMD extension interface, allowing for a modular synthesis flow. This will also facilitate our future work to move to a run-time partial reconfiguration platform.

Assuming that there are M distinct types of execution units (i.e., adders, multipliers, fused multiply-add units), a *configuration* E is defined as the tuple $(e_1, \ldots, e_M)$ where each e_i is the number of execution units of type EU_i to be instantiated. The extension implements the instructions using N instruction control blocks $\mathbf{I} = \{\mathbf{I}_1, \ldots, \mathbf{I}_N\}$. Note that an instruction and its control block have the same vector length, denoted by $\|\mathbf{I}_k\|$, that is implicitly encoded. The pair $(E, \mathbf{I})$ fully characterizes our SIMD extension.

A single register file is used by all the vector instructions, irrespective of their vector lengths. It is configured such that it can store the longest supported vectors. Instructions handling shorter vectors will use only the lower bits of each register. The register file is implemented using the Virtex-5's block RAMs (BRAMs). To handle the longest vectors, it has to be $W = 32 \times \max_{\mathbf{I}_k \in \mathbf{I}} (\|\mathbf{I}_k\|)$ bits wide since each single precision floating point number occupies 32 bits. Altivec instructions can have up to three input and one output operands. However, the exact position of each in the instruction encoding varies. To avoid the overhead of multiplexing the possible positions to the register file, we implemented a register file with four read ports, and one write port. The amount of BRAM available in the Virtex-5 is large enough to implement four identical copies of the register file, each allowing one synchronous read and write. Read requests from different instruction operands will be serviced concurrently by the different copies of the register file. However, all the register file copies are written concurrently on any update. This ensures that all copies of the register file contain identical data, and hence consistency is enforced.

A variant of scoreboarding is employed throughout the SIMD extension. It manages instruction issue and retirement, enabling out-of-order completion. As soon as instructions appear on the APU interface, they are copied into an *instruction buffer*. A confirmation is immediately returned to the PowerPC core. The only exception is the vector store (STV) instruction, which needs to return data from a vector register to the PowerPC core. This instruction sends out a confirmation signal once it completes.

In the instruction buffer, a vector instruction will wait for its *dispatch* to the corresponding vector instruction control block $\mathbf{I}_k$. The instruction is dispatched only when all its operands are available in the register file, and when the hardware determines, based on the known execution time of $\mathbf{I}_k$, that the write port of the register file is available to commit the result during the clock cycle when the execution completes. These conditions together ensure that, once dispatched, instructions execute and commit their results without blocking. We keep track of when instructions will commit their results to the register file using a set of *commit slots* that correspond, in order, to reservations during future cycles to the write port of the register file. These commit

32-bit FP	Resources		Frequency	Stages
execution unit	LUTs	DSP48E	(MHz)	
add	621	0	188	5
mul	132	2	188	3
mul-add	1101	2	152	7

Table 1: Characteristics of execution units.

slots are maintained consistent by shifting their contents to the previous slot at every clock cycle.

When an instruction is dispatched to a vector instruction control block, its operands are read from the register file. The control block will latch them and execute an internal schedule that accomplishes the desired functionality using the available execution units. If there are enough execution units, all operations can be launched in the same clock cycle (such as I_2 in Figure 4). Otherwise, a folding mechanism, described in Section 4.1, schedules the operations on the available execution units over several clock cycles. Once the execution of the instruction completes, the result is placed on the write bus and the destination register is marked as available in the operand availability table.

Some of our design decisions were driven by the idiosyncrasies of our Virtex-5 development board [15]. Vector load (LV) and store (STV) instructions are handled in a special way so as to account for the fact that the memory APU bus width is a fixed 128 bits, regardless of the vector length. The processor core performs all memory accesses including those made by the extension. Our solution for dealing with this constraint is a special *load-shift semantics* for vector load operations: consecutive loads targeting the same vector register will shift the content of the register before incorporating the incoming data in the lower bit positions. If the instructions require a vector length of 128 bits, a single load is issued, and the corresponding data is placed in the lower 128 bits of the longer vector register, while the rest of the vector register, containing shifted data, becomes irrelevant. If instructions require longer vectors, multiple 128 bit loads are issued. Each of these loads will shift the previously loaded data to more significant positions. If loads are issued in the correct order, the long vector load can be replaced by a sequence of regular loads.

Unfortunately, vector stores cannot be handled transparently. Stores may be canceled and reissued by the PowerPC due to branch mispredictions or page faults. There is therefore no easy way to check if a previous store has succeeded or not that is also compatible with our extension. To work around this issue, we implemented an explicit bank selection instruction that specifies which part of the longer vector needs to be stored via the 128 bit APU bus. The bank index is initially reset, thereby making this mechanism transparent to the x4 instructions.

The overall extension is *feasible* if the total resources (i.e., LUTs) occupied by all the instruction control blocks, execution units and other logic, including the scalar FP unit fit the resources of the FPGA. Because we implement the register file in BRAM, we freed up a significant number of additional LUTs. We use post-synthesis resource information for individual modules of our design, and account for the additional LUTs used for multiplexers, in order to derive the total requirement of our design. Besides resource constraints, the scalability of our design is also limited by the critical path of multiplexing the results back to the register file's write port via a single result bus. Nonetheless, we have

successfully placed and routed extensions with as many as 32 multiplexed write sources.

We designed our own execution units, including the single-precision floating point adder, multiplier and fused multiply-adder. Their post-synthesis resource usage and performance are shown in Table 1. The multiply-adder unit fuses the two operations without the intermediary result normalization, and hence is equivalent to its standard AltiVec counterpart. Note that this does not preclude the use of other arithmetic unit designs.

4.1 Folding of SIMD operations

Folding is the mechanism used by the vector instruction control blocks to schedule the execution of vector operations on a smaller set of execution units. Our implementation currently supports folding only for vector lengths and a number of execution units that are powers of two. The folding mechanism sequences the inputs for all operations to the execution units over several clock cycles. Because the execution units are pipelined, we can launch a new set of operations each clock cycle, i.e., the *initiation interval* is one. In particular, for a vector instruction I executed by a control block I_j, the number of consecutive cycles required to place all the operations in the e_k execution pipelines of type E_k is: $\text{fold}(I, E_k) = \|I_j\|/e_k$ if the control block I_j requires the use of the execution units of type E_k. Otherwise, $\text{fold}(I, E_k) = 0$.

Folding requires hardware multiplexers to redirect data from several vector locations to the execution units. These multiplexers are embedded in the instruction control block and driven by state machines. The instruction control block is aware of the number of execution units available in hardware. During instruction execution, after data is fetched from the registers, a sequence of data insertions into the pipeline of the execution units is initiated. We choose to allow the instruction to drive the folding based on a run-time configuration, which leads to slightly larger (generic) multiplexers inside the vector instruction control block. Nevertheless, we believe that this is a small price to pay for design modularity and reuse.

Folding affects the rate at which the instruction control block can handle incoming instructions. If the operators are not folded, the entire instruction execution is fully pipelined, and a new instruction can be initiated every cycle. Otherwise, the instruction control block flags the execution units as busy, and this is an additional factor that may block the dispatch of the next instruction from the instruction buffer. The total execution latency of an instruction $L(I)$ is also affected by folding. This latency consists of a fixed number of clock cycles spent in the instruction control block and in the execution pipeline, and a variable number of clock cycles required to fold the instruction. The latter depends on the vector length of the instruction and the number of execution units available to it.

5. PERFORMANCE PROJECTION MODEL

A key component of our design flow is the static evaluation of design points. In this section, we shall describe the model by which we project the performance of each kernel. Without such a model, it would be impossible to offer an automated *single-pass* design flow that selects the best possible hardware configuration without trial synthesis of many candidate configurations.

The SIMD extension described in the previous section has two degrees of flexibility. We can adjust the number of execution units of each type. We can also choose whether or not to implement instructions of various vector lengths. Recall that while a kernel can only be of one vector length, different kernels in a single application are allowed to have different vector lengths. We can estimate the performance of each kernel on a configuration E and use this metric to drive the instruction selection and implementation in Section 6.

We start by identifying the sequence of vector instructions $I = \{I_1, \ldots, I_n\}$ for each loop body in the kernel k. For most practical situations, there is usually only one loop body in the kernel. These instructions will be issued by the PowerPC processor in program order to the SIMD extension. We assume that the remaining scalar instructions execute out-of-order and have no impact on the execution time. Furthermore, the PowerPC processor is able to start prefetching the data for all the vector loads as soon as they are encountered. The PowerPC core maintains a look ahead window of δ instructions, prefetching additional instructions while it attempts to issue an instruction to the SIMD extension. In our performance model we assumed that memory accesses will hit the cache and that a 128-bit load or store transaction takes d cycles, based on the processor memory bandwidth. We also determine the execution time $L(I_p)$ of instruction I_p. Any folding will also be accounted for in $L(I_p)$ as previously described.

Based on the above assumptions, we estimate the number of clock cycles $T(E, k)$ required to execute one iteration of a loop in kernel k on a configuration E using Algorithm 1. For each instruction I_p, we derive the following timings relative to the beginning of the iteration: (a) the time when the instruction reaches the look-ahead window (α_p), (b) the time when it is issued to the SIMD extension (β_p), and (c) the time when it finishes execution (γ_p). We also track the time when the memory bus becomes available (Ξ), and the time when execution units of each type i are available (F_i). The timing obtained at the end of an iteration is used to seed the computation of the next iteration. We then iterate till we reach a fixed point, and return that as the result. In the description, 'in(I_p)' are the predecessor instructions of I_p in the data dependency graph, and 'fold(I_p, E)' was defined in the previous section.

Let V be a set of vector lengths. In our current context, $V = \{4, 8, 16\}$. The different versions of the kernel k_x are denoted by the set $\{k_x^{v_i}\}$, $v_i \in V$. The Eigen library is modified so that we can obtain the relative iteration counts of the kernel loops compiled for each of the vector lengths. If a kernel has more than one loop, then we apply Algorithm 1 to each loop inside the kernel. We derive a combined per-iteration execution time for each kernel by summing the per-iteration execution times of each loop weighed by their relative counts. We also combine the relative counts of different kernels with actual profiling data from a scalar execution of the application to project the normalized weight $\omega_x^{v_i}$ of each vectorized kernel $k_x^{v_i}$. Profiling needs to be done only once for the non-vectorized application and can be accomplished with a regular GCC compiler and `gprof`.

The performance estimate $T(E, k)$ has to be recomputed for all kernels over all the configurations as the latency of the instructions varies as a function of the folding factor. Even though we can reuse some of the estimations, the number of design points and combination of kernels is large. In our

---

Algorithm 1 $T(E, k)$ for a single loop in a kernel

Require: A configuration $E = (e_1, \ldots, e_M)$ and the sequence of vector instructions $I = \{I_1, \ldots, I_n\}$ that forms the loop body inside kernel k

1: $\Xi = F_1 = \ldots F_n = -\infty$
   // These hold the previous iteration's issue times:
2: $\beta_{-\delta} = \ldots = \beta_{-1} = -\infty$
3: **repeat**
4:   **for** $I_p \in I$ **do**
5:     $\alpha_p = \beta_{p-\delta} + 1$ // models PowerPC lookahead
6:     $t = \max(0, \beta_{p-1} + 1, \alpha_p, \max\limits_{m \in \text{in}(I_p)} \gamma_m)$
7:     $\beta_p = \max\limits_{E_i \text{ used by } I_p} (t, (F_i))$; // models blocking
8:     **for** functional unit type i used by I_p **do**
9:       $F_i = \beta_p + \text{fold}(I_p, E_i)$
10:      **if** I_p is memory transfer **then**
11:        $\Xi = \max(\Xi, \alpha_p) + d$
12:        $\beta_p = \max(\beta_p, \Xi)$
13:    $\gamma_p = \beta_p + L(I_p)$ // instruction ready time
14:    $\tau = \gamma_n$ // ready time of last instruction
15:    **for** $j < \delta$ **do**
16:      $\beta_{-j} = \beta_{n-1-j} - \tau$
17:    **for** E_i **do**
18:      $F_i = F_i - \tau$
19:    $\Xi = \Xi - \tau$
20: **until** τ does not increase
    return τ

---

experimental setup, for example, we had 25 configurations, and 36 instruction candidates. We can prune the exploration space based on the timing relationships between the configurations. Suppose there are two configurations, $E_1 = \{e_1^1, \ldots, e_M^1\}$ and $E_2 = \{e_1^2, \ldots, e_M^2\}$. For a configuration E_i, the minimum overall execution time $\mathcal{T}(E_i)$ is reached when the version selected for each kernel k_x has the lowest execution time. In other words, $\mathcal{T}(E_i) = \sum_x \min\limits_{v_i \in V} (\omega_x^{v_i} \times T(E_i, k_x^{v_i}))$. However, this lower bound on execution time may not be achieved if some of the required instructions are not accommodated by the resource constraint.

6. EXTENSION SELECTION

The selection of the best extension (shown in Algorithm 2) is based on statically projecting the performance achievable by the entire application on the feasible extension configurations. As its input, it takes the independently vectorized kernel versions of the application. It also requires the set of possible vector lengths, the relative weights of the kernels in the execution time, and a resource constraint.

The output of the algorithm consists of a recommended configuration and the subset of our extended AltiVec instruction set to finally instantiate. In particular, for the latter, suppose there are N distinct instructions control blocks in the set $\mathbf{I}$, and that the set of possible vector lengths is V. The algorithm outputs a Boolean decision matrix $\Phi = \{\{\phi_1^{v_1}, \ldots, \phi_N^{v_1}\}, \ldots, \{\phi_1^{v_{|V|}}, \ldots, \phi_N^{v_{|V|}}\}\}$. $\phi_j^{v_i} = 1$ if the control block of instruction j for vector length v_i is to be supported in hardware. The resource usage of this instruction is denoted by $a_j^{v_i}$.

The design space is explored using a *dominance relationship*. Let $E_1 = (e_1^1, \ldots, e_M^1)$ and $E_2 = (e_1^2, \ldots, e_M^2)$ be two configurations. We say that E_1 is dominated by E_2 (denoted

Algorithm 2 SIMD extension selection

Require: A set of vector lengths (V), all kernels vectorized by the various vector lengths ($K = \{k_j^{v_i}\}, v_i \in V$), the relative weight of all kernels ($\{\omega_j^{v_i}\}, k_j^{v_i} \in K$), and a resource constraint (A)

Output A configuration (Π), and the subset of instructions to be implemented (Φ)

1: $SFU = \{E | \nexists E', E \prec E' \wedge res(E) \leq A\}$;
2: $\hat{R} = \infty; \Pi = \Phi = \emptyset$;
3: **while** $SFU \neq \emptyset$ **do**
4:    $E = pop(SFU)$;
5:    $\mathcal{T}(E) = \sum_j \min_{v_i \in V}(\omega_j^v \times T(E, k_j^{v_i}))$
6:    **if** $\mathcal{T}(E) < \hat{R}$ **then**
7:        $\Phi' = \{\{\phi_1^{v_1}, \ldots, \phi_N^{v_1}\}, \ldots, \{\phi_1^{v_{|V|}}, \ldots, \phi_N^{v_{|V|}}\}\}$.
8:        **SATslv minimize** $R = \sum_{j, v_i \in V}(T(E, k_j^{v_i}) \cdot \omega_j^{v_i} \cdot s_j^{v_i})$
         subject to
9:            $\sum_{j, v_i \in V} \phi_j^{v_i} \cdot a_j^{v_i} \leq A - res(E)$
10:           $\forall j \forall v_i \in V, s_j^{v_i} \leq \phi_x^{v_i}$ if instruction x of length v_i is needed in the implementation of kernel $k_j^{v_i}$.
11:           $\forall j, \sum_{v_i \in V} s_j^{v_i} = 1$
12:       **if** $R < \hat{R}$ **then**
13:           $\Pi = E; \Phi = \Phi'; \hat{R} = R$;
14:       **if** $R > \mathcal{T}(E)$ **then**
15:           $SFU = SFU \cup \{E' | E' \prec E \wedge \nexists E'' s.t. E'' \prec E' \wedge E'' \prec E\}$;
      return Π and Φ

as $E1 \prec E_2$) if $\exists i, e_i^1 < e_i^2$ and $\forall j, j \neq i, e_j^1 \leq e_j^2$. In other words, configuration E_1 has strictly less number of units of type i than E_2, and at most the same number of units as E_2 for all other types. In a dominated configuration, i.e. E_1 here, one may implement even more vector instructions using the difference in the resource of E_2 and E_1. Even so, we note that $E_1 \prec E_2 \Rightarrow \mathcal{T}(E_1) \geq \mathcal{T}(E_2)$ regardless of what instructions are added to E_1. This means that if the current configuration is E, and $\mathcal{T}(E)$ is larger than the best found so far ($\hat{R}$ in Algorithm 2), then none of the configurations dominated by E can do better, and so can be discarded.

Algorithm 2 starts with considering the configurations that use less resources than the given resource constraint, and are not dominated by any other configuration (line 1), one at a time. For each configuration E being explored, we compute $\mathcal{T}(E)$ by selecting the best version of each kernel without any resource constraints (line 5). If this unconstrained lower bound (i.e., $\mathcal{T}(E)$) is no better than what has been already found, we discard E as well as all the configurations dominated by E, and proceed to the next candidate. Otherwise, E is a possible solution. A set of resource-based constraints (lines 9-11) is built, and we invoke a SAT solver to generate feasible solutions with the help of an evolutionary optimizer [17] with the goal of deriving a solution with the minimum execution time. The binary decision variable $s_j^{v_i}$ indicates whether kernel j vectorized with length v_i is part of the solution. $\phi_j^{v_i}$ indicates if instruction j with vector length v_i is to be part of the final extension ISA. The constraint in line 10 is to ensure that if a particular vectorized kernel is chosen, then all the instructions used by the kernel are also chosen. The auxiliary function 'res(E)' es-

timates the resources used by configuration E. If the SAT solver is able to arrive at a solution R that is faster than the existing best solution ($\hat{R}$) (line 12), then the newly found solution replaces it (line 13). Furthermore, if R is worse than the unconstrained bound of $\mathcal{T}(E)$ (line 14), it would imply that there is room for improvement. We will then add all configurations immediately dominated by E to the list of configurations to be considered (line 15). The idea here is that in one of these (say E'), it may be possible to obtain an improved execution time by implementing additional instructions using the resource difference between E and E'.

The algorithm is guaranteed to terminate because (a) we limit the number of iterations of the optimizer, and (b) only smaller configurations are added for future consideration. In practice, for the benchmarks reported in Section 7, it took no more than a minute on a Intel Core 2.

The solution returned by the algorithm is fed into an application of ours that puts together a mix of Verilog and VHDL modules that is then pushed through the Xilinx synthesis flow to obtain the bitstream of the SIMD extension. The solution is also used in our modified version of the GNU assembler which is utilized in conjunction with our modified GCC-LTO compiler to generate the executable.

7. RESULTS

We implemented our extensions on a Xilinx ML510 system [15]. The Virtex-5 VFX130 FPGA on board includes a PowerPC 440 core, and 81,920 look-up tables (LUTs). All the experiments reported here are based on the HDL code generated automatically by our toolchain that consists of our modified versions of Eigen and GCC. 18.5% of the LUTs were used for a system wrapper, a scalar FP unit from the Xilinx library and the SIMD extension interface. We selected a set of linear algebra benchmarks that would be ideal candidates for vectorization in embedded applications such as media processing [16], sensor array data processing, global positioning systems and beamforming solutions [14]. Several vector and matrix benchmarks are provided in Eigen. These benchmarks are compute intensive functions and reach performance comparable to BLAS on standard architectures. Furthermore, we used Eigen to vectorize benchmarks from the Iterative Template Library [13], which provides iterative methods for solving linear systems. We explored an extensive range of design points for the SIMD extension, allocating up to 67% additional LUTs. For all these points we were able to synthesize extensions with the same frequency constraints. The core processor runs at 400 MHz, while the extension runs at 133 MHz.

Figure 5 shows the speedup achieved by our co-synthesized design compared to scalar FP execution using the Xilinx IP core. We present the performance for three design points for each benchmark: (1) a design that utilizes a very low amount of resources, hence the execution units and instructions are constrained to 10% of the total LUTs, (2) an x4 mapping where the number of execution units matches the vector length (no folding, would correspond to a naive implementation), and (3) a design using the optimal mix of x4/x8/x16 instructions, constrained only by the maximum available resources. The minor performance improvement observed between the former two designs, which use x4 instructions, supports the observation that, for short vectors, the bottleneck is at instruction issue, and merely adding ex-

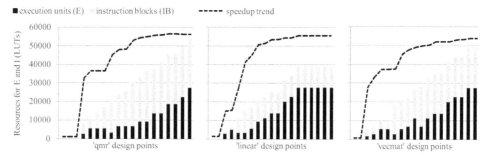

■ execution units (E)   ▦ instruction blocks (IB)   - - - - speedup trend

Figure 6: Resources used by execution units vs. instructions throughout the design space.

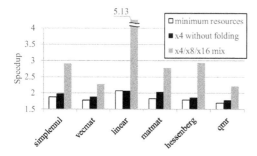

Figure 5: Speedup of different design points compared to scalar FP execution.

ecution units has a limited impact on performance. Instead, using longer vectors led to up to 5.13× improvement.

There is a non-trivial balance between the execution units configuration E, and the instructions control blocks implemented I. x16 instructions encapsulate larger multiplexers and hence use significantly more resources than the shorter vector versions, but deliver better performance. However, there are numerous cases where, due to resource constraints, the optimal solution involves using a smaller set of possibly shorter vector instructions complemented by a higher number of execution units. In Figure 6 we present performance and resource utilization for three benchmarks, for a set of design points when the resource constraints are relaxed. This figure presents only the total amount of resources used for each of the two configurable portions of the design (E, I). While performance increases monotonically, the non-trivial distribution of resources between the instructions and the execution units shows the need for our search algorithm. In addition, Figure 7 gives the composition of the instructions implemented for 'qmr' at the given design points. It shows the resource usage associated with instructions of different vector lengths. x4 instructions use significantly less resources than x16.

Beside speedup, using vector instructions also leads to significant energy savings. We compare the total energy of the fastest design to that of a design using solely the scalar FP Xilinx IP core. The result reflects the total energy consumption of the FPGA core, which includes the energy of the PowerPC embedded processor. We used the current sensor provided on the ML510 board and measured its average value during program execution using a multimeter. Table 2 reports the energy consumption derived from our measurements using the best mix of instructions. The energy consumption of the best mix can be as low as 22% of the original scalar version.

8. RELATED WORK

There are a number of customized vector processor architectures [8, 21, 23] that have been proposed or are available on the market. They provide a rich set of reconfigurable parameters. However, the final result is a monoltihic processor instance with all instructions tightly integrated into the base pipeline. As such, resulting processors are implemented exclusively either in silicon or as soft-cores.

A more modular approach can be found in the sizable body of prior work on *custom instructions*, including a number of commercial products such as those developed by Tensilica [8] and Stretch [19]. They also provide SIMD custom instructions for integer applications. The typical approach used in custom instructions involves the analysis of data flow graphs obtained as a result of compilation, followed by the selection of dataflow subgraphs as candidates for custom instructions implementation [4, 24]. While the selected subgraphs are identified during compilation, platform-dependent optimizations that simplify or share resources are applied during hardware mapping. This phased approach prevents compiler optimizations from fully taking advantage of resource sharing opportunities. This is particularly important for floating point computation because the number of execution units that can be implemented in hardware is small, and a co-optimization approach can potentially yield better designs.

As shown in Section 2, issuing the instructions to the hardware extension leads to significant overhead. Specialized hardware *loop accelerators* [18, 25] have been proposed, relieving the processor of the permanent issue of instructions and operands. Using this approach, loop specific optimizations such as unrolling and pipelining can be used to improve the efficiency of the execution units. Several tools [3, 10] exist that are capable of deriving dedicated loop accelerators from source code applying static transformations to extract the necessary parallelism. This approach, however, does not support irregular loop structures or complex control flow. Also, dedicated memory connections are required to provide data for the loops. Our approach, on the other hand, relies on the core processor to resolve all control flow issues and data transfers, issuing scheduled vector instructions and operands in the proper order to the hardware.

Lastly, some vendors already offered SIMD floating point coprocessors for their embedded processors [14]. This is evidence for its growing importance in the embedded space. The iPhone, for example, includes such a core [11]. However, these offerings are silicon-based, and hence do not possess the flexibility of our solution.

		Benchmarks					
data size		simplemul	vecmat	linear	matmat	hessenberg	qmr
		256	128	1024	128	128	1024
Best time (sec)		2.45	3.11	2.42	1.45	2.22	14.98
Best energy (joule)		7.5	9.1	7.6	5.7	8.2	42.2
Scalar energy (joule)		18.4	18.3	34.1	13.9	14.3	83.4
Best / Scalar energy ratio		41%	50%	22%	41%	57%	51%

Table 2: Execution time and energy.

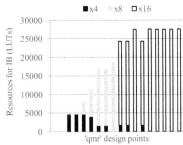

Figure 7: Distribution of resources among x4, x8 and x16 instructions for 'qmr'.

9. CONCLUSION

In this paper, we have examined the issues involved in the acceleration of floating-point computation on a hybrid reconfigurable architecture consisting of standard (integer) processor cores and a FPGA-like reconfigurable fabric. We observed that obtaining good performance for compute intensive applications on such extensions depends on a number of issues including the amount of parallelism available in the application, the structure of the loops, the processor cores' issue rate, memory bandwidth, and the reconfigurable resources available. Due to the intricate balances involved, we found that a 'one size fits all' approach to SIMDization is not always optimal. In fact, we found that for a SIMDizable application, we require a mix of vector lengths. Furthermore, this mix differs from application to application.

Based on the above insights, we built what we believe is the first fully automated toolchain that co-optimizes and co-synthesizes an application and its custom floating point SIMD extension. The toolchain leverages the latest compiler techniques in SIMDization and link-time optimization, and determines the best vector length mix for each individual kernel in a single pass, requiring only hotspot profiling.

The novel SIMD extension architecture proposed for the toolchain is able to share SIMD execution units, so as to meet a given resource constraint. Our co-synthesis toolchain has been implemented on a Xilinx Virtex-5 board. The output of the experiments were checked for correctness and the results reported are actual measurements. The experiments showed that our approach yielded up to 5.13× speedup when compared to the use of the standard Xilinx floating point IP cores. This also translated into an energy consumption that is as low as 22% of the scalar execution. As future work, we would like to examine how *partial* reconfiguration and the fusing of operations can yield even better designs.

10. REFERENCES

[1] Nios 2 processor. http://www.altera.com/literature/lit-nio2.jsp.
[2] M. O. Cheema and O. Hammami. Application-specific SIMD synthesis for reconfigurable architectures. *Microproc. and Microsys.*, 30(6):398 – 412, 2006.
[3] N. Clark, A. Hormati, and S. Mahlke. VEAL: Virtualized execution accelerator for loops. In *ISCA*, 2008.
[4] N. T. Clark, H. Zhong, and S. A. Mahlke. Automated custom instruction generation for domain-specific processor acceleration. *IEEE Transactions on Computers*, 54:1258–1270, 2005.
[5] K. Diefendorff, P. K. Dubey, R. Hochsprung, and H. Scales. Altivec extension to PowerPC accelerates media processing. *IEEE Micro*, 20:85–95, 2000.
[6] From Matlab to Embedded C. www.mathworks.com/products/featured/embeddedmatlab.
[7] J. A. Fisher, P. Faraboschi, and G. Desoli. Custom-fit processors: letting applications define architectures. In *MICRO*, pages 324–335, 1996.
[8] R. E. Gonzalez. Xtensa: A configurable and extensible processor. *IEEE Micro*, 20(2):60–70, 2000.
[9] G. Guennebaud and B. Jacob. Eigen library. http://eigen.tuxfamily.org.
[10] Z. Guo, W. Najjar, and B. Buyukkurt. Efficient hardware code generation for FPGAs. *ACM Trans. Archit. Code Optim.*, 5(1):1–26, 2008.
[11] VFPmathLibrary. http://code.google.com/p/vfpmathlibrary/.
[12] Link time optimization. http://gcc.gnu.org/projects/lto/lto.pdf.
[13] A. Lumsdaine, L.-Q. Lee, and J. Siek. The iterative template library. http://osl.iu.edu/research/itl.
[14] D. Lutz and C. Hinds. Accelerating floating-point 3D graphics for vector microprocessors. In *Signals, Systems and Computers,*, volume 1, pages 355 – 359, 2003.
[15] Virtex-5 ML510 development platform. http://xilinx.com/support/documentation/ml510.htm.
[16] V. Moya, C. González, J. Roca, A. Fernández, and R. Espasa. A single (unified) shader GPU microarchitecture for embedded systems. *HiPEAC*, 2005.
[17] Opt4J meta-heuristic optimization framework for Java. http://www.opt4j.org.
[18] R. Schreiber, S. Aditya, S. Mahlke, V. Kathail, B. R. Rau, D. Cronquist, and M. Sivaraman. PICO-NPA: High-level synthesis of nonprogrammable hardware accelerators. *J. VLSI Signal Process. Syst.*, 31(2):127–142, 2002.
[19] Stretch: Software reconfigurable processors. http://www.stretchinc.com.
[20] R. C. Whaley and A. Petitet. Minimizing development and maintenance costs in supporting persistently optimized BLAS. *Software: Practice and Exp.*, 35(2):101–121, 2005.
[21] M. Woh, Y. Lin, S. Seo, S. Mahlke, T. Mudge, C. Chakrabarti, R. Bruce, D. Kershaw, A. Reid, M. Wilder, and K. Flautner. From SODA to scotch: The evolution of a wireless baseband proc. In *MICRO*, pages 152–163, 2008.
[22] N. Woods. Integrating FPGAs in high-performance computing: the architecture and implementation perspective. In *FPGA*, pages 132–132, 2007.
[23] P. Yiannacouras, J. G. Steffan, and J. Rose. VESPA: portable, scalable, and flexible FPGA-based vector processors. In *CASES*, pages 61–70, 2008.
[24] P. Yu and T. Mitra. Scalable custom instructions identification for instruction-set extensible processors. In *CASES*, pages 69–78, 2004.
[25] M. Zuluaga, T. Kluter, P. Brisk, N. Topham, and P. Ienne. Introducing control-flow inclusion to support pipelining in custom instruction set extensions. *Symp. on App. Specific Processors*, pages 114–121, 2009.

Memory-Efficient and Scalable Virtual Routers Using FPGA

Hoang Le, Thilan Ganegedara and Viktor K. Prasanna
Ming Hsieh Department of Electrical Engineering
University of Southern California
Los Angeles, CA 90089, USA
{hoangle,ganegeda,prasanna}@usc.edu

ABSTRACT

Router virtualization has recently gained much interest in the research community. It allows multiple virtual router instances to run on a common physical router platform. The key metrics in designing network virtual routers are: (1) number of supported virtual router instances, (2) total number of prefixes, and (3) ability to quickly update the virtual table. Limited on-chip memory in FPGA leads to the need for memory-efficient merging algorithms. On the other hand, due to high frequency of combined updates from all the virtual routers, the merging algorithms must be highly efficient. Hence, the router must support quick updates. In this paper, we propose a simple merging algorithm whose performance is not sensitive to the number of routing tables considered. The performance solely depends on the total number of prefixes. We also propose a novel *scalable, high-throughput* linear pipeline architecture for IP-lookup that supports *large virtual routing tables* and *quick non-blocking update*. Using a state-of-the-art Field Programmable Gate Array (FPGA) along with external SRAM, the proposed architecture can support up to 16M IPv4 and 880K IPv6 prefixes. Our implementation shows a sustained throughput of 400 million lookups per second, even when external SRAM is used.

Categories and Subject Descriptors

C.2 [**Computer Communication Networks**]: Internetworking routers

General Terms

Algorithms, Design

Keywords

FPGA, IP Lookup, Virutal Routers, Pipeline

1. INTRODUCTION

1.1 IP Lookup

IP packet forwarding, or simply, IP-lookup, is a classic problem. In computer networking, a routing table is an electronic table or database that is stored in a router or a networked computer. The routing table stores the routes and metrics associated with those routes, such as next hop routing indices, to particular network destinations. The IP-lookup problem is referred to as *"longest prefix matching"* (LPM), which is used by routers in IP networking to select an entry from a routing table. To determine the outgoing port for a given address, the longest matching prefix among all the prefixes needs to be determined. Routing tables often contain a default route, in case matches with all other entries fail.

Most hardware-based solutions for network routers fall into two main categories: TCAM-based and dynamic/static random access memory (DRAM/SRAM)-based solutions. In TCAM-based solutions, each prefix is stored in a word. An incoming IP address is compared in parallel with all the active entries in TCAM in one clock cycle. TCAM-based solutions are simple, and therefore, are de-facto solutions for today's routers. However, TCAMs are *expensive, power-hungry*, and offer little adaptability to new addressing and routing protocols [8]. These disadvantages are more pronounced when we move from IPv4 to IPv6, as the address length increases from 32 to 128 bits.

SRAM-based solutions, on the other hand, require multiple cycles to process a packet. The common data structure in algorithmic solutions for performing LPM is some form of a tree. Pipelining is used to improve throughput. These approaches, however, suffer from either inefficient memory utilization (in trie-based solutions), lack of support for quick updates (in tree-based solutions), or both. Additionally, *overlap* in prefix ranges prevent IP lookup from employing tree search algorithms without modification. Limited on-chip memory also becomes an important factor in supporting large routing tables. Due to these constraints, state-of-the-art SRAM-based designs do not scale to simultaneously support the increased table size and quick update requirement.

1.2 Network Virtualization

Network virtualization is a technique to consolidate multiple networking devices onto a single hardware platform. The main goal of virtualization is to make efficient use of the networking resources. It can be thought of as an abstraction of

Table 1: Sample virtual routing tables (maximum prefix length = 8)

	Virtual table 1 (VID = 0)			Virtual table 2 (VID = 1)	
	Prefix	Next Hop		Prefix	Next Hop
P_{11}	0*	1	P_{21}	10*	2
P_{12}	01*	3	P_{22}	101*	3
P_{13}	101*	2	P_{23}	111*	4
P_{14}	111*	4	P_{24}	100*	1
P_{15}	0010*	5	P_{25}	1*	5
P_{16}	00*	3	P_{26}	0*	2

the network functionality away from the underlying physical network.

Device consolidation of routers at the physical layer results in consolidation up to the network layer where IP lookup is performed. Since router hardware is virtualized in such an environment, they are called virtualized routers, or simply virtual routers. Serving multiple virtual networks on the same routing hardware is a challenge for the research community.

Several ideas have been proposed to realize router virtualization on a single hardware networking platform [2, 6, 12, 18, 22]. These ideas mainly focus on how to implement a memory-efficient virtualized router, while guaranteeing the basic requirements of network virtualization. These requirements are: fair resource usage, fault isolation, and security.

Two existing approaches in the literature for network virtualization are *Separated* and *Merged* approach. The *separated* approach instantiates multiple virutal router instances on the same hardware routing platform by partitioning router resources. In contrast, the *merged* approach combines or merges all the routing tables into a single table to serve packets from different virtual networks.

These approaches have their own advantages and drawbacks. For example, the separated approach requires much more router hardware resources than the merged one, but it provides perfect traffic isolation, security, and avoids single point of failure. On the other hand, the merged approach requires much less hardware resources; yet, the traffic and fault isolation are not as strong as those of the separated approach.

The key issues to be addressed in designing an architecture for IP lookup in virtual routers are: (1) quick update, (2) high throughput, and (3) scalability with respect to the size of the virtual routing table. To address these challenges, we propose and implement a *scalable high-throughput, SRAM-based* linear pipeline architecture for IP-lookup in virtual router that supports *quick* update. This paper makes the following contributions:

- A simple merging algorithm results in the total amount of required memory to be *less sensitive* to the number of routing tables, but to the total number of virtual prefixes (Section 4).

- A tree-based architecture for IP lookup in virtual router that achieves high throughput and supports quick update (Section 5).

- Use of external SRAMs to support large virtual routing table of up to 16M virtual prefixes (Section 6).

- A scalable design with linear storage complexity and resource requirements (Section 5.4).

- A sustained throughput of 400 million lookups per second, even when external SRAM is used (Section 7).

The rest of the paper is organized as follows. Section 2 covers the background and related work. Section 3 gives a formal definition of the problem. Section 4 introduces the proposed merging and IP lookup algorithm. Section 5 and 6 describe the architecture and its implementation. Section 7 presents implementation results. Section 8 concludes the paper.

2. BACKGROUND AND RELATED WORK

2.1 IP Lookup in Virtual Router

Two sample routing tables with the maximum prefix length of 8 are illustrated in Table 1. These sample tables will be used throughout the paper. Note that the next hop values need not be in any particular order. In these routing tables, binary prefix P_{13} (101*) matches all destination addresses that are destined to virtual router 1 and begin with 101. Similarly, prefix P_{24} matches all destination addresses that are destined to virtual router 2 and begin with 100. The 8-bit destination address **IP**= 10100000 from virtual network 2 is matched by the prefixes P_{21}, P_{22}, and P_{25} in virtual table 2. Since $|P_{21}| = 2$, $|P_{22}| = 3$, $|P_{25}| = 1$, P_{22} is the longest prefix that matches **IP** ($|P|$ is defined as the length of prefix P). In longest-prefix routing, the next hop index for a packet is given by the table entry corresponding to the longest prefix that matches its destination IP address. Thus, in the example above, the next hop of 3 is returned.

2.2 Related Work

Network virtualization is a broad research area. It has proved itself to be a powerful scheme to support the coexistence of heterogenous networks on the same physical networking substrate. From research standpoint, this has been a great opportunity for the networking researchers to test their algorithms and/or protocols in production networks. This was not possible in the traditional IP networks due to the protocol rigidity of networking devices. However, this problem can be overcome by using mechanisms like Multi-Protocol Label Switching (MPLS) [3]. The Layer-3 routing information is encapsulated using the MPLS header. The packet switching is done based on the label rather than using the destination IP. Hence, packet routing is independent of the routing information in the virtual network [11].

Although much work has been done for IP lookup ([21, 9, 20]), only a few have been targeted for virtual routers. In the industry, Juniper has introduced router virtualization in their JCS1200 router [2]. This router can support up to 192 virtual networks, where each virtual network is severed by a logical router (i.e. separated approach). Cisco has also proposed solutions for router virtualization in provider networks, using hardware and software isolated virtual routers [6]. They give a comprehensive comparison of the pros and cons of each approach, and the applicability of each for different networking environments.

Chowdhry et. al [11] has surveyed the opportunities and challenges associated with network virtualization from the networking and implementation perspectives. In [10], the authors evaluated the issues and challenges in the virtualized commercial operator environments.

Several solutions for router virtualization have been recently proposed by the research community. In [12, 18], the authors employed the merged approach, whereas in [22], the separated approach was used. In [22], the authors implemented the virtualized router on a hardware-software hybrid platform. They support up to four hardware virtual routers on a NetFPGA [4] platform. The rest of the virtual routers, which were implemented using the Click modular router[15], resided on a general purpose computer, and are virtualized using OpenVZ. The authors described an interesting idea of network adaptive routers. In their idea, a router is dynamically moved on to the hardware platform from the software platform, when the network traffic level for a particular virtual network increases beyond a threshold. The throughput of the implementation is relatively low ($\sim$ 100 Mbps), compared with the rates at which network links operate in production networks (multi Gbps). Moreover, due to extensive hardware utilization, the NetFPGA hardware cannot support more than 4 virtual router instances.

Fu et. al in [12] used a shared data structure to realize router virtualization in the merged approach. They employed a simple overlaying mechanism to merge the virtual routing tables into a single routing table. By using the shared data structure, they have achieved significant memory saving, and showed the scalability of their solution for up to 50 routing tables. For this algorithm to achieve memory saving, the virtual routing tables must have *similar structure*. Otherwise, simple overlaying will result in the increase of memory usage significantly.

Trie braiding [18] is another algorithm introduced for the merged approach. The authors presented a heuristic to merge multiple virtual routing tables in an optimal way, in order to increase the overlap among different routing tables. They introduced a *braiding bit* at each node for each routing table to identify the direction of traversal along the trie. The number of nodes in the final trie is used as a metric to evaluate the performance of their algorithm. Even though the number of nodes are minimized, the memory requirement at each non-leaf node becomes $O(m+2P)$, where m is the number of virtual routers and P is the size of a pointer in bits. It is clear that the memory consumption grows linearly with m. Therefore, reduction in the total number of nodes does not necessarily lead to the reduction of the overall memory consumption. However, the authors claimed that they were able to store 16 routing tables with a total of 290K prefixes using only 36 Mbits. This scheme performs well only when the routing tables have different structure.

3. PROBLEM DEFINITION

The problem of merging and searching multiple virtual routing tables is defined as follows. Given m virtual routing tables $R_i, i = 0, .., m-1$, each having N_i number of prefixes, find (1) an algorithm that can efficiently merge these virtual tables to minimize the total memory requirement and (2) a search data structure that can support high throughput and quick update.

4. IP LOOKUP ALGORITHM FOR VIRTUAL ROUTER

4.1 Definitions

Definition Any node, for which the path from the root of the trie to that node represents a prefix in the routing table, is called a *prefix node*.

Definition Two distinct prefixes are said to be *overlapped* if and only if one is a proper prefix of the other.

Definition A set of prefixes is considered *disjoint* if and only if any 2 prefixes in the set do not overlap with each other.

Definition Prefixes that are at the leaves of the trie are called *leaf prefixes*. Otherwise, they are called *internal prefixes*.

Definition The memory footprint is defined as the size of the memory required to store the entire routing table. The terms *storage*, *memory requirement*, *memory footprint*, and *storage memory* are used interchangeably in this paper.

Definition Each virtual router instance has a routing table, which is called *virtual routing table*, or simply *virtual table*. Additionally, each virtual instance is associated with a *virtual network ID*, or simply *virtual ID*.

Definition *Prefix update* can either be (1) modification to the existing prefixes, (2) insertion of new prefixes, or (3) deletion of existing prefixes. It can also be referred as *incremental update*.

4.2 Set-Bounded Leaf-Pushing Algorithm

Tree search algorithm is a good choice for IP forwarding engine as the lookup latency does not depend on the length of the prefix, but on the number of prefixes in the routing table. In case of tree search, the latency is proportional to log of the number of prefixes. Note that the trie-based approaches can also reduce the latency by using multi-bit trie. However, this reduction comes at the cost of memory explosion, and thus, results in a very *poor* memory efficiency. Furthermore, our experiment shows that the number of nodes in the trie drastically expands as the prefix length increases from 32 bits to 128 bits. Path compression techniques ([16, 17]) work well to contain the number of trie nodes. Nonetheless, they increase the computational complexity at the nodes and reduce the look-up performance.

In order to use tree search algorithms, the given set of prefixes needs to be processed to eliminate the overlap between prefixes. This elimination process results in a set (or sets) of *disjoint* prefixes. There are many approaches proposed to eliminate overlap, such as leaf-pushing, prefix expansion [20], prefix partitioning [14], and prefix merging [9]. Among these approaches, leaf-pushing is the most popular one due to its simplicity. However, as mentioned before, these approaches either increase the number of prefixes, the number of sets of disjoint prefixes, or both. What we are interested in is an algorithm that can bound the number of sets (to 2 in our work), while keeping the increase in number of prefixes minimal.

In the leaf pushing approach, the initial step is to build a trie from the given routing table. Leaf pushing first grows the trie to a full tree (i.e. all the non-leaf nodes have two child nodes), and then pushes all the prefixes to the leaf nodes. All the leaf nodes are then collected to build a *search tree*. Since the set of leaf nodes are disjoint, any tree search algorithm can be employed to perform the lookup. While leaf pushing eliminates overlap between prefixes, it has the negative effect of expanding the size of the prefix table. For all publicly available routing tables, the prefix tables expand about 1.6 times after leaf pushing [19].

From our analysis with real-life routing tables, we observe that about 90% of the prefixes in these public tables are *leaf prefixes* (Section 7.1). Moreover, if these leaves are removed and the non-prefix leaves are trimmed off the trie, the resulting trie still has the same properties as the original trie. This observation gives us a way to control the number of prefixes by partitioning the original routing table into *exactly* 2 sets of prefixes. Set 1 consists of all the leaf prefixes of the original trie, which are *disjoint*. Set 2 includes all the leaf-pushed prefixes of the trimmed trie, which are also *disjoint*. The process of partitioning the prefix table into 2 sets of disjoint prefixes is called "*set-bounded leaf-pushing*" (SBLP). Due to the disjoint prefixes, at most *one* match can be found in each set for each incoming IP address. In case each set has their own match, the longer match is chosen as the final matched prefix, which is from Set 1 as it is longer.

There are 3 steps involved in the algorithm:

1. Move the leaves of the trie into Set 1
2. Trim the leaf-removed trie
3. Leaf-push the resulting trie and move the leaf-pushed leaves into Set 2

The following notations are used in the analysis:

- N: the number of prefixes in the given routing table
- N': the number of prefixes after processing
- k: the leaf-pushing expansion coefficient, defined as the ratio of the total number of prefixes after and before leaf-pushing
- l: the leaf percentage, defined as the ratio of the number of leaf-prefixes and the total number of prefixes

The number of prefixes in the two sets can be expressed as:

$$N_{S_1} = lN \tag{1}$$

$$N_{S_2} = kN(1 - l) \tag{2}$$

$$N' = N_{S_1} + N_{S_2} = kN + lN(1 - k) = N(k + l - kl) \tag{3}$$

Our analysis on IPv4 routing tables showed that $l = 0.9$ and $k = 1.6$ for IPv4, hence, $N' = 1.06N$. Therefore, by using the set-bounded leaf-pushing algorithm, the total number of prefixes in 2 sets is just slightly larger than the total number of original prefixes (by 6%). For IPv6 routing tables, the result is even better, with $N' \approx N$. The experimental results of the real and synthetic routing tables agree with our analysis and are presented in Section 7.

Complexity: The first step of the algorithm is to build a trie from a given routing table consisting of N prefixes. This step has a complexity of $O(N)$. The leaf-prefixes are then moved to Set 1. This step has a complexity of $O(N)$. The trie is then trimmed and leaf-pushed, with a complexity of $O(N)$. In the final step, the leaf-prefixes are moved to Set 2, also with a complexity of $O(N)$. Since all the steps are sequential, the overall complexity of the set-bounded leaf-pushing algorithm is $O(N)$.

4.3 2-3 Tree

We propose a memory efficient data structure based on a 2-3 tree [1], which is a type of B-tree with order of 3. A 2-3 tree is a balanced search tree that has the following properties:

1. There are three different types of nodes: a leaf node, a 2-node and a 3-node (Figure 1).
2. A leaf node contains one or two data fields.

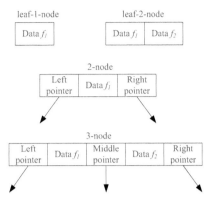

Figure 1: Different types of nodes of a 2-3 tree

3. A 2-node is the same as a binary search tree node, which has one data field and references to two children.
4. A 3-node contains two data fields, ordered so that the first is less than the second, and references to three children. One child contains values less than the first data field, another child contains values between the two data fields, and the last child contains values greater than the second data field.
5. All of the leaves are at the lowest level.

A 2-3 tree with n nodes never has a height greater than $\log_2(n + 1)$. Traversing in 2-3 tree can be performed in a similar way as in a binary search tree: compare and move down the correct link until a leaf node is reached. The search algorithm in 2-3 tree runs in $O(\log_2 n)$ time, where n is the total number of elements in the tree.

The 2-3 tree is chosen as our search data structure over other data structures due to its advantages: (1) a 2-3 tree is always balanced, (2) search in a 2-3 tree is performed the same way as in a binary search tree, and (3) the number of nodes in each level of the tree grows exponentially as we move further from the root. Moreover, insertion and deletion in a 2-3 tree take $O(\log n)$ steps. It will be clearer in the later sections that this complexity can be brought down to $O(1)$ by utilizing the parallelism in hardware.

4.4 Merging Algorithm

We argue that any merging algorithm designed for virtual router need to have the following characteristics:

- The algorithms should be simple and have fast execution time. The main reason is the frequency of updates. In a single routing table, update does not tend to occur frequently. However, when multiple routing tables are considered, the updates are aggregated; therefore, the update rate increases dramatically.
- The algorithms should not be routing-table sensitive. For different routing tables, the total required memory should not have a large variance as it is difficult to allocate memory at design time. Another reason is that new prefixes can break the optimal point of the algorithm and adversely affect the memory footprint.
- The algorithms should not depend on the number of virtual routing tables, but on the total number of prefixes.

Table 2: Merged virtual routing table

	Virtual prefix	Length	Next Hop
P_{11}	**00***	2	1
P_{12}	**001***	3	3
P_{13}	**0101***	4	2
P_{14}	**0111***	4	4
P_{15}	**00010***	5	5
P_{16}	**000***	3	3
P_{21}	**110***	3	2
P_{22}	**1101***	4	3
P_{23}	**1111***	4	4
P_{24}	**1100***	4	1
P_{25}	**11***	2	5
P_{26}	**10***	2	2

We propose a simple algorithm for merging m virtual routing tables $R_i, i = 0, 1, .., m-1$. All the virtual routing tables are combined into a single virtual routing table R_{all}. Each prefix in table R_{all} is a structure consisting of 3 values: (1) virtual prefix value, (2) prefix length, and (3) next hop information. The *virtual prefix* is the concatenation of the virtual ID and the prefix value of each prefix in that order. Each prefix structure is identified by this *virtual prefix*. The maximum length of the virtual prefix is $(L + L_{VID})$, where L_{VID} is the length of the virtual ID and L is the maximum prefix length (32 for IPv4 and 128 for IPv6). The terms *prefix* and *prefix structure* are used interchangeably in this paper.

A *single* binary trie is built for *all* the virtual prefixes in R_{all}. We then apply the *set-bounded leaf-pushing* algorithm (Section 4.2) to generate 2 sets of *disjoint* prefixes, namely S_1 and S_2. Each prefix is padded with 0 up to the maximum length. The number of padded 0s is $(L - L_P)$, where L_P is the length of the prefix. The padded prefix is then attached with a prefix length. Note that each prefix in 2 sets can appear in more than one virtual table. However, these duplicated prefixes have different virtual ID associated with the virtual table that they belong to.

We use an example to illustrate the idea. Consider 2 sample virtual routing tables as depicted in Table 1. The merged routing table is shown in Table 2. Using this merged table, a single binary trie is built and its leaf-prefixes are moved to Set S_1. The leaf-removed trie is trimmed and then leaf-pushed. All the leaf-prefixes are collected in Set S_2. These 3 steps are shown in Figure 2, 3 and 4, respectively. All the prefixes in each set are padded with 0 to form the virtual padded prefixes, which are shown in Table 3.

Complexity: All the prefixes are prepended with its virutal ID in the first step with a complexity of $O(N)$, where N is the total number of prefixes. We then apply the set-bounded leaf-pushing algorithm to the combined virtual routing table. The complexity of this step is $O(N)$ (Section 4.2). Therefore, the complexity of the merging algorithm is $O(N)$.

The merging algorithm can also be parallelized to reduce the execution time. Each virtual routing table can be processed independently. For each virtual table i, 2 sets of disjoint prefixes are generated, S_1^i, S_2^i. The final step is to simply combine all the corresponding sets into a single set:

$$S_1 = \sum_{i=0}^{m-1} S_1^i, S_2 = \sum_{i=0}^{m-1} S_2^i$$

4.5 IP Lookup Algorithm for Virtual Router

Using our merging algorithm described above, m virtual

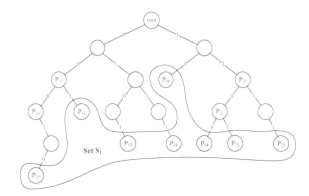

Figure 2: Trie is built and leaves are moved to Set S_1

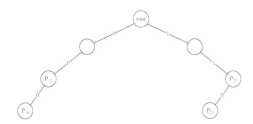

Figure 3: Trie is trimmed

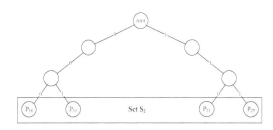

Figure 4: Trie is leaf-pushed and leaves are moved to Set S_2

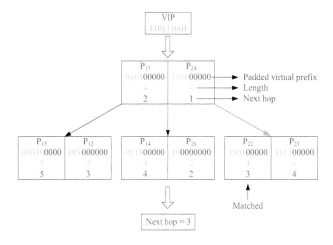

Figure 5: Corresponding 2-3 tree of Set S_1

Table 3: Padded virtual prefixes in 2 sets

	Padded virtual prefix	Length	Next Hop
	Set S_1		
P_{12}	001000000	3	3
P_{13}	010100000	4	2
P_{14}	011100000	4	4
P_{15}	000100000	5	5
P_{22}	110100000	4	3
P_{23}	111100000	4	4
P_{24}	110000000	4	1
P_{26}	100000000	2	2
	Set S_2		
P_{11}	001000000	3	1
P_{16}	000000000	3	3
P_{21}	110000000	3	2
P_{25}	111000000	3	5

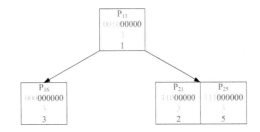

Figure 6: Corresponding 2-3 tree of Set S_2

Table 4: List of notations used in the paper

Notation	Meaning
m	Number of virtual routing tables
R_i	Virtual routing table i
N_i	The number of prefixes in R_i
N	The total number of prefixes in all the virtual routing tables
L	Maximum prefix length (32 for IPv4, 128 for IPv6)
L_P	Prefix length = $\lceil \log L \rceil$
L_{VID}	Length of the virtual ID = $\lceil \log m \rceil$
L_{NHI}	Length of the next hop information
M	Size of the required memory
L_{Ptr}	Address length
$|S_i|$	Number of prefixes in set S_i

routing tables, $R_0, .., R_{m-1}$, are merged and processed to generate 2 sets of prefixes, S_1 and S_2. For each set we build a 2-3 tree using the padded virtual prefix as the key ($S_1 \mapsto T_1, S_2 \mapsto T_2$). Note that since all the prefixes in each set are disjoint, any tree search algorithm can be used to search for the matching prefix. Figure 5 and 6 show the corresponding 2-3 trees of the 2 sample sets in Table 3. After building the 2 trees, IP-lookup operation can be performed as follows. The IP address and virtual ID are extracted from the incoming packet. The virtual ID is appended with the IP address to form the *virtual IP address* (VIP). The VIP is searched in both T_1 and T_2 to find a possible match.

In each step of the comparison, the virtual IP address is compared against the virtual prefix of the current node. There are 2 types of comparison. The first type is to determine if the virtual prefix matches the virtual IP address. The second comparison is to determine the direction of traversal. If the node is a 2-node, which has one 1 data field f_1, then the direction is *left* (if **VIP** $\leqslant f_1$), or *right* otherwise. If the node is a 3-node, which has 2 data fields f_1 and f_2 ($f_1 < f_2$), then the direction can be *left* (if **VIP** $\leqslant f_1$), *middle* (if $f_1 <$ **VIP** $\leqslant f_2$), or *right* otherwise.

The search results from both T_1 and T_2 are combined to give the matching result. Note that T_1 has higher priority than T_2 due to the longer matched prefix. Hence, if there are matches in both trees, the one from tree T_1 is returned as the final result. For instance, assume that a packet with a destination address of $IP = 10111001$ with a virtual ID of 1 arrives. The virtual IP address (VIP) of this packet is 110111001. At the root of T_1, VIP is compared with node values 010100000 and 110000000, yielding no match and a "greater" result. Thus, the packet traverses to the right branch. The comparison with the prefix in this node results in a match with *matched prefix =*

110100000, *matched length* = 4, *next hop* = 3, which is the final outcome.

4.6 Memory Requirement

We now analyze the merging and searching algorithm. Recall that there are 2 types of nodes in a 2-3 tree: 2-node and 3-node. A 2-node has one data field and 2 pointers, or 2 pointers per data field. The 3-node has 2 data fields and 3 pointers, or 1.5 pointers per data field. Note that each data field holds one prefix. It is obvious that the average number of pointers per prefix is between 1.5 and 2. Therefore, for the sake of simplicity, we will assume that the number of pointers per prefix is 2 in our calculation. The list of notations used in the analysis are shown in Table 4.

The memory requirement M_1 and M_2 of the first and second search trees are:

$$M_1 = |S_1|(L + L_P + L_{VID} + L_{NHI} + 2L_{Ptr_1}) \quad (4)$$
$$M_2 = |S_2|(L + L_P + L_{VID} + L_{NHI} + 2L_{Ptr_2}) \quad (5)$$

Where

$$L_P = \log L$$
$$L_{Ptr_1} = \log |S_1|$$
$$L_{Ptr_2} = \log |S_2|$$

The total memory requirement M is:
$$M = M_1 + M_2$$
$$= (|S_1| + |S_2|)(L + L_P + L_{VID} + L_{NHI})$$
$$+ 2|S_1|L_{Ptr_1} + 2|S_2|L_{Ptr_2} \quad (6)$$

In reality, nodes in the last level of the tree need not contain any pointer as they have no children. Additionally, the number of leaf-nodes is at least half the total number of nodes of the tree. Therefore, the total memory requirement can be rewritten as:

$$M = (|S_1| + |S_2|)(L + L_P + \log m + L_{NHI})$$
$$+ |S_1|L_{Ptr_1} + |S_2|L_{Ptr_2} \quad (7)$$

From the formula, we can observe that the total memory requirement M is not sensitive to the number of routing tables m. In fact, M is proportional to $L_{VID} = \lceil \log m \rceil$. As we learned in Section 3, for IPv4, $|S_1| = 0.9N$, $|S_2| = 0.16N$, $|S_1| + |S_2| = 1.06N$, where N is the total number of prefixes in all the routing tables. Thus, the storage complexity is $O(N \times \log m)$. If we fix the number of virtual routers, then M grows linearly with N.

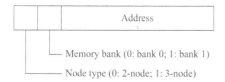

Figure 7: Content of the pipeline forwarded address

5. ARCHITECTURE

5.1 Overall Architecture

Pipelining is used to produce one lookup operation per clock cycle, and thus increase the throughput. The number of pipeline stages is determined by the height of the 2-3 tree. Each level of the tree is mapped onto a pipeline stage, which has its own memory (or table).

Figure 9(a) describes the overall architecture of the proposed IP lookup engine for virtual routers. There are 2 pipelines (one for each set of prefixes). The IP address and virtual ID are extracted from the incoming packet and concatenated to form the virtual IP address (VIP). The VIP is routed to all branches. The searches are performed in parallel in all the pipelines. The results are fed through a priority resolver to select the next hop index of the longest matched prefix. The variation in the number of stages in these pipelines results in latency mismatch. The delay block is appended to the shorter pipeline to match with the latency of the longer pipeline.

The block diagram of the basic pipeline and a single stage are shown in Figure 9(b). The on-chip memory of FPGA is dual-ported. To take advantage of this, the architecture is configured as dual-linear pipelines. This configuration doubles the lookup rate. At each stage, the memory has 2 sets of Read/Write ports so that two virtual IP addresses can be input every clock cycle. In each pipeline stage, there are 3 data fields forwarded from the previous stage: (1) *Virtual IP address*, (2) *next hop*, and (3) *memory address*. The memory address, whose content is shown in Figure 7, is used to retrieve the node stored on the local memory. The node value is compared with the input virtual IP address to determine the match status and the direction of traversal. The *memory address* is updated in each stage depending on the direction of traversal. However, the *next hop information* is only updated if a match is found at that stage. In this case, search in subsequent stages is unnecessary as all the prefixes with a set are disjoint. Hence, those subsequent stages can be turned off to save power consumption. Furthermore, if a match has been found in Set 1 (or pipeline 1), search in Set 2 (or pipeline 2) can also be terminated as Set 1 has a higher priority compared with Set 2.

5.2 Memory Management

The major difficulty in efficiently realizing a 2-3 tree on hardware is the difference in the size of the 2-node and 3-node. The space allocated for a 2-node cannot be reused later by a 3-node. The available memory management is also more complicated. To overcome this problem, a 3-node is divided into two 2-nodes (Figure 8). The left pointer of the first node points to the left child. The right pointer of the first node and the left pointer of the second node both point to the middle child. Finally, the right pointer of the second node points to the right child. Although a pointer

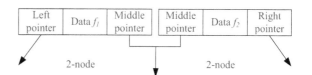

Figure 8: The modified 3-node

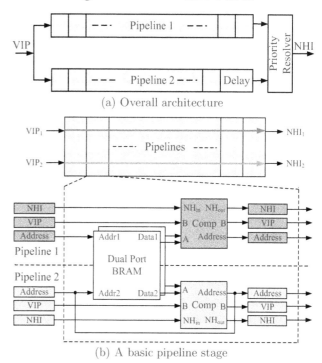

(a) Overall architecture

(b) A basic pipeline stage

Figure 9: Block diagram of the proposed IP-lookup architecture (NIH-Next hop information; VIP-Virtual IP address)

is redundant, the benefit is justifiable. It creates *uniformity* in the size of the nodes, and simplifies the memory management. Additionally, this node-splitting scheme allows us to precisely estimate the amount of required memory, as each prefix is stored in one *effective* 2-node.

Two memory banks are used to support the node-splitting scheme. A 2-node can be placed in any bank, while a 3-node spans over 2 banks. Note that when a 3-node is split into two 2-nodes, each of them must be placed in the same memory location in each bank. This placement allows us to use a single address to access both nodes.

5.3 Virtual Routing Table Update

A virtual routing table update can be any of three operations: (1) modification of an existing prefix (i.e. change of the next hop information), (2) deletion of an existing prefix, and (3) insertion of a new prefix. The first update requires changing the next hop indices of the existing prefixes in the routing table, while the others require inserting a prefix into, or deleting a prefix from a given routing table.

The first type of update can easily be done by first finding the correct node that contains the prefix. Once the node is found, the next hop information is updated. However, the second and third type of updates require extra work. The

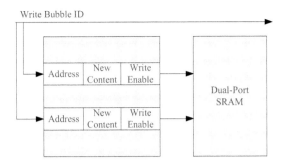

Figure 10: Route update using dual write-bubbles

insertion and deletion cause changes in *at most two nodes* at each level of the tree, in the worst case [24]. For the insertion, the first task is to find the (non-leaf) node that will be the parent p of the newly inserted node n. There are 2 cases: (1) p has only 2 children and (2) p has 3 children. In the first case, n is inserted as the appropriate child of p; p becomes a 3-node. A new 2-node needs to be added for p, and a new 2-node is allocated for n in the next level. In the second case, n is still inserted as the appropriate child of p. However, p has 4 children. An internal node m is created with p's two rightmost children. m is then added as the appropriate new child of p's parent (i.e., add m just to the right of p). If p's parent had only 2 children, insertion is done. Otherwise, new nodes are created recursively up the tree. If the root is given 4 children, then a new node m is created as above, and a new root node is created with p and m as its children. The deletion process is similar, with merging instead of splitting.

Once all the changes in each level of the tree are precomputed, the update operation is performed starting from the root of the tree. Since at most two nodes are modified in each level, this update can easily be done by inserting *only one* write bubble, as shown in Figure 10. There is one dual-ported write bubble table (WBT) in each stage. Each table consists of at least 2 entries. Each entry composes of (1) the memory address to be updated in the next stage, (2) the new content for that memory location, and (3) a write enable bit. The new content of the memory is computed offline in $O(\log_2 N)$ time, where N is the number of nodes. However, it is not necessary to download a new forwarding table for every route update. Route updates can be frequent, but routing protocols need time, in the order of minutes, to converge. Thus, the offline update computation can also be done at the control plane.

When a prefix update is initiated, the memory content of the write bubble table in each stage is updated, and a write bubble is inserted into the pipeline. When it arrives at the stage prior to the stage to be updated, the write bubble uses the new content from the WBT to update the memory location. At most 2 nodes can be simultaneously updated at each stage, using the dual-ported memory. When the bubble moves to the next level (stage), the tree up to that level is fully updated, and the subsequent lookup can be performed properly. This updating mechanism supports non-blocking prefix updates at system speed.

5.4 Scalability

The use of the 2-3 tree leads to a linear storage com-

plexity in our design, as each *effective* 2-node contains exactly one virtual prefix. The height of a 2-3 tree is at most $(1 + \lfloor \log_2 N \rfloor)$, where N is the number of nodes. Since each level of the tree is mapped to a pipeline stage, the height of the tree determines the number of stages. Our proposed architecture is simple, and is expected to utilize a small amount of logic resource. Hence, the major constraint that dictates the number of pipeline stages, and in turn the size of the supported virtual routing table, is the amount of on-chip memory. As mentioned before, the per-level required memory size grows exponentially as we go from one level to the next of the tree. Therefore, we can move the last few stages onto external SRAMs. However, due to the limit on the number of I/O pins of FPGA devices, we can fit only a certain number of stages on SRAM, as described in detail in Section 6.

The scalability of our architecture relies on the close relationship between the size of the virtual routing tables and the number of required pipeline stages. As the number of prefixes increases, extra pipeline stages are needed. To avoid reprogramming the FPGA, we should allocate the maximum possible number of pipeline stages.

6. IMPLEMENTATION

As analyzed in Section 4.6, the total required memory is:

$$M = (|S_1| + |S_2|)(L + L_P + L_{VID} + L_{NHI})$$
$$+ |S_1|L_{Ptr_1} + |S_2|L_{Ptr_2}$$

For the sake of simplicity, let $L_{Ptr_1} = L_{Ptr_2} = L_{Ptr}$ and $(|S_1| + |S_2|) = N_S$, then

$$M = N_S(L + L_P + L_{VID} + L_{NHI} + L_{Ptr})$$

In IPv4, $L = 32$, $L_P = 5$, whereas in IPv6, $L = 128$, $L_P = 7$. We assign $L_{VID} = 5$ to support up to 32 virtual routing tables, $L_{NHI} = 6$ to support up to 64 next hop information, and $L_{Ptr} = 20$. Note that the unit of storage size is in bits unless otherwise stated. The total required memory is:

$$M_{IPv4} = N_S(32 + 5 + 5 + 6 + 20) = 68N_S \quad (8)$$
$$M_{IPv6} = N_S(128 + 7 + 5 + 6 + 20) = 164N_S \quad (9)$$

Therefore, a state-of-the-art FPGA device with 36 Mb of on-chip memory (e.g. Xilinx Virtex6) can support up to 530K prefixes (for IPv4), or up to 220K prefixes (for IPv6), *without* using external SRAM. Note that the total number of nodes is approximately equal to the number of supported virtual prefixes (Section 4.6).

In our design, external SRAMs can be used to handle even larger routing tables, by moving the last stages of the pipelines onto external SRAMs. Currently, SRAM is available in $2 - 32$ Mb chips [7], with data widths of 18, 32, or 36 bits, and a maximum access frequency of over 500MHz. Each stage uses dual port memory, which requires two address and two data ports. Hence, each external stage requires ≈ 180 and ≈ 560 I/O pins for IPv4 and IPv6, respectively. Note that Quad Data Rate (QDR) SRAM can also be used in place of SRAM to provide higher chip-density and access bandwidth.

The largest Virtex package, which has 1517 I/O pins, can interface with up to 6 banks of dual port SRAMs for IPv4, and up to 2 banks for IPv6. For each additional pipeline

Table 5: Number of prefixes and leaf-prefixes of real-life and synthetic routing tables

Core IPv4 routing tables			Edge IPv4 routing tables			Edge IPv6 routing tables		
Table	# prefixes	# leaf prefixes	Table	# prefixes	# leaf prefixes	Table	# prefixes	# leaf prefixes
rrc00	332117	300764 (90.56%)	rrc00_e	95048	71923 (75.67%)	rrc00_e6	95048	95039 (99.99%)
rrc01	324172	294148 (90.74%)	rrc01_e	98390	83445 (84.81%)	rrc01_e6	98390	98388 (99.99%)
rrc03	321617	291885 (90.76%)	rrc03_e	90867	63887 (70.31%)	rrc03_e6	90867	90844 (99.99%)
rrc04	347231	317282 (91.37%)	rrc04_e	95358	72790 (76.33%)	rrc04_e6	95358	95346 (99.99%)
rrc05	322996	293099 (90.74%)	rrc05_e	98305	83188 (84.62%)	rrc05_e6	98305	98297 (99.99%)
rrc06	321577	292260 (90.88%)	rrc06_e	97410	78853 (80.95%)	rrc06_e6	97410	97404 (99.99%)
rrc07	322557	292918 (90.81%)	rrc07_e	95007	71969 (75.75%)	rrc07_e6	95007	95002 (99.99%)
rrc10	319952	290608 (90.83%)	rrc10_e	97376	78685 (80.81%)	rrc10_e6	97376	97369 (99.99%)
rrc11	323668	293810 (90.78%)	rrc11_e	91031	64089 (70.4%)	rrc11_e6	91031	91000 (99.99%)
rrc12	320015	290742 (90.85%)	rrc12_e	97386	78715 (80.83%)	rrc12_e6	97386	97378 (99.99%)
rrc13	335153	303923 (90.68%)	rrc13_e	95163	72338 (76.01%)	rrc13_e6	95163	95153 (99.99%)
rrc14	325797	295613 (90.74%)	rrc14_e	95032	71923 (75.68%)	rrc14_e6	95032	95023 (99.99%)
rrc15	323986	293921 (90.72%)	rrc15_e	91019	64085 (70.41%)	rrc15_e6	91019	91000 (99.99%)
rrc16	328295	297486 (90.62%)	rrc16_e	94780	71801 (75.76%)	rrc16_e6	94780	94767 (99.99%)

stage, the size of the supported routing table at least doubles. Thus, the architecture can support up to 16M prefixes, or 880K prefixes for IPv4 and IPv6, respectively. Moreover, since the access frequency of SRAM is twice that of our target frequency (200 MHz), the use of external SRAM will not adversely affect the throughput of our design.

Employing DRAM in our design requires some modifications to the architecture. Due to its structural simplicity, DRAM has very high density and very high access bandwidth. The major drawback is its high access latency. Therefore, the design needs to have enough memory requests to DRAM in order to hide this expensive latency. One possible solution is to have multiple pipelines sharing the same DRAM module. However, these pipeline must stall when waiting for the requested data coming back from the DRAM module.

7. PERFORMANCE EVALUATION

7.1 Experimental Setup

Fourteen experimental IPv4 core routing tables were collected from Project - RIS [5] on 06/03/2010. These core routing tables were used to evaluate our algorithm for a real networking environment. However, as mentioned before, router virtualization mainly happens at provider edge networks. Therefore, synthetic IPv4 routing tables generated using FRuG [13] were also used as we did not have access to any real provider edge routing tables. FRuG takes a seed routing table and generates a synthetic table with the same statistic as that of the seed. From these synthetic edge routing tables, we generated the corresponding IPv6 edge routing tables using the same method as in [23]. The IPv4-to-IPv6 prefix mapping is *one-to-one*. Hence, the number of prefixes in an IPv4-IPv6 (i.e. rrc00_e and rrc00_e6) table pair is identical. The number of prefixes and leaf-prefixes of the experimental routing tables are shown in Table 5.

There are 3 groups of routing tables: Group 1 (core IPv4 routing tables), Group 2 (edge IPv4 routing tables), and Group 3 (edge IPv6 routing tables). The tables in each group are merged using our merging algorithm and the results are reported in Table 6. We observe that total number of prefixes in 2 sets is only 1.12×, 1.17×, 1.01× the total number of original prefixes in Group 1, 2, 3, respectively. These results agree with our analysis in the previous sections. With regard to memory footprint, Group 1 and 2

Table 6: Merging results of 2 groups of routing tables

	Number of prefixes			
Group	Original	Set 1	Set 2	Total
1	4569133	4148459	962492	5110951(1.12×)
2	1332172	1027691	543135	1570826(1.17×)
3	1332172	1332010	2622	1334632(1.01×)

require 40 MB and 11 MB, while Group 3 needs 27 MB of memory. The reported memory requirement is for both on-chip and off-chip memory combined.

7.2 Throughput

The proposed architecture was implemented in Verilog, using Synplify Pro 9.6.2 and Xilinx ISE 11.3, with Virtex-6 XC6VSX475T as the target. The implementation showed a maximum frequency of 200 MHz, while utilizing less than 10% of the on-chip logic resource. Using dual-ported memory, the design can support 400 million packets per second (MLPS). This result surpasses the worst-case 150 MLPS required by the standardized 100GbE line cards [19]. Note that our solution can also be implemented on other platforms, such as ASIC and multicore. However, it is out of the scope of this paper, and therefore is not presented.

7.3 Performance Comparison

Four key comparisons were performed with respect to (1) the time complexity of the merging algorithm, (2) memory efficiency, (3) quick-update capability, and (4) throughput. We compare our merging algorithm and lookup architecture with the state-of-the-art designs. These candidates are the trie-overlapping [12] (A1) and the trie braiding [18] (A2) approaches. Note that it is difficult to make a fair and meaningful comparison with these approaches due to the lack of common experimental set of routing tables.

Time complexity: Our merging algorithm has the time complexity of $O(N)$. Scheme A1 has the time complexity of $O(N \log N)$ due to the quick-sort algorithm applied on the forwarding information base. Scheme A2 has the time complexity of $O(N^2)$ due to the linear programming algorithm performed at each node of the trie. Therefore, our merging algorithm has a better time complexity compared with other schemes.

Memory efficiency: When all the routing tables contain the similar set of prefixes, scheme A1 performs extremely well and is effective. However, when the similarity is low, this scheme does not lead to any gains over storing the tries separately. In this case, scheme A2 performs better than A1. It was reported in [18] that for 16 routing tables consisting of 290K prefixes, scheme A2 and A1 require up to 36 Mb (4.5 MB) and 72 Mb (9 MB), respectively. On the other hand, our scheme requires only 15 MB for 14 routing tables consisting of over 1.3M prefixes. Note that our scheme is not sensitive to the number of routing tables, but to the total number of prefixes. Thus, if we need to support 290K prefixes, our scheme utilizes only 2.4 MB of memory.

Quick-update capability: All the 3 schemes support quick incremental update. However, scheme A1 may not be memory and lookup efficient after a large number of updates. Therefore, it is occasionally required to reconstruct the entire lookup data structure for optimal lookup efficiency. In scheme A2, new prefix insertion can easily break the optimal trie structure. Hence, it is also required to be re-computed over a longer period of time in order to minimize the trie size. The recomputing period should not be frequent due to the computational-intensive braiding processing. In contrast, our scheme does not require any reconstruction over time. New prefix can quickly be merged using our simple merging algorithm, and the new prefix can be inserted into the tree by injecting the update bubbles into the traffic stream.

Throughput: We cannot directly compare the throughput with the other 2 schemes as they were not implemented on hardware. However, our implementation on FPGA shows a sustained throughput of 400 million lookups per second, even when external SRAM is used. This translates to the worst-case throughput of 128 Gbps (for a minimum packet size of 40 bytes, or 320 bits).

8. CONCLUDING REMARKS

In this paper, we have described a simple algorithm to merge a number of virtual routing tables. The proposed algorithm is not sensitive to the number of routing tables, but to the total number of prefixes. Hence, a virtual router can be shared by as many virtual router instances as desired, as long as the total number of prefixes is less than a threshold set by the amount of available memory. Along with the merging algorithm, a high-throughput, memory-efficient linear-pipeline architecture has also been proposed and implemented. Also, the architecture can easily interface with external SRAM to handle larger virtual routing tables. Using a state-of-the-art Field Programmable Gate Arrays (FPGA) with external SRAM, the proposed architecture can support up to 16M and 880K prefixes for IPv4 and IPv6, respectively. Our post place-and-route results show that the architecture can sustain a throughput of 400 million lookups per second. With these advantages, our algorithm and architecture can be used in virtual routers that require the following criteria: (1) fast internet link rates up to and beyond 100 Gbps, (2) large size of virtual routing tables, (3) large number of virtual router instances, and (4) quick update to minimize interruption in operation. One drawback of the proposed merging algorithm is that it completely disregards the similarities between routing tables. For future work, we plan to exploit these similarities in order to improve the memory efficiency.

9. REFERENCES

[1] 2-3 Tree [Online]. [http://en.wikipedia.org].
[2] Control plane scaling and router virtualization [Online]. [http://www.juniper.net/us/en/local/pdf/whitepapers/2000261-en.pdf].
[3] MPLS [Online]. [http://en.wikipedia.org].
[4] NetFPGA [Online]. [http://netfpga.org/].
[5] RIS RAW DATA [Online]. [http://data.ris.ripe.net].
[6] Router virtualization in service providers [Online]. [http://www.cisco.com/en/US/solutions/collateral/ns341/ns524/ns562/ns573/white_paper_c11-512753.pdf].
[7] SAMSUNG SRAMs [Online]. [http://www.samsung.com].
[8] F. Baboescu, S. Rajgopal, L. Huang, and N. Richardson. Hardware implementation of a tree based IP lookup algorithm for oc-768 and beyond. In *Proc. DesignCon '05*, pages 290–294, 2005.
[9] M. Behdadfar, H. Saidi, H. Alaei, and B. Samari. Scalar prefix search - a new route lookup algorithm for next generation internet. In *Proc. INFOCOM '09*, 2009.
[10] J. Carapinha and J. Jiménez. Network virtualization: a view from the bottom. In *VISA '09: Proceedings of the 1st ACM workshop on Virtualized infrastructure systems and architectures*, pages 73–80, New York, NY, USA, 2009. ACM.
[11] N. M. K. Chowdhury and R. Boutaba. A survey of network virtualization. *Comput. Netw.*, 54(5):862–876, 2010.
[12] J. Fu and J. Rexford. Efficient ip-address lookup with a shared forwarding table for multiple virtual routers. In *CoNEXT '08: Proceedings of the 2008 ACM CoNEXT Conference*, pages 1–12, 2008.
[13] T. Ganegedara, W. Jiang, and V. Prasanna. Frug: A benchmark for packet forwarding in future networks. In *IPCCC '10: Proceedings of IEEE IPCCC 2010*, 2010.
[14] H. Le and V. K. Prasanna. Scalable high throughput and power efficient ip-lookup on fpga. In *Proc. FCCM '09*, 2009.
[15] R. Morris, E. Kohler, J. Jannotti, and M. F. Kaashoek. The click modular router. *SIGOPS Oper. Syst. Rev.*, 33(5):217–231, 1999.
[16] D. R. Morrison. Patricia—practical algorithm to retrieve information coded in alphanumeric. *J. ACM*, 15(4):514–534, 1968.
[17] K. Sklower. A tree-based packet routing table for berkeley unix. In *Winter Usenix Conf.*, pages 93–99, 1991.
[18] H. Song, M. Kodialam, F. Hao, and T. V. Lakshman. Building scalable virtual routers with trie braiding. In *INFOCOM'10: Proceedings of the 29th conference on Information communications*, pages 1442–1450, Piscataway, NJ, USA, 2010. IEEE Press.
[19] H. Song, M. S. Kodialam, F. Hao, and T. V. Lakshman. Scalable ip lookups using shape graphs. In *Proc. ICNP '09*, 2009.
[20] V. Srinivasan and G. Varghese. Fast address lookups using controlled prefix expansion. *ACM Trans. Comput. Syst.*, 17:1–40, 1999.
[21] D. Taylor, J. Turner, J. Lockwood, T. Sproull, and D. Parlour. Scalable ip lookup for internet routers. *Selected Areas in Communications, IEEE Journal on*, 21(4):522 – 534, may. 2003.
[22] D. Unnikrishnan, R. Vadlamani, Y. Liao, A. Dwaraki, J. Crenne, L. Gao, and R. Tessier. Scalable network virtualization using fpgas. In *FPGA '10: Proceedings of the 18th annual ACM/SIGDA international symposium on Field programmable gate arrays*, pages 219–228, New York, NY, USA, 2010. ACM.
[23] M. Wang, S. Deering, T. Hain, and L. Dunn. Non-random generator for ipv6 tables. In *HOTI '04: Proceedings of the High Performance Interconnects, 2004. on Proceedings. 12th Annual IEEE Symposium*, pages 35–40, 2004.
[24] Y.-H. E. Yang and V. K. Prasanna. High throughput and large capacity pipelined dynamic search tree on fpga. In *Proc. FPGA '10*, 2010.

FPGA Side-Channel Receivers

Ji Sun
University of Alberta
Edmonton, AB, Canada
ji.sun@ualberta.ca

Ray Bittner
Microsoft Research
Redmond, WA, USA
raybit@microsoft.com

Ken Eguro
Microsoft Research
Redmond, WA, USA
eguro@microsoft.com

ABSTRACT

The popularity of FPGAs is rapidly growing due to the unique advantages that they offer. However, their distinctive features also raise new questions concerning the security and communication capabilities of an FPGA-based hardware platform. In this paper, we explore some of the limits of FPGA side-channel communication. Specifically, we identify a previously unexplored capability that significantly increases both the potential benefits and risks associated with side-channel communication on an FPGA: an in-device receiver. We designed and implemented three new communication mechanisms: speed modulation, timing modulation and pin hijacking. These non-traditional interfacing techniques have the potential to provide reliable communication with an estimated maximum bandwidth of 3.3 bit/sec, 8 Kbits/sec, and 3.4 Mbits/sec, respectively.

Categories and Subject Descriptors

B.4.2 [**Input/Output and Data Communications**]: Input/Output Devices – *channels and controllers*

General Terms

Design, Security.

Keywords

FPGA, side-channel receiver, thermal, phase shift, DDR2, I2C.

1. INTRODUCTION

Prior work on side-channel communication has primarily focused on side-channel attacks [2][4][5][8][9][10]. Side-channel attacks gain information from systems that are assumed to be secure. However, these exploits do not rely on vulnerabilities in the frontline security protocols that are used, but rather on the fact that systems may emanate information via mechanisms that designers may not anticipate. For example, hackers may be able to extract the key used by an encryption chip simply by closely monitoring the power consumption.

That said, centering the discussion on side-channels as an unintentional source of information does not address two important considerations. First, system developers may purposely want to implement side-channel communication. For instance,

ICs are often pin-limited and a normally out-of-band communication technique could add valuable I/O capacity [18]. Similarly, such unconventional communication vectors may be able to fix board-level design errors or defects in I/O resources after fabrication and assembly. Side-channels may even be used as a latent signature to watermark a system [3][6].

The second issue that should be considered is the possibility of a side-channel receiver. Although many prior research projects have investigated the information that may *leave* a device, to the best of our knowledge, no prior work has looked at feasible side-channel mechanisms by which information may *enter* a device. Bi-directional communication is not only necessary for side-channels to become generally applicable to the positive (white-hat) uses previously mentioned, we must also consider its impact on the potential negative (black-hat) uses. For example, Trojan covert channels are side-channels created by system developers to victimize end users [1][10]. Although an end user might believe that a system is only transmitting approved information (because they can monitor the in-band communications), the system may also be sending private data via a side-channel. The addition of a side-channel receiver would enable much more sophisticated and stealthy attacks. For instance, transmissions that are conditionally triggered would be far more difficult to detect than those that are either always on or statically triggered.

The mechanisms and implications of side-channel communication are particularly important for the FPGA community. This is because the inherent reprogrammability of FPGAs adds a new opportunity to use, or to fall victim to, a side-channel. For example, although the board-level design of an FPGA-based system may be fixed early in the development cycle, the circuit within the FPGA itself can be updated at any point. Thus, as compared to an ASIC-based system, it is easier to take advantage of the I/O and post-fabrication advantages offered by side-channel communication. On the other hand, reprogrammability also may make FPGAs more vulnerable than ASICs to attack. For instance, a Trojan covert channel does not have to be inserted at the level of the transistor layout, it can be added to a system firmware update.

While FPGAs offer an entry point for side-channel communication late in the development process, they also present their own challenges to actually implementing a functional system. Unlike ASICs, that can be customized to offer a wide range of different and finely-tuned structures (including arbitrary analog circuits), FPGAs have very specific pre-defined resources. These structures either may not be customizable or may only be modified within a given range / in specific increments.

In this paper, we investigate techniques to communicate between an external transmitter and an FPGA-based side-channel receiver.

We present three general mechanisms of communication and demonstrate specific proof-of-concept implementations for each. Highlighted in Section 3, speed modulation techniques use a transmitter that can change the intrinsic operational speed of components inside an FPGA. The focus of Section 4, timing modulation approaches communicate by modifying the delay of an FPGA's I/O signals. In Section 5, we discuss pin hijacking techniques in which we co-opt a wire already in use by an FPGA I/O signal to carry additional side-channel data. We also discuss analytical models for their respective bandwidth to provide some measure of the associated functionality or risk.

2. SIDE-CHANNEL EVALUATION

Although we will demonstrate specific working examples of FPGA-based side-channel receivers, we would also like to get some idea of their more general potential. The viability of any particular side-channel technique will largely hinge upon three factors: the difficulty or cost associated with building the external transmitter, the area required or constraints imposed building the receiver in the FPGA, and the maximum transfer rate that the channel can achieve.

Unfortunately, the cost and convenience of implementing a transmitter or receiver is somewhat subjective and likely depends upon the details of the specific use-case. Thus, while we can report factors such as the resource requirements of our proof-of-concept implementations, the first two considerations that we mentioned above are largely qualitative. On the other hand, we can analyze the data bandwidth potential much more objectively.

As shown in Eq. 1, the maximum transfer rate in bits per second of a given communication mechanism (B) is limited by the number of unique symbols we can express (S), the sampling rate of the technique (F), and the number of independent channels that we can create (C). As we describe each of the communication mechanisms in the following sections, we will also discuss how S, F, and C are affected by the specific characteristics of the various approaches.

$$B = log_2(S) * F * C \qquad (1)$$

3. SPEED MODULATION

In this section, we focus on communication side-channels in which a transmitter causes changes in the speed of the underlying logic inside an FPGA-based receiver. One mechanism that such approaches can use is that the performance of any integrated circuit is affected by three factors: process, voltage, and temperature (PVT). Although it may be difficult or impossible to externally modulate the technical process parameters and physical structures created on an FPGA during manufacturing, it is relatively easy to manipulate the supply voltage and temperature of the chip.

Intentionally heating or cooling the chip is significant because, in typical operational ranges, there is an inverse relationship between the temperature and propagation delay of a transistor. Increased temperature decreases the mobility of electrons and holes. This results in the reduction of current, which in turn increase RC delay. Similarly, changing the supply voltage of a chip also changes the propagation delay. This is because, in traditional CMOS circuitry, the supply voltage determines the maximum drain-source voltage (V_{ds}). Increasing V_{ds} increases the switching current, which, in turn, reduces RC delay.

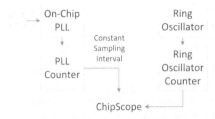

Figure 1: Block diagram of temperature modulation platform

3.1 Case Study – Temperature Modulation

In this paper, we concentrate on temperature modulation. Although theoretically either voltage or temperature could be used for communication, in practice it is likely easier to build a temperature transmitter. This is for two reasons. First, it may be non-trivial to find or build a power system that can actively modulate the voltage provided to the FPGA with sufficient accuracy. Furthermore, such a system would probably require replacing or modifying the existing voltage regulators typically found on FPGA system boards. As will be shown later, the thermal transmitter we built does not require any precision equipment to operate and any modifications made to the FPGA board itself are easily and fully reversible.

To implement a temperature-based side-channel, we borrow a concept from [14] and [17] and use a ring oscillator to detect changes in the temperature of the FPGA. Figure 1 shows a block diagram of our initial testing platform. A ring oscillator provides the clock for a counter (right side of Figure 1). A separate counter, driven from a known frequency clock (left side of Figure 1), is used to sample the ring oscillator counter at a fixed time interval. As the speed of the ring oscillator increases or decreases in response to temperature, the sampled count will correspondingly increase or decrease. These sampled values can be tracked over time to detect changes in temperature.

While the frequency of any given ring oscillator depends upon temperature, how strongly and reliably it reacts to changes in temperature depends upon several factors: the physical characteristics of the FPGA, the number of stages in the oscillator, the relative placement/routing of the LUTs used, and the physical location of the oscillator within the FPGA. As discussed in [14] and [17], these dependencies mean that painstaking chip-specific profiling and calibration is required before ring oscillators can be used as accurate thermometers. However, such calibration is not necessary in our case when temperature is used as a means of communication. This is because we can use changes in temperature rather than absolute values to denote symbols. As will be shown later, this only requires very rough device family-level profiling and calibration.

3.2 Temperature Modulation Bandwidth

As mentioned earlier, the maximum transfer rate that any communication mechanism can achieve is related to the number of communication symbols used (S), the sampling frequency (F), and the number of independent channels implemented (C).

In the case of temperature modulation, S_{Therm} is the number of distinct changes in temperature level used for communication. If we assume that an external transmitter can equally heat or cool the FPGA, we can assign half of the symbols to increases in temperature and half to decreases in temperature. As shown in Eq. 2, the maximum number of usable symbols is defined by the

$$S_{Therm} = T_{Range}/T_{\Delta Min} \qquad (2)$$

$$T_{\Delta Min} = (N_{Therm} * \sigma_{Therm})/Slope_{Therm} \qquad (3)$$

$$F_{Therm} = \min(F_{\Delta Count}, F_{\Delta Temp}) \qquad (4)$$

$$F_{\Delta Count} = N_{Therm} * \sigma_{Therm} \qquad (5)$$

$$Voltage(t) = V_{in}\left(1 - e^{-t/RC}\right) \qquad (6)$$

$$Temp(t) = (P * R)\left(1 - e^{-t/RC}\right) = T_{\Delta Max} \qquad (7)$$

$$F_{\Delta Temp} = \left(-R * C * ln\left(1 - \frac{T_{\Delta Max}}{P * R}\right)\right)^{-1} \qquad (8)$$

operational temperature range that is used (T_{Range}) divided by the minimum change in temperature that the receiver can reliably detect (T_{1Min}).[1] As we will show later, the relationship between temperature and ring oscillator speed is highly linear. Thus, the symbols can be evenly spaced within the temperature range used for communication.

As shown in Eq. 3, the minimum discernable temperature change (T_{1Min}) is defined by the minimum change in ring oscillator speed we can reliably detect divided by how strongly the ring oscillator responds to changes in temperature. The minimum discernable change in ring oscillator speed is related to the measurement error in the system ($N_{Therm}*\sigma_{Therm}$). This is an arbitrary constant noise margin factor multiplied by the maximum standard deviation in the speed of the ring oscillator when the temperature is held constant at any given point in the operational range, as measured by the sampled ring oscillator counter. $Slope_{Therm}$ is the average change in ring oscillator speed per degree.

As shown in Eq. 4, the maximum sampling frequency (F_{Therm}) is determined by the smaller of two rates. The first term in Eq. 4 ($F_{\Delta Count}$) is the rate at which we can accurately detect changes in temperature – i.e. how long does the ring oscillator counter have to run before we can reliably discern if there was a change in temperature? The second term in Eq. 4 ($F_{\Delta Temp}$) is the rate at which we can change the temperature of the FPGA itself – i.e. considering physical factors, how quickly can heat flow between the transmitter and the packaged FPGA core?

Shown in Eq. 5, the rate at which we can detect temperature changes ($F_{\Delta Count}$) is equal to the minimum change in ring oscillator speed we expect to see between different symbols. That is, if we want to detect an X Hz change in the frequency of a ring oscillator, the counter must run for $1/X$ seconds for the difference in the sampled count to be at least one. Thus, we will be able to take a new measurement every $1/X$ seconds, or at a rate of X Hz.

The rate at which we can change the temperature of the FPGA ($F_{\Delta Temp}$) is determined by how quickly the transmitter can dissipate heat into or remove heat from the FPGA. As described in [12], the heat transfer between an IC and an attached heatsink can be modeled by making an equivalent "thermal RC circuit". By investigating the impulse response of this circuit, we can predict the temperature response of the FPGA as the thermal transmitter cycles, either heating or cooling.

Looking at Eq. 6 and Eq.7, we can see the similarities between the more familiar electrical RC equation and the thermal RC equation, respectively. In Eq.7, R is the thermal resistance of the FPGA package and the interface between the thermal transmitter and the FPGA package. C is the thermal capacitance of the FPGA and its package. P is the power that the transmitter can either generate or absorb. T_{1Max} is the maximum change in temperature corresponding to any symbol used for communication. Rearranging this equation, we can solve for time and determine the minimum time required for the transmitter to overcome the FPGA's thermal inertia and raise or lower the temperature by the maximum necessary amount. Eq. 8 is Eq. 7 solved for the inverse of the time period.

Finally, the maximum number of communication channels (C_{Therm}) equals the number of independent temperature zones we can create on the FPGA. For a variety of practical and mechanical reasons, we will assume that subdividing the FPGA is too difficult and C_{Therm} equals one.

4. TIMING MODULATION

In this section, we focus on side-channel communication mechanisms in which a transmitter overlays its own data on top of an unrelated FPGA I/O signal. This is accomplished by phase shifting the signal or changing its delay. These small differences in signal timing are interpreted by an FPGA-based receiver, separately from the data in the conventional signal that it is piggybacking upon. One potential mechanism that timing modulation side-channels can exploit is a system-level design characteristic found in many devices: timing adaptive or self-aligning I/O. This key feature is included by developers when they cannot be certain, at design time, of the delay of the physical transmission pathway used to carry a signal.

This same general timing issue manifests itself in many different ways. For example, the uncertainty in delay could be at a macro or micro scale. Similarly, the communication could involve either round-trip request/acknowledgements or purely uni-directional communication. Regardless of the specifics, though, all of these situations require two features that also enable side-channel communication. The first characteristic is that designers must use I/O protocols that allow for a range of different signal delays. This creates room for a side-channel transmitter to modulate the delay for communication, on top of whatever data the signal is carrying in the more conventional sense. Second, these I/O protocols must include calibration or alignment capabilities to identify the amount of delay currently present in a signal. This evaluation gives a side-channel receiver a direct way to extract the time-based information.

As a simple example of uncertainty in coarse-grain two-way communication, consider a typical client/server network transfer. Because a client PC cannot predict the network latency for any packet to or from any server, the protocol must keep track of request flight times and allow for a fairly wide time-out window. Any network node between the client and server (or the server itself) could communicate with a latent receiver on the client by purposely adding delay or reordering packets to change the arrival time of the data at the client, beyond the variations that occur in the nominal case. Notice that this modulation can be performed on either outgoing requests or incoming acknowledgments. As long as the total round-trip delay of the data remains within legal bounds, the transfer is otherwise unaffected (we consider introducing errors an entirely different class of communication).

---

[1] The accuracy, switching speed, and output quantization of the transmitter will also affect real-world performance. However, for our analysis will assume that these issues will not be the limiting factor, given a well-designed transmitter.

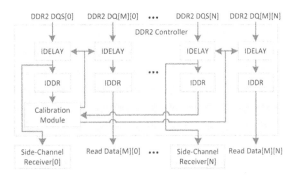

Figure 2: Phase delay detection/re-alignment and phase delay modulation receiver

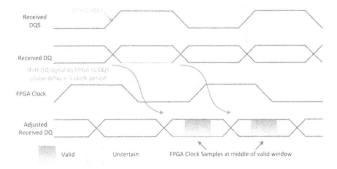

Figure 3: Aligning DQ using DQS and DQ/DQS misalignment

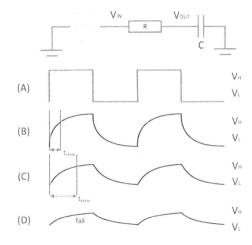

Figure 4: Slew rate with respect to trace capacitance

4.1 Case Study – Phase Delay Modulation

In this paper, we explore the possibility of fine-grain timing modulation implemented on high speed communication lines. Specifically, we add a delay-based signal to a DDR2 memory interface. We exploit a feature built into the interface that is intended to allow circuit designers to compensate for minor differences in timing due to board-level constraints, manufacturing variability, or unpredictable factors that change over time.

A typical DDR2 memory interface consists of clock, control, address and data lines. Precisely controlling the absolute and relative timing of these signals is critical due to the high switching rates that are used. As explained in [7], the data (DQ) bus of a DDR2 module is separated into several smaller logical buses.

Each of these buses also typically includes its own data strobe (DQS) line. Although the entire data bus theoretically operates off of a common clock, this global clock is only used for coarse-grain synchronization. The precise alignment of the data in each of these smaller buses is performed with respect to its own DQS signal. This smaller-scale DQ/DQS bundling is implemented to ease a variety design problems. For example, only the board-level traces within each sub-bus need to be path-length matched, rather than all of the traces for the entire data bus.

The lack of global bus synchronization means that when the FPGA receives incoming data from the DDR2 module, the data in each of the smaller DQ/DQS buses is potentially out of phase with respect to all of the others. Thus, each of these buses needs to be individually re-aligned so that the data can be sampled by a single local clock on the FPGA. As seen in Figure 2, the open-source memory controller [7] we used in our proof-of-concept system has on-board calibration and delay circuitry to perform this re-alignment. As seen in Figure 3, the controller determines the current phase delay on each DQ/DQS bus with respect to the FPGA clock by locating the rising edge of its DQS signal. As seen in Figure 2, the DQ signals are sent through IDELAY blocks (fine-grain delay elements), so the calibration module can arbitrarily phase shift the input data by changing the setting of the IDELAY blocks. As seen in Figure 3, the controller sets the IDELAY blocks so that the FPGA will sample the input data near the center of its valid window.

One key characteristic of this alignment process is that, even during normal operation, the controller must periodically re-evaluate the phase delay of the incoming DQ/DQS buses and adjust the IDELAY settings to maintain proper alignment with the FPGA clock. This dynamic adjustment is required to handle factors that might change the signal timing during runtime, such as temperature (as discussed in Section 3).

An external side-channel transmitter can also impose its own influence on the timing of I/O signals. For example, Figure 4 shows an RC circuit. Increasing the capacitance on the output node increases the slew rate of the output signal. Looking at the system from a digital standpoint, this delays the point at which the output crosses V_H, the threshold voltage for an input logic "1". The same holds true for the transition to V_L, the threshold voltage for an input logic "0". Thus, when we add capacitance to a wire (at least up to some limit), it is perceived by any digital circuit that uses this signal as an input as an increase in timing skew.

Applying this concept to the connection between an FPGA and a DDR2 module, a phase delay transmitter could modulate the capacitance on the board traces used by a DQ/DQS bus. As shown in Figure 2, these changes in capacitance could be detected within the FPGA by monitoring the IDELAY settings. As long as the added capacitance does not overwhelm the driver on the memory module, the conventional data transfer between the memory module and the FPGA would not be interrupted.

4.2 Phase Delay Modulation Bandwidth

When we look at the factors that determine the achievable bandwidth of a phase delay modulation communication channel, we can see parallels to our earlier analysis of temperature modulation channels. For example, Eq. 9 is very similar to Eq. 2 – i.e. the number of symbols that can be used (S_{Phase}) is defined by the range of capacitance that can be added to an existing I/O trace by the transmitter (C_{Range}) divided by the minimum capacitance that can be measured by the receiver, in the form of phase delay

$$S_{Phase} = C_{range}/C_{\Delta min} \qquad (9)$$

$$C = \frac{-t}{R*\ln\left(1-\frac{V(t)}{V_{in}}\right)} \qquad (10)$$

$$C_{max} = C_{range} + C_{Para} = \frac{-t_{\Delta max}}{R_{Drive}*\ln\left(1-\frac{(V_H-V_L)}{V_{dd}}\right)} \qquad (11)$$

$$t_{\Delta max} = \min\left(t_{1/2signal}, \; t_{\Delta Thres}\right) \qquad (12)$$

$$C_{\Delta min} = \frac{-(t_{\Delta min})}{R_{Drive}*\ln\left(1-\frac{(V_H-V_L)}{V_{dd}}\right)} \qquad (13)$$

$$t_{\Delta min} = t_{minQuant} * \lceil N_{Phase} * \sigma_{Phase}\rceil \qquad (14)$$

($C_{\Delta min}$). However, unlike temperature modulation, phase delay communication must piggyback upon an existing I/O signal. The characteristics of this signal heavily affect the transfer rate that can be achieved.

The range of capacitance that can be used for phase delay communication (C_{Range}) is determined by several factors: the frequency of the signal it is overlaid on and the physical attributes of the signal driver, the board-level trace, and the FPGA's input pad. If we model the connection between the driver on the DDR2 module and the input pin of the FPGA as a simple RC circuit, we can illustrate the relationship between these terms.

Eq. 10 is the basic voltage equation for an RC circuit (Eq. 6), solved for capacitance. If we substitute a few variables into Eq. 10, we get Eq. 11. In this case, the maximum load capacitance that the memory module can drive without causing errors is C_{Max}, or the sum of the maximum capacitance that can be added by the transmitter (C_{Range}) and the inherent parasitic capacitance of the connection itself (C_{Para}). C_{Max} is dependent upon the maximum timing skew that can be introduced ($t_{\Delta max}$), the drive voltage of the memory (V_{dd}), the voltage gap between a logic "1" and a logic "0" on the FPGA's input pin (V_H - V_L), and the effective resistance of the memory module driver (R_{Drive}).

As shown in Eq. 12, the maximum allowable timing skew ($t_{\Delta max}$) is the minimum of two periods. The first factor is ½ the period of the signal we are piggybacking upon ($t_{1/2signal}$). That is, if the input pad on the FPGA does not need any setup time, the input signal can reach V_H just as the driver is switching from a logic "1" to a logic "0". On the other hand, the skew may be limited by some internal threshold built into the calibration logic within the communication controller ($t_{\Delta Thres}$). For example, the DDR2 controller that we use in our proof-of-concept system does sanity-checking after the system is initially calibrated, somewhat limiting the maximum allowable skew after this point.

Looking at Eq. 13, we can see that the minimum change in capacitance that can be detected by the receiver ($C_{\Delta min}$) is dependent upon (V_H - V_L), V_{dd}, and R, the same as C_{range}. However, it is also dependent upon the minimum phase delay that can be accurately measured ($t_{\Delta min}$). As shown in Eq. 14, $t_{\Delta min}$ is the minimum time quantum that the calibration system can implement ($t_{minQuant}$) multiplied by an arbitrary constant noise margin factor (N_{Phase}) times the maximum standard deviation in the phase delay when the capacitive load is held constant, as measured by the calibration circuitry (σ_{Phase}). In most systems, $t_{minQvantum}$ will be defined by the timing granularity of the I/O delay elements. In the case of our proof-of-concept system, this is the minimum timestep of the IDELAY blocks. ($N_{Phase}*\sigma_{Phase}$) must be rounded up to the nearest integer because, by definition, we cannot detect or implement fractional $t_{minQvantum}$.

Completing our bandwidth analysis, the maximum sampling frequency (F_{Phase}) is equal to the rate at which recalibration is performed by the receiver. The maximum number of communication channels (C_{Phase}) is equal to the number of independently calibrated signals.

5. PIN HIJACKING

In this section we focus on side-channel communication mechanisms in which a transmitter inserts its own data onto an I/O wire that has already being used by another signal. These communication techniques rely on the fact that there is often "dead time" in a signal or on a bus – i.e. time when the connection is not actively being used for communication. A pin hijacking side-channel transmitter can listen for this idle time (or otherwise know when it will occur) and transmit its own data during this interval. The side-channel can detect and capture the incoming data on the FPGA with its own receiver. As with the timing modulation side-channels, this general concept can be applied on a macro or micro scale.

As a simple example of micro-scale "idle time", consider a typical connection between an external data source and a receiver inside an FPGA. The source and destination must be synchronized, so the FPGA-based receiver might be designed to capture the input data on the rising edge of some common clock. This signal likely wastes at least some portion of the intrinsic bandwidth of the underlying connection. We say this because, unless the signal is running near the limit of the effective setup and hold times of the receiver, the receiver is "ignoring" the input for some portion of the clock period. If the source driver and board-level traces had sufficient headroom to do so, the transmitter could send data on both the rising and falling edges of the clock. Essentially, we can transmit in a double-data rate manner, but time-multiplex between the data from the original signal and data from an entirely new signal. The original receiver would not perceive any difference, but we could add a new receiver to the FPGA that samples on the falling edge of the clock to capture the side-channel data. This same general double-data rate concept can be extended to an N-way data rate connection, only limited by the signaling capability of the physical connection.

5.1 Case Study – I²C Interface Hijacking

In this paper, we looked at a bus that displays very coarse-grain segments of idle time. We built a pin hijacking communication side-channel on top of the dedicated I²C bus that connects the DDR2 memory controller on the FPGA with the Serial Presence Detect (SPD) chip on the memory module itself. In addition to simply demonstrating the feasibility of a pin hijacking side-channel, it also shows that such communication techniques do not require pure input data lines, but can be built from bi-directional pins as well.

DDR2 memories generally contain an SPD EEPROM. This chip stores timing information for the memory, including the maximum clock rate, CAS latency, required refresh rate, etc. The SPD data is normally only accessed when the system is booting so that the FPGA can properly configure the memory controller. After this point, the I²C connection is typically left idle.

The I²C protocol was first introduced by NXP [11]. The simplest I²C structure consists of a master node, a slave node and two open collector, bidirectional signals: the Serial Clock (SCL) line and the Serial Data (SDA) line. The master node first initiates communication with the slave by actively driving the SCL and

SDA lines. It transmits control and address information, then relinquishes control of the SDA line. The slave node listens for this data and, if it is responsible for the provided address, sends back an acknowledgement, actively driving SDA. This establishes a connection between the master and slave until a stop signal is sent. After the transfer is complete, the SCL and SDA lines return to a floating state. Figure 5a shows the normal connection between the memory controller and the SPD module.

Our side-channel connects an additional I²C master to the SDA and SCL lines and adds a small amount of logic to the memory controller that makes it first act as an I²C master (to obtain the timing information from the SPD module) and then as an I²C slave (to obtain data from the side-channel transmitter). Figure 5b shows the modified system. The side-channel transmitter merely waits for the memory controller to complete its transaction with the SPD module and go dormant. After this point, the side-channel transmitter can re-activate the bus and create a new connection between itself and the side-channel receiver.

This same mechanism can be implemented on any standard interface that uses a high impedance state. For example, the data pins of the DDR2 interface are generally tri-stated during normal operation. During that time, it would be possible to set up a side-channel with a very wide bus (64-bits or more) running at high speed. As long as the side-channel has some sort of negotiation so that it can relinquish control of the bus when the rightful user wishes to read or write to the DDR2 memory, it will not impede normal operation. Naturally, as the complexity of this sort of side-channel increases, so does the logic and power requirements for its implementation.

5.2 Pin Hijacking Bandwidth

As with any other digital signal, the number of symbols ($S_{PinHijack}$) and channels ($C_{PinHijack}$) of a pin-hijacking side-channel is determined by the characteristics of the wire or bus that it is based upon. Similarly, so is the sampling rate. However, unique to side-channel communication, we must take into account the fraction of time that the side-channel can actually communicate. As seen in Eq. 15, the effective sampling frequency ($F_{PinHijack}$) is dictated by the maximum allowable clock rate of the basic channel ($F_{Channel}$) multiplied by the fraction of time that the channel is typically unused (*FracIdle*).

$$F_{PinHijack} = F_{channel} * FracIdle \qquad (15)$$

6. Implementation and Results

To demonstrate the feasibility of the three communication mechanisms introduced in this paper, we built proof-of-concept implementations. All of the side-channel receivers were built on a Xilinx Virtex-5 XUPV5-LX110T prototype board. All of the transmitters were built from materials easily obtained from an electronics parts supplier for less than roughly 100 USD.

6.1 Temperature Modulation

Our experimental thermal communication system is shown in Figure 6. The external transmitter consists of a Peltier thermoelectric device, a standard benchtop power supply, and a water-cooled heatsink. When a Peltier device is driven by a DC current, it actively pumps heat from one side of the device to the other. When the Peltier device is cooling the FPGA, the amount of heat that it removes is proportional to the current provided by the power supply and how efficiently the heat is taken away from the other side of the device. The water-cooled heatsink provides a

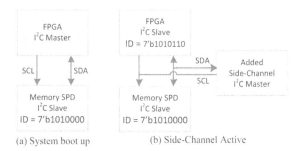

(a) System boot up   (b) Side-Channel Active

Figure 5: SPD I²C connectivity

Figure 6: Temperature modulation platform

Table 1: Experimentation variables

# of stages	2, 3, 4, 5, 6, 8, 10, 14 and 20
Physical Location	25 uniformly spaced locations
Temperature	-15 to 85°C, in 10° intervals

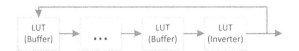

Figure 7: N-Stage Ring Oscillator

thermal mass into which the Peltier device can dump heat. Peltier devices are sensitive to polarity and the transmitter can be switched from cooling the FPGA to heating it simply by reversing the power connection. In this case, the mass of the heatsink provides a source of heat that can be driven into the FPGA. Although we used a water-cooled heatsink because it provided a very large thermal mass so that we could conduct extended heating and cooling experiments, a more conventional heatsink would likely be sufficient for a typical thermal transmitter.

Based on our discussion in Section 3.2, how reliably we can measure the speed of a ring oscillator and how strongly it responds to changes in temperature play a key role in determining the achievable bandwidth of the system. Thus, we performed a series of experiments to determine how the structure and location of the ring oscillator affects these considerations.

As seen in Table 1, we varied the number of stages in the ring oscillator from 2 to 20. As seen in Figure 7, the number of stages in the ring oscillator can be varied arbitrarily by using one inverter and inserting (*N*-1) buffers. We also looked at the effect that location had on the ring oscillators. To ensure the largest degree of consistency and the fastest operational speed, we hand-placed the ring logic as densely as possible and positioned the associated counter in an adjacent column. Each CLB in the Virtex-5 contains two slices, each slice contains four LUTs, and each of the LUTs can implement two independent one-input functions. Thus, all of the ring oscillators that we looked at could fit into a

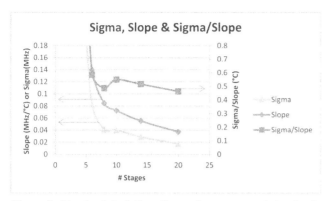

Figure 8: Standard deviation, thermal response and standard deviation/thermal response as a function of the # of ring oscillator stages

Table 2: Characteristics of top 3 ring oscillator candidates

# Stages	20	10	8
Avg. RO Freq @ 25°C (MHz)	62.06	119.9	142.0
σ_{Therm} (MHz)	0.46	0.55	0.49
Avg. $Slope_{Therm}$ (MHz/°C)	0.037	0.073	0.085
$T_{\Delta Min}$ (°C for N_{Therm}=2)	0.93	1.09	0.97
$F_{\Delta Count}$ (KHz for N_{Therm}=2)	34.3	79.6	82.2
$F_{\Delta Temp}$ (Hz for N_{Therm}=2)	3.48	2.89	3.31
B_{Therm} (bits/sec)	3.48	2.89	3.31

Table 3: Resource requirements of thermal receiver

Slices*	117	0.6% of LX110T
6-Input LUTs*	295	0.4% of LX110T
Registers	246	0.4% of LX110T
PLL	1	16% of LX110T (assuming an independent PLL is used)

Assuming an 8-stage ring oscillator

maximum of two CLBs, not including the counter. To determine if there was any regional variation in performance across the chip (either due to manufacturing variation or a possible temperature gradient), we implemented 25 independent ring oscillator/counter pairs spread uniformly across the die in a 5x5 pattern. The components within each of these instrumentation rigs had the same relative placement and routing.

As seen in Figure 1, the duration that the ring oscillator counter runs between samples is determined by the reference clock frequency of the onboard PLL and the constant value used by the reference counter to trigger the sampling logic. We used a 200 MHz reference clock sampling every 65,535 (0xFFFF) clock cycles in our testing. We measured each different type of ring oscillator at each of the 25 locations 4,096 times at temperatures between -15°C and 85°C.

Even when comparing very preliminary ring oscillator testing results with an estimate based upon reasonable values for R, C, and P^2, it is immediately clear that the sampling rate of the system is heavily dominated by how quickly we can change the temperature of the FPGA ($F_{\Delta Temp}$). As we will discuss later, while the ring oscillators can detect temperature changes on the order of

1°C at a sampling rate on the order of kilohertz, the Peltier device requires hundreds of milliseconds to transfer enough heat into or out of the FPGA to discernibly change the temperature. It is unlikely that the "drive capability" of the thermal transmitter will change drastically across smaller and larger devices. This is because both the power that can be absorbed or emitted by the Peltier device and the thermal capacitance of the FPGA plus packaging are roughly proportional to the surface area of the chip. Similarly, the thermal resistance of the FPGA/Peltier interface is roughly inversely proportional to the surface area of the chip. Thus, looking at Eq. 8, the ($R*C$) and ($P*R$) terms will largely remain constant regardless of the size of the FPGA package.

Since we now know that F_{Therm} will be determined by $F_{\Delta Temp}$, we can consider the relationship between the number of symbols ($log_2(S_{Therm})$) we have and the sampling frequency – i.e. we can try to maximize ($log_2(S_{Therm}) * F_{Therm}$). While $log_2(S_{Therm})$ grows linearly when T_{Range} is doubled (assuming that $T_{\Delta Min}$ is fixed for a given ring oscillator), according to Eq. 8 $F_{\Delta Temp}$ shrinks super-linearly when $T_{\Delta Max}$ is doubled. Thus, the bandwidth of the system is highest when we minimize the maximum change in temperature used for communication. This means that $T_{\Delta Max}$ should equal $T_{\Delta Min}$. By extension, this means that we should only use two symbols for communication (+/-$T_{\Delta Min}$) and we should prioritize ring oscillators with the smallest variability and the largest thermal response (minimize $\sigma_{Therm}/Slope_{Therm}$).

In Figure 8, we graph the results of our thermal modulation experiments. The vertical axis represents either the maximum standard deviation of the ring oscillator speed across all 11 temperatures and all 25 locations, the average thermal response (slope) across all locations, or the maximum standard deviation divided by the average slope, respective to the corresponding green, blue and red lines. The horizontal axis represents the various ring topologies in increasing order of the number of stages. Table 2 shows the various characteristics of the three ring oscillators with the smallest $T_{\Delta Min}$. We use these experimentally determined $T_{\Delta Min}$ values to calculate $F_{\Delta Temp}$ and, assuming that S_{Therm} and C_{Therm} both equal one, the potential achievable bandwidth of a communication channel that uses one of these rings (B_{Therm}).

Looking at these results, we can draw several conclusions. First, the variability in the speed ring oscillators (σ_{Therm}) decreases as the size of the ring oscillator grows. This is likely because more stages allows the random jitter that is present in the delay of each individual stage to be averaged, creating a more uniform period overall. Second, the thermal response ($Slope_{Therm}$) also decreases as a function of the number of stages. This is somewhat surprising, although it may be caused by the fact that the delay along larger rings contains a greater fraction of interconnect to logic delay – i.e. the interconnect resources may be far less sensitive to temperature as compared to the LUTs. No matter the cause of this phenomenon, since both σ_{Therm} and $Slope_{Therm}$ decrease as a function of the number of oscillator stages, $T_{\Delta Min}$ is roughly constant when more than about eight stages are used. A ring oscillator with eight stages is particularly attractive because it can be implemented entirely within a single Virtex-5 slice. Since this represents the best combination of size and minimum $T_{\Delta Min}$, we use this ring to report the resource requirements shown in Table 3.

Lastly, unlike the FPGA-based thermometer systems in [14] and [17], none of the equations from Eq. 2 to Eq. 8 contain a reference to the absolute intrinsic operating frequency of the ring oscillator.

---

[2] From the information in [15] and [16], we estimate R, C, and P as 0.13 °C/W, 8.13 J/°C, 30 W, respectively. The thermal capacitance is calculated assuming that the specific heat and density of the IC package are roughly equal to that of solid Al.

We are only concerned with the change in frequency as a function of temperature, or $Slope_{Therm}$. If we combine this with the fact that we only use symbols represented by $+/-T_{\Delta Min}$ (and thus can use conservative positive and negative thresholds), we eliminate the need for chip-specific calibration. Although larger noise margins may affect the achievable bandwidth to a certain degree, it is likely that very approximate testing can determine a reasonable range for $Slope_{Therm}$ that can be used across an entire device family or possibly even all chips made with a given fabrication process.

6.2 Phase Modulation

The XUPV5 board has one DDR2 SO-DIMM socket with eight DQ/DQS sub-buses. Every sub-bus contains one DQS signal that provides synchronization across eight DQ data signals. Our proof-of-concept phase delay transmitter only adds capacitance to the DQS lines rather than all the signals in the DQ/DQS buses. This still creates perceived phase shift across the entire bus because, as discussed in Section 4, the calibration mechanism in the memory controller only examines the DQS signal when determining the phase delay of the bus. We only modulate the capacitance on the DQS signals because it greatly simplifies the physical implementation of the transmitter. Although adding delay unsymmetrically alters the strobe/data signal alignment, we found that we could add almost ¼ of a clock period of phase delay without causing read errors. This is because, as shown in Figure 3, the effective valid window for the data driven by the DDR2 module is fairly wide, even when the memory interface is running at 200MHz (DDR2-800).

Each DQS strobe is actually a differential signal that provides more reliable high-speed communication: DQS and its logical complement, DQS#. As shown in Figure 9, there are two different capacitor topologies that can be used to add delay to the strobe signal. On the left we show a "differential-mode" connection with two capacitors separately connecting DQS and DQS# to ground. On the right we show a "common-mode" connection with one capacitor connected between the drivers. In our early testing, we found that a single capacitor connected between the differential lines provided a much more significant loading effect as compared to the dual capacitor arrangement. This phenomenon is due to the fact that the common mode connection results in two active drivers pulling in opposite directions at all times, essentially doubling the change in voltage that the capacitor experiences during each transition.

The "common-mode" connection topology also had an important advantage over the "differential-mode" technique – it simplified the construction of the phase delay transmitter because we did not have to build a ground plane and did not have to make as many connections to the SO-DIMM. As we will discuss later, simplifying the structure of the transmitter greatly reduced the amount of error introduced into the system.

Figure 10 shows our experimental phase modulation communication setup. We built a phase delay transmitter by mounting a small perfboard on top of the DDR2 SO-DIMM on our FPGA board. This allowed us to attach sockets to the DQS and DQS# pins of the memory module. The red circles in Figure 10 highlight the small wires soldered between the SO-DIMM and the perf-board. We used these sockets to modulate the capacitive load on the strobe lines by manually swapping in and out discrete ceramic capacitors with different values. As mentioned earlier, the effect of the attaching these various capacitors was measured

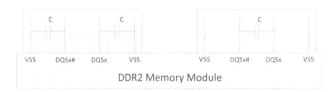

Figure 9: Two capacitor topologies

Figure 10: Phase modulation platform

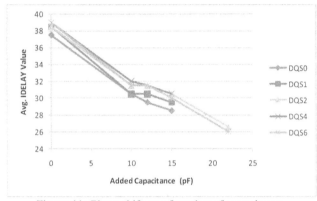

Figure 11: Phase shift as a function of capacitance

Table 4: Characteristics of phase modulation prototype

σ_{Phase}	0.5771 IDELAY units (0.451 ps)
$t_{\Delta Min}$ (N_{Phase}=2)	3 IDELAY units (23.44 ps)
$t_{\Delta Max}$*	12 IDELAY units (93.25 ps)
S_{Phase}	2
F_{Phase}	1KHz

Assuming that the system is not limited by the accuracy of the transmitter
*Determined graphically

Table 5: Resource requirements of phase modulation receiver

Slices	68	0.4% of LX110T
6-Input LUTs	72	0.1% of LX110T
Registers	132	0.2% of LX110T

by looking at the change in IDELAY settings from the calibration circuitry in the FPGA.

The results of our testing are shown in Figure 11 and Table 4. The phase shift detected by the calibration module was measured 1,000 times on each DQS signal for each capacitance value. We only experimented using five of the eight DQS strobes (0, 1, 2, 4, and 6) on the DDR2 memory. This is because these signals were simply more readily accessible. The memory slot on the XUPV5 board is mounted parallel to the system board and the I/O pins for these strobe signals were located on the exposed side of the SO-DIMM rather than the side facing the main PCB.

Looking at Figure 11, we see that the phase shift increases approximately linearly as a function of the applied capacitance (notice, as the memory controller perceives more intrinsic phase delay on the strobe line, it shifts the data less using the IDELAY blocks to achieve the same total phase delay). This linear relationship is predicted by Eq. 10, if we solve for time rather than capacitance. This confirmation gives us confidence that we can use the data from our experiments to determine relative trends between capacitance and phase shift. That said, we did not apply this data directly to Eq. 9, Eq. 11, and Eq. 13 (the equations that involve specific values for the capacitance that is added to a signal). Our uncertainty regarding plugging our experimental data directly into these equations is caused by the fact that there is a large and somewhat unpredictable difference between the capacitance that is physically applied to a wire in our experimental setup and the capacitance that is actually perceived by the DDR2 module and the FPGA.

The effective capacitive load on the DDR2 drivers is heavily affected by the length of the wires used to connect the capacitors to the board-level traces. This is because, due to the high clock frequency of the DDR2 interface, wire inductance is a significant concern. In our initial testing, we found that leads as short as 0.75" created enough inductance to completely isolate the capacitors from the board traces. That is, no matter how large a capacitor we applied, there was no significant change in the signal phase. In our prototype transmitter design, the wires between the SO-DIMM and the perf-board need to be at least 0.25" for mechanical reasons. Furthermore, due to the fact it was constructed by hand, there is visible variation in the length of these connections. Put together, these factors make it very difficult to determine exactly how much capacitance is actually perceived by the memory module and the FPGA. A full implementation of a phase modulation communication system would need to address inductance. Precise capacitors, a fully electronic switching network, and a more elegant method of attachment would be helpful to achieve consistent communication and maximum bandwidth.

Despite our uncertainty regarding the exact applied capacitance, we can still use the results from our experiments to gain insight into the bandwidth potential of this approach – at the very least, this system represents a lower bound. As seen in Table 4, the maximum standard deviation in the phase delay measured by the memory controller (σ_{Phase}) across all of our experiments was 0.58 IDELAY units (one IDELAY unit is $t_{minQuantum}$, or 78.125ps). If we assume N_{Phase} equals three, by Eq. 14 the minimum phase delay that can be accurately measured ($t_{\Delta min}$) equals ($3 * t_{minQuantum}$) or 234.4ps. Thus, looking at Figure 11, we are able to clearly distinguish at least two symbols: applying or not applying a 10pF capacitor. Given two symbols of data per DQ/DQS bus and eight pairs of DQS lines[3] in the test system, ($log_2(S_{Phase}) * C_{Phase}$) equals 8 bits. F_{Phase} is equal to the recalibration rate of the memory controller. The default setting in the memory controller from [7] is 1 KHz. Thus, the maximum bandwidth into the chip would be 8 Kbits per second. Table 5 shows the resource requirements of the phase modulation receiver.

6.3 Pin Hijacking

Our proof-of concept implementation of a pin hijacking side-channel is shown in Figure 12. As discussed earlier, a conventional I²C slave is on the SPD chip on the DDR2 module. The dual-mode I²C master-turned-slave for our side-channel receiver is instantiated in the memory controller on the FPGA.

---

[3] A DDR2 DIMM (rather than SO-DIMM) has 16 DQ/DQS buses. DIMMs with ECC add an additional two channels.

Figure 12: Pin hijacking platform

Table 6: Resource requirements of pin hijacking receiver

Slices	90	0.5% of LX110T
6-Input LUTs	162	0.2% of LX110T
Registers	86	0.1% of LX110T

These two modules communicate via the onboard traces of the XUPV5 board.

Although the side-channel transmitter I²C master would normally be implemented on a separate device, for simplicity sake we built it on the same FPGA as the rest of the system. The I/O signals for the side-channel transmitter are fed through two GPIO pins of the XUPV5 board. These are the red and yellow wires in Figure 12 connecting the GPIO pins on the bottom side of the board with the DDR2 module board traces on the top side. We tapped into the I²C signals of the DDR2 module using the same perfboard and socket technique described in Section 6.2. These connections are highlighted with the blue circle in Figure 10.

The number of symbols ($S_{PinHijack}$) for an I²C connection is two – it is inherently binary since there is only one data wire, SDA. As per the official specification of I²C, $F_{Channel}$ is between 100 KHz and 3.4 MHz, although modern devices are generally capable of communicating at a faster rate. If the FPGA only queries the SPD timing data when the system is booted, the active time of this connection is amortized to zero. Thus, $FracIdle$ is nearly one. Lastly, since we only have one I²C bus, the number of channels ($C_{PinHijack}$) is one. Thus, the maximum achievable bandwidth of our side-channel ($B_{PinHijack}$) equals 3.4 Mbits per second. The resource requirements for our pin hijacking side-channel receiver are shown in Table 6.

Overall, the structure of the I²C interface helps us implement this type of signal hijacking in two ways. First, the protocol has a built-in notion of addressing, so we can send data between the side-channel transmitter and receiver without activating other I²C slaves that might be attached to the bus. Second, the protocol explicitly shuts out other I²C devices once a connection has been established, until the stop signal is sent. This gives us the ability to transfer an infinite-sized payload without violating the bus protocol.

7. Future Work

Although we have demonstrated the feasibility of using speed modulation, timing modulation and pin-hijacking to communicate with an FPGA, there are still many issues that we would like to investigate looking forward.

First, our prototype implementations showed that these communication mechanisms can transmit and receive a coherent signal. However, we have not addressed the issues that surround how we might encode real data. For example, our thermal modulation uses two symbols for communication, an increase or decrease in temperature. However, we cannot use direct binary translation to encode data, because this cannot handle an input data stream with an unbalanced number of zeros and ones. A straightforward technique to avoid runaway temperatures would be a return-to-zero encoding scheme, but might there be a more efficient solution?

We would also like to look at how these communication techniques might interact with each other. On one hand, different methods of information transfer might interact negatively with one another. For example, variations in temperature might change the real-world noise margins for a communication channel that uses phase modulation. On the other hand, combining different approaches into a hybrid mechanism may significantly increase the achievable bandwidth and/or the difficulty in detecting that a side-channel receiver is present.

Along the same lines, we touched on the general concept of noise and how it could be introduced into the system by any number of factors – even simple things like the length of certain wires might be important. Thus, communication errors are bound to occur. We would like to look at what kinds of error correction might best suit our side-channel communication mechanisms.

Furthermore, much more extensive testing is required to determine the real-world operational limitations of these side-channel mechanisms. For example, our thermal receiver was not tested alongside a real working circuit. While we assumed that the heat created by most host circuits would be relatively constant on the time-scale used by our thermal communication system (and thus would be a "DC" component to the temperature modulation), is there anything that can be done to lower the potential influence of the rest of the system? Could an active feedback thermal transmitter help?

Lastly, in this paper we considered the difficulties in creating side-channels. However, we should also look at how we might break them. For example, since side-channels might be used for nefarious purposes such as leaking private information, what countermeasures might be deployed to protect users? On the other hand, if we use these techniques to watermark our IP, how might pirates try to obfuscate these identifiers?

8. Conclusions

It is unclear whether side-channel communication represents a benefit or a liability to system developers and end users. While side-channels have been classically profiled as a security risk, they have the potential to add new unique capabilities to critical FPGA concerns. Either way, though, the increasing popularity and the inherent flexibility of FPGAs puts them at the forefront of this discussion. It is important that we expand our understanding of side-channels and explore potential mechanisms that might be used to implement them.

In this paper we introduced three novel side-channel communication mechanisms: speed modulation, timing modulation and pin hijacking. We used these approaches to highlight an aspect of side-channels that, to the best of our knowledge, has been previously unexplored: the potential of an FPGA-based side-channel receiver. A side-channel receiver is significant because, taken together with prior work on how FPGAs can emit side-channel information, it enables two-way communication.

Our experiments on prototype side-channel receivers demonstrated that we could achieve reliable and, potentially, high bandwidth communication with minimal overhead. While there are still many issues we would like to address, these results prove that reliable bi-directional side-channel communication is possible. This leads the way to practical white-hat applications such as post-fabrication bug fixes and IP watermarking. However, it also enables powerful black-hat attacks such as conditionally triggered covert channels.

9. References

[1] Adamov, A., Saprykin, A., Melnik, D. and Lukashenko, O. The problem of Hardware Trojans detection in System-on-Chip. *International Conference of CAD Systems in Microelectronics* 2009. 178 – 179.

[2] Agrawal, D., Archambeault, B., Rao, J. R. and Rohatgi, P. The EM Side–Channel(s):Attacks and Assessment Methodologies. *International Workshop on Cryptographic Hardware and Embedded Systems* 2002.

[3] Agrawal, D., Baktır, S., Karakoyunlu, D., Rohatgi, P. and Sunar, B. Trojan Detection using IC Fingerprinting. *IEEE Symposium on Security and Privacy*. 296 – 310.

[4] Bar-El, H. "*Introduction to Side-channel Attacks*," White Paper, http://www.discretix.com

[5] Bar-El, H., Choukri, H., Naccache, D., Tunstall, M. and Whelan, C. The Sorcerer's Apprentice Guide to Fault Attacks. Proceeding of IEEE, Vol. 94, No. 2, (Feb. 2006), 370 – 382.

[6] Becker, G. T., Kasper, M. and Paar, C. 2010. Side-Channel based Watermarks for IP Protection. *International Workshop on Constructive Side-Channel Analysis and Secure Design* 2010.

[7] Bittner, R. The Speedy DDR2 Controller For FPGAs. *International Conference on Engineering of Reconfigurable Systems & Algorithms*. 2009.

[8] Chari, S., Rao, J. R. and Rohatgi, P. 2002 Template Attacks. *International Workshop on Cryptographic Hardware and Embedded Systems* 2002

[9] Collins, D. DARPA "TRUST in IC's" Effort. *Microsystems Technology Symposium Enabling the Future*. 2007.

[10] De Mulder, E., Buysschaert, P., Ors, S.B., Delmotte, P., Preneel, B., Vandenbosch, G. and Verbauwhede, I. Electromagnetic Analysis Attack on an FPGA Implementation of an Elliptic Curve Cryptosystem. *International Conference on Computer as a Tool*. EUROCON 2005. 1879 – 1882.

[11] *The I2C-bus Specification Version 2.1*. NXP, Jan. 2000.

[12] Lenz, M., Striedl, G. and Fröhler, U. 2000. *Thermal Resistance: Theory and Practice*. Infineon Technologies AG. (Jan. 2000)

[13] Lin, L., Kasper, M., Güneysu, T., Paar, C. and Burleson, W. Trojan Side-Channels: Lightweight Hardware Trojans through Side-Channel Engineering. *International Workshop on Cryptographic Hardware and Embedded Systems* 2009. 382 – 395.

[14] Lopez-Buedo, S., Garrido, J. and Boemo, E. I. Dynamically Inserting, Operating, and Eliminating Thermal Sensors of FPGA-Based Systems. *IEEE Transactions on Components and Packaging Technologies*, Vol. 25, No. 4, (Dec. 2002), 561 – 566.

[15] *Virtex-5 FPGA Packaging and Pinout Specification UG195 (v4.7)*. Xilinx Inc., Dec. 2009.

[16] *Part Number CP85338*, datasheet, V-Infinity Inc., Aug. 2009

[17] Zick, K. M. and Hayes, J. P. On-line sensing for healthier FPGA systems. *International Symposium on Field Programmable Gate Arrays*. 2010. 239 – 248.

[18] Ziener, F., Baueregger, F. and Teich, J. Using the Power Side Channel of FPGAs for Communication. *International Symposium on Field Programmable Custom Computing Machines*. 2010. 237-244.

FPGA 2011 Poster Session 1

An Accelerated and Energy-Efficient Traffic Monitor using the NetFPGA

Alfio Lombardo, Diego Reforgiato,
Giovanni Schembra, University of Catania, Italy
alombard@diit.unict.it, schembra@diit.unict.it,
diegoref@diit.unict.it

[1]A traffic monitor system has been implemented on the NetFPGA. The NetFPGA is an open networking platform accelerator that enables researchers and instructors to build working prototypes of high-speed, hardware-accelerated networking systems. The traffic monitor application allows network packets to be captured and analyzed from up to all four of the Gigabit Ethernet ports. A graphical user interface showing the traffic of any port has been implemented on top of it. The project has been implemented as a fully open-source project and serves as an exemplar project on how to build and distribute NetFPGA applications. All the code (Verilog, hardware, system software, verification scripts, makefiles, and support tools) can be freely downloaded from the NetFPGA.org website. System performance has been compared with other two implementations: one using the same NetFPGA architecture but implementing the reference router with port mirroring, and the other being a software implementation built on top of the Click Modular Router.

ACM Categories & Descriptors: C.2.6 InternetWorking, C.2.1 Network Architecture and Design, D.2.2 Netowrk Protocols

General Terms: Design, Algorithms

Keywords: NetFPGA, Traffic Monitor, Packet Sniffer, Port Mirroring, Click Modular Router

[1] This work was partially supported by the Italian MIUR PRIN project ``Sorpasso". Moreover, the work leading to this invention has benefited from a fellowship of the Seventh Framework Programme of the European Community [7° PQ/2007-2013] regarding the Grant Agreement n. PIRG03-GA-2008-231021.

Low Power Interconnect Design for FPGAs with Bidirectional Wiring Using Nanocrystal Floating Gate Devices

Daniel Schinke, W. Shepherd Pitts, Neil Di Spigna, Paul Franzon, North Carolina State University
djschink@ncsu.edu

New architectures for the switch box and connection block are proposed for use in an energy efficient field programmable gate array (FPGA) with bidirectional wiring. Power-hungry SRAMs are replaced by non-volatile nanocrystal floating gate (NCFG) devices that retain their state while the system power is off and do not need to be configured at boot up. The NCFG-based FPGA is benchmarked against both a traditional bidirectional

and a modern unidirectional SRAM-based FPGA using a 32-tap FIR Filter designed in HSPICE based on predictive BSIM4.0 CMOS with 45nm gate length technology and a previously developed physical model of the NCFG device. Compared to the traditional bidirectional and the modern unidirectional SRAM-based interconnect the total gate area is reduced by 87% and 63%, respectively. Simulations demonstrate a reduction of 58% in static and 34% in dynamic power consumption compared to the traditional bidirectional SRAM-based FPGA while the signal propagation delay through a switch box is decreased by 28%. When compared to the modern unidirectional SRAM-based FPGA the proposed design has roughly comparable power consumption but the circuit complexity is greatly reduced as a result of doubling the available routing channels. Alternatively the number of the routing channels may be reduced to save area and power whereas the complexity remains similar. The potential benefits from choosing the proposed design can be summarized as small area, low power consumption, high speed and high functionality, which typically trade off and cannot be achieved by the SRAM-based counterparts simultaneously. Compared to previous designs that use continuous floating gate devices in FPGAs, the approach described in this work requires less overhead, lower voltages, and offers improved reliability.

ACM Categories & Descriptors: B.6.1 Design Styles: Memory used as logic

General Terms: Design, Performance

Keywords: FPGA, Nanocrystal, Floating Gate, Low Power, High Speed, Bidirectional Wiring, Switch Box, Connection Block

Dealing with the "Itanium Effect"

Steve Richfield, Consultant, Edgewood, WA
Steve.Richfield@gmail.com

The "Itanium Effect" is a subtle organizational phenomenon leading to the wide adoption of a few widely applicable technologies, and the abandonment of many powerful but more narrowly applicable technologies. This results in potential technological revolutions simply dying on the vine due to a general lack of knowledge about potential enabling technologies. The main elements of the Itanium Effect are:

1. Technology loops, where a limited set of methods results in recreating products from the past, often without correcting their architectural errors
2. Compartmentalized conferences, e.g. FPGA, that work to inhibit designs that merge disciplines
3. Little PhD student participation, that chokes off the supply of fresh ideas
4. Procedural exclusion of futurist and top-down discussions, so that the entire industry proceeds without futurist goals
5. Keeping problems secret, so that no one else can help

The Itanium Effect has become the leading barrier to advancement of high performance computing. We now appear to be on the verge of a computational singularity, where a hundredfold performance gain is available from architectural changes alone, due to the elimination of various sorts of choke points. Unfortunately, there is presently a high threshold to overcome, as there are several enabling technologies that must be simultaneously developed. This can't come from CPU, GPU, or FPGA manufacturers acting alone. These areas must be merged, and somewhat obscure enabling technologies added to glue it all together. The prospective glue technologies examined in this paper include:

1. Logarithmic arithmetic
2. Medium-grained and multi-grained FPGAs
3. Coherent memory mapping
4. Variable data chaining
5. Fast aggregation across ALUs
6. Blurring the SIMD/MIMD distinction using small local program memories
7. A simple horizontal microcoding interface for applications
8. Failsoft configuration on power-up
9. Failsoft partial reconfiguration during execution
10. Physically symmetrical pinout to facilitate the use of defective components.
11. An architecture-independent universal compiler to compile a new APL-level language

ACM Category and Subject Descriptor: B.0 [Hardware]: General

General Terms: Algorithms, Management, Performance, Design, Economics, Reliability, Languages, Theory

Keywords: Aggregation, ALU, APL, Befuddlement, Coherent Memory Mapping, CPU, Data Chaining, Fail-soft Reconfiguration, Flops/Transistor, FPGA, Genetic Algorithm, GPU, Horizontal Microcoding, Instruction Look-ahead, Itanium Effect,Logarithmic Arithmetic, Medium Granularity, Mentoring, Multi-grain, SECDED, SIMD/MIMD, Symmetrical Pinout, Universal Compiler

On Timing Yield Improvement for FPGA Designs Using Architectural Symmetry

Haile Yu, Qiang Xu,
The Chinese University of Hong Kong
Philip H. W. Leong, The University of Sydney
hlyu@cse.cuhk.edu.hk

As semiconductor manufacturing technology continues towards reduced feature sizes, timing yield will degrade due to increased process variation. Previous variation aware design (VAD) methodologies address this problem by using chipwise placement and routing optimizations given the variation distribution is obtained. However, it is very time-consuming to do chipwise variation characterization and optimization. Therefore, this work proposes the use of symmetry in FPGA architectures so that a large range of timing-equivalent configurations can be derived from a single initial implementation by configuration rotation and flipping, allowing the application of post-silicon tuning to mitigate the effects of process variation. Additionally, logic element swaps further improve timing performance. An FPGA design methodology is presented which combines configuration-level redundancy and fine-grained design tuning. The proposed methodology does not need variation characterization and customized placement and routing for each individual FPGA. Compared to other variation aware design methods, it is more cost-efficient in terms of run-time, especially for design implementation on a large amount of FPGAs. Twenty MCNC benchmark circuits in different process technologies were used to show that the proposed method is effective in improving yield and timing in the presence of process variation.

ACM Categories & Descriptors: B.8.2 Performance Analysis and Design Aids

General Terms: Design, Reliability

Keywords: FPGA, Process Variation, Symmetrical Architecture, Yield

High Level Synthesis for FPGAs Applied to a Sphere Decoder Channel Preprocessor

Sven van Haastregt[1], Stephen Neuendorffer[2], Kees Vissers[2], Bart Kienhuis[1],
[1] LIACS, Leiden University, Leiden, The Netherlands
{svhaastr,kienhuis}@liacs.nl
[2] Xilinx Research Labs, San Jose, CA, USA
{stephenn,keesv}@xilinx.com

During the 1990s, High Level Synthesis (HLS) slowly started emerging to allow designers to cope with the ever-increasing complexity of digital signal processing systems such as wireless receivers. Only recently, a new generation of high-quality commercial HLS tools capable of generating decent RTL architectures from algorithmic-style code has become available. Although these tools are now starting to be adopted for actual designs, detailed experiences and results for these tools in significant designs is still lacking. In this work we have analyzed the design process of a significant portion of a wireless communication application using AutoESL's AutoPilot HLS tool. We target a Xilinx Virtex-5 FPGA device and a clock frequency of 225 MHz. We have compared our HLS implementation to a reference implementation obtained using manual RTL design methods. We found that our HLS implementation is competitive to this reference implementation in terms of throughput and resource cost. The time needed to obtain a first HLS implementation matching throughput and resource cost aspects of the reference implementation is similar to the design time of the reference implementation. After obtaining a first HLS implementation, we were able to explore and implement different application architectures with HLS in only a couple of hours, thereby gaining significant savings in design time over manual RTL design, where architectural exploration may take weeks.

ACM Categories & Descriptors: B.5.2 Automatic Synthesis

General Terms: Design

Keywords: FPGA, High Level Synthesis, Sphere Decoder

Resolving Implicit Barrier Synchronizations in FPGA HLS

Jason Cong and Yi Zou,
University of California, Los Angeles
{cong, zouyi}@cs.ucla.edu

Existing C-to-FPGA high-level synthesis (HLS) tools are good at exploiting instruction-level and loop-level parallelism, but not effcient at exploiting task-level parallelism (or requires extensive manual re-write). In this paper, we present an automated °ow and architecture template to map task-level data-model (coarse-grain task graphs) onto FPGAs. We automatically generate multiple communicating FSMDs (nite-state machine with datapath) based on the architecture template to manage the required synchronization and communication. The key architectural components in our approach include a progress table that traces task execution, an automatic memory duplication scheme that enables a larger parallelism and provides isolation between different tasks, and a memory lifetime analysis and reuse scheme to reduce the on-chip memory consumption. Through data- °ow driven execution, the presented °ow can reduce the total latency by 30%, with moderate area overhead, when compared with the RTL implementation using a single hierarchical FSMD generated by a state-of-art HLS tool.

ACM Categories and Subject Descriptors: B.7.1 [Integrated Circuits]: Types and Design Styles; Algorithms implemented in hardware; C.3 [Special-Purpose and Application-Based Systems]: Real-time and embedded systems

General Terms: Algorithms, Performance, Design

Keywords: Barrier, Template, FPGA

A Prototype FPGA for Subthreshold-Optimized CMOS

Peter Grossmann, Miriam Leeser,
Northeastern University
grossmann.p@husky.neu.edu

Field-programmable gate arrays (FPGAs) are frequently used in low power systems because they can implement the same functionality as a microprocessor in a more energy-efficient manner while still offering the benefits of low development time and cost relative to an ASIC. Similar advantages for FPGAs may be found in ultra-low power applications operating at subthreshold supply voltages, where performance is sacrificed in favor of increased energy efficiency. Process technology research has demonstrated the benefits of tailoring device design to subthreshold operation. Subthreshold FPGA research is only beginning, and has yet to consider use of subthreshold-optimized devices. A simplified FPGA implemented in subthreshold-optimized CMOS is presented. The results obtained show that this technology provides the capability to implement an FPGA suitable for ultra-low power applications consuming tens to hundreds of microwatts of average power.

ACM Categories & Descriptors: B.7.1 [Hardware]: Design Types and Style – advanced technologies, gate arrays, VLSI

General Terms: Performance, Design

Keywords: subthreshold, FPGA

The Lincoln Laboratory portion of this work was sponsored by the United States Government under Air Force contract number FA8721-05-C-0002. The opinions, interpretations, conclusions and recommendations are those of the authors and are not necessarily endorsed by the United States Government.

Fault Modeling and Characteristics of SRAM-Based FPGAs

Naifeng Jing[1], Ju-Yueh Lee[2], Chun Zhang[3],
Jiarong Tong[3], Zhigang Mao[1], Lei He[2]
[1] Shanghai Jiao Tong University, China,
jingnaifeng@ic.sjtu.edu.cn
[2] UCLA, USA lhe@ee.ucla.edu
[3] Fudan University, China,
chun.zhang.cz@gmail.com

The reliability of SRAM-based Field Programmable Gate Array (FPGA) is susceptible to Single Event Upset (SEU) fault. To investigate the fault impact, particular the fault in interconnects on FPGA functionality, this paper proposes a SEU fault analysis framework by evaluating the fault with a unified metric. This metric, termed as criticality, quantifies the sensitivity of FPGA functional failure to the SEU fault on logical and interconnect configuration bits. Considering the post layout information, our framework can characterize the SEU fault with respect to different FPGA architectures and CAD algorithms, such that the sensitivity of FPGA functional failure can be investigated in detail during design phase. The experiment result quantitatively shows that the configuration bits in interconnects dominate those in LUTs, several times both in bit number and criticality contribution. The ratio of their criticalities is even higher when LUT input size increases from 4 to 6. The higher criticality of interconnects than their LUT counterpart is due to their natural sensitivity to functional failure instead of their majority of bits. In addition, it is also shown that, among the three common types of switch boxes, the Subset switch box is less fault tolerant than Wilton and Universal.

ACM Categories & Descriptors: B.8.1 [Performance and Reliability]: Reliability, Testing, and Fault-Tolerance

General Terms: Reliability, Design, Measurement

Keywords: SEU, interconnects, Fault Tolerance, FPGA, Reliability

FPGA 2011 Poster Session 2

A Streaming FPGA Implementation of a Steerable Filter for Real-time Applications

Srinidhi Kestur, Dharav Dantara,
Vijaykrishnan Narayanan,
The Pennsylvania State University
kesturvy@cse.psu.edu

Oriented filters are used in many early vision and image processing tasks for feature extraction at arbitrary orientations. Steerable filters are a class of filters in which a filter of arbitrary orientation is synthesized as a linear combination of a set of basis filters. In this work, we describe a streaming implementation of a steerable filter on FPGAs, which includes a two-dimensional convolution filter and a modulator for modulation by a set of oriented sine waves. We present a highly configurable streaming 2D convolution implementation and a novel separable look-up-table based implementation of the modulation step. This steerable filter has been extended to multiple resolutions to realize a steerable pyramid filter. Experimental results on a Virtex6 FPGA show that the steerable pyramid filter provides up to 14X and 21X speedups over related FPGA and CPU implementations respectively. This work was supported in part by a grant from NSF 0916887 and DARPA Neovision2 programs.

ACM Categories & Descriptors: B.7.1 Types and Design Styles: Algorithms implemented in hardware

General Terms: Design

Keywords: Steerable Filter, Pyramid Filter, FPGA Implementation, Convolution, Modulation, Gabor Filter, ML605

Using Many-Core Architectural Templates for FPGA-based Computing

Mingjie Lin, Shaoyi Cheng, Ilia Lebedev,
John Wawrzynek, University of California, Berkeley,
mingjie.lin@gmail.com

Truly unleashing the computing potential of FPGAs, as well as widening their applicability, demands alleviating cumbersome HDL programming and relieving laborious manual optimization. Towards this end, we propose a Many-core Approach to Reconfigurable Computing (MARC) that enables efficient high-performance computing for applications expressed with imperative programming languages such as C/C++ without constructing FPGA computing machines from scratch when targeting various applications within the same or similar problem domains. A MARC system achieves high computing performance by leveraging a many-core architectural template, sophisticated logic synthesizing techniques, and state-of-art compiler optimization technology.

In addition, MARC exploits abundant special FPGA resources such as distributed block memories and DSP blocks to implement complete single-chip high efficiency many-core micro-architectures. The key benefits of MARC include (i) allowing programmers to easily express parallelism through a high-level programming language, (ii) supporting coarse-grain multithreading and dataflow-style fine-grain threading while permitting bit-level resource control, and (iii) greatly reducing the effort required to re-purpose the hardware system for different algorithms or different applications.

ACM Categories & Descriptors: C.3 Special-purpose and Application-based Systems: Microprocessor/microcomputer Applications

General Terms: Design

Keywords: Many-core, Computing, FPGA, Template

A Chip-Level Path-Delay-Distribution Based Dual-VDD Method for Low Power FPGA

Jianfeng Zhu, Dong Wu, Yaru Yan, Xiao Yu, Hu He,
Liyang Pan, Tsinghua University
dongwu@tsinghua.edu.cn

Dual-V_{DD} FPGA architecture has been proposed to reduce the FPGA's power consumption, where a low V_{DD} (V_{DDL}) is assigned to non-critical resources and unused resources are power-gated. In this paper, a path-delay-distribution (PDD) based design method of supply voltage in dual-V_{DD} FPGA is developed, which gives an estimated optimal V_{DD} solution for the required applications. Meanwhile, an improved tree-based V_{DD} assignment algorithm is accordingly designed. Thus chip-level optimization of dual-V_{DD} FPGA is achieved on the chosen granularity with the power consumption minimized. Based on MCNC benchmark circuits at 90nm technology node, our experimental result shows that: the power reduction rate depends on V_{DDL} level; the design method proposed in this work gives the optimal one automatically. This design method could be utilized to guide the FPGA automatic design, saving the time to search for the system's optimal supply voltage, and the proposed assignment algorithm is more efficient in dynamic power reduction.

ACM Categories & Descriptors: B.7.2 Design Aids

General Terms: Algorithm, Theory

Keywords: Dual-VDD, FPGA, Path Delay Distribution

A Comparison of FPGAs, GPUs and CPUs for Smith-Waterman Algorithm

Yoshiki Yamaguchi, University of Tsukuba, JP,
Kuen Hung Tsoi, Wayne Luk,
Imperial College London, UK
yoshiki@cs.tsukuba.ac.jp, khtsoi@doc.ic.ac.uk,
wl@doc.ic.ac.uk

The Smith-Waterman algorithm is a key technique for comparing genetic sequences. This paper presents a comprehensive study of a systolic design for Smith-Waterman

algorithm. It is parameterized in terms of the sequence length, the amount of parallelism, and the number of FPGAs. Two methods of organizing the parallelism, the line-based and the lattice-based methods, are introduced. Our analytical treatment reveals how these two methods perform relative to peak performance when the level of parallelism varies. A novel systolic design is then described, showing how the parametric description can be effectively implemented, with specific focus

on enhancing parallelism and on optimizing the total size of memory and circuits; in particular, we develop efficient realizations for compressing score matrices and for reducing affine gap cost functions. Promising results have been achieved showing, for example, a single XC5VLX330 FPGA at 131MHz can be three times faster than a platform with two NVIDIA GTX295 at 1242MHz.

ACM Categories & Descriptors: C.3 Signal Processing systems, I.2.8 Dynamic Programing

General Terms: Performance

Keywords: FPGA, GPGPU, Performance Comparison, Sequence Alignment, Smith-Waterman Algorithm

Variation Tolerant Asynchronous FPGA

Hock Soon Low, Delong Shang, Fei Xia,
Alex Yakovlev, Newcastle University, UK
h.s.low1@ncl.ac.uk, delong@ncl.ac.uk,
fei.xia@ncl.ac.uk, alex.yakovlev@ncl.ac.uk.

This paper describes the realization of an interconnect Delay Insensitive (DI) FPGA architecture with distributed asynchronous control. This architecture maintains the basic block structure of traditional FPGAs allowing the potential use of existing FPGA design tools in block design. This asynchronous FPGA architecture is mainly aimed at tolerating the unpredictable delay variations caused by process and environment variations in current and future VLSI technology nodes and also targets low power operations, including modes such as dynamic voltage scaling and variable Vdd, as in applications featuring energy harvesting. This is achieved by making the longer inter-block interconnects DI, keeping the computational logic single-rail, and removing global clocks.

ACM Categories & Descriptors: B.8.1 Reliability, Testing, Fault-Tolerance; B.6.1 Design Styles

General Terms: Design, Reliability

Keywords: Asynchronous, FPGA, Process Variation, Variability, Distributed control

FPGA 2011 Poster Session 3

MicroBlaze: An Application-Independent FPGA-based Profiler

Fadi Obeidat, Robert Klenke,
Virginia Commonwealth University
{obeidatfh,rhklenke}@vcu.edu

Monitoring the functional behavior of an application is an important capability that assists in exploring the performance of a target application against different SW/HW implementations. Recently, there have been efforts to exploit the ability to trace the internal signals of the soft-core processors for developing FPGA-based profiling tools to monitor programs running on these processors. However, these previously developed techniques are application-dependent, i.e., they require the designer either to edit the HDL code or the application code to obtain the desired trace information when targeting new applications. In this research, we propose an application-independent profiling technique using the MicroBlaze/FPGA platform where profiling library or user-defined functions can be achieved by tracing the unique instruction flow that distinguishes functions from each other rather than monitoring the program counter value (the addresses of the functions). Hence, modifying the application code or targeting new application does not require reconfiguring the FPGA or modifying the application code for targeting the same functions. This technique can be used to analyze the target application at the source code level, observing the dominant operations and demanded resources that characterize the system behavior. In addition, this technique can assist in selecting the appropriate processor architecture for a given application by considering MicroBlaze as a reference architecture from which the functional behavior of the target application can be mapped to the performance of other architectures.

ACM Categories & Descriptors: C.4 Performance of Systems

General Terms: Measurement, Performance, Design

Keywords: FPGA-based Profiling, HW/SW Codesign, Performance Modeling

FPGA-based Fine-grain Parallel Computing

Andrew W. Hill, Andrea Di Blas, Richard Hughey,
University of California, Santa Cruz
{awhill|andrea|rph}@soe.ucsc.edu

FPGAs are increasing in computing power at a significant rate while the non-recurring engineering costs and time-to-market remain significant lower than those for application-specific integrated circuits (ASICs), encouraging FPGAs to be used in areas previous dominated by ASICs. In this study, we examine the appropriateness of FPGAs for high-performance, low-volume prodution parallel computing by mapping an existing ASIC-based massively parallel single-instruction, multiple data (SIMD) computer, the UCSC Kestrel, to a variety of FPGAs.

The design has a raw peak performance of over 187 billion 8-bit operations per second (OPS), 48 times faster than the original ASIC-based Kestrel, using a Xilinx Virtex-6, and a cost efficiency of up to 81 MOPS/$ using a Xilinx Spartan-3. We also show that we can implement the entire original Kestrel (512 processing elements) as a system on a single programmable chip.

ACM Categories & Descriptors: B.7.1 Types and Design Styles: Gate arrays; C.1.2 Multiple Data Stream Processors (Multiprocessors)

General Terms: Design, Economics, Performance

Keywords: SIMD, Parallel Computing, System on a Programmable Chip

Memory Based Computing: Reshaping the Fine-grained Logic in a Reconfigurable Framework

S. Paul, S. Bhunia, Case Western Reserve University
{sxp190, skb21}@case.edu

Conventional Field Programmable Gate Array (FPGA) architectures leverage on the purely spatial computing model where a design is realized in the form of a small multiple-input single-output lookup tables (LUTs) connected through programmable interconnect switches. However, such a model incorporates an elaborate programmable interconnect network which becomes a major performance bottleneck and leads to poor scalability across process technology nodes. In this paper we evaluate an alternative two-dimensional static random access memory (SRAM) array based reconfigurable computing fabric, referred to as "Memory Based Computing" (MBC) that departs from a purely spatial architecture by advocating multi-cycle evaluation at each computational element. Within a computational element, it uses a dense two-dimensional SRAM array to map large multi-input multi-output functions as LUT and evaluate them in time-multiplexed topological fashion. Multi-cycle execution at each computing node is accomplished using a local interconnect architecture. The proposed framework substantially reduces the requirement for global interconnects by folding computational resources onto a single computational element. We explore the design space for MBC to optimize the major design parameters and compare the performance, power dissipation and energy-delay product for benchmark applications between MBC and conventional SRAM-based FPGA. Simulation results show that compared to a clustered FPGA model, the proposed framework achieves *57%* improvement in performance, *30%* improvement in Energy Delay Product (EDP) and *10%* improvement in technological scalability of performance for standard benchmark circuits. Finally, we validate the functionality of MBC framework and timing of different operations by mapping several small applications on a Cyclone III FPGA platform from Altera.

ACM Categories & Descriptors: B.6.1 Design Styles; B.3.1 Semiconductor Memories; C.1.3 Other Architecture Styles

General Terms: Design, Performance

Keywords: Recongurable Hardware, Field Programmable Gate Array (FPGA), Memory Based Computation

"Health Monitoring" of Live Circuits in FPGAs Based on Time Delay Measurement

Joshua M. Levine, Edward Stott,
George A. Constantinides, Peter Y.K. Cheung,
Imperial College London
josh.levine05@imperial.ac.uk

Literature suggests that timing performance degradation in VLSI could be a major concern in future process technologies. FPGAs are well suited to cope with this challenge, due to their flexibility at design-, manufacture- and run-time.

Existing timing measurement techniques allow for the measurement of delay while the circuit is not operating, and reliability techniques allow for the detection of faults as they occur in operating circuits. Neither allows for the health of an operating circuit to be measured. The ability to monitor the health of a system can provide an early warning of impending failure. This information will enable measures to reduce the impact of, or avoid altogether, the failure. A good indication of the degree of degradation in an operating circuit is the available timing slack in a combinatorial circuit path, between registers, while the circuit is operating at speed.

This work proposes a new time delay measurement technique that does not interfere with the circuit's normal operation. This is achieved by sweeping the phase of a secondary clock signal, driving additional shadow registers. These are connected to each circuit node to be measured, typically those on the most critical paths. The technique is able to measure the timing slack available in the circuit-under-test, while it is performing its usual function.

The technique is demonstrated using a 12-stage LUT chain, and on an 8-bit ripple-carry adder, implemented on an Altera Cyclone III FPGA. It is able to measure the timing slack with a best case resolution of 96ps. The additional circuitry has minimal overhead in terms of area, power consumption, and timing. The increase in circuit delay due to extra fan-out load was measured to be 0.25% in the first example circuit.

ACM Categories & Descriptors: B.8.1 Reliability, Testing, and Fault-Tolerance

General Terms: Experimentation, Measurement, Reliability

Keywords: Recongurable Hardware, Field Programmable Gate Array (FPGA), Memory Based Computation

FPGA Placement by Graph Isomorphism

Hossein Omidian Savarbaghi, Islamic Azad
University, Iran
Kia Bazagran, University of Minnesota
h_omidian_sa@yahoo.com

FPGA placement and routing are still challenging problems. Given the increased diversity of logic and routing resources on FPGA chips, it seems appropriate to tackle the placement problem as a mapping between the nodes and edges in a circuit graph to compatible resources in the architecture graph. We explore utilizing graph isomorphism algorithms to perform FPGA placement. We use a hierarchical approach in which the circuit and architecture graphs are simultaneously clustered to reduce the size of the search space, and then a novel reductive graph product method is used to solve the isomorphism problem. The graph product algorithm is called reductive as it eliminates a

linear number of candidates at every step of the search process, reducing the number of candidate nodes by approximately 1/3. Compared to the annealing-based placement tool VPR 5.0, we achieve approximately 40% improvement in placement runtime, while improving the critical path delay by about 7% and wire length by 5%, while demanding 1.3% more channels on average.

ACM Categories & Descriptors: J.6 [COMPUTER-AIDED ENGINEERING]: Computer-aided Design; B.7.2 [INTEGRATED CIRCUITS]: Design Aids- Placement and Routing

General Terms: Algorithms, Design, Theory

Keywords: Placement, Graph Isomorphism, Graph Product, Clustering

Regular Fabric for Regular FPGA

Xun Chen, Jianwen Zhu, University of Toronto
xchen@eecg.toronto.edu, jzhu@eecg.toronto.edu

In the sub-wavelength regime, design for manufacturability (DFM) becomes increasingly important for field programmable gate arrays (FPGAs). In this paper, we report an automated tile generation flow targeting micro-regular fabric, this flow automatically generate the basic FPGA tile building block in a standard cell format and then form the whole tile with the help of commercial placing and routing tools. Using a publicly accessible, well-documented academic FPGA as case study, we found that comparing to the tile generators previously reported, our generated micro-regular tile incurs less than 10% area overhead, which could be potentially recovered by process window optimization thanks to its superior printability. In addition, we demonstrate that on 45nm technology, the generated FPGA tile reduces lithography induced process variation by 33%; and reduce probability of failure by 21.2%. If further overhead of 10% area can be recovered by enhanced resolution, we can achieve the variation reduction of 93.8% and reduce probability of failure by 16.2%.

ACM Categories & Descriptors: B.7.1 Types and Design Style; B.7.2 Design Aids; B.7.3 Reliability and Testing

General Terms: Design

Keywords: FPGA, Layout Atutomation, Design for Manufacturability, Regular Design Fabric.

FPGA-Based NAND Flash Memory Error Characterization and Solid-State Drive Prototyping Platform

Yu Cai, DSSC, Carnegie Mellon University,
Erich F. Haratsch, LSI
Mark McCartney, Mudit Bhargava, Ken Mai,
Carnegie Mellon University
yucai@andrew.cmu.edu

NAND Flash memory has been widely used for data storage due to its high density, high throughput, low cost, and low power. Howver, as the storage cells become smaller and with more bits programmed per cell, they are expected to suffer from reduced reliability and limited endurance. Wear-leveling and signal processing can signicicantly improve both reliability and endurance. However, finding optimal algorithms would require a quick and accurate characterization of Flash memory providing an insight into the error patterns. To this end, we have designed and implemented an FPGA-based framework for quick, accurate, and comprehensive characterization of Flash memories to allow efficient algorithm explorations.

ACM Categories & Descriptors: B.7.3 [Reliability and Testing]: Error-checking; B.7.1 [Types and Design Styles]: Memory Technologies; B.3.2 [Design Styles]: Mass Storage

General Terms: Design, Experimentation, Performance, Reliability

Keywords: FPGA, NAND Flash, Flash controller, Solid State Drive

Towards Automated Optimisation of Tool-generated HW/SW SoPC Designs

Ravikesh Chandra, Oliver Sinnen,
The University of Auckland
r.chandra@auckland.ac.nz

Currently C-to-hardware (C2H) compilation tools have the potential to generate high-performing and efficient hardware functions from application source code. But often this is not realised without expensive manual code modifications to massage the input source code into a form whereby the compiler can extract maximum meaning from it, thus improving the quality of generated hardware. These modifications represent a significant hurdle for software developers; to improve this we present our work towards a semi-automated compilation framework that attempts to streamline this design flow. The proposed framework consists of an extensible analysis phase of input source code and automated generation of code-mutations that serve as trial candidates. These are then automatically combined within the greater SoPC environment and passed through a parallel compilation stage through the C2H tool. Based on the compilation results the process can be refined and re-executed after manually-assisted candidate pruning. In experimental results, a significant performance speedup has been demonstrated when applying these techniques to simple examples which were compiled out-of-the-box with the same C2H tool. Moreover, minimal extra development effort was necessary to achieve these results. Open challenges still remain, but we believe the promise of such an augmented approach to tool-generated SoPC designs is clear.

ACM Categories & Descriptors: B.5.2 Design Aids: Automatic Synthehsis

General Terms: Design, Performance

Keywords: FPGA, Compilers, C-to-Hardware, Design Space Exploration, SoPC

BBFex: A Bloom-Bloomier Filter Extension for Long Patterns in FPGA-based Pattern Matching System

Bui Trung Hieu, Nguyen Duy Anh Tuan,
Tran Ngoc Thinh,
Vietnam National University – Ho Chi Minh City
University of Technology
bth2909@yahoo.com.vn, duyatuan@gmail.com,
tnthinh@cse.hcmut.edu.vn

There are many pattern matching engines in Network Intrusion Detection Systems (NIDS) have been developed on FPGA-based platforms to accelerates the performance of pattern matching process in order to keep up with the gradually increasing in speed of current networks. However, those systems only support small number of short patterns which are not appropriate to large database such as Clam Antivirus patterns. In this paper, we propose *Bloom-Bloomier Filter Extension* (*BBFex*) as a practical pattern matching engine that handles *large various-length* pattern database. The basic idea in designing BBFex is the combination of Bloom Filter and Bloomier Filter to index patterns and an efficient pattern fragmenting method to split and to merge long patterns. Therefore, BBFex can recognize nearly *84,000* Clam Antivirus static patterns of which lengths vary from *4* to *255* characters with rather low on chip memory density, approximately *0.4* bits per character while keeping the off-chip memory access rate *5X* lower compared to previous similar system and achieving throughput of *1.36 Gbps*. In addition, BBFex is not only limited to Clam Antivirus database because its architecture is designed in respect to general character-based database. Moreover, as a hash-based system, BBFex does not require entire system reconfiguration when updating database.

ACM Categories & Descriptors: B.6.0 General

General Terms: Design

Keywords: Bloom Filter, Bloomier Filter, Clam Antivirus, Hashing, Long Pattern, Pattern Matching

Author Index

NOTES

NOTES

NOTES

NOTES

NOTES

NOTES

www.ingramcontent.com/pod-product-compliance
Lightning Source LLC
Chambersburg PA
CBHW080354060326
40689CB00019B/4011